MATHEMATICAL METHODS IN LINGUISTICS

Studies in Linguistics and Philosophy

Volume 30

The titles published in this series are listed at the end of this volume.

MATHEMATICAL METHODS IN LINGUISTICS

by

BARBARA H. PARTEE

Department of Linguistics,
University of Massachusetts, Amherst

ALICE TER MEULEN

Department of Linguistics,
University of Washington, Seattle

and

ROBERT E. WALL

Department of Linguistics,
University of Texas, Austin

KLUWER ACADEMIC PUBLISHERS

DORDRECHT / BOSTON / LONDON

ISBN 90-277-2245-5 (Pallas pbk.)

Published by Kluwer Academic Publishers,
P.O. Box 17, 3300 AA Dordrecht, The Netherlands.

Kluwer Academic Publishers incorporates
the publishing programmes of
D. Reidel, Martinus Nijhoff, Dr W. Junk and MTP Press.

Sold and distributed in the U.S.A. and Canada
by Kluwer Academic Publishers,
101 Philip Drive, Norwell, MA 02061, U.S.A.

In all other countries, sold and distributed
by Kluwer Academic Publishers Group,
P.O. Box 322, 3300 AH Dordrecht, The Netherlands.

Hardbound edition is published in the series
Studies in Linguistics and Philosophy, Vol. 30
ISBN 90-277-2244-7

Printed in the Netherlands

Table of Contents

PART B: LOGIC AND FORMAL SYSTEMS

PART C: ALGEBRA

PART D: ENGLISH AS A FORMAL LANGUAGE

List of Symbols

Symbol	Meaning	Page
$b \in A$	b is a member of set A	4
$b \notin A$	b is not a member of set A	4
$\{a,b\}$	(unordered) set with members a and b	5
$\{X\vert...\}$	set of all X such that...	6
$A = B$	sets A and B are equal (identical)	9
$\vert A \vert$	cardinality of set A	9
$\#(A)$	cardinality of set A	9
$\aleph_0$	aleph-zero (cardinality of set of natural numbers)	9
$\emptyset$	empty set	9
$A \subseteq B$	A is a subset of B	9
$A \subset B$	A is a proper subset of B	10
$A \not\subseteq B$	A is not a subset of B	10
$\wp A$	power set of A	11
2^A	power set of A	11
$A \cup B$	union of sets A and B	11
$\cup A$	union of all sets in A	12
$A \cap B$	intersection of sets A and B	12
$\cap A$	intersection of all sets in A	14
$A\text{-}B$	difference of sets A and B	14
A'	complement of set A	16
U	universe of discourse	16
$x+y$	arithmetic addition	20
$x*y$	arithmetic multiplication	20
$A+B$	symmetric difference of sets A and B	25
$\langle a,b \rangle$	ordered pair	27
$A \times B$	Cartesian product of sets A and B	28
R^{-1}	inverse of relation R	29
$F: A \rightarrow B$	F is a function from A to B	31
$F(a)$	value of F at argument a	31
$G \circ F$	composition of functions F and G	33
id_A	identity function in set A	34
$x > y$	x is greater than y	43
$x \ngtr y$	x is not greater than y	43
$[[x]]$	equivalence class containing x	45
$A \sim B$	sets A and B are equivalent	55
$\mathbf{N}$	set of natural numbers	57
A^*	set of all strings on A	58
$\mathbf{Z}$	set of integers	59
$2^{\aleph_0}$	cardinality of $\wp \mathbf{N}$	63
$[0,1]$	set of real numbers between 0 and 1	64
$\alpha \oplus \beta$	cardinal addition	73
$\alpha \otimes \beta$	cardinal multiplication	73
$x \cdot y$	arithmetic multiplication	78

Preface

This book grew out of two previous introductory texts: *Fundamentals of Mathematics for Linguists* by Barbara Hall Partee and *Introduction to Mathematical Linguistics* by Robert Wall, both of which had gone out of print in the U.S by the mid 1980's. Faced with the daunting prospect of revising and updating each of these books for re-publication, the authors decided to pool their resources and soon after Alice ter Meulen joined them in the project of producing this book, *Mathematical Methods in Linguistics*.

Like its predecessors, this book is designed primarily for students in linguistics, but it can of course be used by anyone wanting an introduction to the kind of discrete mathematics which finds application in many areas of contemporary linguistic theory. We have tried to make this a gentle introduction in that nearly all the basic material on set theory and logic (Parts A and B) presuppose no mathematical skills beyond the high school level. Indeed, since the mathematics covered here deals with discrete entities–for example, strings of letters from some alphabet–rather than with continuous structures such as lines and areas, the reader will find that it bears a stronger resemblance to high school algebra than to calculus or analytic geometry. One aim, then, is to provide a kind of basic literacy course in set theory and formal logic, which are essential to understanding formalizations in a broad and ever-increasing range of work in linguistics (and in many other fields as well).

The largest portion of this book, however, shows how more complex and interesting structures can be built out of the set-theoretic and logical bases, and, within the limits of space available in these already dense pages, we have tried to indicate how these structures can prove useful in certain linguistic domains. Part C, for example, leads from the notions of order and operation to algebraic structures such as groups, semigroups, and monoids, and on to lattices and Boolean and Heyting algebras, which have played a central role in much recent work in the semantics of events, mass terms, collective vs. distributive actions, etc. In Part D, the model-theoretic semantics of predicate logic is extended and applied to a limited, but interesting, fragment of English, and this leads into a discussion of work on generalized quantifiers and the problems posed by intensional constructions. Part E deals with an area which has traditionally been labelled "mathematical lingusitics," i.e., formal languages and automata theory. This section includes proofs of the non-regularity of English and of the non-context freeness of Swiss German as well as material on formal languages –e.g., indexed languages, tree adjoining languages, and categorial languages– lying between the context free and context sensitive classes. There is also a brief discussion of the mathematical properties of "standard theory" transformational grammars.

As is perhaps evident from these cursory descriptions, Parts C, D, and E each form nearly independent sequels to the introductory material in Parts A and B. There is far more material here than can be covered in a one semester course (or perhaps even a one year course), so an instructor will necessarily have to make a selection according to the background and interests of the class. For those approaching the subject matter for the first time, it might be wise not to try to read the first eight chapters in sequence but to take the elementary sections on set theory and logic in parallel, leaving the more advanced material on axiomatic systems, Chapter 8, for later. The exercises at the end of most chapters and sections (with answers to many of them supplied at the back of the book) will help both students enrolled in a class and those working on their own to check their understanding of the concepts introduced. Some relevant but not, strictly speaking, essential material has been relegated to appendices, and there are, of course, references and suggestions for further reading to be found with each section.

A word should be said about what is not included. We have not tried to cover probability and statistics (used in glottochronology, frequency counts of words and constructions in texts, and in fact relevant to the analysis of any sort of experimental data), the mathematics of wave theory (used in acoustic phonetics), and the mathematics of computation beyond basic automata theory (used in computational linguistics in the study of parsing and machine translation, for example). There is virtually no limit to the mathematical tools which might eventually prove useful in solving linguistic problems, and so a book such as this one can never hope to be completely comprehensive.

Beyond the specific aims just outlined, we have an even broader purpose in mind in puttting this textbook together. To quote from the Preface of *Fundamentals of Mathematics for Linguists*:

A further and even more general aim of the book is to make mathematical concepts and mathematical reasoning more accessible, less formidable, and hopefully even pleasurable, to those students who have stayed away from mathematics out of a perceived insecurity or distaste for the subject. Many of the best textbooks on subjects treated here presuppose a considerable degree of mathematical sophistication, not because the subject matter requires it, but just because in most curricula such topics as formal systems and automata theory are not standard first-year fare and are more likely to be taken up by students who have studied a considerable amount of other logic or mathematics first. And it is certainly true that this book by itself does not provide [all] the tools to become a creative researcher in mathematical linguistics or in any of the branches of mathematics here covered; but [we] believe it does provide a solid grounding to enable the student to understand much of the basis of the formalization encountered in linguistics and other social and behavioral sciences, and to go on to study further mathematics and logic with confidence.

Many people contributed to the preparation of this book. We would especially like to thank Fred Landman, David Dowty, Pauline Jacobson, John Etchemendy, Tom Hukari, Arnold Zwicky, Craige Roberts, and Peter Lasersohn for reading earlier versions of the manuscript and field-testing parts of it in the classroom. Their suggestions and criticisms have led to many improvements, for which we are very grateful. Kathy Adamczyk, Louis Conover, John Brolio, Avery Andrews, and Krzysiek Rozwadowski worked uncountably many hours putting the text into computer-readable form and LATEXing it into camera-ready copy. Their patience and dedication knows no bounds, and they are to be thanked for the fact that the price of the book is a finite and relatively reasonable amount. A special debt of gratitude is owed to Lauri Karttunen, Annie Zaenen, Mark Aronszajn, and Steven Weisler for their support, encouragement, and generous hospitality. We would also like to express our sincere appreciation to Martin Scrivener of Kluwer Academic Publishers for his continued patience, understanding, and unfailing support during the long process of getting this book into print. And we gratefully acknowledge the help of the System Development Foundation for Grant No. 650 to Barbara Partee during part of the time the manuscript was being prepared, and a research grant from the University of Groningen during 1985-86 to Alice ter Meulen.

For any mistakes, omissions, or other deficiencies remaining, the authors have agreed to blame each other.

Part A

SET THEORY

Chapter 1

Basic Concepts of Set Theory

1.1   The concept of a set

A *set* is an abstract collection of distinct objects which are called the *members* or *elements* of that set. Objects of quite different nature can be members of a set, e.g. the set of red objects may contain cars, blood-cells, or painted representations. Members of a set may be concrete, like cars, blood-cells or physical sounds, or they may be abstractions of some sort, like the number two, or the English phoneme /p/, or a sentence of Chinese. In fact, we may arbitrarily collect objects into a set even though they share no property other than being a member of that set. The subject matter of set theory and hence of Part A of this book is what can be said about such sets disregarding the actual nature of their members.

Sets may be large, e.g. the set of human beings, or small, e.g. the set of authors of this book. Sets are either finite, e.g. the readers of this book or the set of natural numbers between 2 and 98407, or they are infinite, e.g. the set of sentences of a natural language or the set of natural numbers: zero, one, two, three, ... Since members of sets may be abstract objects, a set may in particular have another set as a member. A set can thus simultaneously *be* a member of another set and *have* other sets as members. This characteristic makes set theory a very powerful tool for mathematical and linguistic analysis.

A set may be a legitimate object even when our knowledge of its membership is uncertain or incomplete. The set of Roman Emperors is well-defined even though its membership is not widely known, and similarly the set of all former first-grade teachers is perfectly determined, although it may be hard to find out who belongs to it. For a set to be well-defined it must be clear *in principle* what makes an object qualify as a member of it. For our present purposes we may simply assume that, for instance, the set of red objects is well-defined, and disregard uncertainties about the exact boundary between red and orange or other sources of vagueness.

A set with only one member is called a *singleton*, e.g. the set consisting of you only, and there is one special set, the *empty* set or the *null* set, which has no members at all. The empty set may seem rather startling in the beginning, but it is the only possible representation of such things as the set of square circles or the set of all things not identical to themselves. Moreover, it is a mathematical convenience. If sets were restricted to having at least one member, many otherwise general statements about sets would have to contain a special condition for the empty set. As a matter of principle, mathematics strives for generality even when limiting or trivial cases must be included.

We adopt the following set-theoretic notation: we write A, B, $C, \ldots$ for sets, and $a, b, c, \ldots$ or sometimes $x, y, z, \ldots$ for members of sets. The membership relation is written with a special symbol $\in$, so that $b \in A$ is read as 'b is a member of A'. It is convenient also to have a notation for the denial of the membership relation, written as $\notin$, so that $b \notin A$ is read as 'b is not a member of A'. Since sets may be members of other sets we will sometimes write $A \in B$, when the set A is a member of set B, disregarding the convention that members are written with lower case letters.

1.2   Specification of sets

There are three distinct ways to specify a set: (1) by listing all its members, (2) by stating a property which an object must have to qualify as a member of it, and (3) by defining a set of rules which generate its members. We discuss each method separately.

List notation: When a set is finite, its members can in principle be listed one by one until we have mentioned them all. To specify a set in list notation, the names of the members, written in a line and separated by commas, are enclosed in braces. For example, the set whose members are the world's longest river, the first president of the United States and the number three could be written as

(1-1) {The Amazon River, George Washington, 3}

Several things must be noted here. First, in specifying a set, we use a name or some definite description of each of its members, but the set consists of the *objects named*, not of the names themselves. In our example, the first president of the United States, whose name happens to be 'George Washington', is a member of the set. But it is the man who belongs to the set, not his name. Exactly the same set could have been described in the following way

(1-2) {The Amazon River, the first president of the United States, 3}

by using an alternative description for this individual. Of course, a set may also contain linguistic objects like names. To avoid confusion, names which are members of sets in their own right are put in single quotes. The set

(1-3) {The Amazon River, 'George Washington', 3}

should hence be distinguished from the set in (1-1), as it contains a river, a name and a number, but not the man who was the first president of the United States. It is important to realize that one and the same set may be described by several different lists, which *prima facie* have nothing in common except that they denote the same individuals.

Second, insofar as sets are concerned, it is an accidental feature of our left to right writing convention that the members are listed in a particular order. Contrary to what this notation may suggest, there is no first, second or third member in the set (1-1). A less misleading notation, which we sometimes use, is shown in (1-4) below; it avoids the suggestion of any ordering of its members (see the Venn diagrams in Sec. 6 below).

(1-4)

The list notation is obviously more convenient to write and typeset, and is therefore usually preferred.

Another point about the list notation for sets is that writing the name of a member more than once does not change its membership status. Should we write

(1-5) $\{a, b, c, d, e, e, e, e\}$

we would have described exactly the same set as by writing

(1-6) $\{a, b, c, d, e\}$

This is a consequence of a fundamental principle of set theory: for a given object, either it is a member of a given set or it is not. There is no such thing as halfway, multiple or gradual membership in our set theory (although there have been attempts to construct theories of "fuzzy sets"; see Zadeh (1987)).

For large finite sets the list notation may be impractical and is abbreviated if some obvious pattern can be recognized in the list. For example, to list all multiples of five between zero and one hundred, we may write:

(1-7) $\{0, 5, 10, 15, \ldots, 95, 100\}$

Predicate notation: The list notation can be used, strictly speaking, only for finite sets, although it is sometimes used in elliptical form for well-known infinite sets such as the various sets of numbers. For example, the set of positive integers (whole numbers) is sometimes denoted by $\{1, 2, 3, 4, \ldots\}$. A better way to describe an infinite set is to indicate a property the members of the set share. The so-called predicate notation for this type of set description is illustrated by

(1-8) $\{x \mid x$ is an even number greater than $3\}$

The vertical line following the first occurrence of the variable x is read 'such that'. The whole expression in (1-8) is read 'the set of all x such that x is an even number greater than 3.' Here x is a variable, which we may think of as an auxiliary symbol that stands for no particular object, but it indicates what the predicate is applied to. Note that the predicate notation describes finite and infinite sets in the same way (e.g., the predicate 'x is an even number between 3 and 9' specifies the finite set $\{4, 6, 8\}$) and that two predicates, if they are coextensive, will specify the same set. For example,

(1-9) $\{x \mid x$ is evenly divisible by 2 and is greater than or equal to $4\}$

is the same set as (1-8).

A predicate may also define its members in relation to something else. For instance, the set

(1-10) $\{x \mid x$ is a book and Mary owns $x\}$

contains the books that Mary owns.

Russell's Paradox: In the early years of set theory any conceivable property was thought to be a defining property of a set. But Bertrand Russell discovered in 1901 that a paradox could be obtained from an apparently acceptable set specification of that sort.

Russell observed first that if sets are defined by properties of their members, some sets will turn out to be members of themselves and other sets will not. For example, the set of all elephants is not itself an elephant, and therefore is not a member of itself. But the set of all abstract concepts must contain itself as member, since a set is an abstract concept. The properties 'is a member of itself' and 'is not a member of itself' should therefore also be defining properties of sets. In particular, then, one could define a set U as the set of all those sets which are not members of themselves: $U = \{x \mid x \notin x\}$. Then we may ask of U whether it is a member of itself. Now two cases may obtain: (i) if U is *not* a member of itself, then it satisfies the defining characteristic of members of U, and therefore it must be a member of U, i.e., of itself; or (ii) if U *is* a member of itself, then it does not satisfy the defining property, hence it is *not* a member of U, i.e., of itself. Since U either is or is not a member of U, the result is a logical paradox. The evident conclusion from this paradox is that there is no such set U, but nothing in Cantor's set theory excluded such a possible defining property. The discovery of the Russell paradox was therefore of great importance (many different but essentially equivalent versions have since been formulated), but it was all the more significant in light of the fact that logicians and mathematicians had been attempting to show that set theory could serve as a foundation for all of mathematics. The appearance of a paradox in the very foundations of set theory made some people doubtful of long-used and familiar mathematical notions, but mathematical practice continued as usual without being hampered by this foundational crisis. Many inventive and innovative solutions have been proposed to avoid the paradox, to resolve it or to make its consequences harmless. One such way, initially suggested by Russell, was *type theory*, which has found fruitful applications to natural language (e.g. in Montague Grammar; see Part D), as well as in the context of programming languages and their semantics, but it is beyond the scope of this book to discuss the type theories in general or any of the various other solutions to the set-theoretic paradoxes (see, however, the axiomatization of set theory in Chapter 8, section 2.8).

Recursive rules: Since finite sets specified simply by listing their members can never lead to such paradoxes, no changes had to be made for them. For infinite sets, the simplest way to avoid such paradoxes and still be able to define most sets of relevance to ordinary mathematics is to provide a rule for generating elements "recursively" from a finite basis. For example, the set $E = \{4, 6, 8, \ldots\}$ (=(1-8)=(1-9)) can be generated by the following rule:

(1–11)   a) $4 \in E$
         b) If $x \in E$, then $x + 2 \in E$
         c) Nothing else belongs to E.

The first part of the rule specifies that 4 is a member of E; by applying the second part of the rule over and over, one ascertains that since $4 \in E$, then $6 \in E$; since $6 \in E$, then $8 \in E$; etc. The third part insures that no number is in E except in virtue of a and b.

A rule for generating the members of a set has the following form: first, a finite number of members (often just one) are stated explicitly to belong to the set; then a finite number of if-then statements specifying some relation between members of the set are given, so that any member of the set can be reached by a chain of if-then statements starting from one of the members specified in the first part of the rule, and nothing that is not in the set can be reached by such a chain. We will consider such recursive devices in more detail in Chapter 8, section 1.1.

The earlier method of specifying a set by giving a defining property for its members has not been abandoned in practice, since it is often quite convenient and since paradoxical cases do not arise in the usual mathematical applications of set theory. Outside of specialized works on set theory itself, both methods are commonly used.

1.3   Set-theoretic identity and cardinality

We have already seen that different lists or different predicates may specify the same set. Implicitly we have assumed a notion of identity for sets which is one of the fundamental assumptions of set theory: two sets are identical if and only if they have exactly the same members. For instance,

(1–12) $\{1, 2, 3, 4, 5, 6\}$

and

(1–13) $\{x \mid x$ is a positive integer less than 7$\}$

and

(1–14) a) $1 \in A$
b) if $x \in A$ and x is less than 6, then $x + 1 \in A$
c) nothing else is in A

are three different kinds of specifications, but because each picks out exactly the same members, we say that they specify *the same set*. We use the equals sign '=' for set-theoretic identity. Thus we may write, for example,

(1–15) $\{1, 2, 3, 4, 5, 6\} = \{x \mid x$ is a positive integer less than 7$\}$

The equals sign is also used in naming sets. For example, we might write 'let $B = \{1, 2, 3, 4, 5, 6\}$' to assign the name 'B' to the set in (1-12). The context will make it clear whether '=' is being used to stipulate the name of a set or to assert that two previously specified sets are identical.

A consequence of this notion of set-theoretic identity is that the empty set is unique, as its identity is fully determined by its absence of members. Thus the set of square circles and the set of non-self-identical things are the *same* set. Note that the empty list notation '{}' is never used for the empty set, but we have a special symbol '∅' for it.

The number of members in a set A is called the *cardinality* of A, written $|A|$ or $\#(A)$. The cardinality of a finite set is given by one of the natural numbers. For example, the set defined in (1-12) has cardinality 6, and since (1-13) and (1-14) describe the same set, they describe sets of the same cardinality (of course distinct sets may also have the same cardinality). Infinite sets, too, have cardinalities, but they are not natural numbers. For example, the set of natural numbers itself has cardinality 'aleph-zero', written $\aleph_0$, which is not a natural number. We will take up the subject of infinite sets in more detail in Chapter 4.

1.4   Subsets

When every member of a set A is also a member of a set B we call A a *subset* of B. We denote such a relation between sets by $A \subseteq B$. Note that

B may contain other members besides those of A, but this is not necessarily so. Thus the subset relation allows any set to be a subset of itself. If we want to exclude the case of a set being a subset of itself, the notion is called *proper subset*, and written as $A \subset B$. For the denial of the subset relation we put a slash across the subset symbol, e.g. $A \nsubseteq B$ means that A is not a subset of B, hence that A has at least one member which is not a member of B.

The following examples illustrate these concepts.

(1–16)   a) $\{a, b, c\} \subseteq \{s, b, a, e, g, i, c\}$
         b) $\{a, b, j\} \nsubseteq \{s, b, a, e, g, i, c\}$
         c) $\{a, b, c\} \subset \{s, b, a, e, g, i, c\}$
         d) $\emptyset \subset \{a\}$
         e) $\{a, \{a\}\} \subseteq \{a, b, \{a\}\}$
         f) $\{\{a\}\} \nsubseteq \{a\}$
         g) $\{a\} \nsubseteq \{\{a\}\}$, but $\{a\} \in \{\{a\}\}$ (!!)

A curious consequence of the definition of subset is that the null set is a subset of every set. That is, for any set A whatever, $\emptyset \subseteq A$. Since $\emptyset$ has no members, the statement that *every* member of $\emptyset$ is also a member of A holds, even if vacuously. Alternatively, we could reason as follows. How could $\emptyset$ fail to be a subset of A? According to the definition of subset, there would have to be some member in $\emptyset$ that is not also a member of A. This is impossible since $\emptyset$ has no members at all, and so we cannot maintain that $\emptyset \nsubseteq A$. Since the argument does not depend in any way on what particular set is represented by A, it is true that $\emptyset \subseteq A$ for every A.

Note, however, that while $\emptyset \subseteq \{a\}$, for example $\{\emptyset\} \nsubseteq \{a\}$. The set $\{\emptyset\}$ has a member, namely $\emptyset$, and therefore is not the empty set. It is not true that every member of $\{\emptyset\}$ is also a member of $\{a\}$, so $\{\emptyset\} \nsubseteq \{a\}$.

Members of sets and *subsets* of sets both represent relationships of a part to a whole, but these relationships are quite different, and it is important not to confuse them. Subsets, as the name suggests, are *always sets*, whereas members may or may not be. Mars is a member of the set {Earth, Venus, Mars} but not a subset of it. The set containing Mars as its only member, {Mars}, *is* a subset of {Earth, Venus, Mars} because every member of the former is also a member of the latter. Further, whereas every set is a subset of itself, it is not clear whether a set can ever be a member of itself, as we saw above in the discussion of Russell's Paradox. Note how important it is here to distinguish between Mars, the planet, and {Mars}, the set.

Sets with sets as members provide the most opportunities for confusion. Consider, for example, the set $A = \{b, \{c\}\}$. The members of A are b and $\{c\}$. From the considerations in the preceding paragraph we see that $b \not\subseteq A$ and $\{b\} \subseteq A$. Similarly, $\{c\} \not\subseteq A$ because c is not a member of A, and $\{\{c\}\} \subseteq A$ because every member of $\{\{c\}\}$, namely, $\{c\}$, is a member of A. The reader should also verify the following statements concerning this example: $\{b\} \notin A$; $c \notin A$; $\{\{c\}\} \notin A$; $\{b, \{c\}\} \subseteq A$; $\{b, \{c\}\} \notin A$; $\{\{b, \{c\}\}\} \not\subseteq A$.

Another difference between subsets and members has to do with our previous remarks about sets of sets. We have seen that if $b \in X$ and $X \in C$, it does not necessarily follow that $b \in C$. The element b *could* be a member of C, but if so this would be an accidental property of C, not a necessary one. With inclusion, however, if $A \subseteq B$ and $B \subseteq C$, it is *necessarily true* that $A \subseteq C$; that is, if every member of A is also a member of B, and further if every member of B is also a member of C, then it must be true that every member of A is also a member of C. For example, $\{a\} \subseteq \{a, b\}$ and $\{a, b\} \subseteq \{a, b, c\}$ so it follows that $\{a\} \subseteq \{a, b, c\}$. On the other hand, $a \in \{a\}$ and $\{a\} \in \{\{a\}, b\}$, but $a \notin \{\{a\}, b\}$ (assuming of course that a and b are distinct).

1.5   Power sets

Sometimes we need to refer to the set whose members are all the subsets of a given set A. This set is called the power set of A, which we will write as $\wp(A)$. Suppose $A = \{a, b\}$; then the power set of A, $\wp(A)$, is $\{\{a\}, \{b\}, \{a, b\}, \emptyset\}$. The name 'power set' derives from the fact that if the cardinality of A is some natural number n, then $\wp(A)$ has cardinality 2^n, i.e., 2 raised to the n power, or $2 \times 2 \times 2 \times \ldots \times 2$ (n times). Sometimes the power set of A is denoted as 2^A.

1.6   Union and intersection

We now introduce two operations which take a pair of sets and produce another set.

The *union* of two sets A and B, written $A \cup B$, is the set where members are just the objects which are members of A or of B or of both. In the predicate notation the definition is

(1-17) $A \cup B =_{def} \{x \mid x \in A \text{ or } x \in B\}$

Note that the disjunction 'or' in (1-17) allows an object to be a member of both A and B. For this reason, the 'or' is an *inclusive* disjunction; (see Chapter 6, section 2). For example,

(1-18)   Let $K = \{a, b\}$, $L = \{c, d\}$ and $M = \{b, d\}$, then

$$
\begin{aligned}
K \cup L &= \{a, b, c, d\} \\
K \cup M &= \{a, b, d\} \\
L \cup M &= \{b, c, d\} \\
(K \cup L) \cup M &= K \cup (L \cup M) &= \{a, b, c, d\} \\
K \cup \emptyset &= \{a, b\} &= K \\
L \cup \emptyset &= \{c, d\} &= L
\end{aligned}
$$

Set-theoretic union can easily be generalized to apply to more than two sets, in which case we write the union sign in front of the set of sets to be operated on: e.g. $\bigcup \{K, L, M\}$ = the set of all elements in K or L or $M = \{a, b, c, d\}$. There is a nice method for visually representing set-theoretic operations, called *Venn diagrams*. Each set is drawn as a circle and its members are represented by points within it. The diagrams for two arbitrarily chosen sets are represented as partially intersecting – the most general case – as in Figure 1-1. The region designated '1' contains elements which are members of A but not of B; region 2, those things in B but not in A; and region 3, members of both B and A. Points in region 4 outside the diagram represent elements in neither set. Of course in particular instances one or more of these regions might turn out to be empty.

The Venn diagram for the union of A and B is then made by delineating all the regions contained in this set – shown in Figure 1-2 by shading areas 1, 2, and 3.

The second operation on arbitrary sets A and B produces a set whose members are just the members of *both* A and B. This operation is called the *intersection* of A and B, written as $A \cap B$. In predicate notation this operation would be defined as

(1-19) $A \cap B =_{def} \{x \mid x \in A \text{ and } x \in B\}$

For example, the intersection of the sets K and M of (1-18) is simply the singleton $\{b\}$, since b is the only object which is both a member of K and a member of M. Here are some more examples:

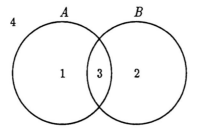

Figure 1-1: Venn diagram of two arbitrary sets A and B.

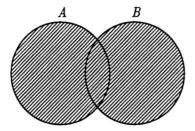

Figure 1-2: Set-theoretic union $A \cup B$.

$(1\text{-}20)$

$$\begin{aligned}
K \cap L &= \emptyset \\
L \cap M &= \{d\} \\
K \cap K &= \{a, b\} \qquad = K \\
K \cap \emptyset &= \emptyset \\
(K \cap L) \cap M &= K \cap (L \cap M) = \emptyset \\
K \cap (L \cup M) &= \{b\}
\end{aligned}$$

The general case of intersection of arbitrary sets A and B is represented by the Venn diagram of Figure 1-3.

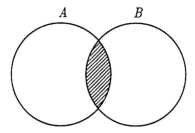

Figure 1-3: Set-theoretic intersection $A \cap B$.

Intersection may also be generalized to apply to three or more sets; e.g., $\bigcap \{K, L, M\} = \emptyset$. The intersection of three arbitrary sets A, B and C is shown in the Venn diagram of Figure 1-4. Here the black area represents what is common to the regions for $A \cap B$, $B \cap C$ and $A \cap C$. Obviously when more than three sets are involved, the Venn diagrams become very complex and of little use, but for simple cases they are a valuable visual aid in understanding set-theoretic concepts.

Problem: Construct a Venn diagram for the union of three arbitrary sets.

1.7   Difference and complement

Another binary operation on arbitrary sets A and B is the difference, written $A - B$, which 'subtracts' from A all objects which are in B. The predicate notation defines this operation as follows:

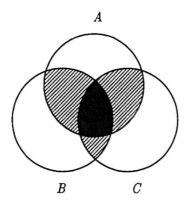

Figure 1–4: Venn diagram for $\bigcap\{A, B, C\}$
$(A \cap B,\ B \cap C$ and $A \cap C$ (shaded) and
$\bigcap\{A, B, C\}$ (black)).

(1–21) $A - B =_{def} \{x \mid x \in A$ and $x \notin B\}$

$A - B$ is also called the *relative complement of A and B*. For instance for the particular sets L and M, given in (1-18), $L - M = \{c\}$, since c is the only member of L which is not a member of M. If A and B have no members in common, then nothing is taken from A; i.e., $A - B = A$. Note that although for all sets A, B: $A \cup B = B \cup A$ and $A \cap B = B \cap A$, it is not generally true that $A - B = B - A$. If one thinks of difference as a kind of subtraction, the fact that the order of the sets matters in this case is quite natural.

The Venn diagram for the set-theoretic difference $A - B$ is shown in Figure 1-5.

Some more examples:

(1–22) $\begin{aligned}
K - M &= \{a\} \\
L - K &= \{c, d\} &= L \\
M - L &= \{b\} \\
K - \emptyset &= \{a, b\} &= K \\
\emptyset - K &= \emptyset
\end{aligned}$

This operation is to be distinguished from the *complement* of a set A,

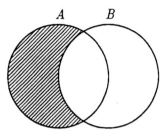

Figure 1–5: Set-theoretic difference $A - B$.

written A', which is the set consisting of everything not in A. In predicate notation

(1-23) $A' = \operatorname{def} \{x \mid x \notin A\}$

Where do these objects come from which do not belong to A? The answer is that every statement involving sets is made against a background of assumed objects which comprise the *universe* (or *domain*) *of discourse* for that discussion. In talking about number theory, for example, the universe might be taken as the set of all positive and negative real numbers. A truly universal domain of discourse fixed once and for all, which would contain literally 'everything' out of which sets might be composed, is unfortunately impossible since it would contain paradoxical objects such as 'the set of all sets'. Therefore, the universe of discourse varies with the discussion, much as the interpretation of the English words 'everything' and 'everyone' tends to be implicitly restricted by the context of discourse. When no other specified name has been given to the universe of discourse in a particular discussion, we conventionally use the symbol U for it. When it is clear from the context or irrelevant to the discussion at hand, the universe of discourse may not be explicitly mentioned at all, but the operation of complement is not well-defined without it. The complement of a set A, then, is the set of all objects in the universe of discourse which are not in A, i.e.,

(1-24) $A' = U - A$

We see that in (1-23) the variable x in the predicate notation is implicitly understood to range over (i.e., take its values from) the set- theoretic universe U (and the same is true, incidentally, in (1-17) and (1-19)).

The Venn diagram with a shaded section for the complement of A is shown in Figure 1-6.

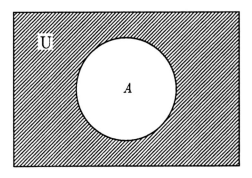

Figure 1–6: The set-theoretic complement A'.

1.8   Set-theoretic equalities

There are a number of general laws pertaining to sets which follow from the foregoing definitions of union, intersection, subset, etc. A useful selection of these is shown in Figure 1-7, where they are grouped (generally in pairs – one for union, one for intersection) under their more or less traditional names. We are not yet in a position to offer formal proofs that these statements really do hold for any arbitrarily chosen sets X, Y, and Z (we will take this up in Chapter 7, section 6), but for now we may perhaps try to convince ourselves of their truth by reflecting on the relevant definitions or constructing some Venn diagrams.

It is easy to see that for any set X, $X \cup X$ is the same as X, since everything which is in X *or* in X simply amounts to everything which is in X. And similarly for everything which is in X *and* in X, so $X \cap X = X$.

Likewise, everything which is in X or in Y (or both) is the same as everything which is in Y or in X (or both); thus, $X \cup Y = Y \cup X$. The argument for intersection is similar.

1. *Idempotent Laws*
   (a) $X \cup X = X$ (b) $X \cap X = X$

2. *Commutative Laws*
   (a) $X \cup Y = Y \cup X$ (b) $X \cap Y = Y \cap X$

3. *Associative Laws*
   (a) $(X \cup Y) \cup Z = X \cup (Y \cup Z)$ (b) $(X \cap Y) \cap Z = X \cap (Y \cap Z)$

4. *Distributive Laws*
   (a) $X \cup (Y \cap Z) = (X \cup Y) \cap (X \cup Z)$
   (b) $X \cap (Y \cup Z) = (X \cap Y) \cup (X \cap Z)$

5. *Identity Laws*
   (a) $X \cup \emptyset = X$ (c) $X \cap \emptyset = \emptyset$
   (b) $X \cup U = U$ (d) $X \cap U = X$

6. *Complement Laws*
   (a) $X \cup X' = U$ (c) $X \cap X' = \emptyset$
   (b) $(X')' = X$ (d) $X - Y = X \cap Y'$

7. *DeMorgan's Law*
   (a) $(X \cup Y)' = X' \cap Y'$ (b) $(X \cap Y)' = X' \cup Y'$

8. *Consistency Principle*
   (a) $X \subseteq Y$ iff $X \cup Y = Y$ (b) $X \subseteq Y$ iff $X \cap Y = X$

Figure 1–7: Some fundamental set-theoretic
equalities.

The Associative Laws state that the order in which we combine three sets by the operation of union does not matter, and the same is true if the operation is intersection. To see that these hold, imagine the construction of the appropriate Venn diagrams. We have three intersecting circles labelled X, Y, and Z. We shade $X \cup Y$ first and then shade Z. The result is shading of the entire area inside the three circles, and this corresponds to $(X \cup Y) \cup Z$. Now we start over and shade $Y \cup Z$ first and then X. The result is the same.

The construction of the Venn diagrams to illustrate the Distributive Laws is somewhat trickier. In Figure 1-8 we show a Venn diagram for $X \cap (Y \cup Z)$. To make it more perspicuous, X has been shaded with vertical lines and $Y \cup Z$ horizontally. The intersection of these two sets is then represented by the cross-hatched area. Figure 1-9 shows the corresponding diagram for $(X \cap Y) \cup (X \cap Z)$. $X \cap Y$ is shaded vertically and $X \cap Z$ horizontally; thus, the union is represented by the area shaded in either (or both) directions. The reader should now be able to construct the Venn diagram for case (a) of the Distributive Laws.

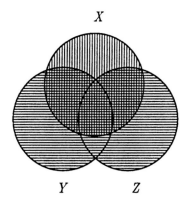

Figure 1–8: Venn diagram for $X \cap (Y \cup Z)$
(X shaded vertically, $Y \cup Z$ shaded
horizontally, $X \cap (Y \cup Z)$ cross-hatched).

The Identity Laws are evident from the definitions of union, intersection, the null set, and the universal set. Everything which is in X or in $\emptyset$ just amounts to everything which is in X, etc. The Complement Laws are likewise easily grasped from the definitions of complement with perhaps a look at

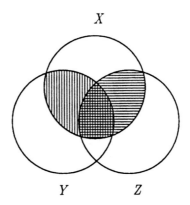

Figure 1–9: Venn diagram for
$(X \cap Y) \cup (X \cap Z)$ $(X \cap Y$ shaded vertically,
$X \cap Z$ shaded horizontally,
$(X \cap Y) \cup (X \cap Z)$ the entire shaded area).

the Venn diagram in Figure 1-6. Case (d) becomes less baffling if we look at Figure 1-5 and consider the area corresponding to the intersection of A with the complement of B.

DeMorgan's Laws are a symmetrical pair. Case (a): everything which is in neither X nor Y is the same as everything which is not in X and not in Y. Case (b): everything which is not in both X and Y is either not in X or not in Y (or in neither). This case is less immediately evident, and a Venn diagram will help.

The Consistency Principle is so called because it is concerned with the mutual consistency of the definitions of union, intersection, and subset. If we think of a Venn diagram in which the circle for X lies entirely inside the circle for Y (representing $X \subseteq Y$), then it is easy to see that $X \cup Y = Y$. On the other hand, if we know that $X \cup Y = Y$, then in the standard Venn diagram the region corresponding to elements which are in X but not in Y must be empty (otherwise, the union would not be equal to Y). Thus, X's members lie entirely in the Y circle; so $X \subseteq Y$. The (b) case is similar.

It may help in getting a grasp on some of these laws if one considers analogues from algebra. The operation of $+$ (addition) and $*$ (multiplication) obey a commutative law:

(1-25) for all numbers x, y, $x + y = y + x$ and $x * y = y * x$

and an associative law:

(1-26) for all numbers x, y, z, $(x + y) + z = x + (y + z)$ and $(x * y) * z = x * (y * z)$

but neither is idempotent: in general it is not true that $x + x = x$ nor that $x * x = x$. However, there is a distributive law relating $*$ and $+$ as follows:

(1-27) for all numbers x, y, z, $x * (y + z) = (x * y) + (x * z)$

but no such law holds if $*$ and $+$ are interchanged; i.e., it is not in general true that $x + (y * z) = (x + y) * (x + z)$. (For example, let $x = 1$, $y = 2$, and $z = 3$; then the left side is 7 and the right side is 12.)

Arithmetic analogues of the Identity Laws are $x + 0 = x$, $x * 0 = 0$, and $x * 1 = x$ with 0 playing the role of the null set and 1 that of the universal set. (But this analogy, too, breaks down: $x + 1$ does not equal 1.)

What we have seen then is that there is an algebra of sets which is in some respects analogous to the familiar algebra involving addition and multiplication but which has its own peculiar properties as well. We will encounter this structure once more when we take up the logic of statements in Chapter 6, and we will discover in Chapter 12 that both are instances of what is called a Boolean algebra.

For the moment our concern is not with the structure of this algebra but rather to show how these equalities can be used in the manipulation of set-theoretic expressions. The idea is that in any set-theoretic expression a set may always be replaced by one equal to it. The result will then be an expression which denotes the same set as the original expression. For example, in $A \cap (B \cup C)'$ we may replace $(B \cup C)'$ by its equivalent, $B' \cap C'$ (citing DeMorgan's Laws), to obtain $A \cap (B' \cap C')$. Since $(B \cup C)'$ and $B' \cap C'$ have the same members, so do $A \cap (B \cup C)'$ and $A \cap (B' \cap C')$.

This technique can be used to simplify a complex set-theoretic expression, as in (1-28) below, or to demonstrate the truth of other statements about sets, as in (1-29) and (1-30). It is usually convenient to arrange such demonstrations as a vertical sequence in which each line is justified by reference to the law employed in deriving it from the preceding line.

(1-28) *Example:* Simplify the expression $(A \cup B) \cup (B \cap C)'$

1.	$(A \cup B) \cup (B \cap C)'$	
2.	$(A \cup B) \cup (B' \cup C')$	DeM.
3.	$A \cup (B \cup (B' \cup C'))$	Assoc.
4.	$A \cup ((B \cup B') \cup C')$	Assoc.
5.	$A \cup (U \cup C')$	Compl.
6.	$A \cup (C' \cup U)$	Comm.
7.	$A \cup U$	Ident.
8.	U	Ident.

(1-29) *Example:* Show that $(A \cap B) \cap (A \cap C)' = A \cap (B - C)$.

1.	$(A \cap B) \cap (A \cap C)'$	
2.	$(A \cap B) \cap (A' \cup C')$	DeM.
3.	$A \cap (B \cap (A' \cup C'))$	Assoc.
4.	$A \cap ((B \cap A') \cup (B \cap C'))$	Distr.
5.	$(A \cap (B \cap A')) \cup (A \cap (B \cap C'))$	Distr.
6.	$(A \cap (A' \cap B)) \cup (A \cap (B \cap C'))$	Comm.
7.	$((A \cap A') \cap B) \cup (A \cap (B \cap C'))$	Assoc.
8.	$(\emptyset \cap B) \cup (A \cap (B \cap C'))$	Compl.
9.	$(B \cap \emptyset) \cup (A \cap (B \cap C'))$	Comm.
10.	$\emptyset \cup (A \cap (B \cap C'))$	Ident.
11.	$(A \cap (B \cap C')) \cup \emptyset$	Comm.
12.	$A \cap (B \cap C')$	Ident.
13.	$A \cap (B - C)$	Compl.

(1-30) *Example:* Show that $X \cap Y \subseteq X \cup Y$.

By the Consistency Principle this expression is true iff $(X \cap Y) \cap (X \cup Y) = X \cap Y$. We demonstrate the latter.

1.	$(X \cap Y) \cap (X \cup Y)$	
2.	$((X \cap Y) \cap X) \cup ((X \cap Y) \cap Y)$	Distr.
3.	$(X \cap (X \cap Y)) \cup ((X \cap Y) \cap Y)$	Comm.
4.	$((X \cap X) \cap Y) \cup ((X \cap Y) \cap Y)$	Assoc.
5.	$((X \cap X) \cap Y) \cup (X \cap (Y \cap Y))$	Assoc.
6.	$(X \cap Y) \cup (X \cap Y)$	Idemp. (twice)
7.	$X \cap Y$	Idemp.

Such arrays constitute formal proofs (of the fact that, in each of these cases, the set in the last line is equal to that in the first line.) We will take up the topic of proofs in due course, but the reader who attempts such

derivations in the exercises will no doubt encounter a notoriously troublesome problem connected with proofs; namely, while it is relatively simple to
verify that a given proof is correct, it may be very difficult to find the one
one wants. So if presented with a problem such as (1-29), one might have
to try many unsuccessful paths before finding one that leads to the desired
final expression. A certain amount of cutting and trying is therefore to be
expected.

Exercises

1. Given the following sets:

$$A = \{a, b, c, 2, 3, 4\} \quad E = \{a, b, \{c\}\}$$
$$B = \{a, b\} \quad F = \emptyset$$
$$C = \{c, 2\} \quad G = \{\{a, b\}, \{c, 2\}\}$$
$$D = \{b, c\}$$

classify each of the following statements as true or false

(a) $c \in A$ (g) $D \subset A$ (m) $B \subseteq G$
(b) $c \in F$ (h) $A \subseteq C$ (n) $\{B\} \subseteq G$
(c) $c \in E$ (i) $D \subseteq E$ (o) $D \subseteq G$
(d) $\{c\} \in E$ (j) $F \subseteq A$ (p) $\{D\} \subseteq G$
(e) $\{c\} \in C$ (k) $E \subseteq F$ (q) $G \subseteq A$
(f) $B \subseteq A$ (l) $B \in G$ (r) $\{\{c\}\} \subseteq E$

2. For any arbitrary set S,

(a) is S a member of $\{S\}$?
(b) is $\{S\}$ a member of $\{S\}$?
(c) is $\{S\}$ a subset of $\{S\}$?
(d) what is the set whose only member is $\{S\}$?

3. Write a specification by rules and one by predicates for each of the
following sets. Remember that there is no order assumed in the list,
so you cannot use words like 'the first' or 'the latter'. Recall also that
a recursive rule may contain more than one if-then statement.

(a) $\{5, 10, 15, 20, \ldots\}$
(b) $\{7, 17, 27, 37, \ldots\}$
(c) $\{300, 301, 302, \ldots, 399, 400\}$
(d) $\{3, 4, 7, 8, 11, 12, 15, 16, 19, 20, \ldots\}$

(e) $\{0, 2, -2, 4, -4, 6, -6, \ldots\}$

(f) $\{1, 1/2, 1/4, 1/8, 1/16, \ldots\}$

4. Consider the following sets:

$$
\begin{array}{llll}
S1 & = & \{\{\emptyset\}, \{A\}, A\} & \qquad S6 = \emptyset \\
S2 & = & A & \qquad S7 = \{\emptyset\} \\
S3 & = & \{A\} & \qquad S8 = \{\{\emptyset\}\} \\
S4 & = & \{\{A\}\} & \qquad S9 = \{\emptyset, \{\emptyset\}\} \\
S5 & = & \{\{A\}, A\}
\end{array}
$$

Answer the following questions. Remember that the members of a set are the items separated by commas, if there is more than one, between the outermost braces only; a subset is formed by enclosing within braces zero or more of the members of a given set, separated by commas.

(a) Of the sets $S1$ - $S9$ which are members of $S1$?

(b) which are subsets of $S1$?

(c) which are members of $S9$?

(d) which are subsets of $S9$?

(e) which are members of $S4$?

(f) which are subsets of $S4$?

5. Specify each of the following sets by listing its members:
   (a) $\wp\{a, b, c\}$ (d) $\wp\{\emptyset\}$
   (b) $\wp\{a\}$ (e) $\wp\wp\{a, b\}$
   (c) $\wp\emptyset$

6. Given the sets $A, \ldots, G$ as in Exercise 1, list the members of each of the following:

   (a) $B \cup C$ (g) $A \cap E$ (m) $B - A$
   (b) $A \cup B$ (h) $C \cap D$ (n) $C - D$
   (c) $D \cup E$ (i) $B \cap F$ (o) $E - F$
   (d) $B \cup G$ (j) $C \cap E$ (p) $F - A$
   (e) $D \cup F$ (k) $B \cap G$ (q) $G - B$
   (f) $A \cap B$ (l) $A - B$

7. Given the sets in Exercise 1, assume that the universe of discourse is $\bigcup\{A, B, C, D, E, F, G\}$. List the members of the following sets:

(a) $(A \cap B) \cup C$ (h) $D' \cap E'$

(b) $A \cap (B \cup C)$ (i) $F \cap (A - B)$

(c) $(B \cup C) - (C \cup D)$ (j) $(A \cap B) \cup U$

(d) $A \cap (C - D)$ (k) $(C \cup D) \cap U$

(e) $(A \cap C) - (A \cap D)$ (l) $C \cap D'$

(f) G' (m) $G \cup F'$

(g) $(D \cup E)'$ (n) $(B \cap C)'$

8. Let $A = \{a, b, c\}$, $B = \{c, d\}$ and $C = \{d, e, f\}$.

(a) What are:

     (i) $A \cup B$ (v) $B \cup \emptyset$

     (ii) $A \cap B$ (vi) $A \cap (B \cap C)$

     (iii) $A \cup (B \cap C)$ (vii) $A - B$

     (iv) $C \cup A$

(b) Is a a member of $\{A, B\}$?

(c) Is a a member of $A \cup B$?

9. Show by using the set-theoretic equalities in Figure 1-7 for any sets A, B, and C,

(a) $((A \cup C) \cap (B \cup C')) \subseteq (A \cup B)$

(b) $A \cap (B - A) = \emptyset$

10. Show that the Distributive Law 4(a) is true by constructing Venn diagrams for $X \cup (Y \cap Z)$ and $(X \cup Y) \cap (X \cup Z)$.

11. The *symmetric difference* of two sets A and B, denoted $A + B$, is defined as the set whose members are in A or in B but not in both A and B, i.e.

$$A + B =_{def} (A \cup B) - (A \cap B)$$

(a) Draw the Venn diagram for the symmetric difference of two sets.

(b) Show that $A + B = (A - B) \cup (B - A)$ by means of the set-theoretic equalities in Figure 1-7. Verify that the Venn diagram for $(A - B) \cup (B - A)$ is equivalent to that in (a).

(c) Show that for all sets A and B, $A + B = B + A$.

(d) Express each of the following in terms of union, intersection, and complementation, and simplify using the set-theoretic equalities.

    (i) $A + A$ (iv) $A + B$, where $A \subseteq B$

    (ii) $A + U$ (v) $A + B$, where $A \cap B = \emptyset$

    (iii) $A + \emptyset$

(e) Show that $((A - B) + (B - A)) = A + B$

(f) Show that $(A + B) \subseteq B$ iff $A \subseteq B$

12. Call adjectives which are correctly predicated of themselves 'autological' and those which are not, 'heterological.' For example, 'English' and 'short' are autological, but 'French' and 'long' are heterologial. Show that when we ask whether the adjective 'heterological' is heterological or autological we are led to a contradiction like that in Russell's Paradox. This is known as Grelling's Paradox.

Chapter 2

Relations and Functions

2.1 Ordered pairs and Cartesian products

Recall that there is no order imposed on the members of a set. We can, however, use ordinary sets to define an *ordered pair*, written $\langle a, b \rangle$ for example,
in which a is considered the *first member* and b is the *second member* of the
pair. The definition is as follows:

(2-1) $\langle a, b \rangle =_{def} \{\{a\}, \{a, b\}\}$

The first member of $\langle a, b \rangle$ is taken to be the element which occurs in
the singleton $\{a\}$, and the second member is the one which is a member of
the other set $\{a, b\}$, but not of $\{a\}$. Now we have the necessary properties
of an ordering since in general $\langle a, b \rangle \neq \langle b, a \rangle$. This is so because we have
$\{\{a\}, \{a, b\}\} = \{\{b\}, \{a, b\}\}$ (that is, $\langle a, b \rangle = \langle b, a \rangle$), if and only if we have
$a = b$. Of course, this definition can be extended to ordered triples and
in general ordered n-tuples for any natural number n. Ordered triples are
defined as

(2-2) $\langle a, b, c \rangle =_{def} \langle \langle a, b \rangle, c \rangle$

It might have been intuitively simpler to start with ordered sets as an additional primitive, but mathematicians like to keep the number of primitive
notions to a minimum.

If we have two sets A and B, we can form ordered pairs from them by
taking an element of A as the first member of the pair and an element of B

as the second member. The *Cartesian product* of A and B, written $A \times B$, is the set consisting of all such pairs. The predicate notation defines it as

(2-3) $A \times B =_{def} \{ \langle x, y \rangle \mid x \in A \text{ and } y \in B \}$

Note that according to the definition if either A or B is $\emptyset$, then $A \times B = \emptyset$. Here are some examples of Cartesian products:

(2-4) Let $K = \{a, b, c\}$ and $L = \{1, 2\}$, then

$$
\begin{aligned}
K \times L &= \{ \langle a, 1 \rangle, \langle a, 2 \rangle, \langle b, 1 \rangle, \langle b, 2 \rangle, \langle c, 1 \rangle, \langle c, 2 \rangle \} \\
L \times K &= \{ \langle 1, a \rangle, \langle 2, a \rangle, \langle 1, b \rangle, \langle 2, b \rangle, \langle 1, c \rangle, \langle 2, c \rangle \} \\
L \times L &= \{ \langle 1, 1 \rangle, \langle 1, 2 \rangle, \langle 2, 1 \rangle, \langle 2, 2 \rangle \}
\end{aligned}
$$

It is important to remember that the members of a Cartesian product are *not* ordered with respect to each other. Although each member is an ordered pair, the Cartesian product is itself an unordered set of them.

Given a set M of ordered pairs it is sometimes of interest to determine the smallest Cartesian product of which M is a subset. The smallest A and B such that $M \subseteq A \times B$ can be found by taking $A = \{a \mid \langle a, b \rangle \in M \text{ for some } b\}$ and $B = \{b \mid \langle a, b \rangle \in M \text{ for some } a\}$. These two sets are called the *projections of M onto the first and the second coordinates*, respectively. For example, if $M = \{ \langle 1, 1 \rangle, \langle 1, 2 \rangle, \langle 3, 2 \rangle \}$, the set $\{1, 3\}$ is the projection onto the first coordinate, and $\{1, 2\}$ the projection onto the second coordinate. Thus $\{1, 3\} \times \{1, 2\}$ is the smallest Cartesian product of which M is a subset.

2.2   Relations

We have a natural understanding of relations as the sort of things that hold or do not hold between objects. The relation 'mother of' holds between any mother and her children but not between the children themselves, for instance. Transitive verbs often denote relations; e.g., the verb 'kiss' can be regarded as denoting an abstract relation between pairs of objects such that the first kisses the second. The subset relation was defined above as a relation between sets. Objects in a set may be related to objects in the same or another set. We write Rab or equivalently aRb if the relation R holds between objects a and b. We also write $R \subseteq A \times B$ for a relation between objects from two sets A and B, which we call a relation *from A to*

B. A relation holding of objects from a single set *A* is called a relation *in*
A. The projection of *R* onto the first coordinate is called the *domain* of *R*
and the projection of *R* onto the second coordinate is called the *range* of *R*.
A relation *R* from *A* to *B* thus can be viewed as a subset of the Cartesian
product *A* × *B*. (There are unfortunately no generally accepted terms for
the sets *A* and *B* of which the domain and the range are subsets.) It is
important to realize that this is a *set-theoretic* reduction of the relation *R* to
a set of ordered pairs, i.e. $\{\langle a, b \rangle \mid aRb\}$. For example, the relation 'mother
of' defined on the set *H* of all human beings would be a set of ordered pairs
in *H* × *H* such that in each pair the first member is mother of the second
member. We may visually represent a relation *R* between two sets *A* and *B*
by arrows in a diagram displaying the members of both sets.

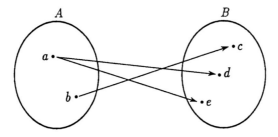

Figure 2–1: Relation *R*: *A* → *B*.

In Figure 2-1, $A = \{a, b\}$ and $B = \{c, d, e\}$ and the arrows represent a
set-theoretic relation $R = \{\langle a, d \rangle, \langle a, e \rangle, \langle b, c \rangle\}$. Note that a relation may
relate one object in its domain to more than one object in its range. The
complement of a relation $R \subseteq A \times B$, written R', is set-theoretically defined
as

(2-5) $R' =_{def} (A \times B) - R$

Thus R' contains all ordered pairs of the Cartesian product which are not
members of the relation *R*. Note that $(R')' = R$. The *inverse* of a relation
$R \subseteq A \times B$, written R^{-1}, has as its members all the ordered pairs in *R*, with
their first and second elements reversed. For example, let $A = \{1, 2, 3\}$ and
let $R \subseteq A \times A$ be $\{\langle 3, 2 \rangle, \langle 3, 1 \rangle, \langle 2, 1 \rangle\}$, which is the 'greater than' relation in
A. The complement relation R' is $\{\langle 1, 1 \rangle, \langle 1, 2 \rangle, \langle 1, 3 \rangle, \langle 2, 2 \rangle, \langle 2, 3 \rangle, \langle 3, 3 \rangle\}$,

the 'less than or equal to' relation in A. The inverse of R, R^{-1}, is $\{\langle 2,3 \rangle, \langle 1, 3 \rangle, \langle 1,2 \rangle\}$, the 'less than' relation in A. Note that $(R^{-1})^{-1} = R$, and that if $R \subseteq A \times B$, then $R^{-1} \subseteq B \times A$, but $R' \subseteq A \times B$.

We have focused in this discussion on *binary* relations, i.e., sets of ordered pairs, but analogous remarks could be made about relations which are composed of ordered triples, quadruples, etc., i.e., *ternary*, *quaternary*, or just n-place relations.

2.3   Functions

A function is generally represented in set-theoretic terms as a special kind of relation. A relation R from A to B is a function if and only if it meets both of the following conditions:

1. Each element in the domain is paired with just one element in the range.

2. The domain of R is equal to A.

This amounts to saying that a subset of a Cartesian product $A \times B$ can be called a function just in case every member of A occurs exactly once as a first coordinate in the ordered pairs of the set.

As an example, consider the sets $A = \{a, b, c\}$ and $B = \{1, 2, 3, 4\}$. The following relations from A to B are functions:

$$(2\text{--}6) \quad \begin{aligned} P &= \{\langle a, 1\rangle, \langle b, 2\rangle, \langle c, 3\rangle\} \\ Q &= \{\langle a, 3\rangle, \langle b, 4\rangle, \langle c, 1\rangle\} \\ R &= \{\langle a, 3\rangle, \langle b, 2\rangle, \langle c, 2\rangle\} \end{aligned}$$

The following relations from A to B are not functions:

$$(2\text{--}7) \quad \begin{aligned} S &= \{\langle a, 1\rangle, \langle b, 2\rangle\} \\ T &= \{\langle a, 2\rangle, \langle b, 3\rangle, \langle a, 3\rangle, \langle c, 1\rangle\} \\ V &= \{\langle a, 2\rangle, \langle a, 3\rangle, \langle b, 4\rangle\} \end{aligned}$$

S fails to meet condition 2 because the set of first members, namely $\{a, b\}$, is not equal to A. T does not satisfy condition 1, since a is paired with both 2 and 3. In relation V both conditions are violated.

Much of the terminology used in talking about functions is the same as that for relations. We say that a function that is a subset of $A \times B$ is a function *from A to B*, while one in $A \times A$ is said to be a function *in A*. The notation '$F: A \rightarrow B$' is used for 'F is a function from A to B.' Elements in the domain of a function are sometimes called *arguments* and their corre-spondents in the range, *values*. Of function P in (2-6), for example, one may say that it takes on the value 3 at argument c. The usual way to denote this fact is $P(c) = 3$, with the name of the function preceding the argument, which is enclosed in parentheses, and the corresponding value to the right of the equal sign.

'Transformation,' 'map,' 'mapping,' and 'correspondence' are commonly used synonyms for 'function,' and often '$F(a) = 2$' is read as 'F maps a into 2.' Such a statement gives a function the appearance of an active process that changes arguments into values. This view of functions is reinforced by the fact that in most of the functions commonly encountered in mathematics the pairing of arguments and values can be specified by a formula contain-ing operations such as addition, multiplication, division, etc. For example, $F(x) = 2x + 1$ is a function which, when defined on the set of integers, pairs 1 with 3, 2 with 5, 3 with 7, and so on. This can be thought of as a rule which says, "To find the value of F at x, multiply x by 2 and add 1." Later in this book it may prove to be necessary to think of functions as dynamic processes transforming objects as their input into other objects as their output, but for the present, we adhere to the more static set-theoretic perspective. Thus, the function $F(x) = 2x + 1$ will be regarded as a set of ordered pairs which could be defined in predicate notation as

(2-8) $\quad F = \{\langle x, y \rangle \mid y = 2x + 1\}$ (where x and y are integers)

Authors who regard functions as processes sometimes refer to the set of ordered pairs obtained by applying the process at each element of the domain as the *graph* of the function. The connection between this use of "graph" and a representation consisting of a line drawn in a coordinate system is not accidental.

We should also note that relations which satisfy condition 1 above but perhaps fail condition 2 are sometimes regarded as functions, but if so, they are customarily designated as 'partial functions.' For example, the function which maps an ordered pair of real numbers $\langle a, b \rangle$ into the quotient of a divided by b (e.g., it maps $\langle 6, 2 \rangle$ into 3 and $\langle 5, 2 \rangle$ into 2.5) is not defined when $b = 0$. But it is single-valued – each pair for which it is defined is

associated with a unique value – and thus it meets condition 1. Strictly
speaking, by our definition it is not a function, but it could be called a
partial function. A partial function is thus a total function on some subset
of the domain. Henceforth, we will use the term 'function,' if required, to
indicate a single-valued mapping whose domain may be less than the set A
containing the domain.

It is sometimes useful to state specifically whether or not the range of a
function from A to B is equal to the set B. Functions from A to B in general
are said to be *into* B. If the range of the function equals B, however, then the
function is *onto* B. (Thus *onto* functions are also *into*, but not necessarily
conversely.) In Figure 2-2 three functions are indicated by the same sort
of diagrams we introduced previously for relations generally. It should be
apparent that functions F and G are *onto* but H is not. All are of course
into.

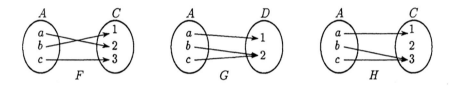

Figure 2–2: Illustration of onto and into
functions.

A function $F\colon A \to B$ is called a *one-to-one* function just in case no member of B is assigned to more than one member of A. Function F in Figure
2-2 is one-to-one, but G is not (since both b and c are mapped into 2), nor
is H (since $H(b) = H(c) = 3$). The function F defined in (2-8) is one-to-one
since for each odd integer y there is a unique integer x such that $y = 2x + 1$.
Note that F is not onto the set of integers since no even integer is the value
of F for any argument x. Functions which are not necessarily one-to-one
may be termed *many to one*. Thus all functions are many-to-one strictly
speaking, and some but not all of them are one-to-one. It is usual to apply
the term "many-to-one", however, only to those functions which are not in
fact one-to-one.

A function which is both one-to-one and onto (F in Figure 2-2 is an
example) is called a *one-to-one correspondence*. Such functions are of special

interest because their inverses are also functions. (Note that the definitions of the inverse and the complement of a relation apply to functions as well.) The inverse of G in Figure 2-2 is not a function since 2 is mapped into both b and c, and in H^{-1} the element 2 has no correspondent.

   Problem: Is the inverse of function F in (2-8) also a function? Is F a one-to-one correspondence?

2.4   Composition

Given two functions $F: A \to B$ and $G: B \to C$, we may form a new function from A to C, called the *composite*, or *composition* of F and G, written $G \circ F$. In predicate notation function composition is defined as

(2-9) $G \circ F =_{def} \{\langle x, z \rangle \mid$ for some $y, \langle x, y \rangle \in F$ and $\langle y, z \rangle \in G\}$

Figure 2-3 shows two functions F and G and their composition.

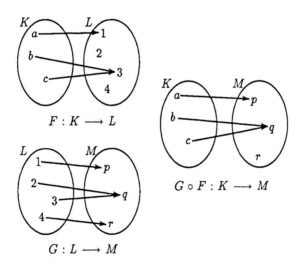

$F : K \longrightarrow L$

$G : L \longrightarrow M$

$G \circ F : K \longrightarrow M$

Figure 2-3: Composition of two functions F and G.

Note that F is into while G is onto and that neither is one-to-one. This shows that compositions may be formed from functions that do not have these special properties. It could happen, however, that the range of the first function is disjoint from the domain of the second, in which case, there is no y such that $\langle x, y \rangle \in F$ and $\langle y, z \rangle \in G$, and so the set of ordered pairs defined by $G \circ F$ is empty. In Figure 2-3, F is the first function and G is the second in the composition. Order is crucial here, since in general $G \circ F$ is not equal to $F \circ G$. The notation $G \circ F$ may seem to read backwards, but the value of a function F at an argument a is $F(a)$, and the value of G at the argument $F(a)$ is written $G(F(a))$. By the definition of composition, $G(F(a))$ and $(G \circ F)(a)$ produce the same value.

A function $F: A \rightarrow A$ such that $F = \{\langle x, x \rangle \mid x \in A\}$ is called the *identity function*, written id_A. This function maps each element of A to itself. Composition of a function F with the appropriate identity function gives a function that is equal to the function F itself. This is illustrated in Figure 2-4.

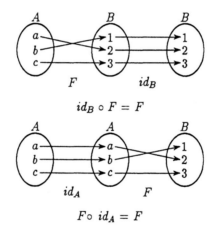

$$id_B \circ F = F$$

$$F \circ id_A = F$$

Figure 2–4: Composition with an identity
function.

Given a function $F: A \rightarrow B$ that is a one-to-one correspondence (thus the inverse is also a function), we have the following general equations:

$$(2\text{-}10) \quad \begin{aligned} F^{-1} \circ F &= id_A \\ F \circ F^{-1} &= id_B \end{aligned}$$

These are illustrated in Figure 2-5.

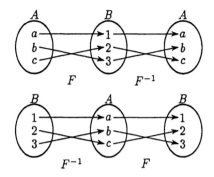

Figure 2–5: Composition of one-to-one
correspondence with its inverse.

The definition of composition need not be restricted to functions but can be applied to relations in general. Given relations $R \subseteq A \times B$ and $S \subseteq B \times C$ the composite of R and S, written $S \circ R$, is the relation $\{\langle x, z \rangle \mid$ for some $y, \langle x, y \rangle \in R$ and $\langle y, z \rangle \in S\}$. An example is shown in Figure 2-6.

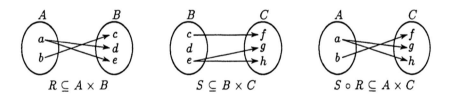

Figure 2–6: Composition of two relations R
and S.

For any relation $R \subseteq A \times B$ we also have the following:

$$(2\text{–}11) \quad \begin{aligned} id_B \circ R &= R \\ R \circ id_A &= R \end{aligned}$$

(Note that the identity function in A, id_A, is of course a relation and could equally well be called the identity relation in A.)

The equations corresponding to (2-10) do not hold for relations (nor for functions which are not one-to-one correspondences). However, we have for any *one-to-one* relation $R: A \rightarrow B$:

(2–12) $\quad R^{-1} \circ R \;\; \subseteq \;\; id_A$
$\qquad\quad R \circ R^{-1} \;\; \subseteq \;\; id_B$

We should note here that our previous remarks about ternary, quaternary, etc. relations can also be carried over to functions. A function may have as its domain a set of ordered n-tuples for any n, but each such n-tuple will be mapped into a unique value in the range. For example, there is a function mapping each pair of natural numbers into their sum.

Exercises

1. Let $A = \{b, c\}$ and $B = \{2, 3\}$.

   (a) Specify the following sets by listing their members.
   - (i) $A \times B$ (iv) $(A \cup B) \times B$
   - (ii) $B \times A$ (v) $(A \cap B) \times B$
   - (iii) $A \times A$ (vi) $(A - B) \times (B - A)$

   (b) Classify each statement as true or false.
   - (i) $(A \times B) \cup (B \times A) = \emptyset$
   - (ii) $(A \times A) \subseteq (A \times B)$
   - (iii) $\langle c, c \rangle \subseteq (A \times A)$
   - (iv) $\{\langle b, 3 \rangle, \langle 3, b \rangle\} \subseteq (A \times B) \cup (B \times A)$
   - (v) $\emptyset \subseteq A \times A$
   - (vi) $\{\langle b, 2 \rangle, \langle c, 3 \rangle\}$ is a relation from A to B
   - (vii) $\{\langle b, b \rangle\}$ is a relation in A

   (c) Consider the following relation from A to $(A \cup B)$:
   $$R = \{\langle b, b \rangle, \langle b, 2 \rangle, \langle c, 2 \rangle, \langle c, 3 \rangle\}$$

   - (i)   Specify the domain and range of R
   - (ii) Specify the complementary relation R' and the inverse R^{-1}
   - (iii) Is $(R')^{-1}$ (the inverse of the complement) equal to $(R^{-1})'$ (the complement of the inverse)?

2. Let $A = \{a, b, c\}$ and $B = \{1, 2\}$. How many distinct relations are there from A to B? How many of these are functions from A to B? How many of the functions are onto? one-to-one? Do any of the functions have inverses that are functions? Answer the same questions for all relations from B to A.

3. Let

$$R_1 = \{\langle 1,1 \rangle, \langle 2,1 \rangle, \langle 3,4 \rangle, \langle 2,2 \rangle, \langle 3,3 \rangle, \langle 4,4 \rangle, \langle 4,1 \rangle\}$$

$$R_2 = \{\langle 3,4 \rangle, \langle 1,2 \rangle, \langle 1,4 \rangle, \langle 2,3 \rangle, \langle 2,4 \rangle, \langle 1,3 \rangle\}$$

(both relations in A, where $A = \{1, 2, 3, 4\}$).

(a) Form the composites $R_2 \circ R_1$ and $R_1 \circ R_2$. Are they equal?

(b) Show that $R_1^{-1} \circ R_1 \neq id_A$ and that $R_2^{-1} \circ R_2 \not\subseteq id_A$.

4. For the functions F and G in Figure 2-3:

(a) show that $(G \circ F)^{-1} = F^{-1} \circ G^{-1}$.

(b) Show that the corresponding equation holds for relations R and S in Figure 2-6.

Chapter 3

Properties of Relations

3.1 Reflexivity, symmetry, transitivity, and connectedness

Certain properties of binary relations are so frequently encountered that it is useful to have names for them. The properties we shall consider are *reflexivity*, *symmetry*, *transitivity*, and *connectedness*. All these apply only to relations *in* a set, i.e., in $A \times A$ for example, not to relations from A to B, where $B \neq A$.

Reflexivity

Given a set A and a relation R in A, R is *reflexive* if and only if all the ordered pairs of the form $\langle x, x \rangle$ are in R for every x in A.

As an example, take the set $A = \{1, 2, 3\}$ and the relation $R_1 = \{\langle 1, 1 \rangle, \langle 2, 2 \rangle, \langle 3, 3 \rangle, \langle 3, 1 \rangle\}$ in A. R_1 is reflexive because it contains the ordered pairs $\langle 1, 1 \rangle, \langle 2, 2 \rangle$, and $\langle 3, 3 \rangle$. The relation $R_2 = \{\langle 1, 1 \rangle, \langle 2, 2 \rangle\}$ is non-reflexive since it lacks the ordered pair $\langle 3, 3 \rangle$ and thus fails to meet the definitional requirement that it contains the ordered pair $\langle x, x \rangle$ *for every* x *in* A. Another way to state the definition of reflexivity is to say that a relation R in A is reflexive if and only if id_A, the identity relation in A, is a subset of R. The relation 'has the same birthday as' in the set of human beings is reflexive.

A relation which fails to be reflexive is called nonreflexive, but if it contains *no* ordered pair $\langle x, x \rangle$ with identical first and second members, it is said to be *irreflexive*. $R_3 = \{\langle 1, 2 \rangle, \langle 3, 2 \rangle\}$ is an example of an irreflexive relation in A. Irreflexivity is a stronger condition than nonreflexivity since

39

every irreflexive relation is nonreflexive but not conversely. The relation 'is taller than' in the set of human beings is irreflexive (therefore also nonreflexive), while the relation 'is a financial supporter of' is nonreflexive (but not irreflexive, since some people are financially self-supporting). Note that a relation R in A is nonreflexive if and only if $id_A \not\subseteq R$; it is irreflexive if and only if $R \cap id_A = \emptyset$.

Symmetry

Given a set A and a binary relation R in A, R is *symmetric* if and only if for every ordered pair $\langle x, y \rangle$ in R, the pair $\langle y, x \rangle$ is also in R. It is important to note that this definition does not require every ordered pair of $A \times A$ to be in R. Rather for a relation R to be symmetric it must always be the case that *if* an ordered pair is in R, *then* the pair with the members reversed is also in R.

Here are some examples of symmetric relations in $\{1, 2, 3\}$:

(3–1) $\{\langle 1, 2 \rangle, \langle 2, 1 \rangle, \langle 3, 2 \rangle, \langle 2, 3 \rangle\}$
$\{\langle 1, 3 \rangle, \langle 3, 1 \rangle\}$
$\{\langle 2, 2 \rangle\}$

$\{\langle 2, 2 \rangle\}$ is a symmetric relation because for every ordered pair in it, i.e., $\langle 2, 2 \rangle$, it is true that the ordered pair with the first and second members reversed, i.e., $\langle 2, 2 \rangle$, is in the relation. Another example of a symmetric relation is 'is a cousin of' on the set of human beings. If for some $\langle x, y \rangle$ in R, the pair $\langle y, x \rangle$ is not in R then R is *nonsymmetric*. The relation 'is a sister of' on the set of human beings is nonsymmetric (since the second member may be male. It is, however, a symmetric relation defined on the set of human females).

The following relations in $\{1, 2, 3\}$ are nonsymmetric:

(3–2) $\{\langle 2, 3 \rangle, \langle 1, 2 \rangle\}$
$\{\langle 3, 3 \rangle, \langle 1, 3 \rangle\}$
$\{\langle 1, 2 \rangle, \langle 2, 1 \rangle, \langle 2, 2 \rangle, \langle 1, 1 \rangle, \langle 2, 3 \rangle\}$

If it is *never* the case that for any $\langle x, y \rangle$ in R, the pair $\langle y, x \rangle$ is in R, then the relation is called *asymmetric*. The relation 'is older than' is asymmetric on the set of human beings. Note that an asymmetric relation must be irreflexive (because nothing in the asymmetry definition requires x and y to be distinct). The following are examples of asymmetric relations in $\{1, 2, 3\}$:

(3-3) $\{\langle 2,3 \rangle, \langle 1,2 \rangle\}$
$\{\langle 1,3 \rangle, \langle 2,3 \rangle, \langle 1,2 \rangle\}$
$\{\langle 3,2 \rangle\}$

A relation is *anti-symmetric* if whenever both $\langle x, y \rangle$ and $\langle y, x \rangle$ are in R, then $x = y$. This definition says only that *if* both $\langle x, y \rangle$ and $\langle y, x \rangle$ are in R, then x and y are identical; it does not require $\langle x, x \rangle \in R$ for all $x \in A$. In other words, the relation need not be reflexive in order to be anti-symmetric.

The following relations in $\{1, 2, 3\}$ are anti-symmetric.

(3-4) $\{\langle 2,3 \rangle, \langle 1,1 \rangle\}$
$\{\langle 1,1 \rangle, \langle 2,2 \rangle\}$
$\{\langle 1,2 \rangle, \langle 2,3 \rangle\}$

Transitivity

A relation R is *transitive* if and only if for all ordered pairs $\langle x, y \rangle$ and $\langle y, z \rangle$ in R, the pair $\langle x, z \rangle$ is also in R.

Because there is no necessity for x, y, and z all to be distinct, the following relation meets the definition of transitivity,

(3-5) $\{\langle 2,2 \rangle\}$

where $x = y = z = 2$.

The relation given in (3-6) is not transitive,

(3-6) $\{\langle 2,3 \rangle, \langle 3,2 \rangle, \langle 2,2 \rangle\}$

because $\langle 3,2 \rangle$ and $\langle 2,3 \rangle$ are members, but $\langle 3,3 \rangle$ is not.

Here are some more examples of transitive relations:

(3-7) $\{\langle 1,2 \rangle, \langle 2,3 \rangle, \langle 1,3 \rangle\}$
$\{\langle 1,2 \rangle, \langle 2,1 \rangle, \langle 1,1 \rangle, \langle 2,2 \rangle\}$
$\{\langle 1,2 \rangle, \langle 2,3 \rangle, \langle 1,3 \rangle, \langle 3,2 \rangle, \langle 2,1 \rangle, \langle 3,1 \rangle, \langle 1,1 \rangle, \langle 2,2 \rangle, \langle 3,3 \rangle\}$

The relation 'is an ancestor of' is transitive in the set of human beings. If a relation fails to meet the definition of transitivity, it is *nontransitive*. If for no pairs $\langle x, y \rangle$ and $\langle y, z \rangle$ in R, the ordered pair $\langle x, z \rangle$ is in R, then the relation is *intransitive*. For example, the relation 'is the mother of' in the set of human beings is intransitive.

Relation (3-6) is nontransitive, as are the following two:

(3–8) $\{\langle 1,2 \rangle, \langle 2,3 \rangle\}$
       $\{\langle 1,2 \rangle, \langle 2,3 \rangle, \langle 1,3 \rangle, \langle 3,1 \rangle\}$

The first of these relations is also intransitive, as are the following relations:

(3–9) $\{\langle 3,1 \rangle, \langle 1,2 \rangle, \langle 2,3 \rangle\}$
       $\{\langle 3,2 \rangle, \langle 1,3 \rangle\}$

Connectedness

A relation R in A is *connected* (or *connex*) if and only if for every two *distinct* elements x and y in A, $\langle x,y \rangle \in R$ or $\langle y,x \rangle \in R$ (or both).

Note that the definition of connectedness refers, as does the definition of reflexivity, to all the members of the set A. Further, the pairs $\langle x,y \rangle$ and $\langle y,x \rangle$ mentioned in the definition are explicitly specified as containing nonidentical first and second members. Pairs of the form $\langle x,x \rangle$ are not prohibited in a connected relation, but they are irrelevant in determining connectedness.

The following relations in $\{1,2,3\}$ are connected:

(3–10) $\{\langle 1,2 \rangle, \langle 3,1 \rangle, \langle 3,2 \rangle\}$
        $\{\langle 1,1 \rangle, \langle 2,3 \rangle, \langle 1,2 \rangle, \langle 3,1 \rangle, \langle 2,2 \rangle\}$

The following relations in $\{1,2,3\}$, which fail the definition, are nonconnected.

(3–11) $\{\langle 1,2 \rangle, \langle 2,3 \rangle\}$
        $\{\langle 1,3 \rangle, \langle 3,1 \rangle, \langle 2,2 \rangle, \langle 3,2 \rangle\}$

It may be useful at this point to give some examples of relations specified by predicates and to consider their properties of reflexivity, symmetry, transitivity, and connectedness.

(3–12) *Example*: R_f is the relation 'is father of' in the set H of all human beings. R_f is irreflexive (no one is his own father); asymmetric (if x is y's father, then it is never true that y is x's father); intransitive (if x is y's father and y is z's father, then x is z's grandfather but not z's father); and nonconnected (there are distinct individuals x and y in H such that neither 'x is the father of y' nor 'y is the father of x' is true).

(3-13) *Example*: R is the relation 'greater than' defined in the set $Z = \{1,2,3,4,\ldots\}$ of all the positive integers. Z contains an infinite number of members and so does R, but we are able to determine the relevant properties of R from our knowledge of the properties of numbers in general. R is irreflexive (no number is greater than itself); asymmetric (if $x > y$, then $y \not> x$; transitive (if $x > y$ and $y > z$, then $x > z$), and connected (for every distinct pair of integers x and y, either $x > y$ or $y > x$.

(3-14) *Example*: R_a is the relation defined by 'x is the same age as y,' in the set H of all living human beings. R_a is reflexive (everyone is the same age as himself or herself); symmetric (if x is the same age as y, then y is the same age as x); transitive (if x and y are the same age and so are y and z, then x is the same age as z); and nonconnected (there are distinct individuals in H who are not of the same age).

3.2   Diagrams of relations

It may be helpful in assimilating the notions of reflexivity, symmetry and transitivity to represent them in relational diagrams. The members of the relevant set are represented by labeled points (the particular spatial arrangement of them is irrelevant). If x is related to y, i.e. $\langle x, y \rangle \in R$, an arrow connects the corresponding points. For example,

Figure 3-1: Relational diagram.

Figure 3-1 represents the relation

$$R = \{\langle 1, 2 \rangle, \langle 2, 1 \rangle, \langle 2, 2 \rangle, \langle 1, 1 \rangle, \langle 2, 3 \rangle, \langle 3, 3 \rangle\}$$

It is apparent from the diagram that the relation is reflexive, since every point bears a loop. The relation is nonsymmetric since 3 is not related to 2 whereas 2 is related to 3. It cannot be called asymmetric or antisymmetric, however, since 1 is related to 2 and 2 is related to 1. It is nontransitive since 1 is related to 2 and 2 is related to 3, but there is no direct arrow from 1 to 3. The relation cannot be intransitive because of the presence of pairs such as $\langle\, 1,1 \,\rangle$.

If a relation is connected, every pair of distinct points in its diagram will be directly joined by an arrow. We see that R is no connected since there is not direct connection between 1 and 3 in Figure 3-1.

3.3   Properties of inverses and complements

Given that a relation R has certain properties of reflexivity, symmetry, transitivity or connectedness, one can often make general statements about the question whether these properties are preserved when the inverse R^{-1} or complement R' of that relation is formed.

For example, take a reflexive relation R in A. By the definition of reflexive relations, for every $x \in A$, $\langle\, x,x \,\rangle \in R$. Since R^{-1} has all the ordered pairs of R, but with the first and second members reversed, then every pair $\langle\, x,x \,\rangle$ is also in R^{-1}. So the inverse of R is reflexive also. The complement R' contains all ordered pairs in $A \times A$ that are not in R. Since R contains every pair of the form $\langle\, x,x \,\rangle$ for any $x \in A$, R' contains none of them. The complement relation is therefore irreflexive.

As another example, take a symmetric relation R in A. Does its complement have this property? Let's assume that the complement R' is not symmetric, and see what we can derive from that assumption. If R' is not symmetric, then there is some $\langle\, x,y \,\rangle \in R'$ such that $\langle\, y,x \,\rangle \notin R'$, by the definition of a nonsymmetric relation. Since $\langle\, y,x \,\rangle \notin R'$, $\langle\, y,x \,\rangle$ must be in the complement of R', which is R itself. Because R is symmetric, $\langle\, x,y \,\rangle$ must also be in R. But one and the same ordered pair $\langle\, x,y \,\rangle$ cannot be both in R *and* in its complement R', so the assumption that the complement R' is not symmetric leads to an absurd conclusion. That means that the assumption cannot be true and the complement R' must be symmetric after all. If R is a symmetric relation in A, then the complement R' is symmetric and vice versa (the latter follows from essentially the same reasoning with R' substituted for R). This mode of reasoning is an instance of what is called a *reductio ad absurdum* proof in logic. It is characterized by making an assumption which leads to a necessarily false conclusion; you may then conclude that the negation of that assumption is true. In Chapter 6 we will introduce rules of inference which will allow such arguments to be made completely precise.

For sake of easy reference the table in Figure 3-2 presents a summary of properties of relations and those of their inverses and complements. These can all be proved on the basis of the definitions of the concepts and the laws of set theory. Since we have not yet introduced a formal notion of proof, we will not offer proofs here, but it is a good exercise to convince yourself of the facts by trying out a few examples, reasoning informally along the lines illustrated above.

R (not $\emptyset$)	R^{-1}	R'
reflexive	reflexive	irreflexive
irreflexive	irreflexive	reflexive
symmetric	symmetric $(R^{-1} = R)$	symmetric
asymmetric	asymmetric	non-symmetric
antisymmetric	antisymmetric	depends on R
transitive	transitive	depends on R
intransitive	intransitive	depends on R
connected	connected	depends on R

Figure 3–2: Preservation of properties of a
relation in its inverse and its complement.

3.4   Equivalence relations and partitions

An especially important class of relations are the *equivalence relations*. They are relations which are reflexive, symmetric and transitive. Equality is the most familiar example of an equivalence relation. Other examples are 'has the same hair color as', and 'is the same age as'. The use of equivalence relations on a domain serves primarily to structure a domain into subsets whose members are regarded as equivalent with respect to that relation.

For every equivalence relation there is a natural way to divide the set on which it is defined into mutually exclusive (disjoint) subsets which are called *equivalence classes*. We write $[\![x]\!]$ for the set of all y such that $\langle x, y \rangle \in R$.

Thus, when R is an equivalence relation, $[\![x]\!]$ is the equivalence class which contains x. The relation 'is the same age as' divides the set of people into age groups, i.e., sets of people of the same age. Every pair of distinct equivalence classes is disjoint, because each person, having only one age, belongs to exactly one equivalence class. This is so even when somebody is 120 years old, and is the only person of that age, consequently occupying an equivalence class all by himself. By dividing a set into mutually exclusive and collectively exhaustive nonempty subsets we effect what is called a *partitioning* of that set.

Given a non-empty set A, a *partition* of A is a collection of non-empty subsets of A such that (1) for any two distinct subsets X and Y, $X \cap Y = \emptyset$ and (2) the union of all the subsets in the collection equals A. The notion of a partition is not defined for an empty set. The subsets that are members of a partition are called *cells* of that partition.

For example, let $A = \{a, b, c, d, e\}$. Then, $P = \{\{a, c\}, \{b, e\}, \{d\}\}$ is a partition of A because every pair of cells is disjoint: $\{a, c\} \cap \{b, e\} = \emptyset$, $\{b, e\} \cap \{d\} = \emptyset$, and $\{a, c\} \cap \{d\} = \emptyset$; and the union of all the cells equals A: $\bigcup \{\{a, c\}, \{b, e\}, \{d\}\} = A$.

The following three sets are also partitions of A:

(3–15) $P_1 = \{\{a, c, d\}, \{b, e\}\}$
$P_2 = \{\{a\}, \{b\}, \{c\}, \{d\}, \{e\}\}$
$P_3 = \{\{a, b, c, d, e\}\}$

P_3 is the trivial partition of A into only one set. Note however that the definition of a partition is satisfied.

The following two sets are not partitions of A:

(3–16) $C = \{\{a, b, c\}, \{b, d\}, \{e\}\}$
$D = \{\{a\}, \{b, e\}, \{c\}\}$

C fails the definition because $\{a, b, c\} \cap \{b, d\} \neq \emptyset$ and D because $\bigcup \{\{a\}, \{b, e\}, \{c\}\} \neq A$

There is a close correspondence between partitions and equivalence relations. Given a partition of set A, the relation $R = \{\langle x, y \rangle \mid x$ and y are in the same cell of the partition$\}$ is an equivalence relation. Conversely, given a reflexive, symmetric, and transitive relation R in A, there exists a partition of A in which x and y are in the same cell if and only if x and y are related by

R. The equivalence classes specified by R are just the cells of the partition. An equivalence relation in A is sometimes said to *induce a partition of A*.

As an example, consider the set $A = \{1,2,3,4,5\}$ and the equivalence relation

$$(3\text{-}17) \quad R = \{\langle 1,1 \rangle, \langle 1,3 \rangle, \langle 3,1 \rangle, \langle 3,3 \rangle, \langle 2,2 \rangle, \langle 2,4 \rangle, \langle 4,2 \rangle, \langle 4,5 \rangle,$$
$$\langle 4,4 \rangle, \langle 5,2 \rangle, \langle 5,4 \rangle, \langle 5,5 \rangle, \langle 2,5 \rangle\}$$

which the reader can verify to be reflexive, symmetric, and transitive. In this relation 1 and 3 are related among themselves in all possible ways, as are 2, 4, and 5, but no members of the first group are related to any member of the second group. Therefore, R defines the equivalence classes $\{1,3\}$ and $\{2,4,5\}$, and the corresponding partition induced on A is

$$(3\text{-}18) \quad P_R = \{\{1,3\},\{2,4,5\}\}$$

Given a partition such as

$$(3\text{-}19) \quad Q = \{\{1,2\},\{3,5\},\{4\}\}$$

the relation R_Q consisting of all ordered pairs $\langle x,y \rangle$ such that x and y are in the same cell of the partition is as follows:

$$(3\text{-}20) \quad R_Q = \{\langle 1,1 \rangle, \langle 1,2 \rangle, \langle 2,1 \rangle, \langle 2,2 \rangle, \langle 3,3 \rangle, \langle 3,5 \rangle, \langle 5,3 \rangle, \langle 5,5 \rangle, \langle 4,4 \rangle\}$$

R_Q is seen to be reflexive, symmetric, and transitive, and it is thus an equivalence relation.

Another example is the equivalence relation 'is on the same continent as' on the set $A = \{$France, Chile, Nigeria, Ecuador, Luxembourg, Zambia, Ghana, San Marino, Uruguay, Kenya, Hungary$\}$. It partitions A into three equivalence classes: (1) $A_1 = \{$France, Luxembourg, San Marino, Hungary$\}$, (2) $A_2 = \{$Chile, Ecuador, Uruguay$\}$ and (3) $A_3 = \{$Nigeria, Zambia, Ghana, Kenya$\}$.

3.5 Orderings

An *order* is a binary relation which is transitive and in addition either (i) reflexive and antisymmetric or else (ii) irreflexive and asymmetric. The former are *weak* orders; the latter are *strict* (or *strong*).

To illustrate, let $A = \{a, b, c, d\}$. The following are all weak orders in A:

(3-21) $R_1 = \{\langle a, b\rangle, \langle a, c\rangle, \langle a, d\rangle, \langle b, c\rangle, \langle a, a\rangle, \langle b, b\rangle, \langle c, c\rangle, \langle d, d\rangle\}$
            $R_2 = \{\langle b, a\rangle, \langle b, b\rangle, \langle a, a\rangle, \langle c, c\rangle, \langle d, d\rangle, \langle c, b\rangle, \langle c, a\rangle\}$
            $R_3 = \{\langle d, c\rangle, \langle d, b\rangle, \langle d, a\rangle, \langle c, b\rangle, \langle c, a\rangle, \langle a, a\rangle, \langle b, b\rangle, \langle c, c\rangle,$
                 $\langle d, d\rangle, \langle b, a\rangle\}$

These are represented in Figure 3-3 as relational diagrams, from which it can be verified that each is indeed reflexive, antisymmetric, and transitive.

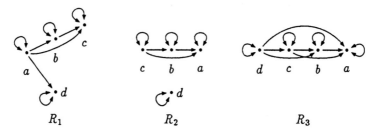

Figure 3–3:
Diagrams of the weak orders in (3-21).

To these weak orders there correspond the strict orders S_1, S_2 and S_3, respectively:

(3-22) $S_1 = \{\langle a, b\rangle, \langle a, c\rangle, \langle a, d\rangle, \langle b, c\rangle\}$
            $S_2 = \{\langle b, a\rangle, \langle c, b\rangle, \langle c, a\rangle\}$
            $S_3 = \{\langle d, c\rangle, \langle d, b\rangle, \langle d, a\rangle, \langle c, b\rangle, \langle c, a\rangle, \langle b, a\rangle\}$

These can be gotten from the weak orders by removing all the ordered pairs of the form $\langle x, x\rangle$. Conversely, one can make a strict order into a weak order by adding the pairs of the form $\langle x, x\rangle$ for every x in A.

As another example of an order, consider any collection of sets C and a relation R in C defined by $R = \{\langle X, Y\rangle \mid X \subseteq Y\}$ We have already noted in effect (Chapter 1, section 4) that the subset relation is transitive and reflexive. It is also antisymmetric, since for any sets X and Y, if $X \subseteq Y$ and $Y \subseteq X$, then $X = Y$ (this will be proved in Chapter 7). The corresponding strict order is the 'proper subset of' relation in C.

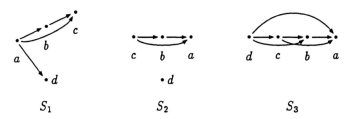

S_1 S_2 S_3

Figure 3–4:
Diagrams of the strict orders in (3-22).

Further, we saw in Example (3-13) that the relation R 'greater than' in the set of positive integers is irreflexive, asymmetric and transitive. It is therefore a strict order. (*Problem*: What relation defines the corresponding weak order?)

Some terminology: if R is an order, either weak or strict, and $\langle x, y \rangle \in R$, we say that x *precedes* y, x *is a predecessor of* y, y *succeeds* (or *follows*) x, or y *is a successor of* x, these being equivalent locutions. If x precedes y and $x \neq y$, then we say that x *immediately precedes* y or x is an *immediate predecessor* of y, etc., just in case there is no element z distinct from both x and y such that x precedes z and z precedes y. In other words, there is no other element between x and y in the order. Note that no element can be said to immediately precede itself since x and y in the definition must be distinct.

In R_1 and S_1 in (3-21) and (3-22), b is between a and c; therefore, although a precedes c, a is not an immediate predecessor of c. In R_2 and S_2, c is an immediate predecessor of b, and b is an immediate predecessor of a.

In diagramming orders it is usually simpler and more perspicuous to connect pairs of elements by arrows only if one is an immediate predecessor of the other. The remaining connection can be inferred from the fact that the relation is transitive. In order to distinguish weak from strict orders, however, it is necessary to include the 'reflexive' loops in weak orders. Diagrammed in this way, the orders in (3-21) would appear as in Figure 3-5. The diagrams of the corresponding strict orders would be identical except for the absence of the loops on each element.

There is also a useful set of terms for elements which stand at the ex-

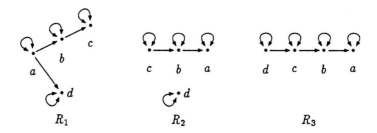

Figure 3-5: Immediate predecessor diagrams
of the orders in (3-21).

tremes of an order. Given an order R in a set A,

1. an element x in A is *minimal* if and only if there is no other element
   in A which precedes x (examples: a in R_1 and S_1; c and d in R_2 and
   S_2; d in R_3 and S_3)

2. an element x in A is *least* if and only if x precedes every other element
   in A (examples: a in R_1 and S_1; d in R_3 and S_3)

3. an element x in A is *maximal* if and only if there is no other element
   in A which follows x (examples: c and d in R_1 and S_1; a and d in R_2
   and S_2; a in R_3 and S_3)

4. an element x in A is *greatest* if and only if x follows every other element
   in A (examples: a in R_3 and S_3).

Note that a in R_1 and S_1 is both a minimal and a least element, while
c and d in these same orders are both maximal but not greatest (c does
not follow d, for example). Element d in R_2 and S_2 is both minimal and
maximal but neither greatest nor least. The order defined by R in Example
(3-13) has 1 as a maximal and greatest element (it follows all other elements
and has no successors) but there is no minimal or least element in the order.
Observe here that the form 'greatest' as used technically about orders need
not coincide with the notions 'greater than ' or 'greatest' in the realm of
numbers.

A least element, if there is one in an order, is unique (if there were
two, each would have to precede the other, and this would violate either

asymmetry or antisymmetry), and similarly for a greatest element. There may be more than one minimal element, however (e.g., c and d in R_2 and S_2 above), and more than one maximal element. An order might have none of these; the relation 'greater than' in the set of all positive and negative integers and zero, $\{0, 1, -1, 2, -1, \ldots\}$ has no maximal, minimal, greatest or least elements.

If an order, strict or weak, is also connected, then it is said to be a *total* or *linear* order. Examples are R_3 and S_3 above and the relation R of Example (3-13). Their immediate predecessor diagrams show the elements arranged in a single chain. Order R_1 is not total since d and c are not related, for example. Often orders in general are called *partial orders* or *partially ordered sets*. The terminology is unfortunate, since it then happens that some partial orders are total, but it is well established nonetheless, and we will sometimes use it in the remainder of this book.

Finally, we mention some other frequently encountered notions pertaining to orders. A set A is said to be *well-ordered* by a relation R if R is a total order and, further, every subset of A has a least element in the ordering relation. The set of natural numbers $\mathbf{N} = \{0, 1, 2, 3, \ldots\}$ is well-ordered by the 'is less than' relation (it is a total order, and every subset of $\mathbf{N}$ will have a least element when ordered by this relation). The set of integers $\mathbf{Z} = \{0, 1, -1, 2, -2, \ldots\}$, on the other hand, is not well-ordered by that relation, since the negative integers get smaller 'ad infinitum'. Note that every finite linearly ordered set must be well-ordered.

A relation R in A is *dense* if for every $\langle x, y \rangle \in R$, $x \neq y$, there exists a member $z \in A$, $x \neq z$ and $y \neq z$, such that $\langle x, z \rangle \in R$ and $\langle z, y \rangle \in R$. Density is an important property of the real numbers which we can think of as all the points lying on a horizontal line of infinite extent. The relation 'is greater than' is not dense on the natural numbers, but it is dense on the real numbers.

Exercises

1. (a) Determine the properties of the following relations on the set of all people. In each case, make the strongest possible statement, e.g. call a relation irreflexive whenever possible rather than non-reflexive.

   (i) is a child of
   (ii) is a brother of

(iii) is a descendant of

(iv) is an uncle of (assuming that one may marry one's aunt or uncle)

(b) Which of your answers would be changed if these relations were defined in the set of all male human beings?

2. Investigate the properties of each of the following relations. If any one is an equivalence relation, indicate the partition it induces on the appropriate set. (If you do not know the concepts, try to find some reasonable assumptions, state them explicitly, and do the exercise based on those).

(a) $M = \{\langle x,y \rangle \mid x$ and y are a minimal pair of utterances of English$\}$

(b) $C = \{\langle x,y \rangle \mid x$ and y are phones of English in complementary distribution$\}$

(c) $F = \{\langle x,y \rangle \mid x$ and y are phones of English in free variation$\}$

(d) $A = \{\langle x,y \rangle \mid x$ and y are allophones of the same English phoneme$\}$

(e) Q is the relation defined by 'X is a set having the same number of members as Y' in some appropriate collection of sets.

3. Let $A = \{1,2,3,4\}$.

(a) Determine the properties of each of the following relations, its inverse and its complement. If any of the relations happens to be an equivalence relation, show the partition that is induced on A.

$$R_1 = \{\langle 1,1 \rangle, \langle 2,1 \rangle, \langle 3,4 \rangle, \langle 2,2 \rangle, \langle 3,3 \rangle, \langle 4,4 \rangle, \langle 4,1 \rangle\}$$
$$R_2 = \{\langle 3,4 \rangle, \langle 1,2 \rangle, \langle 1,4 \rangle, \langle 2,3 \rangle, \langle 2,4 \rangle, \langle 1,3 \rangle\}$$
$$R_3 = \{\langle 2,4 \rangle, \langle 3,1 \rangle, \langle 3,4 \rangle, \langle 2,2 \rangle, \langle 1,3 \rangle, \langle 4,3 \rangle, \langle 4,2 \rangle\}$$
$$R_4 = \{\langle 1,1 \rangle, \langle 2,4 \rangle, \langle 1,3 \rangle, \langle 2,2 \rangle, \langle 3,1 \rangle, \langle 4,4 \rangle, \langle 3,3 \rangle, \langle 4,2 \rangle\}$$

(b) Give the equivalence relation that induces the following partition on $A: P = \{\{1\}, \{2,3\}, \{4\}\}$.

(c) How many distinct partitions of A are possible?

4. What is wrong with the following reasoning that reflexivity is a consequence of symmetry and transitivity? (Birkhof & MacLane (1965)). If $\langle x,y \rangle \in R$, then $\langle y,x \rangle \in R$, since we assume R is symmetric. If both $\langle x,y \rangle$ and $\langle y,x \rangle$ are in R, then $\langle x,x \rangle$ must be in R by transitivity.

5. Let $A = \{1, 2, 3, 5, 6, 10, 15, 30\}$ and let R be a relation in A defined as follows:

$$R = \{\langle x, y \rangle \mid x \text{ divides } y \text{ without remainder}\}$$

   (a) List the members of R, and show that it is a weak partial order but not a total order.
   (b) Construct an immediate predecessor diagram for this order and identify any maximal, minimal, greatest, and least elements.
   (c) Do the same for the set $\wp(B)$, where $B = \{a, b, c\}$, and the relation 'is a subset of'.

Chapter 4

Infinities

In the preceding chapters we have occasionally dealt with sets, such as the set of positive integers, which we intuitively regard as infinite. We now want to examine the concept of infinity in more detail.

Some initially plausible approaches to the problem of characterizing infinity are not satisfactory. A definition employing the terms 'never-ending' or 'impossible, in principle, to list exhaustively,' for example, would be defective, since these expressions are themselves no clearer than the term 'infinite' that is to be explicated. What is needed is a definition that makes use of set-theoretic concepts already at hand and that accords with our intuitions about what sets should be regarded as infinite. Since an infinite set is in some sense "larger" than any finite set, we start by defining what it means for two sets to be of equal or unequal size.

4.1 Equivalent sets and cardinality

We say that two sets A and B have the same number of members, or are *equivalent*, if and only if there exists a one-to-one correspondence between them. Since a one-to-one correspondence is a function that is one-to-one and onto, every member of A is paired with exactly one member of B, and vice versa. In such a situation it would certainly be reasonable to say that the sets are of equal size. We denote the equivalence of A and B by $A \sim B$.

The terms *equal* and *equivalent* must not be confused. Equal sets have *the same members* while equivalent sets have *the same number of members*. Equal sets, are therefore, necessarily equivalent but the converse is, in general, not true. Further, nothing is said in the definition of equivalence about the exact nature of the one-to-one correspondence between the sets – only that one exists.

For the case of finite sets this definition of equivalence leads to the expected conclusion. A set with just four distinct members, for example, can be put into one-to-one correspondence with any other set having exactly four distinct members, but not with any set with more or fewer members. The relation of equivalence of sets is, as the name implies, an equivalence relation with the property that all of the sets with the same number of members are put into the same equivalence class. To each equivalence class we can assign a number, called the *cardinal number*, denoting the size of each set in the class. For finite sets, the cardinal numbers correspond exactly to the natural numbers. Thus a set A with just four members is said to have a *cardinality* of 4, written $|A| = 4$, as we indicated in Chapter 1.

In the case of infinite sets something rather surprising happens. Consider, for example, the set of positive integers P, the set E of positive even integers (without zero), and the function F from P to E that maps every integer x into $2x$ as indicated in Figure 4-1.

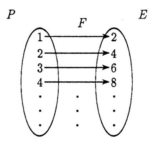

Figure 4–1:   A one-to-one mapping from the
positive integers to the positive even integers.

Every positive integer can be multiplied by 2 to give as a unique value a positive even integer. This shows that F is a function whose range is in E. The function F is one-to-one because for any integers x and y, if $2x = 2y$, then $x = y$. Further F is onto, since every member of E can be represented as $2x$, for some positive integer x. Thus, F is a one-to-one correspondence, and P and E, being equivalent sets, have the same number of members. This result is surprising in view of the fact that E is a proper subset of P (3, for example, is in P but not in E). We are accustomed to thinking of a set as being "larger" than any of its proper subsets, but if we adopt the notion of equivalence as the criterion for equal size of sets, then we are inescapably led to conclude that sometimes a set and a proper subset of that set may have the same number of members. If, on the other hand, we were to say that a set is always "larger" than a proper subset of itself, we would have to accept the puzzling consequence that sets of different size can be put into one-to-one correspondence. Either way the situation seems paradoxical. When we examine the sets that exhibit this unusual behavior, however, we find that they are just the ones that we would intuitively call infinite. Accordingly, we define an infinite set in the following way:

DEFINITION 4.1 *A set is* infinite *iff it is equivalent to a proper subset of itself.*   ∎

(4-1) *Example:* The set of natural numbers $N = \{0, 1, 2, 3, \ldots\}$ is infinite. Consider the set $P = \{1, 2, 3, 4, \ldots\}$, which is a proper subset of N and establish the mapping indicated in Figure 4-2 in which each natural number n is carried into $n + 1$. To each member of N there corresponds a unique member of P, and vice versa. Therefore, G is a one-to-one correspondence, and $P \sim N$.

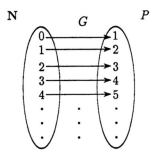

Figure 4–2: Mapping showing that the set
N is equivalent to a proper subset of itself.

(4–2) *Example:* The set of all (finite) strings A^* on the alphabet
       $\{a, b\}$ is infinite. Take as a proper subset of A^* the set $B =$
       $\{b, ba, bb, baa, bab, bba, \ldots\}$ i.e., all strings in A^* beginning with b.
       The mapping h shown in Figure 4-3 is a one-to-one correspondence
       because for every string x in A^* there is a unique string bx in B,
       and vice versa (e is the empty string of zero length).

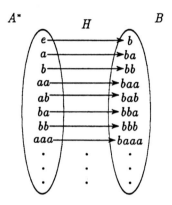

Figure 4–3:   A one-to-one mapping of
$\{a, b\}^*$ onto a proper subset of itself.

It should be easy to see that no finite set can be equivalent to one of
its proper subsets (take, for example, the set $\{a, b, c\}$ and any of its proper
subsets). One point about the definition of *infinite sets* sometimes causes
confusion: Only the *existence* of at least one equivalent proper subset is
required. The definition does not say that an infinite set is equivalent to
every proper subset of itself, a condition that in fact could never be met.
For example, N is not equivalent to its proper subset $\{0, 3, 18\}$.

4.2   Denumerability of sets

We have said that we can associate with each finite set a natural number
that represents its cardinality, and that sets with the same cardinality form
an equivalence class. Equivalent infinite sets can also be grouped into equivalence classes, all members of which have the same cardinality, but there is

no positive integer that can be associated uniquely with such an equivalence class as its cardinal number. This follows from the fact that every integer is the cardinal number of a class of finite sets, and no infinite set can be equivalent to a finite set, since no one-to-one correspondence between them is possible. Nonetheless, it is convenient to have symbols denoting the cardinality of infinite sets; the one conventionally adopted as the cardinal number of the set of natural numbers (and all sets equivalent to it) is $\aleph_0$ (aleph null or aleph zero). It must be emphasized as we have said, that $\aleph_0$ is not a natural number, i.e., not a member of the set $N = \{0, 1, 2, 3, \ldots\}$. Each natural number has a corresponding cardinal number, but there are cardinal numbers, e.g. $\aleph_0$ that correspond to no natural number. A cardinal number can be regarded as an answer to a question about the number of members in a set. If we ask 'How many natural numbers are there?' or 'How many positive integers are there?', the answer is the cardinal number $\aleph_0$.

By definition, a set with cardinality $\aleph_0$, i.e., one that is equivalent to the set of natural numbers, is called *denumerable* or *denumerably infinite* or *countably infinite*. A set that is either finite or denumerably infinite is called *countable*. We have already seen that the set of positive even integers (E in Figure 4-1) is denumerable. Here are some other examples:

(4–3) *Example:* The set of integers, including zero, $Z = \{0, +1, -1, +2, -2, +3, -3, \ldots\}$, is denumerably infinite. One possible one-to-one correspondence with N is

$$Z = \{0, \quad +1, \quad -1, \quad +2, \quad -2, \quad +3, \quad -3, \quad \ldots\}$$
$$F \downarrow \quad \downarrow \quad \downarrow \quad \downarrow \quad \downarrow \quad \downarrow \quad \downarrow$$
$$N = \{0, \quad 1, \quad 2, \quad 3, \quad 4, \quad 5, \quad 6, \quad \ldots\}$$

The function $F: Z \to N$ is defined by

$$F(x) = \begin{cases} 0 & \text{when } x = 0 \\ 2x - 1 & \text{when } x \text{ is positive} \\ -2x & \text{when } x \text{ is negative} \end{cases}$$

That F is indeed a one-to-one correspondence can be seen by noting that positive numbers in Z correspond to odd numbers in N, and negative numbers in Z correspond to even numbers in N (with 0 corresponding to 0).

(4-4) *Example:* The set of reciprocals of the natural numbers without
       zero $S = \{\frac{1}{1}, \frac{1}{2}, \frac{1}{3}, \frac{1}{4}, \frac{1}{5}, \frac{1}{6}, \ldots\}$ is denumerably infinite, as shown by
       the following one-to-one correspondence with **N**:

$$S = \{\frac{1}{1}, \quad \frac{1}{2}, \quad \frac{1}{3}, \quad \frac{1}{4}, \quad \frac{1}{5}, \quad \frac{1}{6}, \quad \ldots\}$$

$$G \downarrow \quad \downarrow \quad \downarrow \quad \downarrow \quad \downarrow \quad \downarrow \qquad\qquad G(x) = \frac{1}{x} - 1$$

$$N = \{0, \quad 1, \quad 2, \quad 3, \quad 4, \quad 5, \quad \ldots\}$$

(4-5) *Example:* The set of odd positive integers $F = \{1, 3, 5, 7, 9, \ldots\}$ is
       denumerably infinite. One possible one-to-one correspondence with
       N is

$$F = \{1, \quad 3, \quad 5, \quad 7, \quad 9, \quad \ldots\}$$

$$H \downarrow \quad \downarrow \quad \downarrow \quad \downarrow \quad \downarrow \qquad\qquad H(x) = \frac{x-1}{2}$$

$$N = \{0, \quad 1, \quad 2, \quad 3, \quad 4, \quad \ldots\}$$

We have seen that the set of positive integers P, the set of even positive
integers E, and the set of odd integers F all have the same cardinality. Since
$P = E \cup F$ one might have supposed that P would have more members than
either E or F, but this is not the case. Thus, the union of two infinite sets
is not necessarily a set with greater cardinality.

Are there sets larger than the set of positive integers? One that might
intuitively seem so is the set of ordered pairs in the Cartesian product $N \times N$.
When the pairs are listed in the order indicated by the arrow in Figure 4-
4, however, we find that the following one-to-one correspondence between
$N \times N$ and N can be established, although in this case it is somewhat more
difficult to prove that the correspondence is actually one-to-one.

One would also tend to think that there are more rational numbers than
natural numbers, since there are an infinite number of rational numbers
between any two natural numbers (recall that a rational number is one which
can be represented as the ratio of two integers x/y where $y \neq 0$). However,
a one-to-one correspondence can be established, proving that the sets are
actually of the same cardinality.

To set up a correspondence, we write down the positive rational numbers
in an array of the following form:

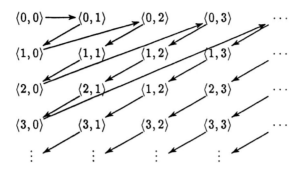

Figure 4–4: An enumeration of the members
of N × N.

$$\mathbf{N} \times \mathbf{N} = \{\langle 0,0\rangle, \langle 0,1\rangle, \langle 1,0\rangle, \langle 0,2\rangle, \langle 1,1\rangle, \langle 2,0\rangle, \langle 0,3\rangle, \langle 1,2\rangle, \langle 2,1\rangle, \ldots\}$$

$$F \qquad \downarrow \quad \downarrow \quad \downarrow \quad \downarrow \quad \downarrow \quad \downarrow \quad \downarrow \quad \downarrow \quad \downarrow$$

$$\mathbf{N} = \{\ \ 0, \quad 1, \quad 2, \quad 3, \quad 4, \quad 5, \quad 6, \quad 7, \quad 8, \ \ldots\}$$

Figure 4–5: A one-to-one correspondence
between N × N and N.

$1/1, 2/1, 3/1, 4/1, 5/1, 6/1, \ldots$

$1/2, 2/2, 3/2, 4/2, 5/2, \ldots$

$1/3, 2/3, 3/3, 4/3, \ldots$

$1/4, 2/4, 3/4, \ldots$

$1/5, 2/5, \ldots$

$1/6, \ldots$

$\ldots$

We first set up a correspondence between the elements of this array and
the positive integers as follows: starting in the upper left-hand corner, count
down the successive diagonals from the top row to the leftmost column. The
first few terms of this correspondence are: 1/1 to 1, 2/1 to 2, 1/2 to 3, 3/1 to

4, 2/2 to 5, 1/3 to 6, 4/1 to 7, ..., etc. This is similar to the enumeration we gave in Figure 4-4. Next we pair the negative rationals with negative integers and 0 with 0 to give a complete correspondence between the integers and the rationals. We then make use of the established correpondence between the natural numbers and the integers to obtain a correspondence between the natural numbers and the rationals. (The rational numbers will each have been written down more than once by this procedure; e.g., 1/2 will also appear as 2/4, 3/6, etc. But having shown a one-to-one correspondence between this larger set and the natural numbers, it is easy enough to go through the list striking out each occurrence of a rational number which has already appeared in another form, moving the succeeding terms higher up in the list to fill in the gaps.) Putting the members of a set in a one-to-one correspondence with the natural numbers by means of some well-defined procedure such as this one is sometimes called *effectively listing* the members of that set.

4.3   Nondenumerable sets

Not only is there a procedure for effectively listing the ordered pairs of integers, one can also effectively list the ordered triples, quadruples, etc., *i.e.*, the set of n-tuples for any given n. (*Problem:* Give a systematic method for listing the ordered triples of integers as a linear sequence.) Thus, a set with cardinal number greater than $\aleph_0$ will not be found by taking successive Cartesian products of **N**. At one time it was suppposed that there were no sets with cardinality greater than $\aleph_0$, but Georg Cantor (1845-1918), the mathematician who developed a large part of the theory of sets, proved that for any set A, the power set of A always has greater cardinality than A. Thus, the power set of **N** will have cardinality greater than **N**.

THEOREM 4.1 (*Cantor*): *For any set A, $|A| < |\wp(A)|$*   ∎

Proof: There is a function from $\wp(A)$ to A that maps every set containing just one element into that element in A, and maps all the other sets into some fixed element of A. This function is onto since every member of A has at least one correspondent in $\wp(A)$. Thus $|A| < |\wp(A)|$ or $|A| = |\wp(A)|$, *i.e.*, $\wp(A)$ is at least as large as A. We next show that there is no one-to-one and onto function F from A to $\wp(A)$, and thus that the sets cannot be equivalent. Assume that there is such an $F : A \rightarrow \wp(A)$. Then every member of A is mapped onto some subset of A. In general, some members of A will be mapped into a subset of which they are also members, and some will not. In the example in Fig. 4-6, 0 and 2 are each mapped by F into a set which

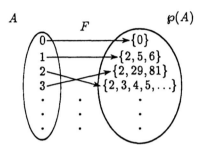

Figure 4–6: Illustration of an alleged one-to-one correspondence between a set and its power set.

has that element as a member, but 1 and 3 are not. Now form the set B by taking every member of A that is mapped into a subset not containing that member. That is, $B = \{x \in A \mid x \notin F(x)\}$. B is some subset of A and is therefore one of the members of $\wp(A)$. By hypothesis, F is onto, so there is at least one member of A that is mapped into B. Call this member y. Now we ask whether y is in B or not.

1. if $y \in B$ then it is not a member of the set it is mapped into, B. Thus if $y \in B$ then $y \notin B$. Contradiction!

2. if $y \notin B$ then it is one of those elements not in the set it is mapped into, so by definition it must be in B. So if $y \notin B$, then $y \in B$. Contradiction again! ■

This two-fold contradiction, which is reminiscent of Russell's Paradox (see Chapter 1.2), shows that the assumption that F is one-to-one and onto is false. Therefore it cannot be the case that $|A|=|\wp(A)|$, so we conclude that $|A|<|\wp(A)|$. A corollary of this important theorem is that there is a cardinal number greater than aleph-zero, which is commonly called $2^{\aleph_0}$, by analogy with the finite cardinals, where the power set of a set with n members has 2^n

members. $2^{\aleph_0}$ does not denote an integer or any other real number, however, since raising 2 to the power $\aleph_0$ is not a meaningful arithmetic operation.

Forming the power set of $\wp(\mathbf{N})$ leads to a cardinal number $2^{2^{\aleph_0}}$ that is larger than $2^{\aleph_0}$; $\wp(\wp(\wp(\mathbf{N})))$ has cardinality $2^{2^{2^{\aleph_0}}}$, and so on. Cantor's Theorem thus yields an infinite sequence of ever greater infinite cardinal numbers: $\aleph_0 < 2^{\aleph_0} < 2^{2^{\aleph_0}} < \ldots$

Another example of a nondenumerable set is the set of all real numbers between 0 and 1 (including 0 and 1 themselves), which we denote $[0,1]$. The real numbers consist of (1) the integers, (2) the other rational numbers and (3) the *irrational* numbers such as $\sqrt{5}$, π, $\frac{1}{3}\sqrt[3]{2}$, etc., which are not expressible as the ratio of two integers. In number theory it is proved that all real numbers, whether rational or irrational, can be written as an integer (possibly 0) followed by an infinitely long decimal fraction to the right of the decimal point. The fraction $\frac{1}{3}$, for example, can be written as $0.3333333\ldots$, where the ellipsis indicates that the sequence of 3's is infinite. Fractions such as $\frac{1}{2}$ can be represented as 0.5 or 0.50 or 0.500, etc., or else as the infinite repeating decimal $0.499999\ldots$. Proof of this last statement would require an excursus into geometric series, but it can be made at least more plausible by considering the following: $\frac{1}{9} = 0.11111\ldots$; $1 = 9(\frac{1}{9}) = 9(0.11111\ldots) = 0.99999\ldots$ The decimal fraction of an irrational number is also infinitely long, but unlike a rational number it does not have repeating digit sequences.

Cantor's proof of the nondenumerability of $[0,1]$ begins with the assumption that every number in this set is uniquely represented by a sequence composed of 0 and an infinitely long decimal fraction. To assure that this representation is unique for each member of the set, we also take every rational number that might be written with an infinite string of 0's, e.g., $0.5000\ldots$, in the form having an infinite string of 9's, e.g., $0.4999\ldots$. We now make the assumption that is to be proved false, namely, that the set $[0,1]$ is denumerable. If so, then its members can be put into a linear sequence with a first member, etc., and this sequence will contain every member of $[0,1]$. In Figure 4-7, this sequence $x_1, x_2, x_3, \ldots, x_n, \ldots$, is indicated as running vertically down the page with the decimal representation of each x_i to the right of the equals sign. The a's are the individual digits in each decimal fraction; a_{13}, for example, is the third digit in the decimal part of the first number in the sequence.

We now show that there is a number y in the set $[0,1]$ that is not in the sequence $x_1, x_2, x_3, \ldots, x_n, \ldots$. This number has the following characteristics: the integer part is 0; the first decimal digit, a_{y1}, is different from

$$x_1 = 0.a_{11}a_{12}a_{13}\cdots a_{1n}\cdots$$
$$x_2 = 0.a_{21}a_{22}a_{23}\cdots a_{2n}\cdots$$
$$x_3 = 0.a_{31}a_{32}a_{33}\cdots a_{3n}\cdots$$
$$\vdots \qquad\qquad \vdots$$
$$x_n = 0.a_{n1}a_{n2}a_{n3}\cdots a_{nn}\cdots$$
$$\vdots \qquad\qquad \vdots$$

Figure 4-7: Putative enumeration of $[0,1]$.

a_{11}; its second decimal digit, a_{y2}; is different from a_{22}; and in general the nth decimal digit a_{yn} is different from a_{nn}. Therefore, y cannot be equal to x_1 because they differ in the first decimal place (and we have agreed that each number has a unique representation in the array); likewise, y cannot be equal to x_2 because they differ in the second decimal place; and in general, y cannot equal any number x_n in the array because it differs from y in (at least) the nth decimal place. Yet y is a number between 0 and 1 because it is of the form $y = 0.a_{y1}a_{y2}a_{y3}\cdots a_{yn}\cdots$. Thus, our assumption that the elements of $[0,1]$ can be put into a linear sequence cannot be maintained, and the set is nondenumerable. This particular form of *reductio ad absurdum*, the so-called *diagonal argument* (y is constructed to be distinct from the integer $0.a_{11}a_{22}a_{33}\cdots a_{nn}\cdots$ on the diagonal of the square array), is encountered frequently in proofs involving infinite sets.

This proves that the cardinality of the set $[0,1]$ is greater than $\aleph_0$ but does not determine just what it is. Cantor was able to show (by a proof we will not reproduce here) that $[0,1]$ is equivalent to the power set of the integers, and thus its cardinal number is $2^{\aleph_0}$. Other sets with this cardinality are the set of all real numbers, the set of all points on a line (of whatever length), the set of all points on a plane, the set of all points in n-dimensional space (for any finite n), and the set of all subsets of the integers.

A problem that remained unsolved for many years was whether there are any infinite cardinal numbers other than $\aleph_0, 2^{\aleph_0}, 2^{2^{\aleph_0}}$, etc. Is there, for example, a cardinal number β such that $\aleph_0 < \beta < 2^{\aleph_0}$ or, to put it another way, is there a set intermediate in size between N and $\wp(N)$? The conjecture that the answer to this question was negative is known as the *Continuum Hypothesis*. It was not until 1963 that the matter was finally resolved (an event sufficiently newsworthy that it was reported in the *New York Times* (Nov. 14, 1963, p. 37)), when P.J. Cohen showed that the

Continuum Hypothesis can be neither proved nor disproved on the basis
of the usual assumptions about set theory. The Continuum Hypothesis is
therefore *independent*, and either it or its negation could be added to set
theory without being redundant or creating a contradiction.

The following examples further illustrate the diagonal method and some
other methods of showing that a set has cardinality greater than $\aleph_0$.

(1) *The set of all real numbers x, $0 \leq x < 1$, written in binary notation.*
The diagonal method can be applied to this set exactly as to the set of real
numbers between 0 and 1 in decimal notation. Since every digit is either a
0 or a 1, one simply sets $y_{nn} = 1$ if $a_{nn} = 0$, and $y_{nn} = 0$ if $a_{nn} = 1$. The
only reason for giving special mention to the binary notation case is that
it is often easier to relate other sets to the real numbers in binary notation
than to the real numbers in decimal notation.

(2) *The set of all subsets of the set of natural numbers, i.e., $\wp(N)$.* For
this example, we will use a method which is not overtly "diagonal", although
it is closely related. (We already know from Theorem 4-1 that this set has
cardinality greater than $\aleph_0$; we use the example to illustrate a method of
proof.)

Assume that $\wp(N)$ has the same cardinality as the natural numbers, i.e.
$\aleph_0$. Then it would be possible to list all the members of $\wp(N)$, i.e. all the
subsets of N, in some linear order, as $S_0, S_1, S_2, \ldots$. Suppose that we had a
complete list of this sort. We could then construct a new subset of N, to be
called S^*, as follows:

> Let the natural number 0 be a member of S^* if and only if 0 is not a
> member of S_0.
>
> Let $1 \in S^*$ if and only if $1 \notin S_1$.
>
> Let $2 \in S^*$ if and only if $2 \notin S_2$.
>
> In general, let $n \notin S^*$ if and only if $n \notin S_n$.

Then S^* is a set of natural numbers, i.e., a subset of N, which is different
from each subset in the list by at least one member. If $n \in S_n$ for all n, then
$S_0 = \emptyset$, and $\emptyset$ was not in the list. Therefore the list could not have been
complete after all, and the cardinality of $\wp(N)$ must be greater than $\aleph_0$.

(3) *The set of all languages on a finite alphabet.* Given an alphabet
$V = \{a_0, a_1, a_2, \ldots a_n\}$, define a *sentence* on V to be any finite string of

elements of V (allowing repetitions). Define a *language* on V to be any set of sentences on V.

As a preliminary step, we will show that the set of all *sentences* on V has cardinality $\aleph_0$, by showing how the sentences can be listed in a single linear list. We will list first all the 1-symbol sentences, and then all the 2-symbol sentences, etc. Within each group, the sentences can be listed in alphabetical order, letting a_0 be the first symbol and a_n the last. Thus the list will begin as follows:

a_0

a_1

$\vdots$

a_n

$a_0 a_0$

$a_0 a_1$

$\vdots$

$a_0 a_n$

$a_1 a_0$

$a_1 a_1$

$\vdots$

$a_1 a_n$

$a_2 a_0$

$\vdots$

$a_n a_n$

$a_0 a_0 a_0$

$\vdots$

$a_n a_n a_n$

$a_0 a_0 a_0 a_0$

$\vdots$

Since all the sentences are clearly included in the list, they can be numbered $0, 1, 2, \ldots$, thus establishing a one-one correspondence between the set of sentences and the natural numbers.

Having established that the set of all *sentences* on V has cardinality $\aleph_0$, we can now show that the set of all *languages* on V has a greater cardinality. We will show three different methods of proof which can be used.

(i) (Diagonal proof.) Assume that the set of all languages on V has cardinality $\aleph_0$, so that the languages can be listed $L_0, L_1, L_2, \ldots$. We have already established a means of listing all the sentences on V as $s_0, s_1, s_2, \ldots$. Then we can set up an infinite square array of 0's and 1's as shown below, where an entry x_i^k is 0 if s_i is not in L_k and x_i^k is 1 if s_i is in L_k.

$$
\begin{array}{c|cccccc}
      & s_0   & s_1   & s_2   & s_3   & s_4   & \cdots \\
\hline
L_0   & x_0^0 & x_1^0 & x_2^0 & x_3^0 & x_4^0 & \cdots \\
L_1   & x_0^1 & x_1^1 & x_2^1 & x_3^1 & x_4^1 & \cdots \\
L_2   & x_0^2 & x_1^2 & x_2^2 & x_3^2 & x_4^2 & \cdots \\
L_3   & x_0^3 & x_1^3 & x_2^3 & x_3^3 & x_4^3 & \cdots \\
L_4   & x_0^4 & x_1^4 & x_2^4 & x_3^4 & x_4^4 & \cdots \\
\vdots & \vdots & \vdots & \vdots & \vdots & \vdots &
\end{array}
$$

Thus for instance the language consisting of all and only the odd-numbered sentences would be represented by a row $010101\ldots$; the language consisting of all the 1-symbol sentences (a_0 through a_n) would be represented by a row whose first $n + 1$ entries were 1's, with all the remaining entries 0's.

Then we can construct a representation of a language L^* different from any in the list as follows: Let $x_0^* = 0$ if $x_0^0 = 1$; $x_0^* = 1$ if $x_0^0 = 0$. In the same way make x_1^* different from x_1^1, x_2^* different from x_2^2, etc.; in general, $x_m^* = 0$ if $x_m^m = 1$, and $x_m^* = 1$ if $x_m^m = 0$. Then by the given interpretation of 0's and 1's, it follows that s_m is in L^* if and only if s_m is not in L_m, and thus that L^* differs by at least one sentence from every language in the list. Since the procedure applies to any such putative list of all languages, it follows that there cannot be such a list, and therefore that the set of all languages on V has a cardinality greater than $\aleph_0$.

(ii) The second proof is analogous to the proof used for the set $\wp(N)$ given as example (2) above. Let S be the name of the set of all *sentences* on V. Then since every language on V is a set of sentences on V, and every set of sentences on V is a language on V, the set of all languages on V is exactly the set of all subsets of S, i.e. $\wp(S)$. Then suppose that the set of all languages on V had cardinality $\aleph_0$. We could then list all the languages, i.e. all the members of $\wp(S)$, in a single list, $L_0, L_1, L_2, \ldots$. But then we could immediately construct a new language L^* as follows (using the enumeration of the sentences of S previously established): let $s_0 \in L^*$ if and only if

$s_0 \notin L_0$, $s_1 \in L^*$ if and only if $s_1 \notin L_1$, etc.; in general, $s_m \in L^*$ if and only if $s_m \notin L_m$. Thus L^* is a subset of S which differs from every language in the list by at least one member, and the list, therefore, could not have been complete. Therefore, the set of all languages, $\wp(S)$, cannot have cardinality $\aleph_0$.

(iii) The third proof is an example of a general method: to show that a given set has cardinality greater than $\aleph_0$, it is sufficient to show that it can be put into a one-one correspondence with a set already known to have cardinality greater than $\aleph_0$. Since the set of real numbers between 0 and 1 in binary notation is already known to have cardinality greater than $\aleph_0$, we will set up a one-one correspondence between it and the set of all languages on V.

Let each language be represented as an infinite sequence of 0's and 1's in the manner described in the first method of proof above. (We do not, however, assume that the languages can be listed in a linear order, since we have already seen that such an assumption leads to a contradiction.) Then each language can be paired with a unique real number between 0 and 1, since the infinite decimal is also an infinite sequence of 0's and 1's designating exactly one language and exactly one real number.

The establishment of the correspondence completes the proof.

The three methods of proof outlined above are equally valid. The first two have the advantage of not requiring prior knowledge of any sets with cardinality greater than $\aleph_0$, but once such knowledge is at hand, the third method is often more convenient. Furthermore, only the third method, setting up a one-one correspondence, can establish exactly what the cardinality of a set is, and then only when the cardinality of the corresponding set is known. In the examples above, all the sets with cardinality greater than $\aleph_0$ have the same cardinality as the set of real numbers, but we have not proved the fact for any of the sets, and we cannot take it for granted because, as we have seen, there are in fact infinitely many different cardinalities greater than $\aleph_0$.

A set which is not countable is called *uncountable* or *non-denumerable* or *non-denumerably infinite*.

4.4   Infinite vs. unbounded

There is sometimes confusion over the difference between the terms 'infinite' and 'unbounded', particularly with respect to statements like 'The length

of English sentences is unbounded', or 'English has sentences of unbounded
length.' *Unbounded* means 'having no upper bound', i.e. having no limiting
value such that every value is at or under that limit. Both of the cited
sentences mean simply that there is no fixed length such that all English
sentences are of that length or less, and this is perfectly consistent with the
statement that every English sentence is finite in length. One can argue
validly from the premise that the length of English sentences is unbounded
to the conclusion that the *set* of English sentences is infinite (see problem
4 in the following exercises), but one cannot validly argue from that to the
conclusion that the *length* of some English sentence is infinite.

Further examples

(1) The number of sides of regular polygons is unbounded, since for any
polygon with n sides, there is another with $n + 1$ sides; but the number of
sides is always finite. The *set* of such polygons is infinite.

(2) Consider the set of real numbers x such that $0 < x < 1$. Although
there is no largest real number in that set (1 itself is excluded from the set,
and for every real number less than 1, there is a larger real number that
is less than 1), the size of the real numbers in that set is *bounded*, since 1
serves as an upper bound. In this case, the size of the members of the set is
bounded, but the set itself is nevertheless infinite.

(3) Starting with the words in some given English dictionary, the length
of English sentences that do not use any word more than once is bounded.
(The number of distinct words in the given dictionary would provide an
upper bound; it is irrelevant to the question of boundedness whether an
English sentence of that length could actually be constructed.)

As can be seen from the examples, the terms 'bounded' and 'unbounded'
apply to values of functions, or to measures of various sorts applied to members of a set; these terms do not describe cardinalities of sets, as do 'finite'
and 'infinite'. It is never strictly meaningful to speak of an 'unbounded
set', although such a phrase may sometimes be interpretable in context as
elliptical for some longer phrase. Confusion can be most easily avoided by
eschewing the use of the term 'unbounded' altogether, and replacing statements like the first two above by statements like 'There is no upper bound
on the length of English sentences'. For the reader who encounters the term
'unbounded' in a statement, it may be advisable to ascertain whether the
statement can be unambiguously recast in such a form before proceeding.

Exercises

1. Show that the relation of equivalence of sets is in fact an equivalence relation.

2. Show that the set of integral powers of 10 $\{10, 100, 1000, 10,000, 100,000, \ldots\}$ is denumerably infinite.

3. Show that the set of all negative integers is infinite.

4. Suppose that the following assumptions are true of English:

   (i)   There is a finite alphabet for writing sentences, consisting of 26 letters, a set of punctuation marks and a space.

   (ii)   Every sentence is a finite string in the alphabet given in (i).

   (iii) There is no upper bound on the length of sentences of English. E.g. given any sentence, a longer one can be made by conjoining it with another one.

   What then is the cardinality of the set of all sentences of English?
   Motivate your answer.

5. A hotelkeeper has a hotel with a denumerably infinite number of rooms, all single rooms, numbered $1, 2, 3, 4, 5 \ldots$. On Saturday night the hotel was full, but Joe Doe came in asking for lodging. The obliging hotelkeeper, using his intercom, asked each guest to move into the room $n + 1$ when his present room was numbered n. So Joe Doe was given room 1. But on Sunday everyone stayed for another night. Now a denumerably infinite football team came in asking for lodgings one room per person. How could the obliging hotelkeeper accommodate them?

6. Assume that the earth rests on the back of a giant turtle, and that the turtle sits on the back of two giant turtles, and those two on three, etc. 'all the way down' (i.e. there is no bottom layer of turtles).[1]

---

[1] This problem was inspired by a legendary anecdote reported in the preface of an equally legendary, but actual Ph.D. dissertation, *Constraints on Variables in Syntax* by J. R. Ross, MIT 1967. Since only parts of the dissertation are published, we repeat the anecdote here as told by Ross for historically accurate preservation:

(a) Suppose each turtle is the sole deity of some monotheistic sect
(exactly one sect per turtle). What is the cardinality of the set
of all such sects?

(b) Suppose each *subset* of the set of all these earth-supporting turtles
forms the deity-group of some one sect (a-, mono- or polytheis-
tic, with the latter including both finite and infinite numbers of
deities). What is the cardinality of the set of all such sects?

After a lecture on cosmology and the structure of the solar system, William James was
accosted by a little old lady. "Your theory that the sun is the center of the solar system,
and that the earth is a ball which rotates around it has a very convincing ring to it, Mr.
James, but it's wrong. I've got a better theory", said the little old lady. "And what is
that, madam?" inquired James politely. "That we live on a crust of earth which is on
the back of a giant turtle". Not wishing to demolish this absurd little theory by bringing
to bear the masses of scientific evidence he had at his command, James decided to gently
dissuade his opponent by making her see some of the inadequacies of her position. "If
your theory is correct, madam," he asked, "what does this turtle stand on?" "You are a
very clever man, Mr. James, and that's a very good question" replied the little old lady,
"but I have an answer to it. And it's this: the first turtle stands on the back of a second,
far larger turtle, who stands directly under him". "But what does this second turtle stand
on?" persisted James patiently. To this the little old lady crowed triumphantly. "It's no
use, Mr. James - it's turtles all the way down."

(Note that two different sects may of course worship some turtles in common as long as they do not worship exactly the same set.)

7. Cardinal numbers form their own numerical system in which we can do *cardinal arithmetic*. This exercise gives the basic notions. Let A and B be disjoint sets, finite or infinite, and let $a = |A|$ and $b = |B|$. We define cardinal addition, written $\oplus$, and cardinal multiplication, written $\otimes$, as follows:

$$a \oplus b = |(A \cup B)|$$
$$a \otimes b = |(A \times B)|$$

When A and B are both finite, cardinal addition and multiplication produce the same results as the corresponding arithmetic operations on integers. When at least one is infinite, however, the operations are no longer parallel in all respects. Find examples of sets A and B for which the following hold:

(a) $\aleph_0 \oplus 1 = \aleph_0$
(b) $\aleph_0 \otimes 2 = \aleph_0$
(c) $\aleph_0 \oplus \aleph_0 = \aleph_0$
(d) $\aleph_0 \otimes \aleph_0 = \aleph_0$

Do the operations $\oplus$ and $\otimes$ appear to be commutative and associative?

8. It can be proved that $\aleph_0$ is the smallest infinite cardinal number. Consider the following putative counterexample to this claim. Choose a cardinal number x such that $2^x = \aleph_0$. x cannot be finite, since 2 raised to any finite power is finite; but x cannot be equal to $\aleph_0$ either, since $2^{\aleph_0} > \aleph_0$ by Cantor's Theorem. Therefore x is an infinite cardinal number less then $\aleph_0$. What is wrong with this argument?

Appendix A

Set-Theoretic Reconstruction of Number Systems

In this appendix we represent the structures of the natural numbers, the integers, and the rationals in pure set-theoretic terms. This set-theoretic representation of numbers gives us first of all a good impression of the power of set theory in representing other structures or mathematical systems. To represent a number structure in pure set-theoretic terms means to define its primitives, operations and relations in set-theoretic terms only. To define the notion number in terms of sets may seem strange at first, since we are so much more familiar with numbers than with sets. The set-theoretic representation of numbers is in fact quite artificial and and the one given here is also not the only conceivable one. It is sufficiently cumbersome that it is never used in practice for ordinary manipulation of numbers. So its function is purely theoretical: it is a necessary step in establishing the interesting claim that set theory is the universal foundation of all of mathematics.

A.1 The natural numbers

First we define 0 as the empty set:

$$0 =_{def} \emptyset$$

Then for the number 1 let us find a set with exactly one member which is built from sets already constructed, i.e. built from $\emptyset$. Such a set is $\{\emptyset\}$. So we define

$$1 =_{def} \{\emptyset\}$$

As a result of these two definitions we see that

$$1 = \{0\}$$

We continue in the same way

$$2 =_{def} \{\emptyset, \{\emptyset\}\} = \{0, 1\}$$

$$3 =_{def} \{\emptyset, \{\emptyset\}, \{\emptyset, \{\emptyset\}\}\} = \{0, 1, 2\}$$

We can proceed indefinitely in this way, defining each successive number as the set of all its predecessors. This can be expressed formally in either of two ways:

for all n (i) $n + 1 = \{0, 1, 2, ..., n\}$
       or (ii) $n + 1 = n \cup \{n\}$

Given any set of finite elements of any sort, the way to tell how many elements it has is to compare it with each of these 'number' sets in turn until one is found whose members can be put in a one-to-one correspondence with the members of the set in question. An analogy can be drawn to the method of telling that something is a meter long by comparing it to the standard meter, a physical object preserved in Paris.

Each natural number has a unique representation in our scheme, but it remains to be shown that the numbers, as reconstructed, have the properties that we expect them to have. In particular, our reconstruction should exhibit the required behavior in relations such as equality and greater-than, and under operations such as addition and multiplication.

The notion of a *successor* of a natural number is defined as:

$$\text{successor of } x =_{def} x \cup \{x\}.$$

We indicate the successor of x by $s(x)$.

Equality between natural numbers is defined as set equality, i.e., having identical membership. Thus, 5 and $s(4)$ are the same number, each being $\{0, 1, 2, 3, 4\}$.

The linear *order* 'less than' is defined by set inclusion: $x < y$ iff $x \subset y$; also, $x \leq y$, 'less than or equal to,' iff $x \subseteq y$, and similarly for $x > y$ and $x \geq y$.

Addition can be defined by a pair of rules using the notion of successor:

for all x (i) $x + 0 = x$
           (ii) $x + s(n) = s(x + n)$

For example, to add two numbers, the second part of the definition is repeated until the first part becomes applicable. The steps for $4 + 3$ are:

$$
\begin{aligned}
4 + 3 \ &= \ 4 + s(2) && \text{def. successor} \\
&= \ s(4 + 2) && \text{def. addition} \\
&= \ s(4 + s(1)) && \text{def. successor} \\
&= \ s(s(4 + 1)) && \text{def. addition} \\
&= \ s(s(4 + s(0))) && \text{def. successor} \\
&= \ s(s(s(4 + 0))) && \text{def. addition} \\
&= \ s(s(s(4))) && \text{def. addition} \\
&= \ s(s(5)) && \text{def. successor} \\
&= \ s(6) && \text{def. successor} \\
&= \ 7 && \text{def. successor}
\end{aligned}
$$

Subtraction can also be defined by a pair of rules, but it is only defined when a set is being subtracted from one which contains it:

for all x (i) $x - x = 0$
           (ii) $s(x) - n = s(x - n)$

For example,

$$
\begin{aligned}
4 - 2 \ &= \ s(3) - 2 && \text{def. of successor} \\
&= \ s(3 - 2) && \text{def. of subtraction} \\
&= \ s(s(2) - 2) && \text{def. of successor} \\
&= \ s(s(2 - 2)) && \text{def. of subtraction} \\
&= \ s(s(0)) && \text{def. of subtraction} \\
&= \ s(1) && \text{def. of successor} \\
&= \ 2 && \text{def. of successor}
\end{aligned}
$$

Multiplication can be defined by a pair of rules involving addition, which has been already defined:

for all x (i) $x \cdot 1 = x$

(ii) $x \cdot s(n) = (x \cdot n) + x$

For example,

$$
\begin{aligned}
2 \cdot 3 &= 2 \cdot s(2) & \text{def. of successor} \\
&= 2 \cdot 2 + 2 & \text{def. of multiplication} \\
&= 2 \cdot s(1) + 2 & \text{def. of successor} \\
&= (2 \cdot 1 + 2) + 2 & \text{def. of multiplication} \\
&= (2 + 2) + 2 & \text{def. of multiplication} \\
&= 4 + 2 = 6 & \text{by addition, as} \\
& & \text{previously defined}
\end{aligned}
$$

A.2 Extension to the set of all integers

Mathematicians (and scientists in general) strive to develop concepts with as wide a range of application as possible. Looking at the system above, one detects a gap: the concepts of equality, addition and multiplication are defined for any two natural numbers, but subtraction is not. It would desirable to extend the number system so as to have subtraction defined everywhere.

What does it mean to 'extend' a system? It means to create a new system with additional elements and possibly additional operations or relations in such a way that the new system contains a *subsystem which is isomorphic to the old system*. In other words, there is some subset of the elements, operations and relations of the new system which can be put in one-to-one correspondence with the elements, operations and relations of the old system, so that the corresponding operations on corresponding elements yield corresponding elements, and the corresponding relations contain corresponding ordered pairs of elements. This guarantees in effect that nothing of the old system has been lost in constructing the new one.

In this case, where we are concerned with an operation, subtraction, which is not defined on certain elements, we would much prefer, for purposes of conceptual economy, that the operation in the new system be given a single definition on all the elements. We will construct a new number system in which subtraction has a uniform definition on all elements, and which contains a subsystem which is isomorphic to the original system. The new number structure is called the *integers*. Remember that the set-theoretic representation of number structures is not in any sense a definition of what the numbers are in absolute terms, but rather of how they can be represented by set-theoretic constructions or *re*-constructions.

The representation of the integers does not bear any resemblance to the ordinary integers $\ldots - 2, -1, 0, 1, 2, \ldots$. They are here defined in a special way so that the operations and relations on them can be defined in terms of the operations and relations already defined for the natural numbers.

DEFINITION A.1 *An integer is an ordered pair $\langle a, b \rangle$ of natural numbers.* ∎

(Intuitively, the ordered pair $\langle a, b \rangle$ will correspond to the integer which is the difference $a - b$; i.e., $\langle 5, 3 \rangle$ represents 2; $\langle 2, 4 \rangle$ represents -2. Thus, many oredered pairs represent the same integer.)

Equality: $\langle a, b \rangle = \langle c, d \rangle$ if and only if $a + d = c + b$, using the definition of $+$ for the natural numbers. Note first that equality is an equivalence relation in the new system. Note also that under this definition $\langle a, b \rangle = \langle a + k, b + k \rangle$ for any k. Hence,

$$\begin{aligned}
\langle 7, 3 \rangle &= \langle 6, 2 \rangle &= \langle 5, 1 \rangle &= \langle 4, 0 \rangle \\
\langle 3, 7 \rangle &= \langle 2, 6 \rangle &= \langle 1, 5 \rangle &= \langle 0, 4 \rangle \\
\langle 3, 3 \rangle &= \langle 2, 2 \rangle &= \langle 1, 1 \rangle &= \langle 0, 0 \rangle
\end{aligned}$$

Every integer is therefore equal to some integer of one of these three forms:

1. $\langle a - b, 0 \rangle$

2. $\langle 0, a - b \rangle$

3. $\langle 0, 0 \rangle$

where a and b are natural numbers and '$-$' is as defined for the natural numbers. By convention, all integers equal to some integer of the first type will be called *positive integers*, the second type *negative integers* and the third type *zero*.

Ordering 'greater than': $\langle a, b \rangle > \langle c, d \rangle$ if and only if $a + d > c + b$ where $>$ on the right is the relation 'greater than' defined on the natural numbers. For example, $\langle 6, 3 \rangle > \langle 2, 1 \rangle$ (i.e., $3 > 1$) because $(6 + 1) > (2 + 3)$; similarly, $\langle 4, 4 \rangle > \langle 2, 5 \rangle$ (i.e., $0 > -3$) since $(4 + 5) > (2 + 4)$.

Addition: $\langle a, b \rangle + \langle c, d \rangle = \langle a + c, b + d \rangle$ where addition on the right is addition as already defined on natural numbers. For example, $\langle 6, 3 \rangle + \langle 4, 2 \rangle = \langle 10, 5 \rangle$ (i.e., $3 + 2 = 5$); also, $\langle 2, 5 \rangle + \langle 2, 1 \rangle = \langle 4, 6 \rangle$ (i.e., $-3 + 1 = -2$).

Subtraction: $\langle a, b \rangle - \langle c, d \rangle = \langle a, b \rangle + \langle d, c \rangle = \langle a + d, b + c \rangle$. For example, $\langle 4, 2 \rangle - \langle 6, 3 \rangle = \langle 4, 2 \rangle + \langle 3, 6 \rangle = \langle 4 + 3, 2 + 6 \rangle = \langle 7, 8 \rangle$ (i.e., $2 - 3 = -1$). (To subtract, one adds the 'negative' of the subtrahend, i.e., $2 - 3 = 2 + (-3)$.) Note further that $\langle a, b \rangle = \langle a, 0 \rangle - \langle b, 0 \rangle$. Since we call numbers of the form $\langle a, 0 \rangle$, $\langle b, 0 \rangle$ positive, we may now interpret this result as showing that any integer $\langle a, b \rangle$ can be represented as the difference of two positive integers $\langle a, 0 \rangle - \langle b, 0 \rangle$.

Multiplication: $\langle a, b \rangle \cdot \langle c, d \rangle = \langle (a \cdot c) + (b \cdot d), (a \cdot d) + (b \cdot c) \rangle$, where multiplication on the right side is multiplication as already defined on natural numbers. For example, $\langle 6, 3 \rangle \cdot \langle 4, 2 \rangle = \langle (6 \cdot 4) + (3 \cdot 2), (6 \cdot 2) + (3 \cdot 4) \rangle = \langle 24 + 6, 12 + 12 \rangle = \langle 30, 24 \rangle$ (i.e., $3 \cdot 2 = 6$); similarly, $\langle 2, 5 \rangle \cdot \langle 1, 2 \rangle = \langle (2 \cdot 1) + (5 \cdot 2), (2 \cdot 2) + (5 \cdot 1) \rangle = \langle 2 + 10, 4 + 5 \rangle = \langle 12, 9 \rangle$ (i.e., $(-3) \cdot (-1) = 3$). This definition has the desired result for positive integers: $\langle a, 0 \rangle \cdot \langle c, 0 \rangle = \langle a \cdot c, 0 \rangle$; and for negative integers: $\langle 0, b \rangle \cdot \langle 0, d \rangle = \langle bd, 0 \rangle$; $\langle a, 0 \rangle \cdot \langle 0, d \rangle = \langle 0, ad \rangle$.

The natural numbers are not themselves a subset of this set-theoretic representation of the integers. Rather, the set of all integers contains a subset consisting of the positive integers and zero which is isomorphic to the set of natural numbers. Although in many applications the distinction between natural numbers and non-negative integers is not important, the concepts can be seen to differ by virtue of the total systems of which they are part. For example, while the positive integer $+5$ can be subtracted from the positive integer $+3$, the corresponding natural number 5 cannot be subtracted from the natural number 3.

A.3 Extension to the set of all rational numbers

The operations of addition, subtraction and multiplication are now defined on all the integers. We have not said anything yet about division. The question 'What number multiplied by x gives y?' does not always have an answer in the integers. The next extension of this system will be to a number structure in which this question is always answered: the *rationals*. There is one notable exception: division by 0 is always impossible. (It is instructive to attempt to extend the system to one which includes division by 0 and observe the difficulties one encounters.) The elements of the new system will be defined in terms of integers, for convenience written as usual $\ldots -2, -1, 0, 1, 2, \ldots$. The operations and relations of the new system will be defined in terms of the operations and relations on the integers. An isomorphism can then be shown between the integers and a subsystem of the rationals.

DEFINITION A.2   *A rational number is an ordered pair $\langle a, b \rangle$ of integers where $b \neq 0$.*   ∎

The pair $\langle a, b \rangle$ may be interpreted in the language of ordinary arithmetic as the fraction $\frac{a}{b}$. Note that since each integer is defined as a pair of natural numbers a rational will be a pair of pairs of natural numbers.

Equality: $\langle a, b \rangle = \langle c, d \rangle$ if and only if $a \cdot d = c \cdot b$.

Ordering 'greater than': $\langle a, b \rangle > \langle c, d \rangle$ if and only if $a \cdot d > c \cdot b$.

Addition: $\langle a, b \rangle + \langle c, d \rangle = \langle a \cdot d + c \cdot b, b \cdot d \rangle$.

Subtraction: $\langle a, b \rangle - \langle c, d \rangle = \langle a \cdot d - c \cdot b, b \cdot d \rangle$.

Multiplication: $\langle a, b \rangle \cdot \langle c, d \rangle = \langle a \cdot c, b \cdot d \rangle$.

Division: $\langle a, b \rangle : \langle c, d \rangle = \langle a \cdot d, c \cdot b \rangle$.

(All operations on the right sides are as defined for the integers.)

It will be noted that attempting to divide by 0 yields an ordered pair whose second member is 0; by definition, such ordered pairs are not rational numbers and hence division by 0 is impossible within the system.

To define the isomorphism between the integers and a substructure of the rationals (except division), let the rational number $\langle x, 1 \rangle$ correspond with the integer x, and all the operations for the rationals (except division) correspond to operations with the same name for the integers and similarly for the ordering. It can be verified that this is an isomorphism.

A.4 Extension to the set of all real numbers

This section does not actually come within the realm of discrete mathematics, which deals with set of cardinality no larger than $\aleph_0$. The real numbers, as we saw in Chapter 4, form a larger set, and its properties are different in many ways. Most of the subject of calculus, for example, depends on some of the essential properties of the real number system.

This extension of the number system in its set-theoretic representation allows us to obtain a system in which we always have an answer to a question like 'Which number multiplied by itself gives 2?'. There are two fundamental ways of constructing the real number system, one due to Cantor, the other to Dedekind. We give here Cantor's construction. Consider sequences

$$A = \frac{1}{2}, \frac{2}{3}, \frac{3}{4}, \frac{4}{5}, \frac{5}{6}, \frac{6}{7}, \ldots$$

and

$$B = \frac{2}{1}, \frac{3}{2}, \frac{4}{3}, \frac{5}{4}, \frac{6}{5}, \frac{7}{6}, \ldots$$

Both of these sequences converge to 1; i.e., the more a sequence is developed, the closer one gets to 1, even though 1 is never actually reached. This is expressed more precisely by saying that a sequence $a_0, a_1, a_2, \ldots$ converges to x if for any positive number ϵ (epsilon), no matter how small, we can find an index N such that $|a_n - x| < \epsilon$ for all $n > N$. Some sequences of rational numbers converge to a number which is itself not representable as a rational number. The above definition cannot be used to test convergence in such cases, since we have no means of expressing the point of convergence. Another definition of convergence can be given which is equivalent to the former but which does not depend on the nature of x.

DEFINITION A.3 *A sequence $a_0, a_1, a_2, \ldots$ converges if for any positive number ϵ no matter how small we can find an index N such that $|a_n - a_m| < \epsilon$ for all $m > N$ and $n > N$.*   ∎

In other words, we are stating that the terms far out in the series must get closer and closer to each other, which has the same effect as saying that they must all get closer and closer to some particular point of convergence. Cantor defined a real number as a convergent sequence of rational numbers. The rational numbers themselves can be represented in this system as sequences of the form $r, r, r, \ldots$ where r is a rational number, since a sequence all of whose members are identical cerainly satisfies the definition of convergence. If one thinks of real numbers as infinite decimals, one way of representing real numbers would be as the limit of a sequence of finite decimals (which are rational numbers) of the form $x_1., x_1.x_2, x_1.x_2x_3, x_1.x_2x_3x_4$, i.e., $\frac{x_1}{1}, \frac{x_1x_2}{10}, \frac{x_1x_2x_3}{100}, \ldots$ Operations must all be defined anew for the real numbers, but this is quite simple. To give just one example, addition is defined by: $a_0, a_1, a_2, \ldots + b_0, b_1, b_2, \ldots = a_0 + b_0, a_1 + b_1, a_2 + b_2, \ldots$

Review Exercises

1. Consider the following sets:

$$
\begin{aligned}
A_1 &= \{\emptyset, \{B\}, \{\emptyset, B\}\} \\
A_2 &= \{B\} \\
A_3 &= \{\emptyset\} \\
A_4 &= \{\emptyset, \{\emptyset, B\}\} \\
A_5 &= \{\{B\}, \{\emptyset, B\}\} \\
A_6 &= \{\emptyset, B\}
\end{aligned}
$$

Determine the following sets:

(a) $A_1 \cap A_4$

(b) $(A_2 \cup A_3) - A_6$

(c) $\wp(A_6) \cap A_5$

(d) $A_4 - A_2$

2. On the integers specify a relation which is :

(a) symmetric and irreflexive

(b) transitive and asymmetric

3. Consider the set N of all natural numbers in set-theoretic representation.

(a) Let R be the subset relation on N. Is R symmetric and/or transitive and/or reflexive ?

(b) If $n \in N$ and $x \in n$, is necessarily $x \subset n$? Motivate your answer.

4. Suppose that, starting with a single common ancestor, Adam, each man has some finite positive number of sons, each of his sons has some finite positive number of sons etc. forever. Suppose that for each

man other than Adam we know who his father was and also what his chronological order is amongst his brothers (no simultaneously born twins, no women either).

(a) Show how a one-to-one correspondence between the set of all men and the natural numbers may be constructed, including an illustration of how the beginning of the list might look.

(b) Let every distinct set of men (finite or infinite, and spanning arbitrary stretches of time) be called a 'club'. Show without using any of the results of Chapter 4 that the set of all clubs is non-denumerably infinite.

5. Determine whether the following systems are partially ordered, linearly ordered or well-ordered.

(a) the set of all positive and negative rational numbers; the relation 'is equal to or less than'

(b) the set of all negative rational numbers; same relation as (a)

(c) the set of all negative rational numbers and zero; the relation 'is equal to or greater than'

(d) the set A of all strings finite in length formed by concatenating elements a, b, c; the relation 'is at least as long as'

(e) the same set A as in (d); the relation R described by 'xRy if either y is longer than x or x and y are the same length but x does not come after y alphabetically'

*(f) the set of natural numbers; the relation R described by 'xRy if x and y are both even and $x \leq y$ or, if x and y are both odd and $x \leq y$'.

*(g) as (f) but R is: 'xRy if x and y are both even and $x \leq y$ or, if x and y are both odd and $x \leq y$ or x is even and y is odd'.

*(h) as (f) but R is: 'xRy if x and y are both even and $x < y$ or, if x and y are both odd and $x \leq y$ or x is odd and y is even'.

6. Show that for any sets A, B, C, if $|A| \leq |B|$, and $|B| \leq |C|$, then $|A| \leq |C|$.

Part B

LOGIC AND FORMAL SYSTEMS

Chapter 5

Basic Concepts of Logic and Formal Systems

5.1   Formal systems and models

Formalization or axiomatization is an outgrowth of the broader goals of scientific systematization. Euclid systematized geometry by showing how a great many statements known to be true about geometrical figures could be logically derived from a small set of principles assumed to be true, called the *axioms*. Newton systematized mechanics by showing how the known laws of motion, both planetary and terrestrial, could be derived from three basic statements. In both cases, the initial assumptions had the status of true statements, 'self-evident' in the Euclidean system, empirically discovered truths in the Newtonian system. In both cases the system was concerned with particular objects, points and lines in the one case, physical objects in the other.

The realization that a strict separation of the formal, *syntactical* aspects of a system from any of its meaning assignments or interpretations, i.e. its *semantics*, is both possible and desirable was one of the consequences of the discovery of non-Euclidean geometries.

Euclid's axioms included one known as the 'Parallel Postulate' which can be stated as follows.

Parallel Postulate: *Given a line L and a point P not on line L, one and only one line L' can be drawn through P parallel to the line L (i.e., not intersecting no matter how far extended.)*

Since this particular postulate had always seemed less 'self-evident' than the others, numerous attempts, all unsuccessful, were made to derive it from the remaining axioms. N. Lobachevsky and (independently) J. Bolyai in the early 19th century made such an attempt, trying to use the method of *reductio ad absurdum*, which we have illustrated in our reasoning about properties of complement relations in Section 3.3. They began by assuming that more than one line parallel to L could be drawn through point P, but instead of deriving a contradiction as intended, they discovered or invented the first non-Euclidean geometry. The revised axiom system turned out to be perfectly consistent (a notion we discuss in Chapter 8). Later, Riemann constructed another non-Euclidean geometry, in this case by replacing the Parallel Postulate by a postulate stating that *no* lines parallel to a given line L could be drawn through a given point P not on L, i.e. that *all* distinct lines intersect eventually. Again, no contradiction arose. These discoveries in no sense refuted Euclidean geometry, but they did lead to a fundamental change in our attitude towards the axioms. Earlier the axiomatic approach was thought to systematize a body of absolute truths, but after Bolyai, Lobachevsky and Riemann it began to be appreciated that while the derived statements were valid, i.e. logically necessary consequences of the axioms, the axioms themselves were simply assumptions. We now no longer ask whether certain axioms are true in any absolute sense, but what, if anything, they might be *true of*. That question is equivalent to asking what *models*, if any, the set of axioms has.

Euclidean geometry may seem by its usual terminology to have presupposed a particular model, namely the abstract set of points and lines and the figures that can be constructed with compass and straightedge. However, to look at it as a genuinely formal system we must first replace the occurrences of the words 'point' and 'line' by undefined primitives such as 'p' and 'l', making corresponding changes in the definitions of subsequent terms, since notions of 'parallel', 'triangle' etc. can be defined in terms of 'point' and 'line'. We then find that, for instance, if we start with a fixed circle in a plane and interpret 'p' as 'point in the interior of the circle' and 'l' as 'open-ended chord of this circle' (an 'open-ended chord of a circle' is a straight line within the circle which approaches indefinitely closely, but does not touch the circumference), then through a given point, more than one parallel can be drawn to a given line. This is illustrated in Figure 5-1.

Starting with line AB and point C, we can construct lines DCE and FCG, among others. DCE and FCG are both parallel to AB since neither will intersect AB 'no matter how far extended', i.e. no matter how close to

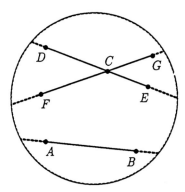

Figure 5–1: Open-ended chords in a circle

the circumference of the circle they get. This interpretation therefore does not satisfy the Euclidean axioms and does not provide a model for them. It does provide a model for the Bolyai-Lobachevsky non-Euclidean geometry. In fact, it is often by constructing a model for a set of axioms that we prove them to be consistent (see Ch. 8, Sec. 2 for the connection between these two important notions 'consistency' and 'having a model'). Any system or structure in which all of Euclid's axioms are true is called a model of Euclid's system; plane geometry is the *standard* or *intended* model, since it was with that "in mind" that Euclid developed the formal system in the first place.

The development of quantum mechanics has similar consequences for the attitude we have towards Newton's physical system. It is still true that all of the laws of mechanics which Newton derived follow from three basic principles. But the laws are now seen to hold only in certain macroscopic situations. The actual physical universe is no longer held to be a model of the Newtonian system.

In the cases of geometry and mechanics the model came first and the formalization later. This is the usual case in empirical research and in mathematics, but it is not the only one. It proves to be very fruitful to study formal systems in the abstract, since insofar as distinct systems have a similar structure, their formalizations are alike. Direct study of a formal system can yield results which can be applied generally to all systems which are models of it. Also, once we show that a certain system is equivalent in its formal structure to another better known system, what we know about the latter may transfer to new insights about the former.

In general, a formal system consists of:

(i) a non-empty set of *primitives*

(ii) a set of statements about the primitives, the *axioms*

(iii) a means of deriving further statements from the axioms, either:

> (a) an explicit set of recursive rules of derivation; or
>
> (b) appeal to a background logic for the language in which the axioms are stated, usually predicate logic; or
>
> (c) no explicit means of derivation; one is to derive "whatever logically follows" from the axioms.

Some of the more "syntactic" formal systems that we will illustrate in Chapter 8 follow option (iiia) above.

In most formalizations of scientific theories and branches of mathematics, it is taken for granted or assumed to be given what the permitted background logic or forms of reasoning are. But forms of reasoning themselves are the subject matter of logic, to which most of this part of this book is devoted. Hence we use logic or a logical language to reason *about* other systems like set theory, geometry or physics. We call the language which we use to talk and reason about another system the *meta-language*, and the system reasoned and talked about the *object language*. The distinction is of course a relative one, since we can use set theory, for instance, in its turn as a meta-language to talk about physical systems. Natural languages are the only kind of languages rich enough to incorporate their own meta-language. We talk *in* English *about* English, although in linguistics we also develop specialized formal languages to talk about sentence structure or word meaning, for instance.

In the last chapter of this part of the book, Chapter 8, we will return to the subject of formal systems, axiomatization, and model theory, after we have introduced enough logic to present some interesting examples. We will also see how a system of logic can itself be axiomatized. In the case of logic, an axiomatization will consist of:

(i) a syntax defining the expressions of the language.

(ii) a set of axioms (themselves among the formulas of the language)

(iii) a set of explicit rules of inference for deriving further formulas from the axioms. The axioms plus all further formulas so derivable are the *theorems* of the system.

5.2   Natural languages and formal languages

The languages we speak and use naturally to communicate with each other are what we call *natural* languages. Natural languages are acquired as first languages in childhood and are suited to just about any communicative goal we may have. Formal languages, on the other hand, are usually designed by people for a clear, particular purpose, but, although these languages are constructed, in use they may to a certain extent change and evolve. Examples of formal languages are the language of set theory with which you got acquainted in Part A, the language of logic which we introduce in Chapters 6 and 7, the language of ordinary arithmetic, and programming languages like Pascal, Fortran, Prolog, Lisp and all their 'dialects'. There are many other notational systems with conventional meaning which may deserve the name 'language' as well, like musical notation, traffic light systems, Morse code and so on, but we will leave these out of our present considerations. One of the most important uses linguists and especially semanticists make of formal languages is to *represent meaning* of natural languages. Characterizing meaning is the main goal of the semantic component of a grammar, whether it be a grammar of a formal language or a grammar of a natural language. Like any scientific enterprise, semantics chooses particular aspects and parts of meaning as objects of study and employs formal languages as analytic tools. Logic is a branch of the foundations of mathematics which has developed a number of particularly useful formal languages, of which the first-order logic introduced in this part of the book is perhaps the best known and most often used. As we already suggested in the previous section, logical languages can be used as meta-languages in which we reason about set theory as object language or about set theoretic objects. But logical languages can be applied to any other object language and formalize the reasoning from axioms to theorems in that domain. One of our interests in this book is in developing the background for applications of logic and formal languages to natural languages, such as English. Part D is devoted to such applications and to a number of current topics in the semantics of natural language. But first we have to study the language of logic, and learn how to use it. And of course the study of logic has many other important applications both within and outside of the field of linguistics.

5.3   Syntax and semantics

The distinction between the *syntax* and the *semantics* of a language or a
formal system is essentially a distinction between on the one hand talking
about properties of expressions of the system itself, such as its primitives,
axioms, rules of inference or rewrite rules, and theorems, and on the other
hand talking about relations between the system and its models or interpretations. Although the separation of form and content is itself ancient, it is
not always possible to draw a hard and fast line between the purely syntactic and the purely semantic aspects of a language or system, especially since
many properties of a system are likely to be reflected in both its syntax and
its semantics. But there is general agreement that syntax and semantics
have some clear distinctions among their core notions. For instance, the
construction of proofs from premises or axioms according to formal rules of
inference or rewriting rules is a syntactic activity, while demonstrating that
a certain set of axioms is consistent by showing that it has a model (see
Chapter 8) is giving a semantic argument. On the syntactic side are well-
formedness rules, derivations, proofs, and other notions definable in terms
of the forms of expressions. On the semantic side are notions like truth and
reference, properties which expressions may have relative to one model or
interpretation and fail to have with respect to another.

Both syntactic and semantic methods of argumentation and tools of analysis have proved valuable in the study of formal systems. Neither is inherently superior or more legitimate; one may be more direct or handy than the
other for answering a particular question or showing that a given formal system has some property or other. Many important results in the metatheory
of logic concern the relation between syntax and semantics, and the discipline of *model theory* is expressly concerned with the application of semantic
tools to logic and mathematics. (See Chapter 8)

The program of studying only the syntax of a system without making
any appeal, explicit or tacit, to its meaning constitutes the *formalist research program*, which is known as Hilbert's program in the foundations of
mathematics and, stretching the concept perhaps, as Chomsky's program of
studying syntax autonomously in the theory of generative grammar. Modern
generative syntax is in fact rooted in the mathematical theory of formal languages and automata, a syntactic enterprise on the above characterization,

since it deals with the properties of string rewriting and symbol manipulating in systems. Semantics in the "formal semantics" tradition is rooted in logic and model theory, and borrows many of its tools from those developed by logicians for the study of the formal languages of logic. It is ironic that the name "formal semantics" has become the standard name of the model-theoretic approach to semantics, which is decidedly not a formalist program in the above sense.

Outside of logic the term *semantics* is often used in a much broader sense, roughly as anything relating to meaning. In linguistics one finds a range of uses along with ongoing debates concerning where theoretical boundaries can most usefully be drawn. So in one sense, issues concerning scope ambiguity are certainly among the concerns of semantic theories of natural languages; at the same time one can distinguish among theories that treat certain scope ambiguities "in the syntax" or "in the semantics." In the chapters which follow, we will stick to the rather clearly regimented usage that has become customary in logic, reserving the term *semantics* for the study of the relations of formal systems to their interpretations.

5.4   About statement logic and predicate logic

In Chapters 6 and 7 we will examine two systems of logic: *statement logic* (also called the *propositional calculus* or *statement calculus*) and *predicate logic* (also known as *(first-order) predicate calculus*). Each will be treated as a formal language with its own vocabulary, rules of syntax, and semantics (or system of interpretation). But as we will see, the syntactic and semantic components of these languages are very much simpler than those of any natural language; indeed, that is their virtue, since they have been purposely constructed to avoid ambiguities and many complicated features contained in natural languages. For instance, the sentences of our logical languages are all declaratives—there are no interrogatives, imperatives, performatives, etc.—and, further, the means of joining sentences together to form compound sentences is severely limited. We will find sentential connectives corresponding (roughly) to English *and, or, not, if . . . then,* and *if and only if,* but nothing to answer to *because, while, after, although,* and many other conjunctions. In predicate logic we will in addition find counterparts of a few determiners of English—*some, all, no, every,*—but not *most, many, a few, several, one half,* etc. As a discipline, logic is the study of reasoning (the product not the process—the latter is the province of psy-

chology), with the objective of identifying correct, or *valid*, instances and
distinguishing them from those that are incorrect, or *invalid*. We recognize
intuitively for example, that the reasoning exhibited in argument (5–1) is
valid, in that the conclusion (the sentence below the horizontal line) is a
necessary consequence of the premises above the line. To put it another
way, if we grant the truth of the premises in (5–1), we cannot, logically,
deny the truth of the conclusion.

(5–1)   All men are mortals.
                          Socrates is a man.
         Therefore, Socrates is a mortal.

In contrast, the reasoning in argument (5–2) is easily seen to be invalid:

(5–2)   All cats are mammals.
                          All dogs are mammals.
              Therefore, All cats are dogs.

That is, in (5–2) even if we accept the premises we may logically reject the
conclusion.

A system of formal logic—for these examples it will be predicate logic—is
intended to give a systematic account of what underlies these intuitions. In
this enterprise the logical language serves as a model, or image, of the natural language (albeit a much simplified one), but it is designed so that one
can give an explicit account of validity for any arguments expressed in it. An
argument couched in natural language can then be assessed by translating it
into the logical language and determining the validity of the translation. Argument (5–1), for example, could be translated into the following argument
in predicate logic, which, as we will see in Chapter 7, is valid:

(5–3) $(\forall x)(H(x) \rightarrow M(x))$
           $H(s)$
   $\therefore \overline{M(s)}$

Clearly the success of such a program will depend heavily on the adequacy
of the translations (assuming a satisfactory characterization of validity and
invalidity in the logical language).

One motivation for proceeding in this way is that many arguments in
natural language, while superficially distinct, appear to be instances of the

same underlying *argument form.* We observe, for example, that (5–1) produces another valid argument under systematic replacement of its proper and common nouns:

(5–4)   All rabbits are rodents.
                   Peter is a rabbit.
      Therefore, Peter is a rodent.

Evidently the validity of (5–1) and (5–4) does not rest on the meanings of words such as *man, Socrates,* and *rabbit,* but rather results from the framework in which these words are embedded, i.e., the *form* of the argument. We also observe that the word *all* is an integral part of of this form; replacing it by *some,* for example, yields an invalid argument:

(5–5)   Some men are mortals.
                   Socrates is a man.
      Therefore, Socrates is a mortal.

(Note that the conclusion of (5–5), while true, does not follow necessarily from the premises.) We might then say that (5–1) and (5–4) are instances of the (valid) argument form (5–6):

(5–6)   All X's are Y's
                   a is an X
      Therefore, a is a Y

and similarly, (5–2) is an instance of the following invalid argument form:

(5–7)   All X's are Y's
                   All Z's are Y's
      Therefore, All X's are Z's

A logical language, then, is designed to provide effective translations and an account of validity or invalidity for a certain range of argument forms. Predicate logic treats the two forms just mentioned, for example, but statement logic, as we will see presently, does not, since it is constructed to deal only with argument forms whose validity hinges of the meanings of sentential connectives such as *and, or,* and *if ... then,* but not on quantifier words such as *all,* and *some.*

Chapter 6

Statement Logic

6.1 Syntax

The syntax of statement logic is very simple: We assume an infinite basic vocabulary of *atomic statements* represented by the symbols $p, q, r, s, \ldots$, with primes or subscripts added as needed.

DEFINITION 6.1

1. *Any* atomic statement *itself is* a sentence or well-formed formula *(wff).*

2. *Any wff preceded by the symbol '$\sim$' (negation) is also a wff.*

3. *Any two (not necessarily distinct) wffs can be made into another wff by writing the symbol '&' (conjunction), '$\vee$' (disjunction), '$\rightarrow$' (conditional), or '$\leftrightarrow$' (biconditional) between them and enclosing the result in parentheses.*

∎

Here are some examples of wff's of statement logic constructed according to these rules:

(6–1) p

     q'

     $(p \vee q)$

     $\sim (p' \leftrightarrow p')$

     $\sim r$

     $\sim \sim r$

     $((((p \mathbin{\&} q) \vee \sim q') \rightarrow r) \leftrightarrow s)$

The following are not wff's:

(6–2) pq
    $\vee\, p$
    $\sim \vee pq$
    $p \vee q$ (lacks outer parentheses)
    $\sim (p)$ (no parentheses around atomic statements)

Note: we will occasionally omit outer pairs of parentheses in the interest of increased legibility, e.g., $p \vee (q\ \&\ r)$ instead of $(p \vee (q\ \&\ r))$. The former can be regarded as an informal abbreviation for the latter.

As we have said, logical languages are typically designed to mirror certain natural language constructions. In the present case, the connectives &, ∨, →, ↔, are intended as the couterparts of English *and, or, if ... then,* and *if and only if,* when used to conjoin declarative sentences, e.g., the *and* of *John smokes and Mary snores.* Atomic wff's are the logical representatives of simple declarative sentences, i.e., those which do not contain instances of the sentential connectives *and, or, if ... then, if and only if,* or *not.* The negation symbol '∼', is a unary operator rather than a binary connective in that it applies to only one wff to produce a wff. Its English counterpart is the *not* in *John will not leave* or the more formal *It is not the case that* (e.g., *It is not the case that John will leave*). Note that what the logic regards as a "simple" declarative sentence may in fact be quite complex syntactically. For example, *John's incessant smoking has caused Mary to consider strangling him* contains none of our designated sentential connectives and so would be represented as an atomic sentence in statement logic.

A word about terminology. We will say that an English sentence such as *John smokes* makes, or expresses, a *statement.* We ignore, for the present, pragmatic concerns such as speaker and context. We use 'statement' as a neutral term to avoid using the more common 'proposition,' since the latter has acquired a number of different meanings over time which we would prefer to avoid sorting out. Synonymous sentences, e.g., *Paris is the capital of France* and *France's capital is Paris* express the same statement, while ambiguous sentences, e.g., *Visiting relatives can be annoying* express more than one statement.

6.2   Semantics: Truth values and truth tables

The semantics of statement logic is nearly as simple as its syntax. Each atomic statement is assumed to have assigned to it one of the *truth values*: 1 (also called *true*) or 0 (*false*). We are thus working with a two-valued logic; systems with more than two values have also been studied, but they will not concern us here (but see Appendix BII). Each complex wff also receives a truth value, which is determined by (1) the truth values of its syntactic component statements, and (2) the syntactic structure of the complex wff; i.e., its connectives and their arrangement in the formula. For example, the truth value of $(p\ \&\ q)$ will be determined by the truth values of p and q and by the so-called *truth-functional* properties of the connective $\&$. The latter is given by a *truth table* saying how the truth value of a formula is a function of the truth values of its immediate constituents when the principal connective is the conjunction $\&$. We now give the truth tables for the five connectives along with some remarks on how they compare with their English counterparts. In the following, P, Q, etc., will stand for any arbitrary wff, atomic or complex.

6.2.1   Negation

Negation reverses the truth value of the statement to which it is attached. For any formula P, if P is true, then $\sim P$ is false, and, conversely, if P is false, then $\sim P$ is true. This is summarized in the truth table of Table 6–1.

P	$\sim P$
1	0
0	1

Table 6–1: Truth table for negation

Logical negation is of course intended to mirror sentential negation in natural language. In English, this is often expressed by the insertion of *not* into the verb phrase (*John is here, John is not here*), sometimes with the addition of a form of *do* (*John smokes, John does not smoke*). The semantic effect is generally to produce a sentence opposite in truth value to the original, but there are cases where this is not so: *John must leave, John must not leave.* Here then is a case in which the English and the logical connectives are not exact correspondents. Closer to the behavior of the logical connective is the circumlocution *it is not the case that* (cf., *John must leave, It is not the case that John must leave*).

6.2.2   Conjunction

If we conjoin two declarative English sentences by *and*, the result is, by and large, true if both conjuncts are true, and false if one or both of the conjuncts are false. For example, if *John smokes* is true and *Jane snores* is also true, then *John smokes and Jane snores* is true; if either or both of the constituent sentences are false, the entire conjunction is false. The truth table for the logical connective & is constructed accordingly:

P	Q	$(P \ \& \ Q)$
1	1	1
1	0	0
0	1	0
0	0	0

Table 6–2: Truth table for conjunction

Note that P and Q are variables denoting any wff whatsoever and that there are four rows in the table corresponding to the four ways of assigning two truth values independently to two statements.

As we have now come to expect, there are instances in which & does not correspond exactly to the English sentential conjunction *and*. The latter, for example, sometimes carries a temporal connotation which is absent from the logical connective (cf., *John took a shower and he got dressed, John got dressed and he took a shower*). In the logic of statements $(p \ \& \ q)$ always has the same truth value as $(q \ \& \ p)$. Furthermore, while $(p \ \& \ p)$ is perfectly well formed (and has the same truth value as p itself), a sentence such as *John smokes and John smokes* is distinctly odd and could be appropriately used only in rather special circumstances (perhaps as a colorful way of saying that John smokes incessantly).

In translating from English into statement logic the sentential connective *but* is often rendered as &; thus, *John smokes but Jane snores* might be translated into $(p \ \& \ q)$, where the & carries none of the connotations of contrast or unexpectedness of the English connective. Similar remarks could be made about *however, although, despite the fact that*, and so on.

English *and* can of course be used to conjoin noun phrases, verb phrases, etc. as well as sentences (*John and Mary, smokes and drinks*), and nothing in our logical language corresponds to this usage (remember that we are ignoring the internal structure of simple sentences). Sometimes sentences containing phrasal conjunction can be treated as elliptical forms of sentential conjunction; e.g., *John and Mary smoke* might be regarded as an abbreviated form of *John smokes and Mary smokes* and thus could be translated into something like $(p \, \& \, q)$. Not all cases of phrasal conjunction can be so treated, however, as we can see by examples such as *John and Mary met in New York* or *Mary mixed red and blue paint*.

6.2.3   Disjunction

The logical connective ∨ has the following truth table:

P	Q	$(P \lor Q)$
1	1	1
1	0	1
0	1	1
0	0	0

Table 6–3:   Truth table for disjunction

Thus the disjunction of two statements is true if at least one of the disjuncts is true; it is false only if both are false. The rough English correspondent is the sentential connective *or* as in *John smokes or Jane snores*. The logical connective is the so-called *inclusive* disjunction, which is true when both disjuncts are true. It is commonly supposed that English *or* also has an *exclusive* sense, which excludes the possibility that both disjuncts are true; cf., *You may have soup or you may have salad, but not both*, but it is controversial whether the English word is actually ambiguous or whether the inclusive vs. exclusive sense of such disjunction sentences is determined by matters of context and other pragmatic factors. Latin *vel* and *aut* have often been cited as natural language examples of disjunctions which bear, respectively, the inclusive and exclusive senses, but even here the facts are not entirely clear. In any event, the logical connective ∨ is unambiguously inclusive, as evidenced by the first row of its truth table. (There is no standard symbol for exclusive logical disjunction, but if there were, its truth table would be like that in Table 6–3 except for having the value 0 in the first row).

Similar remarks about phrasal disjunction can be made here as in the case of of phrasal conjunction. For example, *(Either) John or Mary smokes* can be regarded as elliptical for *John smokes or Mary smokes* and therefore represented as $(p \lor q)$. A problematic case is *A doctor or a dentist can write prescriptions*, where the intended interpretation is that *both* doctors and dentists can write prescriptions (it would be false if doctors could but dentists couldn't, for example). Thus, the best translation for this sentence would be of the form $(p \& q)$, not $(p \lor q)$.

6.2.4   The Conditional

The discontinuous connective *if... then* in English is used in a host of different ways and has been the subject of much discussion. The correspondent in our logical language, $\rightarrow$, shares one crucial feature with all the natural language uses, *viz.*, when the *if*-clause (the antecedent) is true, and the *then*-clause (the consequent) is false, the entire conditional statement is false. For instance, *If Mary is at the party, then John is at the party (too)* is clearly false if Mary is at the party but John isn't. This is reflected in the second row of the truth table for $\rightarrow$:

P	Q	$(P \rightarrow Q)$
1	1	1
1	0	0
0	1	1
0	0	1

Table 6–4: Truth table for the conditional

$(P \rightarrow Q)$ is true in all other cases, and it is this aspect of the semantics of the conditional which is most controversial. When asked for the truth value of *If Mary is at the party, then John is at the party (too)* in case Mary is *not* at the party, we may be puzzled. We might be inclined to say that the conditional sentence has no clearly defined truth value or that the question of its truth value does not arise. Even in the case where both Mary and John are at the party, we might hesitate to say that the conditional is true since we would expect some logical or causal connection between antecedent and consequent be determined before we could determine the actual truth value. Here we seem to have a case where the logical and the English connectives are greatly at variance. How can we justify our choice of 1 (true) in these cases?

The answer goes along two lines: (1) In a two-valued logic, if a statement is not false, then it must be true: there is no other choice. (2) This definition of the conditional suffices for the analysis of valid and invalid arguments in mathematics and thus carries the weight of tradition. It is not without its troublesome and sometimes paradoxical side effects, however.

6.2.5 The Biconditional

The truth table for the biconditional is shown in Table 6-5.

P	Q	$(P \leftrightarrow Q)$
1	1	1
1	0	0
0	1	0
0	0	1

Table 6–5: Truth table for the biconditional

English expressions translated by the biconditional are 'if and only if', 'just in case that', and 'is a necessary and sufficient condition for.' It is sometimes difficult to tell whether some statements in ordinary language should be represented by the conditional or the biconditional. For example the sentence *I will leave tomorrow if I get the car fixed* might mean that getting the car fixed is a sufficient condition for leaving tomorrow (although I might leave tomorrow anyway), but it might be intended to mean that getting the car fixed is not only a sufficient but also a necessary condition for leaving tomorrow (I won't leave unless the car gets fixed). The latter interpretation is forced when the connective is 'if and only if': *I will leave tomorrow if and only if I get the car fixed.* In mathematics this connective is frequently abbreviated 'iff.' Formal definitions of mathematical terms always employ it. The usual form is

(6–3) *X* is called a *Y* (or is a *Y*) iff *X* has property *P*.

Using 'if' instead of 'iff' would leave open the possibility that *X* might also be called a *Y* (the term being defined) in other circumstances as well. The 'if and only if' makes it a proper definition by restricting *X*'s being called *Y* to *only* those cases in which *X* has property *P*.

The truth tables provide a general and systematic method of computing the truth value of any arbitrarily complex statement. The number of lines in the truth table is determined by the requirement that all possible combinations of truth values of atomic statements must be considered. In general, there are 2^n lines when there are n atomic statements. The order of evaluating the constituent statements is from the most deeply embedded one to the outermost. So to construct a truth table for $((p \mathrel{\&} q) \to \sim (p \lor r))$, one would proceed as follows:

(i) construct columns for the atomic statements p, q and r,

(ii) construct columns for $(p \mathrel{\&} q)$ and for $(p \lor r)$,

(iii) construct a column for $\sim (p \lor r)$ reversing the values for $(p \lor r)$,

(iv) construct the truth table for the entire statement, applying the conditional table to the table for $(p \mathrel{\&} q)$ and the table for $\sim (p \lor r)$.

The entire process is laid out in the following table.

p	q	r	$(p \mathrel{\&} q)$	$(p \lor r)$	$\sim (p \lor r)$	$((p \mathrel{\&} q) \to \sim (p \lor r))$
1	1	1	1	1	0	0
1	1	0	1	1	0	0
1	0	1	0	1	0	1
1	0	0	0	1	0	1
0	1	1	0	1	0	1
0	1	0	0	0	1	1
0	0	1	0	1	0	1
0	0	0	0	0	1	1

Table 6–6: Truth table for
$((p \mathrel{\&} q) \to \sim (p \lor r))$

Obviously truth tables can get very complex when more than three atomic statements are involved, and clerical errors are easily made. But in principle we can compute the entire table for any complex statement.

6.3   Tautologies, contradictions and contingencies

Statements can be classified according to their truth tables. A statement is called a *tautology* if the final column in its truth table contains nothing but 1's, i.e. the statement is always true, whatever the initial assignment of truth values to its atomic statements. Such statements are true simply because of the meaning of the connectives. A statement is called a *contradiction* if the final column in its truth table contains nothing but 0's, i.e. it is always false, whatever the initial assignment of truth values to its atomic statements. All other statements with both 1 and 0 in their truth table are called *contingent* statements or *contingencies*. Their truth or falsity does depend on the initial truth value assignment to their atomic statements.

Some examples of each type, which the reader may verify, are:

- tautologies: $(p \lor \sim p)$, $(p \to p)$, $(p \to (q \to p))$, $\sim (p \mathbin{\&} \sim p)$

- contradictions: $\sim (p \lor \sim p)$, $(p \mathbin{\&} \sim p)$, $\sim ((p \lor q) \leftrightarrow (q \lor p))$

- contingencies: p, $(p \lor p)$, $((p \lor q) \to q)$, $((p \to q) \to p)$

Here, for example, are truth tables for $(p \lor \sim p)$ and $(p \mathbin{\&} \sim p)$:

p	$\sim p$	$(p \lor \sim p)$
1	0	1
0	1	1

Table 6–7: Truth table for tautology
$(p \lor \sim p)$

p	$\sim p$	$(p \mathbin{\&} \sim p)$
1	0	0
0	1	0

Table 6–8: Truth table for contradiction
$(p \mathbin{\&} \sim p)$

An important property of tautologies and contradictions is that any statements whatever may be substituted for the atomic statements without affecting the truth value of the original expression. For example, if in the
tautology $(p \lor \sim p)$ we replace p by $(q \to r)$, the resulting expression
$((q \to r) \lor \sim (q \to r))$ is still a tautology, as shown in Table 6–9. In
general, the substitution of any statement Q for p in $(p \lor \sim p)$ produces
a statement of the form $(Q \lor \sim Q)$. Whatever the truth value of Q in any
particular line, the truth value of $\sim Q$ is the opposite; thus, one must be
true and the other false. The disjunction of Q and $\sim Q$ is therefore true on
every line of the truth table. Since Q may be any statement at all, elementary or complex, we see that this tautology (and all tautologies in fact) is
true by virtue of its *form*, i.e., the arrangement of statements and connectives, and not because of the particular statements it is made of. The same
considerations apply, *mutatis mutandis*, to contradictions.

q	r	$(q \to r)$	$\sim (q \to r)$	$((q \to r) \lor \sim (q \to r))$
1	1	1	0	1
1	0	0	1	1
0	1	1	0	1
0	0	1	0	1

Table 6–9: Truth table showing that
$((q \to r) \lor \sim (q \to r))$ is a tautology

It is often very important to know whether a certain statement is a
tautology or not, but since long truth tables are cumbersome, there is a
simple "quick falsification" test which searches systematically for a line on
a truth table whose final value is 0. If the search is completed and no such
line is found, then we know for sure the statement under investigation is
a tautology. The test is an application of the general reasoning strategy
of *reductio ad absurdum*. We assume there is a line whose final value is 0,
and reason "backwards" from that assumption to see whether we can find
an assignment of truth values to the atomic statements without running
into contradictory or conflicting assignments. The procedure is illustrated
first with a simple example: $(p \to (q \to p))$. Assume there is a line whose
final value is 0. We enter the truth value directly under the principal or
"highest" connective i.e., the last one added in the syntactic construction of
the formula.

$$(p \rightarrow (q \rightarrow p))$$
$$0$$

Then reasoning from that assumption, we know that the antecedent of this conditional must be true and the consequent false, since that is the only 0-case for conditionals.

$$(p \rightarrow (q \rightarrow p))$$
$$1 \quad 0 \qquad 0$$

Now we simply fill out the 1-assignment for the atomic p in the consequent: (since the assignment of truth values to the atomic statement must be uniform, i.e., the same throughout the entire formula).

$$(p \rightarrow (q \rightarrow p))$$
$$1\,0 \qquad 0 \ 1$$

Looking at the truth table for conditionals we see now that we run into conflicting assignments: on the one hand, the consequent $(q \rightarrow p)$ should be false, but on the other hand that cannot be the case, since p is true and $(q \rightarrow p)$ can only be false if p is false, given the table for conditionals. Hence we may conclude that the assumption that there is a line on the truth table for this statement which ends in false is itself false. Thus all lines must be 1; $(p \rightarrow (q \rightarrow p))$ is a tautology.

Let's work through another example with the very similar, but contingent $((p \rightarrow q) \rightarrow p)$.

 Step 1. $((p \rightarrow q) \rightarrow p)$
$$0$$
 Step 2. $((p \rightarrow q) \rightarrow p)$
$$1 \qquad 0\,0$$
 Step 3. $((p \rightarrow q) \rightarrow p)$
$$0 \ 1 \qquad 0\,0$$

(The antecedent $(p \rightarrow q)$ must be true, while p is false, and that is admissable.)

 Step 4. $((p \rightarrow q) \rightarrow p)$
$$0 \ 1\,0 \quad 0\,0$$

or

Step 4'. $((p \to q) \to p)$
                0 1 1   0 0

Thus the truth value of q may be either 1 or 0, and the procedure is completed without running into conflicting assignments. So $((p \to q) \to p)$ must be at least contingent, though it may even be a contradiction. We cannot now do a similar short-cut test to see whether it is a contradiction, since we end up writing the complete truth table checking for all the other cases. Note that this method may not always save time if there turn out to be many possible assignments which we have to check for a line ending in 0.

6.4   Logical equivalence, logical consequence and laws

If a biconditional statement is a tautology, the two constituent statements so connected are *logically equivalent*. For example, the truth table in Table 6-10 shows the statements $\sim (p \lor q)$ and $(\sim p \,\&\, \sim q)$ to be logically equivalent since $(\sim (p \lor q) \leftrightarrow (\sim p \,\&\, \sim q))$ is a tautology:

p	q	$(p \lor q)$	$\sim (p \lor q)$	$\sim p$	$\sim q$	$(\sim p \,\&\, \sim q)$	$(\sim (p \lor q) \leftrightarrow (\sim p \,\&\, \sim q))$
1	1	1	0	0	0	0	1
1	0	1	0	0	1	0	1
0	1	1	0	1	0	0	1
0	0	0	1	1	1	1	1

Table 6–10: Truth table showing the logical
equivalence of $\sim (p \lor q)$ and $(\sim p \,\&\, \sim q)$

Logically equivalent statements may also be characterized by saying that they have the same truth value for any assignment of truth values to the atomic statement (note the fourth and seventh columns in Figure 6–10). It is of course just this fact which insures that the biconditional connecting the two formulas will always be true.

   Logically equivalent statements are important for the analysis of valid patterns of reasoning because they may freely replace one another in any statement without affecting its truth value. For example, in the statement $(p \lor q)$, replacement of p by the logically equivalent complex statement $(p \,\&\, p)$ yields a statement $((p \,\&\, p) \lor q)$ whose truth value is exactly the same as the original statement, whatever that may happen to be. Substitution of logically equivalent expressions always preserves truth value, i.e. preserves *both* truth and falsity. To denote logical equivalence between two arbitrary statements P and Q we write $P \Longleftrightarrow Q$. Note that this "double arrow" is not a new connective for statements, but rather a convenient notation for expressing that $P \leftrightarrow Q$ is a tautology.

If a conditional statement is a tautology, we say that the consequent is a *logical consequence* of the antecedent or, equivalently, that the antecedent *logically implies* the consequent. An example is shown in the truth table of Table 6–11, which demonstrates that q is a logical consequence of $((p \rightarrow q) \, \& \, p)$.

p	q	$(p \rightarrow q)$	$((p \rightarrow q) \, \& \, p)$	$(((p \rightarrow q) \, \& \, p) \rightarrow q)$
1	1	1	1	1
1	0	0	0	1
0	1	1	0	1
0	0	1	0	1

Table 6–11: Truth table showing that q is a
logical consequence of $((p \rightarrow q) \, \& \, p)$

In contrast to logical equivalence, the relation of logical consequence preserves truth but not necessarilly falsity. That is, is the antecedent of a tautologous conditional is true, then the consequent must be true also (cf. line 1 of Table 6–11, for example). If the antecedent is false, then nothing can be guaranteed about the truth value of the consequent (cf. lines 3–4 of Table 6–11). The relation of logical consequence is important, as we will see in the next section, since it is the basis for the construction of valid arguments. We write $P \Rightarrow Q$ to indicate that Q is a logical consequence of P.

Note that when $P \Rightarrow Q$ we cannot in general substitute Q for P in a larger formula and be guaranteed that truth will be preserved. For example, given that $(p \, \& \sim p) \Rightarrow p$ (which the reader may quickly verify by a truth table), we cannot conclude that $((p \, \& \sim p) \rightarrow q) \Rightarrow (p \rightarrow q)$, replacing $(p \, \& \sim p)$ by its logical consequence p. In fact, if p is true and q is false, then $((p \, \& \sim p) \rightarrow q)$ will be true and $(p \rightarrow q)$ false. Thus, our remarks about truth preservation by logical consequence pertain only to replacement of *an entire formula* by a logical consequence of that formula. This is in

Laws of statement logic

1. Idempotent Laws
(a) $(P \vee P) \iff P$
(b) $(P \mathbin{\&} P) \iff P$

2. Associative Laws
(a) $((P \vee Q) \vee R) \iff (P \vee (Q \vee R))$
(b) $((P \mathbin{\&} Q) \mathbin{\&} R) \iff (P \mathbin{\&} (Q \mathbin{\&} R))$

3. Commutative Laws
(a) $(P \vee Q) \iff (Q \vee P)$
(b) $(P \mathbin{\&} Q) \iff (Q \mathbin{\&} P)$

4. Distributive Laws
(a) $(P \vee (Q \mathbin{\&} R)) \iff ((P \vee Q) \mathbin{\&} (P \vee R$
(b) $(P \mathbin{\&} (Q \vee R)) \iff ((P \mathbin{\&} Q) \vee (P \mathbin{\&} R$

5. Identity Laws
(a) $(P \vee F) \iff P$
(b) $(P \vee T) \iff T$
(c) $(P \mathbin{\&} F) \iff F$
(d) $(P \mathbin{\&} T) \iff P$

6. Complement Laws
(a) $(P \vee \sim P) \iff T$
(b) $\sim \sim P \iff P$
   (also called *double negation*)
(c) $(P \mathbin{\&} \sim P) \iff F$

7. DeMorgan's Laws
(a) $\sim (P \vee Q) \iff (\sim P \mathbin{\&} \sim Q)$
(b) $\sim (P \mathbin{\&} Q) \iff (\sim P \vee \sim Q)$

8. Conditional Laws
(a) $(P \to Q) \iff (\sim P \vee Q)$
(b) $(P \to Q) \iff (\sim Q \to \sim P)$
   (also called *contraposition*)
(c) $(P \to Q) \iff \sim (P \mathbin{\&} \sim Q)$

9. Biconditional Laws
(a) $(P \leftrightarrow Q) \iff ((P \to Q) \mathbin{\&} (Q \to P))$
(b) $(P \leftrightarrow Q) \iff ((\sim P \mathbin{\&} \sim Q) \vee (P \mathbin{\&} Q))$

Table 6–12

contrast to the relation of logical equivalence where, as we noted above, replacement of *any subformula* by a logically equivalent expression preserves the truth value of the entire formula.

It is convenient to have at hand a small number of logical equivalences from which all others may be derived. Table 6–12 gives those "laws" most frequently used, together with their names. This list is redundant in that some equivalences are derivable from others, but it is a convenient set to work with. Since we will refer to them repeatedly in this and the next chapter, it is worthwhile to memorize them. We write T for any arbitrarily chosen tautology and F for any contradiction, and P, Q, R for any statements whatever, whether atomic of complex.

We may verify that these equivalences do indeed hold by the truth table method. As an example, take an instance of the equivalence 8(a) of this table: $(p \rightarrow q) \iff (\sim p \lor q)$. If these two statements are equivalent, their corresponding biconditional must be a tautology. We may check that with a truth table as shown in Table 6–13. Furthermore, in view of our remarks in the preceding section about the preservation of tautologousness under uniform substitution of atomic statements, we know that $(P \rightarrow Q) \leftrightarrow (\sim P \lor Q)$ is a tautology, for any statements P and Q whatever; hence, the (a) case of the Conditional Laws.

p	q	$(p \rightarrow q)$	$\sim p$	$(\sim p \lor q)$	$((p \rightarrow q) \leftrightarrow (\sim p \lor q))$
1	1	1	0	1	1
1	0	0	0	0	1
0	1	1	1	1	1
0	0	1	1	1	1

Table 6–13: Truth table verifying a logical
equivalence.

Since logically equivalent statements may be substituted for each other with preservation of truth values, we may use these laws to transform a statement into one which is logically equivalent but perhaps of lesser complexity. The procedure may be illustrated with a simple example, showing that $(p \rightarrow (\sim q \lor p))$ reduces to T, i.e. it is a tautology. We write the law used in each step of the derivation at the right.

(6-4) 1. $(p \rightarrow (\sim q \vee p))$
       2. $(\sim p \vee (\sim q \vee p))$ Conditional law
       3. $((\sim q \vee p) \vee \sim p)$ Commutative law
       4. $(\sim q \vee (p \vee \sim p))$ Associative law
       5. $\sim q \vee T$ Complement law
       6. T Identity law

As we have said, substitution of logical equivalents can be carried out on subformulas contained within larger formulas. For example, $(p \ \& \ (q \rightarrow r))$ is logically equivalent to $(p \ \& \ (\sim q \vee r))$, where the latter is derived from the former by replacing the subformula $(q \rightarrow r)$ by its logical equivalent $(\sim q \vee r)$. Since logically equivalent formulas have the same truth values on every line of their truth tables, they will contribute in the same way to the truth values of larger formulas in which they are embedded. Therefore, the truth value of a larger formula will be unaffected by the substitution of logically equivalent subformulas. This principle is sometimes referred to as the Rule of Substitution.

This rule applies only to the substitution of subformulas, i.e., wff's which are syntactic constituents of a larger formula. It would not be allowed, for example, to convert $(p \ \& \ (q \rightarrow r))$ into $(q \ \& \ (p \rightarrow r))$, citing the logical equivalence of $(p \ \& \ q)$ and $(q \ \& \ p)$, since $(p \ \& \ q)$ is not a subformula (constituent) of $(p \ \& \ (q \rightarrow r))$.

In the following derivation the application of the Rule of Substitution is explicitly noted by "(Sub.)" at line 4. This derivation does not achieve a simplification of the original formula but shows how one of the logical equivalences, contraposition, can be established using some of the other ones. P and Q here are arbitrary wffs.

(6-5) 1. $P \rightarrow Q$
       2. $\sim P \vee Q$ Cond.
       3. $Q \vee \sim P$ Comm.
       4. $\sim \sim Q \vee \sim P$ Compl. (Sub.)
       5. $\sim Q \rightarrow \sim P$ Cond.

Note that essentially the same derivation could have been given to convert $(p \rightarrow q)$ into the logically equivalent $(\sim q \rightarrow \sim p)$, but since the equivalence holds under any uniform substitutions of formulas for p and q, we may as well carry out the derivation for the general case, i.e., as a *derivation schema*.

6.5 Natural deduction

We have shown thus far how statements are combined syntactically, how truth tables represent the semantics of connectives and how we use them to compute the truth value of a complex statement, and how logical laws allow rewriting a statement as a logically equivalent one. We are now ready to take up an analysis of valid patterns of reasoning.

An *argument* consists of (1) a number of statements called *premises*, which are assumed to be true, even if just for the sake of the argument, and (2) a statement which is called the *conclusion*, whose truth is alledged to follow necessarily from the assumed truth of the premises. We are interested in characterizing the valid forms of argument by defining a number of inference rules which guarantee truth preservation (but which may or may not preserve falsehood). An argument is called *valid* if and only if there is no uniform assignment of truth values to its atomic statements which makes all its premises true but its conclusion false; if there is such an assignment we call the argument *invalid*.

The criterion for validity can be formulated differently, but equivalently, by requiring that, if $P_1, P_2, \ldots, P_n$ are the premises, and Q the conclusion, the statement $((P_1 \mathbin{\&} P_2 \mathbin{\&} \ldots \mathbin{\&} P_n) \to Q)$ is a tautology. This is so because the conditional is tautologous just in case there is no possibility of a true antecedent and a false conclusion. Relating the validity of arguments to tautologies allows us to use the laws from the previous section to infer that any uniform substitution for the atomic statements in a valid argument produces another valid argument.

Let's take a simple example of a natural language argument we all intuitively judge to be valid. We use .∴. to indicate the conclusion, read as 'therefore'.

(6-6)   If John loves Mary, then Mary is happy
         John loves Mary
  ∴. ‾‾‾‾‾‾‾‾‾‾‾‾‾‾‾‾‾‾‾‾‾‾‾‾‾‾‾‾‾‾‾‾‾‾‾‾‾‾
     Mary is happy

Translating this argument to the formal language with the following key:
p—John loves Mary,
q—Mary is happy,
we have:

(6–7) $p \to q$

           p
           _____
$\therefore\, q$

The truth table we constructed as Table 6–11 shows this argument to be
valid. The table demonstrates that q is a logical consequence of $((p \to$
$q)$ & $p)$. By the principle of uniform substitution in tautologies, we can
say that $(((P \to Q)$ & $P) \to Q)$ is a tautology for any formulas P and Q
whatever, and thus

(6–8) $P \to Q$

           P
           _____
$\therefore\, Q$

is a valid argument form. It is traditionally called *Modus Ponens*. Here is a
more complicated instance:

(6–9) $((\sim (r \lor s) \to t) \to (r$ & $t))$
           $(\sim (r \lor s) \to t)$
           _____
$\therefore\, \overline{(r\ \&\ t)}$

Here is an example of an invalid argument:

(6–10) $p \to q$

           q
           _____
$\therefore\, p$

The test of validity by truth table (Table 6–14), shows that the corresponding
conditional is not a tautology; thus, it is possible for the premises to be true
and the conclusion false, namely, when p is false and q is true.

p	q	$(p \to q)$	$((p \to q)$ & $q)$	$(((p \to q)$ & $q) \to p))$
1	1	1	1	1
1	0	0	0	1
0	1	1	1	0
0	0	1	0	1

Table 6–14: Truth table for
$(((p \to q)$ & $q) \to p)$

An English example which would be translated into the argument in (6–10) is as follows:

(6–11)   If John loves Mary, then Mary is happy
         Mary is happy
         ∴ John loves Mary

It is easy to see in this simple case that the truth of the premises does not logically imply the truth of the conclusion, but in more complex instances one can sometimes be deluded into thinking that the argument is valid. Such seductive invalid argument forms are called *fallacies*. This one is known as *the fallacy of affirming the consequent*. A similar one, the *fallacy of denying the antecedent*, reasons from $(p \to q)$ and $\sim p$ to the conclusion $\sim q$.

Although the validity of any argument form may be determined by constructing a truth table, it is often inconvenient to do so, particularly if it contains a large number of elementary statements. An argument which contains five elementary statements would require a truth table of 2^5 or 32 lines, for example.

An alternative is to analyze the argument into a sequence of simpler arguments, and if these simpler arguments have already been shown to be valid, we can be sure that the original argument is also valid. For example, to demonstrate the validity of the argument in (6–12)

(6–12) $(p \to (q \to (r \ \& \ s)))$
         p
         q
         ∴ $(r \ \& \ s)$

we could show that the conclusion follows from the premises by a sequence of two applications of the valid argument form *Modus Ponens*. This is shown in (6–13).

(6–13)   1. $(p \to (q \to (r \ \& \ s)))$
         2. p
         3. q
         4. $(q \to (r \ \& \ s))$ from lines 1 and 2 by *Modus Ponens*
         5. $(r \ \& \ s)$ from lines 3 and 4 by *Modus Ponens*

Simple valid argument forms which can be used in the way we just used

Modus Ponens are known as *rules of inference*. The seven listed in Table 6–15 will suffice for all of the arguments we will encounter in this section. Like the table of logical equivalences given above, this list is redundant: some of the rules can be derived from others, together with the logical equivalences. As an exercise, the reader may wish to check each one for validity by means of a truth table.

Rules of Inference

Name & Abbr.	*Form*	*Example*
Modus Ponens (M.P.)	$P \rightarrow Q$ P $\therefore Q$	If John loves Mary, Mary is happy John loves Mary $\therefore$ Mary is happy
Modus Tollens (M.T.)	$P \rightarrow Q$ $\sim Q$ $\therefore \sim P$	If John loves Mary, Mary is happy Mary is not happy $\therefore$ John does not love Mary
Hypothetical Syllogism (H.S.)	$P \rightarrow Q$ $Q \rightarrow R$ $\therefore P \rightarrow R$	If Fred lives in Paris, then Fred lives in France If Fred lives in France, then Fred lives in Europe $\therefore$ If Fred lives in Paris, then Fred lives in Europe
Disjunctive Syllogism (D.S.)	$P \lor Q$ $\sim P$ $\therefore Q$	Fred lives in Paris, or Fred lives in London Fred does not live in Paris $\therefore$ Fred lives in London
Simplification (Simp.)	$P \& Q$ $\therefore P$	Roses are red, and violets are blue $\therefore$ Roses are red
Conjunction (Conj.)	P Q $\therefore P \& Q$	Roses are red. Violets are blue. $\therefore$ Roses are red, and violets are blue
Addition (Add.)	P $\therefore P \lor Q$	Roses are red $\therefore$ Roses are red, or cigarettes are a health hazard

Table 6–15: Common rules of inference for
statement logic

Here is an example of an argument using these rules. The lines are numbered for convenience in referring to them, and every line other than the premises is justified by a rule of inference and the lines used by that rule.

(6–14)   1. $p \rightarrow q$
         2. $p \lor s$
         3. $q \rightarrow r$
         4. $s \rightarrow t$
         5. $\sim r$
         6. $\sim q$ 3,5 M.T.
         7. $\sim p$ 1,6 M.T.
         8. s 2,7 D.S.
         9. t 4,8 M.P.

The derivation in (6–14) is said to be a *proof* of t from the premises in lines 1-5. Since the premises also logically imply the statements in lines 6, 7, and 8, these have also been proved, and in fact we could have stopped after any one of these lines and called the derivation a proof of $\sim q$, $\sim p$, or s; it all depends on where we focus our attention. Note, however, that given some premises and an alleged conclusion, we are not assured that there is some derivation leading from the premises to that conclusion (there won't be when the argument form is invalid), and even when there is one, we cannot be sure that we will be able to find it. On the other hand, given an alleged proof such as (6–14), it is a simple matter to check whether it is in fact a proof by verifying the derivation of each line. In general, logic provides us with methods for checking proofs but not for discovering them. It is true that in statement logic one can always determine whether a given conclusion follows from given premises (we could always construct the truth table for the corresponding conditional), but in more complex systems such as that of the next chapter there is no general method for determining this.

Here is a more challenging proof, whose difficulty resides in the fact that the premises are not of the right form to apply any rule of inference directly.

(6–15)   Prove $(p \to q)$ from the premises $(p \to (q \lor r))$ and $\sim r$.

$\quad$ 1. $(p \to (q \lor r))$
$\quad$ 2. $\sim r$
$\quad$ 3. $\sim p \lor (q \lor r)$ $\qquad$ 1 Cond.
$\quad$ 4. $(\sim p \lor q) \lor r$ $\qquad$ 3 Assoc.
$\quad$ 5. $r \lor (\sim p \lor q)$ $\qquad$ 4 Comm.
$\quad$ 6. $\sim p \lor q$ $\qquad$ 2, 5 D.S.
$\quad$ 7. $p \to q$ $\qquad$ 6 Cond.

By converting the first premise to an equivalent statement by the Conditional, Associative and Commutative Laws, we are finally able to apply D.S. as the sole rule of inference in this proof. Recall that substitution of logical equivalents preserves truth value, and so in particular it preserves truth. Thus, in a proof we can never pass from truth to falsity by replacing a formula by its logical equivalent, and validity will not be affected.

$\quad$ The following proof makes use of the Rule of Substitution in deriving logical equivalents:

(6–16) $\quad$ 1. $\sim (p \to \sim q)$
$\qquad$ 2. $\sim r$
$\qquad$ 3. $\sim (\sim (p \mathbin{\&} \sim \sim q))$ $\qquad$ 1 Cond. (Sub.)
$\qquad$ 4. $(p \mathbin{\&} \sim \sim q)$ $\qquad$ 3 Comp.
$\qquad$ 5. $(p \mathbin{\&} q)$ $\qquad$ 4 Comp. (Sub.)
$\qquad$ 6. $((p \mathbin{\&} q) \mathbin{\&} \sim r)$ $\qquad$ 2,5 Conj.
$\qquad$ 7. $(p \mathbin{\&} (q \mathbin{\&} \sim r))$ $\qquad$ 6 Assoc.
$\qquad$ 8. $(p \mathbin{\&} \sim \sim (q \mathbin{\&} \sim r))$ $\qquad$ 7 Comp. (Sub.)
$\qquad$ 9. $(p \mathbin{\&} \sim (q \to r))$ $\qquad$ 8 Cond. (Sub.)

$\quad$ (Henceforth we will not mention the Rule of Substitution explicitly in the annotation of a proof but merely refer to the logical equivalence used in deriving that line.)

6.5.1 Conditional Proof

Certain proofs whose conclusions contain a conditional as the main connective are more easily proved by a method of *conditional proof*. Suppose an argument has $P_1, P_2, \ldots, P_n$ as premises and $Q \to R$ as conclusion. In a conditional proof we add the antecedent Q of the conclusion as an additional *auxiliary* premise and then from Q together with the other premises derive

R. The conditional proof is concluded by cancelling the auxiliary premise Q and writing the conclusion $Q \to R$. The validity of this method of proof is based on the fact (which you should check for yourself) that

$$((P_1 \,\&\, P_2 \,\&\, \ldots \,\&\, P_n) \to (Q \to R))$$

is logically equivalent to

$$((P_1 \,\&\, P_2 \,\&\, \ldots \,\&\, P_n \,\&\, Q) \to R))$$

(where $P_1, \ldots, P_n, Q$, and R are any wff's.) As an example we construct a conditional version of (6–15).

(6–17) Prove $(p \to q)$ from the premises $(p \to (q \lor r))$ and $\sim r$.

1.	$(p \to (q \lor r))$	
2.	$\sim r$	
3.	p	Auxiliary Premise
4.	$q \lor r$	1, 3 M.P.
5.	$r \lor q$	4 Comm.
6.	q	2, 5 D.S.
7.	$p \to q$	3–6 Conditional Proof

In writing a conditional proof we indicate with a bar each line which is based on the auxiliary premise in order to remind ourselves that we are working under a special additional assumption. A conditional proof must always cancel that auxiliary premise by the rule of Conditional Proof before ending the entire proof. It is for obvious reasons forbidden to use any lines of the conditional part of the proof after this cancellation. The following proof shows how conditional proofs may be embedded.

(6–18) Prove $((q \to s) \to (p \to s))$ from $(p \to (q \,\&\, r))$

1.	$(p \to (q \,\&\, r))$	
2.	$q \to s$	Auxiliary Premise
3.	p	Auxiliary Premise
4.	$q \,\&\, r$	1, 3 M.P.
5.	q	4 Simpl.
6.	s	2, 5 M.P.
7.	$p \to s$	3–6 Conditional Proof
8.	$((q \to s) \to (p \to s))$	2–7 Conditional Proof

Comparable restrictions apply in more deeply embedded conditional proofs. The exit from one level to the next higher one is always accompanied by the formation of a conditional whose antecedent is the auxiliary premise from the lower level and whose conclusion is the formula just derived (see line 7 in (6–18), for example). Using lines from lower levels in lines of the proof at higher levels is also forbidden (e.g., q in line 5 is not available for use after we leave the lowest level at line 7). Note, however, that lines from higher levels *are* available in lower levels (e.g., line 1 is used in the derivation of line 4).

Auxiliary premises can be any wff whatsoever, so long as they prove useful towards our final goal. In (6–18) the statement s did not occur anywhere in the initial premise, but it is perfectly legitimate as part of an auxiliary premise.

6.5.2   Indirect Proof

The inferences we have introduced up till now are direct proofs: the conclusion is produced as the final line of the proof by a series of valid inferences. In an *indirect* proof, we introduce the negation of the desired conclusion as an auxiliary premise and reason to a contradiction. Given the assumption that the other premises are all true, this contradiction shows that the auxiliary premise to be false, so its positive form, *i.e.*, the desired conclusion, must be true. This is the method of proof we have called *reductio ad absurdum*. We now have the means to make this reasoning formally precise as a rule of inference. It is a special form of conditional proof, as it uses an auxiliary premise, but that auxiliary premise is not chosen freely; rather it is the negation of the desired conclusion. The conclusion is not necessarily of conditional form, and may even be atomic. Here is an example of *reductio ad absurdum*:

(6–19)   Prove p from $(p \lor q)$, $(q \to r)$ and $\sim r$

1.	$p \lor q$	
2.	$q \to r$	
3.	$\sim r$	
4.	$\sim p$	Auxiliary Premise
5.	q	1, 4 D.S.
6.	r	2, 5 M.P.
7.	$r \,\&\, \sim r$	3, 6 Conj.
8.	p	4–7 Indirect Proof

Line 7 is a contradiction, and hence the auxiliary premise in line 4 is false.

Indirect proof can be shown to be a special form of conditional proof in the following way. Adding the auxiliary premise $\sim p$ in the proof above, for example, we derive $(r \;\&\; \sim r)$. By the rule of conditional proof we get $(\sim p \rightarrow (r \;\&\; \sim r))$. As the next line we add the tautology $\sim (r \;\&\; \sim r)$: a tautology can be written down as a valid step anywhere in any proof since it can never be false. Then we derive $\sim \sim p$ by Modus Tollens and then p by the Complement Law.

Indirect proofs can have other indirect proofs and conditional proofs embedded in them, and likewise they can be embedded in conditional proofs. In all such cases, lines from a more deeply embedded section cannot be assumed true in a less deeply embedded section.

Indirect proofs are used very frequently in mathematics, where they are often much easier to construct than a direct proof. We encountered an instance of it, for example, in showing that the null set is a subset of every set. By assuming the negation of this statement, we were led to the conclusion that the null set has a member, which, taken with the definition of the null set, forms a contradiction. Thus, the assumption that the null set is not a subset of every set reduces to an absurdity and cannot be maintained.

6.6   Beth Tableaux

In current research in theoretical computer science and logic, machines are being developed which automatically prove theorems, so called 'theorem provers'. The main motivation is to simulate human theorem provers (which you are becoming). But a straightforward implementation of the proof procedures we have introduced for this elementary logical system is not possible. If you attempt to derive a statement mechanically from a given set of premises, you may start trying to substitute equivalent statements for the premises or for parts of them. It is obviously not feasible to check *all* possible substitutions as there are infinitely many equivalent statements to consider. You rely often on a certain intuition or heuristic to determine which statements are particularly useful to try and which are not. At present, such heuristics are too little understood to consider implementing them in an automated theorem prover. But if there is a clear procedure to list all substitutions that should be taken into account for any given statement to be proven, its derivation from the premises becomes feasible also for a machine. Such a procedure exists and is known as the *Beth method of Semantic Tableaux*, after the Dutch logician Evert Beth. The finite number of substitutions this method needs in deducing a statement are:

1. the statement itself

2. all of its constituent statements

3. certain simple combinations of these statements, depending on the given premises.

It is one of the most attractive features of (closed) semantic tableaux, considered as a method of proof, that all statements which appear in a proof of a statement P are constituent statements of P. In this section we will present the method for statements, and in the next chapter we will extend the method to include some of the internal structure of statements.

Beth Tableaux are based on the idea that a conditional statement is proven when all attempts to find a counterexample, falsifying its consequent while verifying its premises, are shown to fail. If there is a counterexample, this method will find it, and what is more, if there is no counterexample, we will always find out after a finite number of steps. A proof consists always of a number of premises P_1 & P_2 & ... & P_{n-1} and the conclusion P_n, connected by the conditional connective. A Beth Tableau attempts to make the premises true and the conclusion false, hence making the entire statement $((P_1$ & P_2 & ... & $P_{n-1}) \rightarrow P_n)$ false. If it is not successful, the tableau is 'closed', and no interpretation of the substatements provides a counterexample to the validity of the argument. But if it is successful, the tableau will show how to construct a counterexample. The procedure is quite simple, and we will introduce it by some elementary examples before giving the complete set of rules for construction of tableaux.

Example 1. Prove $\sim\sim p$ from $(p$ & $q)$.

The notation of Beth Tableaux we use here is as follows:

1) Set up two columns, separated by a straight vertical line (use plenty of paper in the beginning, a tableaux might turn out to be rather more complex than you anticipated).

2) Write TRUE on the left and FALSE on the right side of the line.

3) Insert the premise(s) under TRUE on line 1, and the conclusion under FALSE.

	TRUE	FALSE
1.	$(p$ & $q)$	$\sim\sim p$

We reason as follows, knowing the semantics of the connectives from their truth tables. If the premise is $(p \,\&\, q)$, then this is assumed to be true in any attempt to prove the conclusion $\sim\sim p$ from it. Since a conjunction can only be true when both its constituent formulas are true, we can infer that p is true and that q is true. That information we write on the next two lines.

2. p
3. q

Since we have only atomic statements under TRUE now, we have to turn to the statement under FALSE to develop the tableau further. We reason that since the double negation is false, a single negation must be true, because negation simply reverses the truth value of any statement. That is recorded by inserting $\sim p$ under TRUE on the next line.

4. $\sim p$

If a negation is true, that statement without that negation must be false, for the same reason that motivated step 4. So we now get

5. p

We have only atomic statements now, and the tableau cannot be further developed. But if we look back to the information we have extracted from the given premise and conclusion, we see that on line 2 we inferred that p is true, but on line 5 that the same statement p is false. But that is impossible, given the central assumption of logic that a statement cannot be both true and false at the same time. So the otherwise sound reasoning we used in developing the tableau has led us into a contradiction! You may now think that hence the tableau method is of no use at all, but then you jump to conclusions too rashly. For we have set up the tableau from the beginning under a certain assumption: namely, that there exists an assignment of truth values which verifies the premises and falsifies the conclusion. That is why we put the premise under TRUE and the conclusion under FALSE. On that assumption, we ran into a contradiction, just as in a *reductio ad absurdum* proof. This means that our assumption was illegitimate to start with. In other words, there is no way to make the premise true and the conclusion false, i.e. there is no counterexample to the claim that the conclusion follows validly from the premise. The tableaux which run into contradiction by having one and the same statement listed under TRUE and under FALSE

are 'closed' by writing a double line under both sides of the tableau. Note
that the statement which gives closure does not have to be atomic, as it is in
this simple example. Any complex statement which is supposedly both true
and false leads to a contradiction, giving closure. The entire tableau for this
example is as follows:

	TRUE	FALSE
1.	$(p \mathbin{\&} q)$	$\sim\sim p$
2.	p	
3.	q	
4.	$\sim p$	
5.		p
	======	======

To show which connective is 'decomposed' in a line, we can annotate
each line after the first one with the connective symbol subscripted to the
line number, indicating also whether it occurs under TRUE or under FALSE.
The above tableau would have had respectively 2. $_{\&\,T}$, 3. $_{\&\,T}$, 4. $_{\sim F}$ and 5. $_{\sim T}$.
It is a good practice to annotate the following examples for yourself in this
way.

Example 2. Prove $\sim p \lor q$ from $\sim (p \to q)$.

To make the premise $\sim (p \to q)$ true and the conclusion $\sim p \lor q$ false, we
open the tableau as follows:

	TRUE	FALSE
1.	$\sim (p \to q)$	$\sim p \lor q$

Next the statement $\sim p \lor q$ is simplified giving rise to lines 2 and 3.

	TRUE	FALSE
2.		$\sim p$
3.		q

These lines are motivated by the truth table for disjunction, which tells
us that a disjunction is false only when both disjuncts are. Now 2 can be
simplified, since a negation is false when the statement without negation is
true. So the next step is

	TRUE	FALSE
4.	p	

Similarly the premise can be simplified by cancelling the negation and listing
the statement without negation under FALSE.

$$5. \qquad\qquad\qquad | \quad (p \to q)$$

We know that a conditional statement is false just in case its antecedent is true and its consequent is false. So from 5 we get to

$$6. \qquad p \qquad | \qquad q$$

Now all statements have been simplified and no complex statements remain. The tableau shows that when we interpret the atomic statement p as true and the atomic statement q as false, we obtain a counterexample to the original statement $\sim (p \to q) \to \sim p \lor q$. This claim can be verified with the quick falsification method based on truth tables:

$$
\begin{array}{ccccccccc}
\sim(p & \to & q) & \to & \sim p & \lor & q \\
1\ 1 & 0 & 0 & 0 & 0\,1 & 0 & 0
\end{array}
$$

When one and the same atomic statement occurs on both sides of the tableau, we assume that no counterexample can be based on it. This is obviously based on the law that a statement cannot be both true and false.

Example 3 is an illustration of a closing tableau, proving the statement $q \to \sim p \lor q$ valid.

Example 3. Prove $\sim p \lor q$ from q

	TRUE	FALSE
1.	q	$\sim p \lor q$
2.		$\sim p$
3.		q
	======	======

Closure obtained on the statement q is indicated by the ====== line on both sides. If there is a non-atomic statement on either side after closure which may still lead to simplification, this only means that the truth value of that statement does not matter to the validity of the entire sentence, as is clearly the case in this example for $\sim p$. Hence closed tableaux may still contain complex statements, but we cannot and need not apply any more rules to them.

The construction of tableaux may get more complex when there are alternative interpretations to consider. For instance, when a disjunction $p \lor q$ is true, then p may be true or q may be true (or both). In such cases the tableau will split into alternative interpretations. Consider the tableau for $(\sim p \lor q) \to (p \to q)$.

Example 4.

	TRUE	FALSE
1.	$(\sim p \lor q)$	$(p \to q)$
2.	p	
3.		q

```
4.    4.₁  ~p  │ 4.₂  q   │ 4.₁        │ 4.₂
                │ ======   │            │ ======
5.              │          │     p      │
      ======    │          │ ======     │
```

Lines 2 and 3 are just as in Example 1. Line 4 leads to a split into subtableaux 4_1 and 4_2, since the disjunction may be true on the basis of the truth of either disjunct. Each disjunct is hence entered into its 'own' subtableau and we simplify and check for possible closure of each subtableau. In 4, the second subtableau is closed on each side as q occurred under FALSE in 3. Then 5 simplifies the true negation $\sim p$, and again this subtableau closes since p occurred under TRUE in 2.

A (sub)tableau closes only if a statement occurs both under TRUE and under FALSE. A complex tableau closes only if *all* its subtableaux close. If we do not obtain such a statement on both sides in the tableau construction, then we find an assignment of truth values to the atomic statements which constitutes a counterexample to the alledged validity of the tested statement. The entire method of construction is given by the following construction rules.

Construction Rules for Beth Tableaux

		If statement occurs under TRUE	If statement occurs under FALSE
negation	$\sim p$	put p under FALSE	put p under TRUE
conditional	$p \to q$	SPLIT! put q under TRUE, and p under FALSE	put p under TRUE and q under FALSE

conjunction $p \,\&\, q$ put p and q SPLIT!
                under TRUE   put p under FALSE
                                       and q under FALSE

disjunction $p \lor q$ SPLIT!   put p and q under FALSE
                put p under TRUE
                and q under TRUE

Note that the development of one open subtableau suffices to find a counterexample. In constructing subtableaux all statements from the earlier steps in the tableau before it split count in finding closure possibilities. In general, it is a good strategy to apply splitting rules only after you have used all other applicable rules.

Here is an example of a tableau which splits twice.

Example 5. Prove $(p \,\&\, q)$ from $(p \rightarrow q)$

	TRUE			FALSE		
1.	$(p \rightarrow q)$			$(p \,\&\, q)$		
2.	$2._1$	$2._2$	$2._1$ $\quad p$	$2._2$ $\quad q$		
3.	$3._{1.1}$ q $\mid$ $3._{1.2}$	$3._{2.1}$ q $\mid$ $3._{2.2}$	$3._{1.1}$ $\mid$ $3._{1.2}$ p	$3._{2.1}$ $\mid$ $3._{2.2}$ p		
		$===$		$===$		

The split on the second line is constructed by the false conjunction, which makes each of the two conjuncts false. The next line continues this split, and introduces a second split by the true conditional, which makes the consequent true and the antecedent false. Since we have to consider this situation under each of the two assumptions in line 2, we split each subtableau and apply the rule for a true conditional in each subtableau. In attempting to close any subtableau, all statements that occur on lines above a given subtableau must be taken into consideration. The subscripting of subtableaux indicates which higher subtableaux are relevant, e.g., in this example $2._2$ is relevant to $3._{2.1}$, but $2._1$ is not relevant to $3._{2.2}$. Closure can only be obtained for the subtableau $3._{2.1}$, hence we obtain the following counterexamples:

1) $p = 0$ and $q = 1$ $(3._{1.1})$
2) $p = 0$ and $q = 1$ or 0 $(3._{1.2})$
3) $p = 0$ and $q = 0$ $(3._{2.2})$

In each of these cases the premise of this example is true and the conclusion false.

The method of semantic tableaux for the logic of statements constitutes a 'decision procedure' for the validity of statements. This notion will be central in Chapter 8, but we may make a few preliminary remarks about it in the context of the tableau construction. Any statement consists of a finite number of connectives and atomic statements. The rules guarantee that any tableau construction comes to an end: it either closes or it provides a counterexample. Any tableau hence consists of a finite number of steps corresponding to the number of connectives in the statement tested, and a circular or looping tableau is never possible. The only respect in which the procedure is not fully automatic yet is in the order of application of the rules.

Exercises

1. Translate the following sentences into statement logic. Use lower case letters for atomic statements and give the "key" to the translation, i.e., say which atomic statements are the correspondents of which English sentences. (In some cases you may want to use a syntactically different version of the English sentence.) Example: "If John is at the party, then Mary is, too." Translation: $(p \rightarrow q)$. Key: p: "John is at the party"; q: "Mary is at the party".

   (a) Either John is in that room or Mary is, and possibly they both are.

   (b) The fire was set by an arsonist, or there was an accidental explosion in the boiler room.

   (c) When it rains, it pours.

   (d) Sam wants a dog, but Alice prefers cats.

   (e) If Steve comes home late and has not had any supper, we will reheat the stew.

   (f) Clarence is well educated only if he can read Chuvash.

   (g) Marsha won't go out with John unless he shaves off his beard and stops drinking.

   (h) The stock market advances when public confidence in the economy is rising and only then.

   (i) A necessary but perhaps not sufficient condition for negotiations to commence is for Barataria to cease all acts of agression against Titipu.

In each case say what, if anything, has been "lost in translation"; that is, what semantic properties of the English sentence are not represented in the logical formula.

2. The following sentences contain various sorts of ellipsis, so that some of the connectives appear not to be connecting whole statements. Reformulate them so that the connectives connect statements (using different connectives if necessary) and translate into symbolic notation as above.

   (a) John and Bill are going to the movies, but not Tom.

   (b) Susan doesn't like squash or turnips.

   (c) If neither Peter nor Fred is going to the party, then neither will I.

   (d) If Mary hasn't gotten lost or had an accident, she will be here in five minutes.

   (e) A bear or a wolf frightened the boys.

   (f) A party or a softball game would have amused the children.

3. Let p, q and r be true and let s be false. Find the truth values of the following statements.

   (a) $((p \mathbin{\&} q) \mathbin{\&} s)$

   (b) $(p \mathbin{\&} (q \mathbin{\&} s))$

   (c) $p \to s$

   (d) $s \to p$

   (e) $((p \mathbin{\&} q) \leftrightarrow (r \mathbin{\&} \sim s))$

   (f) $(p \to (q \leftrightarrow (r \to s)))$

4. Construct truth tables for each of the following statements. Note whether any are logically equivalent.

   (a) $(p \lor \sim q)$

   (b) $\sim (\sim p \mathbin{\&} q)$

   (c) $((p \leftrightarrow q) \mathbin{\&} p)$

   (d) $((p \to (q \lor \sim r)) \mathbin{\&} (p \to (q \lor \sim r)))$

   (e) $(((p \to q) \to p) \to q)$

5. For each of the following, use the "quick falsification" method to find an assignment of truth values to the atomic statements which makes the entire statement false.

   (a) $(p \lor q)$
   (b) $((p \lor q) \rightarrow (p \,\&\, q))$
   (c) $(\sim (\sim q \lor p) \lor (p \rightarrow q))$
   (d) $((((p \rightarrow q) \rightarrow r) \rightarrow s) \rightarrow (p \rightarrow q))$
   (e) $(((p \lor q) \,\&\, (r \,\&\, s)) \leftrightarrow (((p \,\&\, q) \,\&\, r) \,\&\, s))$

6. Let p, q and r be atomic statements. Which of the following are tautologies, contradictions or contingent statements?

   (a) $(p \lor \sim p)$
   (b) $(p \lor q)$
   (c) $((p \,\&\, q) \rightarrow (p \lor r))$
   (d) $(\sim p \,\&\, \sim (p \rightarrow q))$
   (e) $((p \lor r) \rightarrow \sim p)$

7. Certain of the logical connectives can be defined in terms of others. For example, $(p \rightarrow q)$ can be defined as an abbreviation for $(\sim p \lor q)$, since the two statements are logically equivalent. Hence, all formulas containing the connective $\rightarrow$ could be replaced by formulas containing $\lor$ and $\sim$.

   (a) Define $\rightarrow$ in terms of $\&$ and $\sim$.
   (b) Define $\&$ in terms of $\lor$ and $\sim$.
   (c) Define $\leftrightarrow$ in terms of $\rightarrow$ and $\&$.
       (Thus, the five connectives could ultimately be reduced to two: $\lor$ and $\sim$).
   (d) Show how the five connectives could be reduced to just $\&$ and $\sim$.

8. Use the laws in Table 6–12 to reduce each of the following statements to the simplest equivalent statement.

   (a) $(\sim p \lor (p \,\&\, q))$

(b) $((\sim p \,\&\, q) \lor \sim (p \lor q))$

(c) $(\sim p \,\&\, ((p \,\&\, q) \lor (p \,\&\, r)))$

(d) $((\sim p \,\&\, q) \leftrightarrow (p \lor q))$

(e) $(((p \lor q) \,\&\, (r \lor \sim q)) \rightarrow (p \lor r))$

9. Give a formal proof of validity for each of the following argument forms. (A conditional or indirect proof will be much easier in some.)

(a)
$$p \rightarrow q$$
$$q \rightarrow r$$
$$\sim r$$
$$\therefore \sim p$$

(b)
$$p$$
$$\sim r$$
$$(p \,\&\, \sim r) \rightarrow q$$
$$\therefore q$$

(c)
$$p \lor q$$
$$\sim q$$
$$r \rightarrow \sim p$$
$$\therefore \sim r$$

(d)
$$p \rightarrow \sim q$$
$$r \rightarrow q$$
$$\sim r \rightarrow s$$
$$\therefore p \rightarrow s$$

(e)
$$\sim p \lor q$$
$$\sim q \,\&\, r$$
$$\sim (p \lor q) \rightarrow s$$
$$\therefore r \,\&\, s$$

(f)
$$p \lor (q \,\&\, r)$$
$$\sim t$$
$$(p \lor q) \rightarrow (s \lor t)$$
$$\sim p$$
$$\therefore r \,\&\, s$$

(g)
$$p \leftrightarrow q$$
$$\sim p$$
$$(q \,\&\, \sim r) \lor t$$
$$(s \lor t) \rightarrow r$$
$$\therefore r \,\&\, \sim q$$

(h)
$$\sim p \rightarrow q$$
$$r \rightarrow (s \lor t)$$
$$s \rightarrow \sim r$$
$$p \rightarrow \sim t$$
$$\therefore r \rightarrow q$$

(i)
$$p \rightarrow (q \,\&\, r)$$
$$q \rightarrow s$$
$$r \rightarrow t$$
$$(s \,\&\, t) \rightarrow \sim u$$
$$u$$
$$\therefore \sim p$$

(j)
$$p \rightarrow q$$
$$r \rightarrow s$$
$$\sim q \lor \sim s$$
$$p$$
$$(t \,\&\, u) \rightarrow r$$
$$\therefore \sim t \lor \sim u$$

(k) $(p \,\&\, q) \to (p \to (r \,\&\, s))$ (l) p
        $(p \,\&\, q) \,\&\, u$ $(p \,\&\, q) \vee (p \,\&\, r)$
      $\overline{\therefore \, r \vee s}$ $(p \vee q) \to \sim r$
                                                        $\overline{\therefore \, p \leftrightarrow q}$

10. Express the following arguments in symbolic form, and determine whether they are valid.

   (a) The butler or the cook or the chauffeur killed the baron. If the cook killed the baron, then the stew was poisoned, and if the chauffeur killed the baron, there was a bomb in the car. The stew wasn't poisoned, and the butler didn't kill the baron. Therefore, the chauffeur killed the baron.

   (b) If the subject has not understood the instructions or has not finished reading the sentence, then he has pressed the wrong button or has failed to answer. If he has failed to answer, then the timer hasn't stopped. The subject has pressed the right button, and the timer has stopped. Therefore, the subject understood the instructions.

   (c) If the pressure is 1 atm, the water is boiling only if the temperature is at least 100°C. If the pressure is 1 atm, then the water is frozen only if the temperature is at most 0°C. The pressure is 1 atm and either the temperature is at least 100°C or it is at most 0°C. The water is not boiling. Therefore, the temperature is at most 0°C.

   (d) If I am honest, then I am naive. Either I am honest or naive, or else Sam was right and that magazine salesman is a crook. I am not naive, and that magazine salesman is certainly a crook. Therefore, Sam was right.

   (e) A certain consonantal segment, if it occurs initially, is prevocalic, and if it is noninitial, it is voiceless. If it is either prevocalic or voiceless, it is continuant and strident. If it is continuant, then if it is strident, it is tense. If it is tense, then if it occurs initially, it is palatalized. Therefore, the segment is palatalized and voiceless.

11. Let the set $S = \{p, (p \vee q), (p \vee p), (p \vee \sim p), (p \,\&\, (q \vee \sim q)), (\sim q \to p), (p \to (q \to p)), (\sim p \to q), (p \vee (q \,\&\, \sim q)), (p \vee (q \vee \sim q))\}$. Let the relation $R = \{\langle x, y \rangle \mid x \in S$ and $y \in S$ and $x \Leftrightarrow y\}$

(a) Show that R is an equivalence relation.

(b) Find the equivalence classes into which R partitions S.

12. Construct Beth tableaux to test the validity of each of the following arguments:

(a) $p \to (q \to r))$
   $\sim (\sim p \lor r)$
   _____
   $p \,\&\, \sim q$

(b) $p \to q$
   $q \,\&\, r$
   _____
   $p \,\&\, q$

(c) $(p \to q) \,\&\, (s \lor t)$
   $t \to q$
   _____
   $(p \to q) \lor \sim (s \to q)$

13. Expressions in the propositional calculus may be written in "Polish parenthesis-free notation," which places the connective to the left of the propositions it connects rather than between them. In this notation the connectives are N (negation), A (alternation), K (conjunction), C (conditional), and E (biconditional). The last four extend over the next two well-formed expressions to the right; negation extends over only one. The expressions in standard notation in the left column below would written in Polish notation as shown in the right column.

Standard	Polish
$\sim p$	Np
$p \lor q$	Apq
$p \,\&\, q$	Kpq
$p \to q$	Cpq
$p \leftrightarrow q$	Epq
$(p \,\&\, q) \lor r$	$AKpqr$
$p \,\&\, (q \lor r)$	$KpAqr$

Observe that parentheses are unnecessary in Polish notation to distinguish between formulas such as $(p \,\&\, q) \lor r$ and $p \,\&\, (q \lor r)$.

(a) Translate into Polish notation:

   (i) $((p \vee q) \& (q \vee r)) \& (p \vee s)$

   (ii) $(\sim p \& (\sim p \rightarrow q)) \rightarrow q$

   (iii) $(p \vee q) \rightarrow ((r \leftrightarrow s) \& p)$

(b) Translate into standard notation:

   (i) ApCKNpNqKpEqr

   (ii) KANKAKEE$pqrspqrs$

   (iii) NCAKE$pqrst$

(c) Express DeMorgan's Laws in Polish notation.

Chapter 7

Predicate Logic

7.1 Syntax

We now turn to the second of the logical languages we will examine: predicate logic. In it we will be able to analyze arguments such as (5-1) and (5-2) as well as all the arguments of the statement calculus.

In predicate logic an elementary statement can be composed of a *predicate* and a number of *terms*. For example, $H(s)$ contains a (one-place) predicate H and the term s; the statement $L(j, m)$ is composed of a (two-place) predicate L and two terms, j and m. The former might serve, for example, as the translation of *Socrates is human*, where *Socrates* is represented by s and *is human* by the predicate H. Similarly, $L(j, m)$ might be the predicate logic counterpart of *John loves Mary*.

Predicates are specified as one-place, two-place, etc. according to the number of terms they require to form a statement. In the examples above, H was one-place and L was two-place. Combining a predicate with the wrong number of terms results in an expression which is not well formed, e.g., $H(j, m); L(s)$. Predicates will typically be represented by upper case letters but will not ordinarily carry any explicit indication of the number of terms they require. There is no limit on the number of places for a predicate so long as the number is finite.

We should note here, incidentally, that a predicate in the logical language need not correspond to a predicate in the grammatical sense in a natural language. Although the (logical) predicate H above was used to translate the (grammatical) predicate *is human* in the sentence *Socrates is human*,

137

the logical predicate L corresponds to the transitive verb *loves* in *John loves Mary*, and indeed nothing prevents us from translating *John loves Mary* into predicate logic as $G(m)$, where G is a one-place predicate corresponding to *John loves*, which presumably is not a grammatical constituent at all.

Terms come in two varieties. The first is *individual constants* exemplified by s, m, and j above. As the name suggests, in the semantics of the predicate logic these will denote specific individuals, and in translating natural language statements they will typically show up as the correspondents of proper names such as *John, Mary*, and *Socrates*. The second kind of term is the *individual variable* (or simply *variable*), for which we use lower case letters from the end of the alphabet—*v, w, x, y, z*—with primes and/or subscripts attached if we need to mention more of them. When a predicate is combined with one or more variables, e.g., $H(x)$, $L(m, y)$, the result is not a statement but an expression called an *open statement* or *propositional function*.

An open statement can be made into a statement by prefixing an appropriate number of quantifiers, thus: $(\forall x)H(x)$, $(\exists y)L(m, y)$. The *universal quantifier* is denoted by $\forall$ and is the correspondent of English expressions such as *all, each*, and *every*. The existential quantifier, represented by $\exists$, corresponds to *some* (in the sense of "at least one, possibly more"). The x written alongside the universal quantifier in $(\forall x)H(x)$ indicates that the quantification is with respect to that variable in the expression which follows. This labelling of quantifiers is necessary since an expression may in general contain more than one quantifier and more than one variable. For example, in $(\forall x)(\exists y)L(x, y)$ the first position in $L(x, y)$ is universally quantified and the second existentially, but in $(\exists x)(\forall y)L(x, y)$ it is the other way around.

Letting H correspond once again to *is human*, we might gloss $(\forall x)H(x)$ as *Every individual is human* or *Everything is human*. $(\exists x)H(x)$ would correspond to *Some (at least one) individual is human*, or briefly, *Something is human*. Letting m correspond to *Mary* and L to *loves*, $(\exists y)L(m, y)$ could be the translation of *There is at least one individual whom Mary loves*, or more briefly, *Mary loves something* (or *someone*, if all individuals we happen to be talking about are human). Similarly, $(\forall y)L(m, y)$ would correspond to *Mary loves every individual*, or, again, if all the individuals happen to be human, *Mary loves everyone*.

Note incidentally that in many instances the particular choice of variable letters is not important. Instead of $(\forall x)H(x)$ we could equally well have written $(\forall y)H(y)$ or $(\forall z)H(z)$, etc. Similarly, $(\exists x)L(m, x)$ would do just as well as $(\exists y)L(m,y)$. Of course when more than one variable is involved, we must use different letters for variables which may be distinct, e.g., in $(\forall x)(\exists y)L(x,y)$. To write $L(x,x)$ and then quantifiy, say existentially, to produce $(\exists x)L(x,x)$ would give a statement which we might gloss as *There is at least one individual which loves itself* (or *himself*). Here the same term, x, occupies both positions required by the two-place predicate L. In $(\exists x)(\forall y)L(x,y)$, *There is at least one individual who loves every individual*, the x and the y may take on values which are distinct individuals but they may also be the same; indeed, this statement will be true only if there is at least one individual who loves every individual, including that individual itself (or himself). Still, we should keep in mind that the choice of variable letter is immaterial so long as the same quantifiers are associated with the same predicate positions; i.e., $(\exists y)(\forall x)L(y,x)$ is an alphabetic variant of $(\exists x)(\forall y)L(x,y)$; but $(\exists y)(\forall x)L(y,x)$ and $(\exists x)(\forall y)L(y,x)$ would *not* be alphabetic variants because the quantifiers are associated with different positions in the predicate L.

We will return to further details of the use of quantifiers and variables below, but let us now observe that statements and open statements may be joined by the connectives $\sim, \&, \vee, \rightarrow$, and $\leftrightarrow$; for example:

(7-1)   (i) $\sim H(x)$
           (ii) $\sim H(s)$
           (iii) $((\forall x)H(x) \,\&\, L(j,m))$
           (iv) $(\sim H(s) \rightarrow \sim(\forall x)H(x))$

Expressions (ii), (iii), and (iv) might translate, respectively, *Socrates is not human*, *Everything is human and John loves Mary*, and *If Socrates is not human, then not everything is human*. Formula (i) is not a statement but an open statement since it contains an unquantified variable, and, not being a statement, it would presumably not serve as the translation of any declarative English sentence (perhaps *He is not human*, where the referent of *he* is not specified would come closest).

An open statement, even if internally complex, may always have quantifiers prefixed, so we may, if we choose, convert $\sim H(x)$ into $(\forall x)\sim H(x)$ or $(\exists x)\sim H(x)$ (corresponding to *Every individual is not human* — which is ambiguous for many speakers, but the intended sense here is that each individual fails to be human — and *At least one individual is not human*, respectively.)

Now that we have informally introduced the syntax of the language of
predicate logic by illustration and example, we give a precise formulation of
the syntactic rules.

The vocabulary consists of

(7-2)   (i)   individual constants: $j, m, \ldots$
         (ii)   individual variables: $x, y, z, \ldots$ (sometimes subscripted)
                The individual constants and variables together are called
                the set of *terms*.
         (iii) predicates: $P, Q, R, \ldots$, each with a fixed finite number of
                argument places, called its *arity*.
         (iv)   the five connectives of the logic of statements: $\sim, \vee, \&, \to, \leftrightarrow$
         (v)   two quantifiers: $\forall$ and $\exists$
         (vi)   auxiliary symbols: (,) and [,]

The syntactic rules generate the set of *formulas* of the language of predicate logic. We will define the set of *statements* as a proper subset of this
set of formulas.

(7-3)   (i)   If P is an n-ary (i.e., n-place) predicate and $t_1, \ldots, t_n$
                are terms, then $P(t_1, \ldots, t_n)$ is a formula.
         (ii)   If φ and ψ are formulas, then $\sim\varphi$, $(\varphi \,\&\, \psi)$, $(\varphi \vee \psi)$, $(\varphi \to \psi)$,
                and $(\varphi \leftrightarrow \psi)$ are formulas.
         (iii) If φ is a formula and x is an individual variable, then $(\forall x)\varphi$
                and $(\exists x)\varphi$ are formulas.
         (iv)   The formulas of the language of predicate logic can only be
                generated by finite numbers of applications of rules (i)–(iii).

The first rule generates *atomic* formulas (containing no connectives or
quantifiers) like $R(x, y)$, $P(c)$, $K(m, x)$, and $S(x, z, m)$. Note that connectives may combine formulas with or without quantifiers, and that any quantifier plus variable may be prefixed to a formula, even when that variable does
not occur within the formula (e.g., $(\forall x)P(y)$ is well-formed.) The syntax
thus allows *"vacuous"* quantification. (Some systems do not allow vacuous
quantification, but they pay a price: the set of generative rules is more
complex if quantifier prefixes are allowed only when the quantified variable
occurs inside the formula. We prefer to have a simpler syntax and render
vacuous quantification meaningless or harmless in the semantics.)

If x is any variable and φ is a formula to which a quantifier is attached
by rule (iii) above to produce $(\forall x)\varphi$ or $(\exists x)\varphi$, then we say that φ is the

scope of the attached quantifier and that φ or any part of φ *lies in the scope*
of that quantifier. We also refer to the φ as the *matrix* of the expression
$(\forall x)\varphi$ or $(\exists x)\varphi$. Some examples are given in (7-4) below, where the scope
of each quantifier is underlined.

(7-4)   (i) $(\exists x)\underline{P(x)}$
         (ii) $(\exists y)\underline{R(x,y)} \,\&\, P(y)$
         (iii) $(\exists y)\underline{(R(x,y) \,\&\, P(y))}$
         (iv) $(\exists x)\underline{(P(m) \,\&\, R(j,y))}$
         (v) $(\exists x)\underline{(\forall y)(R(x,y) \to K(x,x))}$ (scope of $(\exists x)$)
                $\underline{}$ (scope of $(\forall y)$)
         (vi) $(\exists x)\underline{[Q(x) \,\&\, (\forall y)(P(y) \to (\exists z)S(x,y,z))]}$ (scope of $(\exists x)$)
                $ \underline{}$ (scope of $(\forall y)$)
                $ \underline{}$ (scope of $(\exists z)$)

In (ii) note that $(\exists y)$ was attached to $R(x,y)$, which is therefore the
scope of the existential quantifier, and the result conjoined with $P(y)$, which
is outside the scope of $(\exists y)$. In (iii), on the other hand, the existential quantifier was attached to $(R(x,y) \,\&\, P(y))$, which thereby becomes its scope.
Note that in (iv) a quantifier has the following formula as its scope even if
the quantification is vacuous. In (v) and (vi) we see cases involving quantification of formulas which already contain quantifiers. Thus the scope of
one quantifier may be contained within the scope of another.

This notion of quantifier scope is crucial in the following definition.

(7-5)   DEFINITION 7.1 *An occurrence of a variable x is* bound *if it occurs
         in the scope of* $(\exists x)$ *or* $(\forall x)$. *A variable is* free *if it is not bound.* ∎

Binding is hence a relation between a prefixed quantifier and an occurrence of a variable. For example, in $P(x)$ the x is free, but it is bound in
$(\exists x)P(x)$. In (7-4)(ii), the y in $R(x,y)$ is bound (by the $(\exists y)$) but the y in
$P(y)$ is free. In (iii) both occurrences of y are bound. In both (ii) and (iii)
the x in $R(x,y)$ is free, not being in the scope of a quantifier associated with
x. Similarly, the y in (iv) is free because the only quantification is by $(\exists x)$.
We now see that what we have called "vacuous" quantification is vacuous in
the sense that it does not give rise to any binding of variables. Note incidentally that constants, e.g., m and j in (iv), are not said to be bound or free;
binding applies only to variables. In (v) and (vi) all variable occurrences are

bound. Note that a variable which may be free in a subformula may become bound in a larger formula, e.g., the x and y in $S(x, y, z)$ in (vi).

Any occurrence of a variable in a formula is either bound or free; there is no middle ground. A variable may only be bound once, however. We might wonder, for example, whether the x in the $M(x)$ of the formula $(\forall x)(P(x) \rightarrow (\exists x)M(x))$ is bound both by the $(\exists x)$ and again by the $(\forall x)$. It is not; it is bound by the $(\exists x)$ only, and the x in $P(x)$ is then bound by the $(\forall x)$. The formula would surely be less confusingly written if we had chosen different variables, thus: $(\forall x)(P(x) \rightarrow (\exists y)M(y))$, which is an alphabetic variant of the original. In general, it is good practice in writing formulas to avoid using the same variable letter for distinct variables, even in cases such as this one where the intervening quantification assures their distinctness. We will return to the subject of alphabetic variants in Sec 7.3.

A *statement* of the predicate logic is defined as a formula that does not contain any free variables. Every occurrence of a variable in a statement is hence bound by some quantifier in the formula. The set of statements is sometimes called the set of *sentences, propositions*, or *closed formulas* of the predicate logic. A formula with at least one free variable is, as we have said, called an *open formula*, or *propositional function*.

7.2   Semantics

We give here an informal account of the semantics of predicate logic. A more formal treatment will be presented in Part D (Chapter 13).

As with propositional logic, a statement in the predicate calculus bears one of the truth values 1 (true) or 0 (false). If the statement is composed of predicates and terms, and possibly quantifiers also, then its truth value is determined by the *semantic values* (which are not necessarily truth values) of its components. For example, the statement $H(s)$, composed of the one-place predicate H and the constant s, receives its truth value in the following way: s has as its semantic value some individual chosen from a set D of individuals presumed to be fixed in advance. (D is like the domain of discourse of set theory and is often referred to in that way). Suppose, for example, that D is the set of all human beings, living or dead, and the individual assigned to s is Socrates. The predicate H has as its semantic value some *set* of individuals from D—let us say, for example, {Socrates, Aristotle, Plato, Mozart, Beethoven}. The statement $H(s)$ now gets the truth value *true* by virtue of the fact that the individual corresponding to s is a member of the set corresponding to H. On the other hand, had H had as its value the set {Mahler, Proust, Michelangelo}, $H(s)$ would have been false, Socrates not being a member of this set.

We use the double brackets $[\![\alpha]\!]$ to indicate the semantic value of the expression α. Thus, in the preceding example $[\![s]\!]$ = Socrates , $[\![H]\!]$ = {Socrates, Aristotle, Plato, Mozart, Beethoven}, and $[\![H(s)]\!] = 1$.

A two-place predicate L has as its semantic value a *set of ordered pairs* of individuals from D, i.e., a subset of $D \times D$. A statement such as $L(j, m)$ is true just in case the ordered pair of individuals $\langle x, y \rangle$ is in this set, where x is the semantic value of j and y is the semantic value of m. For example, if $[\![j]\!]$ is John Donne and $[\![m]\!]$ is Mary Queen of Scots, then $L(j, m)$ is true if $\langle$John Donne, Mary Queen of Scots$\rangle$ is in the set which is the semantic value of L; otherwise $L(j, m)$ is false. In general symbolic terms, for any two-place predicate K and terms a and b, $[\![K(a, b)]\!] = 1$ iff $\langle [\![a]\!], [\![b]\!] \rangle \in [\![K]\!]$.

Clearly the truth value of any statement in predicate logic will depend on the domain of discourse and the choice of semantic values for the constants and predicates. When these are fully specified, we say that we have a *model* for predicate logic. More specifically, a model consists of a set D and a function F which assigns:

(i)   to each individual constant   a member of D

(ii)   to each one-place predicate   a subset of D

(iii)   to each two-place predicate   a subset of $D \times D$

and in general

(iv)   to each n-place predicate   a subset of $\underbrace{D \times D \times \ldots \times D}_{n}$

(i.e., a set of ordered n-tuples of elements from D)

Thus, a statement in predicate logic such as $H(s)$ or $L(j, m)$ is not simply true or false, but true or false *relative to a particular model M*. If we want to emphasize this fact in our notation, we can add the name of the model as a superscript, thus: $[\![H(s)]\!]^M = 1, [\![s]\!]^M$ = Socrates, etc. Certain statements will turn out to be true or false irrespective of the model chosen, and such statements constitute the tautologies and contradictions, respectively, of predicate logic. Inasmuch as the connectives &, $\vee$, etc. have the same truth tables as in statement logic, it follows at once that an expression such as $H(s) \vee {\sim}H(s)$ is a tautology in this system, and $H(s) \,\&\, {\sim}H(s)$ is a contradiction. That is, whatever the model, $H(s)$ and ${\sim}H(s)$ will have opposite truth values, thus $H(s) \vee {\sim}H(s)$ will always be true, etc. A statement such as $H(s)$ or $L(j,m)$, whose truth value varies from model to model, is contingent. We will shortly encounter examples in the predicate calculus which are not such straightforward analogs of tautologies and contradictions in the logic of statements.

The semantics of quantified expressions is somewhat more complex than that of statements composed simply of predicates and terms. We sketch the basic ideas here informally and defer the detailed formalism to Chapter 13.

A formula in which all occurrences of variables are bound, such as $(\forall x)$ $H(x)$ or $(\exists y)L(m,y)$, is a statement and should accordingly be true or false with respect to the chosen model. Such statements, however, are composed syntactically of a quantifier (plus variable) and an open statement, e.g., $H(x)$ or $L(m,y)$, which is not a statement and does not, strictly speaking, have a truth value. In evaluating quantified expressions we nonetheless let these propositional functions take on truth values temporarily by letting the quantified variable range over all the individuals in the domain D one by one and determining the truth value the propositional function *would have* for each of those individuals. For example, to determine the truth value of $(\forall x)H(x)$ we let x range over all individuals in D and for each such assignment of a value to x determine the truth value $H(x)$ would have: true if $[\![x]\!]$ is in $[\![H]\!]$ in the model and false otherwise. Then $(\forall x)H(x)$ is true iff $[\![x]\!]$ is in $[\![H]\!]$ for *all* individuals in D. If for some individual, $[\![x]\!] \notin [\![H]\!]$, then $(\forall x)H(x)$ is false. To put it another way, $(\forall x)H(x)$ is true (in a particular model) iff $H(x)$ is true as x takes on as successive values every individual in D. Correspondingly, $(\exists x)H(x)$ is true iff $H(x)$ is true *for at least one* individual in D when x assumes that value.

Let us consider a small partial model. Predicates and terms not mentioned are also assumed to have values in the model, but for clarity we ignore them.

(7-6)   Let $D = \{$Socrates, Aristotle, Plato, Mozart, Beethoven, Tolstoy$\}$
    $F(s) = $ Socrates $F(m) = $ Mozart
    $F(a) = $ Aristotle $F(b) = $ Beethoven
    $F(p) = $ Plato $F(t) = $ Tolstoy
    $F(H) = \{$Socrates, Aristotle, Plato$\}$
    $F(M) = \{$Socrates, Aristotle, Plato, Mozart,
            Beethoven, Tolstoy$\} = D$
    $F(L) = \{\langle$Socrates, Socrates$\rangle$, $\langle$Socrates, Aristotle$\rangle$,
            $\langle$Mozart, Beethoven$\rangle$, $\langle$Beethoven, Mozart$\rangle$,
            $\langle$Tolstoy, Plato$\rangle$, $\langle$Plato, Mozart$\rangle$, $\langle$Aristotle, Tolstoy$\rangle\}$

The reader may now verify that the following statements, among others, are true in this model:

$$H(s), H(a), H(p), M(s), M(b), L(s,s), L(t,p)$$

while the following are false:

$$H(m), H(b), H(t), L(a,s), L(m,m)$$

The statement $(\forall x)M(x)$ is true in this model since $M(x)$ is true whenever x takes as its value each of the members of D, i.e., $M(s)$, $M(a)$, $M(p)$, $M(m)$, $M(b)$, and $M(t)$ are all true. The statement $(\exists x)H(x)$ is true, since $H(x)$ is true for at least one value of x—in fact, it is true when $[\![x]\!]$ is Socrates or Aristotle or Plato. (Note carefully that the semantic values x takes are individuals from the set D and not constant letters s, a, p, etc., of the language.) Similarly, it is easy to see that since $(\forall x)M(x)$ is true (and the universe of discourse is not empty), $(\exists x)M(x)$ is true also.

The statement $(\exists y)L(m,y)$ is true since there is at least one value of y (just Beethoven, in fact) such that the ordered pair $\langle$ Mozart, $[\![y]\!]\rangle$ is in the set assigned to L, i.e., $[\![L]\!]$. However, $(\forall y)L(m,y)$ is false since $\langle$ Mozart, $[\![y]\!]\rangle$ is not in $[\![L]\!]$ for every value of y ($\langle$ Mozart, Socrates $\rangle$ is lacking, for example).

Given the truth values of the statements already mentioned, we can determine the truth values of complex statements such as $(H(s)\ \&\ H(m))$, $((\forall x)M(x)\lor H(a))$, and $(H(p) \to (\exists y)L(m,y))$ in the usual way according to the truth tables for the sentential connectives. The reader should verify that these three examples are, respectively, false, true, and true in the assumed model.

Evaluating an expression such as $(\exists x)(H(x)\ \&\ M(x))$ in which the connective lies inside the scope of the quantifier is not quite so straightforward. By the rule for evaluating existentially quantified expressions, we must determine whether there is any value of x in D which makes the complex propositional function $H(x)\ \&\ M(x)$ true. Here we must try each individual in D as a value for x and determine whether both $H(x)$ and $M(x)$ are true for that value. If at least one such value is found, $(\exists x)(H(x)\ \&\ M(x))$ is true; otherwise, it is false. In the model given, this formula is true since there are in fact three individuals—Socrates, Aristotle, and Plato—which are both in $[\![H]\!]$ and $[\![M]\!]$. On the other hand, $(\forall x)(H(x)\ \&\ M(x))$ is false; not every individual is in both $[\![H]\!]$ and $[\![M]\!]$. We see, however, that $(\forall x)(H(x) \to M(x))$

is true in this model. There is no individual which, when assigned to x, makes the conditional $H(x) \rightarrow M(x)$ false; i.e., no individual which is in $[\![H]\!]$ but not in $[\![M]\!]$.

Problem: What is the truth value in this model of $(\forall x)(L(m, x) \rightarrow H(x))$? of $(\forall x)(L(m, x) \rightarrow M(x))$?

Expressions containing quantifiers within the scope of other quantifiers add an extra degree of complexity in the evaluation. The same rules apply, but the expression is evaluated, so to speak, from the outside in. $(\forall x)(\exists y) L(x, y)$, for example, will be true just in case for every possible value of x in D the expression $(\exists y)L(x, y)$ is true. When is the latter true? If there is at least one value of y for which $L(x, y)$ is true, where x has the value fixed in the previous step. That is, we let x range over all the individuals in D, and at each value we determine the truth value of $(\exists y)L(x, y)$ by again letting y range over all the individuals in D. $(\exists y)L(x, y)$ might be true for some values of x and false for others, but the entire expression $(\forall x)(\exists y)L(x, y)$ is true only if $(\exists y)L(x, y)$ is true for every value of x.

In the chosen model, $(\forall x)(\exists y)L(x, y)$ happens to be true. To see this, let x be Socrates; then $(\exists y)L(x, y)$ is true when y is Socrates or Aristotle. If x is Aristotle, then $(\exists y)L(x, y)$ is true when y is Tolstoy, and so on. We find ultimately that for each value of x we can always find some value of y which makes $L(x, y)$ true. Or to put it another way, each member of D appears at least once as first member in the set of ordered pairs assigned to L. Thus, $(\forall x)(\exists y)L(x, y)$ is true in this model.

Note, on the other hand, that in this model $(\exists y)(\forall x)L(x, y)$ is false. For this formula to be true, we would have to find at least one value of y for which $(\forall x)L(x, y)$ is true, i.e., some individual which appears as second member with every individual in D as first member in the set of ordered pairs assigned to L. It is easy to see from inspection of $[\![L]\!]$ that no such individual exists, so $(\exists y)(\forall x)L(x, y)$ is false in this model.

These last two examples demonstrate that the order in which quantifiers appear in an expression when one is universal and the other existential can have semantic significance. That is to say that there may in general be models, as here, in which one statement is true and the other, with the order of quantifiers reversed, is false. This is immediately evident if we choose a slightly less artificial model. Let D be the set of all living persons and let $L = \{\langle x, y \rangle \mid x \text{ loves } y\}$. Then $(\forall x)(\exists y)L(x, y)$ is true if for each person there is at least one individual (possibly himself or herself) whom that person loves, but $(\exists y)(\forall x)L(x,y)$ would be true only if there were at least one person who is universally loved, i.e., loved by everyone. It is easy to imagine that the former could be true while the latter is false.

We can now see how to translate certain types of English statements into predicate logic. For *All cats are mammals*, for example, we will need one-place predicates, call them C and M, to correspond to *is a cat* and *is a mammal*. We can then represent the English statement by $(\forall x)(C(x) \rightarrow M(x))$, which we can gloss roughly as follows: for every individual in the universe of discourse, if that individual is a cat, then it is also a mammal; or more briefly, everything which is a cat is a mammal. (Note, by the way, that in our predicate calculus rendition the statement is true in case there are no cats in the universe of discourse, for then $C(x)$ will be false for all values of x and hence the conditional will always be true.) In the same vein, *No cats are mammals* might come out as $(\forall x)(C(x) \rightarrow \sim M(x))$: everything which is a cat fails to be a mammal. Again, this is true in case the universe of discourse contains no cats, unlike the English statement, which we might well regard as inappropriate or nonsensical in such an instance. We are once again in familiar territory where English statements and their nearest logical correspondents do not match up perfectly.

Some cats are mammals could be translated as $(\exists x)(C(x) \& M(x))$, which is true iff there is at least one individual in the domain of discourse which is both a cat and a mammal. In this case the absence of cats from the universe of discourse makes the predicate calculus statement false, whereas we might say that the English statement suffers from presupposition failure (with whatever consequences attach to this defect). Note that $(\exists x)(C(x) \rightarrow M(x))$, with a conditional as in the translation of the universal statement, would not do. This statement is true when there are no cats (the antecedent is always false) or when there is at least one mammal (the consequent is true). Although we are prepared to accept a certain amount of disparity between English statements and their logical translations, we would not want to say that *Some cats are mammals* gets the same translation as *Either there are no cats or there is at least one mammal*.

The negative existential statement *Some cats are not mammals* could be rendered as $(\exists x)(C(x) \& \sim M(x))$, (which is also false when the universe of discourse contains no cats).

7.3   Quantifier laws and prenex normal form

Based on this set-theoretic semantics of predicate logic there are a number of important equivalences, which we may consider as laws of predicate logic. They will be very useful when constructing proofs and also in recognizing formulas which are equivalent to translations of English sentences but which do not resemble them structurally. In the following we write $\varphi(x), \psi(x)$, etc. for any formula which contains at least one free instance of the variable x, e.g. $H(x), L(x,x), (\forall y)L(x,y), (\exists y)(H(x) \rightarrow L(x,y))$, etc., and similarly for $\varphi(y), \psi(y)$, and so on.

A statement of the form $(\exists x) \sim \phi(x)$ asserts that there is at least one individual which makes $\sim\phi(x)$ true; this individual therefore makes $\phi(x)$ false. Thus $(\forall x)\phi(x)$ could not be true, because the universal quantifier would require all instances of $\phi(x)$ to be true; therefore $\sim(\forall x)\phi(x)$ is true.

This reasoning can also be applied in the reverse direction, and the result is the first quantifier law:

(7–7)   Law 1 Quantifier Negation: $\sim(\forall x)\phi(x) \Leftrightarrow (\exists x)\sim\phi(x)$

A possible pair of English correspondents would be: *Not everyone passed the test* and *Someone did not pass the test.*

Because of the Law of Double Negation, i.e., $\sim\sim\phi \Leftrightarrow \phi$, Law 1 could also be written in the following equivalent forms:

(7–8)   Law 1′ $(\forall x)\phi(x) \Leftrightarrow \sim(\exists x)\sim\phi(x)$
         Law 1″ $\sim(\forall x)\sim\phi(x) \Leftrightarrow (\exists x)\phi(x)$
         Law 1‴ $(\forall x)\sim\phi(x) \Leftrightarrow \sim(\exists x)\phi(x)$

English correspondents for these versions are also easy to construct. For Law 1‴, for example, we could have *Everyone did not pass the test* (i.e., everyone failed the test) and *No one passed the test.*

A consequence of Law 1 (and the Law of Double Negation) is that either quantifier could be entirely eliminated from predicate logic in favor of the other and the result would be an equivalent system.

The next group of laws are analogs of the Distributive Laws for & and ∨ in the statement calculus, although we should note that two of those that follow are only logical implications and not logical equivalences.

(7-9) **Laws of Quantifier Distribution**

Law 2 $(\forall x)(\varphi(x) \,\&\, \psi(x)) \Leftrightarrow (\forall x)\varphi(x) \,\&\, (\forall x)\psi(x)$

Law 3 $(\exists x)(\varphi(x) \vee \psi(x)) \Leftrightarrow (\exists x)\varphi(x) \vee (\exists x)\psi(x)$

Law 4 $(\forall x)\varphi(x) \vee (\forall x)\psi(x) \Rightarrow (\forall x)(\varphi(x) \vee \psi(x))$

Law 5 $(\exists x)(\varphi(x) \,\&\, \psi(x)) \Rightarrow (\exists x)\varphi(x) \,\&\, (\exists x)\psi(x)$

The left side of Law 2 is true iff every individual in the domain of discourse makes both $\phi(x)$ and $\psi(x)$ true. The right side is true iff every individual makes $\phi(x)$ true and every individual makes $\psi(x)$ true. These are fairly obviously equivalent statements. The similar reasoning involved in verifying Law 3 is left as an exercise for the reader.

The left side of Law 4 is true iff everything (in the universe of discourse) makes $\phi(x)$ true or everything makes $\psi(x)$ true. In such a case it follows that everything makes $\phi(x)$ or $\psi(x)$ true. The reverse implication does not hold, however. The statement that everything in the universe of discourse is either male or female does not imply that everything is male or everything is female. Similar reasoning can be applied to Law 5.

Laws 2 and 3 suggest a fundamental connection between the universal quantifier and conjunction and between the existential quantifier and disjunction. $(\forall x)\phi(x)$ is true just in case $\phi(a)$ is true *and* $\phi(b)$ is true *and* ..., where $a, b, \ldots$ name all the members of the universe of discourse. Similarly, $(\exists x)\phi(x)$ is true just in case $\phi(a)$ is true *or* $\phi(b)$ is true *or* .... Thus a universally quantified statement is equivalent to a (possibly infinite) conjunction $\phi(a) \,\&\, \phi(b) \,\&\, \ldots$, while an existential statement is equivalent to the disjunction $\phi(a) \vee \phi(b) \vee \ldots$. From this perspective, Law 1 resembles a kind of generalized DeMorgan's Law:

(7-10) $\sim(\phi(a) \,\&\, \phi(b) \,\&\, \ldots) \Leftrightarrow \sim\phi(a) \vee \sim\phi(b) \vee \ldots$

The next group of laws pertains to the linear order of quantifiers in doubly quantified statements. If both quantifiers are universal or both are existential, their linear order in the statement is irrelevant (Laws 6 and 7). This much is probably evident from the semantic treatment of the quantifiers outlined earlier. The extension of these laws to cases of three or more quantifiers of the same type is then immediate. For these reasons, a statement of the form $(\forall x)(\forall y)\phi(x, y)$ is often abbreviated as $(\forall x, y)\phi(x, y)$. Similarly, $(\exists x)(\exists y)(\exists z)\phi(x, y, z)$ is abbreviated to $(\exists x, y, z)\phi(x, y, z)$, etc.

(7–11) **Laws of Quantifier (In)Dependence**
    Law 6 $(\forall x)(\forall y)\varphi(x,y) \Leftrightarrow (\forall y)(\forall x)\varphi(x,y)$

    Law 7 $(\exists x)(\exists y)\varphi(x,y) \Leftrightarrow (\exists y)(\exists x)\varphi(x,y)$

    Law 8 $(\exists x)(\forall y)\varphi(x,y) \Rightarrow (\forall y)(\exists x)\varphi(x,y)$

We have already seen above that reversing the order of existential and universal quantifiers produces a non-equivalent statement. Yet the logical implication given in Law 8 holds. If everyone has someone whom he or she loves, $(\forall x)(\exists y)L(x,y)$, it is not necessarily true that each loves the same person; i.e., $(\exists y)(\forall x)L(x,y)$ may be false. On the other hand, if there is someone who is loved by everyone, i.e., the latter statement is true, then it does follow that the former statement is true: for each person there is someone whom that person loves—the object of universal adoration, at the least. The reading with the existential preceding the universal quantifier is sometimes called the *stronger* reading of the two, as it excludes situations which are included by the weaker reading.

In applying these laws to particular closed formulas, it is sometimes necesssary to make an alphabetic change of variable. For example, $(\forall x)F(x)$ & $(\forall y)G(y)$ is not of the correct form to be converted to $(\forall x)(F(x)$ & $G(x))$ by Law 2.

It can be put into the required form, however, by replacing the subformula $(\forall y)G(y)$ by the equivalent formula $(\forall x)G(x)$. This gives $(\forall x)F(x)$ & $(\forall x)G(x)$ for the whole formula, which is then equivalent to $(\forall x)(F(x)$ & $G(x))$ by Law 2. An alphabetic change of variable is permissible if (1) the same new letter is substituted for *every* occurrence of the letter being replaced, and (2) the replacements do not change the overall binding configuration of the entire formula. Under these conditions, the new formula, called an *alphabetic variant*, is logically equivalent to the original one. Consider the example just mentioned.

(7–12) $(\forall x)F(x)$ & $(\forall y)G(y) : (\forall x)F(x)$ & $(\forall x)G(x)$

In the formula on the left, the y's can be replaced by x's because all occurrences of variables remain bound to the same quantifier.

Here is another example of alphabetic variants:

(7–13) $(\forall x)((\forall z)F(x,z) \rightarrow (\exists y)H(y,x)) :$
    $(\forall x)((\forall y)F(x,y) \rightarrow (\exists y)H(y,x))$

Note that the overall binding configuration is unchanged.

The following formulas are *not* equivalent and hence are *not* alphabetic variants.

(7–14) $(\forall x)(F(x) \rightarrow (\exists y)G(x,y)) : (\forall x)(F(x) \rightarrow (\exists x)G(x,x))$

The x in $G(x,y)$ is bound first by the $(\forall x)$, afterward by the $(\exists x)$.

(7–15) $(\forall x)(F(x) \rightarrow (\exists y)G(x,y)) : (\forall z)(F(z) \rightarrow (\exists y)G(x,y))$

x has not been replaced everywhere in the formula (and the x in $G(x,y)$ becomes free).

It will sometimes be convenient, especially in carrying out the rules of inference outlined in the next section, to move all quantifier symbols to the left of the formula. The following laws characterize when a quantifier prefix may be moved while preserving truth value.

(7–16) **Laws of Quantifier Movement**

Law 9 $(\varphi \rightarrow (\forall x)\psi(x)) \Leftrightarrow (\forall x)(\varphi \rightarrow \psi(x))$

provided that x is not free in φ.

Law 10 $(\varphi \rightarrow (\exists x)\psi(x)) \Leftrightarrow (\exists x)(\varphi \rightarrow \psi(x))$

provided that x is not free in φ.

Law 11 $(\forall x)\varphi(x) \rightarrow \psi \Leftrightarrow (\exists x)(\varphi(x) \rightarrow \psi)$

provided that x is not free in ψ.

Law 12 $(\exists x)\varphi(x) \rightarrow \psi \Leftrightarrow (\forall x)(\varphi(x) \rightarrow \psi)$

provided that x is not free in ψ.

These laws are used to find the *Prenex Normal Form* of any formula, which is its alphabetic variant with all quantifiers preceding a quantifier-free matrix. For example, to convert

(7–17) $(\exists x)F(x) \rightarrow (\forall y)G(y)$

to PNF, we apply Law 9 to get

(7–18) $(\forall y)[(\exists x)F(x) \rightarrow G(y)]$

This is allowed since the variable y in the moved quantifier has no free occurrences in the antecedent $(\exists x)F(x)$. The resulting formula is still not in

PNF because $(\exists x)$ has only $F(x)$ as its scope. We need to move $(\exists x)$ from inside the formula $(\exists x)F(x) \rightarrow G(y)$, which we can do by Law 12 since x does not occur free in the consequent $G(y)$. The result is $(\forall x)(F(x) \rightarrow G(y))$, which is equivalent to the bracketed subexpression in (7-18). Thus, the desired equivalent to (7-17) in PNF is:

(7–19) $(\forall y)[(\forall x)(F(x) \rightarrow G(y))]$

The square brackets may now be dropped to give

(7–20) $(\forall y)(\forall x)(F(x) \rightarrow G(y))$

The reader may wish to verify that if Law 12 had been applied to (7-17) and then Law 9 to the result, we would have obtained $(\forall x)(\forall y)(F(x) \rightarrow G(y))$, which is of course equivalent to (7-20) (and thus to (7-17) also).

As in the case of other laws, it may sometimes be necessary to replace a formula by an alphabetic variant before proceeding. If (7-17) had been given in the form $(\exists x)F(x) \rightarrow (\forall x)G(x)$, for example, we could have applied Law 9 to give

(7–21) $(\forall x)[(\exists x)F(x) \rightarrow G(x)]$

(Note that x does not occur *free* in $(\exists x)F(x)$.) But now when we try to move $(\exists x)$ outside the square brackets by Law 12, we cannot do so because x now does occur free in the consequent $G(x)$. (The fact that it is bound by the $(\forall x)$ outside is irrelevant here; we are working on the subformula $(\exists x)F(x) \rightarrow G(x)$, and in this subformula, x occurs free in the consequent.) The solution is to convert $(\exists x)F(x) \rightarrow G(x)$ to an alphabetic variant, say, $(\exists y)F(y) \rightarrow G(x)$, and then apply Law 12, legally, to give $(\forall y)(F(y) \rightarrow G(x))$. The final result is:

(7–22) $(\forall x)(\forall y)(F(y) \rightarrow G(x))$

which is, of course, equivalent to $(\exists x)F(x) \rightarrow (\forall x)G(x)$ (and to (7-20) and (7-17)).

Given any formula, we can bring it into prenex form by the following procedure.

1. atomic formulas are already in *PNF*.

2. if φ is equivalent to φ' which is in *PNF*, then $(\forall x)\varphi$ is equivalent to $(\forall x)\varphi'$ which is in *PNF*.

3. if φ is equivalent to φ' which is in *PNF*, then $\sim\varphi$ is equivalent to $\sim\varphi'$. If φ' contains quantifiers, apply Law 1 to $\sim\varphi'$ to obtain a *PNF*.

4. if the formula is of the form $\varphi \to \psi$, the procedure is more complex. Assume that we have the *PNF's* φ' and ψ', which are equivalent to φ and ψ, respectively. Convert to alphabetic variants to make sure that any variable which occurs bound by a quantifier in either φ' or ψ' does not occur at all in the other. Then we may use the quantifier movement rules to obtain a *PNF* equivalent to $\varphi' \to \psi'$.

This procedure guarantees that there is a *PNF* for any formula, since we can define all other connectives and quantifiers in terms of $\sim$ and $\to$ and the universal quantifier.

The use of *Prenex Normal Forms* is primarily to compare the complexity of the quantificational structure of formulas. But when an ordinary English sentence is translated into predicate logic, the most natural rendition often has the quantifiers embedded, since in ordinary English the quantifiers occur inside NP's. For example, to translate a sentence such as *Some person likes every book* into predicate logic we will have to assume a universe of discourse which contains both persons and books. Therefore a translation such as $(\exists x)(\forall y)L(x,y)$ will not do since it is true only if some individual stands in the L relation to every individual in D, i.e., persons, books, and whatever else may happen to be included. We need (one-place) predicates corresponding to 'is a person' and 'is a book,' say P and B, and then the most natural translation (for the reading of the sentence in which there is at least one person who likes all books) would be:

(7–23) $(\exists x)(P(x) \,\&\, (\forall y)(B(y) \to L(x,y)))$

This form might serve our purposes very well, but the rules of inference in the following section are much more conveniently applied if the formula is first converted to *PNF*. For example, (7-23) could be converted to *PNF* by the following steps:

(7-24)   1. $(\exists x)(P(x) \,\&\, (\forall y)(B(y) \to L(x,y)))$
          2. $(\exists x) \sim\sim(P(x) \,\&\, (\forall y)(B(y) \to L(x,y)))$ 1, Double Neg.
          3. $(\exists x) \sim(\sim P(x) \lor \sim(\forall y)(B(y) \to L(x,y)))$ 2, DeM.
          4. $(\exists x) \sim(\sim P(x) \lor (\exists y)\sim(B(y) \to L(x,y)))$
                                                              3, Quant. Neg. (Law 1)
          5. $(\exists x) \sim(P(x) \to (\exists y)\sim(B(y) \to L(x,y)))$ 4, Cond.
          6. $(\exists x) \sim(\exists y)(P(x) \to \sim(B(y) \to L(x,y)))$
                                                              5, Quant. Mvt. (Law 10)
          7. $(\exists x)(\forall y) \sim(P(x) \to \sim(B(y) \to L(x,y)))$
                                                              6, Quant. Neg. (Law 1)
          8. $(\exists x)(\forall y) \sim(\sim P(x) \lor \sim(B(y) \to L(x,y)))$ 7, Cond.
          9. $(\exists x)(\forall y)(\sim\sim P(x) \,\&\, \sim\sim(B(y) \to L(x,y)))$ 8, DeM.
          10. $(\exists x)(\forall y)(P(x) \,\&\, (B(y) \to L(x,y)))$ 9, Double Neg.

7.4   Natural deduction

We need to add very little to our rules of inference to handle arguments
containing quantified formulas and statements. Remember that valid arguments are characterized by rules which preserve only truth. The main idea
is to introduce rules which strip away the quantifier prefix, then apply the
rules of inference to the remaining matrix and finally introduce quantifiers
back into the formula. We require two new rules for removing quantifiers—
Universal Instantiation (U.I.) and *Existential Instantiation* (E.I.)—and two
for introduction of quantifiers—*Universal Generalization* (U.G.) and *Existential Generalization* (E.G.). To avoid incorrect inferences, some of the new
rules carry additional conditions on application. In these inference rules
$(\forall x)\varphi(x)$ and $(\exists x)\varphi(x)$ are used to indicate explicitly that the variable x
occurs in the arbitrarily complex formula φ, i.e., the rules cannot be applied
to vacuously quantified formulas.

A universally quantified formula is true if and only if *every instantiation*
of an object from the universe of discourse for the quantified variable in the
matrix is true. Therefore we can infer from the truth of $(\forall x)\varphi(x)$ that some
particular instantiation given by an assignment to the variable x is true.
From a universally quantified sentence *All men are mortal*, we may hence
infer *If John is a man, he is mortal*. The new rule U.I. can be formulated
as:

Universal Instantiation (U.I.)

$$(\forall x)\varphi(x)$$
$$\therefore \overline{\varphi(c)}$$

where c is an individual constant substituted for every free occurrence of x in $\varphi(x)$ of the premise (and having as its semantic value an object in the universe of discourse). With U.I. we have all we need to demonstrate the validity of the argument (5-3). Here is the proof.

$$
\begin{array}{llll}
(7\text{-}25) & 1. & (\forall x)(H(x) \to M(x)) & \\
& 2. & H(s) & \\
& 3. & H(s) \to M(s) & 1, \text{ U.I.} \\
& 4. & M(s) & 2, 3 \text{ M.P.}
\end{array}
$$

Since the second premise introduces a particular individual constant s, and the conclusion mentions the same constant, we use it in this application of U.I. The formula in line 3 is not quantified anymore, and hence the rules of the logic of statements can be used. Here *Modus Ponens* detaches the consequent of line 3, which is the desired conclusion.

To prove that some formula is true of every member of a set, one can *arbitrarily* choose an individual from that set and prove that the formula holds of it. If the proof depends only on the fact that this individual is a member of that set and not on any additional properties it may have, it can be validly inferred that the statement holds of all individuals in the set. This line of reasoning is made precise in the rule of Universal Generalization: what is true of an arbitrarily selected object is true of every object in the universe of discourse. We reserve the individual constant v as a special symbol for such an arbitrarily selected object, indexing it $v_1, v_2, \ldots, v_n, \ldots$ when more are needed. Note that v is an individual constant, so $\varphi(v)$ is an atomic statement and not an open formula. Yet v is like a variable in that it stands for an arbitrary individual, and not for any specific one in the universe of discourse. U.G. is formulated as:

Universal Generalization (U.G.)

$$\varphi(v)$$
$$\therefore \overline{(\forall x)\varphi(x)}$$

This rule is used in the following argument form, of which we give first the English and then the formal language version.

(7–26)   Every rabbit is a quadruped
            Every quadruped is warm-blooded
       ∴. Every rabbit is warm-blooded

(7–27) $(\forall x)(R(x) \to Q(x))$
            $(\forall x)(Q(x) \to W(x))$
       ∴. $(\forall x)(R(x) \to W(x))$

The proof is as follows:

    1. $(\forall x)(R(x) \to Q(x))$
    2. $(\forall x)(Q(x) \to W(x))$
    3. $R(v) \to Q(v)$ 1, U.I.

The first premise is instantiated by the arbitrarily selected constant v. Recall that every constant produces a true instantiation of a universally quantified formula; thus, $R(v) \to Q(v)$ is a legitimate instantiation of line 1.

    4. $Q(v) \to W(v)$ 2, U.I.

Here we have instantiated the second premise with the same constant we selected in line 3.

    5. $R(v) \to W(v)$ 3, 4, H.S.
    6. $(\forall x)(R(x) \to W(x))$ 5, U.G.

Since v has been arbitrarily selected, the proposition containing it can be universally generalized to the conclusion in line 6.

    Here is another example of the use of U.I. to remove a universal quantifier and of U.G. to replace the quantifier afterward.

(7–28)   1. $(\forall x)(P(x) \,\&\, Q(x))$
            2. $(\forall x)(R(x) \to {\sim}P(x))$
            3. $P(v) \,\&\, Q(v)$ 1, U.I.
            4. $R(v) \to {\sim}P(v)$ 2, U.I.
            5. $P(v)$ 3, Simp.
            6. ${\sim}{\sim}P(v)$ 5, Compl.
            7. ${\sim}R(v)$ 4, 6, M.T.
            8. $Q(v)$ 3, Simp.
            9. $Q(v) \,\&\, {\sim}R(v)$ 7, 8, Conj.
           10. $(\forall x)(Q(x) \,\&\, {\sim}R(x))$ 9, U.G.

When $\varphi(c)$ is true, where c is a constant, it constitutes a true instantiation of the open formula $\varphi(x)$. So we may conclude $(\exists x)\varphi(x)$ from the true $\varphi(c)$. For example, if we already know (or hold as true) that John is a human being, we may infer that there is some human being or that a human being exists. The rule of Existential Generalization is formulated as:

Existential Generalization (E.G.)

$$\varphi(c)$$
$$\therefore \overline{(\exists x)\varphi(x)}$$

The following proof employs E.G.

(7–29) 1. $H(c)$
      2. $(\forall x)(H(x) \rightarrow M(x))$
      3. $H(c) \rightarrow M(c)$ 2, U.I.
      4. $M(c)$ 1, 3, M.P.
      5. $(\exists x)M(x)$ 4, E.G.

If an existentially quantified statement is true, there is at least one assignment to its variable which provides an instantiation for the matrix. Therefore we can infer from the truth of $(\exists x)\varphi(x)$ that $\varphi(w)$ for some constant w interpreted by an object in the universe of discourse. In general some instantiations of the matrix may be false, because the object assigned to the variable is not a true instantiation, and other assignments provide true instantiations. So w is like v introduced in U.I. in that it does not refer to a specific individual, but it is different in that the range of individuals to which it can possibly refer is not in general the entire universe of discourse, but a subset of individuals, those that form true instantiations of the matrix in question. Because of this restriction on w we must be particularly careful in applying E.I. For example, suppose that $(\exists x)\varphi(x)$ and $(\exists x)\psi(x)$ are two premises of an argument and that in the proof the former has been instantiated by $\varphi(w)$ using E.I. Now it is not valid to use w again in inferring $\psi(w)$, because we have no guarantee that the same object will verify both matrices. The correct inference must use two distinct constants, w_1 and w_2, deriving $\varphi(w_1)$ and $\psi(w_2)$ from the premises. We therefore impose a restriction on E.I. that the constant introduced cannot have occurred previously in the same proof. The rule E.I. is formulated as:

Existential Instantiation (E.I.)

$$(\exists x)\varphi(x)$$
$$\therefore \overline{\varphi(w)}$$

(where w is a new constant)

Now $\varphi(w)$ cannot be a basis for universal generalization to $(\forall x)\varphi(x)$, since w has not been selected totally arbitrarily, but rather from a possibly smaller set of individuals which happen to form true instantiations of the matrix. Here is a proof involving E.I.:

(7-30)   1. $(\exists x)(P(x)\,\&\,Q(x))$
        2. $P(w)\,\&\,Q(w)$ 1, E.I.
        3. $P(w)$ 2, Simp.
        4. $(\exists x)P(w)$ 3, E.G.

This step is valid since w is a constant that forms a true instantiation of $P(x)$.

        5. $Q(w)$ 2, Simp.
        6. $(\exists x)Q(x)$ 5, E.G.
        7. $(\exists x)P(x)\,\&\,(\exists x)Q(x)$ 4, 6, Conj.

The following proof illustrates an important point about the rules of E.I. and U.I.:

(7-31)   1. $(\exists x)(T(x)\,\&\,P(x))$
        2. $(\forall x)(P(x)\rightarrow H(x))$
        3. $T(w)\,\&\,P(w)$ 1, E.I.
        4. $P(w)\rightarrow H(w)$ 2, U.I.

Since $P(x)\rightarrow H(x)$ is verified by every individual in the domain of discourse, it is legitimate to choose w to form the instantiation. The proof would be technically incorrect if we had first instantiated line 2 as $P(w)\rightarrow H(w)$ by U.I. and then instantiated line 1 as $T(w)\,\&\,P(w)$ by E.I. since w would then have occurred in a previous line.

        5. $P(w)$ 3, Simp.
        6. $H(w)$ 4, 5, M.P.
        7. $T(w)$ 3, Simp.
        8. $T(w)\,\&\,H(w)$ 6, 7, Conj.
        9. $(\exists x)(T(x)\,\&\,H(x))$ 8, E.G.

Note that it would have been incorrect to derive $(\forall x)(T(x)\,\&\,H(x))$ from line 8 by U.G. because w was introduced by E.I.

An English counterpart of this argument form is the following:

(7–32)   Some toadstools are poisonous.
            All poisonous things are harmful.
            ∴ Some toadstools are harmful.

The following "proof" is erroneous because the restriction on E.I. has been ignored.

(7–33)   1. $(\exists x)(C(x)\,\&\,V(x))$
         2. $(\exists x)(D(x)\,\&\,V(x))$
         3. $C(w)\,\&\,V(w)$ 1, E.I.
         4. $D(w)\,\&\,V(w)$ 2, E.I. *(incorrect)*
         5. $C(w)$ 3, Simp.
         6. $D(w)$ 4, Simp.
         7. $C(w)\,\&\,D(w)$ 5, 6, Conj.
         8. $(\exists x)(C(x)\,\&\,D(x))$ 7, E.G.

This argument form is easily seen to be invalid by examining the following English version:

(7–34)   Some cats are vicious.
            Some dogs are vicious.
            ∴ Some cats are dogs.

In order for a quantifier to be removed by E.I. or U.I. it must stand at the left side of the expression with no other quantifiers or connectives preceding it, and it must have the rest of the expression as its scope. Thus, $\sim(\forall x)(P(x)\,\&\,Q(x))$ cannot be instantiated as $\sim(P(v)\,\&\,Q(v))$ by U.I. because the negation sign precedes the quantifier. To instantiate this expression it should first be transformed to $(\exists x)\sim(P(x)\,\&\,Q(x))$ by Quantifier Negation, and then E.I. can be applied to give $\sim(P(w)\,\&\,Q(w))$. Similarly, $P(c) \rightarrow (\exists x)Q(x)$ cannot be directly instantiated to $P(c) \rightarrow Q(w)$ by E.I. because the existential quantifier is not at the extreme left of the expression, but it can produce this result after being converted to the equivalent statement $(\exists x)(P(c) \rightarrow Q(w))$ by Law 9. Neither quantifier in $(\forall x)P(x)\,\&\,(\exists y)Q(y)$ can be removed by instantiation; $(\forall x)$ is at the left but does not have the remainder of the entire expression within its scope. The solution is to convert the expression to PNF and then apply E.I. or U.I.

In the reverse process, the quantifier is attached to the left of the proposition being generalized and takes that entire expression as its scope. Thus $P(v) \lor Q(v)$ cannot be generalized to $P(v) \lor (\exists x)Q(x)$ by inserting a quantifier internally, and $P(v) \lor Q(v)$ cannot be generalized by U.G. to $(\forall x)P(x) \lor Q(v)$ since the scope of the universal quantifier does not include $Q(v)$.

Recall that the method of Conditional Proof allows us to introduce a premise P, which is temporarily assumed to be true, and upon deriving Q from P and the original premises to state that $P \to Q$ is logically implied by the original premises. Since the truth of P is not asserted but only accepted provisionally for the sake of deriving $P \to Q$ and then abandoned, P may be any proposition at all. In the predicate calculus, the first line of a conditional proof can be a quantified formula, e.g., $(\forall x)P(x)$ or $(\forall x)(\exists y)Q(x,y)$, or a predicate with constant terms, e.g., $P(s)$ or $L(a,b)$. In particular, the constant terms v and w may appear, e.g., $P(v), L(w,v)$, where, as before, v is an arbitrarily selected constant and w is a constant that forms a true instantiation of some existentially quantified expression. In the following example the conditional proof begins with $P(v)$.

(7–35)   1. $(\forall x)((P(x) \lor Q(x)) \to R(x))$
         2. $(P(v) \lor Q(v)) \to R(v)$ 1, U.I.
         3. $\quad P(v)$ Aux. Premise
         4. $\quad P(v) \lor Q(v)$ 3, Add.
         5. $\quad R(v)$ 2, 4, M.P.
         6. $P(v) \to R(v)$ 3–5, Cond. Proof
         7. $(\forall x)(P(x) \to R(x))$ 6, U.G.

The following is a possible English version of this argument form:

(7–36)   **Everyone who is polite or quarrelsome is right-handed.**
         $\therefore$ **Everyone who is polite is right-handed.**

The temporarily assumed premise in the following conditional proof is $P(c)$, where c is a specific constant term.

(7-37) 1. $(\forall x)(P(c) \rightarrow Q(x))$
      2. $P(c) \rightarrow Q(v)$ 1, U.I.
      3. $P(c)$ Aux. Premise
      4. $Q(v)$ 2, 3, M.P.
      5. $(\forall x)Q(x)$ 4, U.G.
      6. $P(c) \rightarrow (\forall x)Q(x)$ 3–5, Cond. Proof
      7. $(\exists y)(P(y) \rightarrow (\forall x)Q(x))$ 6, E.G.

Note that in line 7 the existential quantifier has the entire conditional as its scope. To conclude $(\exists y)P(y) \rightarrow (\forall x)Q(x)$ from line 6 by E.G. would be technically incorrect since the existential quantifier binds only the variable in the antecedent of the conditional. E.g., let $(\forall x)Q(x)$ be false, and $(\exists y)P(y)$ and $(\exists y)\sim P(y)$ both be true. Then $(\exists y)(P(y) \rightarrow (\forall x)Q(x))$ is true, but $(\exists y)P(y) \rightarrow (\forall x)Q(x)$ is false.

Compare the following English version of this argument form:

(7-38)   **If Chauncey is a priest, then everyone is qualified**
      ∴ **There is someone such that, if he is a priest,**
              everyone is qualified.

It would be invalid to conclude: If there is at least one priest, then everyone is qualified.

The derivation in (7-39) constitutes part of the proof of one of the Laws of Quantifier Distribution.

(7-39) 1. $(\forall x)(P(x) \,\&\, Q(x))$ Aux. Premise
      2. $P(v) \,\&\, Q(v)$ 1, U.I.
      3. $P(v)$ 2, Simp.
      4. $(\forall x)P(x)$ 3, U.G.
      5. $Q(v)$ 2, Simp.
      6. $(\forall x)Q(x)$ 5, U.G.
      7. $(\forall x)P(x) \,\&\, (\forall x)Q(x)$ 4, 6, Conj.
      8. $(\forall x)(P(x) \,\&\, Q(x)) \rightarrow ((\forall x)P(x) \,\&\, (\forall x)Q(x))$
                                        1–7, Cond. Proof

This illustrates another aspect of conditional proof, namely, that it may proceed from no premises except the one that begins the conditional proof. In such a case the truth of the derived conditional statement is independent of any other propositions, which is another way of saying that the conclusion is tautologous. To see this, recall that for any valid argument form

$$(7\text{-}40) \qquad \varphi_1$$
$$\varphi_2$$
$$\varphi_3$$
$$\vdots$$
$$\therefore \overline{\psi}$$

the conditional $(\varphi_1 \,\&\, \varphi_2 \,\&\, \varphi_3 \ldots) \to \psi$ is a tautology. We could think of the first seven lines of (7-39) not as a conditional proof but as a direct proof of $(\forall x)P(x) \,\&\, (\forall x)Q(x)$ from the single premise $(\forall x)(P(x) \,\&\, Q(x))$, and thus $(\forall x)(P(x) \,\&\, Q(x)) \to ((\forall x)P(x) \,\&\, (\forall x)Q(x))$ is tautologous. In general, for every valid argument form (7-40) there is a corresponding conditional proof

$$(7\text{-}41)$$

1.	$(\varphi_1 \,\&\, \varphi_2 \,\&\, \varphi_3 \,\&\, \ldots)$		Aux. Premise
2.	φ_1		1, Simp.
3.	φ_2		1, Simp.
4.	φ_3		1, Simp.
	$\vdots$		
n.	ψ		
n+1.	$(\varphi_1 \,\&\, \varphi_2 \,\&\, \varphi_3 \,\&\, \ldots) \to \psi$		1–n, Cond. Proof

that takes all the premises as provisional rather than assumed and derives a tautologous conditional as a conclusion. In both cases the same statement is being made: The premises $\varphi_1, \varphi_2, \varphi_3, \ldots$ taken together logically imply the conclusion ψ. The difference is only in whether or not the premises are assumed to be true.

To prove arguments containing multiply quantified propositions, e.g., $(\forall x)(\exists y)P(x, y)$ or $(\forall x)P(x) \to (\exists y)Q(y)$, we employ essentially the same procedure as that used with singly quantified statements: remove the quantifiers by U.I. and E.I., apply the rules of inference to the resulting formula, and then replace the quantifiers by U.G. and E.G. In applying U.I. or E.I. to multiply quantified expressions, the quantifiers are removed one by one, beginning with the leftmost quantifier, and, as before, only a quantifier having the entire expression as its scope is removable. To this end, it may be necessary first to convert an expression into one logically equivalent by means of the laws in Sec. 7.3. The complication comes in making sure that

distinct variables do not become confused during successive applications of
U.I. or E.I. For example, from $(\forall x)(\forall y)P(x,y)$ we get $(\forall y)P(v,y)$ by U.I.,
but if we further instantiate this by v to get $P(v,v)$, then the information that $P(x,y)$ is a propositional function in two variables, not one, has
been lost. $P(v,v)$ could be generalized by U.G. only to $(\forall x)P(x,x)$, not to
$(\forall x)(\forall y)P(x,y)$, since we cannot bind some occurrences of a variable by one
quantifier and some by another. In instantiating $(\forall x)(\forall y)P(x,y)$ we could
use two different symbols, v_1 and v_2, say, each representing an arbitrarily
chosen constant, which, by being distinct, preserve the form of the propositional function $P(x,y)$. Although it is *permitted* to use distinct symbols
in such a case to instantiate distinct variables, it is not *necessary* to do so.
$P(v,v)$, for example, is a legitimate instantiation of $(\forall x)(\forall y)P(x,y)$, and
thus $(\forall x)(\forall y)P(x,y)$ logically implies $(\forall x)P(x,x)$. The latter does not imply the former, however, and thus in a proof if distinct variables are allowed
to merge, the original distinction cannot be subsequently recaptured in the
generalization steps.

Consider, for example, the following proof:

$(7\text{--}42)$ 1. $(\forall x)(\forall y)(P(x,y) \to Q(y,x))$
             2. $(\forall x)(\forall y)(Q(y,x) \to R(x))$
             3. $(\forall y)(P(v_1,y) \to Q(y,v_1))$ 1, U.I.
             4. $P(v_1,v_2) \to Q(v_2,v_1)$ 3, U.I.
             5. $(\forall y)(Q(y,v_1) \to R(v_1))$ 2, U.I.
             6. $Q(v_2,v_1) \to R(v_1)$ 5, U.I.

The instantiations in lines 5 and 6 could have been made with any constants whatever, but the choice of v_1 and v_2, the same constants used in
lines 3 and 4, allows H.S. to be applied to lines 4 and 6.

             7. $P(v_1,v_2) \to R(v_1)$ 4, 6, H.S.
             8. $(\forall y)(P(v_1,y) \to R(v_1))$ 7, U.G.
             9. $(\forall x)(\forall y)(P(x,y) \to R(x))$ 8 U.G.

The order in which v_1 and v_2 are generalized in lines 8 and 9 is immaterial
since both quantifiers are universal, and, of course, the particular choice of
variable symbols — x for v_1 and y for v_2— is arbitrary. The conclusion could
equally well be written $(\forall y)(\forall x)(P(y,x) \to R(y))$.

If the premises had been instantiated everywhere by v, then line 7 would
have been $P(v,v) \to R(v)$, which can be generalized in one step to $(\forall x)$

$(P(x,x) \rightarrow R(x))$. Again, this is a valid conclusion from the premises but a weaker one than the conclusion actually derived in (7-42).

As another example of an argument involving multiply quantified statements, consider the following.

(7-43)   **Whoever forgives at least one person is a saint.**
          There are no saints.
          ∴ **No one ever forgives anyone.**

We represent 'x forgives y' by $F(x,y)$ and 'x is a saint' by $S(x)$.

(7-44)   1. $(\forall x)(\forall y)(F(x,y) \rightarrow S(x))$
          2. $\sim(\exists x)S(x)$
          3. $(\forall y)(F(v_1,y) \rightarrow S(v_1))$ 1, U.I.
          4. $F(v_1,v_2) \rightarrow S(v_1)$ 3, U.I.
          5. $(\forall x)\sim S(x)$ 2, Quant. Neg.
          6. $\sim S(v_1)$ 5, U.I.
          7. $\sim F(v_1,v_2)$ 4, 6, M.T.
          8. $(\forall y)\sim F(v_1,y)$ 7, U.G.
          9. $(\forall x)(\forall y)\sim F(x,y)$ 8, U.G.

Statements containing both universal and existential quantifiers present a special problem in the order in which the quantifiers are reattached by E.G. and U. G. Suppose, for example, that $(\exists x)(\forall y)L(x,y)$ has been instantiated first by E.I. and then by U.I. to $L(w,v)$. The quantifiers can now be replaced, and either order of applying E.G. and U.G. yields a valid consequence. U.G. first and then E. G. produces the original expression, and generalizing in the opposite order gives $(\forall y)(\exists x)L(x,y)$, which is logically implied by $(\exists x)(\forall y)L(x,y)$. (*There is someone who loves everyone* implies *Everyone is loved by at least one individual.*) If we instantiate $(\forall x)(\exists y)L(x,y)$, however, where the universal stands before the existential quantifier, and then generalize, replacing the quantifiers in the opposite order yields an incorrect conclusion. $(\forall x)(\exists y)L(x,y)$, *Everyone has someone whom he loves* does not logically imply $(\exists y)(\forall x)L(x,y)$, *There is at least one individual who is loved by everyone.* Thus, in order to generalize a proposition containing both v and w it is necessary to know the order in which these constants were originally introduced by U.I. and E.I. If U.I. came before E.I., then the generalizations must be carried out in the order E.G. before U.G. If E.I. was applied before U.I., then either order of E.G. and U.G. is permitted. This restriction is illustrated in the proof of the following argument:

(7–45)   **Every human has a father.**
            All Bulgarians are humans.
            ∴. **Every Bulgarian has a father.**

$H(x)$ represents 'x is a human'; $F(x,y)$, 'x is the father of y'; and $B(x)$, 'x is a Bulgarian', in the following proof.

(7–46)   1. $(\forall y)(\exists x)(H(y) \rightarrow F(x,y))$
         2. $(\forall x)(B(x) \rightarrow H(x))$
         3. $(\exists x)(H(v) \rightarrow F(x,v))$ 1, U.I.
         4. $H(v) \rightarrow F(w,v)$ 3, E.I.
         5. $B(v) \rightarrow H(v)$ 2, U.I.
         6. $B(v) \rightarrow F(w,v)$ 4, 5, H.S.

Since v was introduced by U.I. before w was introduced by E.I. (lines 3 and 4), they must be generalized in the opposite order.

         7. $(\exists x)(B(v) \rightarrow F(x,v))$ 6, E.G.
         8. $(\forall y)(\exists x)(B(y) \rightarrow F(x,y))$ 7, U.G.

Generalizing in the other order would have given $(\exists x)(\forall y)(B(y) \rightarrow F(x,y))$, *There is at least one individual who is the father of all Bulgarians.*

7.5   Beth Tableaux

The Beth Tableaux for statements were designed as a strategy for finding a *valuation* or assignment of truth values to the atomic subformulas of a statement which verifies the premises and falsifies the conclusion and hence constitutes a counterexample to its supposed validity (truth in all valuations). Now we present an extension of that strategy to quantified formulas, seeking an assigment to individual variables which falsifies the formula. The principles remain the same as for the case of statements. A quantificational argument is valid if and only if *every* (sub)tableau for that argument leads to closure. To construct tableaux for quantified formulas we need four new rules, two for each quantifier depending on its occurrence under TRUE or under FALSE. We will first discuss some examples and then formulate the rules precisely.

Consider the (valid) argument with the premise $(\forall x)(F(x) \rightarrow G(c))$ and conclusion $(\exists x)F(x) \rightarrow G(c)$.

We know that a true universal statement is verified by checking all assignments to its variables, which is a never–ending task in an infinite universe of discourse. For that reason it is better to try first to come to closure of the tableau by starting to decompose the conclusion, which we assume to be false, trying to reason towards an assignment falsifying the claimed validity. Note that the existential quantifier has only the antecedent of the conditional in its scope. The conditional is therefore the main connective, and we apply the conditional rule for statements under FALSE. A false conditional must have a true antecedent and a false consequent, so $(\exists x)F(x)$ is entered under TRUE, and $G(c)$ under FALSE. If $(\exists x)F(x)$ is assumed true, then there must be an object in the domain which has the property F. Let's call that object a, and continue the tableau with $F(a)$ assumed true. Now the only formula left for decomposition is the initial universal premise. As in the rule of inference U.I. we know that for some arbitrary object the predicate must be true; so it must be true for a as well. We use a in instantiating the universal quantifier, obtaining $F(a) \rightarrow G(c)$ under TRUE. Now the conditional rule for true statements can be applied, which produces a split and puts $G(c)$ under TRUE and $F(a)$ under FALSE, in different subtableaux. But now the two subtableaux close, since $G(c)$ occurs under both TRUE and FALSE, and $F(a)$ occurs under TRUE and FALSE. So we cannot find an assignment which makes the premise true and the conclusion false; hence the entire argument is valid. The complete tableau is (7-47):

$$D = \{c, a\}$$

(7–47)

	TRUE		FALSE	
1.	$(\forall x)(F(x) \rightarrow G(c))$		$(\exists x)F(x) \rightarrow G(c)$	
2.	$(\exists x)F(x)$		$G(c)$	
3.	$F(a)$			
4.	$F(a) \rightarrow G(c)$			
5.	$5._1$	$5._2 \quad G(c)$	$5._1 \quad F(a)$	$5._2$
	======	======	======	======

The subset of the universe of discourse we actually checked consists in this case just of the objects denoted by the individual constants a and c. But since a was arbitrarily chosen we could make exactly the same tableau for any other constant. This would not have been so had we used c in instantiating the premise, since that constant is obviously not arbitrarily chosen. In constructing tableaux for quantified formulas we keep track of the set of objects used in the construction by listing them on the side of the tableau; this is for convenience of reference in case some rule we apply carries restrictions on the constant we may use in it.

Here is a slightly more complex example of a valid argument. The premises are $(\forall x)(F(x) \rightarrow {\sim}G(x))$ and ${\sim}(\forall x){\sim}F(x)$ and the conclusion is $(\exists x){\sim}G(x)$. First we try to apply rules for connectives, in this case just true negation on ${\sim}(\forall x){\sim}F(x)$, bringing $(\forall x){\sim}F(x)$ under FALSE. Continuing with that formula, since it is a false universal, we know there must be an object which falsifies the matrix ${\sim}F(x)$; let's call it a. So ${\sim}F(a)$ is false, and using the rule for false negation, we bring $F(a)$ under TRUE. Now we look at the existential conclusion, which, if false, says that there is no object satisfying ${\sim}G(x)$. Well, then ${\sim}G(a)$ is false, too, and hence $G(a)$ must be true. Next we decompose the first premise, using a as arbitrary object for instantiation of the universal quantifier: $F(a) \rightarrow {\sim}G(a)$ is true. With an application of the rule for a true conditional, we get a split with $F(a)$ under FALSE and ${\sim}G(a)$ under TRUE. Then we bring $G(a)$ under FALSE, and obtain closure for both subtableaux.

$$D = \{a\}$$

(7–48)

	TRUE	FALSE
1.	$(\forall x)(F(x) \rightarrow {\sim}G(x))$	$(\exists x){\sim}G(x)$
	${\sim}(\forall x){\sim}F(x)$	
2.		$(\forall x){\sim}F(x)$
3.		${\sim}F(a)$
4.	$F(a)$	
5.		${\sim}G(a)$
6.	$G(a)$	
7.	$F(a) \rightarrow {\sim}G(a)$	
8.	$8._1$ $\mid$ $8._2 \ {\sim}G(a)$	$8._1 \ F(a)$ $\mid$ $8._2$
	====== $\mid$ ======	====== $\mid$ ======

This tableau shows us clearly that it is a good strategy to choose constants we have already introduced in the universe of discourse in developing the potentially falsifying assignment. Had we chosen a new constant in Step 7, we could have continued the tableau without obtaining closure, but we would have to check all assignments instantiating the first premise, hence sooner or later we would have checked for a anyway. So it's best to check assignments with "old" constants first before introducing new ones. This strategy will provide us with the *smallest* possible counterexample, if there is one.

The next example shows that even when a tableau leads to closure for a number of constants, in checking truth or falsity of a universal statement we have to continue introducing new constants to instantiate the matrix, until we find a counterexample. We can never be *sure* that no such counterexample exists, since we can always introduce a new constant. Is the inference $(\exists x)F(x) \rightarrow (\forall x)F(x)$ valid? Obviously not, since if something has a property, we can't conclude that everything has that property. Let's construct a tableau providing us with a counterexample. The premise $(\exists x)F(x)$ must be true, so there is an a such that $F(a)$ is true. Now we use a again in instantiating the universally quantified conclusion, and close the tableau. But this does not mean that we cannot find a counterexample; we have simply looked at a very special situation, a "world" with only one object, and we have not yet checked all objects in the domain. So we introduce a new object b and instantiate the universal quantifier. This leads to a counterexample and the tableau will not close anymore! So the counterexample consists of a model with the universe of discourse $D = \{a, b\}$ and the interpretation of F in this model $= \{a\}$.

(7–49)

	TRUE	$D = \{a,b\}$ FALSE
1.	$(\exists x)F(x)$	$(\forall x)F(x)$
2.	$F(a)$	
3.		$F(a)$
		======
4.		$F(b)$

Note that a universe of discourse with just one element would not constitute a counterexample, and that the smallest counterexample must have a universe with two elements. You may wonder why we did not introduce a new object in Step 3 right away. The reason is that we have adopted the strategy of checking "old" objects before introducing new ones. Although we can foresee that at first we get closure and then have to introduce a new object, it is an important property of Beth Tableaux that they provide a mechanical procedure to prove validity of arguments, and we can't rely on "foresight" in mechanical procedures. We are now ready to formulate the new rules for quantifiers in Beth Tableaux.

Quantifier Rules for Beth Tableaux

	quantifier occurs under TRUE	quantifier occurs under FALSE
universal	instantiate any object in D^*	instantiate old objects and then add new objects to D
existential	instantiate old objects and then add new objects to D	instantiate any object in D^*

* If D is empty and we cannot first introduce objects by applying the rules for false universals or true existentials, then introduce a new object. Also update these quantifiers whenever a new object is introduced.

Note the similarity between true universal quantifiers and false existential quantifiers; these two rules never add a new object to D except when the domain is empty and we cannot first introduce objects with the other quantifiers. If D is empty, we introduce an arbitrary object before applying these rules for true universals and false existentials. In applying them to non-empty domains, we always check all old objects. But if the other two rules (false universal and true existential) later introduce new elements, we have to check again for closure with these new elements, "updating" the application of true universal and false existential. The other pair of rules (false universal and true existential) may introduce new objects even after closure was obtained with all old ones.

It is best to apply all connective rules before using the quantifier rules, and to remember to check all subtableaux for closure when a split occurs. A subtableau has its own universe of discourse, as potential counterexamples may differ in the cardinality of D. If an argument contains individual constants, you may start with a universe with the same number of distinct objects as there are distinct individual constants in the formulas of the argument, but that will no longer guarantee that you get the *smallest possible* counterexample.

We give two more instructive examples, after which you should be able to construct tableaux for any argument formalizable in predicate logic.

$$D = \{a,b\}$$

(7–50)		TRUE	FALSE
	1.	$(\exists x)(\forall y)R(x,y)$	$(\forall x)R(x,x)$
	2.$_{\exists T}$	$(\forall y)R(a,y)$	
	3.$_{\forall T}$	$R(a,a)$	
	4.$_{\forall F}$		$R(a,a)$
		======	======
	BUT!!!		
	5.$_{\forall F}$		$R(b,b)$
	6.$_{\forall T}$	$R(a,b)$	

We have no more rules to apply, and we obtain a counterexample consisting of the model with a domain $D = \{a,b\}$, assignments $g(x) = a, g(y) = a$, and $g'(x) = b$ and $g'(y) = b$, and the extension of $R = \{\langle a,a\rangle, \langle a,b\rangle\}$. We assume that anything which is not listed in the extension of a predicate is in the complement of the predicate. This could have been made explicit by giving a positive and a negative extension for any predicate. Note that we "update" the true universal quantifier of 2 in 6, instantiating the newly introduced b of 5 for the formula in 2.

$$D = \{a,\ldots\}$$

(7–51)		TRUE	FALSE
	1.	$(\forall x)(F(x) \to \sim G(x))$	$(\exists x)\sim G(x)$
		$\sim(\exists x)\sim F(x)$	
	2.$_{\exists T}$	$\sim F(a)$	
	3.$_{\forall T}$	$(F(a) \to \sim G(a))$	
	4.$_{\exists F}$		$\sim G(a)$
	5.$_{\sim T}$		$F(a)$
	6.$_{\sim F}$	$G(a)$	
	7.	7.$_1$ | 7.$_2$ $\sim G(a)$	7.$_1$ $F(a)$ | 7.$_2$
		======	======

In Sec. 8.3 we will return to some important points of difference between tableaux for statements and tableaux for quantified arguments.

7.6   Formal and informal proofs

We may apply the principles developed in the preceding section on Natural Deduction to the proof of statements about sets. Note that $A \subseteq B$, for example, is a statement which asserts that a certain two-place predicate, 'is a subset of', holds of a particular pair of sets, A and B. That this is customarily written $A \subseteq B$ instead of $\subseteq (A, B)$ is merely a notational convention of set theory. Similarly, $x \in A$ is an open statement containing the variable x in which "$\in A$" functions as a one-place predicate. $(\exists x)(x \in A)$ is then a statement asserting that A is not empty. The Axiom of Extension (two sets are equal if they have the same members) might be written as $(\forall X, Y)(X = Y \leftrightarrow (\forall x)(x \in X \leftrightarrow x \in Y))$.

The following is a proof showing formally that $(\forall X, Y)(X = Y \leftrightarrow (X \subseteq Y \,\&\, Y \subseteq X))$ (two sets are equal iff each is a subset of the other) follows from the Axiom of Extension as premise:

(7-52) 1. $(\forall X, Y)(X = Y \leftrightarrow (\forall x)(x \in X \leftrightarrow x \in Y))$
        2. $V_1 = V_2 \leftrightarrow (\forall x)(x \in V_1 \leftrightarrow x \in V_2)$ 1, U.I. (twice)
        3. $V_1 = V_2 \leftrightarrow (\forall x)((x \in V_1 \rightarrow x \in V_2) \,\&\, (x \in V_2 \rightarrow x \in V_1))$
                                                          2, Bicond.
        4. $V_1 = V_2 \leftrightarrow ((\forall x)(x \in V_1 \rightarrow x \in V_2) \,\&\, (\forall x)(x \in V_2 \rightarrow x \in V_1))$
                                         3, Quant. Distr. (Law 4)
        5. $V_1 = V_2 \leftrightarrow (V_1 \subseteq V_2 \,\&\, V_2 \subseteq V_1)$ 4, Definition of $\subseteq$

In step 5 we have simply replaced two subexpressions of line 4 by their abbreviated forms.

        6. $(\forall X, Y)(X = Y \leftrightarrow (X \subseteq Y \,\&\, Y \subseteq X))$5, U.G. (twice)

Line 6 thus can be added to our stock of true statements about sets in general (cf. Fig. 1-7).

As another illustration of a proof of a set-theoretic proposition we demonstrate the following (which was asserted without proof in Ch. 1, Sec. 4):

For any sets X, Y, and Z, if X is a subset of Y and Y is a subset of Z, then X is a subset of Z.

In symbols,

(7-53) $(\forall X, Y, Z)((X \subseteq Y \,\&\, Y \subseteq Z) \rightarrow X \subseteq Z)$

Our demonstration uses a conditional proof:

(7–54)   1. | $V_1 \subseteq V_2 \& V_2 \subseteq V_3$ Aux. Premise
         2. | $(\forall x)(x \in V_1 \rightarrow x \in V_2) \& (\forall x)(x \in V_2 \rightarrow x \in V_3)$
                                                          1, Def. of $\subseteq$
         3. | $(\forall x)((x \in V_1 \rightarrow x \in V_2) \& (x \in V_2 \rightarrow x \in V_3))$
                                                          2, Quant. Distr. (Law 2)
         4. | $(v \in V_1 \rightarrow v \in V_2) \& (v \in V_2 \rightarrow v \in V_3)$ 3, U.I.
         5. | $v \in V_1 \rightarrow v \in V_2$ 4, Simp.
         6. | $v \in V_2 \rightarrow v \in V_3$ 5, Simp.
         7. | $v \in V_1 \rightarrow v \in V_3$ 5, 6, H.S.
         8. | $(\forall x)(x \in V_1 \rightarrow x \in V_3)$ 7, U.G.
         9. | $V_1 \subseteq V_3$ 8, Def. of $\subseteq$
        10. | $(V_1 \subseteq V_2 \& V_2 \subseteq V_3) \rightarrow V_1 \subseteq V_3$ 1–9, C.P.
        11. | $(\forall X, Y, Z)((X \subseteq Y \& Y \subseteq Z) \rightarrow X \subseteq Z)$
                                                          10, U.G. (three times)

7.7   Informal style in mathematical proofs

Mathematicians rarely present proofs in the completely formal style we have been using since they can assume that their audience is familiar enough with logical equivalences and rules of inference to require only an outline of the essential steps. We have already used this style of presentation in earlier sections (see, for example, Chapter 3, Sec. 6). Such an informal proof should be easily expanded into a fully formal version that can be checked step by step if there is any doubt concerning its validity. Thus, the term "informal", when applied to proofs, does not mean "sloppy", only "condensed".

To illustrate, we give (7-54) as a mathematician might write it:

(7–55)   Let X, Y, and Z be arbitrary sets such that $X \subseteq Y$ and $Y \subseteq Z$. Let x be an arbitrary member of X. Because $X \subseteq Y, x \in Y$; and because $Y \subseteq Z$, $x \in Z$. Therefore, $x \in X \rightarrow x \in Z$, and thus $X \subseteq Z$.

Observe that no explicit mention is made of U.I. and U.G., it being understood from the context and use of the word 'arbitrary' that the result is true of all sets. In the last two sentences of the proof it is assumed that the reader knows the definition of $\subseteq$ and the inference rule of Hypothetical Syllogism. The whole is in the form of a conditional proof headed by the statement $X \subseteq Y \,\&\, Y \subseteq Z$, but it is left to the reader to draw the conclusion $(X \subseteq Y \,\&\, Y \subseteq Z) \to X \subseteq Z$ and to generalize it universally.

As another example, we state the definition of 'proper subset' and give both formal and informal proofs of a theorem containing this predicate.

(7-56) $(\forall X, Y)(X \subset Y \leftrightarrow (X \subseteq Y \,\&\, X \neq Y))$

The expression $X \neq Y$ is an alternative notation for $\sim(X = Y)$. Similarly, $X \not\subseteq Y, X \not\subset Y$, and $x \notin Y$ can be written in place of $\sim(X \subseteq Y)$, $\sim(X \subset Y)$, and $\sim(x \in Y)$, respectively. The predicate $\subset$ in (7-56) is defined in terms of the predicates $\subseteq$ and $=$, which can in turn be expressed in terms of the predicate $\in$, thus:

(7-57) $(\forall X, Y)(X \subset Y \leftrightarrow ((\forall x)(x \in X \to x \in Y) \,\&$
         $\sim(\forall x)(x \in X \leftrightarrow x \in Y)))$

We wish to prove:

For any sets X and Y, if X is a proper subset of Y, there is some member of Y that is not a member of X.

That is,

(7-58) $(\forall X, Y)(X \subset Y \to (\exists x)(x \in Y \,\&\, x \notin X))$

(7-59)   *Proof* (formal):

1.	$V_1 \subset V_2$	Aux. Premise
2.	$V_1 \subseteq V_2 \,\&\, V_1 \neq V_2$	1, Def. of $\subset$
3.	$V_1 \neq V_2$	2, Simp.
4.	$\sim(V_1 \subseteq V_2 \,\&\, V_2 \subseteq V_1)$	3, (7-52) above
5.	$V_1 \not\subseteq V_2 \lor V_2 \not\subseteq V_1$	4, DeM.
6.	$V_1 \subseteq V_2$	2, Simp.
7.	$V_2 \not\subseteq V_1$	5, 6, D.S.
8.	$\sim(\forall x)(x \in V_2 \to x \in V_1)$	7, Def. of $\subseteq$
9.	$(\exists x)\sim(x \in V_2 \to x \in V_1)$	8, Quant. Neg.
10.	$(\exists x)\sim(x \notin V_2 \lor x \in V_1)$	9, Cond.
11.	$(\exists x)(x \in V_2 \,\&\, x \notin V_1)$	10, DeM.
12.	$V_1 \subset V_2 \to (\exists x)(x \in V_2 \,\&\, x \notin V_1)$	1–11, Cond. Proof
13.	$(\forall X, Y)(X \subset Y \to (\exists x)(x \in Y \,\&\, x \notin X))$	12, U.G. (twice)

(7-60)   *Proof* (informal): Let X and Y be arbitrary sets such that $X \subset Y$.
Then, by definition, $X \subseteq Y$ and $X \neq Y$. $X = Y$ iff $X \subseteq Y$ and
$Y \subseteq X$. Therefore, since $X \neq Y$ and $X \subseteq Y$, it follows that $Y \not\subseteq X$,
which implies that there is some x in Y that is not in X.

As a final example we give formal and informal versions of a proof involving binary relations:

For any binary relation R, $R = (R^{-1})^{-1}$.

We make use of the result proved in (7-52), i.e., for all sets X and Y,
$X = Y$ iff $(X \subseteq Y \,\&\, Y \subseteq X)$. Thus we first prove $R \subseteq (R^{-1})^{-1}$, then that
$(R^{-1})^{-1} \subseteq R$. (This is the customary procedure in showing equality of two
sets.)

(7-61)   *Proof* (formal):

1.	$\langle v_1, v_2 \rangle \in V$	Aux. Premise

$[\langle v_1, v_2 \rangle$ is an arbitrarily chosen ordered pair in the
arbitrarily chosen binary relation $V]$

2.	$(\forall R)(\forall x, y)(\langle x, y \rangle \in R \leftrightarrow \langle y, x \rangle \in R^{-1})$	Def. of inverse
3.	$(\forall x, y)(\langle x, y \rangle \in V \leftrightarrow \langle y, x \rangle \in V^{-1})$	2, U.I.
4.	$\langle v_1, v_2 \rangle \in V \leftrightarrow \langle v_2, v_1 \rangle \in V^{-1}$	3, U.I. (twice)
5.	$(\langle v_1, v_2 \rangle \in V \rightarrow \langle v_2, v_1 \rangle \in V^{-1}) \,\&\,$	4, Bicond.
	$(\langle v_2, v_1 \rangle \in V^{-1} \rightarrow \langle v_1, v_2 \rangle \in V)$	
6.	$\langle v_1, v_2 \rangle \in V \rightarrow \langle v_2, v_1 \rangle \in V^{-1}$	5, Simp.
7.	$\langle v_2, v_1 \rangle \in V^{-1}$	1, 6, M.P.
8.	$(\forall x, y)(\langle x, y \rangle \in V^{-1} \leftrightarrow \langle y, x \rangle \in (V^{-1})^{-1})$	2, U.I.

[generalizing line 2 again, this time with respect to V^{-1}]

9.	$\langle v_2, v_1 \rangle \in V^{-1} \leftrightarrow \langle v_1, v_2 \rangle \in (V^{-1})^{-1}$	8, U.I. (twice)
10.	$(\langle v_2, v_1 \rangle \in V^{-1} \rightarrow \langle v_1, v_2 \rangle \in (V^{-1})^{-1}) \,\&\,$	9, Bicond.
	$(\langle v_1, v_2 \rangle \in (V^{-1})^{-1} \rightarrow \langle v_2, v_1 \rangle \in V^{-1})$	
11.	$\langle v_2, v_1 \rangle \in V^{-1} \rightarrow \langle v_1, v_2 \rangle \in (V^{-1})^{-1}$	10, Simp.
12.	$\langle v_1, v_2 \rangle \in (V^{-1})^{-1}$	7, 11, M.P.
13.	$\langle v_1, v_2 \rangle \in V \rightarrow \langle v_1, v_2 \rangle \in (V^{-1})^{-1}$	1-12, C.P.
14.	$(\forall x, y)(\langle x, y \rangle \in V \rightarrow \langle x, y \rangle \in (V^{-1})^{-1})$	13. U.G. (twice)
15.	$V \subseteq (V^{-1})^{-1}$	14, Def. of $\subseteq$
16.	$(\forall R)R \subseteq (R^{-1})^{-1}$	15, U.G.

The proof of the other half, i.e. $(R^{-1})^{-1} \subseteq R$, is quite similar and is left
as an exercise for the reader.

Here is an informal version of the part just proved:

(7-62) *Proof* (informal): Let R be an arbitrarily chosen binary relation. Assume $\langle x, y \rangle \in R$. Then by the definition of inverse, $\langle y, x \rangle \in R^{-1}$. Again, by the definition of inverse, if $\langle y, x \rangle \in R^{-1}$, then $\langle x, y \rangle \in (R^{-1})^{-1}$. Thus, if $\langle x, y \rangle \in R, \langle x, y \rangle \in (R^{-1})^{-1}$, and so $R \subseteq (R^{-1})^{-1}$.

In fact, if the proof were intended for readers assumed to be very familiar with these notions, it might appear in even more condensed form:

(7-63) *Proof*: Let R be a relation and let $\langle x, y \rangle$ be in R. Then $\langle y, x \rangle \in R^{-1}$ and $\langle x, y \rangle \in (R^{-1})^{-1}$. $\therefore R \subseteq (R^{-1})^{-1}$.

or even

(7-64) *Proof*: Obvious.

A proof is in part a demonstration that some statement follows by logical steps from assumed premises, but it is also an attempt to convince *some actual or imagined audience* of this logical connection. Therefore, what counts as an adequate proof depends to a certain extent on the level of sophistication of one's audience. Of course, as a minimal condition it must be valid, but a proof at the level of detail appropriate for an introductory logic textbook would strike an experienced mathematician as tedious and pedantic, whereas condensed proofs omitting many logical steps appear incomprehensible to beginners. In subsequent proofs in this book we will aim for an informal level which we hope will be neither condescending nor obscure.

Exercises

1. Translate the following English sentences into predicate logic; choose your own variables and predicate letters, giving the key. If you think more than one translation is suitable, give the alternatives and discuss their differences. Represent as much as possible of the structure relevant to quantificational arguments.

    (a) Everything is black or white.

    (b) Either everything is black or it is white.

  (c) A dog is a quadruped.
  (d) Fido is a dog.
  (e) Everybody loves somebody.
  (f) Someone is loved by everyone.
  (g) There is someone whom everyone loves.
  (h) If someone loves someone, John loves himself.
  (i) No one loves himself, unless it is John.
  (j) Anyone either loves himself or some woman.
  (k) If you love a woman, kiss her or lose her.
  (l) If no one kisses John, Mary will.
  (m) People who live in New York love it.
  (n) If John does not love New York, he does not live there (i.e., in it).
  (o) If someone does not love New York, he does not know it.
  (p) If a tableau closes, there are no counterexamples.
  (q) Give him a finger, and he takes the whole hand. (Dutch proverb)
  (r) Someone who is noisy annoys everyone but himself.
  (s) If someone is noisy, he annoys everybody.
  (t) Although no one made noise, John was annoyed.
  (u) Someone owns a car but rides his bike as well.
  (v) Only drunk drivers under 18 cause bad accidents.
  (w) Don't drink and drive!
  (x) Driving is risky, if you are drunk.
  (y) All is well that ends well.

2. As a translation of the sentence *Everyone answered all the questions*,
   the statement $(\forall x)(\forall y)A(x,y)$ is not adequate, when $A(x,y)$ translates
   'x answered y', since, as we saw in Sec. 7.3, the universe of discourse
   must contain both people and questions. We have to represent the two
   distinct sets by two predicates in the antecedent of a conditional formula. In the light of this discussion, translate the following sentences.

  (a) No one answered every question.
  (b) For every question there was someone who answered it.

(c) Everyone answered at least one question.

(d) Some people didn't answer any questions.

(e) Everyone likes Mary except Mary herself. (use $I(x, y)$ for identity)

(f) Everyone but Fred answered at least one question.

(g) Everyone who answered a question attempted some question or other.

(h) No one answered any question that everyone attempted.

(i) Everyone who attempted a question answered it.

3. In each of the following expressions, identify all bound and free occurrences of variables, and underline the scope of the quantifiers.

(a) $(\forall x)P(x) \vee Q(x, y)$

(b) $(\forall y)(Q(x) \rightarrow (\forall z)P(y, z))$

(c) $(\forall x){\sim}(P(x) \rightarrow (\exists y)(\forall z)Q(x, y, z))$

(d) $(\exists x)Q(x, y) \,\&\, P(y, x)$

(e) $(\forall x)(P(x) \rightarrow (\exists y)(Q(y) \rightarrow (\forall z)R(y, z)))$

4. Each part of this exercise consists of an English sentence followed by a translation of it in predicate logic and a number of additional formulas. Indicate which of the formulas are equivalent to the translation and give the laws or rules necessary to show this equivalence. If a formula is not equivalent to the translation, give a rendition of it in English.

(a) Everything has a father and all odd numbers are integers.
(*Note*: While it would be tempting to read the given formula as *everyone* has a father ...', this would be inaccurate, since we have not restricted the universe to the set of people and cannot do so if we want the predicates odd and integer to apply to some elements in the universe. To render *everyone* in predicate logic, we would have to add an antecedent with the predicate person.)

$$(\forall x)(\exists y)F(y, x) \,\&\, (\forall z)(O(z) \rightarrow I(z))$$
(1) $(\forall z)(\forall x)(\exists y)(F(y, x) \,\&\, (O(z) \rightarrow I(z)))$
(2) $(\forall z)(\exists y)(\forall x)(F(y, x) \,\&\, (O(z) \rightarrow I(z)))$
(3) $(\forall x)(\forall z)(\exists y)(F(y, x) \,\&\, (O(z) \rightarrow I(z)))$

(b) If Adam is a bachelor, then not all men are husbands.

$$B(a) \rightarrow \sim(\forall x)(M(x) \rightarrow H(x)$$

(1) $(\forall x)(B(a) \rightarrow \sim(M(x) \rightarrow H(x)))$

(2) $(\exists x)(B(a) \rightarrow \sim(M(x) \rightarrow H(x)))$

(3) $\sim(B(a) \rightarrow (\forall x)(M(x) \rightarrow H(x)))$

(4) $B(a) \rightarrow (\exists x)(M(x) \& \sim H(x))$

(c) If there is anything that is evil, then God is not benevolent.

$$(\exists x)E(x) \rightarrow \sim B(g)$$

(1) $\sim((\exists x)E(x) \& B(g))$

(2) $(\forall x)(E(x) \rightarrow \sim B(g))$

5. Find two equivalent but different formulas translating each of the sentences below, using the predicates given.

(a) For every integer, there is a larger integer.
$(I(x), L(x,y))$

(b) Either every prime number is odd or some integers are even, or both.
$(P(x), I(x), O(x))$

(c) If there is a prime number which is even, then all prime numbers greater than 7 are odd.
$(P(x), O(x), G(x,y))$

(d) If all men are mortal, then Socrates is mortal.
$(H(x), M(x))$

6. Give the Prenex Normal Forms of these formulas:

(a) $((\exists x)A(x) \& (\exists x)B(x)) \rightarrow C(x)$

(b) $(\forall x)A(x) \leftrightarrow (\exists x)B(x)$

7. Prove the validity of the following argument forms:

(a) $\sim(\exists x)(P(x) \& Q(x))$
$(\exists x)(P(x) \& R(x))$
$\therefore \overline{(\exists x)(R(x) \& \sim Q(x))}$

(b) $(\forall x)(P(x) \rightarrow Q(x))$
$(\exists x)(R(x) \& \sim Q(x))$
$\therefore \overline{(\exists x)(R(x) \& \sim P(x))}$

(c) $(\forall x)(P(x) \rightarrow Q(x))$
        $(\exists x)(P(x) \,\&\, R(x))$
∴ $\overline{(\exists x)(R(x) \,\&\, Q(x))}$

(d) $(\forall x)(P(x) \rightarrow Q(x))$
        $\sim(\forall x)(P(x) \qquad \rightarrow$
        $R(x))$
∴ $\overline{(\exists x)(\sim R(x) \,\&\, Q(x))}$

(e) $(\forall x)(P(x) \rightarrow Q(x))$
        $P(a)$
        $R(a)$
∴ $\overline{(\exists x)(R(x) \,\&\, Q(x))}$

(f) $(\forall x)((P(x) \vee Q(x)) \rightarrow R(x))$
        $(\forall x)((R(x) \vee S(x)) \rightarrow T(x))$
∴ $\overline{(\forall x)(P(x) \rightarrow T(x))}$

8. Construct proofs of validity for the following English arguments. ((a)-
   (c) are adapted from the author of *Alice in Wonderland*, Lewis Caroll
   [C. L. Dodgson], *Symbolic Logic*, (1896).)

   (a) Babies are illogical. Nobody who is despised can manage a crocodile.
       Illogical persons are despised. Therefore, babies cannot manage
       crocodiles.

   (b) Everyone who is sane can do logic. No lunatics are fit to serve on
       a jury. None of your sons can do logic. Therefore, none of your
       sons is fit to serve on a jury.

   (c) No ducks waltz. No officers ever decline to waltz. All my poultry
       are ducks. Therefore, my poultry are not officers.

   (d) All vowels are sonorants. All stops are obstruents. Nothing is
       both a sonorant and an obstruent. Therefore, nothing is both a
       vowel and a stop.

   (e) No linguist believes in the parity principle. Everyone believes in
       the parity principle or is a behaviorist. Every dietician renounces
       behaviorism. My aunt is a dietician. Therefore, there is someone
       who is neither a linguist nor a behaviorist.

9. Test the validity of the following arguments with Beth Tableaux. Provide a counterexample, if invalid.

    (a) $\sim(\exists x)F(x) \Rightarrow (\forall x)\sim F(x)$

    (b) $(\forall x)(\exists y)R(x,y) \Rightarrow (\exists y)(\forall x)R(x,y)$

    (c) $(\exists y)(\forall x)R(y,x) \Rightarrow (\forall x)(\exists y)R(y,x)$

10. Give a formal proof of each of the following:

    (a) If $A \subseteq B$ and $B \subset C$, then $A \subset C$.

    (b) If $A \subseteq B$ and $A \not\subseteq C$, then $B \not\subseteq C$.

11. Give informal proofs of each of the following statements:

    (a) $(A - B) \subseteq A$

    (b) $((A - B) \cup (B - A) = \emptyset)$ iff $A = B$

    (c) $B' \supseteq A$ iff A and B are disjoint.

    (d) $A \subseteq B$ iff $A \cup (B - A) = B$

    (e) $\wp(A) \cap \wp(B) = \wp(A \cap B)$

    (f) $\wp(A) \cup \wp(B) \subseteq \wp(A \cup B)$

12. Give informal proofs of the properties of binary relations in Fig. 3-2 not already proved in the text. (If the property is "not determined", give examples which show why this is so.)

Chapter 8

Formal Systems, Axiomatization, and Model Theory

8.1   The syntactic side of formal systems

In this section and the next, we return in greater detail to the study of formal systems from syntactic and semantic perspectives. In this section we focus on the syntactic side, and our aim will be to link together the notion of recursive definition which we introduced in Chapter 1 as a means of specifying sets with the closely related notions of *inductive proof*, new in this chapter, and of axiomatic system. Some of the close connections between grammars and formal systems will be illustrated, and various string operations will be formalized, although grammars as a topic in their own right will not be taken up until Part E. The discussion in this section will be purely syntactic (in part so as to illustrate what that means); we will return to a semantic investigation of some of the formal systems discussed here in the next section.

8.1.1   Recursive definitions

Consider the set M of all mirror-image strings on $\{a, b\}$. A mirror-image string is one that can be divided into halves, the right half consisting of the same sequence of symbols as the left half but in the reverse order. For example, *aaaa*, *abba*, *babbab*, and *bbabbabb* are mirror-image strings, but *babb*, *aaab*, and *bab* are not. The following is a possible recursive definition of *M*.

(8–1)   1. *aa* ∈ *M* & *bb* ∈ *M*
        2. $(\forall x)(x \in M \to (axa \in M\ \&\ bxb \in M))$
        3. *M* contains nothing but those members it has by virtue of lines 1 and 2

Line 1, which is called the *base* of the recursive definition, asserts that $x \in M$ is true of the specific string *aa* and *bb*. Line 2, called the *recursion step* or simply the *recursion*, says that for any string *x* if $x \in M$ is true, then it is also true of the strings formed from *x* by concatenating an *a* at both ends or a *b* at both ends. Line 3, the *restriction*, rules out any true instances of $x \in M$ other than those covered by lines 1 and 2. Without the restriction, the definition would specify a class of sets meeting the conditions of lines 1 and 2 but possibly containing other members as well.

The recursion step of a recursive definition is characteristically a conditional in which what is being defined occurs in both the antecedent and the consequent. This makes recursive definitions look like alleged definitions that are circular and, consequently, not really definitions at all. For example, the putative definition of 'subset' in (8-2)

(8–2)   For any sets *A* and *B*, *A* is a *subset* of *B* iff every subset of *A* is also a subset of *B*.

contains a vicious circularity in which the notion 'subset' is characterized by appealing to that notion itself. That is, one could not know what a subset is until one had already determined what a subset is. If 'subset' had already been adequately defined in the customary way in terms of the predicate ∈, then (8-2) would be a perfectly sensible, in fact, true statement; but as a statement introducing the term 'subset' for the first time (8-2) is defectively circular.

In a recursive definition this circularity is avoided by the presence of the base, which makes a nonconditional statement about the thing being defined. Given the base, one can take an appropriate substitution instance of the recursion step and by *Modus Ponens* derive the consequent of that substitution instance. From the base and recursion of (8-1), for example, the following inference can be carried out:

(8-3)   1. $aa \in M \ \& \ bb \in M$

       2. $(\forall x)(x \in M \to (axa \in M \ \& \ bxb \in M))$

       3. $aa \in M$ 1, Simp.

       4. $aa \in M \to (aaaa \in M \ \& \ baab \in M)$ 2, U.I.

       5. $aaaa \in M \ \& \ baab \in M$ 3,4, M.P.

       6. $baab \in M$ 5, Simp.

From this line and another substitution instance of the recursion step

       7. $baab \in M \to (abaaba \in M \ \& \ bbaabb \in M)$ 2, U.I.

we can derive

       8. $abaaba \in M \ \& \ bbaabb \in M$ 6, 7, M.P.

Such a series of steps constitutes a proof that certain strings are in M, given the base and recursion of the recursive definition (8-1) as premises. The fact that such a proof is possible for every string asserted to be in M by the definition serves to convince us that this recursive definition really does define something and is not circular. Without the base, however, no such proofs are possible. From the recursion step alone one can derive only a series of conditionals.

(8-4)   1. $(\forall x)(x \in M \to (axa \in M \ \& \ bxb \in M))$

       2. $aa \in M \to (aaaa \in M \ \& \ baab \in M)$ 1, U.I.

       3. $(aa \in M \to aaaa \in M) \ \& \ (aa \in M \to baab \in M)$ 2, Log. Equiv.

       4. $aa \in M \to aaaa \in M$ 3, Simp.

       5. $aaaa \in M \to (aaaaaa \in M \ \& \ baaaab \in M)$ 1, U.I.

       6. $aa \in M \to (aaaaaa \in M \ \& \ baaaab \in M)$ 4, 5, H.S.

The conclusions that can be derived are statements that *if* certain strings are in M, then so are certain others. Lacking the base, the definition would not assert that M contain any strings at all.

We also note that the close connection between sets and predicates allows us to regard a recursive definition either as defining a predicate, e.g., the predicate 'is a member of M' in the preceding example, or, equivalently, as defining a set that is the extension of that predicate, e.g., the set M.

A slightly more complex example is the recursive definition of the set of well-formed formulas (*wff*'s) in statement logic (cf. Sec. 6.1). The following definition divides those strings constructed from the alphabet

$$C = \{p, q, r, \& , \lor, \sim, \to, \leftrightarrow, (,)\}$$

that are legitimate expressions in this system of logic, e.g., $((p \& q) \vee r) \rightarrow s)$, from those, e.g., $(p \& \rightarrow r)$, which are not.

(8-5)   1. p is a *wff*; q is a *wff*; r is a *wff*

2. For all α and β, if α and β are *wff*'s then so is

    (a) $(\alpha \& \beta)$

    (b) $(\alpha \vee \beta)$

    (c) $(\alpha \rightarrow \beta)$

    (d) $(\alpha \leftrightarrow \beta)$

    (e) $\sim \alpha$

3. Nothing is a *wff* except as a consequence of lines 1 and 2.

Using this definition we can prove that some particular expression, say $((p \& q) \vee r)$, is a *wff*.

(8-6)
1. p is a *wff* & q is a *wff*   (1), Simp.
2. $(p$ is a *wff* & q is a *wff*) $\rightarrow$ $(p \& q)$ is a *wff*   (2a), U.I.
3. $(p \& q)$ is a *wff*   1, 2, M.P.
4. r is a *wff*   (1), Simp.
5. $((p \& q)$ is a *wff* & r is a *wff*) $\rightarrow$ $((p \& q) \vee r)$ is a *wff*   (2b), U.I.
6. $(p \& q)$ is a *wff* & r is a *wff*   3, 4, Conj.
7. $((p \& q) \vee r)$ is a *wff*   5, 6, M.P.

The definition in (8-5) does not characterize all the *wff*'s of statement logic since it allows no more than three distinguishable atomic statements p, q, and r. Of course more symbols could be added to the alphabet and the base of the recursive definition could be appropriately expanded, but for any given finite number of symbols for atomic statements there is some *wff* in statement logic containing more than this number of distinct atomic statements. Thus, it would appear that there must be an infinite number of symbols for atomic statements in the alphabet and that the base of the definition must consist of an infinite conjunction of the form p is a *wff* & q is a *wff* & $\cdots$. This raises anew the problem of specifying the members of an infinite set—here, the set of conjuncts in the base of the recursive definition. The solution is to precede the recursive definition of *wff* by a recursive definition of 'atomic statement' (more precisely, the set of symbols denoting atomic statements). One symbol, say p, is chosen and other symbols are created by adding primes successively: p, p', p'', p''', etc. Each such symbol is considered distinct, designating an atomic statement potentially distinct from all others. The recursive definition is as follows:

(8-7) 1. p is (or denotes) an atomic statement
       2. For all x, if x is an atomic statement, then so is x'
       3. Nothing else is an atomic statement

The recursive definition of *wff* is now as in (8-5) except that the base is replaced by:

      1. Every atomic statement is a *wff*.

It is also understood, of course, that the definition of *wff* now applies to strings on the finite alphabet $C' = \{p, ', \&, \vee, \sim, \rightarrow, \leftrightarrow, (,)\}$.

Nothing essentially new is involved in framing one recursive definition in terms of another. We have already seen many examples of definitions in which previously defined concepts appear; for example, the definition of 'power set' in terms of 'subset' in Chapter 1. If recursive definition is a legitimate mode of definition, then there can be no objection to using one recursively defined predicate in the recursive definition of another.

8.2   Axiomatic systems and derivations

Recursive definitions and axiomatic systems have a similar logical structure. From a finite number of statements given initially an infinite number of additional statements are derivable by repeated application of a specified set of rules. The statements assumed at the outset are the *axioms*, and the additional statements, called *theorems*, are derived from the axioms and previously derived theorems by interated applications of the *rules of inference*. The set of axioms, the set of rules of inference, and the alphabet in which all these are written constitute an *axiomatic system*. Viewed in this way, a recursive definition is like an axiomatic system in which the base states the axioms and the recursion step constitutes the rules of inference. The members of the set specified by the recursive definition, aside from those given by the base, comprise the theorems of the system.

DEFINITION 8.1 *An axiomatic system is an ordered triple* (A, S, P) *in which*

1. A *is a finite set of symbols, called the* alphabet.

2. S *is a set of strings on* A, *called the* axioms.

3. P *is a set of n-place relations in A^*, the set of all strings made from the alphabet A, where $n \geq 2$ (i.e., the n-tuples in P must be at least ordered pairs.) The members of P are called* productions *or* rules (of inference).

■

We now indicate how the productions are to be employed in deriving additional strings.

DEFINITION 8.2 *Given an axiomatic system* (A, S, P), *if*

$$(x_1, x_2, \ldots, x_{n-1}, x_n)$$

is a production in P, we say that x_n follows from $(x_1, x_2, \ldots, x_{n-1})$. *We also use $x_1, x_2, \ldots, x_{n-1} \to x_n$ as an equivalent notation for $(x_1, x_2, \ldots, x_{n-1}, x_n)$.*

■

DEFINITION 8.3 *Given an axiomatic system* (A, S, P), *a linearly ordered sequence of strings $y_1, y_2, \ldots, y_m$ is called a* derivation *or* proof *of y_m if and only if every string in the sequence is either (1) an axiom, or (2) follows one of the productions in P from one or more strings preceding it in the sequence. If there is a derivation of y in a given axiomatic system, y is called a* theorem *of that system.*

■

We can illustrate these definitions by reinterpreting the recursive definition in (8-1) of mirror-image strings on $\{a, b\}$ as an axiomatic system.

(8-8) $A = \{a, b\}$
        $S = \{(aa, bb)\}$
        $P = \{(x, y) \in A^* \times A^* \mid y = axa \vee y = bxb\}$

The productions are thus the infinite set of ordered pairs

(8-9) $\{(e, aa), (e, bb), (a, aaa), (a, bab), (b, aba), (b, bbb), (aa, aaaa), \ldots\}$

or in the alternative notation,

(8–10) $\{e \rightarrow aa, e \rightarrow bb, a \rightarrow aaa, a \rightarrow aba, b \rightarrow bbb, aa \rightarrow aaaa, \ldots\}$

In this axiomatic system, we see that the sequence of lines

(8–11) $bb, abba, aabbaa$

is a derivation of $aabbaa$ since the last string follows from preceding strings (in fact, from just the one immediately preceding) by the production $abba \rightarrow aabba$; similarly, $abba$ follows from bb by the production $bb \rightarrow abba$; and bb is an axiom. Therefore, $aabbaa$ is a theorem of this axiomatic system. The sequence

(8–12) $bb, baab$

is not a derivation since $baab$ does not follow from bb by the rules of P. This does not necessarily mean that the string $baab$ is not a theorem since there may exist some derivation in the system in which $baab$ is the last line. It happens in this case that there is, viz.,

(8–13) $aa, baab$

and thus $baab$ is a theorem.

One consequence of the definition is that the first line of a derivation must be an axiom since there are no lines preceding the first from which it could follow. Thus, a sequence such as

(8–14) $ab, aaba, baabab$

is not a derivation because ab is not an axiom. A derivation may, however, consist of only one line and, if so, that line must necessarily be an axiom.

The set of productions P in (8-8) is an infinite set of all ordered pairs of the form (x, axa) and (x, bxb), where x is a variable whose values are all the strings in A^*. P, therefore, contains productions such as $L(a, aaa)$ and $(ab, babb)$ that will never actually be used in the derivation of any theorems in this system from the given set of axioms. Further, because x is a variable symbol and not a member of the alphabet A, the expressions (x, axa) and (x, bxb) are not themselves productions but rather *production schemata* or

formulas for constructing productions. This finite set of schemata specifies
an infinite set of productions in which the variable symbol x is replaced by
any constant string on A^*. To be completely formal, we could, of course,
give a recursive definition of the set of productions, thus embedding one
recursive specification within another as we did in (8-5) and (8-7).

The axioms may also be specified by schemata containing variable symbols (or by recursive definition). For example, in the axiomatic system given
in (8-15), whose theorems are all the *wff*'s of statement logic, S is an axiom
schema specifying as an axiom any string consisting of the symbol p followed
by any number of primes [cf. (8-7)]. P is also a schema for the infinite set
of productions of this system.

(8-15) $A = \{\&, \vee, \sim, \to, \leftrightarrow, (,), p, '\}$
$S = \{px \mid x \in \{'\}^*\}$
$P = \{(x, \sim x), (x, y, (x \& y)), (x, y, (x \vee y)), (x, y, (x \leftrightarrow y))\}$ where
x and y are strings in A^*

Problem: Which of the following sequences are derivations in the axiomatic
system of (8-15)?

1. $p, \sim p, \sim\sim p$

2. $p, p', (p \vee p'), ((p \vee p') \& p'')$

3. $(p \vee p), p', (p' \to (p \vee p))$

4. $p, \sim p, p'$

8.2.1   Extended axiomatic systems

From a syntactic perspective, it is not uncommon to extend the definition
of an axiomatic system somewhat to allow two kinds of symbols in the alphabet. Specifically, we have a *basic alphabet* and an *auxiliary alphabet*,
which are disjoint sets. Symbols from both sets may appear in the lines of
a derivation, *but the theorems contain only symbols from the basic alphabet*.
An axiomatic system with two disjoint alphabets of this sort will be called
an *extended axiomatic system* (e.a.s.). (Note: We are here dangerously close
to blurring the line between axiomatic systems and grammars; model theo-
rists would probably not countenance these extended axiomatic systems as
genuine axiomatic systems.)

DEFINITION 8.4 *An* extended axiomatic system *is an ordered quadruple* (A, B, S, P) *where*

1. A *is a finite set of symbols, the* auxiliary alphabet.

2. B *is a finite set of symbols, the* basic alphabet; A *and* B *are disjoint.*

3. S *is a set of strings on* $(A \cup B)^*$, *the* axioms. S *may be specified by a finite set of axiom schemata.*

4. P *is a set of* n-*place relations* $(n \geq 2)$ *on strings of* $(A \cup B)^*$ *called* productions *or* rules of inference. P *may be specified by a finite set of production schemata. If* $(x_1, x_2, \ldots, x_{n-1}, x_n)$ *is a production in* P, *we say that* x_n follows from $x_1, x_2, \ldots, x_{n-1}$, *which can also be denoted by* $x_1, x_2, \ldots, x_{n-1} \to x_n$.

∎

In an e.a.s. we distinguish between a derivation and a proof, since not every derivation ends in a theorem. The definition of derivation is just as before.

DEFINITION 8.5 *Given an e.a.s.* (A, B, S, P), *a linearly ordered sequence of strings,* $y_l, y_2, \ldots, y_m$ *is called a* derivation *of* y_m *if every string in the sequence (1) is an axiom, or (2) follows by one of the productions in* P *from one or more strings preceding it in the sequence.* ∎

DEFINITION 8.6 *Given an e.a.s.* (A, B, S, P), *a string* y *is a* theorem *iff (1) there is a derivation of* y *in* (A, B, S, P), *and (2)* $y \in B^*$. *When* y *is a theorem, a derivation of* y *is called a* proof *of* y. ∎

We note that by our definitions every axiomatic system is also an e.a.s. with the null set as the auxiliary alphabet, but not every e.a.s. is an axiomatic system. An e.a.s. with a nonnull auxiliary alphabet is a *proper* e.a.s.

An example of a proper e.a.s., whose theorems are the mirror-image strings on a, b, is the following (cf. (8-8)):

$$(8\text{–}16) \quad A = \{M\}$$
$$B = \{a, b\}$$
$$S = \{M\}$$

$$P = \begin{cases} \alpha M \beta & \to & \alpha a M a \beta \\ \alpha M \beta & \to & \alpha b M b \beta \\ \alpha M \beta & \to & \alpha a a \beta \\ \alpha M \beta & \to & \alpha b b \beta \end{cases} \quad \begin{array}{l} \text{where } \alpha \text{ and } \beta \text{ are any strings} \\ \text{on } (A \cup B)^* \end{array}$$

The following sequence of lines

$(8\text{–}17)\quad M, aMa, aaMaa, aabMbaa$

is a derivation of $aabMbaa$ but not a proof in this system, since $aabMbaa$ contains a symbol of the auxiliary alphabet and therefore cannot be a theorem. The following is a proof of $aabbaa$.

$(8\text{–}18)\quad M, aMa, aaMaa, aabbaa$

Two systems having the same set of theorems are said to be *equivalent*. Thus, the e.a.s. of (8-16) is equivalent to the axiomatic system of (8-8).

The following e.a.s. is equivalent to the axiomatic system (8-15), which generates the *wff*s of statement logic.

$(8\text{–}19)\quad A = \{E, F\}$
$\qquad\qquad B = \{\&, \vee, \sim, \rightarrow, \leftrightarrow, (,), p,'\}$
$\qquad\qquad S = \{F\}$

$$P = \left\{ \begin{array}{rcl} \alpha F\beta & \rightarrow & \alpha \sim F\beta \\ \alpha F\beta & \rightarrow & \alpha(F \,\&\, F)\beta \\ \alpha F\beta & \rightarrow & \alpha(F \vee F)\beta \\ \alpha F\beta & \rightarrow & \alpha(F \rightarrow F)\beta \\ \alpha F\beta & \rightarrow & \alpha(F \leftrightarrow F)\beta \\ \alpha F\beta & \rightarrow & \alpha E\beta \\ \alpha E\beta & \rightarrow & \alpha E'\beta \\ \alpha E\beta & \rightarrow & \alpha p\beta \end{array} \right\}$$ where α and β are any strings on $(A \cup B)^{*}$

(The symbol $\rightarrow$, unfortunately, is used for two different purposes in this system: to signify 'follows from' in the production schemata and in the fourth schema as a symbol in the alphabet of statement logic.)

The following sequence is a proof of $((p' \,\&\, p'') \vee p)$ in this system:

(8-20)   1. F
          2. $(F \lor F)$
          3. $((F \& F) \lor F)$
          4. $((E \& E) \lor F)$
          5. $((E \& E) \lor F)$
          6. $((E \& E) \lor E)$
          7. $((E' \& E) \lor E)$
          8. $((E' \& E') \lor E)$
          9. $((E' \& E'') \lor E)$
         10. $((p' \& E'') \lor E)$
         11. $((p' \& p'') \lor E)$
         12. $((p' \& p'') \lor p)$

The axiom set of the e.a.s. in (8-19) contains only the single symbol F, not an infinite set of strings specified by axiom schemata. Rather, the last two production schemata in the list generate the symbols for atomic statements, p, p', p'', p''', etc. Note that a rather natural interpretation of this system is possible in which F is a 'well-formed formula' and E is an 'atomic statement'. The production schemata could then be interpreted as statements such as 'if F is a well-formed formula, then so is its negation,' 'an atomic statement is a well-formed formula,' 'p is an atomic statement,' etc.

Problem: Describe the theorems of the following e.a.s.

(8-21) $A = \{Q\}$
         $B = \{a\}$
         $S = \{aQa\}$
         $P = \begin{cases} \alpha Q \beta & \rightarrow & \alpha a Q \alpha a \beta \\ \alpha Q \beta & \rightarrow & \beta \end{cases}$ where α and β are any strings on $(A \cup B)^*$

8.3   Semi-Thue systems

One way in which axiomatic systems can be classified is according to some property of their production schemata. One could, for example, distinguish systems with only binary productions, i.e., of the form $\varphi \rightarrow \psi$, where φ and ψ are strings, or one could consider the class of systems in which for every production $x_1, x_2, \ldots, x_{n-1} \rightarrow x_n$ the number of symbols in x_n is greater than or equal to the sum of the number of symbols in $x_1, x_2, \ldots, x_{n-1}$. Any formal property of the productions could, in principle, serve as a basis for such a classification. The systems to which we now direct our attention are the semi-Thue systems (after the Norwegian mathematician Axel Thue, who first studied them). These are extended axiomatic systems whose productions are restricted in a manner specified by the following definition.

DEFINITION 8.7 *A semi-Thue system is an e.a.s.* (A, B, S, P) *in which every production schema is binary and of the form*

$$\alpha x \beta \rightarrow \alpha y \beta$$

where x *and* y *are strings on* $(A \cup B)^*$ *and* α *and* β *are variables taking as values strings on* $(A \cup B)^*$. ∎

Thus, the change effected by any production is restricted to the replacement of some fixed string of symbols by another fixed string. Of the axiomatic systems we have examined thus far, (8-8), (8-16), and (8-19) are semi-Thue systems. (In (8-8) each production is of the form $x \rightarrow y$, where both α and β are the null string.) The system given in (8-15) is not semi-Thue since some of its productions are ternary and not binary. The e.a.s. in (8-21) fails the definition because in neither of its production schemata is a fixed string replaced by a fixed string. In $\alpha Q \beta$, the variable string αQ is replaced by e, and in $\alpha Q \beta \rightarrow \alpha a Q \alpha a \beta$, the fixed string Q is replaced by the variable string $a Q \alpha a$.

The fact that all productions in a semi-Thue system are binary allows us to narrow the definition of 'derivation' somewhat.

DEFINITION 8.8 ∎

Given a semi-Thue system (A, B, S, P), a linearly ordered sequence of strings $y_1, y_2, \ldots, y_m$ is called a derivation of y_m iff (1) y_1 is an axiom, and (2) each string except y_1 follows from the immediately preceding string by one of the productions in P.

The definitions of 'theorem' and 'proof' remain as in an e.a.s.

A *Thue system* differs from a semi-Thue system in that for every production schema $\alpha x \beta \rightarrow \alpha y \beta$ in P, a Thue system also contains the inverse schema $\alpha y \beta \rightarrow \alpha x \beta$. We shall not be concerned with such systems here.

Although it may appear that the restrictions on the productions of a semi-Thue system are rather severe, these systems can in fact generate any set of theorems that can be generated by an arbitrary e.a.s. In other words, there is no loss in generality in restricting e.a.s.'s in the manner of semi-Thue systems because for any e.a.s. there is an equivalent semi-Thue system. (The converse is, of course, trivially true, since every semi-Thue system is an e.a.s.) However, a semi-Thue system may be rather more complex than a nonsemi-Thue e.a.s. to which it is equivalent. To illustrate, we exhibit a semi-Thue system that is equivalent to the e.a.s. in (8-21). Since all semi-Thue production schemata are of the same form, it is generally accepted practice to omit the variables α and β in writing them; thus, we write $x \to y$ instead of $\alpha x \beta \to \alpha y \beta$.

(8-22) $A = \{C, D, E, F, G, H\}$
$B = \{a\}$
$S = \{HFGa\}$

The schemata in P are numbered for convenience in referring to them.

$$P = \begin{cases} 1. & FG \to DGaa \\ 2. & FD \to DF \\ 3. & HD \to HC \\ 4. & CD \to FC \\ 5. & CG \to FFGa \\ 6. & HF \to E \\ 7. & EF \to E \\ 8. & EG \to E \\ 9. & Ea \to a \end{cases}$$

(8-23) and (8-24) show the derivations of a and $aaaa$, respectively.

(8-23) HFGa   Axiom
EGa   by 6.
Ea   by 8.
a   by 9.

(8-24) $HFGa$ Axiom
         $HDGaaa$ by 1.
         $HCGaaa$ by 3.
         $HFFGaaaa$ by 5.
         $EFGaaaa$ by 6.
         $EGaaaa$ by 7.
         $Eaaaa$ by 8.
         $aaaa$ by 9.

8.4   Peano's axioms and proof by induction

Peano's axioms for the natural numbers, actually due to Dedekind, are not only one of most well-known axiomatic systems in the history of mathematics, but they give rise to the *Principle of Mathematical Induction* and the technique of *proof by induction* or *inductive proof*, a conceptually important tool which further helps to highlight the close affinity between recursive definitions and axiomatic systems.

In this section we introduce Peano's axioms and the method of proof by induction; we will come back to Peano's axioms from a model-theoretic perspective in 8.5.7.

In Part A, Appendix A, we saw a *constructive* approach to the natural numbers, with set theory assumed as a basis. We review that construction here, putting it in the form of a recursive definition of NN.

(8-25)   1. $\emptyset \in NN$
         2. For all X, if $X \in NN$, then $X \cup \{X\} \in NN$
         3. Nothing else is in NN

The set NN defined in this way has many useful properties which make it a reasonable, if artificial, set-theoretic reconstruction of the natural numbers. Zero is identified with $\emptyset$, 1 with $\{\emptyset\}$, 2 with $\{\emptyset, \{\emptyset\}\}$, and so on, each natural number n being identified with the unique member of NN having n members. The definition endows the natural numbers with appropriate structure and can be used as the basis for defining further arithmetical relations and operations and extending the number system as discussed in Appendix A.

In the axiomatic approach to natural numbers, the aim was rather to set forth some essential properties of the natural numbers from which all their other properties should be derivable as theorems, just as in the Euclidean axiomatization of plane geometry. In stating the basic axioms, only logical concepts (including, in this case, equality) are assumed, and a set of axioms involving two primitive predicates and one primitive constant is given. The primitives are (1) the one-place predicate 'is a natural number' and the two-place predicate 'is the successor of' and (2) the constant 0. It is to be emphasized that these are primitives; the only meaning they have is given to them in the axiomatization. The concept of a natural number is, therefore, implicitly defined by the axioms: they are those things of which, in some model of the system, the interpretation of the predicate 'is a natural number' is true. Let us write Nx for 'x is a natural number' and Sxy for 'x is a successor of y'. The axioms are:

P1) $N0$ (zero is a natural number)

P2) $(\forall x)(Nx \rightarrow (\exists y)(Ny \,\&\, Syx \,\&\, (\forall z)(Szx \rightarrow z = y)))$ (every natural number has a unique successor)

P3) $\sim (\exists x)(Nx \,\&\, S0x)$ (0 is not the successor of any number)

P4) $(\forall x)(\forall y)(\forall z)(\forall w)((Nx \,\&\, Ny \,\&\, Szx \,\&\, Swy \,\&\, z = w) \rightarrow x = y)$ (no two distinct natural numbers have the same successor

P5) If Q is a property such that

   (i) $Q0$ (zero has Q), and

   (ii) $(\forall x)(\forall y)((Nx \,\&\, Qx \,\&\, Ny \,\&\, Syx) \rightarrow Qy)$, (if a natural number has Q then its successor has Q, i.e. Q is a 'hereditary' property)

   then $(\forall x)(Nx \rightarrow Qx)$ (every natural number has Q)

These axioms together characterize the set of all natural numbers in certain important respects in which they differ from other infinite sets. Although we will not go into the proof here, it can be shown that this axiomatization of the natural numbers is also sufficient for proving the equivalence of the notions *ordinary infinite* and *Dedekind infinite*, which used only the notion of one-to-one correspondence, defined in Section 4.2.

The fifth Peano postulate is very important. It introduces the notion of *mathematical induction*. Intuitively, this axiom says that the natural numbers are subject to the 'domino-effect': whenever you find a property that knocks down zero, and makes each number knock down its successor, you can conclude that all numbers are knocked down. There are no natural numbers outside this single infinite chain. The first four axioms guarantee the existence of an infinite chain of successors starting at zero, but do not preclude the existence of additional natural numbers, e.g. a second infinite chain unconnected to the first. The fifth axiom precludes the existence of any more numbers than are required by the first four axioms.

Now let us look more closely at the Principle of Mathematical Induction and its application. Let us first restate the principle, i.e. Peano's fifth axiom, in a slightly simpler form by (i) suppressing the predicate N and assuming that our domain of quantification is restricted to just the natural numbers, and (ii) using the notation $S(x)$ to denote the successor of x, something we can legitimately do since the first four axioms guarantee that the successor-of relation is a function.

For any predicate Q, if the following statements are both true of Q:

(8–26)   1. $Q0$
             2. $(\forall x)(Qx \rightarrow Q(S(x)))$

then the following statement is also true of Q:

             3. $(\forall x)Qx$

The similarity between (8-26) 1 and 2 and the base and recursion step, respectively, of a recursive definition is readily apparent. The Principle of Mathematical Induction is not a definition, however, but a rule of inference to be applied to statements about the integers. A proof that employs this rule of inference is known as a *proof by induction* or an *inductive proof*.

Let us examine the structure of such a proof in more detail. Suppose we have been given a predicate $P(x)$ such that (8-27) 1 and 2 hold. These form the premises of the argument.

(8–27)   1. $P(0)$
             2. $(\forall x)(P(x) \rightarrow P(x+1))$

From $P(0)$ and a substitution instance of line 2

             3. $P(0) \rightarrow P(1)$ 2, U.I.

we can derive

             4. $P(1)$ 1, 3, M.P.

and from this and another substitution instance of line 2

      5. $P(1) \rightarrow P(2)$ 2, U.I.

we can derive

      6. $P(2)$ 4, 5, M.P.

and so on.

To prove the statement $(\forall x)P(x)$ would require an infinite number of steps, and we would ordinarily not want to consider an infinitely long sequence of lines a proof, if for no other reason than that it would be impossible to examine it in order to verify its correctness. Thus, there is no proof of $(\forall x)P(x)$ that can be constructed by using only the rules of inference we have considered up to now. Nevertheless, (8-26) 3 is intuitively a valid conclusion to draw from the premises (8-26) 1 and 2, and the Principle of Mathematical Induction is a formal assertion that this inference is legitimate. It should be noted that the Principle of Mathematical Induction itself is not susceptible of proof but only acceptance or rejection on the grounds of its effectiveness in separating intuitively valid from intuitively invalid arguments. With this additional rule of inference, the proof of $(\forall x)P(x)$ is simply as follows:

(8–28)   1. $P(0)$

          2. $(\forall x)(P(x) \rightarrow P(x+1))$

          3. $(\forall x)(P(x))$ 1, 2, Math. Ind.

As an example we prove by induction that for every integer n the sum of the series $0 + 1 + 2 + \ldots + (n-1) + n$ equals $[n(n+1)]/2$.

The premises of the argument are the propositions stating all the usual arithmetic properties of the integers (the commutativity of addition, etc.), which can be deduced as theorems from Peano's Axioms. As is usual in inductive proofs almost all the work comes in establishing the truth of the statements corresponding to (8-28) 1 and 2, known as the *base* and the *induction step*, respectively. Once these have been derived, the remainder of the proof consists of just one inferential step justified by the Principle of Mathematical Induction. We begin by demonstrating the truth of the base, i.e., that $0 + 1 + \ldots + n = [n(n+1)]/2$ is true for $n = 0$. In this case the sequence to the left of the equals sign consists of just 0, and the expression to the right becomes $[0(0+1)]/2$, which is equal to 0.

The induction step to be established is

$$(8\text{--}29) \quad (\forall n)\left(0 + 1 + \ldots + n = \frac{n(n+1)}{2} \rightarrow \right.$$
$$\left. 0 + 1 + \ldots + n + (n+1) = \frac{(n+1)(n+1+1)}{2}\right)$$

that is, if the equation is true for any integer n, it is also true for $n + 1$, the successor of n. To prove (8-29) we use a conditional proof in which we assume the antecedent of the conditional in (8-29) for an arbitrary integer k.

(8-30)   1. $0 + 1 + \ldots + k = \dfrac{k(k + 1)}{2}$ C.P.

2. $0 + 1 + \ldots + k + (k + 1) = \dfrac{k(k + 1)}{2} + (k + 1)$
     1, adding $(k + 1)$ to both sides

3. $0 + 1 + \ldots + k + (k + 1) = \dfrac{k(k + 1) + 2(k + 1)}{2}$
     2, converting right side to common denominator

4. $0 + 1 + \ldots + k + (k + 1) = \dfrac{(k + 1)(k + 2)}{2}$
     3, factoring $(k + 1)$ in numerator

5. $0 + 1 + \ldots + k + (k + 1) = \dfrac{(k + 1)((k + 1) + 1)}{2}$
     4, expressing $k + 2$ as $(k + 1) + 1$

6. $0 + 1 + \ldots + k = \dfrac{k(k + 1)}{2} \rightarrow$
     $0 + 1 + \ldots + k + (k + 1) = \dfrac{(k + 1)(k + 1) + 1}{2}$

Since k was chosen arbitrarily, line 6 can be universally generalized to (8-29). Having now established the truth of the base and the induction step, the Principle of Mathematical Induction allows us to conclude:

(8-31) $(\forall n)\left(0 + 1 + \ldots + n = \dfrac{n(n + 1)}{2}\right)$

Proof by induction can be applied not only to theorems about the set of integers but to theorems about any set that can be put into one-to-one correspondence with the integers, i.e., the denumerably infinite sets. As an example of this sort we prove a generalized form of the Distributive Law for union and intersection of sets.

(8-32) $A \cup (B_1 \cap B_2 \cap \ldots \cap B_n) = (A \cup B_1) \cap (A \cup B_2) \cap \ldots \cap (A \cap B_n)$

The form in which the Distributive Law was given in Chapter 2 is a special case of (8-32) in which $n = 2$; that is

(8–33) $\quad A \cup (B_1 \cap B_2) = (A \cup B_1) \cap (A \cup B_2)$

Equation (8-32) is meaningless for $n = 0$ and trivial for $n = 1$. We take as the base of the inductive proof that (8-32) holds for $n = 2$, i.e., that (8-33) is true. This is easily shown by expressing the sets in terms of predicates and applying the Distributive Law of disjunction over conjunction in statement logic.

To prove the induction step we assume that (8-32) holds for an arbitrarily chosen integer k:

(8–34) $\quad A \cup (B_1 \cap B_2 \cap \ldots \cap B_k) = (A \cup B_1) \cap (A \cup B_2) \cap \ldots \cap (A \cup B_k)$

We wish to show that (8-34) implies (8-35).

(8–35) $\quad A \cup (B_1 \cap B_2 \cap \ldots \cap B_{k+1}) = (A \cup B_1) \cap (A \cup B_2) \cap \ldots \cap (A \cup B_k) \cap (A \cup B_{k+1})$

The left side of (8-35) can be rewritten by the Associative Law as

(8–36) $\quad A \cup ((B_1 \cap B_2 \cap \ldots \cap B_k) \cap B_{k+1})$

which is equal to

(8–37) $\quad (A \cup (B_1 \cap B_2 \cap \ldots \cap B_k)) \cap (A \cup B_{k+1})$

by an application of the Distributive Law for the case $n = 2$, which has already been proved. By the induction hypothesis (8-34), expression (8-37) is equal to

(8–38) $\quad ((A \cup B_1) \cap (A \cup B_2) \cap \ldots \cap (A \cup B_k)) \cap (A \cup B_{k+1})$

By the Associative Law we can omit one set of parentheses to obtain the right side of (8-35). This shows that (8-35) holds if (8-34) does. From this and the base by the Principle of Mathematical Induction the generalized form of the Distributive Law is shown to be true for all n equal to or greater than 2 (or greater than 1 if we include this trivial case).

In this last example induction is used to prove a theorem about a class of equations of the form given in (8-32), which can be put into one-to-one correspondence with the integers. The mapping is between an equation and an integer n representing its length—specifically, the number of terms in the expression $B_1 \cap B_2 \cap \ldots \cap B_n$. Proof by induction on the length of a string is the commonest use of this method of proof in mathematical linguistics.

Problem: Prove by induction the following generalized form of one of DeMorgan's Laws:

$$(A_1 \cap A_2 \cap \ldots \cap A_n)' = A_1' \cup \ldots \cup A_n'$$

8.5 The semantic side of formal systems: model theory

8.5.1 Theories and models

As we said in Chapter 5, the distinction between syntax and semantics in the logical tradition is closely tied to the distinction between formal systems and their interpretations. Model theory, the study of the interpretations of formal systems, focuses on the relation between *theories* and *models*, with these terms understood in a technical sense which we will now describe.

A set of axioms together with all the theorems derivable from them is called a *theory*. Or equivalently, a theory is a set of statements that is closed under logical consequence, i.e. is such that any logical consequence of any statement in the set is again in the set.

Finding a *model* for a theory requires finding some abstract or concrete structured domain and an interpretation for all of the primitive expressions of the theory in that domain such that on that interpretation, all of the statements in the theory come out *true* for that model on that interpretation. If a theory has an axiomatic characterization, something is a model for that theory iff it is a model for the axioms.

Plane geometry is the standard model of the Euclidean axioms; before the discovery of the non-Euclidean geometries discussed in 5.1 it was believed to be the only model. The natural numbers are the standard or intended model of the Peano axioms; we will see some non-standard models in section 8.5.7 below.

In exploring theories and models, one can start at either end, and mathematical discoveries and advances have been made in both directions. One can start with a given set of phenomena as intended models and try to write down axioms that will best characterize them - this often forces one to sharpen up one's conception of the intended coverage of the theory, and of course helps to uncover various consequences of one's initial assumptions. (One can take the whole enterprise of linguistics as trying to formally characterize the class of possible human languages; the starting point is then a somewhat vaguely specified set of intended models.) One can also start from a set of axioms and see what sorts of models it has. In the model-theoretic perspective, these two complementary activities constantly feed each other. Different axiomatic systems may be discovered to characterize exactly the same set of models, and hence to be equivalent from a semantic point of view; or two quite disparate domains may be discovered to have virtually identical axiomatizations, revealing a hitherto unsuspected structural similarity.

A note of warning: the term "model", especially in the verbal form "modelling", has another very different sense as well, one in which it actually comes closer to what logicians mean by *theory* than to what they mean by *model*, and outside of logic and model theory this other sense may in fact be more common. When one speaks of modelling some physical phenomenon, or constructing an abstract model of some biological or cognitive process, the intent is generally some form of theory building or at least some step in that direction. One important clue to help resolve the ambiguity comes from looking at what the model in question is a model *of*: models in the sense of model theory are always models of axioms or other expressions in some language, never of concrete objects. Models themselves in model theory may be either concrete or abstract objects, so the nature of the things modelled is a more reliable clue to the relevant sense of "model" than is the nature of the models.

In the remaining subsections of this section, we will first look at some fundamentally important properties that relate formal systems and theories to their models, and then look into some examples of axiomatic systems and models for them, some very simple and some quite rich, illustrating the interplay between axioms and models as we go. In these sections we take the logic as a given; in 8.6 we will broach the issue of axiomatizing the logic itself.

8.5.2   Consistency, completeness, and independence

A formal system is *consistent* if it is not possible to derive from its axioms both some statement and the denial of that same statement. An inconsistent system cannot have a model, since no actual statement can be simultaneously true and false; hence one way to show that a system is consistent is to exhibit a model for it.

It is useful that we have both a syntactic and a semantic characterization of consistency known to be equivalent, since one is easier to apply in some cases and the other in others. In particular, when a system is inconsistent, it's usually easier to demonstrate that syntactically than semantically. That is, it's usually easier to derive a contradiction from the axioms than to prove by a meta-level argument that the system has no models. Conversely, when a system is consistent, it's usually easier to show that semantically, by finding a model, than to demonstrate that it's impossible to derive a contradiction from the given axioms. When one doesn't know the answer in advance, it may be necesary to try both methods alternately until one of them succeeds.

The term *completeness* is used in various senses. What all notions of completeness have in common is that for a formal system to be complete in some sense, it must be possible to derive within the formal system all the statements satisfying some given criterion; different notions of completeness reflect different criteria for the desired statements. Among the most commonly encountered notions of completeness is one which is syntactic, since it is defined in terms of formal systems alone, and one which is semantic, defined in terms of the relations between formal systems and their models. A formal system is called *formally complete* if every statement expressible in the system, i.e. expressible using only the primitives of the system including a given formalized logic, can either be proved or disproved (its negation proved) in the system. Other terms for the same or very similar notions are *deductively complete* (Copi), *complete with respect to negation* (Thomason), and *syntactically complete*. A formal system is *semantically complete with respect to a model M*, or *weakly semantically complete* (Thomason), if every statement expressible in the system which is true in the model M is derivable in the formal system.

The notion of *independence* concerns the question of whether any of the axioms are superfluous. An axiom is *independent* if it cannot be derived from the other axioms of the system. A whole system is said to be *independent* (a slight abuse of language) if all of its axioms are independent. That was a syntactic characterization of independence (why?); a semantic chracterization is the following: A given axiom is independent of the other axioms of a system S if the system S' that results from deleting that axiom has models which are not models of the whole system S. In any reasonably "well-behaved" framework, the two notions of independence will be provably equivalent and one can use whichever one is easier to apply in a given case. As in the case of consistency, which is easier often depends on whether the answer is positive or negative. Determining precisely what it takes for a framework to be sufficiently "well-behaved" for the syntactic and semantic characterizations of independence to determine the same notion is one kind of question studied in the metamathematical side of model theory.

The three notions of consistency, completeness, and independence are not all of equal importance. Consistency is of fundamental importance, since it is obviously a minimal condition of adequacy on any set of axioms designed to formalize any system that is not meant to be self-contradictory. Completeness is often of theoretical importance to logicians, but (a) proving completeness for a system of any complexity generally requires a fairly high level of mathematical sophistication (and many important formal systems are provably incomplete); and (b) it is not obvious that completeness is ever any issue that linguists need to be concerned with. Questions of completeness will therefore be relatively neglected here. Independence of axioms is simply a matter of "elegance"; it is generally considered desirable in an axiom system, but has no significant consequences for the system as a whole.

8.5.3   Isomorphism

The notion of isomorphism, the relation of "having the same structure", is of fundamental importance in any attempt to set up a concrete model of an abstract system or a mathematical theory of a family of concrete systems. Informally speaking, two systems are isomorphic if some specified part of their structure is identical and they differ only in interpretation or content or in unspecified parts of their structure. For example, a paper pattern for a dress may be said to be isomorphic to the cut-out cloth with respect to size and shape; they differ only in their material. Japanese and Korean are sometimes said to be isomorphic with respect to syntactic structure, a claim which would be true if the two languages differed in their morphemes but sentences could be put into morpheme-by-morpheme correspondence preserving syntactic configurations and permitting the same syntactic operations.

The formal definition applies to a pair of systems A and B, each consisting of a set of elements on which are defined one or more operations and/or one or more relations. (Such systems will be studied in more detail in Part C, where we will look at them as algebras and see many more examples of isomorphisms.)

DEFINITION 8.9 *An isomorphism between two such systems is a one-one correspondence between their elements and a one-one correspondence between their operations and relations which satisfies the following conditions:*

1. *If a relation R holds between two elements of A, the corresponding relation R' holds between the corresponding elements of B; if R does not hold between two elements of A, R' does not hold between the corresponding elements of B.*

2. *Whenever corresponding operations are performed on corresponding elements, the results are corresponding elements.*

∎

If there exists an isomorphism between two systems A and B, the systems are said to be *isomorphic*. Note that for two systems not to be isomorphic, it must be the case that there is *no* isomorphism between them, not simply that some particular one-one correspondence fails to be an isomorphism.

(8–39) *Examples*:
(1) The set 1,2,3,4,5 with the relation "greater than" ($>$) can be shown to be isomorphic to the set -1,-2,-3,-4,-5 with the relation "less than" ($<$) by letting each number in the first set correspond to its negative in the second set, since for any two positive integers n and n', if $n > n'$, then $-n < -n'$.
(2) The set $A = \{0, 1\}$ with the operation of "absolute value of difference" defined in the first table below is *not* isomorphic to the set $B = \{0, 1\}$ with the operation of ordinary multiplication, shown in the second chart.

A:

	y	
$\lvert x - y \rvert$	0	1
0	0	1
1	1	0

x

B:

	y	
$x \cdot y$	0	1
0	0	0
1	0	1

x

Neither of the two possible one-one correspondences between the two sets can give an isomorphism, since (1) in set A, the result of the operation on two of the pairs of elements is one element and on the other two pairs is the other element, while in set B, one element is the result in three cases and the other in only one; and (2) in set B, the result of operating on one element and itself $(0 \cdot 0$ and $1 \cdot 1)$ is always that same element, while in set A this is not the case. Either of these reasons alone is actually sufficient to show that no one-one correspondence can be set up so that the operations performed on corresponding elements would yield corresponding elements as results.

Isomorphism plays an important role in model theory. If we ask how many different models there are for a given axiomatic theory, we generally mean different in the sense of non-isomorphic with respect to relevant structure; isomorphic models are alike in relevant structure. In the next section, we will see a model-theoretic application of the notion of isomorphism.

Note that the relation of isomorphism is an equivalence relation in the sense of section 3.4.

8.5.4 An elementary formal system

The following system is described in Hao Wang's *Survey of Mathematical Logic*, pp. 14-18. The system, called L, consists of a set S and a single two-place predicate (binary relation) R defined on S. The axioms of L are as follows:

A1: $(x)(x = 1 \lor x = 2 \lor x = 3) \& 1 \neq 2 \& 1 \neq 3 \& 2 \neq 3$; i.e., S contains only the three distinct elements 1, 2, and 3.

A2: $(x) \sim Rxx$; i.e., R is irreflexive.

A3: $(x)(y)(z)((Rxy \,\&\, Rxz) \supset y = z)$; i.e., R is not one-many.

A4: $(x)(y)(z)((Ryx \,\&\, Rzx) \supset y = z$; i.e., R is not many-one. (i.e., A3 and A4 together require R to be one-one.)

A5: $(x)(\exists y)Rxy$; i.e., every element of S bears R to at least one element.

A6: $R12$; 1 bears R to 2.

A model for L must therefore meet the following conditions:

(a) There must be specified:

    (1) a non-empty set D of objects
    (2) a rule which associates each element of S with an element of D.
    (3) a binary relation R_* defined on the set D

(b) The axioms A1-A6 must be true when interpreted according to (1)-(3) above.

It is quite easy to find a model for L. Let the set D consist of three persons, *Chang*, *Li*, and *Yang*, sitting around a round table with *Chang* immediately to the right of *Li*, associating them with 1, 2, and 3 respectively. Let R^* be the relation "sits immediately to the right of". It can be checked that all the axioms become true statements in this system.

In fact, if we take an arbitrary set D with three objects $1^*, 2^*, 3^*$ which represent 1, 2, 3 respectively, and choose a relation R^* which holds between the pairs $(1^*, 2^*)$, $(2^*, 3^*)$, $(3^*, 1^*)$ and does not hold between any other pairs, we will have a model for L. Furthermore, it can be shown that *every* model for L must have exactly this form. That is, any two models of L must be isomorphic. If all the models of a given formal system are isomorphic, the system is called *categorical*[1].

Once we assume A1, it is easy to find other axioms which yield a categorical system. For example, the following axiom can replace all of A2-A6:

---

[1]The term "categorical" should not be confused with "categorial". The former is a term of long standing, particularly in logic; the latter is a recent coinage applied to a special type of phrase-structure grammar studied by Curry, Lambek, and others, and perhaps can also be used as an adjective corresponding to "category", although that is the etymology of the former.

THE SEMANTIC SIDE OF FORMAL SYSTEMS: MODEL THEORY   207

A2*: R is true of the pairs $(1,2)$, $(2,3)$, and $(1,3)$ and false of the remaining pairs formed from 1, 2, and 3.

The axioms A1 and A2* determine the same interpretations as A1-A6. Other categorical systems can be constructed analogously.

If in the specification of L we had not given specific names to any of the elements of S, we could not state A1 and A6. The effect of A1 could still be gotten from the axiom A1':

A1': There exist only three distinct things:
$$(\exists x)(\exists y)(\exists z)(x \neq y \,\&\, y \neq z \,\&\, x \neq z \,\&\, (w)(w = x \lor w = y \lor w = z)).$$

But nothing resembling A6 could be expressed in the new system. However, the system determined by A1' and A2-A5 is also categorical since as soon as one pair of elements is specified as having the relation R, the rest of the structure is determined by the axioms, and all the models must be isomorphic.

Since the axioms of L specify uniquely (up to isomorphism) the set S and the relaion R, every expressible statement about R and S is either provable or disprovable from A1-A6. Hence L is *formally complete*. It can be shown, in fact, that *every* categorical system is formally complete.

If we were to omit certain of the axioms A1-A6, the resulting system would not be complete or categorical. If, for example, we were to omit the axiom A5, then a possible model for the resulting system could be constructed by letting *Chang, Li*, and *Yang* sit on the same side of a rectangular table with *Chang* at the far right and *Li* in the middle, associating them with 1, 2, and 3 as before and keeping $R*$ as "sits immediately to the right of". This model is not isomorphic to the original one; the new system is not complete, since $R23$ and $R31$ are neither provable nor disprovable in it.

8.5.5   Axioms for ordering relations

Various kinds of orderings were defined in Chapter 3 in terms of such properties of relations as transitivity, antisymmetry, etc. These definitions can be very easily formalized as axiomatic systems, with each relevant property specified by an axiom. What we gave as "examples" of the different kinds of orderings in 3.5 we can now redescribe as *models* of the corresponding axiom systems.

Any ordering relation is a binary relation R on a set S. We assume as part of the "background theory" ordinary set theory, including the representation of binary relations on S as sets of ordered pairs of members of S, and we specify the particular axioms that must be satisfied by particular kinds of orderings.

DEFINITION 8.10 R *is a weak partial order on* S *iff:*

1. Transitivity: $\forall x \forall y \forall z((x \in S \,\&\, y \in S \,\&\, z \in S) \to ((Rxy \,\&\, Ryz) \to Rxz))$

2. Reflexivity: $\forall x (x \in S \to Rxx)$

3. Antisymmetry: $\forall x \forall y((x \in S \,\&\, y \in S) \to ((Rxy \,\&\, Ryx) \to x = y))$

■

Alternatively, we need not explicitly assume set theory or use the language of set membership, but can simply take the domain S as the universe over which the quantified variables in the axioms range. In that case, the previous definition would be recast as follows:

DEFINITION 8.11 R *is a weak partial order on* S *iff:*

1. Transitivity: $\forall x \forall y \forall z((Rxy \,\&\, Ryz) \to Rxz)$

2. Reflexivity: $\forall x(Rxx)$

3. Antisymmetry: $\forall x \forall y((Rxy \,\&\, Ryx) \to x = y)$

■

One will also encounter axiomatizations in which the wide-scope universal quantifiers are omitted and open formulas are understood as universally quantified. We will not take that further step here; but it is worth noting that the prevalence of "pure universal" axioms like those above is not simply an accident. The study of model theory has shown that pure universal theories, all of whose axioms are pure universal ones like those above, have a number of nice relations to their models.

In Chapter 3 it was noted that generally each weak ordering, obeying the axioms of reflexivity and antisymmetry, could be paired with a corresponding strong ordering, with those axioms replaced by irreflexivity and asymmetry.

DEFINITION 8.12 R *is* a strict partial order *on S iff:*

1. Transitivity: $\forall x \forall y \forall z((Rxy \, \& \, Ryz) \to Rxz)$

2. Irreflexivity: $\forall x(\sim Rxx)$

3. Asymmetry: $\forall x \forall y(Rxy \to \sim Ryx)$

∎

The relations R_1, R_2, and R_3 diagrammed in Section 3.5 are all models of the axioms for weak partial orders, and S_1, S_2, and S_3 are models of the axioms for strict partial orders. Another model of weak partial orders is the subset relation on any collection of sets; the 'proper subset' relation provides the corresponding strict order.

What about the relations 'is at least as old as' and 'is older than' on H, the set of humans, assuming there do exist various pairs of people who are the same age? Intuitively, one might suppose that 'is at least as old as' would be a weak partial order on humans, much as 'is a subset of' provides a weak partial order on a set of sets. But while 'is at least as old as' on the set of humans does satisfy the axioms of transitivity and reflexivity, it fails antisymmetry. For let a and b be two individuals of the same age: then Rab and Rba, but $a \neq b$.

Note carefully the role of identity here: $a \neq b$ because a and b are two distinct members of the set H; being the same age makes them equivalent with respect to the relation R (and 'is the same age as' is an equivalence relation), but it doesn't make them equal in the sense required by the antisymmetry condition.

A relation like 'is at least as old as' which satisfies transitivity and reflexivity but possibly fails antisymmetry is called a *preorder* or sometimes a *quasi-order*; we could axiomatize it by writing down just the first two of the three axioms for a weak partial order. Where there's a preorder on S there is always the possibility of defining an order on a suitable partitioning of S. In this example, for instance, intuitively we want to count people of the same age as identical or indistinguishable; the formal technique for achieving that is to define the ordering not directly on the set of all people but on the set of equivalence clases formed under the relation 'is the same age as', in which all the people of a given age will be grouped together in a single equivalence class. In fact, when we step back and look at these equivalence classes, we can see that one might even consider analyzing our talk of ordering people by their ages in terms of ordering people's ages.

What about 'is older than'? Does that similarly fail to be a strict partial order on the given set of humans? Actually, no; it does satisfy all three axioms of Transitivity, Irreflexivity, and Asymmetry. But unlike the corresponding order on *ages*, or the apparently similar relation 'is greater than' on the numbers, it is not a linear order, since it is not connected;[2] see the following definitions.

Note: in examples such as those we have just been discussing, it is not so important to try to learn to remember the names and definitions of particular kinds of orderings or which examples satisfy which axioms; you can always look up the technical details in this or other books when you need them, and details of terminology are not all uniform among different research communities anyway. The important thing to focus on in this chapter are the illustrations of how changes in the axioms relate to changes in the models, and how the interesting properties of a formal system can be explored from both syntactic and semantic perspectives, often most fruitfully by looking at both together.

Linear orderings, both weak and strict, were defined and illustrated in Section 3.5. If we recast them axiomatically, they come out as follows.

DEFINITION 8.13 *R is* a weak linear (or total) order *on S iff:*

1. Transitivity: $\forall x \forall y \forall z ((Rxy \,\&\, Ryz) \rightarrow Rxz)$

2. Reflexivity: $\forall x (Rxx)$

3. Antisymmetry: $\forall x \forall y ((Rxy \,\&\, Ryx) \rightarrow x = y)$

4. Connectedness: $\forall x \forall y (x \neq y \rightarrow (Rxy \lor Ryx))$

■

Given that the first three axioms above constitute the definition of a weak partial order on S, we can abbreviate the definition above as follows.

---

[2]The relation 'is at least as old as' *is* connected, but neither asymmetric nor antisymmetric. It is an example of what Suppes (1957) defines as a *weak ordering*, a relation which is transitive, reflexive, and connected, i.e. a connected preorder. This is not a kind of ordering that is standardly singled out; but one is free to define and name whatever kinds of formal systems one thinks will prove useful for one's purposes.

DEFINITION 8.14 *R is a weak linear (or total) order on S iff:*

1. *R is a weak partial order on S*
2. Connectedness: $\forall x \forall y (x \neq y \rightarrow (Rxy \vee Ryx))$

∎

We give the definition of strict linear order in analogous fashion.

DEFINITION 8.15 *R is a strict linear (or total) order on S iff:*

1. *R is a strict partial order on S*
2. Connectedness: $\forall x \forall y (x \neq y \rightarrow (Rxy \vee Ryx))$

∎

Among the models for these axioms systems, the relations R_3 and S_3 given in Section 3.5 are models of weak and strict linear orderings respectively.

The reader may have noticed a certain degree of systematicity in the relation between the names chosen for various kinds of ordering relations and the selection of axioms used in their definitions. Such systematicity is most prevalent (and most desirable) in contexts where the emphasis is on contrasts among closely related axiomatic systems, as is the case here. Shorter names are often used when differences among similar systems are not at issue; so, for instance, an author may omit the adjectives *weak* and *strict* and talk simply of partial and total orderings if all her orderings are weak or if all of them are strict; definitions usually accompany initial uses of such terms when there could be any doubt. In the case of orderings, watch out for the use of the adjective *strong*, which is used as an antonym sometimes of *weak* and sometimes of *partial*. The lack of perfect standardization in nomenclature is a perfectly reasonable side effect of the useful versatility of axiomatic definitions; be prepared when in doubt to check a given author's definitions.

The definition of *well-ordering* was also given in Section 3.5: a set S is *well-ordered* by a relation R if R is a total order and, further, every subset of S has a least element in the ordering relation. If we try to write down this further condition as an additional axiom to add to the axioms for total orderings, we come across an important difference between it and all the other axioms we have introduced in this section: it cannot be expressed in first-order predicate logic.

If we give ourselves the full expressive power of set theory, including the possibility of quantifying over sets, we can write down the axioms for well-ordering in the same form we used for the first version above of the definition of weak partial orderings.

DEFINITION 8.16 *A relation R is a* well-ordering *of a set S iff:*

1. *R is a total ordering on S.*

2. *Every subset of S has a least element with respect to the order R:*
   $$\forall S'((S' \subseteq S) \to \exists x(x \in S' \,\&\, \forall y((y \in S' \,\&\, x \neq y) \to Rxy)))$$

∎

But we cannot omit the set theory talk this time as we could before. We can recast it so that we are quantifying over one-place predicates instead of over sets, which we do in Section 8.6.7 where we discuss higher-order logics. But what we cannot do is express the second axiom just with ordinary individual variables ranging over the members of the domain S.

The well-ordering axiom, axiom 2 above, turns out to be quite powerful and subtle. If logicians could have found a way to replace it with a first-order axiom having the same effect, they surely would have. What has been proved is that the well-ordering axiom is equivalent to each of several other non-first-order axioms, including Peano's fifth axiom, the induction axiom, which has already been introduced and to which we will return in Section 8.5.7. The relations among these higher-order axioms are discussed in Section 8.6.7. Properties which like transitivity and reflexivity *can* be expressed by first-order axioms are called first-order properties, but the modifier is used only when the contrast with higher-order properties is relevant.

Ordering relations and their axiomatic characterizations provide a rich round for exploring the syntactic and the semantic side of formal systems and their interrelations. Once one sees that each property like reflexivity or antisymmetry can be characterized by an axiom, the possible combinations to be explored become endless. Can an ordering be both asymmetric and antisymmetric? Does the answer to that question vary with the other axioms in the given system? Are there axioms that will force the set ordered to be infinite? To be finite? Are there informally describable kinds of orderings that cannot be characterized by a finite set of axioms? Is that last question well-defined, and if it is not precise, can it still be fruitful?

The rich realm of axiomatizations of ordering relations also leads one to wonder whether there is some single most general characterization of orderings such that all the well-known kinds of orderings are gotten by adding various axioms to some common core of shared axioms. Different authors have different degrees of tolerance on this question; the natural desire for a most general notion of ordering is in conflict with the fact that the standard kinds of ordering relations are required to be, besides transitive, either reflexive and antisymmetric or irreflexive and asymmetric and there seems to be no non-ugly way to say just that. Suppes (1957), noting that transitivity is the one property they all share, makes transitive relations the most general case in a diagram displaying the inclusion relation among several different kinds of ordering relations (an ordering of ordering relations.) Most authors decline to attempt a single most general definition of ordering relations. A wealth of syntactic and semantic arguments establishing various properties of orderings can be found in Suppes (1960).

8.5.6   Axioms for string concatenation

In this section we will axiomatize a very simple structure, the structure of string concatenation. A string concatenation system consists of a set A of strings of symbols from some alphabet together with the operation of *concatenation*, which is an operation that applies to two strings and consists simply of writing the second down after the first so as to combine them into a single longer string. In order for the system to be well-defined, the set A of strings must be closed under the concatenation operation; that is, the result of concatenating any two strings in A must itself be in A.

There are two formally different kinds of string concatenation systems, differing in whether they include an empty string among the strings of the system or not. We can show how that difference corresponds to a difference of one axiom in otherwise identical axiom systems.

For concatenation systems without an empty string, we can axiomatize them as shown below; structures with a binary operation satisfying these axioms are called *semigroups*.

DEFINITION 8.17 *A system consisting of a set A and a binary operation on A is a* semigroup *iff*:

1. *A is closed under* $\frown$: $\forall x\forall y((x \in A \,\&\, y \in A) \to x^\frown y \in A)$

2. *The operation* $\frown$ *is associative:* $\forall x\forall y\forall z((x^\frown y)^\frown z = x^\frown(y^\frown z))$

■

To write these axioms in pure predicate logic form, we would need to eliminate the operator notation "$x^\frown y$". (Similar conversions must be made in going from the function-oriented programming language LISP to the predicate-logic-based language PROLOG.) We can do that by using the notation $Cxyz$ with the intended interpretation "$x^\frown y = z$". That would also force us to stipulate more carefully the existence and uniqueness requirements implicit in the operator notation. The revised first axiom would read as follows:

DEFINITION 8.18 ...

1. *A is closed under C:* $\forall x\forall y\exists z(Cxyz \,\&\, \forall w(Cxyw \to w = z))$

2. ...

■

Axiom 2 of our earlier definition would also have to be revised, of course, but it merely becomes more complicated and harder to read, so we refrain from carrying out the revision.

An example of a concatenation system of this kind, i.e. a model of the above axioms where the set A is indeed a set of strings and the operation $\frown$ is interpreted as concatenation, is the set of all strings of a's, b's, and c's whose total length is even: $A = \{aa, ab, ac, ba, bb, \ldots, abaa, abab, abac, \ldots, cbccab, \ldots\}$. The set A is closed under concatenation and the concatenation operation is associative.

The set A' which is just like A above except that all the strings in A' have odd length, together with the operation of concatenation, would *not* form a model of the axioms, because it does not satisfy Axiom 1. (Why not?)

Turning now to systems that include the empty string, the first question is what that means. The empty string, like the number zero or the empty set, has more formal than intuitive motivation. It has length zero; it is a substring of every string; and it has the property that when concatenated with any string it yields that string itself. This last is its defining property in the axiomatic characterization of concatenation systems with the empty string: letting e designate the empty string, $x \frown e = x$, and $e \frown x = x$, for any string x. The empty string therefore satisfies the definition of being an *identity element* with respect to concatenation, just as 0 is an identity element for addition, 1 is for multiplication, and the empty set is for set union.

A concatenation system with empty string therefore satisfies both of the earlier axioms plus an axiom specifying the existence of an identity element; structures that satisfy these axioms are called *monoids*. A monoid is therefore characterizable in general as a semigroup with an identity element.

DEFINITION 8.19 *A system consisting of a set A and a binary operation* $\frown$ *on A is a* monoid *iff:*

1. *A is closed under* $\frown$: $\forall x \forall y ((x \in A \,\&\, y \in A) \rightarrow x \frown y \in A)$

2. *The operation* $\frown$ *is associative:* $\forall x \forall y \forall z ((x \frown y) \frown z = x \frown (y \frown z))$

3. *A contains an identity element e:* $\exists e \forall x (x \frown e = e \frown x = x)$

■

Both monoids and semigroups are examples of kinds of *algebras*. We will return to them in Chapter 10 in the context of group theory and other related algebras. Some parts of the study of algebras relate closely to the study of model theory, since algebras are usually characterizable with a small set of simple axioms whose models can be shown to share rich and significant structural properties. (Among the algebras to be studied in Chapters 9-12, lattices, Boolean algebras, and Heyting algebras have played a particularly important role in model theoretic investigations.)

8.5.7   Models for Peano's axioms

Peano's axioms, repeated below, were introduced in section 8.4, where we showed their connection to the important concept of proof by mathematical induction. In this section we return to them from a semantic perspective, to consider some of their models in addition to the intended model, the natural numbers. In Section 8.6.7 below we will discuss the relation of Peano's famous fifth axiom to the well-ordering axiom mentioned in 8.5.5. The first four axioms are first-order; the fifth is not.

(8–40) *Peano's axioms.* There are two primitive predicates, N and S. (The intended interpretation of N is 'is a natural number' and that of S is 'is the (immediate) successor of'.) There is one primitive constant, 0, whose intended interpretation is the natural number zero.

P1) $N0$

P2) $\forall x(Nx \rightarrow \exists y(Ny \,\&\, Syx \,\&\, \forall z(Szx \rightarrow z = y)))$

P3) $\sim \exists x(Nx \,\&\, S0x)$

P4) $\forall x \forall y \forall z \forall w((Nx \,\&\, Ny \,\&\, Szx \,\&\, Swy \,\&\, z = w) \rightarrow x = y)$

P5) If Q is a property such that

(a) $Q0$

(b) $\forall x \forall y((Nx \,\&\, Qx \,\&\, Ny \,\&\, Syx) \rightarrow Qy)$,

then $\forall x(Nx \rightarrow Qx)$

Peano, like Euclid, conceived of the primitive terms of the system as already having known meaning, and of the axioms as the smallest set of true statements about the natural number series from which its other properties could be derived. But if we look at the system in the purely formal way described above, we find that other meanings can be given to the primitives, and each of these interpretations would impart another meaning to derived statements about the natural numbers. Russell gives some instructive examples:[3]

(1) Let '0' stand for 100 and let 'natural number' be taken to mean the integers from 100 onward. All the axioms are satisfied, even the third; for although 100 is ordinarily the successor of 99, 99 is not a 'natural number' in this interpretation.

(2) Let '0' be 0 but let 'natural number' be interpreted as 'even number'

---

[3]This is part of an interesting discussion in Waismann, Chapter 9. See also his Chapter 6.

and let the 'successor' of a number be that number obtained by adding 2 to it. The number series will now read

$$0, 2, 4, 6, 8, \ldots$$

and again all five of Peano's axioms are satisfied.

(3) Let '0' be 1, let 'natural number' be any number of the sequence

$$1, 1/2, 1/4, 1/8, 1/16, \ldots$$

and let 'successor of' mean 'half of'. All five axioms also hold on this interpretation.

By contrast, we might consider some interpretations of N and S which do *not* satisfy all five Peano axioms.

(4) Let '0' stand for 0, 'successor' for successor, and let 'natural number' be interpreted as 'natural number less than or equal to 100'. Then axioms P1, P3, P4, and P5 hold, but P2 does not, because 100 does not have a successor in this interpretation. Similarly, *no* finite set can satisfy all of the Peano axioms.

(5) Let '0' stand for 0, let the 'successor' of any number be the number gotten by adding 1 to it (as in the standard interpretation), but let the 'natural numbers' be 0, 0.5, 1, 1.5, 2, 2.5, 3, 3.5, ... Axioms P1, P2, P3, and P4 hold; for instance, the unique successor of 1.5 is 2.5, and of 1 is 2; the unique predecessor of 7.5 is 6.5, and of 8 is 7. No fractional number is the successor of any whole number, and vice versa. The only axiom violated by this interpretation is P5, the induction principle. A property Q could satisfy (i) and (ii) of P5 and still fail to hold of all the 'natural numbers' by failing to hold for 0.5, 1.5, 2.5, ... , which will be missed by the "domino attack" of (i) and (ii).

8.5.8   Axiomatization of set theory

The primitives of set-theory are of course the notions 'set' and 'member'. What are the axioms of set-theory, the assumptions from which we may derive all we know about sets and their members? There are a number of different axiomatizations, characterizing distinct set-theories, but the best known one, which we give here, is known as the Zermelo-Frankel axiomatization (abbreviated ZF). This axiomatization appears to be quite successful

in that its axioms are very intuitive, simple truths about sets, and no contradictions can be derived from them. One axiom, the axiom of *extensionality*,
says that a set is uniquely determined by its members. The other axioms
either state that a certain set exists or that a certain set can be constructed
by application of an operation. These axioms provide the foundation from
which we may derive theorems about sets or set-theoretic concepts and, for
instance, prove the exact relationships between properties of relations, and
properties of their inverses or complements. Notationally we do not distinguish between sets and members, as we did with upper and lower case letters
in the previous chapters, i.e., w, x, y, z are arbitrary set-theoretic objects, but
anything enclosed in braces is a set. The membership relation holds between
a member and the set it is a member of, but $x \in x$ is not excluded.

(8–41) The Zermelo-Frankel Axioms of Set Theory

   Axiom 1. Extensionality *If x and y have the same elements,*
   $x = y$.

   Axiom 2. Regularity *For every non-empty set x there is $y \in x$*
   such that $x \cap y = \emptyset$.

   Axiom 3. Empty set *There is a set with no members.*

   Axiom 4. Pairing *If x and y are sets, then there is a set z such*
   that for all w, $w \in z$ if and only if $w = x$ or $w = y$.

   Axiom 5. Union *For every x there is a y such that $z \in y$ if and*
   only if there is a $w \in x$ with $z \in w$.

   Axiom 6. Power set *For every x there is a y such that for all z,*
   $z \in y$ if and only if $z \subseteq x$.

   Axiom 7. Infinity *There is a set x such that $0 \in x$ and whenever*
   $y \in x$, then $y \cup \{y\} \in x$.

   Axiom 8. Replacement *If P is a functional property and x is a*
   set, then the range of P restricted to x is a set; i.e., there is a set
   y such that for every z, $z \in y$ if and only if there is a $w \in x$ such
   that $P(w) = z$.

   The axiom of Regularity says that, if we are collecting objects into sets,
we may stop at any stage and what we have then collected is a set. It
is perhaps not really 'self-evident' that this is true, but at least it can be
proven to be consistent with all the other axioms, and it is a very powerful axiom in constructing simple and direct proofs of other theorems. The
Empty-set axiom implies together with Extensionality that there is exactly
one empty set. Pairing guarantees that for every x and y the set $\{x, y\}$

exists. Union and Power-set assert existence of these sets formed from arbitrary x. Infinity proves to be essential in representing the natural numbers as sets. Replacement is the one axiom that Frankel added to Zermelo's axiomatization, instead of his axiom of Separation, which says that a definable subset of a set is also a set, i.e. if x is a set and P is a property then there is a subset y of x which contains just the elements of x which have property P. Separation follows from Replacement, but Replacement does not follow from Separation. There are also statements which cannot be proved from the axioms 1-7 with Separation, but which are provable from 1-7 with Replacement.

These axioms are sufficient as foundations of mathematics, and note that the only primitive relation is membership. Yet there are statements which cannot be proved or disproved from this axiomatization. One in particular is often assumed as an additional axiom: the Axiom of Choice. Let A be a set of non-empty sets. A *choice-function* for A is a function F with domain A and $F(X) \in X$ for each $X \in A$. The function F "chooses" an element in each $X \in A$, namely $F(X)$.

(8-42) **Axiom of Choice** Every set of non-empty sets has a choicefunction.

This axiom is often used in set theory, and has a variety of guises. It is not provable from axioms 1-8 as Paul Cohen proved in 1963; it is consistent with them, and no contradiction is derivable from it with 1-8, which Gödel proved in 1938. Yet its acceptance is not universal, and there are theorems which admit of simpler proofs with it but which also have more complicated proofs without using the Axiom of Choice. The results of Gödel and Cohen are milestones in the foundations of mathematics, producing innovative and fruitful proof techniques with wide new applications. For our present purposes it suffices to know that the Axiom of Choice is not universally accepted and granted equal status with the other axioms of set theory, although in the sequel we will implicitly rely on it as an additional axiom. (Axioms 1-8 + the Axiom of Choice are abbreviated to ZFC.)

8.6 Axiomatizing logic

8.6.1 An axiomatization of statement logic

There are a number of axiomatizations of the system of statement logic we introduced in Chapter 6 that equally meet the criteria of completeness and

independence. We present here the axiomatization of Hilbert and Ackermann, which was obtained by deleting one non-independent axiom from the
system of Whitehead and Russell's *Principia Mathematica* (1913).

Remember that we use $p, q, r, \ldots$ as variables for atomic statements and
$P, Q, R, \ldots$ as variables for statements of arbitrary complexity. Only two
connectives are taken as primitives, namely $\sim$ and $\vee$. The other connectives
are introduced by the following definitions:

$P \to Q$ is an abbreviation for $\sim P \vee Q$

$P \& Q$ is an abbreviation for $\sim (\sim P \vee \sim Q)$

$P \leftrightarrow Q$ is an abbreviation for $(P \to Q) \& (Q \to P)$
      i.e., for $\sim (\sim (\sim P \vee Q) \vee \sim (\sim Q \vee P))$

Whenever the three defined connectives occur below, they are to be interpreted as abbreviations for the equivalent expressions with just negations
and disjunctions.

(1) Axioms

  (a) $(p \vee p) \to p$
  (b) $p \to (p \vee q)$
  (c) $(p \vee q) \to (q \vee p)$
  (d) $(p \to q) \to ((r \vee p) \to (r \vee q))$

(2) Rules of Inference

  (a) Rule of Substitution: For a statement variable in any statement Q
      we may substitute a statement P, provided that P is substituted
      for every occurrence of that statement variable in Q.
  (b) Modus Ponens: From P and $P \to Q$ infer Q.

Bear in mind the following important distinction between proofs in this
formal system and proofs *within* statement logic. In the latter, any tautology
could be used to obtain a conclusion from given premises; in the formal
system, the tautologies are what we are trying to prove from the four axioms.
So we cannot use a tautology in the proof of a theorem unless it is one of
the axioms or has been proved earlier to be a theorem.

Not only is it possible to derive theorems in this system, but we can also derive new rules of inference which make the derivations of other theorems more convenient. Derived rules of inference are simply coded shortcuts in proofs. For instance, the first derived rule below says that if $P \vee P$ is a theorem, then P is a theorem. The proof of the derived rule consists simply in showing how, whenever a theorem of the form $P \vee P$ has been established, axioim (a) and the Rule of Substitution can be used to derive a theorem of the form P. Having shown that, we are free in the future to skip straight from $P \vee P$ to P, justifying the step by the derived rule. Since rules of inference are all of the form 'If ... is a theorem, then ... is a theorem," the method of establishing rules of inference is closely related to the rule of conditional proof (see Chapter 6).

(8–43)   Derived rule I: If $P \vee P$ is a theorem, then P is a theorem.
  Proof:
  1. $P \vee P$ Premise
  2. $(p \vee p) \to p$ Axiom (a)
  3. $(P \vee P) \to P$ 2, Substitution
  4. P 1, 3, Modus Ponens

  Derived rule II: If P is a theorem, and Q any statement, then $P \vee Q$ is a theorem.
  Proof:
  1. P Premise
  2. $p \to (p \vee q)$ Axiom (b)
  3. $P \to (P \vee Q)$ 2, Substitution
  4. $(P \vee Q)$ 1, 3, Modus Ponens

  Derived rule III: If $P \vee Q$ is a theorem, then $Q \vee P$ is a theorem.

  Derived rule IV: If $P \to Q$ is a theorem and R is any statement, then $(R \vee P) \to (R \vee Q)$ is a theorem.

The proofs of derived rules III and IV are similar to the proofs for I and II (cf. axioms (c) and (d)).

Two theorems are proved below to illustrate the general method of proofs within axiomatic systems. Each theorem may be used along with the axioms and original and derived rules of inference in proving successive theorems.

(8-44)   Theorem 1. $(p \to q) \to ((r \to p) \to (r \to q))$
      Proof:
         1. $(p \to q) \to ((r \lor p) \to (r \lor q))$ Axiom (d)
         2. $(p \to q) \to ((\sim r \lor p) \to (\sim r \lor q))$ 1, Subst. $\sim r / r$
         3. $(p \to q) \to ((r \to p) \to (r \to q))$ 2, Def. $\to$

The substitution in line 2 perhaps deserves mention. The Rule of Sub-stitution allows any complex statement to replace any atomic statement as long as the substitution is made uniformly throughout the entire formula. The atomic statement replaced is r of line 1. It is of no significance that the same symbol occurs again in the replacing statement $\sim r$. We could as well have taken $\sim s$, and then the resulting theorem would have had s instead of r.

(8-45)   Derived rule V: If $(P \to Q)$ and $(Q \to R)$ are theorems , then
      $(P \to R)$ is also a theorem.
      Proof:
         1. $(P \to Q)$ Premise
         2. $(Q \to R)$ Premise
         3. $(p \to q) \to ((r \to p) \to (r \to q))$ Theorem 1
         4. $(Q \to R) \to ((P \to Q) \to (P \to R))$ 3, Subst.
         5. $(P \to Q) \to (P \to R)$ 2, 4, M.P.
         6. $(P \to R)$ 1, 5, M.P.

In general, there will be a derived rule of inference obtainable from any theorem which has the form of an implication.

(8-46)   Theorem 2. $\sim p \lor p$
      Proof:
         1. $p \to (p \lor q)$ Axiom (b)
         2. $p \to (p \lor p)$ 1, Subst.
         3. $(p \lor p) \to p$ Axiom (a)
         4. $p \to p$ 2, 3, D.R.V.
         5. $\sim p \lor p$ def. $\to$

8.6.2   Consistency and independence proofs

Above we noted that consistency can be proven most easily by specifying a model, and independence by showing semantically what effect dropping the axiom tested for independence has on the set of models of the entire system. The proofs given here of the consistency and independence of the Hilbert and Ackermann axiomatization of statement logic illustrate the possibility of giving syntactic proofs of consistency and independence. The difficulty of finding semantic arguments for the special case of axiomatizing logic itself stems from the difficulty of giving a non-trivial model. A model is anything of which the axioms are true when primitive terms are translated in some specified way; but the axioms in this case are tautologies, hence "true of" anything.

(i) Consistency

Hilbert and Ackermann's consistency proof is a proof that there is no way to derive within the system both a statement and its negation. It is a syntactic argument since it involves only the formal properties of the axioms and rules of inference Superficially it looks semantic in that it appears to be introducing a model, but this "quasi-model," it must be emphasized, is not something of which the axioms are "true". It simply serves to isolate certain formal characteristics of the axioms and rules of inference.

In this "quasi-model" the statement symbols $p, q, r, \ldots$ are not variables for statements, but for the numbers 0 and 1. Disjunction is taken to represent multiplication:

$$0 \lor 0 = 0 \qquad 1 \lor 0 = 0$$
$$0 \lor 1 = 0 \qquad 1 \lor 1 = 1$$

Negation is defined as follows:

$$\sim 0 = 1 \qquad \sim 1 = 0$$

Since the other connectives are defined in terms of these, they are defined now similarly by these numerical equations.

It can be shown now that given this numerical encoding, (1) the axioms all have the value 0 for all values of statement symbols occuring within them, and (2) starting from statements which have the value 0 for all values of their components and applying the rules of inference can only lead to other statements which have 0 as value for all values of their components. It follows that no formula can ever be derived which has value 1. But from the definition of negation, it is clear that if P is 0 then $\sim P$ is 1. Hence, since we can never derive a statement with value 1, we cannot derive both a statement and its negation in the statement logic axiomatization. The system is therefore consistent.

To show that axiom (c), for example, has value 0 for all values of its components, we let p and q each take on the values 0 and 1 and examine each case.

Axiom(c): $(p \lor q) \to (q \lor p)$; i.e., $(\sim (p \lor q)) \lor (q \lor p)$

$\quad p = 0, q = 0 : (\sim (0 \lor 0)) \lor (0 \lor 0) = \sim 0 \lor 0 = (1 \lor 0) = 0$

$\quad p = 0, q = 1 : (\sim (0 \lor 1)) \lor (1 \lor 0) = \sim 0 \lor 0 = (1 \lor 0) = 0$

$\quad p = 1, q = 0 : (\sim (1 \lor 0)) \lor (0 \lor 1) = \sim 0 \lor 0 = (1 \lor 0) = 0$

$\quad p = 1, q = 1 : (\sim (1 \lor 1)) \lor (1 \lor 1) = \sim 1 \lor 1 = (0 \lor 1) = 0$

The other axioms can be handled similarly.

To show that the rules of inference permit only statements whose value is always 0 to be derived from statements whose value is always 0, we can proceed as follows:

Rule of Substitution: A statement p whose value may be 0 or 1 is substituted for some variable whose value can be 0 or 1; if the formula into which p is substituted has the value 0 for either value of the variable p, it will still have the value 0 for either value of p.

Rule of Implication: Assume that $P \to Q$ and P have the value 0 for all values of their components. $P \to Q$ is an abbreviation for $\sim P \lor Q$. Since P has value 0, $\sim P \lor Q$ has value $\sim 0 \lor$ (value of Q), i.e., $1 \lor$ (value of Q). But for $1 \lor$ (value of Q) to equal 0, as given, the value of Q must be 0. Hence if P and $P \to Q$ have value 0 for all values of their components, so does Q.

(ii) Independence

The question of independence of the given set of axioms has been solved by Hilbert and Ackermann and independtnly by Paul Bernays, who first showed that the fifth axiom included by Whitehead and Russell was not independent. Hilbert and Ackermann provide a syntactic proof of independence for each axiom, again using quasi-arithmetical models; one example is included here:

Independence of Axiom (b): $p \to (p \lor q)$; i.e., $\sim p \lor (p \lor q)$

$\quad$ Let $\quad 0 \lor 0 = 0 \lor 1 = 0 \lor 2 = 0 \lor 3 = 0$

$\quad\quad\quad\quad 1 \lor 1 = 1 \lor 2 = 1 \lor 3 = 1$

$\quad\quad\quad\quad 2 \lor 2 = 2 \lor 3 = 2$

$\quad\quad\quad\quad 3 \lor 3 = 3$

and let $\lor$ be commutative. (Thus $p \lor q$ is always the minimum of p and q.)

$\quad$ Let $\quad \sim 0 = 1 \quad\quad \sim 2 = 3$

$\quad\quad\quad\quad \sim 1 = 0 \quad\quad \sim 3 = 2$

It can be shown that axioms (a), (c), and (d) always have the value 0 or 2. It can also be shown that from formulas with value 0 or 2, the rules of inference allow derivation only of other formulas with values 0 or 2.

But if we let $p = 2$ and $q = 1$, axiom (b) has the value 1. Therefore axiom (b) cannot be derived from the other three; it is *independent*.

In each proof of independence of an axiom, a different interpretation of the whole system is required, since in each case we must find a property which is posssessed by all but one of the axioms and which is passed on by the rules of inference.

8.6.3   An axiomatization of predicate logic

First-order prodicate logic has a particularly pleasant property: it allows for axiomatizations that are *complete* and *sound*. Completeness means here that all valid formulas (i.e. formulas that are true in *all* interpretations) are derivable from the axioms using the rules of inference. Soundness of axiomatization is the inverse property: all derivable formulas, i.e. all theorems, are valid. Together these two properties mean that all and only valid formulas are derivable from the axioms.

There are a number of axiomatizations of first-order predicate logic that are complete and sound. The following one is particularly simple in its formulation as it uses only two connectives and two rules of inference. The other connectives can be defined in a way similar to the definitions in 8.6.1. The existential quantifier ($\exists x$) is defined as $\sim(\forall x) \sim$. However, instead of a rule of substitution, this axiomatization uses axiom-schemata. Thus, according to the first schema, any wff of the form $\varphi \rightarrow (\psi \rightarrow \varphi)$ is an axiom, where φ and ψ are arbitrary statements of first-order logic, i.e. formulas without free variables. As before in Section 7.3 we write $\varphi(x)$, $\psi(x)$ etc. for any formula which contains at least one free occurrence of the variable x. We write a for an arbitrary individual constant, $\varphi(a)$ for the statement obtained from $\varphi(x)$ by replacing all free occurrences of x by a, and $\varphi(y)$ for the formulas obtained from $\varphi(x)$ by replacing all free occurrences of x by y. In the latter case it is understood that $\varphi(x)$ does not contain occurrences of the variable y.

Axiomatization of Predicate Logic

Axioms

A1) $(\varphi \to (\psi \to \varphi))$

A2) $(\varphi \to (\psi \to \chi)) \to ((\varphi \to \psi) \to (\varphi \to \chi))$

A3) $(\sim \varphi \to \sim \psi) \to (\psi \to \varphi)$

A4) $(\forall x)\varphi(x) \to \varphi(a)$

Rules of inference

R1) From φ and $\varphi \to \psi$, derive φ (Modus Ponens)

R2) From $\varphi \to \psi(a)$, derive $\varphi \to (\forall x)\psi(x)$ provided that a does not occur in φ

The first three axiom-schemata, together with the rule of inference Modus Ponens provide anther axiomatization of statement logic, different from the one given in 8.6.1, since it uses axiom-schemata. Predicate logic is hence an *extension* of statement logic. We illustrate this axiomatization of predicate logic with the proofs of three theorems.

(8-47)   Theorem 1. $(\forall x)\varphi(x) \to (\forall y)\varphi(y)$ is derivable for any statement $(\forall x)\varphi(x)$ of predicate logic.
  Proof:
    1. $(\forall x)\varphi(x) \to \varphi(a)$ Axiom-schema 4
         where a does not occur in $(\forall x)\varphi(x)$
    2. $(\forall x)\varphi(x) \to (\forall y)\varphi(y)$ 1, R2   ∎

This theorem shows that alphabetic variants are equivalent, and hence that the choice of individual variables is arbitrary.

(8-48)   Theorem 2. $\varphi \to \varphi$ is derivable for any statement φ of predicate logic.
  Proof:
    1. $(\varphi \to ((\varphi \to \varphi) \to \varphi)) \to ((\varphi \to (\varphi \to \varphi)) \to (\varphi \to \varphi))$
         Axiom-schema 2
    2. $\varphi \to ((\varphi \to \varphi) \to \varphi)$ Axiom-schema 1
    3. $(\varphi \to (\varphi \to \varphi)) \to (\varphi \to \varphi)$ 1, 2, Modus Ponens
    4. $\varphi \to (\varphi \to \varphi)$ Axiom-schema 1
    5. $\varphi \to \varphi$ 3, 4, Modus Ponens ∎

As is evident from this proof, to write down actual derivations in this axiomatic system is rather cumbersome. We will use theorem 2 in the proof of the law of the excluded middle for predicate logic.

(8–49)   Theorem 3. $(\forall x)(\varphi(x) \vee \sim\varphi(x))$

Proof:

1. $\sim\varphi(a)\rightarrow\sim\varphi(a)$ by theorem 2
2. $\varphi(a) \vee \sim\varphi(a)$ 1, definition of disjunction
3. $(\varphi(a) \vee \sim\varphi(a)\rightarrow((\psi\rightarrow(\psi\rightarrow\psi))\rightarrow(\varphi(a) \vee \sim\varphi(a))))$
                                                                       Axiom-schema 1
4. $((\psi\rightarrow(\psi\rightarrow\psi))\rightarrow(\varphi(a) \vee \sim\varphi(a)))$ 2, 3, Modus Ponens
5. $((\psi\rightarrow(\psi\rightarrow\psi))\rightarrow(\forall x)(\varphi(x) \vee \sim\varphi(x)))$ 4, R2
6. $(\psi\rightarrow(\psi\rightarrow\psi))$ Axiom-schemata 1
7. $(\forall x)(\varphi(x) \vee \sim\varphi(x)))$ 5, 6, Modus Ponens   ∎

8.6.4   About completeness proofs

This axiomatization of first-order predicate logic is complete, i.e., all and only valid formulas are provable. Although this claim itself has been proven formally by Kurt Gödel and later also by Leon Henkin, these proofs are quite technical and not directly useful for any linguistic purposes. But the notion of completeness is an important meta-theoretical concept and to get an impression of its value we discuss the main ideas of Henkin's proof semi-formally here.

The main stages of Henkin's completeness proof are the following three claims:

(1) if a formula φ is not provable in predicate logic, then the singleton set $\{\sim \varphi\}$ is consistent.

(2) every consistent set of statements M is contained in a maximally consistent set M^*.

(3) every maximally consistent set M^* has an interpretation making exactly all statements in M^* true.

We explain the three claims and the notions used in them non-technically:

ad 1) Suppose that φ is not provable in predicate logic. We reason in a *reductio ad absurdum* argument. If $\{\sim \varphi\}$ is inconsistent, then, according to the definition of inconsistency, we can derive some formula ψ and its negation hence also the contradiction $(\sim \psi \& \psi)$ from it. In that case one can show that $\sim \varphi \rightarrow (\sim \psi \& \psi)$ is provable, and that therefore $\sim (\sim \psi \& \psi) \rightarrow \varphi$ is provable. Since $\sim (\sim \psi \& \psi)$ is provable as well, it follows by Modus Ponens that φ is provable after all, which contradicts the initial assumption that φ is not provable in predicate logic. So the additional assumption that $\sim \varphi$ is inconsistent cannot be right, so $\sim \varphi$. is consistent.

ad 2) A set of formulas M^* is *maximally consistent* if M^* is consistent and for every arbitrary formula φ not in M^*, $M^* \cup \{\varphi\}$ is inconsistent. This means that there is no formula which can be added to M^* while keeping it consistent. Any consistent set of formulas M can be extended to a maximally consistent set M^* which contains all formulas of M. We enumerate the formulas $\varphi_1, \varphi_2, \varphi_3, \ldots$ in M according to their length and by equal length alphabetically and enumerate also all the individual constants. Take $M_0 = M$ and form M_{n+1} for arbitrary n from the set M_n by adding the formula $\psi(a) \rightarrow (\forall x)\psi(x)$ if φ_{n+1} is of the form $(\forall x)\psi(x)$; where a is the first individual constant in the enumeration which does not occur in φ_{n+1} nor in any of the formulas in M_n. If φ_{n+1} is not of the form $(\forall x)\psi(x)$ then $M_{n+1} = M_n$. This procedure produces sequence of consistent sets $M_0, M_1, M_2, \ldots$ Let M^* be the set consisting only of all elements of any M_n. Then M_n is consistent, since there is no finite subset which is inconsistent. M^* is maximal since any formula not in M^* is excluded because it would make it inconsistent by the procedure.

ad 3) Every consistent set of formulas has a model in which all formulas are true. We should describe this precisely for any form of formula, but the details are not particularly illuminating. In case the formula is universally quantified, the procedure of constructing M^* guarantees that all assignments to the quantified variable give formulas which are still in M^*.

Now if $\varphi_1, \ldots, \varphi_n \rightarrow \psi$ is valid in predicate logic, then the proof of ψ from premises $\varphi_1, \ldots, \varphi_n$ must exist in our axiomatization of predicate logic. For if $\varphi_1, \ldots, \varphi_n \rightarrow \psi$ is valid, then $\varphi_1 \rightarrow (\varphi_2 \rightarrow \ldots (\varphi_n \rightarrow \psi)) \ldots)$ is true and hence provable. With Modus Ponens applied n times we prove ψ from $\varphi_1, \ldots, \varphi_n$.

This sketch of Henkin's completeness proof may give you a taste of one of the most important results in predicate logic. It shows that you may safely switch back and forth between model-theoretic arguments and proofs, since they are simply semantic and syntactic counterparts. Perhaps the most important and startling "side effect" of the research on completeness was the discovery of negative results showing the incompleteness of some systems. To that topic we turn briefly in Section 8.6.6.

8.6.5 Decidability

We have seen already that finding a proof for a formula with natural deduction rules often requires ingenuity and insight. There is no foolproof procedure we can prescribe which yields a proof for any provable formula. In the semantics of the statement logic, however, there is the mechanical truth table method which always answers the question whether a statement is a tautology or not. In predicate logic truth tables do only part of the semantic job but we have to consider assignments to variables on possibly infinite domains as well. There is no general procedure which yields a definite yes/no answer to the question whether a predicate-logical statement is valid or provable. No success in finding a proof may mean either that we have to try harder or that the statement is not a theorem, but we never know which is the case!

If you understand the workings of the Beth Tableaux for predicate logic, you have seen that the construction of some tableaux may just never come to an end by closure or counterexample. Neither can we tell from the form of a predicate-logical statement after how many steps we will either find a counterexample or obtain closure. All we know is that if the statement is valid it will eventually end in closure. This is why the tableau method, even though it is more mechanical than natural deduction, does not constitute a general procedure answering 'yes' or 'no' to the question whether an arbitrary statment of predicate logic is a theorem. The fact that membership in the set of theorems of predicate logic cannot be decided for every arbitrary formula by such a mechanical procedure is called the *undecidability* of predicate logic. The statement logic, however, is *decidable*, because of the existence of the mechanical procedures of truth tables or tableaux which characterize the valid statements. Another subsystem of first-order predicate logic, *monadic predicate logic*, where predicates can take only one argument, is also decidable. The proof of the decidability of monadic predicate logic is based on two facts: (1) that any monadic formula can be transformed to a special prenex normal form in which all existential quantifiers precede the universal quantifiers (see below on Skolem Normal Forms) and (2) that a tableau for such formulas always ends after a finite number of steps in closure or in a counterexample by enumerating the domain. Both claims can be proven, but to do so here would lead us too far afield.

The set of theorems of predicate logic is not decidable, but it is enumerable in a systematic way. The Beth Tableaux method provides such an enumeration, since we know that every valid theorem eventually leads to closure. The method does not produce a yes/no answer for any arbitrary formula, but it does produce "yes" answers for all valid theorems. We say that this constitutes an *effective enumeration* of the set of theorems of predicate logic. Of course, the complement of this set, i.e., the set of all non-theorems or invalid arguments, is not effectively enumerable. For if it were, we would have a decision procedure saying "yes" to all theorems and "no" to all non-theorems. The completeness theorem is not in any conflict with the undecidability of predicate logic, for if an argument is valid, there is a finite proof of it, but we have no general method of finding such a proof. We return to the relations between decidability, effectively enumerable sets, different kinds of functions, and computability in Part E.

8.6.6   Gödel's incompleteness theorems

The Peano axioms form the foundation of mathematical number theory. We may wonder whether it is complete with respect to its intended interpretation. In 1931, just after proving the completeness of predicate logic, Kurt Gödel proved the startling theorem that Peano arithmetic is *incomplete*; i.e., there is a true statement about natural numbers which is not provable from the Peano axioms!

The proof of what is known as *Gödel's first incompleteness theorem* constitutes one of the most sophisticated proof techniques in logic. Gödel's first incompleteness result concerned the incompleteness of Peano arithmetic. His second incompleteness result stated that any consistent axiomatization which is strong enough to contain number-theoretic representations of proofs does not yield a proof of its own consistency. The result is shocking when one realizes that it means that the proof of the consistency of arithmetic is as questionable as its consistency itself.

The first incompleteness theorem uses the natural numbers simultaneously as an object-level system and as its own metalanguage in constructing a number-theoretic representation of a statement which says about itself that it is false. The intutitive background stems from the ancient Cretan paradox of the liar, which is easily expressed in natural language by the self-referential statement, *I am a liar*. Anyone making such a statement runs into semantic paradoxes, for if the statement is true, he is not a liar and hence what he says is false, but if the statement is false, then he cannot be a liar and what he says is true. The vicious circularity resides in using a semantic truth predicate (being a liar = not speaking the truth) *in* the statement as well as in applying it *to* the statement itself. The formal proof of the incompleteness theorem is too intricate to even outline here; the interested reader is referred to Hofstadter (1979) for a generally accessible exposition or to Bell and Machover (1977), Enderton (1972), or any other textbook in mathematical logic for all necessary details.

Another surprising consequence of the incompleteness theorem is that, since ZFC is effectively axiomatizable, complete with respect to negation and thought to be consistent, its supposed consistency can never be proven.

Even though the Gödel results deeply shook the foundations of mathematics and logic, mathematical practice never took much notice and proceeded as usual. We may take their metaphysical implications as saying that mathematical reality is too rich ever to get completely captured in a consistent and complete axiomatization; or we may conclude more soberly that formalizations have their limits too, and we had better be aware of them.

8.6.7   Higher-order logic

There are different ways in which we may enrich the language of first-order predicate logic by admitting quantification over predicates or functions. The system we introduced contained quantifiers restricted to individual variables, which constitute the first-order quantification. But there are many nouns and verbs in natural language which are not properties of individuals, but rather properties of properties of individuals. If this vase is blue and blue is a color, we cannot infer that this vase is a color, but rather that this vase if *of* a color. The predicate 'is a color' cannot properly be applied to ordinary individuals, but can be applied to properties of them. Properties and relations of these first-order objects are second-order objects, and so on. A logical system is an n-order logic when it contains at least one n-order variable (free or bound). Note that an n-order logic may contain quantifiers of lower order as well as relations mixing arguments of different orders. The interpretation of second-order quantifiers must consider all or some assignments of subsets of a domain to the second-order variables, since a first-order predicate is interpreted by a subset of the domain. The interpretation of 'is a color', for instance, is a set of subsets of colored objects. The semantics of second-order quantifiers must hence employ the full power-set of the domain of the model. We will not develop a full-fledged syntax and semantics of higher-order systems here but discuss some aspects of second-order logic of interest in linguistic applications.

Two examples of familiar notions illustrate the expressive power of second-order logic.

(1) A well-ordering is an ordering relation in which every non-empty set has a least element. This is expressed in second-order logic by

$$(\forall X)((\exists w)Xw \rightarrow (\exists y)(Xy \,\&\, (\forall z)((Xz \,\&\, z \neq y) \rightarrow y < z)))$$

(2) The induction axiom in Peano's axiomatization of artithmetic can be translated into a second-order formula. It says that a set of natural numbers which contains 0 and is closed under the successor function, constitutes the set of all natural numbers. In a second-order formula, where X is a second-order variable and S is the successor-relation, a relation between a set and a natural number, this is expressed as

$$(\forall X)(X(0) \,\&\, (\forall y(X(y) \rightarrow S(X,y)) \rightarrow (\forall y)X(y)))$$

Any first-order formula can be translated to a logically equivalent second-order formula which has a special form: it is prenex and all existential n-order quantifiers precede universal first-order quantifiers. This is called its *Skolem Normal Form* (SNF) after the logician Skolem who proved the general theorem that such a normal form exists for any first-order formula. We discuss some examples as illustration of the method. The value of Skolem Normal Forms lies in their explicit representation of quantificational dependencies of assignments to variables. The simplest example is the equivalence of $(\forall x)(\exists y)R(x,y) \iff (\exists F)(\forall x)R(x,F(x))$. The individual variable y is assigned a value by a function F depending on the assignment to the universally quantified x.

To see that $(\exists F)(\forall x)R(x,F(x))$ implies $(\forall x)(\exists y)R(x,y)$, suppose we have an interpretation M with an assignment g which verifies $(\forall x)(\exists y)R(x,y)$. We know that for any a in the domain of M there is at least one b such that $[\![R(x,y)]\!]^{M,g}$ is true. We obtain a function f on the domain of M by choosing one such b for each a and taking $f(a) = b$. This uses the Axiom of Choice. Then $[\![(\forall x)R(x,F(x))]\!]^{M,g'}$ is true where g' is exactly like g with f substituted for F. This function f is called a *Skolem function*, or a *choice-function*, for the formula $(\forall x)(\exists y)R(x,y)$ in the interpretation M. This illustrates the general method: an existential first-order quantifier is translated to an existential second-order function quantifier, which binds a function taking as arguments all individual variables bound by universal quantifiers preceding it. One more example of this procedure may suffice as illustration. Suppose we have a formula

$$(\exists y)(\forall x)(\exists z)(\forall u)(\forall y)(\exists w)R(y, z, w)$$

(presumably other variables occur in the matrix, but they are irrelevant for the present example). The first existential quantifier precedes the universal quantifiers, so is already in SNF. Consider the remainder of the formula:

$$(\forall x)(\exists z)(\forall u)(\forall v)(\exists w)R(y, z, w)$$

The second existential quantifier $(\exists z)$ depends on $(\forall x)$, and we translate the formula to

$$(\exists F)(\forall x)(\forall u)(\forall v)(\exists w)R(y, F(x), w)$$

What remains is

$$(\forall x)(\forall u)(\forall v)(\exists w)R(y, F(x), w)$$

This is logically equivalent to

$$(\exists G)(\forall x)(\forall u)(\forall v)R(y, F(x), G(x, u, v))$$

Here G is a Skolem function with three arguments. The original formula is hence equivalent to the SNF

$$(\exists y)(\exists F)(\exists G)(\forall x)(\forall u)(\forall v)R(y, F(x), G(x, u, v))$$

Linguistic applications of Skolem-functions have been primarily in the semantics of question-answering. A multiple question like "Which student got which grade?" is interpreted as a set of statements which constitute true answers to it, which must give a specific grade for each student. The answer to the wh-quantifier "which grade" depends on the answer to "which student". This dependency can be captured by a Skolem-function and implemented in a Montague style semantics or in other model-theoretic frameworks.

The same considerations which showed that first-order predicate logic is undecidable apply to higher-order logics which contain first-order logic. There cannot be a procedure which answers 'no' in every case in which a formula is not a theorem. But we have seen that the Beth Tableaux method provided a procedure to enumerate the valid theorems. No such effective enumeration exists for the theorems of higher-order logics, however. For if there was such an enumeration, it could be turned into a 'no'-answering procedure for first-order logic by replacing names and predicate constants by appropriate variables, universally quantifying these and negating the entire second-order formula. We know first-order logic is undecidable, so there cannot be such a 'no'-answering procedure. So there is no tableau method for second-order logic, no effective procedure identifying all theorems.

Second-order logic, and hence any higher-order logic, is incomplete. The proof cannot be discussed here, but it is based on the fact that an incomplete fragment of arithmetic can be represented in it, showing that Gödel's incompleteness result may be applied to higher-order logics. This means that there are valid theorems which cannot be proven from any axiomatization of higher-order logic. It is an interesting open question just how much higher-order expressive power can be admitted into first-order logic while preserving its completeness.

Type theory is the system of logic with quantifiers and variable of any order. Montague Grammar is based on a type theory but usually employs only a limited fragment with third-order quantification in the interpretation of natural language. New research is developing more flexible forms of type theory which may have important applications in linguistics and computer science.

Exercises

1. Give a recursive definition of the well-formed strings in the statement calculus in Polish parenthesis-free notation (Chapter 6, Exercise 13). Give a proof *CENApppp* is a well-formed string using your definition.

2. Let f be a function that maps each n in $Z = 0, 1, 2, 3, \ldots$ into 2^{2^n}; e.g., $f(1) = 2^{2^1} = 2^2 = 4$. Given a recursive definition of f, and use it to compute the value of $f(4)$.

3. Suppose we were to take the successor of any positive number x as being $x + 2$. Show that the four Peano Axioms (Section 8.4) would

then specify the set of natural numbers as the set of even numbers $0, 2, 4, 6, 8, \ldots$. Would the Principle of Mathematical Induction still be a reasonable rule of inference when defined over this set?

4. Prove by induction that the power set of a set with n members has 2^n members, for any finite positive integer n.

5. Prove by induction the generalized distributive law of multiplication over addition; i.e., for all $n, a \times (b_1 + b_2 + \ldots + b_n) = (a \times b_1) + (a \times b_2) + \ldots + (a \times b_n)$.

6. What is wrong with the following inductive proof that all horses are of the same color? For a set containing only one horse, the base clearly holds, since that horse has only one color. Now assume that all sets of n horses contain only horses of the same color. We show that it follows that the same is true of all sets of $n + 1$ horses. Choose a set of $n + 1$ horses and select any n of them, disregarding the extra horse for the moment. By assumption, these n horses are all of the same color. Now replace one of the n horses by the extra horse, forming a new set of n horses. These again, by assumption, are all of the same color, and so the extra horse is the same color as all the others. Therefore, all horses are of the same color.

7. Consider the following axiomatic system. The "alphabet" consists of all well-formed formulas in the statement calculus plus the symbols $\rightarrow, ($, and $)$. There are three axioms:

(A1) $p \rightarrow (q \rightarrow p)$

(A2) $(p \rightarrow (q \rightarrow r)) \rightarrow ((p \rightarrow q) \rightarrow (p \rightarrow r))$

(A3) $(\sim p \rightarrow \sim q) \rightarrow (q \rightarrow p)$

and two rule schemata:

(R1) From any two expressions of the form $A \rightarrow B$ and A, we can derive B (A and B are variables ranging over the wff's of the statement calculus).

(R2) From any expression A we can derive B, where B is the result of substituting a wff x for every instance of some atomic statement, i.e., p, q, r, etc., in A.

The following is a proof of $p \to p$ in this system:

1. $(p \to (q \to r)) \to ((p \to q) \to (p \to r))$ (A2)
2. $(p \to ((q \to p) \to r)) \to ((p \to (q \to p)) \to (p \to r))$
                  1, (R2) (Substituting $(q \to p)$ for q)
3. $(p \to ((q \to p) \to p)) \to ((p \to (q \to p)) \to (p \to p))$
                  2, (R2) (Substituting p for r)
4. $p \to (q \to p)$ (A1)
5. $p \to ((q \to p) \to p)$
                  4, (R2)(Substituting $(q \to p)$ for q)
6. $(p \to (q \to p)) \to (p \to p)$ 3, 5, (R1)
7. $p \to p$ 4, 6, (R1)

Construct a proof of $\sim p \to (p \to q)$ in this system. *Hint*: Begin by substituting $(\sim q \to \sim p) \to (p \to q)$ for p and $\sim p$ for q in A1. It can be shown that the theorems of this system are all and only the tautologous *wff's* of statement logic [see, for example, Massey (1970, pp. 125-159)]. The connectives & and $\lor$, which do not appear in this system, can be defined in terms of $\sim$ and $\to$.

8. Reformulate the recursive difinition in Exercise 1 as an axiomatic system having the *wff's* n Polish notation as its theorems. Find an equivalent semi-Thue system.

9. Construct an extended axiomatic system whose theorems are all strings in $\{a\}^*$ of length divisible by 2 or by 3. For example, *aa, aaa, aaaa, aaaaaa, aaaaaaaa* are theorems, but *a, aaaaa aaaaaaa* are not. Can you see why there is no equivalent axiomatic system without an auxiliary alphabet?

10. Prove in the axiomatization of predicate logic given in Section 6.3 the following theorems. You may assume that all predicate logical tautologies are provable in this axiomatization.

   (a) $P(a) \to (\exists x)P(x)$
   (b) from premise $(\forall x)(\varphi \to P(x)))$ that $(\varphi \to (\forall x)P(x))$ if x does not occur in φ
   (c) from premise $(\forall x)(P(x) \to Q(x))$ that $(\forall x)P(x) \to (\forall x)Q(x)$

11. If the deletion of a certain axiom from a negation complete system makes it not negation complete, then the axiom is independent. Why?

12. The following systems all satisfy Peano's axioms under appropriate interpretations. For each case state what interpretation must be given to '0', 'is a natural number', and 'is a successor of'.

(a) $0, -1, -2, -3, \ldots$

(b) $5, 10, 15, 20, 25, \ldots$

(c) $+1, -2, +4, -8, +16, -32, \ldots$

13. Consider the following formal system W.
Primitives: set P of objects called "points", a set L of objects called "lines".
Axioms:
(1) every line is a set of points; i.e. $L \in \wp(P)$
(2) there exist at least two distinct points
(3) if p and q are distinct points, then there is one and only one line of which p and q are both members.
(4) if l is a line, there exists a point not in l
(5) if l is a line, and p is a point not in l, then there exists one and only one line containing p and disjoint from l.

(a) Find a model for W in which P has exactly four objects.

(b) Prove from the axioms that every point is in at least two distinct lines

(c) Prove that the empty set cannot be a member of L.

(d) Show that there can be no model for W in which P has exactly two members.

(e) If we added as sixth axiom "every line contains exactly one point" would the resulting system be consistent?

14. Give the Skolem normal forms for the following formulas:

(a) $(\forall x)(\exists y)(\forall z)R(x, y, z)$

(b) $(\forall x)(\exists y)(\exists z)R(x, y, z)$

(c) $(\forall x)(\exists y)(R(x, y) \to (\exists z)(S(x, z) \mathbin{\&} S(y, z)))$

(d) $(\forall x)(\forall y)(\exists z)(R(x, y) \mathbin{\&} \sim P(z) \to (\forall u)S(z, y, x, u))$

Appendix B-I

Alternative Notations and Connectives

The logical language we have studied in this chapter is the best known classical system of logic of statements. There are various alternative symbolic notations for the connectives we introduced, the most common of which are listed below.

Alternative notation for connectives

	our symbol	alternative(s)
negation	~	¬, -, $\bar{p}$
conjunction	&	∧, •
conditional	→	⊃ (called 'horseshoe')

Table B.I.–1:

Furthermore, there are two connectives which we have not introduced, as they are not part of the system most commonly used. One, called "Quine's dagger", ↓ is sufficiently powerful to be the only connective in a system equivalent to the one given. Its truth table is shown in (B.II.-2).

239

P	Q	$P \downarrow Q$
1	1	0
1	0	0
0	1	0
0	0	1

Table B.I.–2:

Its nearest English correspondent is *neither ... nor*. As an interesting exercise one can show that negation can be defined in terms of this connective, and then that disjunction can be defined in terms of negation and this connective. We have already proven (Chapter 6, Exercise 7) that the five-connective system can be reduced to one containing just $\vee$ and $\sim$. Therefore $\downarrow$ suffices alone for the five connectives.

Similarly, there is another connective, written as $|$, which is called the "Sheffer stroke", whose by the truth table is as follows:

P	Q	$P \mid Q$
1	1	0
0	1	1
1	0	1
0	0	1

Table B.I.–3:

Appendix B-II

Kleene's Three-valued Logic

The logic of statements and the predicate logic are two-valued, since there are but two truth values and every formula is either true or false. This is based on the assumption that the semantic assignments used in an interpretation are *total* functions. In some linguistic applications and especially in computational contexts, that assumption seems much too strong, since it requires that there is a clear semantic procedure which decides for any given x whether $[\![\varphi(x)]\!]$ is true or false for any arbitrary φ. But if we allow a *partial* interpretation function of predicates, such a procedure may not always exist since its value on $\varphi(x)$ may be undefined for some x. Kleene developed a semantics for predicate logic with such partial functions which yield values true or false when defined, but which may also be undefined. Since it has certain linguistically useful aspects, we discuss it here briefly.

In case a partial function is undefined for an argument it may be because we lack information, or we may take it to mean that we disregard its value as it is does not matter to our interpretation. The following truth tables represent the strong Kleene semantics for the connectives, where 1 is 'true', 0 is 'false' and * means the truth value is undefined.

p	$\sim p$	p	q	$p \mathbin{\&} q$	$p \lor q$	$p \to q$	$p \leftrightarrow q$
1	0	1	1	1	1	1	1
0	1	1	0	0	1	0	0
*	*	1	*	*	1	*	*
		0	1	0	1	1	0
		0	0	0	0	1	1
		0	*	0	*	1	*
		*	1	*	1	1	*
		*	0	0	*	*	*
		*	*	*	*	*	*

From this table we can see that if sufficient information is available to verify or falsify a statement, the undefined part does not alter it. But if the value of a part must be known to determine the value of a complex statement, the latter remains undefined until we know the value of its parts. This means that the value of a complex statement may be determined even when we do not know the value of *all* of its parts. For instance, as soon as we know that the antecedent of a conditional is false, we know that the conditional is true, irrespective of what the consequent may be. Kleene's operations are monotonic in the sense that any valuation function preserves its initial assignments when the domain is extended and new objects are added to the interpretation of the partial predicates. If we understand the undefined cases as arguments of which we have not yet determined the value, it is an unnatural consequence of these truth tables that a classical tautology such as $p \lor \sim p$ remains undefined until we know the value of p. There are ways to escape such consequences and preserve the classical tautologies and contradictions in a partial truth definition, but we cannot go into such systems here.

Three-valued logics have primarily been applied in linguistics in semantic theories of *presuppositions*. There is a lively controversy surrounding the analysis of presupposition in philosophy and linguistics, which cannot be surveyed here. For illustration we define this notion in semantic terms:

> Any statement p is a *presupposition* of a statement q iff if p is not true (but false or undefined), q is undefined.

The truth of a presupposition p is in some sense an *assertability condition* for q. In our everyday use of natural language we rely uncommonly often on such presuppositions. We use names to refer to people under the assumption that they exist; we use definite NPs like *the students who passed their exams* with the common understanding that we mean to say something about a particular non-empty set of students. We also presuppose that it is raining, when we say *John knows it is raining* or *Jane does not regret that it is raining.* Characteristic of presuppositions is that if p is a presupposition of q, p is also a presupposition of $\sim q$. This means that presuppositions are preserved under negation, and this is captured in the fact that * is preserved under negation according to the truth tables above. It is a major research question how the presuppositions of complex sentences are to be characterized in terms of the presuppositions of its component sentences and this is called the *projection-problem* of presuppositions. Kleene's system goes a long way, since it recognizes that the presuppositions of a complex sentence may not be just the sum of the presuppositions of its parts. Presuppositions of sentences may for example be cancelled in sentences of which they are a constituent. Consider for instance the conditional *If there is a president of the U.S., the president is elected.* This sentence contains two sentences (1) *There is a president of the U.S.* and (2) *The president is elected.* (1) is a presupposition of (2), since if (1) is false, (2) must be undefined, because it does describe anyone in that case. The Kleene interpretation of the conditional captures this nicely, since $p \to q$ is true even when q is undefined and p is false. So the entire conditional sentence does not have (1) as presupposition. But Kleene's interpretation can be seen to lead to problems in the following sentence (3) *If revolutions are unconstitutional, the president is elected.* Now (1) does seem to be a presupposition of (3), since if (1) is false, the consequent of (3) is undefined and hence (3) must be undefined. The antecedent may, however, very well be false, when (1) is false, since they are independent. If the antecedent is false, (3) is true. But if there is an assignment making (3) true and (1) false, (1) cannot be a presupposition of (3). This seems wrong and not in accordance with our intuitions. Generally speaking, in a conditional with a contingent antecedent whose truth value is independent of the presuppositions of its consequent, the presuppositions of the consequent are incorrectly cancelled in the Kleene interpretation of the connectives. There are ways to mend this problem, but none has yet found general acceptance. The suggested further reading for this chapter contains some main references to the literature on presuppositions.

Review Exercises

1. Suppose that $P \longleftrightarrow Q$ is true, what is $P \vee \sim Q$?

    (a) p
           q
         $\therefore \overline{(p \& q) \vee r}$

    (b) $p \leftrightarrow q$
         $\therefore \overline{\sim q \vee p}$

    (c) $p \to (q \to \sim\sim r)$
           $p \& \sim r$
         $\therefore \overline{\sim q}$

    (d) $p \vee q$
           $\sim p \vee r$
           $\sim q$
         $\therefore \overline{r}$

    (e) $p \& (q \to (r \vee \sim\sim s))$
           q
         $\therefore \overline{p \& (s \vee r)}$

    (f) $\sim (p \vee \sim q)$
           $r \vee p$
         $\therefore \overline{q \& r}$

2. Prove:

    (g) $p \to q$
           $p \to (q \to r)$
           $q \to (r \to s)$
         $\therefore \overline{p \to s}$

    (h) $r \to (p \vee s)$
           $q \to (s \vee t)$
           $\sim s$
         $\therefore \overline{(\sim p \& \sim t) \to (\sim r \& \sim q)}$

    (i) $p \to q$
           $\sim q \& r$
         $\therefore \overline{\sim p}$

    (j) $p \vee q$
           $r \& \sim p$
         $\therefore \overline{q}$

    (k) $p \leftrightarrow (\sim q \to r)$
           $\sim r \& \sim (s \to q)$
         $\therefore \overline{\sim p}$

3. Show that the following set of statements is inconsistent

    (a) $r \& (p \vee q)$

    (b) $\sim (p \& r)$

    (c) $\sim (q \& r)$

4. Does conjunction distribute over conditionals? I.e., is $(p \& q) \to (p \& r)$ equivalent to $p \& (q \to r)$?

5. Translate the following expressions to predicate logic.

(a) All horses are quadrupeds, but some quadrupeds are not horses.

(b) Distinct utterances must have distinct phonemic transcriptions.

(c) Not all trees are deciduous.

(d) Some politicians are honest men

(e) No ducks are amphibious

(f) Every cloud has a silver lining

(g) Only Rosicrucians experience complete happiness

(h) Everything I like is immoral, illegal or fattening

(i) I like anything that is immoral, illegal or fattening

(j) Everyone wants everyone to be rich

(k) Everyone wants to be rich

6. For each of the following formulas give an interpretation in a model which makes the formula false.

(a) $((\exists x)F(x) \& (\exists x)G(x)) \to (\exists x)(F(x) \& G(x))$

(b) $(\forall x)(\exists y)(\forall z)H(x,y,z) \to (\exists y)(\forall x)(\forall z)H(x,y,z)$

7. Formalize and prove with natural deduction

(a) All linemen for the Green Bay Packers weigh at least 200 pounds. Mathilda weighs less than 200 pounds. Therefore, Mathilda is not a lineman for the Green Bay Packers.

(b) All cabdrivers and headwaiters are surly and churlish. Therefore, all cabdrivers are surly.

8. Construct Beth Tableaux for

(a) $[(\exists x)F(x) \to (\forall x)G(x)] \implies (\forall x)(F(x) \to G(x))$

(b) $*(\forall x)(G(x) \& (\sim F(x) \lor H(x))) \implies (\forall x)(G(x) \& (\exists x)(F(x) \to (\forall x)H(x))$

Part C

ALGEBRA

Chapter 9

Basic Concepts of Algebra

9.1 Definition of algebra

An *algebra* **A** is a set A together with one or more operations f_i. We may represent an algebra by writing

$$(9\text{--}1) \quad \mathbf{A} = \langle\, A,\ f_1,\ f_2,\ \ldots, f_n\,\rangle$$

or by using particular symbols for the operations, such as

$$(9\text{--}2) \quad \mathbf{A} = \langle\, A,\ +,\ \times\,\rangle$$

The set A may finite or infinite, and there may be either a finite or an infinite number of different operations. However, each operation must be *finitary*, i.e. unary, binary, ternary ..... Each n-ary operation must be a well-defined operation, i.e. defined for all n-tuples of elements of A and yielding a unique element of A as a value for each n-tuple (cf. the mapping condition for functions in Section 2.3).

These requirements on the operations can be stated in the form of two axioms which each operation in an algebra must satisfy. For simplicity, the axioms are stated in terms of a binary operation ∘; their generalization to arbitrary n-ary operations is straightforward.

Axiom 1. *Closure: A is closed under the operation ∘, i.e. for any $a, b \in A$ there is an element $c \in A$ such that $a \circ b = c$.*

Axiom 2. *Uniqueness: If $a = a'$ and $b = b'$ then $a \circ b = a' \circ b'$.*

Closure and uniqueness in appropriate sets are ordinarily considered the minimal requirements for well-behaved operations. Admitting partial operations in an algebra is common in universal algebra and category theory, which are beyond the introductory scope of this book. (See Goldblatt (1979), Grätzer (1971), MacLane and Birkhoff (1983) and for discussion in the context of Montague grammar especially Janssen (1983).) We shall not be concerned with operations that do not satisfy closure and uniqueness. Various kinds of algebras can be obtained by adding further axioms to these two basic requirements. We will study a number of such algebras in this chapter.

We have already encountered many structures which are algebras in this sense. The syntax of the logic of statements, for instance, can be represented as an algebra based on the set of well-formed statements (S) and the connectives as operations: $\mathbf{A} = \langle\, S,\ \sim,\ \&,\ \vee,\ \rightarrow,\ \leftrightarrow\, \rangle$. Similarly, the semantics of the logic of statements can be considered as an algebra, based on the set of truth values and the truth tables, interpreting the connectives as operations: $\mathbf{B} = \langle\, \{0,1\},\ \sim,\ \&,\ \vee,\ \rightarrow,\ \leftrightarrow\, \rangle$, where the connectives are understood as operations on truth values, not as syntactic symbols. We will see below that there is an important connection between the syntactic algebra and the semantic algebra of such formal languages, which serve as models for the syntax and semantics of natural languages.

DEFINITION 9.1 *An algebra* $\mathbf{B}$ *is a subalgebra of an algebra* $\mathbf{A} = \langle\, A,\ f_1^A,\ f_2^A,\ \ldots, f_n^A\, \rangle$ *if* $\mathbf{B}$ *satisfies the following conditions:* $\mathbf{B} = \langle\, B,\ f_1^B,\ f_2^B,\ \ldots, f_n^B\, \rangle$, *where*

(i) $B \subseteq A$

(ii) *For every* i, $f_i^B = f_i^A{\restriction}B$; *i.e.,* f_i^B *yields the same values as* f_i^A *when restricted to elements of* B.

(iii) B *is closed under all operations* f_i^B

∎

9.2   Properties of operations

In Section 1.8 a number of properties of operations on sets were introduced. We repeat certain of these definitions here as properties of operations in algebras for easy reference and add a number of properties of operations which are frequently encountered in algebraic operations.

An operation $\circ$ from $A \times A$ to B is *associative* if and only if for all a, b, c in A, $(a \circ b) \circ c = a \circ (b \circ c)$. In an associative operation it is immaterial in what order repeated applications of it are made. Set-theoretic union and intersection and function composition are associative, as are logical conjunction and disjunction. Examples of non-associative operations are set-theoretic difference and division of real numbers.

An operation $\circ$ from $A \times A$ to B is *commutative* if and only if for all a, b in A, $a \circ b = b \circ a$. Familiar commutative operations are logical conjunction and disjunction; set intersection and union; and addition and multiplication of real numbers. Some non-commutative operations are subtraction, division and function composition.

An operation $\circ$ from $A \times A$ to B is *idempotent* if and only if for all a in A, $a \circ a = a$. Set-theoretic union and intersection are idempotent, as are logical conjunction and disjunction. But most of the operations we have encountered are not: addition, multiplication, subtraction, division, relative complementation and function composition are not idempotent operations.

For two operations $\circ_1$ and $\circ_2$ both from $A \times A$ to B, $\circ_1$ *distributes over* $\circ_2$ if and only if for all a, b, c in A, $a \circ_1 (b \circ_2 c) = (a \circ_1 b) \circ_2 (a \circ_1 c)$. We have seen that set-theoretic union distributes over intersection and vice versa. But, although arithmetic multiplication distributes over addition $(a \times (b + c) = (a \times b) + (a \times c))$, addition does not distribute over multiplication, since in general $a + (b \times c) \neq (a + b) \times (a + c)$.

9.3   Special elements

The next three notions are special properties which certain members of a set may have with respect to some operation defined on the set.

Given an operation $\circ$ from $A \times A$ to B, an element e_l is a *left identity element* of $\circ$ if and only if for all a in A, $e_l \circ a = a$. Similarly, e_r in A is a *right identity element* of $\circ$ if and only if for all a in A, $a \circ e_r = a$. As we saw in Section 2.4, for a function $F : A \to B$, if the operation $\circ$ denotes function composition, then $id_B \circ F = F$ and $F \circ id_A = F$. Thus for the operation of composition of functions the identity functions id_B and id_A are respectively a left and right identity element. Subtraction defined on the set of integers and zero has a right identity element, namely zero itself, since for all n, $n - 0 = n$. But there is no left identity element; i.e., there is no element m in the set such that for all n, $m - n = n$.

For commutative operations, every left identity element is also a right identity element, and vice versa. To see this, consider a left identity e_l . By definition $(\forall a \in A)(e_l \circ a = a)$. Because the operation is commutative, $e_l \circ a = a \circ e_l = a$, for all $a \in A$, and so e_l is also a right identity element. Similarly, every right identity is also a left identity for commutative operations. An element that is both a right and left identity element is called a *two-sided identity* or simply an *identity element*. While commutativity of an operation is a sufficient condition for every right or left identity to be two-sided, it is not a necessary condition; a two-sided identity may exist for some operations that are not commutative. An example of this is found in the operations of composition of functions defined on some set of functions $\mathbf{F} = \{F, G, H, \ldots\}$, each being a function in A. If id_A is one of these function, it is a two-sided identity, since for each $x \in F$, $id_A \circ x = x \circ id_A = x$, but the operation of composition of functions is not in general commutative. For addition the two-sided identity is 0, but for arithmetic multiplication it is 1, since for all n, $n + 0 = 0 + n = n$ and $n \times 1 = 1 \times n = n$. Given some collection of sets, the identity element for intersection is U, the universal set, and for union it is the empty set (verify!). Relative complementation has $\emptyset$ as a right identity but in general it has no left identity. It is provable that if for a given operation a two-sided identity exists, then this element is unique.

Given an operation $\circ$ from $A \times A$ to B with a two-sided identity element e, a given element a in A is said to have a *right inverse* a_r if and only if $a \circ a_r = e$. A given element a in A is said to have a *left inverse* a_l if and only if $a_l \circ a = e$. If a^{-1} is both a left and a right inverse of a, i.e. $a^{-1} \circ a = a \circ a^{-1} = e$, then a^{-1} is called a *two-sided inverse* of a. When the term 'inverse' is used without further qualification, we mean that it is two-sided. Note that inverses are always paired in the following way: b is a right inverse of a if and only if a is a left inverse of b, since both statements follow from $a \circ b = e$. One should observe also that the question of the existence of an inverse can be raised with respect to *each* element in the set on which the operation is defined. In contrast, an identity element, if it exists, is defined for the operation as a whole. To illustrate, let addition be defined in the set Z of all positive and negative integers and zero. As we have seen, 0 is the two-sided identity element for this operation. Consider now the number 3, and let us ask if it has an inverse in Z. Is there an element z in Z that when added to 3 yields 0? The number -3 is such an element, and, furthermore, it is both a right and a left inverse, since $3 + (-3) = (-3) + 3 = 0$. From this it also follows that 3 is a two-sided inverse of -3. For addition, every member of Z has an inverse, since to each integer z, except 0, there corresponds a negative integer $-z$, such that $z + (-z) = 0$. The number 0 is its own inverse, since $0 + 0 = 0$.

Given an operation $\circ$ from $A \times A$ to B, an element 0_l is called a *left zero of* $\circ$ if and only if for all a in A, $0_l \circ a = 0_l$. Similarly, 0_r is called a *right zero of* $\circ$ if and only if for all a in A, $a \circ 0_r = 0_r$. An element that is both a left and a right zero is called a *two-sided zero*, or simply a *zero*. This terminology derives from the fact that the number zero functions as a zero element in arithmetic multiplication. There is no zero element for subtraction or division. The empty set is a zero element for set intersection and the universal set U is the zero element for set union.

9.4 Maps and morphisms

Relations between algebras may be described by functions mapping one algebra in another; $F : \mathbf{A} \to \mathbf{B}$. Such a map is *injective* if some function $F : \mathbf{A} \to \mathbf{B}$ is one-to-one, i.e. $F(a) = F(b)$ implies $a = b$. $F : \mathbf{A} \to \mathbf{B}$ is *surjective* (or *onto*) if $\{F(a) \mid a \in A\} = B$. And $F : \mathbf{A} \to \mathbf{B}$ is *bijective* if F is both injective and surjective (or one-to-one and onto). A *morphism* is a mapping $F : \mathbf{A} \to \mathbf{B}$ conceived of dynamically as a transformation process of $\mathbf{A}$ into $\mathbf{B}$. If $\mathbf{A} = \langle A, f_1, \ldots, f_n \rangle$ and $\mathbf{B} = \langle B, g_1, \ldots, g_n \rangle$ then $\mathbf{A}$ and $\mathbf{B}$ are *isomorphic* if and only if there is a one-to-one correspondence between their operations (we will assume for simplicity that the correspondence is $f_i \leftrightarrow g_i$) and a one-to-one and onto function φ mapping A onto B such that for all $x, y, z, \ldots,$ in A and all $i \leq n$

$$g_i(\varphi(x), \varphi(y), \varphi(z), \ldots) = \varphi(f_i(x, y, z, \ldots)).$$

A *homomorphism* is a correspondence between algebras with all the properties of an isomorphism except that the mapping from A to B may be *many-to-one*; the set B may be smaller than the set A.

An *automorphism* of an algebra $\mathbf{A}$ is an isomorphism of $\mathbf{A}$ with itself. The identity mapping ($\varphi(x) = x$) always provides an automorphism for any algebra (the "trivial" automorphism); the question generally asked of a given algebra is whether it has any other ("non-trivial") automorphisms.

For instance, let $\mathbf{A} = \langle S, \sim, \&, \vee, \to, \leftrightarrow \rangle$, and $\mathbf{B} = \langle \{0,1\}, \sim, \&, \vee, \to, \leftrightarrow \rangle$, as defined above in 9.1.

Any assignment of truth-values to the statements in S is a homomorphism $F : \mathbf{A} \to \mathbf{B}$. *i.e.* distinct statements p, q may be mapped to the same truth-value, but

$$
\begin{aligned}
F(p \,\&\, q) &= F(p) \,\&\, F(q) \\
F(p \vee q) &= F(p) \vee F(q) \\
F(p \to q) &= F(p) \to F(q) \\
F(p \leftrightarrow q) &= F(p) \leftrightarrow F(q) \\
F(\sim p) &= \sim F(p)
\end{aligned}
$$

Construction of truth tables for complex statements can now be understood as based on the fact that, given an assignment to the atomic statements, the composition preserves the homomorphism from the syntactic algebra to the semantic one. This can be considered to be the algebraic counterpart of the Principle of Compositionality, often also espoused in one form or another for the syntax and semantics of natural languages. The principle requires the meaning of a complex expression to be a function of the meaning of its constituent parts and the way in which they are put together (See also Ch. 13). Homomorphisms can, of course, relate semantic algebras, e.g. by embedding a given interpretation into an extension of that interpretation. Extensive applications are made of these embeddings, for instance, in semantic theories based on dynamic interpretations and in Kripke semantics (see Ch. 12).

A simple example of an algebra A' which is isomorphic to A is a syntax of the statment logic which uses instead of p, q, r etc. for statements, a different alphabet, say the Greek letters ϕ, ψ, χ etc., and possibly alternative symbols for the connectives. If alphabetic variance is the only difference between two logical systems they are isomorphic from an algebraic point of view.

Throughout the remainder of this part of the book we will encounter more interesting mathematical examples of homomorphisms and isomorphisms.

Category theory, a relatively recent and flourishing development of algebra, studies properties of algebras that can be expressed in terms of morphisms. It provides a very abstract and universal perspective on the foundations of set theory, algebra and logic, in which cross-fertilization yields many new insights and results. The interested reader is referred to Goldblatt (1979) for an introduction.

Exercises

1. Consider the operation of intersection defined on some arbitrary collection of sets.

   (a) Is there a two-sided identity element?

   (b) Which sets have an inverse element?

2. Given an arbitrary collection of sets, what elements, if any, have inverses with respect to the operation of a) union and b) symmetric difference?

3. If for a given operation in an algebra a two-sided identity exists, it is unique. Prove this for the operation of set-theoretic union.

Chapter 10

Operational Structures

10.1 Groups

A *group* **G** is an algebra which consists of a set G and a single binary operation, which we will usually write as ∘, but which may sometimes be written + or × : **G** = $\langle G, \circ \rangle$. To be a group, **G** must satisfy the following conditions, the group axioms:

G1: **G** is an algebra (i.e. ∘ completely defined and G closed under ∘).
G2: ∘ is associative.
G3: G contains an identity element.
G4: Each element in G has an inverse element.

Note that a group operation does not have to be commutative. A group whose operation is commutative is a *commutative* or *Abelian group*.

We are already acquainted with some models of these group axioms.

a. The positive rational numbers with multiplication form a group: (G1) the product of any two positive rationals is a unique positive rational, (G2) multiplication is associative, (G3) 1 is the identity element, and (G4) every positive rational p/q has an inverse q/p. Furthermore this group is Abelian since multiplication is commutative.

b. The integers $\{0, 1, 2, 3\}$ form a group with the operation of addition modulo 4. (The sum of x and y modulo 4 is the remainder after dividing $x + y$ by 4; e.g. $3 + 7 = 2$ (modulo 4).) The verification of this will be left to the reader.

257

c. The set of all even integers under addition forms a group, but the set of all odd integers does not, since it does not contain an identity element, and it is not closed under addition.

d. The group of 'symmetries of the square' is an example of a different sort, since the elements of the set for this group are not numbers but the following rigid motions of a square:

R - a 90° clockwise rotation about its center O
R' - a 180° clockwise rotation about its center O
R" - a 270° clockwise rotation about its center O
I - a 360° clockwise rotation about its center O
H - a reflection in the horizontal axis through O
        (i.e. flipping the square about the horizontal axis)
V - a reflection in the vertical axis through O
D - a reflection in the diagonal in quadrant I and III
D' - a reflection in the diagonal in quadrants II and IV

The group operation is the successive performing or composition of any of these motions: e.g. $R \circ R = R'$. This group is not commutative, since, for instance, $R \circ H = D$ while $H \circ R = D'$.

The best way to compute the products of this group is to cut out a square of paper and label its sides so that the manipulations can actually be performed. First consider the front of the square:

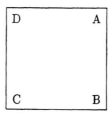

Figure 10–1.

Performing the operation defined as R will give the orientation shown in Figure 10–2:

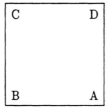

Figure 10-2.

Starting from the original orientation and performing R' gives the orientation shown in Figure 10-3; if we instead perform R'', the result is as shown in Figure 10-4.

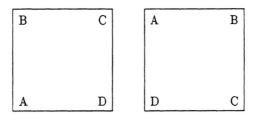

Figure 10-3.   Figure 10-4.

Performing the operation I from the original starting point of Figure 10-1, or from any other configuration, does not change the orientation at all; in fact I is the identity operation for the group. The simplest way to keep track of these operations is to label the front of the square as in Figure 10-5.

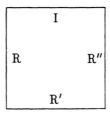

Figure 10-5.

At this point, the reader can verify such products as $R \circ R = R'$, $R \circ R' = R''$, $R' \circ R' = I$.

To label the back of the square, perform each of the reflections, starting each time from the I position, and label the side that comes out on top with the name of the operation. The relevant axes are as shown in Figure 10-6:

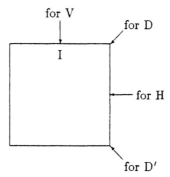

Figure 10-6.

The back of the square will then be labelled as in Figure 7, with V labelling the back of the same side that I labels on the front:

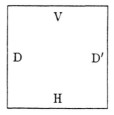

Figure 10-7.

Then the rest of the products can be verified; e.g., $H \circ R' = V$, $V \circ D = R$. Note that when you have, for instance, performed V and then want to perform D, you must find what is *then* the appropriate diagonal axis and reflect the square (i.e., turn it over) through that axis; the product is R, since the two operations in succession lead to the same orientation that R leads to directly.

It is recommended that such a square actually be constructed since this example recurs in several subsequent illustrations and problems.

From the group axioms we can prove the following elementary theorems.

THEOREM 10.1 *In any group, the equations $x \circ a = b$ and $a \circ y = b$ have the unique solutions $x = b \circ a^{-1}$ and $y = a^{-1} \circ b$ respectively.* ∎

Proof:

$$
\begin{aligned}
(b \circ a^{-1}) \circ a &= b \circ (a^{-1} \circ a) &\quad \text{associativity} \\
b \circ (a^{-1} \circ a) &= b \circ e &\quad \text{def. inverse} \\
b \circ e &= b &\quad \text{def. identity}
\end{aligned}
$$

Hence $(b \circ a^{-1}) \circ a = b$, so $x = b \circ a^{-1}$ is a solution of $x \circ a = b$. It is also the unique solution, since

$$x = x \circ e = x \circ (a \circ a^{-1}) = (x \circ a) \circ a^{-1}.$$

So if $x \circ a = b$, substitute b for $(x \circ a)$ in the last member of the equality above and observe that $x = b \circ a^{-1}$. Similarly for the unique solution $y = a^{-1} \circ b$ to $a \circ y = b$. ∎

The theorem provides an answer to the following general question: Consider any two elements of a group, a and b (they need not be distinct); will it be possible to find in the group more elements x such that $x \circ a = b$? The theorem says that there will always be exactly one such an element, namely whatever element is obtained by performing the operation on b and the inverse of a.

The first part of the proof shows that $b \circ a^{-1}$ is indeed such an x, by putting $b \circ a^{-1}$ in for x in the product $x \circ a$ and showing from the group axioms that the result must indeed be b. But this does not show that $b \circ a^{-1}$ is the *only* such x. The second part of the proof does this, in an indirect way. First it is established that for *any* element x of a group, $x = (x \circ a) \circ a^{-1}$. Now consider an arbitrary element x for which $x \circ a = b$. (We know already that there is at least one such element, but so far there could be more than one.) Then since $x = (x \circ a) \circ a^{-1}$ for *any* x, if we have an x for which $x \circ a = b$, we see that for such an x we can deduce $x = b \circ a^{-1}$; i.e., any solution of $x \circ a = b$ must be identical to the original solution, namely $b \circ a^{-1}$, which is to say that the solution is unique.

COROLLARY 10.1 *A group has only one identity element.* ∎

Proof: By the group definition, there is at least one solution to $e \circ x = e$, i.e. $x = e$. By Theorem 10.1, this is the only solution. ∎

Corollary 10.2 *A group has only one inverse a^{-1} for each element a.* ∎

Proof: By the group definition, there is at least one solution $y = a^{-1}$ to $a \circ y = e$. By Theorem 10.1, this solution is unique. ∎

Theorem 10.2 *A group with 4 or fewer elements must be commutative.* ∎

Proof:
    case (i): 1 element - trivial
    case (ii): 2 distinct elements e and a,

$$e \circ a = a \circ e = a \text{ (identity)}$$

    case (iii): 3 distinct elements e, a and b,

$$e \circ a = a \circ e = a \text{ (identity)}$$

$$e \circ b = b \circ e = b \text{ (identity)}$$

But $a \circ b \neq a$ because then b would equal e; and $a \circ b \neq b$ because then a would equal e; hence $a \circ b = e$. Similarly for $b \circ a$ hence $a \circ b = b \circ a = e$.

    case (iv): 4 distinct elements e, a, b and c,

$$e \circ a = a \circ e = a, \ e \circ b = b \circ e = b \text{ and } e \circ c = c \circ e = c \text{ (identity)}$$

Consider any two non-identity elements, e.g. a and b. The product $a \circ b$ cannot be either a or b, as above. If $a \circ b = e$, then $b = a^{-1}$ and hence $b \circ a = e$ also. If $a \circ b = c$, then $b \circ a$ cannot be a or b (violation of uniqueness of identity element), or e; in the last case b would be the inverse of a, so $a \circ b = e$, but we already have $a \circ b = c$. Hence $b \circ a = c$ also. In either case the group is commutative. ∎

    From the fact that the theorem only mentions up to 4-member groups, it should not be inferred that groups with 5 or more members may be non-commutative. In fact, it is provable, but tedious, that all 5-member groups must also be commutative. Groups with 6 or more members need not be commutative, however.

    The operation on a finite group is often given by a matrix. Rows and columns are labelled with members of the set. The value of $a \circ b$ is placed in the cell at the ath row and the bth column. Because of its similarity to

the multiplication table of the natural numbers less than 10, such a matrix
is generally referred to as a 'multiplication table'. Finding the value of $a \circ b$
is called 'multiplying a by b' even when the operation bears no resemblance
to the operation of multiplication. A word of caution: when constructing
an example of a finite group by its multiplication table, it is quite easy to
check for closure, the identity element and inverses by direct inspection of
the table. It is also straightforward to tell from the table whether a group
is commutative or not, i.e. the table is symmetric around the diagonal. But
a group operation must also be associative, and there is no simple way to
check associativity by inspection of the table; rather, one has to check each
instance of the operation.

10.2   Subgroups, semigroups and monoids

We define a subgroup G' as a subalgebra of G which is itself a group. We
give the following examples of subgroups as illustration.

   a. The group of even integers with addition is a proper subgroup of the
   group of all integers with addition.

   b. The group of all rotations of the square $\langle \{I, R, R', R''\}, \circ \rangle$ where $\circ$ is
   composition of operations as described above, is a subgroup of the
   group of all symmetries of the square as in Example (d) above.

   c. The system $\langle \{I, R, R'\}, \circ \rangle$ is *not* a subgroup of the group of all symmetries of the square; it is not a group and it is not even a subalgebra of
   the original group, because the given set $\{I, R, R'\}$ is not closed under
   the operation $\circ$.

   d. The set of all non-negative integers with addition is a *subalgebra* of the
   group of all integers with addition, because the non-negative integers
   are closed under addition. But it is not a *subgroup* because it is not
   itself a group: it is associative, and has an identity element (0), but all
   of the members of the set except 0 lack inverses.

The *order* of any group **G** is the number of members in the set G. An
important theorem of group theory states that the order of any subgroup
exactly divides, i.e. without remainder, the order of the parent group. For
instance, only subgroups of order 1, 2 and 4 are possible for a 4-member

group, these being the integral divisors of 4. The theorem does not guarantee that every subset having the proper number of members will give rise to a subgroup – only that if a subgroup exists, its order is a divisor of the order of the group. An immediate consequence of this theorem is that a group **G** of order 5 has only the trivial subgroups of order 1 (the identity element itself) and of order 5 (itself) as subgroup, since 5 has no other divisors.

A second theorem, of which we omit the proof since it uses notions that are not introduced here, states that if a group is *finite*, then all its non-empty subalgebras are also subgroups. The practical consequence of this theorem is that in checking whether a given system is a subgroup of a finite group, one only needs to verify that the given subset is not empty and is closed under the group operation, i.e. is a subalgebra. If these two conditions are met, there will necessarily be an identity element and inverses for each element. Example (b) above is such a case. Example (d) above shows the failure of a subalgebra to be a subgroup in an infinite case.

A third theorem about subgroups will be proven here.

THEOREM 10.3 *The intersection* $\mathbf{G'} \cap \mathbf{G''}$ *of two subgroups* $\mathbf{G'}$ *and* $\mathbf{G''}$ *of a group* $\mathbf{G}$ *is itself a subgroup of* $\mathbf{G}$.   ■

Proof:

(i) If a, b are in $\mathbf{G'} \cap \mathbf{G''}$, they must both be in both $\mathbf{G'}$ and $\mathbf{G''}$. $\mathbf{G'}$ and $\mathbf{G''}$ are groups, so $a \circ b$ is in both, hence $a \circ b$ is in $\mathbf{G'} \cap \mathbf{G''}$.

(ii) If a is in $\mathbf{G'} \cap \mathbf{G''}$, it is in both $\mathbf{G'}$ and $\mathbf{G''}$. $\mathbf{G'}$ and $\mathbf{G''}$ are groups, so a^{-1} is in both, hence $\mathbf{G'} \cap \mathbf{G''}$ must contain a^{-1}.

(iii) Since $\mathbf{G'}$ and $\mathbf{G''}$ are groups, they both contain e; hence $\mathbf{G'} \cap \mathbf{G''}$ must contain e.   ■

There are some useful algebraic structures which are weaker than groups and satisfy only some of the group axioms.

A *semigroup* is defined as an algebra which consists of a set and a binary associative operation $(G1 + G2)$. There need not be an identity element nor inverses for all the elements.

A *monoid* is defined as a semigroup which has an identity element $(G1, G2, G3)$. There need not be inverses for all the elements. An *Abelian monoid* is a monoid with a commutative operation.

Given these definitions, any group is a subgroup of itself, and a semigroup and a monoid as well. Every monoid is a semigroup, but not vice versa. Here are some telling examples.

  a. The set of all non-negative integers with addition is an Abelian monoid.

  b. The set of all positive integers (excluding zero) with addition is a semigroup but not a monoid.

Since both ordinary addition and ordinary multiplication are associative, it can be deduced that addition and multiplication modulo any n are also associative. Therefore any system with addition or multiplication, either ordinary or modulo some n, is a semigroup if it is closed and is a monoid if it also contains the appropriate identity element 0 or 1.

  c. The set of all positive even integers with ordinary multiplication is a semigroup but not a monoid, since 1 is missing.

  d. The set of all positive odd integers with ordinary multiplication is a monoid. (Closed since multiplication of odd integers yields only odd integers)

  e. The set $\{0,1,2,3,4\}$ with multiplication modulo 5 is a monoid.

  f. The set of all multiples of 10 which are greater than 100, i.e.

$$\{110, 120, 130, \ldots\}$$

with ordinary addition is a semigroup, but not a monoid.

None of the above examples are groups; in each example, one or more elements lack inverses. Note that where multiplication (modulo n) is involved no system which contains 0 can be a group, since 0 has no multiplicative inverse.

Submonoids are defined analogously to subgroups. M is a submonoid of the monoid M' iff M is a monoid and its identity element is the same as in M'. The stipulation that the identity elements must be the same is not necessary for subgroups, since there it is an automatic consequence. It is possible to find subsets of a monoid that themselves form monoids, however, but with different identity elements.

10.3   Integral domains

An *integral domain* **D** is an algebra consisting of a set D and two binary operations called 'addition' and 'multiplication', written $a + b$ and $a \cdot b$, respectively; $\mathbf{D} = \langle D, +, \cdot \rangle$, which satisfies the following axioms:

D1: **D** is an algebra.

D2: The set D with the operation $+$ forms an Abelian group with identity 0.

D3: The set D with the operation $\cdot$ forms an Abelian monoid with identity 1, and $1 \neq 0$.

D4: (Cancellation Law) If $c \neq 0$ and $c \cdot a = c \cdot b$, then $a = b$.

D5: (Distributive Law) For all a, b, c in D, $a \cdot (b + c) = (a \cdot b) + (a \cdot c)$.

The assumption in D3 that $1 \neq 0$ eliminates the 'trivial' case of the set containing only 0, which would otherwise be an integral domain under ordinary addition and multiplication. Axiom D4, which says that multiplication obeys the cancellation law except in the case of the additive identity 0, in effect recaptures a great deal of the structure lost by not requiring multiplicative inverses. In fact, whenever D is a *finite* set, Axiom D4 insures that every element except 0 has a multiplicative inverse.

Note that the distributive law is not symmetric between $\cdot$ and $+$; it will not in general be true that $a + (b \cdot c) = (a + b) \cdot (a + c)$. Aside from the requirement that $1 \neq 0$, the distributive law is the only axiom which requires there to be some connection between the two operations. Because integral domains have two operations, we need to introduce some new notation for inverses. In a group, where there is only one operation, a^{-1} unambiguously designated the inverse of a with respect to the given operation. For integral domains, we will use a^{-1} to designate the multiplicative inverse of a (if it has one; since not all elements need have inverses, this notation can be used only where it can be shown that an inverse exists). We will introduce the notation $-a$ to stand for the additive inverse of a, which by D2 always exists. Thus by definition $-a$ is the element which when added to a gives 0. For all of the infinite models mentioned below, this notation corresponds to our ordinary use of the minus sign, but it would be advisable to regard that correspondence as accidental (although clearly it is not) and throughout this section simply read '$-a$' as 'the additive inverse of a'.

In integral domains, as in ordinary arithmetic, the minus sign is also used as a binary operator, corresponding to the operation of subtraction.

We can define $b - a$ as that element x such that $x + a = b$. By Theorem 10.1 for groups the equation $x + a = b$ has the unique solution $b + (-a)$, so the operation $b - a$ is well defined. Thus the two uses of the minus sign are closely related. We could also have defined subtraction first, and then define $-a$ as $0 - a$. There is never any ambiguity, since subtraction is a binary operation, whereas the sign for the additive inverse is always prefixed to a single element.

The standard model of an integral domain is the set of all integers, positive, negative and 0, with ordinary addition and multiplication. Other examples of infinite integral domains are the set of all rational numbers and the set of real numbers, again with ordinary addition and multiplication. A less obvious model is the set of all rational numbers whose denominator is 1 or a power of 2. Still other models can be constructed. None of these sets form a group with multiplication, because there is no multiplicative inverse for 0 in any of them, i.e. no number which when multiplied by 0 gives 1. In the domain of the rationals or of the reals, 0 is the only element without a multiplicative inverse; in the domain of the integers, however, none of the elements except 1 itself has a multiplicative inverse.

In Section 8.5.5, we introduced an axiomatic characterization of several types of orderings for sets in general. Here we will show a different approach to a linear or simple ordering which can be used only for integral domains, since it makes use of the notions of addition and multiplication. The relation $\leq$ as defined below is a simple linear ordering, although we will not prove that assertion here.

Not all integral domains can be ordered; thus the ordered integral domains are a much more restricted class of systems that the integral domains. More restricted still are the ordered integral domains whose positive elements (to be defined below) are well-ordered. These integral domains in fact turn out to be isomorphic to the set of all integers with ordinary addition and multiplication and, of course, to each other. For this reason, these notions of ordering are of central importance in characterizing axiomatically our ordinary system of arithmetic with integers.

DEFINITION 10.1 *An integral domain* **D** *is said to be ordered by a relation* $\leq$ *if the following axioms hold:*

(i) Addition law. *For all a,b,c and d if $a \leq b$ and $c \leq d$, then $a + c \leq b + d$*

(ii) Multiplication law. *If $a \leq b$ and $0 \leq c$, then $a \cdot c \leq b \cdot c$*

(iii) Law of trichotomy. *For any a and b, one and only one of the following holds: a < b, a = b, or a > b (also called connectedness).*

∎

We have already shown that subtraction can be defined in any integral domain: $b - a$ is equal to $b + (-a)$. We now make use of subtraction to define the properties of being *positive* or *negative* for elements of ordered integral domains.

DEFINITION 10.2 *An element a of an ordered integral domain is* positive *if and only if $a > 0$; a is negative if and only if $a < 0$. The three basic axioms for the ordering relation < are reflected by three similar properties of positive elements:*

(i') Addition. *The sum of two positive elements is positive.*

(ii') Multiplication. *The product of two positive elements is positive.*

(iii') Trichotomy. *For any given element a, one and only one of the following holds: a is positive, $a = 0$ or $-a$ is positive.*

∎

The proof of these is left to the reader.

As remarked above, not all integral domains can be ordered. Among the integral domains which can be ordered are the familiar infinite ones: the set of integers, or the set of all rational numbers, or the set of all real numbers, all with ordinary addition and multiplication and $\leq$ interpreted as 'less than or equal to' in the usual sense. If we add to the axioms for ordering a further axiom for well-ordering for positive elements only, we will have a formal system all of whose models turn out to be isomorphic to the integers with respect to addition, multiplication and $\leq$.

DEFINITION 10.3 *A subset S of an ordered integral domain is* well-ordered *if each non-empty subset S' of S contains a smallest element, i.e. an element a such that $a < x$ for every x in S'.*   ∎

The new axiom for well-orderings, which depends on the prior introduction of the axioms for orderings and on the definition of 'positive' already given, can be stated as follows:

Well-ordering axiom: The positive elements are well-ordered.

To illustrate the use of the well-ordering principle, we prove that in any well-ordered integral domain, there is no element between 0 (the additive identity) and 1 (the multiplicative identity). For the standard model, namely the integers, the theorem may seem obvious, but it is not so obvious how to prove it from the axioms for the well-ordered integral domains.

THEOREM 10.4   *There is no element between 0 and 1 in any well-ordered integral domain.*   ■

Proof: Assume, for a *reductio ad absurdum* proof, that there is at least one element c with $0 < c < 1$, i.e. the class of such elements is not empty. By the well-ordering axiom, there is a *least* element m in this class, and $0 < m < 1$, so $0 < m$ and $0 < (1 - m)$. By the multiplication law for positive elements of an ordered integral domain, $0 < m \cdot (1 - m)$, i.e. $0 < m - m^2$, so $m^2 < m$. By the same axiom, $0 < m \cdot m$, i.e. $0 < m^2$. Then by the transitivity of $<$, $0 < m^2 < m < 1$. The m^2 is another element in the class of elements between 0 and 1, which is, moreover, smaller than m. But m was by definition the minimum element in the class, (contradiction!). So there is no element between 0 and 1.   ■

THEOREM 10.5   *A set S of positive integers which includes 1, and which includes $n + 1$ whenever it includes n, includes every positive integer.*   ■

Proof: We will prove by *reductio ad absurdum* that the set S', consisting of those positive integers not in S, is empty. Assume that S' is not empty, then it contains a least element m. But $m \neq 1$ by hypothesis. By Theorem 4 there is no positive integer smaller than 1, so $m > 1$. That means $m - 1$ is positive. Since m is the smallest positive integer not in the set S, $m - 1$ is in the set S, since $m - 1 < m$. Then, by hypothesis, $(m - 1) + 1$ is also in S, but $(m - 1) + 1 = m$, so m in in S. Contradiction!   ■

We can now prove directly that Peano's fifth postulate (see Sections 8.4 and 8.5.7) holds for the positive integers.

Principle of Finite Induction. Associate with each positive integer n a statement $P(n)$ which is either true or false. If (i) $P(1)$ is true, and (ii) for all k, $P(k)$ implies $P(k + 1)$, then $P(n)$ is true for all positive integers n.

Proof: The set of those integers k for which $P(k)$ is true satisfies the hypothesis, and hence the conclusion of Theorem 10.5.   ∎

To illustrate the application of the principle of finite induction in proofs, we will use it to prove one of the laws of exponents in integral domains, for which we first need to give a definition.

DEFINITION 10.4 *A positive power a^n of a in any integral domain D is defined recursively by (i) $a^1 = a$, (ii) $a^{n+1} = a^n \cdot a$.*   ∎

Using this definition, we can prove by induction that in any integral domain $(a \cdot b)^n = a^n \cdot b^n$ for all n. First of all, we view the statement of the theorem as expressing a property of n; $P(n) = (a \cdot b)^n = a^n \cdot b^n$. This is the first step in setting up any proof by induction, but it is often left implicit.

The proof itself has two parts: first we prove $P(1)$, and then we prove that for arbitrary k, $P(k)$ implies $P(k + 1)$.

(*i*) $P(1)$:

$$
\begin{aligned}
(a \cdot b)^1 &= a \cdot b && \text{by definition} \\
&= a^1 \cdot b^1 && \text{by definition}
\end{aligned}
$$

(*ii*) $P(k) \to P(k + 1)$:

$$
\begin{aligned}
(a \cdot b)^k &= a^k \cdot b^k && \text{cond. premise} \\
(a \cdot b)^{k+1} &= (a \cdot b)^k \cdot (a \cdot b) && \text{by definition} \\
&= (a^k \cdot b^k) \cdot (a \cdot b) && \text{cond. premise} \\
&= a^k \cdot (b^k \cdot (a \cdot b)) && \text{associativity} \\
&= a^k \cdot ((b^k \cdot a) \cdot b) && \text{associativity} \\
&= a^k \cdot ((a \cdot b^k) \cdot b) && \text{commutativity} \\
&= a^k \cdot (a \cdot (b^k \cdot b)) && \text{associativity} \\
&= (a^k \cdot a) \cdot (b^k \cdot b) && \text{associativity} \\
&= a^{k+1} \cdot b^{k+1} && \text{by definition}
\end{aligned}
$$

$[(a \cdot b)^k = a^k \cdot b^k] \to [(a \cdot b)^{k+1} = a^{k+1} \cdot b^{k+1}]$ cond. proof

From (i) and (ii) it follows by the principle of finite induction that $P(n)$ is true for all positive integers n, i.e. that for all positive n, $(a \cdot b)^n = a^n \cdot b^n$.

We have introduced here the well-ordering principle, and hence induction, for the positive integers. An alternative approach is to state both the well-ordering principle and induction for the non-negative integers, in which case the first step in an induction proof would be for the case of $n = 0$. The two approaches are interdefinable.

10.4   Morphisms

Since the notions of homomorphism and isomorphism are defined for algebras in general, it is possible to define a morphism between algebras of different sorts, as long as they have the same number of operations. Here we give an example of a homomorphism between a monoid and a group, and then discuss some group isomorphisms and an isomorphism between two integral domains.

Consider the monoid $M = \langle N, + \rangle$ consisting of all the non-negative integers with the operation of ordinary addition. M is not a group because of the absence of inverses. Let the group $G = \langle G = \{0,1,2,3,4\}, + \bmod 5\rangle$. We can define a homomorphism from M to G by the function $F(n)$ which maps each non-negative integer in N onto the element of G which is congruent with it modulo 5. (Numbers which are congruent mod 5 leave the same remainder after division by 5.) For example, $F(16) = 1$, $F(23) = 3$, $F(45) = 0$, etc. The function F establishes a homomorphism, since $F(x) + F(y)$ $((\bmod 5)) = F(x + y)$. The *kernel* of a homomorphism F is defined as the set of elements of the domain of F which are mapped onto the identity element in the range of F. In this example, the kernel of the homomorphism $F : M \to G$ is the set of all non-negative multiples of $5 : \{0,5,10,15,\ldots\}$.

The definition of isomorphisms for groups is a direct application of the definition of isomorphisms for algebras in general. Since a group has only one operation, we can say simply that an isomorphism between two groups $G = \langle G, \circ \rangle$ and $G' = \langle G', \circ' \rangle$ is a one-to-one correspondence between their elements which preserves the group operation, which may be distinct operations in the two groups. I.e., if a is mapped to a', and b to b' and vice versa, then $a \circ b$ is mapped to $a' \circ' b'$ and vice versa. Putting it more formally, an isomorphism between two groups $G = \langle G, \circ \rangle$ and $G' = \langle G', \circ' \rangle$ is a one-to-one correspondence $F : G \to G'$ such that for all x, y in G, $F(x) \circ' F(y) = F(x \circ y)$. Here are two examples of such group isomorphisms.

Example 1: The group of integers $\{1,2,3,4\}$ under multiplication modulo 5 is isomorphic with the group of the integers $\{0,1,2,3\}$ under addition modulo 4, with the correspondence

$$1 \longleftrightarrow 0, 2 \longleftrightarrow 1, 3 \longleftrightarrow 3, 4 \longleftrightarrow 2$$

This is best illustrated by the group tables

+ (mod 4)	0	1	2	3
0	0	1	2	3
1	1	2	3	0
2	2	3	0	1
3	3	0	1	2

× (mod 5)	1	2	4	3
1	1	2	4	3
2	2	4	3	1
4	4	3	1	2
3	3	1	2	4

Example 2: The group of integers $\{0,1,2,3\}$ under addition modulo 4 is also isomorphic with the group of rotations of the square: let

$$0 \longleftrightarrow I, 1 \longleftrightarrow R, 2 \longleftrightarrow R', 3 \longleftrightarrow R''$$

We can prove that isomorphisms are equivalence relations on the set of all groups.

THEOREM 10.6 *The relation 'is isomorphic to' is a reflexive, symmetric and transitive relation between groups.* ∎

Proof: The reflexive property is trivial, since every group is isomorphic to itself by the identity mapping. As for the symmetric property, let F be an isomorphic correspondence between G and G'. Since F is one-to-one, it has an inverse F^{-1} which is an isomorphism of G' onto G. Finally, if F_1 maps G isomorphically onto G', and F_2 maps G' isomorphically onto G'', then the composition of $F_2 \circ F_1$, the function whose value for a given argument a is the value of F_2 applied to $F_1(a)$, is an isomorphism of G with G''. ∎

An isomorphism between two integral domains **D** and **D'** is a one-to-one correspondence of the elements a of D with the elements a' of D', which satisfies for all elements a, b in D the conditions

1) $(a + b)' = a' + b'$

2) $(a \cdot b)' = a' \cdot b'$

For an example of an isomorphism between two integral domains, let us start from the following facts about reckoning with even and odd numbers.

even + even = odd + odd = even
even + odd = odd + even = odd
even · even = even · odd = odd · even = even
odd · odd = odd

We can regard these identities as definitions of operations of 'addition' and 'multiplication' in a new algebra of the two elements 'even' and 'odd'. This algebra is isomorphic to the finite integral domain I_2 of integers modulo 2, with ordinary addition and multiplication modulo 2, under the correspondence *even* $\longleftrightarrow$ 0 and *odd* $\longleftrightarrow$ 1.

Exercises

1. Show that the integers 0,1,2, and 3 form a group with the operation of addition modulo 4, i.e. show that each of the four group axioms is satisfied. You need not give a full demonstration of associativity—just 2 or 3 examples.

2. Which of the following are groups?

    (a) The integers 1,3,5,7,8 under multiplication modulo 11.

    (b) The integers 1,3,4,5,9 under multiplication modulo 11.

    (c) The system described by the following multiplication table:

$\circ$	a	b	c	d
a	a	b	c	d
b	b	a	d	c
c	c	d	a	a
d	d	c	b	b

    (d) The system described by the following table:

$\circ$	a	b	c	d
a	b	d	a	c
b	d	c	b	a
c	a	b	c	d
d	c	a	d	b

    (e) The set of all subsets of $S = \{x_1, x_2\}$ with the operation of set union.

    (f) The same set S as in (e) with the operation of set intersection.

    (g) The set of rigid motions of a square $\{I, H, V, R'\}$ and the operation of performing them successively.

    (h) The set of rigid motions of a square $\{I, D, R\}$ and the operation of performing them successively.

3. (a) Draw the group operation table for the group of symmetries of
       the square $\{I, R, R', R'', H, V, D, D'\}$.

   (b) There are three different subgroups having exactly four elements.
       Find them and draw their group operation tables.

   (c) There are five different subgroups having exactly two elements.
       Find them and draw their tables.

   (d) Show which of the subgroups in (b) are isomorphic.

   (e) Show a non-trivial automorphism for one of the subgroups of (b).

   (f) Show a homomorphism of one of the subgroups of (b) with one
       of the subgroups of (c).

4. Prove that the set consisting of the identity element alone is a subgroup
   for any group.

5. (a) Does the set $\{1, 2, 3, 4, 5\}$ form a group with multiplication mod-
       ulo 6? Justify your answer.

   (b) Show that the set $\{1, 2, 3, 4, 5, 6\}$ forms a group with multiplica-
       tion modulo 7.

   (c) Find three different proper subgroups of the group in (b).

   (d) Find a set of integers which forms a group with *addition* modulo
       some n which is isomorphic to the group in (b).

   (e) Can you find a general condition on n which will identify all those
       n's for which the set $\{1, 2, \ldots, n - 1\}$ forms a group with multi-
       plication modulo n? Prove your assertion if possible, otherwise
       explain why you think it is correct.

6. Prove that if S is a subgroup of S′ and S′ is a subgroup of S″, then S
   is a subgroup of S″.

7. (a) The set R of all strictly positive rational numbers with multipli-
       cation forms a monoid which is also a group. Find a *sub*-monoid
       R_0 of R such that R_0 is *not* a group.

   (b) Is the set of all rational numbers with multiplication a semigroup?
       A monoid? A group?

8. Determine whether the set-theoretic operation 'symmetric difference' is
   commutative, associative and idempotent. Is there an identity element
   for this operation? What sets, if any, have inverses? Given the set

$A = \{a, b\}$ what sort of operational structure is formed by the power-set of A with the operation of symmetric difference?

9. Let $A = \{a, b\}$. Show that $\langle \wp(A), \cup \rangle$ and $\langle \wp(A), \cap \rangle$ are both semigroups but not groups. Find an isomorphism between them.

10. (a) Prove that if a, b and c are any elements of an integral domain $\mathbf{D}$, then $a + b = a + c$ implies $b = c$. (Hint: make use of the fact that a has an additive inverse.)

    (b) Prove that for all a in D, $a \circ 0 = 0 \circ a = 0$. (Hint: Use $a + 0 = a$ and the distributive law to prove that $a \circ (a + 0) = a \circ a$ and $a \circ (a + 0) = (a \circ a) + (a \circ 0)$. Note: $\circ$ is used here for 'multiplication'.)

    (c) Justify each step in the following proof of $(-a) \circ (-b) = a \circ b$. (Note: $-a$ and $-b$ are names given to the additive inverses of a and b).

    (1) $[a \circ b + a \circ (-b)] + (-a) \circ (-b) = a \circ b + [a \circ (-b) + (-a) \circ (-b)]$

    (2) $[a \circ b + a \circ (-b)] + (-a) \circ (-b) = a \circ b + [a + (-a)] \circ (-b)$

    (3) $[a \circ b + a \circ (-b)] + (-a) \circ (-b) = a \circ b + 0 \circ (-b)$

    (4) $[a \circ b + a \circ (-b)] + (-a) \circ (-b) = a \circ b$

    (5) $[a \circ b + a \circ (-b)] + (-a) \circ (-b) = a \circ [b + (-b)] + (-a) \circ (-b)$

    (6) $[a \circ b + a \circ (-b)] + (-a) \circ (-b) = a \circ 0 + (-a) \circ (-b)$

    (7) $[a \circ b + a \circ (-b)] + (-a) \circ (-b) = (-a) \circ (-b)$

    (8) $(-a) \circ (-b) = a \circ b$

11. Prove the law of transitivity for $<$ in an ordered integral domain, i.e. for any a, b, and c, if $a < b$ and $b < c$ then $a < c$.

12. Using the definition of positive elements, deduce the three basic laws
of positive elements, (i'), (ii') and (iii') in Def. 10.2, from the laws for
$<$.

13. The definition of any positive power a^n of a in any integral domain **D**
is given by:

$$a^1 = a$$
$$a^{n+1} = a^n \circ a$$

(a) Prove by induction that $a^m \circ a^n = a^{m+n}$ in any integral domain.
(Hint: Use induction on n; in the second part of the induction,
assume that $a^m \circ a^n = a^{m+n}$ for all m and for $n = k$ and prove
that it must then hold for all m and for $n = k+1$).

(b) Prove by induction that in any integral domain $(a^m)^n = (a^n)^m$.
(Hint: You will probably want to make use of the theorem that
$a^n \circ b^n = (a \circ b)^n$ which was proven in this chapter.)

Chapter 11

Lattices

11.1 Posets, duality and diagrams

In the previous chapter we have seen that the arithmetical properties of elements of formal systems may be described in operational structures. Operations may serve to generate new elements from a given set of basic elements, and thus we may view an operational or an algebraic structure naturally as a syntactic system which generates elements in a formally precise way. The relation of this dynamic conception of such systems and the linguistic notion of a grammar which generates strings as elements of a natural or formal language will be explored in much more detail in Part E. The present chapter is concerned with certain ordering relations between elements of systems or domains of objects and the order-theoretic or 'topological' properties of such ordered structures. We will see that the concepts introduced in this chapter provide a universal perspective on set theory and algebra in which important correlations between the two mathematical theories can be insightfully described. Recently linguistic applications of lattices have been made primarily to semantic topics such as plural NPs, mass terms and events, using the ordering relations to structure the domains of an interpretation of a language. The potential usefulness in linguistics of syntactic applications of lattice theory is explored in research on feature systems, for instance. In this chapter we will introduce lattice theory without paying attention to any particular linguistic applications or motivations.

In Chapter 3 we pointed out the set-theoretic importance of partial orderings on sets, i.e. sets of objects ordered by a reflexive, anti-symmetric and transitive relation. Here we will call any partially ordered set A together with its ordering $\leq$, i.e. $\langle A, \leq \rangle$, a *poset*, often writing just A and tacitly assuming the intended partial ordering, which is widely accepted practice.

A poset which also satisfies the property of linearity (for all $a, b \in A$: $a \leq b$ or $b \leq a$) is called a *chain*, or a *fully* or *linearly ordered set*. Additional properties and operations may be defined on posets which constitute a stronger structure. Thus the real numbers form a poset, but also a chain, disregarding the arithmetical operations.

If A is a poset and $a, b \in A$, then a and b are *comparable elements* or *comparable objects* if $a \leq b$ or $b \leq a$. If a and b are not comparable, they are *incomparable*, written as $a \parallel b$. In a chain there are of course no incomparable elements.

In an arbitrary poset A we define an upper bound of $B \subseteq A$ as an element $a \in A$, if it exists, such that for all $b \in B$, $b \leq a$. An upper bound a of B is *the least upper bound of B* (abbreviated to *lub* of B) or *the supremum of B* (abbreviated to sup B) if, for any upper bound c of B, we have $a \leq c$. We often write $a = \bigvee B$, or $a = $ sup B, since by antisymmetry of the ordering relation we know that if B has a least upper bound, this is a unique least upper bound.

If $\langle A, \leq \rangle$ is a poset, then inversion of the partial ordering preserves the poset characteristics, i.e. writing $a \geq b$ for $b \leq a$ in the given poset we have defined a new poset $\langle A, \geq \rangle$. Verification of the three requirements on a partial order in this new poset $\langle A, \geq \rangle$ is straightforward: e.g., antisymmetry holds since if $a \geq b$ and $b \geq a$, the definition of $\geq$ gives us $b \leq a$ and $a \leq b$, and we know that in $\langle A, \leq \rangle$ in that case $a = b$. We call $\langle A, \geq \rangle$ the *dual* of $\langle A, \leq \rangle$, which is obviously a symmetric relation between posets. This notion will come in handy in proving statements about posets, since it allows us to replace all occurrences of $\leq$ in a true statement S by $\geq$, thus obtaining the (equally true) dual S' of S, without actually carrying out the entire proof for the inverse of the partial ordering.

To appreciate the importance of this duality in posets, we define the dual of an upper bound of $B \subseteq A$, called a *lower bound of $B \subseteq A$*, as an element $a \in A$ such that for all $b \in B$, $b \geq a$ which is equivalent to $a \leq b$. A lower bound a of B is *the greatest lower bound of B* (abbreviated to *glb* of B) or *the infimum of B* (abbreviated to inf B) if, for any lower bound c of B we have $a \geq c$. We write $a = \bigwedge B$, or $a = $ inf B. Supremum and infimum are thus duals; hence whatever we may prove about one of them holds also of the other. For instance, we proved above that if a subset B in a poset has a supremum, it has a unique supremum, so we know by duality that the infimum of B, if its exists, is unique.

Partial orderings may be represented visually by so called Hasse diagrams. The *diagram* of a poset $\langle A, \le \rangle$ represents the elements or objects by o, and if the ordering relation holds between two elements, they are connected by a line, reflecting the order from bottom to top in the representation.

For instance, writing out the ordering set-theoretically, let the poset $A = \{\langle 0,0 \rangle, \langle 0,a \rangle, \langle 0,b \rangle, \langle 0,1 \rangle, \langle a,a \rangle, \langle a,1 \rangle, \langle b,b \rangle, \langle b,1 \rangle, \langle 1,1 \rangle\}$. Assuming reflexivity and transitivity of the connecting lines, we represent A by the diagram in Figure 11-1 (cf. the immediate successor diagrams of Section 3-5).

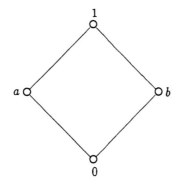

Figure 11–1: The diagram of a poset
$A = \langle \{0, a, b, 1\}, \le \rangle$.

We call a diagram *planar* or *flat* if it does not contain any intersecting lines, as in Figure 11-1. In general greater clarity of representation is obtained if the number of intersecting lines is kept as small as possible. From Figure 11-1 we can read off that $0 \le 1$ since we assumed transitivity of the connecting lines, and also we generally know that $x \le x$ for any arbitrary element x.

We say that a *covers* b (or that b *is covered by* a) if $a > b$ and for no $c : a > c > b$. (Recall that $a < b$ means $a \le b$ and $a \ne b$.) By induction on the length of chains, we may prove that the covering relation determines the partial ordering in a *finite* poset.

Diagrams usually represent finite posets, but infinite posets are sometime partially represented by diagrams and need further explanation in the text. Note that the real and the rational numbers, despite their essential order-theoretic differences, are represented by the same linear diagram, due to the 'poverty' of the covering relation which determines the diagram. Dualization of a given poset turns the diagram upside down, but preserves the connecting lines.

Set-theoretic inclusion induces a natural partial order on the power set of a given set A, i.e., $\wp(A)$ is a poset. We represent this inclusion relation on the power set for the set $A = \{a, b, c\}$ in Figure 11-2.

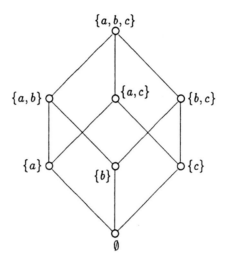

Figure 11–2: The diagram of the poset $\wp(A)$
for $A = \{a, b, c\}$.

Intersecting lines may not define an element. In Figure 11-3 a poset is represented in which all pairs of elements have an upper and lower bound, but these are not always unique. E.g., both c and d are upper bounds for $\{a, b\}$, but neither c nor d is a supremum for $\{a, b\}$.

11.2   Lattices, semilattices and sublattices

There is a special class of posets, called *lattices*, which have proven to be very important in the general study of a variety of mathematical theories including analysis, topology, logic, algebra and geometry. They have led to many

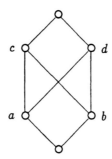

Figure 11–3: The diagram of a poset with
non-unique upper and lower bounds

fruitful interactions and new results in various theories and to a productive development of universal algebra and more recently category theory. Linguistic applications of lattice theory are currently being developed in syntax and semantics.

There are two ways of defining lattices, one from a given poset and the other, more in line with the group-theoretic definitions, by requiring properties on operations. We present the two definitions in this order.

A poset $\langle A, \leq \rangle$ is a *lattice* if $\sup\{a, b\}$ and $\inf\{a, b\}$ exist for all $a, b \in A$. We will introduce two new operations $a \wedge b = \inf\{a, b\}$, calling $a \wedge b$ the *meet* of a and b, and $a \vee b = \sup\{a, b\}$, calling $a \vee b$ the *join* of a and b. In lattices the operations of meet and join are always binary, i.e., we may view them dynamically as maps from $A \times A$ to A. This allows us to characterize a lattice as an algebra, i.e. as a non-empty set with two operations with certain algebraic properties. The four properties characteristic of lattice operations are:

(L1) $a \wedge a = a, a \vee a = a$ idempotent law

(L2) $a \wedge b = b \wedge a, a \vee b = b \vee a$ commutative law

(L3) $(a \wedge b) \wedge c = a \wedge (b \wedge c)$ associative laws
$(a \vee b) \vee c = a \vee (b \vee c)$

The important fourth property of lattice operations connects the two operations. Note first that if $a \leq b$, then $\inf\{a, b\} = a$, i.e. $a \wedge b = a$, and dually, if $a \geq b$, then $\sup\{a,b\} = a$, i.e., $a \vee b = a$. Since $a \leq a \vee b$ by definition of $\sup\{a,b\}$, we let $a \vee b$ substitute for b in the first equations to derive $a \wedge (a \vee b) = a$. Similarly, since $a \geq a \wedge b$ by definition of $\inf\{a,b\}$, we derive from the second equations $a \vee (a \wedge b) = a$. Thus we have the two absorption laws:

(L4) $\quad a \wedge (a \vee b) = a$ $\qquad\qquad$ absorption law
$\qquad\quad a \vee (a \wedge b) = a$

Any algebra with two binary operations that have these four properties (L1)–(L4) constitutes a lattice. It will often be very useful to view lattices as algebras, since all that we know about algebraic structures can readily be transferred to lattices. In fact, we often make use of the following theorem, provable from (L1)–(L4), about the connection between lattices represented as posets and lattices represented as algebras.

THEOREM 11.1

(i) Let the poset $\mathbf{A} = \langle A, \leq \rangle$ be a lattice. Set $a \wedge b = \inf\{a,b\}$ and $a \vee b = \sup\{a,b\}$. Then the algebra $\mathbf{A}^{\mathbf{a}} = \langle A, \wedge, \vee \rangle$ is a lattice.

(ii) Let the algebra $\mathbf{A} = \langle A, \wedge, \vee \rangle$ be a lattice. Set $a \leq b$ iff $a \wedge b = a$. Then $\mathbf{A}^{\mathbf{P}} = \langle A, \leq \rangle$ is a poset and the poset $\mathbf{A}^{\mathbf{P}}$ is a lattice.

(iii) Let the poset $\mathbf{A} = \langle A, \leq \rangle$ be a lattice. Then $(\mathbf{A}^{\mathbf{a}})^{\mathbf{P}} = \mathbf{A}$.

(iv) Let the algebra $\mathbf{A} = \langle A, \wedge, \vee \rangle$ be a lattice. Then $(\mathbf{A}^{\mathbf{P}})^{\mathbf{a}} = \mathbf{A}$.

■

Proof: (i) We leave it to the reader to verify that the meet and join operations as defined in (i) satisfy (L1)–(L4). Absorption becomes $a = \sup\{a, \inf\{a,b\}\}$, which is clearly true since $\inf\{a,b\} \leq a$.
(ii) From $a \wedge a = a$ follows $a \leq a$ (reflexive). If $a \leq b$ and $b \leq a$ then $a \wedge b = a$ and $b \wedge a = b$; hence $a = b$ (anti-symmetry). If $a \leq b$ and $b \leq c$ then $a \wedge b = a$ and $b \wedge c = b$, so $a = a \wedge b = a \wedge (b \wedge c) = (a \wedge b) \wedge c = a \wedge c$; hence $a \leq c$ (transitivity). I.e., $\leq$ is a partial order on A. To show that this poset is a lattice we verify existence of sup and inf for any a,b in A. From $a = a \wedge (a \vee b)$ and $b = b \wedge (a \vee b)$ follows $a \leq a \vee b$ and $b \leq a \vee b$. So $a \vee b$ is an upper bound of both a and b. We now want to show that it is a least upper bound, i.e., if for some c, $a \leq c$ and $b \leq c$, then $a \vee b \leq c$. Suppose

$a \leq c$ and $b \leq c$ then $a \vee c = (a \wedge c) \vee c = c$ and similarly for $b \vee c = c$, so $(a \vee c) \vee (b \vee c) = c \vee c = c$. Hence $(a \vee b) \vee c = c$. Absorption gives us $(a \vee b) \wedge c = (a \vee b) \wedge [(a \vee b) \vee c] = a \vee b$, i.e. $a \vee b \leq c$. Thus $a \vee b = \sup\{a,b\}$. Dual reasoning gives us $a \wedge b = \inf\{a,b\}$.

(iii) and (iv) check to see that the orderings in $(\mathbf{A}^{\mathbf{a}})^{\mathbf{P}}$, $\mathbf{A}$ and $(\mathbf{A}^{\mathbf{P}})^{\mathbf{a}}$ are the same. ∎

These facts guarantee a smooth transition between lattices as posets and as algebras. We may choose whatever perspective is most convenient for our purposes, while knowing that all results will be preserved when the same lattice is represented differently.

Duality in lattices as algebras is simply obtained by exchanging the two operations in any statement about lattices.

Next we consider parts of the structure of a lattice and we will see that the algebraic definition and the order-theoretic definition of a lattice show some discrepancy concerning their substructures.

If $\mathbf{L}$ is a lattice and $\mathbf{L}'$ is a non-empty subset of $\mathbf{L}$ such that for every pair of elements a,b in $\mathbf{L}'$ both $a \wedge b$ and $a \vee b$ are in $\mathbf{L}'$ (where $\wedge$ and $\vee$ are the lattice operations of $\mathbf{L}$), then $\mathbf{L}'$ with the same operations restricted to $\mathbf{L}'$ is a *sublattice* of $\mathbf{L}$. If $\mathbf{L}'$ is a sublattice of $\mathbf{L}$, then for any a,b in $\mathbf{L}'$ $a \leq b$ is in $\mathbf{L}'$ iff $a \leq b$ is in $\mathbf{L}$. But note that for a given lattice $\mathbf{L}$ there may be subsets which as posets are lattices, but which do not preserve the meets and joins of $\mathbf{L}$, and hence are not sublattices of $\mathbf{L}$. An example is given in Figure 11-4 where $\mathbf{L} = \langle \{a,b,c,d,e\}, \leq \rangle$ and $\mathbf{L}' = \langle \{a,c,d,e\}, \leq' \rangle$, which is a lattice as poset but which is not a sublattice of $\mathbf{L}$, since in $\mathbf{L}$ $c \vee d = b$ whereas in $\mathbf{L}'$ $c \vee d = a$.

In the next section we will come to understand the reason for defining the sublattice notion algebraically, rather than on the poset representation of a lattice. For the present it suffices to note that the algebraic sublattice notion is stronger than the sub-poset which is also a lattice. It is important to realize that the above theorem about the equivalences between poset representation and algebraic representation of a lattice may break down once we have to consider parts of their structure. There are lattice-theoretic structures which are 'weaker' in the sense of representing just parts of a lattice with less of its structure. The following notions are special cases of sublattices called *semilattices*. A poset is a *join semilattice* if $\sup\{a,b\}$ exists for any elements a,b. Dually, a poset is a *meet semilattice* if $\inf\{a,b\}$ exists for any a,b. In a diagram, conventionally, a join semilattice is represented top-down, and a meet semilattice bottom-up. There are again equivalent

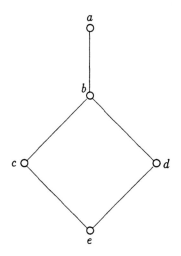

Figure 11–4: The sub-poset
$L' = \langle \{a, c, d, e\}, \leq \rangle$ is a lattice, and a
subalgebra, but not a sublattice.

algebraic definitions: If $\langle A, \circ \rangle$ is an algebra with one binary operation $\circ$, it is a semilattice if $\circ$ is idempotent, commutative and associative. Theorem 11-1 for poset and algebraic representations of lattices holds with the appropriate modifications for both kinds of semilattices.

THEOREM 11.2

(i) Let the poset $\mathbf{A} = \langle A, \leq \rangle$ be a join semilattice. Set $a \vee b = \sup\{a, b\}$. Then the algebra $\mathbf{A^a} = \langle A, \vee \rangle$ is a semilattice.

(ii) Let the algebra $\mathbf{A} = \langle A, \circ \rangle$ be a semilattice. Set $a \leq b$ iff $a \circ b = b$. Then $\mathbf{A^P} = \langle A, \leq \rangle$ is a poset and the poset $\mathbf{A^P}$ is a join semilattice.

(iii) Let the poset $\mathbf{A} = \langle A, \leq \rangle$ be a join semilattice. Then $(\mathbf{A^a})^P = \mathbf{A}$.

(iv) Let the algebra $\mathbf{A} = \langle A, \vee \rangle$ be a semilattice. Then $(\mathbf{A^P})^a = \mathbf{A}$.

■

The proof is deferred to the exercises.

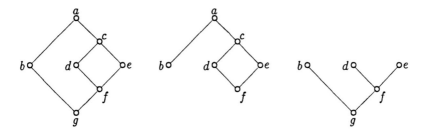

Figure 11-5: A lattice with examples of join
and meet semilattices.

11.3 Morphisms in lattices

Mappings from one lattice to another compare their structures, algebraically
or order-theoretically.

Two lattices $\mathbf{L_1} = \langle L_1, \wedge, \vee \rangle$ and $\mathbf{L_2} = \langle L_2, \wedge, \vee \rangle$ are *(algebraically)*
isomorphic if there is a bijection F from $\mathbf{L_1}$ to $\mathbf{L_2}$ such that for every a, b
in L_1

(i) $F(a \vee b) = F(a) \vee F(b)$, and

(ii) $F(a \wedge b) = F(a) \wedge F(b)$

If two lattices are isomorphic, F is called the *lattice isomorphism*. Note
that F^{-1} is also a lattice isomorphism, if F is, and that if $F : \mathbf{L_1} \longrightarrow \mathbf{L_2}$
and $F' : \mathbf{L_2} \longrightarrow \mathbf{L_3}$ are lattice isomorphisms, then their composition $F' \circ F :$
$\mathbf{L_1} \longrightarrow \mathbf{L_3}$ is also a lattice isomorphism.

Isomorphism of lattices as posets is defined by requiring the bijection to
be order-preserving. If $\mathbf{P_1} = \langle P_1, \leq \rangle$ and $\mathbf{P_2} = \langle P_2, \leq \rangle$ are two posets and
$F : \mathbf{P_1} \longrightarrow \mathbf{P_2}$, F is called an *order-preserving map* if $F(a) \leq F(b)$ holds
in $\mathbf{P_2}$ whenever $a \leq b$ holds in $\mathbf{P_1}$. Sometimes an order-preserving map is
called a *monotone* or an *isotone* mapping.

THEOREM 11.3 *Two posets which are lattices* $\mathbf{L_1} = \langle L_1, \leq \rangle$ *and* $\mathbf{L_2} =$
$\langle L_2, \leq \rangle$ *are* (order-theoretically) *isomorphic iff there is a bijection*

$F : \mathbf{L_1} \to \mathbf{L_2}$ *such that both* F *and* F^{-1} *are order-preserving.*

∎

Proof. ($\Longrightarrow$). If $F : \mathbf{L_1} \to \mathbf{L_2}$ is an isomorphism and $a \leq b$ holds in $\mathbf{L_1}$ then $a = a \wedge b$, so $F(a) = F(a \wedge b) = F(a) \wedge F(b)$, therefore $F(a) \leq F(b)$, and F is order-preserving. Dually, the inverse of an order-preserving isomorphism is also order-preserving.

($\Longleftarrow$). Let $F : \mathbf{L_1} \to \mathbf{L_2}$ and its inverse F^{-1} be order-preserving. If a, b in $\mathbf{L_1}$ then $a \leq a \vee b$ and $b \leq a \vee b$, so $F(a) \leq F(a \vee b)$ and $F(b) \leq F(a \vee b)$, therefore $F(a) \vee F(b) \leq F(a \vee b)$. Suppose $F(a) \vee F(b) \leq c$, then $F(a) \leq c$ and $F(b) \leq c$, and then $a \leq F^{-1}(c)$ and $b \leq F^{-1}(c)$, so $(a \vee b) \leq F^{-1}(c)$ and therefore $F(a \vee b) \leq c$. It follows that $F(a) \vee F(b) = F(a \vee b)$. Dually, it is provable that $F(a) \wedge F(b) = F(a \wedge b)$.   ∎

The diagrams can represent such order-preserving mappings clearly. Figure 11-6 shows an order-preserving bijection $F(a) = a, \ldots, F(d) = d$ from a lattice to a chain which is not an algebraic isomorphism.

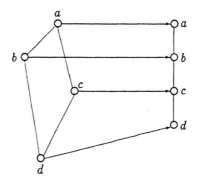

Figure 11–6: An order-preserving bijection
which is not an isomorphism

The following notions are weaker than isomorphisms, and often suffice to characterize the structural similarity between two domains, especially when the mappings are intended to represent information-preserving relations.

A *homomorphism* of the semilattice $\mathbf{S_1} = \langle S_1, \circ \rangle$ into the semilattice $\mathbf{S_2} = \langle S_2, \circ \rangle$ is a mapping $F : \mathbf{S_1} \to \mathbf{S_2}$ such that $F(a \circ b) = F(a) \circ F(b)$. Since any lattice consists of a join and a meet semilattice, this homomorphism notion is split into a *join homomorphism* and a *meet homomorphism*.

A (full) lattice homomorphism is a map that is both a join and a meet homomorphism, i.e. a map F such that $F(a \vee b) = F(a) \vee F(b)$ and $F(a \wedge b) = F(a) \wedge F(b)$.

Note that lattice homomorphisms and join and meet homomorphisms are order-preserving, but the converse is not generally true. In Figure 11-7 the three diagrams show the distinct notions; (11-7.1) is an order-preserving mapping that is neither a join nor a meet homomorphism (cf. Figure 11-6), (11-7.2) a join homomorphism that is not a meet homomorphism and (11-7.3) a (full) lattice homomorphism.

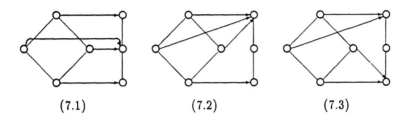

(7.1)   (7.2)   (7.3)

Figure 11–7: An order-preserving mapping,
a join homomorphism and a lattice
homomorphism

Finally we define an *embedding* of a lattice L_1 into a lattice L_2 as an isomorphism F from L_1 into a sublattice of L_2. If such an embedding exists, L_2 contains a *copy* or an *image* of L_1 as sublattice. This notion will be useful in determining whether a given lattice has a special structure, as we will see below in Section 11.5.

11.4 Filters and ideals

In a lattice we may construct various special subsets with nice properties based on their closure under the ordering relation and the operations.

An *ideal* I of a lattice L is a non-empty subset of L such that both of the following hold:

(i) if $a \in I$, $b \in L$ and $b \leq a$, then $b \in I$

(ii) if $a, b \in I$, then $(a \vee b) \in I$

An ideal I is *proper* if $I \neq L$ and I is *maximal* if it is not contained in another proper ideal of **L**.

Dualizing these notions, we define a *filter* F of a lattice **L** as a non-empty set of L such that both of the following hold:

(i) if $a \in F$, $b \in L$ and $b \geq a$, then $b \in F$

(ii) if $a, b \in F$, then $(a \wedge b) \in F$

A filter is *proper* if $F \neq L$ and F is maximal if it is not contained in another proper filter of **L**. Maximal filters are often called *ultrafilters*.

The set of ideals and the set of filters of a lattice are closed under finite intersection, and under arbitrary intersection in case the intersection is not empty (proof is an easy exercise). This *finite intersection property* guarantees existence of the least ideal generated by any non-empty subset $X \subseteq L$, written as $(X]$. If X is a singleton $\{x\} \subseteq L$, then we often write $(x]$ and call this a *principal ideal*. (Dually, the filter $[X)$ generated by $X \subseteq L$, etc.).

If **L** is a lattice and **I(L)** the set of all ideals in **L**, then **I(L)** is a poset with set inclusion and constitutes a lattice, called the *ideal lattice*. Together with the (provable) claim that any non-empty subset of **I(L)** has a supremum, which makes **I(L)** a *complete lattice*, we may prove that **L** can be embedded in **I(L)** by an embedding function $G(x) = (x]$. Sometimes the image of this embedding G is called the *ideal representation* of a lattice (dually, *filter representation*). The proof appeals to a form of the axiom of choice but requires no ingenuity and can be found in any standard reference on lattices (e.g. Grätzer (1971)).

To illustrate this notion of an ideal representation, consider the following simple lattice $\mathbf{L} = \langle \{a, b, c, d\}, \leq \rangle$ in Figure 11-8. The set of all ideals in **L**, **I(L)** , consists of $\{a, b, c, d\}, \{b, c, d\}, \{b, d\}, \{c, d\}$ and the principal ideal $\{d\}$. (Why is e.g. $\{a, b, d\}$ *not* an ideal?) **L** can be embedded into **I(L)** by the following embedding function: $G : \mathbf{L} \to \mathbf{I(L)}$ such that

$G(a) = \{a, b, c, d\}$
$G(b) = \{b, d\}$
$G(c) = \{c, d\}$
$G(d) = \{d\}$

The ideal representation of **L** is $\{\{a, b, c, d\}, \{b, d\}, \{c, d\}, \{d\}\}$.

The following notions provide 'bounds' to a lattice in a very general way. An element a of a lattice **L** is *join-irreducible* if $a = b \vee c$ implies that $a = b$

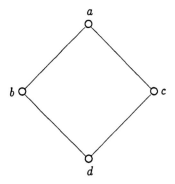

Figure 11–8.

or $a = c$; dually, a is *meet-irreducible* if $a = b \wedge c$ implies that $a = b$ or $a = c$.
We call a lattice $\mathbf{L} = \langle L, \wedge, \vee, 0, 1 \rangle$ a *bounded lattice* if

(i) $\langle L, \wedge, \vee \rangle$ is a lattice

(ii) $x \wedge 0 = 0$ and $x \vee 1 = 1$, for any arbitrary element x.

These notions will again be useful in Chapter 12.

The following is an important theorem establishing a connection between join homomorphisms and ideals.

THEOREM 11.4 I is a proper ideal of the lattice $\mathbf{L}$ iff there is a join homomorphism G from $\mathbf{L}$ onto the two element chain $\mathbf{C} = \langle \{0,1\}, \leq \rangle$ such that $I = G^{-1}(0)$, i.e. $I = \{x \mid G(x) = 0\}$.   ∎

Proof. $(\Longrightarrow)I$ is a proper ideal and let G be defined by $G(x) = 0$ if $x \in I$ and $G(x) = 1$ if $x \notin I$, which obviously is a join homomorphism.
$(\Longleftarrow)$ If $G : \mathbf{L} \to \mathbf{C}$ is a join homomorphism and $I = G^{-1}(0)$, then for any $a, b \in I$, $G(a) = G(b) = 0$. So $G(a \vee b) = G(a) \vee G(b) = 0 \vee 0 = 0$, hence $(a \vee b) \in I$. If $a \in I$ and $x \in L$ with $x \leq a$, then $G(x) \leq G(a) = 0$, i.e. $G(x) = 0$, so $x \in I$. Furthermore, G is onto, so $I \neq L$, i.e I is proper.   ∎

Of course Theorem 11.4 may be dualized for proper filters.

11.5   Complemented, distributive and modular lattices

In this section we will discuss some particularly well-known lattices which have additional properties and operations providing more structure.

In a bounded lattice **L** we call the least element a, i.e. $a \leq b$ for any $b \in L$, the *bottom* or *zero* of **L**, conventionally writing it as 0. Similarly, the greatest element in a bounded lattice is called the *top* or *unit* of **L**, conventionally written as 1. A bounded lattice $\mathbf{L} = \langle L, \wedge, \vee, 0, 1 \rangle$ is said to be *complemented* if for each $a \in L$ there is a $b \in L$ such that

(C1) $a \vee b = 1$

(C2) $a \wedge b = 0$

and b is called the *complement* of a. In general an element in a lattice may have more than one complement or none at all. A lattice **L** is *relatively complemented* if for any $a \leq b \leq c$ in L there exists d in L with

(RC1) $b \wedge d = a$

(RC2) $b \vee d = c$

and d is called the *relative complement* of b in the interval $[a, c]$. A lattice L is *distributive* if it satisfies either one of the distributive laws

(D1) $a \wedge (b \vee c) = (a \wedge b) \vee (a \wedge c)$

(D2) $a \vee (b \wedge c) = (a \vee b) \wedge (a \vee c)$

Since (D1) entails (D2) and vice versa (see exercises), satisfaction of either one suffices for a lattice to be distributive.

It is important to realize that any lattice already satisfies the two lattice inequalities

(LI1) $[(a \wedge b) \vee (a \wedge c)] \leq [a \wedge (b \vee c)]$

(LI2) $[a \vee (b \wedge c)] \leq [(a \vee b) \wedge (a \vee c)]$

Hence to check for distributivity of a lattice it suffices to check the inverses of these inequalities, which together entail (D1) and (D2).

A lattice **L** is *modular* if it satisfies the *modular law*

(M) $a \leq b \rightarrow [a \vee (b \wedge c) = b \wedge (a \vee c)]$

Again since any lattice satisfies $a \leq b \to [b \wedge (a \vee c) \leq a \vee (b \wedge c)]$ checking the inverse inequality suffices to demonstrate modularity in a lattice.

The following theorem is straightforward.

THEOREM 11.5 *Every distributive lattice is modular.*   ∎

Proof: If $a \leq b$, $a \vee b = b$ and use this in (D2).   ∎

Non-modularity and non-distributivity of a lattice can be verified by embedding two special five element lattices into it, represented by the diagrams NM (Non-Modularity) and ND (Non-Distributivity) in Figure 11-9. These results belong to the core of lattice theory, and are due respectively to Dedekind and to the founder of lattice theory, Birkhoff.

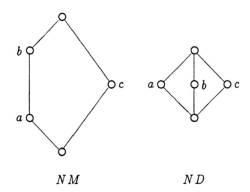

NM ND

Figure 11-9: Diagrams for non-modularity
and non-distributivity

THEOREM 11.6 *(Dedekind)* **L** *is non-modular iff diagram NM can be embedded into* **L**.   ∎

Proof: ($\Leftarrow$) In NM $a \leq b$, but it is not the case that $a \vee (b \wedge c) = b \wedge (a \vee c)$, so **L** contains a copy of a non-modular lattice and hence cannot itself be modular.

($\Longrightarrow$) Suppose **L** does not satisfy the modular law, then we will construct a diagram isomorphic to NM as sublattice. For some a, b, c in L we have $a \leq b$, but $a \vee (b \wedge c) < b \wedge (a \vee c)$. Let $a_1 = a \vee (b \wedge c)$ and $b_1 = b \wedge (a \vee c)$.

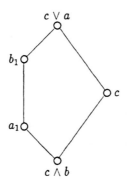

Then $c \wedge b_1$ $= c \wedge [b \wedge (a \vee c)]$

$\qquad\qquad = [c \wedge (c \vee a)] \wedge b$ commutative, associative laws

$\qquad\qquad = c \wedge b$ absorption

and $c \vee a_1$ $= c \vee [a \vee (b \wedge c)]$

$\qquad\qquad = [c \vee (b \wedge c)] \vee a$ commutative, associative laws

$\qquad\qquad = c \vee a$ absorption

Since $c \wedge b \leq a_1 \leq b_1$ we have $c \wedge b \leq c \wedge a_1 \leq c \wedge b_1 = c \wedge b$, so $c \wedge a_1 = c \wedge b_1 = c \wedge b$. Similarly for $c \vee b_1 = c \vee a_1 = c \vee a$. It is easy to see that the above diagram is isomorphic to and hence a copy of NM.   ∎

THEOREM 11.7   *(Birkhoff)* **L** *is a non-distributive lattice iff ND can be embedded into* **L**.   ∎

Proof. ($\Longleftarrow$)$a \vee (b \wedge c) = (a \vee b) \wedge (a \vee c)$ does not hold in ND, so if ND can be embedded in **L**, it cannot be a distributive lattice.

($\Longrightarrow$) Suppose **L** is non-distributive, i.e. for some $a, b, c \in L$, $[(a \wedge b) \vee (a \wedge c)] < [a \wedge (b \vee c)]$. Assume also that L does not contain a copy of NM as sublattice, i.e., L is modular. Define the following elements, in order to construct a sublattice in L which is isomorphic to ND.

$$
\begin{aligned}
d &= (a \wedge b) \vee (a \wedge c) \vee (b \wedge c) \\
e &= (a \vee b) \wedge (a \vee c) \wedge (b \vee c) \\
a_1 &= (a \wedge e) \vee d \\
b_1 &= (b \wedge e) \vee d \\
c_1 &= (c \wedge e) \vee d
\end{aligned}
$$

Now $d \leq a_1, b_1, c_1 \leq e$.

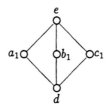

With absorption we derive from $(a \wedge e) = a \wedge (b \vee c)$, that

$$a \wedge d = a \wedge ((a \wedge b) \vee (a \wedge c) \vee (b \wedge c))$$

Modularity allows exchanging a and $(a \wedge b) \vee (a \wedge c)$

$$= ((a \wedge b) \vee (a \wedge c)) \vee (a \wedge (b \wedge c))$$
$$= (a \wedge b) \vee (a \wedge c)$$

Now it follows that $d < e$. To show that the above diagram is a copy of ND in L, we prove $a_1 \wedge b_1 = a_1 \wedge c_1 = b_1 \wedge c_1 = d$ and $a_1 \vee b_1 = a_1 \vee c_1 = b_1 \vee c_1 = d$.

We prove this here for one case only, the others are similar.

$$
\begin{aligned}
a_1 \wedge b_1 = \quad & ((a \wedge e) \vee d) \wedge ((b \wedge e) \vee d) \\
& ((a \wedge e) \wedge ((b \wedge e) \vee d) \vee d) && \text{modularity} \\
& ((a \wedge e) \wedge ((b \vee d) \wedge e) \vee d) && \text{modularity} \\
& ((a \wedge e) \wedge e \wedge (b \vee d)) \vee d) && \text{comm. assoc.} \\
& ((a \wedge e) \wedge (b \vee d)) \vee d && \text{idempotent} \\
& (a \wedge (b \vee c) \wedge (b \vee (a \wedge c))) \vee d && \text{absorption} \\
& (a \wedge (b \vee b \vee c) \wedge a \wedge c))) \vee d && \text{modularity} \\
& (a \wedge (b \vee (a \wedge c))) \vee d && a \wedge c \leq b \vee c \\
& (a \wedge c) \vee (b \wedge a) \vee d && \text{modularity} \\
& d
\end{aligned}
$$

∎

The following theorems indicate clearly the force of complementation in distributive lattices and correlate it to the weaker notion of relative complementation.

THEOREM 11.8 *In a distributive, complemented lattice each element a has a unique complement $a^{\cdot}$.* ∎

Proof. Suppose there were two complements a^* and b^* of a, then $a^* = a^* \wedge 1 = a^* \wedge (a \vee b^*) = (a^* \wedge a) \vee (a^* \wedge b^*) = 0 \vee (a^* \wedge b^*) = a^* \wedge b^*$; similarly $b^* = a^* \wedge b^*$, so $a^* = b^*$. ∎

Theorem 11.9 *In a distributive lattice relative complements are unique, if they exist.* ∎

Proof. Let **L** be a distributive lattice with $a \le b \le c$ in **L**. If d and d' were both relative complements of b in the interval $[a, c]$, then

$$
\begin{aligned}
d = \ & d \wedge c \\
& d \wedge (b \vee d') \\
& (d \wedge b) \vee (d \wedge d') \\
& (d \wedge d')
\end{aligned}
$$

∎

　Similarly, $d' = (d \wedge d')$, so $d = d'$.

Theorem 11.10 *In a distributive lattice, if a has a complement, then it has a relative complement in any interval containing it.* ∎

Proof. Take $b \le a \le c$ and let d be the complement of a and $x = (d \vee b) \wedge c$ the relative complement of a in $[b, c]$. To prove $a \wedge x = b$ and $a \vee x = c$.

$$a \wedge x = a \wedge ((d \vee b) \wedge c) = ((a \wedge d) \vee (a \wedge b)) \wedge c = (0 \vee b) \wedge c = b,$$

$$a \vee x = a \vee ((d \vee b) \wedge c) = (a \vee d \vee b) \wedge (a \vee c) = 1 \wedge (a \vee c) = c$$

∎

Theorem 11.11 *In a distributive lattice, if a and b have complements a^* and b^*, respectively, then $a \wedge b$ and $a \vee b$ have complements $(a \wedge b)^*$ and $(a \vee b)^*$, respectively, and the de Morgan identities hold:*

(i) $(a \wedge b)^* = a^* \vee b^*$

(ii) $(a \vee b)^* = a^* \wedge b^*$

∎

Proof. By Theorem 11.8 we only need to prove (i) by verifying

$$(a \wedge b) \wedge (a^* \vee b^*) = 0 \text{ and } (a \wedge b) \vee (a^* \vee b^*) = 1$$

$$(a \wedge b) \wedge (a^* \vee b^*) = (a \wedge b \wedge a^*) \vee (a \wedge b \wedge b^*) = 0 \vee 0 = 0,$$

$$(a \wedge b) \vee (a^* \vee b^*) = (a \vee a^* \vee b^*) \wedge (b \vee a^* \vee b^*) = 1 \wedge 1 = 1$$

The proof of (ii) is an exercise.

Exercises

1. Which of the posets in the diagrams of figures 11-1, 11-2 and 11-3 are lattices?

2. (i) Which of the following sets of sentences can be formally represented as posets (each name corresponds to an element):

   (a) Alan is a descendant of Bob and Carol. Carol is a descendant of David and Eliza. Bob is a descendant of Fred and Gladys.

   (b) as in (a) adding: Fred and Eliza are descendants of Henry and Isabella.

   (c) as in (a) adding: Everyone is a descendant of Adam.

   (d) David and Eliza, who told Fred about it, were told by Bob and Carol, after Alan told them both.

   (e) Jane told Jim and Joseph, who either told Jenny directly or she heard from Julius who had heard from them.

   (ii) Draw diagrams for the posets in (i) and indicate which are semilattices and/or lattices.

   (iii) For the lattices in (i) compute all meets and joins.

3. Describe the poset formed by the power set of a four-element set and draw its diagram. What corresponds to the set-theoretic operations in an algebraic representation of this lattice? Check whether they satisfy (L4).

4. Formulate and prove the dual of Theorem 11.2 for meet semilattices.

5. Draw a diagram for a meet homomorphism which is not a join homomorphism from a four-element lattice to a four-element chain and prove it does not represent a lattice homomorphism.

6. Prove that the distributive laws (D1) and (D2) are equivalent.

7. Prove that in a complemented distributive lattice $a = (a^*)^*$.

8. Prove the second of the de Morgan identities of Theorem 11.11.

9. Supply the laws used for each of the proofs of Theorems 11.8–11.11.

Chapter 12

Boolean and Heyting Algebras

12.1   Boolean algebras

In this chapter we discuss two well-known algebras as specially structured lattices and prove some of their properties as well as present some semantic interpretations of these structures.

A *Boolean lattice* $\mathbf{BL} = \langle L, \wedge, \vee, *, 0, 1 \rangle$ is a complemented distributive lattice. A *Boolean algebra* is a Boolean lattice in which 0, 1 and $*$ (complementation) are also considered to be operations; i.e. $\mathbf{BA} = \langle B, \wedge, \vee, *, 0, 1 \rangle$ where $\vee$ and $\wedge$ are the usual binary operations, $*$ is a unary operation and 0 and 1 are taken to be nullary operations, which simply pick out an element of B. For easy reference, we repeat and relabel the laws which a $\mathbf{BA} = \langle B, \wedge, \vee, *, 0, 1 \rangle$ obeys:

(B0)   **BA is an algebra**

(B1)   **Associative Laws**

    (i) $a \wedge (b \wedge c) = (a \wedge b) \wedge c$

    (ii) $a \vee (b \vee c) = (a \vee b) \vee c$

(B2)   **Commutative Laws**

    (i) $(a \wedge b) = (b \wedge a)$

    (ii) $(a \vee b) = (b \vee a)$

(B3)   **Distributive Laws**

    (i) $a \wedge (b \vee c) = (a \wedge b) \vee (a \wedge c)$

(ii) $a \vee (b \wedge c) = (a \vee b) \wedge (a \vee c)$

(B4) **Top and Bottom Laws**

  (i) $a \wedge 1 = a$ and $a \wedge 0 = 0$

  (ii) $a \vee 0 = a$ and $a \vee 1 = 1$

(B5) **Complementation Laws**

  (i) $a \wedge a* = 0$

  (ii) $a \vee a* = 1$

Often in the literature a special two-element Boolean algebra, called **BOOL** or **2** is used to represent the two truth values 'false' and 'true' where $0 < 1$, $0 = 1*$ and $1 = 0*$.

In a **BA** an element a is called an *atom* when a covers 0. The dual notion is less frequently encountered, but defined as an element a which covers 1, called the *dual atom*. A **BA** is called an *atomic* **BA** when it contains an atom a for each of its non-zero elements x such that $a \leq x$. Any finite **BA** is atomic and an atomic **BA** may not be dually atomic.

We prove some central theorems about **BA** which illustrate their power and structural elegance.

THEOREM 12.1 *In a* **BA** *an element is join-irreducible iff it is an atom.* ∎

Proof: ($\Leftarrow$) If a is an atom then $a = b \vee c$ means that $b = a$ or $b = 0$; if $b = 0$ then $a = 0 \vee c = c$; so a is join-irreducible.
($\Rightarrow$) Suppose a is not an atom or 0, then $a > x > 0$ for some element x. When $x < a$, $a = a \wedge 1 = a \wedge (x \vee x*) = (a \wedge x) \vee (a \wedge x*) = x \vee (a \wedge x*)$. Since $a \wedge x* \leq a$ and $a \wedge x* = a$ would imply $x = a \wedge x = a \wedge x* \wedge x = 0$, we know $a \wedge x* < a$, hence a would be join-reducible. ∎

The definitions of ideals and filters in a lattice given in Chapter 11 carry over directly to ideals and filters in **BA**, but note the additional fact that in a **BA** 0 is an element of every ideal and 1 is an element of every filter. Due to the strong notion of complementation and the universal top and bottom element in any **BA** we have the following strong correlation between ideals and filters.

THEOREM 12.2 *In any* **BA** *(i) for any $I \subseteq B$, I is an ideal iff $I*$ is a filter; (ii) for any $F \subseteq B$, F is a filter iff $F*$ is an ideal.* ∎

Proof: *(i)* Note that $0 \in I$ iff $1 = 0* \in I*$. Take $a, b \in I$ then $a \vee b \in I$ iff $(a \vee b)* = a* \wedge b* \in I*$. If $a \in I$, we know $b \leq a$ iff $a* \leq b*$; so $b \in I$ iff $b* \in I*$. The proof of *(ii)* is obtained dually. ∎

THEOREM 12.3 *If F is a filter in a $\mathbf{BA}$, then F is an ultrafilter iff for each $b \in B$ either $b \in F$ or $b* \in F$.* ∎

Proof: ($\Leftarrow$) Suppose for any $b \in B$ either $b \in F$ or $b* \in F$ and take F' to be a filter which properly contains F, i.e. there is some $c \in F' - F$. Since $c \notin F$, $c* \in F \subseteq F'$. So F' is not proper. Hence F is a maximal proper filter, an ultrafilter.

($\Rightarrow$) Let F be an ultrafilter and take $b \notin F$. Set $F' = F \cup \{b\}$ which is not proper since F is already maximal. So $F \cup \{b\}$ does not have the finite intersection property and for some finite subset X of F, $\inf(X) \wedge b = 0$. So $\inf(X) \leq b*$. $\mathrm{Inf}(X)$ is in F and hence $b* \in F$. ∎

The following theorem is proven with a form of the axiom of choice, and shows the existence of a rich class of ultrafilters in any $\mathbf{BA}$.

THEOREM 12.4 (The Ultrafilter Theorem) *Each filter in a $\mathbf{BA}$ can be extended to an ultrafilter.* ∎

Proof: Let $\mathbf{F}$ be the non-empty class of all filters in some $\mathbf{BA}$, partially ordered by set-theoretic inclusion. We want to show that every chain in this ordering in $\mathbf{F}$ has an upper bound. Let $C = \{C_i : i \in I\}$ be a chain in $\mathbf{F}$ and let $\mathbf{C} = \cup_{i \in I} C_i$. If $x, y \in \mathbf{C}$, then for some $i, j \in I$, $x \in C_i$ and $y \in C_j$. Since C is a chain, either $C_i \leq C_j$ or $C_j \leq C_i$; take $C_i \leq C_j$. Then $x, y \in C_j$ and since C_j is a filter $x \wedge y \in C_j \in \mathbf{C}$. If $b \in B$ and $x \leq b$ then $b \in C_j \in \mathbf{C}$. Since $0 \notin C_i$ for any $i \in I$, $0 \notin \mathbf{C}$. So $\mathbf{C}$ is a filter, which is the upper bound for C in $\mathbf{F}$. With a form of the axiom of choice (called Zorn's Lemma) we derive that for any filter $\mathbf{F}$, $\mathbf{BA}$ must contain a maximal filter extending that filter. ∎

There is an important connection between ultrafilters and homomorphisms, as indicated by the following theorem.

THEOREM 12.5 *Let $\mathbf{BA_1}$ and $\mathbf{BA_2}$ be two Boolean algebras and consider a homomorphism $F : \mathbf{BA_1} \to \mathbf{BA_2}$. If U is an ultrafilter of $\mathbf{BA_2}$, then $F^{-1}(U)$ is an ultrafilter of $\mathbf{BA_1}$.* ∎

The proof of Theorem 12.5 is not given here, since it requires a number of algebraic concepts which have not been introduced.

12.2   Models of BA

The Boolean laws may already have reminded you of the properties of set-theoretic operations, and, indeed, sets provide simple models of Boolean algebras. Starting from any non-empty set X a model for **BA** can be constructed as follows:

- Let B be $\wp(X)$, the power set of X

- Let $\vee$ be set-theoretic union $\cup$

- Let $\wedge$ be set-theoretic intersection $\cap$

- Let $*$ be set-theoretic complementation $'$ relative to X

- Let 1 be X

- Let 0 be $\emptyset$

We may verify that all Boolean laws are true under this interpretation.

(12–1) Let $X = \{a, b, c\}$ then $B = \{\{a, b, c\}, \{a, b\}, \{a, c\}, \{b, c\}, \{a\}, \{b\}, \{c\}, \emptyset\}$. Union and intersection are as usual and the complements are: $\{a, b, c\}* = \emptyset$, $\{a, b\}* = \{c\}$, $\{a, c\}* = \{b\}$ and $\{b, c\}* = \{a\}$.

Note that by starting from a set with n elements, we construct a **BA** with 2^n elements. Thus for every positive power of 2 there is a Boolean algebra whose set has exactly that cardinality. It can be proven, although we will not do so, that every finite **BA** has a cardinality of 2^n for some positive n. In Section 3 we will prove that every finite model of **BA** is isomorphic to a particular set-theoretic model based on the construction described above. Thus this family of models is particularly important. For infinite models the situation is not so simple. Every infinite set leads to a model for **BA** by the given construction, but not every infinite **BA** is isomorphic to one of these models. There are, for instance, Boolean algebras of cardinality $\aleph_0$, but $\aleph_0$ is not the cardinality of the power of any set, as we know from Cantor's Theorem (see Section 4.4).

We can also show that the logic of statements familiar from Part B constitutes a model of **BA**. Let **L** be the logical language whose syntax was defined in Section 2.1, and S be the set of statements generated by its syntactic rules. For s and $s' \in S$ we write $s \sim s'$ when s and s' are provably logically equivalent in this logic of statements. Now $\sim$ is an equivalence relation on S. For each $s \in S$ we define the equivalence class

$$[\![s]\!] = \{s' \in S \mid s \sim s'\}$$

Let B be the set of all such equivalence classes of logically equivalent statements. Define a partial ordering on B by

$$[\![s]\!] \leq [\![s']\!] \text{ iff } (s \rightarrow s') \text{ is valid}$$

Then $\langle B, \leq \rangle$ is a Boolean algebra called the *Lindenbaum algebra* of L. The Boolean operations on B are defined by

$$[\![s]\!] \wedge [\![s']\!] = [\![s \ \& \ s']\!], \quad [\![s]\!] \vee [\![s']\!] = [\![s \vee s']\!], \quad [\![s]\!]* = [\![\sim s]\!].$$

Top and bottom are then respectively

$1 = [\![s]\!]$ for any tautology s

$0 = [\![s]\!]$ for any contradiction s

An ultrafilter in the Lindenbaum algebra of L can be identified with a maximally consistent set of statements, which would constitute the first step in proving the completeness of L through its ultrafilter representation. Such topics belong to more advanced model theory and are beyond the scope of this book (Reference: Bell and Machover (1977)).

12.3 Representation by sets

The first example we gave of a model of **BA** was the power set algebra of a set. In this section we show that each Boolean algebra is isomorphic to a *subalgebra* of a power set algebra, or, in other words, each Boolean algebra may be *reprsented* as a subalgebra of a power set algebra. This important theorem is due to M.F. Stone and is called Stone Representation. We first need to define two new notions:

DEFINITION 12.1

(1) *A ring of sets is a family of subsets of a set X which contains for any two subsets A and B of X also $A \cup B$ and $A \cap B$.*

(2) *A field of sets is a ring of sets which contains X and the empty set $\emptyset$ and the complement A' of any subset $A \subseteq X$.* ∎

From these definitions it is easy to see that a field of subsets of X is a Boolean *subalgebra* of the Boolean power set algebra of X, but that a ring of subsets is a *sublattice* of the power set algebra of X, considered as a distributive lattice. We will prove that any finite distributive lattice is isomorphic with a ring of sets and that any finite Boolean algebra is isomorphic with the field of all subsets of some finite set. (The proof follows essentially Birkhof and MacLane, 377-380).

From Section 12.1 we need Theorem 12.1 and we define a set $S(a) = \{x \mid x \le a$ and x covers $0\}$ of join-irreducible elements x for an element a in any finite lattice **L**. Consider the mapping F which assigns each element a its $S(a)$.

LEMMA 12.1 *In any finite lattice **L**, F carries meets in L into set-theoretic intersections: $S(a \wedge b) = S(a) \cap S(b)$.* ∎

Proof. By definition of $a \wedge b$ we know that for any join-irreducible element x, $x \le a \wedge b$ iff $x \le a$ and $x \le b$. ∎

LEMMA 12.2 *In any finite distributive lattice **L**, F carries joins in L into set-theoretic unions: $S(a \vee b) = S(a) \cup S(b)$.* ∎

Proof. Take any join-irreducible x, then x is contained in $a \vee b$ iff $x = x \wedge (a \vee b) = (x \wedge a) \vee (x \wedge b)$. Now $x \wedge a = x$ or $x \wedge b = x$. So $(a \vee b)$ contains x iff $S(a)$ contains x or $S(b)$ contains x. The converse is obvious in any lattice. ∎

These two lemmas show that F is a homomorphism from **L** onto a ring of subsets of the set X of join-irreducible elements of L. Together with the result of Exercise 3 at the end of this chapter we know that F is also a one-to-one onto homomorphism. So we know

THEOREM 12.6 *Any finite distributive lattice is isomorphic with a ring of sets.* ∎

In the case of a finite Boolean algebra we know from Theorem 12.1 that each element a is the join of the atoms $x \leq a$. With the above two lemmas we know

$$S(a) \cap S(a') = S(a \wedge a*) = S(0) = \emptyset$$

$$S(a) \cup S(a') = S(a \vee a*) = S(1) = J$$

where J is the set of all join-irreducible element of L. So $[S(a)]* = S(a')$ and F as defined above is an isomorphism from any Boolean algebra to a field of subsets of join-irreducible elements of L. We still need to prove that this field contains *all* sets of join-irreducible elements of L.

THEOREM 12.7 *Any finite Boolean algebra is isomorphic with the Boolean algebra of all sets of its join-irreducible elements.* ∎

Proof. We need to prove that for any two distinct sets of join-irreducible elements of L the joins of each set are distinct. The claim that the join of all elements in such a set contains all the join-irreducible elements of that set and nothing else follows from

LEMMA 12.3 *If A is a set of join-irreducible elements, and there is some join-irreducible element a such that $a \leq \bigvee\{x \mid x \in A\}$, then $a \in A$.* ∎

Proof. $a = a \wedge \bigvee\{x \mid x \in A\} = \bigvee(a \wedge x)$ and since a is join-irreducible for some such $x \in A$, $a \wedge x = a$, so $0 < x \leq a$. But then $a = x$. ∎

The significance of Stone Representations for representing information and structuring models for the semantic interpretation of natural language is discussed in Landman (1986). The mathematical import of Boolean algebras can be illustrated further by relating them to certain topological structures and so called Boolean spaces, but the interested reader should consult the exposition of such topics in Grätzer (1971) or Bell and Machover (1977)

12.4 Heyting algebra

Besides Boolean lattices and algebras which are used to represent such logical systems as the classical logic of Part B, there are other, weaker lattice theoretic structures and corresponding algebras which represent constructive reasoning based on a stricter notion of proof by rejecting any use of reductio arguments. In the semantics of natural language attention has recently been

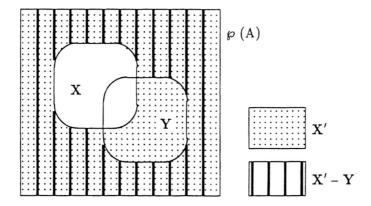

Figure 12-1.

refocused on theories of meaning based on verification/falsification conditions, or more generally, assertability conditions, which subsume the classical
truth conditions and analyze the informative content of an expression in the
context of use. Although an account of the philosophical and mathematical foundations of such constructivist logics and their potential linguistic
applications is outside the scope of this book, it is useful to present some of
the basic syntactic and semantic concepts to develop an initial understanding of more epistemically flavored formal systems. We need to define one
additional lattice-theoretic notion.

In a lattice **L** the (*relative*) *pseudo-complement* of an element a relative
to b is the greatest element c in L such that $a \wedge c \leq b$. Note that this pseudo-
complementation involves only the meet operation. It is easy to see that c
is the pseudo-complement of a relative to b precisely when

(12–2)   for all x in L, $x \leq c$ iff $a \wedge x \leq b$

e.g., in the power set lattice with the inclusion ordering, $\langle \wp(A), \leq \rangle$, for any
sets X, $Y \in \wp(A)$, $X' - Y$ is the pseudo-complement of X relative to Y.
(See Fig. 12-1.) In general, we write $a \Rightarrow b$ for the pseudo-complement of a
relative to b, and we say that a lattice **L** is *relatively pseudo-complemented*
iff $a \Rightarrow b$ exists for every a and b in L.

A relatively pseudo-complemented lattice $\langle H, \wedge, \vee \rangle$ is called a *Heyting
lattice* (or a *pseudo-Boolean lattice*) if it contains a bottom element 0. Define

$a*$ by setting $a* = a \Rightarrow 0$ and note that $a*$ is the lub of $\{x \mid a \wedge x = 0\}$, i.e. $a*$ is the pseudo-complement of a (relative to 0). The dual of a Heyting lattice is called a *Brouwerian lattice*, which is studied in McKinsey and Tarski (1946).

Correspondingly, an algebra $\langle H, \wedge, \vee, \Rightarrow, 0, 1 \rangle$ is a *Heyting algebra* (**HA**) and it has the following properties:

(**H1**) $\langle H, \wedge, \vee \rangle$ is a distributive lattice

(**H2**) $a \wedge 0 = 0$ and $a \vee 1 = 1$

(**H3**) $a \Rightarrow a = 1$

(**H4**) $(a \Rightarrow b) \wedge b = b$; $a \wedge (a \Rightarrow b) = a \wedge b$

THEOREM 12.8 *A Heyting lattice is distributive.* ∎

Proof. In every lattice, $b \leq b \vee c$ and $c \leq b \vee c$, so $a \wedge b \leq a \wedge (b \vee c)$ and $a \wedge c \leq a \wedge (b \vee c)$. Hence $(a \wedge b) \vee (a \wedge c) \leq a \wedge (b \vee c)$. We know $a \wedge b \leq (a \wedge b) \vee (a \wedge c)$, so in a Heyting lattice if $b \leq a$, then $b \leq (a \wedge b) \vee (a \wedge c)$ and if $c \leq a$, then $c \leq (a \wedge b) \vee (a \wedge c)$. So if $b \vee c \leq a$ then $(b \vee c) \leq (a \wedge b) \vee (a \wedge c)$, thus $a \wedge (b \vee c) \leq (a \wedge b) \vee (a \wedge c)$, i.e., $a \wedge (b \vee c) = (a \wedge b) \vee (a \wedge c)$. ∎

The notion of a filter in a Heyting lattice can be characterized as follows:

THEOREM 12.9 *A subset $F \subseteq H$ is a filter of a Heyting lattice* **H** *iff (i) F contains 1 and (ii) if $a \in F$ and $a \Rightarrow b$ then $b \in F$.* ∎

Proof. ($\Leftarrow$) Suppose $1 \in F$ and since in a relatively pseudo-complemented lattice $a \leq b \Rightarrow (a \wedge b)$, we have $a \Rightarrow (b \Rightarrow (a \wedge b)) = 1$. If $a, b \in F$ then $b \Rightarrow (a \wedge b) \in F$ and $a \wedge b \in F$. If $a \in F$ and $a \leq b$ then $a \Rightarrow b = 1 \in F$, so $b \in F$. This proves F is a filter.

($\Rightarrow$) Suppose F is a filter, then $1 \in F$. If $a \in F$ and $a \Rightarrow b \in F$ then $a \wedge b = a \wedge (a \Rightarrow b) \in F$, since $a \wedge (a \Rightarrow b) \leq b$ (by substituting $a \Rightarrow b$ for c in the definition of a relatively pseudo-complemented lattice) and $b \leq a \Rightarrow b$. So $b \in F$. ∎

The notion of a filter in a Heyting lattice is used to capture closure of a set of statements under their implications, as we will see in the following section on the semantics of Heyting algebras. We can define a pre-ordering (reflexive and transitive) on the elements of a filter in a Heyting lattice by

$$a \leq_F b \text{ iff } (a \Rightarrow b) \in F$$

Logically equivalent statements $a \sim b$ for which $a \leq_F b$ and $b \leq_F a$ form again an equivalence class determined by the filter F. A lattice ordering may be defined on elements of such an equivalence class by $|a| \leq |b|$ iff $(a \Rightarrow b) \in F$ and it is provable that the lattice obtained from this ordering is also relatively pseudo complemented. Details can be found in Rasiowa and Sikorski (1970), among others.

12.5 Kripke semantics

In 1965 Saul Kripke published a semantic interpretation of intuitionistic logic based on Heyting algebras as a corollary of his semantics for modal logics (see Chapter 15). Because some fruitful notions for a theory of meaning for natural language based on information conditions may be related to this Kripke semantics we sketch this semantics here informally without entering into the axiomatization or metatheory of intuitionistic logic.

The core idea of Kripke semantics is to relativize the truth of a statement to temporal stages or states of knowledge. So a statement is not simply true but rather true at a stage or in a state of knowledge, which we will generally call an *information-state*. We take these information-states to be ordered temporally, i.e. assuming a partial order which represents the different alternative ways in which we may gradually acquire and extend our knowledge and information. So the set of information-states does not just contain the past stages of information gathering but also all *possible* future states to which we may get from what we now actually know. We also assume that we share such information-states as a community of (formal or natural) language users rather than thinking of them as internal mental representations as the founder of intuitionistic logic, L. Brouwer, suggested.

A sentence which is true at an certain information-state will always be true at later states, since once we have verified a statement we never lose that information (this is the idealization of the language user in semantics!). Hence we require that truth of a statement at an information-state persists through all consecutive information states. More formally, the set of information-states in an interpretation forms a poset under the temporal order called a *Kripke-frame* $\mathbf{P} = \langle P, \leq \rangle$. The interpretation of a statement corresponds to the subset of information-states at which the statement is true. Persistence of truth is tantamount to requiring such subsets to be filters on $\mathbf{P}$ or hereditarily closed under the temporal ordering.

The collection of filters on $\mathbf{P}$ will be written $\mathbf{P}^+$. We define a *Kripke-*

valuation to be a function from the set of statements to the set of filters $V : S \rightarrow \mathbf{P}^+$, assigning to each statement $s \in S$ a filter $V(s) \subseteq P$, i.e. the information-states at which s is true. A *model* based on a Kripke-frame is a pair $\mathbf{M} = \langle \mathbf{P}, V \rangle$ where V is a Kripke-valuation. Now we define recursively the notion of truth at an information-state for all complex statements (we leave the syntax of the statements implicit as it is essentially the syntax of the logic of statements in Chapter 6).

We define a notion $\mathbf{M}| =_p s$ which is to be read as 'the statement s is true at information-state p in the model $\mathbf{M}$.'

(1) $\mathbf{M}| =_p s$ for s an atomic statement iff $s \in V(s)$.

(2) $\mathbf{M}| =_p s$ & s' iff $\mathbf{M}| =_p s$ and $\mathbf{M}| =_p s'$

(3) $\mathbf{M}| =_p s \vee s'$ iff $\mathbf{M}| =_p s$ or $\mathbf{M}| =_p s'$

(4) $\mathbf{M}| =_p \sim s$ iff for all p' such that $p \leq p'$ not $\mathbf{M}| =_{p'} s$

(5) $\mathbf{M}| =_p s \mapsto s'$ iff for all p', $p \leq p'$ if $\mathbf{M}| =_{p'} s$ then $\mathbf{M}| =_{p'} s'$

Thus at information-state p the negation of a statement s is true when the statement can never become true or verified at any later possible stage. A conditional statement is true when at all later stages which verify the antecedent the consquent is verfied as well. The advantage of introducing information-states is that they are used to quantify over possible extensions of the actual information-state in defining verification of negative statements and conditionals.

Unrelativized truth can be defined as truth at all information-states and a statement is valid on a Kripke-frame if it is true on all models based on that frame.

If we extend this definition of truth at an information-state to the full predicate loigc including the universal and existential quantifiers, we need to put some further conditions on the clauses for statements as well. If we analyze the internal structure of statements, we can only verify such quantificational statements when we know 'what they are about,' i.e., when we know the reference of the terms that occur in such quantified statements. More informally speaking, we do not know how to verify (or falsify for that matter) an English sentence *John is old* when we do not know to whom *John* refers or who John is.

For similar reasons we require that (i) each information-state is assigned a non-empty set of objects which act as 'referents' for individual constants

and variables, and (ii) successive states only add referents. Then clause
(1) above is extended to incorporate the requirement that $V(s)$ picks only
objects from this 'referent'-set as interpretations of the individual variables
and constants occurring in s (an atomic formula of a predicate logic). For
disjunction we require that all terms of both disjuncts are interpreted by
objects from the referent-set at the stage of evaluation of the disjunction
and similarly for conditionals and negations. The quantifier clauses to be
added are defined as follows:

(6) $M| =_p (\forall x)\varphi$ iff for every p' such that $p \leq p'$ $M| =_{p'} \varphi(x/t)$ where t
      is an object from the referent-set of p'.

(7) $M| =_p (\exists x)\varphi$ iff $M| =_p \varphi(x/t)$ where t is an object from the referent-
      set of p.

From these recursive clauses we can see that the law of double negation, although valid in classical logic, is not valid in a Kripke semantics. Note however that verification of a formula entails verification of its doubly negated
form but not vice versa (if $M| =_p s$ then $M| =_p \sim\sim s$), and a negative for-
mula is equivalent to its triply negated form ($M| =_p\sim s$ iff $M| =_p\sim\sim\sim s$).
Also the classical law of excluded middle (every formula or its negation is
true) does not hold in Kripke semantics.

   On the basis of a syntactic specification of the intuitionistic logical system and this Kripke semantics we can prove the important completeness and
soundness theorems, and Kripke semantics can also be formulated by semantic tableau rules (as it originally was). We will not discuss such metatheo-
retic issues of intuitionistic logic here, but rather point out the connection
between Kripke semantics and Heyting algebras.

   Since the intersection and union of two filters are filters too, the poset
$\mathbf{P}^+ = \langle \mathbf{P}^+, \leq \rangle$ based on the set of filters with inclusion is a bounded distributive lattice with meets and joins given by intersection and union. $\mathbf{P}^+$
is indeed a Heyting algebra such that for any $A, B \in \mathbf{P}^+ A \Rightarrow B$ is the
pseudo-complement of A relative to B. We have for all filters F,

$$F \leq A \Rightarrow B \text{ iff } A \cap F \leq B$$

and

$$A^* = A \Rightarrow \emptyset$$

Now a Kripke-valuation $V : S \mapsto \mathbf{P}^+$ for a Kripke-frame $\mathbf{P}$ is also a valuation
for the Heyting algebra $\mathbf{P}^+$. This connection can be used to show that

Kripke-validity on the frame $\mathbf{P}$ is the same as validity in a Heyting algebra $\mathbf{P}^+$.

For a semantics of natural language Kripke semantics may have to be extended beyond its verification conditions to include recursive falsification conditions defining falsity of a formula in an information-state. This would allow for a more interesting treatment of positive and negative facts, as well as a more adequate analysis of conditionals. An important current research question is how modal verbs and conditionals may be analyzed as constraining the set of possible extensions of a given information-state as rules or constraints which determine patterns of information growth or restrictions on possible ways of gathering new information. The interested reader will find further references in the suggested further reading for this chapter.

Exercises

1. Prove that in any Boolean algebra if $a \wedge b = 0$ and $a \vee b = 1$ then $a = b^*$.

2. Prove the idempotence of the meet and join operations from the other Boolean laws.

3. Show that in a finite Boolean lattice every element is the join of some join-irreducible elements. (Hint: you need induction on n when n is the number of elements $x \leq a$ for given a, and the base of the induction is the bottom element).

4. Prove for any join-irreducible element a of a distributive lattice, if $a \leq b \vee c$ then $a \leq b$ or $a \leq c$.

5. Prove for any relatively pseudo-complemented lattice with a top element 1 that

   (i) $a \Rightarrow a = 1$
   (ii) $a \leq b$ iff $a \Rightarrow b = 1$
   (iii) $b \leq a \Rightarrow b$

6. Prove that any finite lattice is a Heyting lattice.

7. If $\langle B, \wedge, \vee, {}^*, 0, 1 \rangle$ is a Boolean algebra then for any $a, b \in B$ define $a \mapsto b$ to be $a^* \vee b$. Show that $\langle B, \wedge, \vee, \mapsto, 0, 1 \rangle$ is a Heyting algebra.

Review Exercises

1. Following the procedure used in Theorem 10.1 prove that in a group, $y = a^{-1} \circ b$ is the unique solution of $a \circ y = b$.

2. Construct a commutative group with five elements.

3. Let the operation $x \cdot y$ be defined as $x + (y - 3)$. Show that the set G of all integers forms a group with respect to this operation and that 3 is the identity element of this group. What is the inverse element for an integer x?

4. (a) List four different subgroups of the group of all integers under ordinary addition.

   (b) For each of these subgroups, state whether it is isomorphic to the original group. If so, prove it and if not explain why not.

5. Determine all the possible isomorphisms between the group of the integers $\{0, 1, 2, 3\}$ with addition modulo 4 and the group of rotations of the square $\{I, R, R', R''\}$.

6. Let $A = \{a, b, c\}$. Find all the distinct one-to-one correspondences from A onto A. Construct composites of all pairs of these one-to-one correspondences and express your results in the form of a multiplication table. What sort of mathematical configuration is represented by this multiplication table?

7. Let A^* be the set of all strings formed from some finite set A. For all strings x and y in A^* x is said to be a *conjugate* of y iff there are strings u and v such that $x = uv$ and $y = vu$.

   (a) Show that conjugacy is an equivalence relation and describe the partition it induces on A^*. For a string x_n of length n what are the maximum and minimum number of strings in the equivalence class containing x_n?

(b) Prove that if x is a conjugate of y there is a string z such that $xz = zy$.

(c) Let $T = \{T_1,\ T_2,\ T_3,\ T_4\}$ be the set of functions each of which maps a string in A of length 4 into one of its conjugates, e.g., T_1 maps $a_1a_2a_3a_4$ into $a_1a_2a_3a_4$ and T_2 maps $a_1a_2a_3a_4$ into $a_2a_3a_4a_1$. Show that the operational structure consisting of T and the operation of composition of functions is an Abelian group.

8. Each of the following is a system of the form $\mathbf{A} = \langle\, A, \oplus, \odot\,\rangle$ consisting of a set and two binary operations. For each system, answer the following questions:

(a) Which of the group axioms are satisfied by $\langle\, A, \oplus\,\rangle$?

(b) Which of the group axioms are satisfied by $\langle\, A, \odot\,\rangle$?

(c) Is $\mathbf{A}$ an integral domain? If not, which axioms are not satisfied?

(1) $A =$ the set of all integers
$\oplus =$ ordinary addition
$\odot =$ ordinary multiplication

(2) $A =$ the set of all non-negative integers
$\oplus =$ ordinary subtraction
$\odot =$ ordinary multiplication

(3) $A = \{0, 1, 2, \ldots, 24\}$
$\oplus =$ addition modulo 25
$\odot =$ multiplication modulo 25

(4) $A = \{1, 2, 3, \ldots, 9, 10\}$
$\oplus =$ addition modulo 11
$\odot =$ multiplication modulo 11

(5) $A = \{1, 5, 7, 11\}$
$\oplus =$ addition modulo 12
$\odot =$ multiplication modulo 12

(6) $A =$ the set of all rational numbers p/q with $0 < p/q < 1$
$\oplus =$ ordinary addition
$\odot =$ ordinary multiplication

(7) $A =$ the set of all integers
$\oplus =$ ordinary addition

$\odot$ defined by $a \odot b = 0$ for all $a, b \in A$

9. Prove the following laws for integral domains. (You may use the results of previous problems as well as the axioms and theorems from the text.)

(a) $(a + b) \cdot (c + d) = (ac + bc) + (ad + bd)$ for all a, b, c, d.

(b) $-0 = 0$ (Note: $-x$ stands for "additive inverse of x", x^{-1} stands for "multiplicative inverse of x")

(c) If $a \cdot b = 0$, then either $a = 0$ or $b = 0$.

(d) $-(-a) = a$

10. The following correspondences are many-one mappings of the multiplicative group of all non-zero real numbers on part of itself. Which are homomorphisms? For those which are not, show why not. (*For those which are, *prove* that all the requirements are satisfied.)

(a) $x \mapsto |x|$

(b) $x \mapsto -x$

(c) $x \mapsto 2x$

(d) $x \mapsto 1/x$

(e) $x \mapsto x^2$

11.* Which of the following relations R are equivalence relations? For those which are, describe the equivalence classes.

(a) G is a group, S is a subgroup of G, and R is the set of all ordered pairs (a, b) with a, b in G such that $a^{-1} \cdot b \in S$.

(b) J is the integral domain of all integers and R is the set of all ordered pairs (a, b) with a, b in J such that $a + (-b)$ is even.

(c) J is the integral domain of all integers and R is the set of all ordered pairs (a, b) with a, b in J such that $a + (-b)$ is odd.

12. (a) Construct a group of symmetries of an equilateral triangle analogous to the group of symmetries of the square (There should be six elements altogether).

(b) Find all subgroups of that group.

(c) Construct a homomorphism between the whole group and one of its proper subgroups.

13. Prove using the axioms of Boolean algebras that the set of elements of a Boolean algebra cannot form a group under the union operation.

14. Prove in a relatively pseudo-complemented lattice

(a) $a = b$ iff $a \Rightarrow b = 1 = b \Rightarrow a$

(b) $1 \Rightarrow b = b$

(c) $a \leq b \Rightarrow (a \wedge b)$

Part D

ENGLISH AS A FORMAL LANGUAGE

Chapter 13

Basic Concepts

Richard Montague was the first to seriously propose and defend the thesis that the relation between syntax and semantics in a natural language such as English could be viewed as not essentially different from the relation between syntax and semantics in a formal language such as the language of first-order logic. While Montague's claim was and is a controversial one, both the perspective he offered and the technical apparatus used in developing it have transformed the study of natural language semantics. In this section we focus first on the *principle of compositionality* and its central role in articulating the relation of semantics to syntax in a formal language. The principle is also known as Frege's principle, and Montague took himself to be formalizing a basically Fregean viewpoint in adopting it. The second topic of this chapter is the *lambda calculus*, invented by Alonzo Church in the 1930's but introduced to linguists mainly through Montague's work. The lambda calculus has no intrinsic connection to the principle of compositionality, but it has proved to be one of the most important and fruitful tools in the formal semanticist's toolbox, and without it, it would be much harder to make a plausible case for the compositionality of natural language semantics. For a linguist interested in semantics, we would suggest that a familiarity with the basics of the lambda calculus could be as important as a familiarity with first-order predicate logic.

13.1 Compositionality

The term "semantics" is used in a variety of ways in a variety of fields; probably the only common denominator among these is that semantics must

be concerned with meaning, but "meaning" is if anything an even vaguer
term. Among logicians, however, the term "semantics" has had a relatively
precise usage, at least in the dominant Western tradition reflected, say in
Donald Kalish's article in the *Encyclopedia of Philosophy*, and it is out of
that tradition that Montague's work came. If you remember the discussion of syntax and semantics in Part B: Logic especially the presentation
of the syntax and semantics of statement logic in sections 6.1 and 6.2, and
of predicate logic in 7.1 and 7.2, you might have noted that both systems
are syntactically disambiguated, i.e., no wellformed formula has more than
one derivation. Quantifiers and connectives in formulas always have a de-
terminate and fixed scope. Furthermore, the semantic interpretation of any
statement or predicate logical formula is obtained via a systematic semantic
procedure interpreting its parts and the logical symbols connecting them.
The correspondence between the syntactic structure of a formula and its semantic interpretation is in fact very tight, as we will see in this section. The
principle of compositionality, or Frege's principle, is a way of articulating
the relevant notion of correspondence.

The Principle of Compositionality. The meaning of a complex expression is a function of the meanings of its parts and of the syntactic rules by
which they are combined.

Construed broadly and vaguely enough, the principle is nearly uncontro-
versial, but Montague's precise version of it places rather severe constraints
on admissable systems of syntax and semantics. As the wording given above
suggests, the exact import of the compositionality principle depends on how
one makes precise the notions of *meaning*, of *part*, and of *syntactic rule*, as
well as on the class of functions permitted to instantiate the "is a function
of" requirement.

In the specification of formal languages, the compositionality principle
is generally satisfied in the following way: the syntax is given by a recursive specification, starting with a stipulation of basic expressions of given
categories, and with recursive rules of the following sort:

Syntactic Rule n: If α is a well-formed expression of category A and β is a
well-formed expression of category B, then γ is a well-formed expression of
category C, where $\gamma = F_i(\alpha,\beta)$.

In such a rule, F_i is a syntactic operation such as concatenation; we will
give illustrations of such rules below.

The semantics is then given by a parallel recursive specification, including a stipulation of the semantic values for the basic expressions and for each syntactic rule a single semantic rule of the following form:

Semantic Rule n: If α is interpreted as α' and β is interpreted as β', then γ is interpreted as $G_k(\alpha', \beta')$.

In such a rule, G_k is a semantic operation, examples of which we will see below.

Note the distinction between syntactic and semantic *rules* as schematized above and syntactic and semantic *operations*, the F_i, G_k that appear within the rules. When the compositionality requirement is taken as a constraint on the correspondence between *rules*, as it is here, it does not by itself impose any correspondence requirement on the operations that occur within the rules. One might, for example, formulate a rule of Yes-No Question Formation for English utilizing a complex syntactic operation built up out of a combination of Subject-Aux Inversion, Do-Support, and the imposing of an appropriate intonation contour, deriving a yes-no question from its declarative counterpart. The task of giving a uniform semantic interpretation rule corresponding to such a syntactic rule is obviously very different from the (presumably impossible) task of giving a uniform semantic interpretation of the operation of Subject-Aux Inversion (which occurs in a semantically heterogeneous variety of constructions in addition to Yes-No Questions.)

13.1.1 A compositional account of statement logic

To illustrate, let us recast a part of the syntax and semantics of the statement logic of Chapter 6 and the predicate logic given in Chapter 7 in a form which makes the semantics explicitly compositional.

The syntax of SL, the language of statement logic originally presented in Section 6.1, is restated below.

(13-1) The primitive vocabulary of SL consists of the following:

    (i) a denumerably infinite set of *atomic statements* which we designate by the letters p, q, r, s, with primes or subscripts added when necessary.

    (ii) the following logical constants: $\sim$, $\&$, $\vee$, $\rightarrow$, $\leftrightarrow$. The same symbols are used in the metalanguage to designate these symbols in the object language.

(iii) the punctuation symbols (,). These are also used as names of
themselves in the metalanguage.

(13-2) The set of wffs of SL is defined recursively as follows:

(1) **Basic Clause:** Every atomic statement is a wff.

(2) **Recursive Clauses:**

(2.1) If ϕ is a wff, then the result of prefixing $\sim$ to ϕ is a wff.

(2.2) If ϕ and ψ are wffs, then the result of concatenating (,
ϕ, &, ψ, and) in that order is a wff.

(2.3) If ϕ and ψ are wffs, then the result of concatenating (,
ϕ, $\vee$, ψ, and) in that order is a wff.

(2.4) If ϕ and ψ are wffs, then the result of concatenating (,
ϕ, $\rightarrow$, ψ, and) in that order is a wff.

(2.5) If ϕ and ψ are wffs, then the result of concatenating (,
ϕ, $\leftrightarrow$, ψ, and) in that order is a wff.

The somewhat pedantic way of stating the recursive rules above is intended to emphasize that the operations which apply to wffs to produce
larger wffs include the introduction of logical constants and punctuation
marks. Given this syntax, the only relevant *parts* of a complex wff are its
constituent wffs. In this syntax, the logical constants are not assigned to any
syntactic category; the only category employed in the syntax is the category
of wffs. The semantics will be stated accordingly, assigning semantic values to complex wffs as functions of the semantic values of their constituent
wffs and of the rules by which they were constructed. (The same language
could be given a different syntax in which the logical constants (but not
the punctuation marks) are indeed assigned to categories (e.g. 'one-place
connective' and 'two-place connective') and receive semantic values (which
will be truth-functions); the semantic rules would then treat the connectives
as well as the wffs as *parts* of complex wffs and the semantic rules would
be stated in a correspondingly different way. See Dowty, Wall, and Peters
(1979) or Gamut (1982, vol. 1) for explicit illustration and discussion of this
contrast.

The semantics of SL, as stated in Section 6.1, assigns to every complex
wff a truth value, either 1 (true) or 0 (false), based on the truth values of

its constituent wffs and the syntactic rules by which they were assigned. A specification of the semantics that meets the compositionality requirement must therefore include a specification of semantic values (in this case truth values) for the atomic statements and a recursive semantic rule corresponding to each of the recursive syntactic rules. Such a semantics can be stated as follows.

(13-3) Assignment of semantic values to atomic statements: Let f be a function which assigns to each atomic statement of SL one of the two truth values 0 and 1.

(13-4) The semantic interpretation of the set of all wffs of SL, given an initial valuation f for the atomic statements, is defined recursively as follows.

(1) **Basic Clause:** If ϕ is an atomic statement, then the semantic value of ϕ is $f(\phi)$.

(2) **Recursive Clauses:**

(2.1) (unabbreviated) The semantic value of the result of prefixing $\sim$ to ϕ is 1 iff the semantic value of ϕ is 0.

(2.1) (abbreviated) The semantic value of $\sim \phi$ is 1 iff the semantic value of ϕ is 0. (The remaining rules will be written in their abbreviated form.)

(2.2) The semantic value of $(\phi \,\&\, \psi)$ is 1 iff the semantic values of ϕ and ψ are both 1.

(2.3) The semantic value of $(\phi \lor \psi)$ is 1 iff the semantic value of ϕ is 1 or the semantic value of ψ is 1.

(2.4) The semantic value of $(\phi \to \psi)$ is 1 iff the semantic value of ϕ is 0 or the semantic value of ψ is 1.

(2.5) The semantic value of $(\phi \leftrightarrow \psi)$ is 1 iff the semantic value of ϕ is identical to the semantic value of ψ.

Each of the recursive semantic rules specifies an operation which applies to the truth values of the constituent wffs to determine the truth value of the resulting wff. The operations are those familiar from the truth tables of Section 6.2, although here they are defined implicitly rather than explicitly.

It is clear from the statement of the syntactic rules and of the unabbreviated form of the first recursive semantic rule that plain English makes a rather cumbersome metalanguage and some succinct special-purpose notation could prove useful. Notation in this area is not as standardized as in some other parts of mathematics and logic, but we will introduce some fairly common notational practices below.

The syntax in (13-1) and (13-2) can be used in assigning each SL statement a unique derivation tree similarly to the syntactic trees in a Phrase-Structure component of a grammar of a natural language. The semantic rules in (13-3) and (13-4) will then give each tree a compositional interpretation, following the derivation node by node from the bottom up. Here we only illustrate the kind of tree for this syntax of SL and its semantic interpretation, and defer further discussion and alternative syntaxes to SL to the exercises of this chapter.

The derivation of the statement $\sim (p \vee q)$ is as in (13-5). The tree is annotated with the number of the (sub-) rule used in constructing each node. The compositional interpretation of (13-5) is as given in (13-6), where it is assumed that the truth value of the atomic statements is given: false for p and true for q. Note that the annotation remains exactly the same due to the rule-by-rule compositionality of SL.

Strictly speaking the semantics could either be defined on wffs the way we did in (13-1) and (13-2) with bracketing for disambiguation, or we could do without the auxiliary bracketings and have the syntax generate the derivation-trees. These kinds of derivation-trees would then constitute an equivalent but different way of disambiguating a formal or natural language and the compositional semantics would have to take trees rather than formulas as the objects to be interpreted.

(13–5)

$$\sim (p \vee q) \quad 2.1$$
$$|$$
$$(p \vee q) \quad 2.3$$
$$p,1 \qquad q,1$$

(13-6)

13.1.2   A compositional account of predicate logic

The syntax and semantics of predicate logic introduce several complexities related to the greater expressive power of predicate logic compared with statement logic. We have to recognize the distinct categories of predicates, terms, and formulas, the distinction between constants and variables among the terms, and the semantics of variables and of the binding of variables by quantifiers. The last of these was presented in a somewhat informal manner in Section 7.2, with the detailed formulation deferred to this chapter. It is interesting to reflect on the fact that the category of closed formulas, or statements, plays no essential role in the compositional semantics. It is an insight that can be traced back to Frege that we can compositionally define semantic values for formulas from semantic values for formulas (and predicates and terms), and then define semantic values for statements by an extra step, but that it is impossible to give a compositional semantics for statements using just statements as the recursive category. We return to this issue after presenting the explicit syntax and semantics below.

The syntax of PL, the language of predicate logic presented in Section 7.1, is restated in a different form below.

(13-7)   The primitive vocabulary of PL consists of the following:

(i)   A set of individual constants, which we designate in the meta-language by the letters a, b, c, with and without primes. (Different object languages have their own particular sets of constants, which may be finite or denumerably infinite.)

(ii) A denumerably infinite set of individual variables, $x_0, x_1, x_2, \ldots$ The individual constants and the individual variables together constitute the *terms*.

(iii) A set of predicates, each with fixed arity, which we officially designate in the metalanguage by P_i^n (for the ith n-ary predicate) but more frequently represent as P, Q, R with primes or subscripts as needed and the arity clear from context. As in the case of the individual constants, particular object languages will have their own particular choices of predicates.

(iv) The logical connectives of SL: $\sim, \&, \lor, \rightarrow, \leftrightarrow$.

(v) The quantifier symbols $\forall, \exists$.

(vi) The parentheses $), (, [,]$.

Together these symbols form the vocabulary of PL; more precisely, we should think of PL as a family of languages, one for each choice of individual constants and predicates (the non-logical constants.) Each such language is *a* language of predicate logic; when we speak of *the* language of predicate logic we mean the form that all these languages share, assuming some arbitrary and representative set of individual constants and predicates. (Note that while different languages may use different symbols for the individual variables, this is merely an alphabetic variation. All languages of predicate logic have a denumerably infinite set of individual variables, and their semantics is fixed by the recursive rules of the semantics, not stipulated language by language as the interpretation of the non-logical constants is.)

Given the vocabulary, the set of formulas of PL is defined recursively as in (13-8) below. In the metalanguage for talking about the syntax of PL, we need variables that range over expressions of various categories to use in the recursive rules. As in the statement of the syntax of SL, we use ϕ and ψ as variables over formulas. We use P as a variable over predicates, t, possibly with subscripts, as a variable over terms (including both individual constants and individual variables), and v as a variable over variables. (We don't need to introduce any variable over individual constants in our metalanguage because there are no rules that apply only to individual constants.) Also in our metalanguage for writing syntactic rules, instead of writing out the syntactic operations explicitly with mention of concatenation, prefixing, etc., we follow the common convention already illustrated in Chapters 6 and 7 of indicating the syntactic operation by writing its result.

(13–8) The set PL of formulas of predicate logic is the smallest set satisfying conditions (1)-(8) below: (Note: This "smallest set" locution is equivalent to adding a condition (9) which says that nothing is in the set except by virtue of a finite number of applications of (1)-(8).)

> (1) If P is an n-ary predicate and $t_1, \ldots, t_n$ are all terms, then $P(t_1, \ldots, t_n)$ is a formula. (These are the atomic formulas.)
>
> (2) If ϕ is a formula, then $\sim\phi$ is a formula.
>
> (3) If ϕ and ψ are formulas, then $(\phi \,\&\, \psi)$ is a formula.
>
> (4) If ϕ and ψ are formulas, then $(\phi \vee \psi)$ is a formula.
>
> (5) If ϕ and ψ are formulas, then $(\phi \rightarrow \psi)$ is a formula.
>
> (6) If ϕ and ψ are formulas, then $(\phi \leftrightarrow \psi)$ is a formula.
>
> (7) If ϕ is a formula and v is a variable, then $(\forall v)\phi$ is a formula.
>
> (8) If ϕ is a formula and v is a variable, then $(\exists v)\phi$ is a formula.

The definition just given is nearly identical to that given in Section 7.1 and yields exactly the same set of formulas; the only difference is that we have expanded what was stated as one rule into the five rules (2)-(6) and another rule into the two rules (7) and (8). We did that in order to be able to follow the letter of the compositionality principle and have one semantic interpretation rule for each syntactic rule. We couldn't literally do that if, for instance, rules (2)-(6) were collapsed into one rule, since each of those operations yields a distinct interpretation. In practice it is more common than not to collapse such rules anyway, and only if the compositionality of a certain grammar is challenged or uncertain is it necessary to be very precise about the individuation of the syntactic rules and their correspondence with the semantic rules.

Now we turn to the semantics of PL, which was given in Section 7.2 but not fully formally.

Remember that a model **M** for predicate logic consists of a domain D

of entities or individuals and F an assignment-function which provides the interpretation of the primitive non-logical constants of the language, i.e. a function which maps each individual constant to an individual in D and each n-ary predicate to P^n to a set of n-tuples of individuals. (Note that the domain may be indicated by other capitals; in 13.2.2 we use A, and E is also commonly found.) Besides the interpretation of the non-logical vocabulary, we need a separate function assigning individual variables, call it $g : VAR \rightarrow D$. The reasons why a separate variable-assignment is needed is that the recursive manipulation of these assignment functions plays a separate and distinctive role in the compositional semantic interpretation of quantified formulas. In effect, we generally have to consider all possible assignments to the variable in a formula in arriving at the truth conditions for the whole formula. Hence the semantic rules need to be able to refer to and change the variable-assignments in the course of the interpretation. Any element of the descriptive vocabulary, on the other hand, is interpreted once and for all independently of anything else in the formula in which it occurs, hence they are truly descriptive constants for individuals or for predicates. The interpretation of the entire language of predicate logic can now be formulated compositionally as a rule-by-rule mapping defining the denotation of an arbitrary complex formula relative to a given model and a given variable-assignment.

The *denotation of an expression α relative to a model* M *and an assignment g*, symbolized $[\![\alpha]\!]^{M,g}$, is defined recursively, in parallel to the syntactic rules given in (13-6) above, as follows:

(13–9)   (0) (a) If α is a non-logical constant in CON_A^L, then $[\![\alpha]\!]^{M,g} = F(\alpha)$.
    (b) If α is a variable in VAR_a, then $[\![\alpha]\!]^{M,g} = g(\alpha)$.

   (1) If P is an n-ary predicate and t_1, t_n are all terms, then
      $[\![P(t_1, \ldots, t_n)]\!]^{M,g} = 1$ iff $\langle [\![t_1]\!]^{M,g}, \ldots, [\![t_n]\!]^{M,g} \rangle \in [\![P]\!]^{M,g}$

If $\phi, \psi \in ME_t$, then:

   (2) $[\![\sim\phi]\!]^{M,g} = 1$ iff $[\![\phi]\!]^{M,g} = 0$

   (3) $[\![\phi \& \psi]\!]^{M,g} = 1$ iff $[\![\phi]\!]^{M,g} = 1$ and $[\![\psi]\!]^{M,g} = 1$

   (4) $[\![\phi \vee \psi]\!]^{M,g} = 1$ iff $[\![\phi]\!]^{M,g} = 1$ or $[\![\psi]\!]^{M,g} = 1$

(5) $[\![\phi \rightarrow \psi]\!]^{M,g} = 1$ iff $[\![\phi]\!]^{M,g} = 0$ or $[\![\psi]\!]^{M,g} = 1$

(6) $[\![\phi \leftrightarrow \psi]\!]^{M,g} = 1$ iff $[\![\phi]\!]^{M,g} = [\![\psi]\!]^{M,g}$

(7) If ϕ is a formula an v is a variable, then $[\![\forall v \phi]\!]^{M,g} = 1$ iff for all $d \in D, [\![\phi]\!]^{M,g^{d/u}} = 1$

(8) If ϕ is a formula an v is a variable, then $[\![\exists v \phi]\!]^{M,g} = 1$ iff there is at least one $d \in D$ such that $[\![\phi]\!]^{M,g^{d/u}} = 1$

The rules just given define semantic values for formulas compositionally in terms of the semantic value for their parts; in order to accomplish this, the semantic values for formulas were taken to be truth with respect to a model and an assignment. Having done that, we can now define truth with respect to a model (independent of assignment) for closed formulas, or statements. The easiest way to do it will define truth with respect to a model for all formulas, but it is for the closed formulas that we have the clearest idea of what results the definition shall give. (See exercise 4 for an alternative definition to (13-10) which gives different results for some of the open formulas.

(13–10)   (1) For any formula ϕ, $[\![\phi]\!]^{M}$ (i.e. ϕ is a true *simpliciter* with respect to M) iff for all assignments g, $[\![\phi]\!]^{M,g} = 1$.

(2) For any formula ϕ, $[\![\phi]\!]^{M} = 0$ iff it is not the case that $[\![\phi]\!]^{M} = 1$.

When working out the semantic interpretation of a formula, then, one first proceeds compositionally through the derivation, using rules from (13-9); then the last step is the application of the rules of (13-10).

Since the semantic rules of (13-9) match one-onto-one with syntactic rules we now have a rule-by-rule compositional semantics of Predicate Logic. Let's see how some simple examples of derivations and their compositional interpretation work out.

We will analyze the following three examples:

(i) Mary is reading a book.

(ii) Every student is reading a book.

(iii) No student is reading a book.

Keeping the quantifier prefixes as close as possible to their corresponding predicates, their translations to predicate logic are:

(i) $(\exists x)(\text{book}(x)\,\&\,\text{read}(m, x))$

(ii) $(\forall y)[\text{student}(y) \rightarrow (\exists x)(\text{book}(x)\,\&\,\text{read}(y, x))]$

(iii) $\sim (\exists y)[\text{student}(y)\,\&\,(\exists x)(\text{book}(x)\,\&\,\text{read}(y, x))]$

The derivation tree for (i) according to the syntax in (13-8) is as in (13-11), annotating each node with the number of the rule used in constructing the expression on that node (the lowest nodes are all elements of the primitive vocabulary given in (13-7)).

(13–11)

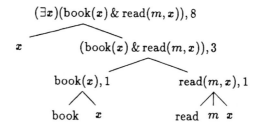

Given this derivation the interpretation of the formula proceeds from the bottom up the tree, determining the interpretation of each higher node by the semantic rule corresponding to its syntactic counterpart. Let us assume we are given the following model M and variable-assignment g for the interpretation

$\mathbf{M} = \langle D, F \rangle$, where $D = \{\text{mary, jane, MMiL}\}$
$\qquad\qquad F(m) = \text{mary}$
$\qquad\qquad F(\text{student}) = \{\text{mary, jane}\}$
$\qquad\qquad F(\text{book}) = \{\text{MMiL}\}$ (i.e. this book you are reading)

$$F(\text{read}) = \{\langle \text{mary}, \text{MMiL} \rangle\}$$
$$g(x) = \text{jane}$$
$$g(y) = \text{mary}$$

Starting at the bottom we determine according to rule (0) in (13-9) that $[\![\text{book}]\!]^{M,g} = F(\text{book}) = \{\text{MMiL}\}$, and $[\![x]\!]^{M,g} = g(x) =$jane. Furthermore, we can determine $[\![\text{book}(x)]\!]^{M,g} = 0$ according to the semantic rule (1) in (13-9), since jane is not an element of the denotation of book. Next we proceed to the interpretation of $[\![\text{read}]\!]^{M,g} = F(\text{read}) = \{\langle \text{mary}, \text{MMiL} \rangle\}$, $[\![m]\!]^{M,g} = F(m) =$mary, and $[\![x]\!]^{M,g} = g(x) =$jane. Applying rule (1) once again we have $[\![\text{read}(m, x)]\!]^{M,g} = 0$, since $\langle \text{mary,jane} \rangle$ is not in $[\![\text{read}]\!]^{M,g}$. Now we have two false formulas each with a free variable x as input to the next node where they are conjoined, and by rule (3) we determine that $[\![(\text{book}(x) \,\&\, \text{read}(m, x))]\!]^{M,g} = 0$ too.

The interesting part of the compositional interpretation of this formula comes in the final node, where the variable is bound existentially by an application of rule 8. According to its semantic counterpart rule 8 $[\![(\exists x)(\text{book}(x) \,\&\, \text{read}(m, x))]\!]^{M,g} = 1$ just in case we can find an assignment to the variable x of an individual in D such that the matrix $(\text{book}(x) \,\&\, \text{read}\,(m, x))$ with that individual assigned to the variable x is true. It is clear that the given variable-assignment g does not fulfill these conditions, since we already found out that it makes the matrix false. So now we are instructed to look beyond the given variable- assignment g that comes with the model, and search among all possible assignment-functions for an alternative g' to g which assigns to x another individual which is a book and is read by Mary. We call a variable-assignment function g' an x-alternative to g if it is identical to g with respect to all variables other than x, differing from g if at all only in the value it assigns to x. Fortunately our simple model makes the search for such an x-alternative of g in this case easy. We choose $g(x) = $ MMiL and determine subsequently that $[\![(\text{book}(x) \,\&\, \text{read}(m, x))]\!]^{M,g'} = 1$, since g' assigns MMil to x and MMil is an element in the denotation of book, and is paired with mary in the denotation of the relation read. So by rule (8) we now have $[\![(\exists x)(\text{book}(x) \,\&\, \text{read}(m, x))]\!]^{M,g} = 1$, since we have shown that there is an x-alternative of g, namely g', which makes the subformula (book $(x) \,\&\,$ read (m, x)) true.

Once we finish working up the tree, however, we still have to apply (13-10) to establish a truth value for the whole formula independent of the assignment. According to (13-10), the formula $(\exists x)(\text{book}(x) \,\&\, \text{read}(m, x))$ is true with respect to M iff it is true for every assignment function. One can

show (with a lot of tedious work; it is more common to just convince oneself
and then assert it) that the choice of starting assignment had no effect on
the outcome in this example. So, since it came out true for our original g,
we can be confident that it will indeed be true for all other possible starting
choices of assignments as well. So we conclude that our formula (which is
indeed a closed formula) is true with respect to M.

This concludes the compositional interpretation of (i). Note at this point
that although we initially used the given variable-assignment g, in the end
it did not play any role in the determination of truth-value of the entire
formula. We will return this remarkable fact below.

The second example we want to consider is

(ii) Every student is reading a book

Despite the syntactic similarity of the English sentences (i) and (ii), their
translations to predicate logic are structurally different. This difference is
primarily due to the fact that universal quantifiers require a conditional
matrix. Of course, these differences will have their consequences for the
interpretation of the formula.

(13–12)

$$(\forall y)[\text{student}(y) \rightarrow (\exists x)(\text{book}(x)\,\&\,\text{read}(y,x))], 7$$

$$y \qquad \text{student}(y) \rightarrow (\exists x)(\text{book}(x)\,\&\,\text{ready}(y,x)), 5$$

$$\text{student}(y), 1 \quad (\exists x)(\text{book}(x)\,\&\,\text{read}(y,x)), 8$$

$$\text{student} \quad y \qquad x \quad (\text{book}(x)\,\&\,\text{read}(y,x)), 3$$

$$\text{book}(x), 1 \qquad\qquad \text{read}(y,x), 1$$

$$\text{book} \quad x \qquad\qquad \text{read} \quad y \quad x$$

We will use the same model and variable-assignment as for (i) for the
interpretation of (ii). The style of presentation is slightly more compact here
as an example of how lay-out may make it easier to follow the compositional

interpretation procedure. Answering the exercises relating this material, you will have an opportunity to develop your own style and improve on this illustration.

Compositional interpretation of (13-12):

(1) like (13-11): $[\![book]\!]^{M,g} = F(book) = \{MMil\}$, and $[\![x]\!]^{M,g} = g(x) =$ jane.

(2) Rule (1): $[\![book(x)]\!]^{M,g} = 0$, as jane is not in denotation of book.

(3) Let $[\![y]\!]^{M,g} = g(y) =$ mary, $[\![read]\!]^{M,g} = F(read) = \{\langle mary, MMiL\rangle\}$

(4) Rule (1): $[\![read(y,x)]\!]^{M,g} = 0$, as $\langle mary, jane\rangle$ is not in $[\![read]\!]^{M,g}$

(5) from steps (2) and (4), rule (3) gives 0

(6) Let $g'(x) = $ MMiL, then $[\![(\exists x)(book(x)\,\&\,read(y,x))]\!]^{M,g'} = 1$.

(7) $[\![student]\!]^{M,g} = F(student) = \{mary, jane\}$

(8) by rule (1), $[\![student(y)]\!]^{M,g} = 1$ since $g(y)$ is in $[\![$ student$]\!]^{M,g}$

(9) from steps (8) and (6), rule (5) gives $[\![student(y) \rightarrow (\exists x)(book(x)$
$\&\,read(y,x))]\!]^{M,g'} = 1$.

(10) Rule (7): $[\![(\forall y)[student(y) \rightarrow (\exists x)(book(x)\,\&\,read(y,x))]]\!]^{M,g} = 0$.

Let $g'(y) = $ jane, then $[\![student(y)]\!]^{M,g'} = 1$, and given $g'(x) = $ MMiL and $[\![book(x)]\!]^{M,g'} = 1$, $[\![read(y,x)]\!]^{M,g'} = 0$, and no x-alternative to g', keeping jane the referent of y, gives a book read by jane. Hence the formula is false in the given model.

(Notes: (1) There is nothing against assigning the same individual to two distinct free variables—functions may be many-to-one! (2) To evaluate a formula containing a 'there is' within the scope of a 'for all' you need to have access not only to all alternatives of the given assignment, but also to all alternatives to any of those. Although in small domains as in our example this remains still feasible, for larger domains the search can get rapidly more complex, but for infinite domains the search may never end. In fact, on infinite domains even the evaluation of a simple universal quantifier may never end, as derivation by exhaustion is impossible, i.e., as long as you have not yet found a counterexample you may be in one of two situations; either a counterexample is still to come, or there is no counterexample. But you never know which situation you are in.)

The final example we will discuss here in detail is (iii) No student is reading a book. The syntactic derivation is given in (13-13).

(13-13) $\sim(\exists y)[\text{student}(y) \,\&\, (\exists x)(\text{book}(x) \,\&\, \text{read}(y,x))], 2$

$$\sim \quad (\exists y)[\text{student}(y) \,\&\, (\exists x)(\text{book}(x) \,\&\, \text{read}(y,x))], 8$$

$$y \quad\quad \text{student}(y) \,\&\, (\exists x)(\text{book}(x) \,\&\, \text{ready}(y,x)), 3$$

$$\text{student}(y), 1 \quad (\exists x)(\text{book}(x) \,\&\, \text{read}(y,x)), 8$$

$$\text{student} \quad y \quad\quad x \quad (\text{book}(x) \,\&\, \text{read}(y,x)), 3$$

$$\text{book}(x), 1 \quad\quad\quad \text{read}(y,x), 1$$

$$\text{book} \quad x \quad\quad\quad \text{read} \quad y \quad x$$

Using the same model and starting variable-assignment as before:

(1) $[\![\text{book}(x) \,\&\, \text{read}(y,x))]\!]^{\text{M},g} = 0$

(2) Let $g'(x) = \text{MMil}$, then $[\![\text{book}(x) \,\&\, \text{read}(y,x))]\!]^{\text{M},g'} = 1$, so $[\![(\exists x)(\text{book}(x)$

     $\&\, \text{read}(y,x))]\!]^{\text{M},g} = 1$

(3) $[\![\text{student}(y)]\!]^{\text{M},g} = 1$

(4) Rule (3): $[\![\text{student}(y) \,\&\, (\exists x)(\text{book}(x) \,\&\, \text{read}(y,x))]\!]^{\text{M},g} = 1.$

(5) Rule (8): $[\![(\exists y)[\text{student}(y) \,\&\, (\exists x)(\text{book}(x) \,\&\, \text{read}(y,x))]\!]^{\text{M},g} = 1.$

(6) Rule (2): $[\![\sim(\exists y)[\text{student}(y) \,\&\, (\exists x)(\text{book}(x) \,\&\, \text{read}(y,x))]\!]^{\text{M},g} = 0.$

(Note: the logically equivalent formula $(\forall y)[\text{student}(y) \rightarrow\, \sim(\exists x)(\text{book}(x)$ $\&\, \text{read}(y,x))]$ would require more interpretation steps, since here we need to consider all y-alternatives to g' to see whether they all falsify the formula in the scope of this universal quantifier (one of them will not, but the others will). From a semantic point of view it is in general simpler to evaluate formulas where the negation has widest scope, which can be obtained by applying the quantifier laws given in (7-7) through (7-16).)

We have seen now that in interpreting a quantified formula you first work with the given variable-assignment, but then you are often required to search for an alternative of it for a particular variable. This interpretive procedure requires not only that all alternatives for any variable to the given assignment are in some direct way available, but whenever the formula contains n successively nested quantifiers, an equal number of distinct levels of alternatives to alternatives needs to be accessed. Despite the compositional formulation we gave this Predicate Logic, in the course of an interpretation you may change what you had, if the given variable- assignment did not give you the right value in the first place (e.g. the application of rule 8 in the interpretation of (i)). It is clear that rule-by-rule compositionality seems at first to be a very strong requirement on the relation between the syntax and the semantics of a formal system. Yet it seems to allow information which is gained first, to be lost later. In other words, it does not require by itself that the meaning of the parts is still a recognizable part of the final result. This seems almost a flagrant contradiction of the Fregean Principle of Compositionality, if it is interpreted in a static way as adding primitive semantic objects to compose the meaning of the whole without any interaction between the parts. Compositionality can be understood more dynamically as a requirement on the process of interpretation, stating that the syntactic structure will guide the semantics, while having access to all possible variable-assignments. Current research in semantic theory explores various forms of interpretation processes which are compositional in different ways to different degrees.

To conclude this subsection we should return to Frege's insight mentioned at the beginning. We have seen in detail now how the compositional interpretation of Predicate Logic defines the denotation of any quantified formula in terms of the denotations of a set of formulas in which the relevant variable is free. At a time that Aristotelian syllogistic logic was still the best available theory of quantification on the market it constituted a tremendous innovation that universal and existential noun-phrases could be treated semantically on a par, if they were 'decomposed' into a variable and a quantifier prefix and the crucial but small difference of the conditional versus the conjunction in the matrix. The conditions for this new understanding were created by the mathematical development a more abstract concept of a function and the fundamental separation of the syntax of a formal system from its semantic interpretation.

13.1.3 Natural language and compositionality

When it comes to natural languages such as English, there are obvious prima facie obstacles to compositionality that make it not surprising that both linguists and philosophers before Montague doubted that English could be given a compositional semantics. One of the most obvious obstacles is the

phenomenon of quantifier scope ambiguity in English: the semantic interpretation is certainly not uniquely determined by the syntax if we take the
relevant syntactic structure to be surface structure (much less deep structure
or D-structure.) Indeed the treatment of quantifier scope has been one of
the most controversial issues within and across theories of syntax and semantics from the time of the generative-interpretive semantics split in the
late 1960's down to the present. Some theories posit a distinct syntactic
level (such as the LF of May (1977) or the underlying representations of
generative semantics) on which quantifier scope is disambiguated and on
which a compositional semantics could potentially be defined (see Cooper
and Parsons (1976)). Montague's rule-by-rule version of the compositionality requirement makes possible a treatment in which the syntactic *derivation*
rather than any *level of representation* disambiguates quantifier scope (see
Partee (1975), Dowty, Wall and Peters (1981).) Other theories (e.g. Cooper
(1983)) opt for a more nearly context-free syntax and a weakening of the
compositionality requirement. We mention these issues to give some indication of the complexity and controversy surrounding the application of the
compositionality principle to natural language semantics.

The mathematical formulation of the compositionality principle in Montague's version of it involves representing both the syntax and the semantics
as *algebras* and the semantic interpretation as a homomorphic mapping from
the syntactic algebra into the semantic algebra. The technical working out
of this idea in the general case is somewhat complex; the details are given in
Montague (1974) and explications can be found in Halvorsen and Ladusaw
(1979), DWP (1981, Chapter 8), Link (1979), Janssen (1983). For the logic
of statements, whose syntax and semantics are quite simple, the relevant
algebras and homomorphism can be specified quite straightforwardly.

(i) The syntax algebra: $\mathcal{A} = \langle A, F_0, \ldots, F_4 \rangle$ is defined as follows: Let X_0
be the set of sentential constants $\{p, q, r, p', q', \ldots\}$; and let $F_0, \ldots, F_4$ be
syntactic operations defined as follows:

$$
\begin{aligned}
F_0(\alpha) &= \sim\tilde{\alpha} \\
F_1(\alpha, \beta) &= \alpha \,\&\, \beta \\
F_2(\alpha, \beta) &= \alpha \lor \beta \\
F_3(\alpha, \beta) &= \alpha \to \beta \\
F_4(\alpha, \beta) &= \alpha \leftrightarrow \beta
\end{aligned}
$$

(Note: Here α and β are variables in the metalanguage for sentential constants. These operations should be read as e.g. 'take a sentential constant
and execute F_0 by prefixing it with the negation-symbol', etc.)

Then the set A, the set of all well-formed expressions of the logic of state-ments, is defined as closure of the set X_0 under the operations $F_0, \ldots, F_4$. Note that this gives exactly the same effect as the corresponding set of five recursive rules, one for each of the operations. This language is particularly simple by virtue of containing only one syntactic category, that of sentences, and in having a one-one correspondence between syntactic rules and syntac-tic operations that allow us to conflate the two notions.

(ii) The semantic algebra: $\mathcal{B} = \langle B, G_0, \ldots, G_4 \rangle$ is defined as follows: $B = \{0, 1\}$, the set of truth values. $G_0, \ldots, G_4$, the semantic operations corre-sponding to the syntactic operations $F_0, \ldots, F_4$, are the unary and binary functions from truth values to truth values defined by the usual truth ta-bles for the respective operations $F_0, \ldots, F_4$. So G_0, for example, is the function from $\{0, 1\}$ to $\{0, 1\}$ defined by (13-13), and G_1 the function from $\{0, 1\} \times \{0, 1\}$ to $\{0, 1\}$ defined by (13-14).

(13–14) $\quad G_0(1) = 0$
$\qquad\quad G_0(0) = 1$

(13–15) $\quad G_1(1, 1) = 1$
$\qquad\quad G_1(1, 0) = 0$
$\qquad\quad G_1(0, 1) = 0$
$\qquad\quad G_1(0, 0) = 0$

(iii) Semantic interpretation as a homomorphism from A to B: An interpretation for the statement logic must assign a truth value to each sentential constant, and must recursively assign truth values to complex statements on the basis of their syntactic structure. Let f be an assignment of truth values to the constants, i.e. a function from X_0 to $\{0, 1\}$, and let g be the interpretation function defined as follows:

If ϕ is a sentential constant, then $g(\phi) = f(\phi)$.

$$
\begin{array}{llllllll}
g(\sim \phi) & = & 1 & \textit{iff} & g(\phi) & = & 0 \\
g((\phi \,\&\, \psi)) & = & 1 & \textit{iff} & g(\phi) & = & 1 \text{ and } g(\psi) & = & 1 \\
g((\phi \vee \psi)) & = & 1 & \textit{iff} & g(\phi) & = & 1 \text{ or } g(\psi) & = & 1 \\
g((\phi \rightarrow \psi)) & = & 1 & \textit{iff} & g(\phi) & = & 0 \text{ or } g(\psi) & = & 1 \\
g((\phi \leftrightarrow \psi)) & = & 1 & \textit{iff} & g(\phi) & = & g(\psi)
\end{array}
$$

We can then see that g is indeed a homomorphism from A to B every formula in A is mapped by g onto a truth value in B, and the mapping is structure-preserving with respect to all the corresponding operators, G_i in B corresponding with F_i in A; this is established by showing that (13-15) and (13-16) below are valid.

(13–16) $g(F_0(\phi)) = G_0(g(\phi))$ *for every formula* ϕ

(13–17) $g(F_i(\phi, \psi)) = G_i(g(\phi), g(\psi))$ *for* $i = 1, \ldots, 4$ *and all formulas* ϕ, ψ

    The homomorphism requirements (13-15) and (13-16) may also be schematized by a pair of diagrams as in (13-17) and (13-18), where $g \times g$ in (13-18) stands for the function mapping pairs of formulas $\langle \phi, \psi \rangle$ onto the corresponding pairs of truth values $\langle g(\phi), g(\psi) \rangle$.

(13–18)

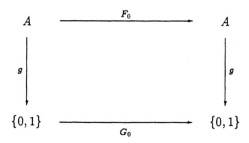

(13–19)

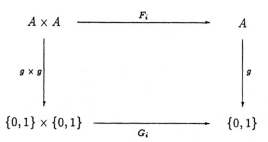

A further important property of grammars that conform to the compositionality principle in this strong homomorphism sense is that it is possible to think of such grammars as generating expressions and their interpretations in tandem; one need not conceive of the syntax generating an entire expression "before" the semantics interprets it. The small piece of a schematic *interpreted derivation* tree in (13-20) illustrates this point.

(13–20)

$$\langle F_2(F_0(F_3(\alpha,\beta)),\gamma), G_2(G_0(G_3(g(\alpha),g(\beta))),g(\gamma))\rangle$$

$$\langle F_0(F_3(\alpha,\beta)), G_0(G_3(g(\alpha),g(\beta)))\rangle$$

$$\langle F_3(\alpha,\beta), G_3(g(\alpha),g(\beta))\rangle$$

$$\langle \alpha, g(\alpha)\rangle \quad \langle \beta, g(\beta)\rangle \qquad \langle \gamma, g(\gamma)\rangle$$

Returning to the issue of compositionality in natural languages, we conclude this section with an informal, intuitive discussion of a core example of quantifier-scope ambiguity and the way in which it is connected to anaphoric binding in discourse. The purpose is here merely to illustrate the importance and extent of the issue, rather than to legislate on the best possible solution. It should be clear from Chapter 7 and this chapter that the syntactic structure of a logical formula determines the set of possible interpretations in which it is true, given an interpretation to the non-logical constants. But syntactically different formulas may have some models, though not all (unless they are logically equivalent), in which they are true in common. For instance, consider (i) and (ii)

(i) $(\forall x)(\exists y)(P(x) \rightarrow R(x,y))$

(ii) $(\exists y)(\forall x)(P(x) \rightarrow R(x,y))$

In a model in which there is at least one variable-assignment to y such that every x which is a P bears the relation R to it, both (i) and (ii) are verified (cf. exercise 3). Of course, (i) is true in other models as well, since (ii) entails (i) but not vice versa. So (i) leaves in a manner of speaking more open or undetermined as to what the model has to look like for it to be true, whereas

(ii) is more demanding. If we use an English sentence corresponding to (i), e.g. *Every student loves someone* (domain : People), we may well mean that every student loves the same person, although we could have expressed that also with *The students all love the same person* or something like this. We should consider it a virtue rather than a vice that natural language allows us different ways of describing the same situation, especially since further context often provides a clue as to which kind of situation is intended. For instance, we could continue with *Maria is her name*. Now we understand that the students must all love the same person, since both the proper name and the possessive pronoun dependent on it require a unique referent. (Let's forego the far fetched interpretation in which *Maria* could name any woman loved by a student as if it was used as a generic proper name for student-loved women). So it is this second sentence that serves to 'disambiguate' the first, and from a semantic point of view cuts down the set of possible models in which just (i) is true to the subset in which (ii) is true as well.

Now we could require that the first English sentence should be represented as the logical formula of (ii), if it is followed by this second sentence. This would mean that the first simple English sentence would be translated to two distinct logical formulas. If we also want to adhere to compositional semantics for English, this would have as a consequence that there should be two distinct syntactic derivations of this English sentence. This option is taken by quite different contemporary theories of quantifier scope e.g. May (1985) and Montague (1974), but not by e.g. Cooper (1983). We should, however, realize that this syntactic disambiguation of English sentences is really a syntactic reflection of a semantic process, namely determining the set of models in which a sentence is true or the set of situations which can be correctly described by the sentence. Quantifier scope can be encoded syntactically in the order of the quantifiers in the prefix or by coindexing in various ways, but it is the choice of variable assignments which do the real work of characterizing the dependencies between individuals.

13.2   Lambda-abstraction

13.2.1   Type theory

The lambda-operator, λ, was introduced by Alonzo Church (Church (1941)) to permit the construction of expressions which unambiguously and compositionally denote functions. Without the λ-operator, function names can only be introduced by contextual definition, as in "Let f be the function from R to R such that $f(x) = x^2 + 3$." There also tends to be equivocation in ordinary notational practice, using expressions like $f(x)$ or $x^2 + 3$ to denote either a function or its value at argument x, an equivocation that is hard to avoid without a systematic way of building descriptive names of functions. In the λ-calculus, the function f such that $f(x) = x^2 + 3$ would be denoted by the expression $\lambda x.x^2 + 3$ (or $\lambda x[x^2 + 3]$ or $(\lambda x(x^2 + 3))$; notation is not uniform), and the application of that function to an argument z would be expressed as $(\lambda x.x^2 + 3)(z)$, which as we shall see below is equivalent to the expression $z^2 + 3$.

What has made λ-abstraction so valuable a tool in contemporary semantics is the recognition that many of the most basic syntactic constructions of English can be interpreted compositionally as involving function-argument application, and that many of the apparently less basic constructions can be given a compositional semantics involving λ-abstraction. We will illustrate some of the linguistic applications at the end of this section.

As a preliminary, we need to introduce some basic notions of *type theory*. (There exist both *typed* and *untyped* versions of the lambda calculus, but it is the typed version that has become familiar to linguists from Montague's work.) A type system is a system of semantically motivated categories designed so that restrictions on well-formedness stated in terms of types can guarantee that any well- formed expression will be semantically well-defined. Russell introduced the notion as a way of regimenting the language of set theory so as to make the paradoxical "sets" mentioned in Chapter 1 unexpressable. The type theory we introduce here is just one among many, but is a common basic one.

The *set of types* is defined recursively as follows:

(13–21)   (1) e is a type.

(2) t is a type.

(3) If a and b are types then $\langle a, b \rangle$ is a type.

Sometimes rule (3) in the formation of types is replaced by the more general rule (3'):

(3') If $a_1, \ldots, a_n$ and b are types, then $\langle a_1, \ldots, a_n, b \rangle$ is a type.

Since functions of more arguments can be reduced to unary functions, the type $\langle a_1, \ldots, a_n, b \rangle$ may be replaced by $\langle a_1, \langle a_2, \langle \ldots \langle a_n, b \rangle \rangle \ldots \rangle \rangle$ and therefore one does not need to postulate types for such n-ary functions explicitly.

A typed language is a language each of whose well-formed expressions is assigned a type by a compositional syntax whose semantics conforms to the following principles, where D_a stands for the set of possible denotations of expressions of type a.

(13–22) Let A be a given domain of entities. Then

      (1) $D_e = A$

      (2) $D_t = \{0, 1\}$, the set of truth-values

      (3) $D_{\langle a,b \rangle}$ = the set of functions from D_a to D_b

In case an n-ary type is defined, its intended interpretation is:

$$D_{\langle a, \ldots, a_n, b \rangle} = \text{the set of functions from } D_{a_1} \times \ldots \times D_{a_n} \text{ to } D_b$$

In other words, expressions of type e denote individuals, expressions of type t denote truth values, and expressions of type $\langle a, b \rangle$ denote functions whose arguments are in D_a and whose value is in D_b.

Examples:

(1) Suppose A, and hence D_e, is the set of real numbers. Then the expression mentioned in the previous section, $(\lambda x(x^2 + 3))$, is of type $\langle e, e \rangle$, since it denotes a function from numbers to numbers.

(2) Sets in a typed language are identified by expressions denoting their characteristic functions. Consider, for instance, the set of numbers greater than 7. Its characteristic function f is defined by (13-23).

(13–23)
$$f(x) = \begin{cases} 1 \text{ if } x > 7 \\ 0 \text{ if } x < 7 \end{cases}$$

In λ-notation, f can be expressed as $(\lambda x(x > 7))$. Since f is a function from numbers to truth-values, the type of the expression is $\langle e, t \rangle$; this is the type for any expression denoting (the characteristic function of) a set of entities.

(3) The predicate calculus can be given as a typed language; individual constants and variables are of type e, formulas are of type t, one-place predicates (which denote sets) are of type $\langle e, t \rangle$, two-place predicates are of type $\langle e, \langle e, t \rangle \rangle$, etc.

13.2.2   The syntax and semantics of λ-abstraction

The λ-operator and the rule of λ-abstraction give us a means for forming compositionally interpretable names of functions. Compare, for example, the schematic letter name f with the structurally descriptive name $(\lambda x(x^2 + 3))$. Now, how in general does one form an expression like the latter? Start with an expression that denotes the *value* of the desired function for a variable argument: in this case, $(x^2 + 3)$. To form the name of the function which applies to an arbitrary number x and gives as value the number $(x^2 + 3)$, we "abstract on" the argument variable x and form the *λ-abstract* $(\lambda x(x^2 + 3))$, consisting of the prefixed *λ-operator* λx and the body $(x^2 + 3)$. More generally, we have the syntactic formation rule in (13-24).

(13–24) *λ-abstraction, Syntax:*
   If u is a variable of type a and α is an expression of type b, then $(\lambda u \alpha)$ is an expression of type $\langle a, b \rangle$.

The λ-operator, like the quantifiers, is a variable-binding operator. And like the quantifiers, its semantics makes crucial appeal to variable assignments.

But note that the λ-operator can change the type of its argument, e.g. from t to some functional type, whereas quantifiers take formulas to make formulas and hence do not change their argument-type.

(13–25) *λ-abstraction, Semantics:*
   Given u of type a, α of type b, $[\![(\lambda u \alpha)]\!]^{M,g}$ is that function f from D_a to D_b such that:

   for any object k in D_a, $f(k) = [\![\alpha]\!]^{M,g'}$,
   where g' is just like g except that $g'(u) = k$.

To take our earlier example, $[\![(\lambda x(x^2 + 3))]\!]^{M,g}$ is that function f such that for any number n in D_e, $f(n) = [\![(x^2 + 3)]\!]^{M,g'}$. That is, we find the value of the function for a given argument n by evaluating the body of the λ-abstract with respect to an assignment that assigns n to x. Suppose $n = 5$. Then $f(5) = [\![(x^2+3)]\!]^{M,g'}$, where $g'(x) = 5$; supposing the expressions in the formula have their standard semantics, the value of the expression $(x^2 + 3)$ on the assignment of 5 to x will be the number 28, where g' is the variable-assignment which assigns exactly the same values to all variables other than x as g does, but assigns the number n to x.

The process we have just illustrated is called *lambda-conversion*: it computes the value of the lambda-expression for the argument the function is applied to. It is important to realize that lambda-conversion is fundamentally different from the syntactic process of substituting a constant for a variable in a formula. The former is a semantic and computational process of executing an algorithm for a given argument, the latter should be viewed as a syntactically defined 'transformation' on formulas or a rule of inference which supposedly guarantees that truth is preserved in a particular deductive system. Lambda-abstraction gives us the important means to distinguish a function from the set of its values, which has proven tremendously useful for linguistic applications, especially where intensional aspects of meaning play a crucial semantic role (cf. section 13.2.5).

There is an important restriction on lambda-conversion that should be adhered to for $(\lambda u \alpha)(\beta)$ to be logically equivalent to α', where α' is just like α but with the assignment of β to the variable u. We have to make sure that in case β contains any free variables of some type, they do not accidentally get bound by any quantifiers occurring in α. For instance, we cannot convert

$$(\lambda\phi\exists x(P(x)\,\&\,\phi))(Q(x))$$

to

$$\exists x(P(x)\,\&\,Q(x))$$

The reason why this conversion would not always be logically equivalent is that $Q(x)$ is interpreted by the given variable assignment in the first formula, but could be interpreted by an x-alternative to it in the second formula resulting in different truth-conditions. Of course, to avoid accidentally binding free variables one seeks recourse to logically equivalent alphabetic variants of the argument the lambda-term is applied to (cf. section 7.3 for the notion of alphabetic variants). Similar restrictions apply when the formal language contains operators which have quantificational force, as the intensional language defined in Chapter 15. But we will not discuss these any further here.

Less accurately but quite mnemonically, one can say that $(\lambda u \alpha)$ denotes a function with $\underline{u}$ as argument and $[\![\alpha]\!]$ as value.

13.2.3   A sample fragment

Drawing together the notions we have introduced thus far, we present the syntax and semantics of a sample formal language-schema TL, a schema for typed languages whose logical constants include all those of the predicate calculus with equality, plus the lambda operator. Particular languages L falling under this schema differ in the choice of (non-logical) constants and their interpretation.

I. Syntax of TL (13–26) The set T of *types* of TL is the smallest set such that

(i) $e, t \in T$

(ii) If $a, b \in T$, then $\langle a, b \rangle \in T$

(13–27) The *primitive vocabulary* of TL consists of the following:

(i) The connectives $\sim$, $\&$, $\vee$, $\rightarrow$, $\leftrightarrow$

(ii) The quantifiers $\forall, \exists$

(iii) The lambda-operator λ

(iv) The equality symbol $=$

(v) The parentheses), (, [,]

(vi) For every type a, a denumerably infinite set VAR_a containing variables $v_{n,a}$ for each natural number n

(vii) For every type a, a (possibly empty) set CON_a^L of (non-logical) constants of type a

Note: the symbols introduced in (i)–(iv) are called logical *constants*; their meaning is fixed for all languages in the family TL. The *non-logical constants* of (vii) are language-particular, and their interpretation must be specified in a model for a particular language L.

(13-28) **Syntactic rules of TL**

The set ME_a of *meaningful expressions of TL of type a* is defined recursively as follows:

(i) For each type a, every variable in VAR_a and every constant in CON_a^L is in ME_a.

(ii) For any types a and b, if $\alpha \in ME_{\langle a,b \rangle}$ and $\beta \in ME_a$, then $\alpha(\beta) \in ME_b$.

(iii) For any types a and b, if u is a variable of type a and $\alpha \in ME_b$, then $(\lambda u \alpha) \in ME_{\langle a,b \rangle}$.

(iv) If ϕ and ψ are in ME_t (are formulas), then the following are also in ME_t: $\sim \phi, (\phi \,\&\, \psi), (\phi \vee \psi), (\phi \rightarrow \psi), (\phi \leftrightarrow \psi)$.

(v) For any type a, if $\phi \in ME_t$ and u is a variable of type a, then $\forall u \phi$ and $\exists u \phi$ are in ME_t.

(vi) For any type a, if α and β are both in ME_a, then $(\alpha = \beta) \in ME_t$.

As a particular instance of this schema which we will use for examples in the text and in the exercises, let TLA ("typed language of arithmetic") be syntactically defined by the following choice of constants:

(13-29) **Constants of TLA.**

$$CON_e^{TLA} = \{\bar{0}, \bar{1}, \bar{2}, \ldots\}$$

$$CON_{\langle e,t \rangle}^{TLA} = \{\textbf{even, odd, prime}\}$$

$$CON_{\langle e, \langle e,t \rangle \rangle}^{TLA} = \{\textbf{gr}\}$$

$$CON_{\langle e,e \rangle}^{TLA} = \{\textbf{succ}\}$$

$$CON_{\langle e, \langle e,e \rangle \rangle}^{TLA} = \{\textbf{plus}\}$$

Note that, e.g., $\bar{0}$ is a syntactic name, not a number. In (13-35) these names are assigned their natural referents.

In practice it is common to drop outermost parentheses, and to drop other parentheses where there is no danger of ambiguity. We will also follow a common practice in using the following, more readable, variables in place of the official ones:

(13–30) **Variable conventions**

Type	Variable
e	x, y, z (also with subscripts or primes)
$\langle e, t \rangle$	P, Q
$\langle e, \langle e, t \rangle \rangle$	R, S
$\langle e, e \rangle$	f

Examples of well-formed expressions of various types of TLA follow.

(13–31)

	Expression	Type
(i)	$odd(x) \vee even(x)$	t
(ii)	$succ(succ(x))$	e
(iii)	$gr(\bar{3})$	$\langle e, t \rangle$
(iv)	$gr(\bar{3})(x)$	t
(v)	$(\lambda x gr(\bar{3})(x))$	$\langle e, t \rangle$
(vi)	$(\lambda x gr(\bar{3})(x))(succ(\bar{3}))$	t

In order to parse a complex λ-expression, it is often helpful to construct a tree that displays its derivation according to the syntax, just like the derivation trees in 13.1.1 and 13.1.2 for the two logical languages. Such a tree structure is sometimes called a *derivation tree* or an *analysis tree*. A derivation tree for (13-31) is given in (13-32).

In the derivation trees for TLA, it is useful to annotate each node first with the type of the expression on that node and, second, with the number of the rule that we applied in constructing that expression. The construction of such a derivation tree can also be valuable aid in working out the semantics of complex expressions, since the semantic interpretation rules correspond rule-by-rule to the syntactic derivation rules. We give the semantics for TL in general below, followed by the language-particular interpretation of the constant of TLA.

(13-32) $(\lambda x\, \mathbf{gr}(\bar{3})(x)), \langle e,t\rangle, 3$

$$x, e \qquad \mathbf{gr}(\bar{3})(x), t, 2$$

$$\mathbf{gr}(\bar{3}), \langle e,t\rangle, 2 \qquad x, e$$

$$\mathbf{gr}, \langle e, \langle e,t\rangle\rangle \qquad \bar{3}, e$$

II. Semantics of TL

(13-33) Given a non-empty set A, the domain of entities, the set D_a of possible denotations of expressions of type a is given by the following definition:

> (i) $D_e = A$
> $D_t = \{$TRUE, FALSE (or 1 and 0 conventionally)$\}$

> (ii) For any $a, b \in T$, $D_{\langle a,b\rangle} = D_b^{D_a}$, i.e. the set of all functions from D_a to D_b.

The denotation of an expression of a language L of the family TL is defined relative to a *model* M and an *assignment* g of values to variables. A *model for L* is an ordered pair $\mathbf{M} = \langle A, F\rangle$, such that A is a domain of entities and F is a function which provides an interpretation to the primitive non-logical constants of L, i.e. a function which maps each constant of type a onto a denotation in D_a. An *assignment* g of values to variables is a function which assigns to each variable $v_{n,a}$ a value from the set D_a.

(13-34) **Semantic rules of TL**

> The *denotation of an expression α relative to a model* M *and an assignment* g, symbolized $[\![\alpha]\!]^{M,g}$, is defined recursively, in parallel to the syntactic rules given in (13-28) above, as follows:

> (i) (a) If α is a non-logical constant in CON_A^L, then $[\![\alpha]\!]^{M,g} = F(\alpha)$.
> (b) If α is a variable in VAR_a, then $[\![\alpha]\!]^{M,g} = g(\alpha)$.

> (ii) If $\alpha \in ME_{\langle a,b\rangle}$ and $\beta \in ME_a$, then $[\![\alpha(\beta)]\!]^{M,g} = [\![\alpha]\!]^{M,g}([\![\beta]\!]^{M,g})$.

(iii) = the λ-rule given in (13-25).

(iv) If $\phi, \psi \in ME_t$, then:

$[\![\sim \phi]\!]^{M,g} = 1$ iff $[\![\phi]\!]^{M,g} = 0$

$[\![\phi \& \psi]\!]^{M,g} = 1$ iff $[\![\phi]\!]^{M,g} = 1$ and $[\![\psi]\!]^{M,g} = 1$

$[\![\phi \lor \psi]\!]^{M,g} = 1$ iff $[\![\phi]\!]^{M,g} = 1$ or $[\![\psi]\!]^{M,g} = 1$

$[\![\phi \to \psi]\!]^{M,g} = 1$ iff $[\![\phi]\!]^{M,g} = 0$ or $[\![\psi]\!]^{M,g} = 1$

$[\![\phi \leftrightarrow \psi]\!]^{M,g} = 1$ iff $[\![\phi]\!]^{M,g} = [\![\psi]\!]^{M,g}$

(v) If $\phi \in ME_t$, $u \in VAR_a$, then

  (a) $[\![\forall u\phi]\!]^{M,g} = 1$ iff for all $d \in D_a, [\![\phi]\!]^{M,g^{d/u}} = 1$

  (b) $[\![\exists u\phi]\!]^{M,g} = 1$ iff there is at least one $d \in D_a$ such that $[\![\phi]\!]^{M,g^{d/u}} = 1$.

(vi) If $\alpha, \beta \in ME_a$, then $[\![\alpha = \beta]\!]^{M,g} = 1$ iff $[\![\alpha]\!]^{M,g} = [\![\beta]\!]^{M,g}$.

Note that the only language-particular part of the interpretation of a language L of the family TL resides in the choice of a model M, i.e. in the choice of a domain A of entities and an interpretation F of the language-particular, i.e. non-logical, constants. The specification of the set of constants and their interpretation F can be thought of as the *lexicon* of the language. Given the model, the semantic interpretation of the infinite set of expressions of the language is fixed by the recursive semantic rules, which are the same for all typed languages of the family TL.

The semantics for the sample language TLA is fixed by the following specification of a model:

(13–35) *A model* M *for TLA.*

M $= \langle A, F \rangle$, where $A =$ the set of natural numbers $\{0, 1, 2, 3, \ldots\}$ and F is specified as follows:

(i) $F(\bar{0}) = 0, F(\bar{1}) = 1$, etc.

(ii) $F(\mathbf{even}) =$ (the characteristic function of) the set of even numbers.

$F(\mathbf{odd}) =$ (the characteristic function of) the set of odd numbers.

$F(\mathbf{prime}) =$ (the characteristic function of) the set of prime numbers.

(iii) $F(\mathbf{gr})$ ("greater than") is that function f such that $f(a)(b) =$ 1 iff b is greater than a. Note that $f(a) =$ the (characteristic function of the) set of numbers greater than a.

(iv) $F(\mathbf{succ}) =$ the successor function.

(v) $F(\mathbf{plus})$ is that function f such that $f(a)(b) = a + b$; $f(a)$ by itself is a function which takes a single argument and adds a to it.

We can now determine the denotation of the expressions given as examples in (13-31); this we do in (13-36). Denotations must be relative to model M and an assignment g; M was given in (13-35), and for g we will choose, arbitrarily, an assignment which assigns the number 2 to every variable. Details are left as an exercise to the reader.

(13–36)

	Expression α	Denotation $[\![\alpha]\!]^{M,g}$
(i)	$\mathbf{odd}(x) \vee \mathbf{even}(x)$	TRUE, independent of assignment
(ii)	$\mathbf{succ}(\mathbf{succ}(x))$	4
(iii)	$\mathbf{gr}\,(\bar{3})$	the set of numbers greater than 3
(iv)	$\mathbf{gr}\,(\bar{3})(x)$	false, since 2 is not greater than 3
(v)	$(\lambda x\,\mathbf{gr}\,(\bar{3})(x))$	the set of numbers greater than 3
(vi)	$(\lambda x\,\mathbf{gr}\,(\bar{3})(x))(\mathbf{succ}\,(\bar{3}))$	TRUE, since 4 is greater than 3

13.2.4   The lambda-calculus

The pure lambda-calculus is a theory of functions as *rules*. It was developed around 1930 to serve as foundation for logic and mathematics in its type-free version, in which any function may be its own argument. (In Zermelo-Fraenkel set-theory such self-application was ruled out by the axiom of foundation.) Despite the paradoxes that arose in such unrestricted type-free systems, a consistent part of the theory has turned out to be extremely useful as a formal theory of (partial) recursive functions. It has more recently been successfully applied in computer science for instance in the semantics of programming languages. In linguistics it is not the entire system of lambda-calculus, but rather its operation of lambda-abstraction and conversion that have proven extremely useful as we will discuss in more detail in the next section. The present section contains a very elementary exposition of the lambda-calculus itself, illustrating how fundamental a theory of functions it really is.

The syntax of the lambda-calculus is very simple. The set Λ of lambda-terms and formulas of the lambda-calculus are defined in (13-37) recursively.

(13–37) **Syntax of the lambda-calculus**

      Lexicon: $x, y, \ldots$ -variable
                λ -lambda-abstractor
                $(,)$ -parentheses
      Rules: (i) $x \in \Lambda$
                (ii) if $M \in \Lambda$ then $(\lambda x M) \in \Lambda$ (abstraction)
                (iii) if $M, N \in \Lambda$ then $(M N) \in \Lambda$ (application)
                (iv) if $M, N \in \Lambda$ then $M = N$ is a formula

The axiomatization of the theory is given in (13-38). Here M, N and Z are arbitrary lambda-terms.

(13–38) **Axiomatization of the lambda-calculus**

    (i) $(\lambda x M) N = M'$ which is M with every occurrence of x replaced by N (conversion)

    (ii) $=$ is reflexive, symmetrical and transitive

    (iii) if $M = N$ then $M Z = N Z$

    (iv) if $M = N$ then $Z M = Z N$

    (v) if $M = N$ then $(\lambda x M) = (\lambda x N)$

If $M = N$ can be proven from these axioms, we say that M and N are *convertible*. It must be noted that there is a certain asymmetry in for instance the equation expressed in (13-39).

(13–39) $(\lambda x \mathrm{succ}(x))(\bar{3}) = 4$

The statement in (13-39) can be interpreted as "4 is the result of computing the successor of 3", but not vice versa. This asymmetry is expressed overtly by calling the computation a *reduction* of $(\lambda x \mathbf{succ}(x))(\bar{3})$ to 4. One of the central theorems of the lambda-calculus, called the *Church-Rosser theorem*, says that if two terms can be converted, then there is a term to which both can be reduced. There are many more notions of conversion and reduction definable in the lambda-calculus than we introduced here. Our rule (13-25) is sometimes called β-conversion.

The lambda-calculus it itself not a logical, inferential system, but we can define the usual predicate logical concepts in lambda-terms as in (13-40). We give here the definitions from Henkin (1963), which are also presented in Gallin (1975). Here we use a typed language merely for convenience and coherence with the previous sections: ϕ and ψ are variables of type t, i.e. formula-variables, and f is a variable of type $\langle t, t \rangle$.

(13–40) $\text{TRUE} =_{def} ((\lambda\phi\phi) = (\lambda\phi\phi))$

$\text{FALSE} =_{def} ((\lambda\phi\phi) = (\lambda\phi\text{TRUE}))$

$\sim =_{def} (\lambda\phi(\text{FALSE}= \phi))$

$\& =_{def} (\lambda\phi\lambda\psi(\lambda f(f(\phi) = \psi) = \lambda f(f(\text{TRUE}))))$

$\rightarrow =_{def} (\lambda\phi\lambda\psi(\phi \,\&\, \psi = \phi)$

$\vee =_{def} (\lambda\phi\lambda\psi(\sim \phi \rightarrow \psi))$

$x_a A =_{def} (\lambda x_a A = \lambda x_a \text{TRUE})$

$\exists x_a A =_{def} \sim x_a \sim A$

In (13-40) the definitions of the disjunction and the existential quantifier are already quite familiar from Chapter 7. In developing an intuition for what the other definitions do, we can understand for instance the definition of conjunction as the operation of assigning the truth-value TRUE to both formulas and of the conditional as stating that the information that ψ is true is already contained in the information that ϕ is true.

Church showed that the part of the lambda-calculus which is concerned only with functions provides a good formalization of the intuitive concept of 'effectively computability' as *lambda-definability*. Alan Turing in 1937 analyzed the notion of machine-computability, which came to be called *Turing-computability*, and proved its equivalence to lambda-definability. It is remarkable that despite the very simple syntax of lambda-calculus the system is strong enough to describe all computable functions. This makes it in fact a paradigmatic programming language, laying out the applicative behavior of the computational procedures in their barest form. But it is for most practical purposes not a very handy programming language, exactly because of its completely transparent structure. Yet several well-known programming languages have some features which resemble the lambda-calculus. In LISP, for instance, procedures can be arguments of procedures, as well as output of procedures.

Due to the fact that functions could take themselves as arguments, i.e. the *type-free character* of the pure lambda-calculus the question arose what models of the theory could look like. A set X was needed into which the entire function space $X \rightarrow X$ could be embedded, which was impossible in ordinary set-theory due to Cantor's theorem (cf. Chapter 4). Dana Scott in 1969 developed models of the type-free lambda-calculus by taking only the *continuous* functions on X. Only then did it become clear how a denotational semantics of programming languages could be constructed. This has opened a vast area for innovative research in the common aspects of the semantics of programming and natural languages. The interested reader is referred to Barendregt (1984) for a complete introduction to the mathematical aspects of lambda-calculus and Scott domains.

13.2.5 Linguistic applications

In this section we will briefly discuss a few of the many applications to natural language semantics that have made lambda-abstraction a basic tool in the development of formal semantics. In general, lambda-expressions provide a means for giving compositionally analyzable names to *functions* of arbitrary types. This can be richly exploited in giving a compositional semantics for natural languages like English which have a large number of syntactic categories and quite a variety of recursive mechanisms that end up embedding expressions of one category in expressions of another or the same category. Lambda-expressions can make explicit how the interpretation of a relative clause is a function of the interpretation of a corresponding open sentence, how predicate negation or conjunction is related to sentential negation or conjunction, how the meaning of a passive verb can be defined in terms of the meaning of a corresponding active verb, etc. Lambdas can also be used to make explicit the interpretation of various grammatical morphemes or function words, such as reflexive clitics and other "argument-manipulating" devices, logical determiners such as *every* and *no*, the comparative morpheme *-er*, etc. We will illustrate just a few of these applications below;

for other illustrations and references to more, see Montague (1973), Cresswell (1973), Partee (1975), Williams (1983), Dowty, Wall and Peters (1981),
Dowty (1979), Janssen (1983), and in fact much of the formal semantics
literature since the mid-1970's. Lambdas became widely known to the linguistic community through the work of Montague, but Montague was not
their inventor (Alonzo Church was: see Church (1941)), and one does not
have to be a "Montague grammarian" or even a formal semanticist to find
them useful.

What does it mean to give compositionally analyzable names to functions? The contrast is similar to that between proper names like *John* and
definite descriptions like *the oldest student in the semantics class*. In much
common mathematical practice, and in most of this book, functions are referred to with proper names, either coined on the spot or established names
like *Meet* or +, or with typical variables in place of names, like f and g. In the
language TL and other such typed languages that include lambda abstraction, we have not only the possibility of including as many proper names
of functions as we wish but also the possibility of building up structured
function- denoting lambda-expressions for which the semantics specifies just
what function each such expression denotes.

I. Phrasal conjunction

One very simple and elegant application of lambda-abstraction which
Montague exploited in PTQ is its use in defining the interpretation of "Boolean"
phrasal conjunction, disjunction, and negation in terms of sentential conjunction, disjunction, and negation respectively. (The term "Boolean" phrasal
conjunction refers, for reasons the reader will appreciate, to the kind of
phrasal conjunction illustrated in the examples below, as opposed to e.g. the
group-forming NP conjunction illustrated by "John and Mary are a happy
couple", or the irreducibly phrasal conjunction of adjectives in "a red and
white dress".)

To illustrate this application, we give below a few syntactic rules in simple phrase-structure-rule form together with corresponding schematic translation rules. We will comment on the nature of such rules after illustrating
them.

Syntactic Rule	Translation Into TL
S → S and S	$S'_1 \mathbin{\&} S'_2$
S → S or S	$S'_1 \vee S'_2$
VP → VP and VP	$\lambda x.(\text{VP}'_1(x) \mathbin{\&} \text{VP}'_2(x))$
NP → NP or NP	$\lambda P.(\text{NP}'_1(P) \vee \text{NP}'_2(P))$

First a note on the NP interpretations presupposed here: as we will discuss later in this subsection, we interpret NPs as *generalized quantifiers*, of type $\langle\langle e,t\rangle,t\rangle$. We use P and Q as variables of type $\langle e,t\rangle$.

Second a note on the nature of these rules: The syntactic rules are given in familiar phrase-structure form, but could easily be recast in the recursive format specified earlier. When dealing with simple context-free grammars, it is straightforward to convert a grammar of one form to one of the other. The translation rules are not semantic interpretation rules as defined above, since they specify expressions in TL as their output rather than model-theoretic objects. The first rule, for instance, says that the translation into TL of any expression formed by application of the first syntactic rule will be formed by taking the translations of the two parts and putting an & between them. (We subscript the S's in the translation simply to distinguish occurrences.) The resulting formula of TL will itself be semantically interpreted according to the semantic rules of the language TL, which we do not repeat here (see Section 13.2.3). As Montague showed, as long as the translation rules are compositional and the semantic interpretation of the intermediate language is compositional, the intermediate language could in principle be eliminated and a compositional model-theoretic semantic interpretation given directly to the source language (in this case a fragment of English.) But the use of an intermediate language is at least convenient; whether such an intermediate language plays a role in capturing "linguistically significant generalizations" is a point of some debate.

In any case we will continue to use the conventions illustrated above in giving short versions of rules, including the convention of using primes (′) to indicate the translations of the parts.

In order to illustrate the workings of the rules above, we need to combine them with a few other rules for simple sentences; these follow Montague's treatment in PTQ except for supressing intensionality.

S	→	NP VP	$NP'(VP')$
NP	→	some/a CN	$\lambda P.(\exists x)(CN'(x)\,\&\,P(x))$
NP	→	every CN	$\lambda P.(\forall x)(CN'(x)\rightarrow P(x))$
NP	→	John, Mary, ...	$\lambda P.P(j)$, etc.
VP	→	walks, talks, ...	walk′, talk′, ...
CN	→	man, woman, ...	man′, woman′, ...

Using these rules and lambda-conversion, the reader can verify equivalences and non-equivalences like the following.

(13–41) (a) John walks and talks   is equivalent to:
         (b) John walks and John talks

(13–42) (a) Some man walks and talks   is **not** equivalent to:
         (b) Some man walks and some man talks

Before linguists had learned to exploit lambdas, Boolean phrasal conjunction was treated syntactically by positing some kind of "conjunction reduction" transformation or schema, which would, for example, derive (13-41a) above from the full conjoined sentence (13-41b). But as (13-41) and (13-42) together illustrate, syntactic conjunction reduction sometimes preserves meaning and sometimes does not. It is now widely appreciated that the actual distributions of forms and meanings in such cases of Boolean phrasal conjunction can be more systematically explained by directly generating the phrasal conjunctions syntactically and using semantic rules like those formulated above with lambdas to interpret them. It thus appears that the intuition that phrasal conjunction is derivative from sentential conjunction is best regarded as based on semantic rather than syntactic generalizations. Direct syntactic generation combined with compositional semantic interpretation can, if all goes well, capture the scopal interactions of conjunction with other scopally relevant parts of the interpretation, without any special stipulations.

Further linguistic research has been and continues to be concerned with exploring the limits and generalizability of such an approach to Boolean conjunction as well as analyzing the various sorts of non-Boolean conjunctions (mentioned above) and their interrelations. One major generalization explored by Keenan and Faltz (1985), Gazdar (1980), and Partee and Rooth (1983) centers on the observation that the particular translation rules given above for VP-conjunction and NP-disjunction should not have to be stipulated: it should be possible to predict them just by knowing (i) the interpretation of sentential conjunction and disjunction and (ii) the semantic types associated with the syntactic categories VP and NP. Partee and Rooth propose a schema for generalized conjunction, recursively defined, which has those properties, and which replaces the individual explicit rules given above, so that the lambdas no longer play an overt role. But the functions that are denoted by those lambda-expressions are playing the same central role in the resulting account, and the lambda notation for denoting them compositionally helped to make the relevant generalizations findable.

II. Relative clauses

Another construction whose semantics has been much better understood since the introduction of lambdas into the linguist's toolbox is the relative clause. While many open problems remain concerning both the syntax and the semantics of relative clauses of various kinds in various languages, we can at least give one very straightforward account of one very basic kind of relative clause construction as another good sample application of lambda-abstraction. The account is probably approximately correct for some real-life cases and at least suggestive of how to proceed for others. We will stick to the syntactically simplest sorts of examples so as to be able to concentrate on the central aspects of the compositional semantics of the construction.

There are two parts to the account of relative clauses: their internal syntax and semantics, i.e. how they are formed and interpreted, and the syntax and semantics of the construction through which they come to modify nouns or noun phrases. Let's look at these in turn.

What we call relative clauses are modifiers which play an adjectival sort of role but which are formed in some sense from sentences. Lambda-abstraction provides an explicit way to say exactly that, as long as we assume that the relevant "underlying sentences" are open sentences, i.e., sentences whose interpretation contains a free variable in the "relativized position" (a position which may end up occupied by a gap or a resumptive pronoun depending on the construction). So, for example, we might take all the relative clauses in (13-43b) and (13-44b) below to be derived from something like the sentences (or almost sentences) in (13-43a) and (13-44a). If the translations of the sentences are as given in (13-43c) and (13-44c), the translations of the relative clauses can be derived by lambda-abstraction on the relativized variable, as shown in (13-43d) and (13-44d). One can read the expression in (13-43d) in quasi-English, a bit loosely, as "the property of being an x_3 such that Mary loves x_3." (This is loose because "property" is normally an intensional notion and the literal interpretation is just the characteristic function of a set; but when talking about the model-theoretic interpretations in English, explicit set-talk simply tends to be cumbersome, and the misrepresentation is harmless as long as the context does not allow real misinterpretation.)

(13–43) (a) Mary loves e_3
        (b) who(m) Mary loves; that Mary loves; such that Mary loves him
        (c) love$'(m, x_3)$
        (d) λx_3.love$'(m, x_3)$

(13–44) (a) e_2 hates John
         (b) who hates John; who$_2$ e_2 hates John;
             such that he/she hates John
         (c) hate$'(x_2, j)$
         (d) $\lambda x_2.\text{hate}'(x_2, j)$

The semantic type of the open sentences is t, so when we do lambda-abstraction with respect to a variable of type e, the type of the resulting expressions in (13-43d) and (13-44d) is $\langle e, t \rangle$, the type of functions from entities to truth values, i.e. the type of characteristic functions of sets of entities. So (13-43d) denotes the set of entities that Mary loves, and (13-44d) the set of entities that hate John. This is the same type that is assigned to simple predicative adjectives like *purple* or *carnivorous*. Lambda-abstraction on open sentences gives us an infinite stock of such predicates.

Note that we have not actually given explicit syntactic and semantic rules for forming relative clauses but have simply specified what the effects of the rules should be. This is for two reasons. The obvious one is to avoid descriptive complications and maintain theoretical neutrality as regards the syntax of relative clauses; the less obvious one is that in the immediately preceding example it was important to be explicit about the interpretation of NPs as generalized quantifiers, while in this example that would just present extraneous complications (though no substantive problems), so we have presented the translations in the form they would have after some steps of lambda conversion had replaced the original translations of the proper names and the gaps or pronouns by expressions of type e. The one addition to the previous fragment that does need to be mentioned is the addition of the gaps or pronouns: the simplest way to add them for our purposes (though this is an area rife with competing approaches) is to assume that the syntax (via the lexicon) contains among its NPs an infinite supply of indexed gaps (here represented as e_1, e_2, etc.) and/or pronouns (he_1, he_2, etc.), whose translations are just like the translations of the proper nouns *John*, *Mary*, etc., given in the previous fragment except containing variables like x_1, x_2, etc. instead of constants like j, m. The relative clause formation rule has to be sensitive to a choice of relativized variable, since an underlying sentence might contain more than one, and the rule would not be compositional if with the same input it could give us two non-synonymous outputs – it would then not be possible to determine the meaning of the whole as a function of the meanings of the parts plus their syntactic mode of combination. Aside from that, the only complications in the rule are the syntactic ones, the semantics being simple lambda- abstraction.

Now how do relative clauses combine with nouns or noun phrases? This is also an area of controversy and possibly of typological diversity as well. But as discussed in Partee (1973), one can make the case that compositionality requires that relative clauses combine with common noun phrases to form common noun phrases in order for a determiner like *no, every,* or *most* to have the relative clause as well as the head noun within its scope. While this claim can be challenged as well, we will assume that the basic external syntax of relative clauses is as given in (13-45a); the corresponding semantic interpretation rule is then just a kind of predicate conjunction, as given in (13-45b). The semantic type of both constituent expressions and of the result is $\langle e, t \rangle$.

(13–45) (a) CN $\rightarrow$ CN REL
(b) $\lambda x.(\text{CN}'(x) \, \& \, \text{REL}'(x))$

We can illustrate the combined results of the relative clause formation rule and the rule in (13-45) by putting the relative clause in (13-44) together with the CN *woman* to form the CN phrase *woman who hates John.* The structure is shown in (13-46a) and the translation in (13-46b). The expression (13-46b) is of a form to which lambda-conversion can apply; applying it gives (13-46c) as an equivalent but simpler expression.

(13–46) (a) [[woman] [who hates John]]
(b) $\lambda x.(\text{woman}'(x) \, \& \, \lambda x_2.(\text{hate}'(x_2, j))(x))$
(c) $\lambda x.(\text{woman}'(x) \, \& \, \text{hate}'(x, j))$

Since (13-46c) cannot be simplified further, it is an example of what is meant by a "reduced translation": an expression logically equivalent to the actual translation but simplified as much as possible by applying lambda-conversion (and any other relevant simplifying rules the given system may contain). Whether there is always a unique reduced form is a question that can be remarkably difficult and which depends in any case on what the full power of a particular system is.

Other constructions exhibiting unbounded dependencies also appear quite generally to have interpretations which include lambda- abstraction on the

position corresponding to the gap or pronoun introduced in the construction (if there is one). One such construction is WH-questions (see especially
Groenendijk and Stokhof 1989). As a first step toward an interpretation,
we might say that the question in (13-47a) is translated as in (13-47b); of
course (13-47b) itself does not specify an interpretation until one provides
an interpretation for the expression *which man*. Much of the debate about
the semantics of interrogatives concerns that last point; most theories agree
on the aspects of the interpretation represented by (13-47b) (with important
differences, however, concerning the possible scope interactions between operators inside the body of the question and expressions that are part of the
wh-phrase).

(13–47) (a) Which man does Mary believe that Susan wants to marry e_1?
         (b) (which man)$'(\lambda x_1.$(Mary believes that Susan
             wants to marry $x_1)')$

Other unbounded dependency phenomena for which analyses using lambda-
abstraction have been proposed include focus phenomena, the comparative
construction (Cresswell 1976), topicalization (Gazdar et al 1985), and the
pseudocleft construction (Partee 1984). Partee (1979) suggests the following
generalization:

(13–48) All and only unbounded syntactic rules are interpreted semantically
         by rules that bind variables which were free in one or more of the
         input expressions.

The generalization as proposed allows that such variable binding may be
either by quantification or by lambda-abstraction; in terms of primitiveness,
it is worth noting that it is possible to have lambda-abstraction as the only
primitive variable-binding operator and define the quantifiers in terms of it
(see (13-40)), but not vice versa. Although the generalization is too theory dependent to admit of direct confirmation or refutation, its plausibility
suggests that lambda-abstraction can provide a valuable tool for capturing
important semantic generalizations.

III. Generalized quantifiers

Generalized quantifiers will be the topic of the next chapter; here we just
introduce them briefly as one of the linguistically very important innovations

that is crucially dependent on having higher types available than are found in predicate logic. Lambda abstraction provides a good way of giving the explicit semantics for generalized quantifiers and for the determiner meanings that may go into building them up.

As indicated implicitly in earlier examples, we can treat NP's as forming a semantic as well as a syntactic constituent within a typed logic like Montague's, and this was one of the most influential of Montague's innovations in his classic paper "PTQ" (Montague 1973). The NP's *every man, some man, John,* and *Mary* given in the earlier fragment are interpreted as generalized quantifiers; the reader should convince herself that their type is $\langle\langle e, t\rangle t\rangle$ (e.g. by drawing a derivation tree for the logical expression which translates each of them and labelling each node with the type of the expression.)

Given those interpretations of *every man* and *some man*, it is possible to abstract on the CN position and get back a statement of the meaning of the Det. We do this for *some* in (13-49a-b) and for *every* in (13-50a-b).

(13–49)   (a)   some CN: $\lambda P.(\exists x)(CN'(x) \& P(x))$
          (b)   some: $\lambda Q.\lambda P.(\exists x)(Q(x) \& P(x))$

(13–50)   (a)   every CN: $\lambda P.(\forall x)(CN'(x) \rightarrow P(x))$
          (b)   every: $\lambda Q.\lambda P.(\forall x)(Q(x) \rightarrow P(x))$

The reader should immediately verify that applying the determiner meaning given for *some* or *every* to a CN translation like *man'* will indeed give an expression equivalent to the specified translation for *some man* or *every man*. One lambda-conversion step should show the equivalence.

We can now replace the two earlier rules which introduced *every* and *some* syncategorematically (i.e. without assigning them to any category) by the single rule "NP → Det CN" together with lexical entries for the specific Dets. More members of the category Det will be discussed in Chapter 14.

We will go through the translation and simplification via lambda conversion of the sentence *Some man walks*, whose syntactic structure is given in (13-51).

(13–51)

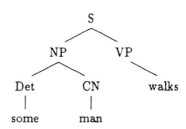

(13–52)   (i)   some: $\lambda Q.\lambda P.(\exists x)(Q(x) \,\&\, P(x))$
          (ii)   man: man$'$
          (iii)   some man: $\lambda Q.\lambda P.(\exists x)(Q(x) \,\&\, P(x))(\text{man}')$
          (reduce by lambda conversion before continuing:)
                                $\lambda P.(\exists x)(\text{man}'(x) \,\&\, P(x))$
          (iv)   walks: walk$'$
          (v)   some man walks: $(\lambda P.(\exists x)(\text{CN}'(x) \,\&\, P(x)))(\text{walk}')$
          (reduces to:) $(\exists x)(\text{man}'(x) \,\&\, \text{walk}'(x))$

We see from the last line that the translation of *Some man walks* in this system ends up, after lambda conversion, the same as its translation in predicate logic. The difference is not in the interpretation but in whether or not that interpretation is arrived at compositionally on the basis of a reasonable natural language syntax. In predicate logic there is no way to view the interpretation of the NP as a **constitutent**; in a more richly typed system there is. The treatment of NPs as generalized quantifiers has turned out to yield a very fruitful domain of research; some of the work in this area is reported in Chapter 14.

IV. VP-deletion

Yet another early recognized application of lambda-abstraction was in the analysis of VP-deletion, and in particular to capture the distinction between the so-called "strict identity" and "sloppy identity" readings of sentences like (13-53).

(13–53) John believes he's sick and Bill does too.

The first step in the analysis is to recognize that the first conjunct, repeated in (13-54), is ambiguous even excluding the possibility of *he* referring to someone other than John, an ambiguity involving a bound variable
reading of the pronoun, as represented in (13-54a), vs. a "pragmatic" or
"coreferential" reading of the pronoun, represented in (13-54b) by simply
translating the pronoun as the constant j. Although (13-54a) and (13-54b)
yield the same truth conditions, they involve differences in what corresponds
to the VP *believe he's sick* that do lead to truth-conditional differences in
VP-deletion sentences like (13-53).

(13–54) John believes he's sick.
      (a) $(\lambda x.\text{believe}'(x, \text{sick}'(x)))(j)$
      (b) $\text{believe}'(j, \text{sick}'(j))$

The corresponding pair of interpretations for the VP *believe he's sick*
are given in (13-55a-b). In effect, the VP in the interpretation in (13-55a)
denotes the property of believing oneself to be sick, while that in (13-55b)
denotes the property of believing John to be sick.

(13–55) believe he's sick
      (a) $\lambda x.\text{believe}'(x, \text{sick}'(x))$: call this P_1
      (b) $\lambda x.\text{believe}'(x, \text{sick}'(j))$: call this P_2

The ambiguity in the original sentence (13-53) is then accounted for by
the ambiguity of the antecedent VP, as represented in (13-55a-b), together
with the principle that the missing VP is interpreted as semantically identical to the antecedent VP. The reader is invited to work out that lambda-
conversion yields the two appropriate readings for *Bill does too* from the
representations in (13-56).

(13–56) Bill does too
      (a) $P_1(b)$
      (b) $P_2(b)$

It has been noted by many semanticists, including Dahl, McCawley, and
Keenan in the early 1970's, that the term "sloppy identity" is a bit of a
misnomer resulting from the early syntactic approaches to the problem (the
term was coined by J.R. Ross) and the possibility of gender differences in

examples like *John finished his homework before Mary did* and that in fact the syntactically "sloppy" identity is a reflection of strict semantic identity.

The semantics of VP-deletion is basically just identity of VP interpretation; lambdas simply help articulate the relevant VP interpretations.

V. Passive

Lambdas are also very useful for expressing the interpretations of various rules or operations which manipulate the argument frames of verbs or verb phrases and other predicates. The passive construction makes an interesting example, since it was generally regarded as a transformation of a sentence structure within transformational grammar but within contemporary formal semantics the debate is more over whether passive is a phrasal or a lexical operation. We will illustrate first the phrasal passive analysis of Bach (1980) and then compare it with the lexical approach of Dowty, Bresnan and others.

In order to focus on the relevant issues, we should make one simplification and remove one earlier simplification. The simplification we will make is to treat all NP's as of type e, and restrict the NP's in examples to proper nouns so that no harm can be done by the simplification. The earlier simplification that we should now undo was never introduced officially but appeared in examples: in examples like (13-43), (13-44), and (13-45) we followed the practice of predicate logic in representing transitive verbs as two-place relations that combine with an ordered pair of arguments. Here we will follow Montague and other semanticists in interpreting a transitive verb as a function which applies to the interpretation of the direct object to yield another function which applies to the interpretation of the subject to yield a truth value. So transitive verbs will be treated as of type $\langle e, \langle e, t \rangle \rangle$ (still assuming that we are treating all NP's as being of type e.) The rule for combining them with their object to make a VP is given in (13-57).

(13–57) VP → TVP NP   Translation: $TVP'(NP)'$

A syntactic derivation tree for the simple sentence *John loves Mary* is given in (13-58a); a corresponding semantic derivation tree with its nodes labeled with the corresponding types and translations is given in (13-58b).

(13–58) (a)

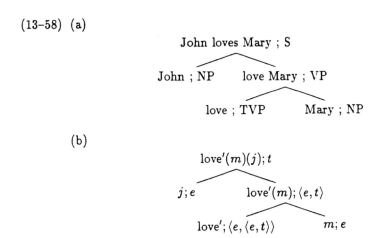

(b)

Note that what is represented in predicate logic as $love'(j, m)$ is now written $love'(m)(j)$, reflecting the order in which the function is combined with its arguments rather than the order of the NP's in the English sentence. It is customary in Montague grammar to retain the former notation as a conventional abbreviation of the latter, however.

Now we can state the phrasal passive rule which derives a passive verb phrase from a transitive verb (phrase) as proposed by Bach (1980). The operation written *EN* in (13-59) is the operation which puts the first verb of its argument into the passive participle form, and adds a *be* before it. Since the passive rule is not a simple phrase structure rule, we have stated it in a form closer to the standard recursive format of the earlier sections of this chapter.

(13–59) **Phrasal passive rule for agentless passives**
Syntax: If α is a TVP, then $EN(\alpha)$ is a PVP (Passive VP).
Semantics: If α translates as α', then $EN(\alpha)$ translates as
$$\lambda x.(\exists y)(\alpha'(x)(y))$$

The passive verb phrase *be loved* is then translated as shown in (13-60).

(13–60) be loved: $\lambda x.(\exists y)(love'(x)(y))$

In the example just given, the TVP was a lexical transitive verb, *love*.

The rule is also intended to apply to what Bach analyzes as phrasal transitive verbs (meaning phrases which function as transitive verbs, not phrases which contain transitive verbs), such as the italicized (discontinuous) TVP's in (13-61).

(13–61)   Phrasal TVP's: *give* a book *to John*
                           give John *a book*
                           persuade John *to leave*
                           buy this book *to read to the children*

A competing hypothesis is that passive is a lexical rule, as proposed by Dowty (1978) and Bresnan. The statement of the rule could be identical in its syntax and its semantics to the phrasal rule given above, but restricted to apply only to lexical items. The difference between the lexical and phrasal versions of the rule is subtle, much less than the difference between a syntactic and a lexical treatment of passive in earlier transformational approaches. The lexical rule in its most basic form does not apply to the phrasal verbs illustrated in (13-71). But it is not difficult to extend it to a schema applying to lexical verbs of all categories TVP/X, i.e. all categories of verbs which take some kind of complement to form a transitive verb (phrase). The basic strategy for doing this is similar to the strategy used in defining phrasal conjunction in the beginning of this subsection. (In the terminology one encounters in the literature on categorial grammar and type-changing operations, we would want to "lift" the passive operation from an operation on TVP-type interpretations to an operation on functions that have TVP-type interpretations as their values. To write this out explicitly in detail is a bit too complicated to do here in this case, since TVP's are already of a slightly complicated type, the semantics of the basic passive operation is slightly complex, and the various complements and adjuncts that enter into phrasal TVP's are of types we have not discussed.)

Whether phrasal or lexical, lambdas help provide an explicit and perspicuous statement of the semantics of the passive construction.

VI. Meaning postulates and lexical rules

Dowty (1978, 1979) discusses a wide variety of other governed rules which he proposes to treat as lexical rules, and lambdas figure prominently in the semantics. In discussing lexical rules, we should discuss meaning postulates at the same time, since the two are often closely related in form, and the choice of which is more appropriate to use in a particular case is generally an empirical linguistic issue.

Among the phenomena that have been analyzed in terms of meaning postulates and/or lexical rules are causative verbs, detransitivization, morphological reflexives, adjectival *un-* prefixation, object raising, "dative movement", the relation between *seek* and *try to find* and that between *want* and *want to have*, and many of the more semantically regular parts of derivational morphology. The best general reference, and the starting point for much work in this area, is Dowty (1979).

We will discuss just one of these phenomena, causative verbs, and use that discussion to illustrate both meaning postulates and lexical rules and the relation between them. This will also give us a good opportunity to show how lambda-expressions are arrived at by specifying what one wants them to do.

Consider the (much-discussed) relation between transitive and intransitive *break* in English. There are differences of opinion as to just what the semantic relation between the two is. Many linguists believe (I) that it is at least true that (13-62a) entails (13-62b). Some believe (II) that (13-62a) and (13-62b) entail one another, i.e. are logically equivalent. Others are doubtful about claim (II) but believe (III) that a similar claim holds true, but with an abstract and possibly universal causative operator "CAUSE" whose interpretation is not exactly identical to that of the English word *cause*. Some believe neither (II) nor (III) but believe that (I) (or a variant of I with *CAUSE* in place of *cause*) is the strongest generalization that can be made; that is, that (13-62b) captures part of the meaning of (13-62a) but does not exhaust it.

(13–62) (a) John broke the window.
         (b) John caused the window to break.

In stating the relevant translations of these sentences, we will use $break_2'$ for the transitive verb and $break_1'$ for the intransitive; we translate *the window* simply as an *e-* type constant w; and we will introduce without motivating it an operator *THAT* which applies to a formula to give a proposition- denoting expression. (Discussion of such an operator would need notions that will be introduced in Chapter 15; but nothing relevant in the present example depends on the occurrence of this operator in it.) Then we can translate (13-62a) (uncontroversially) as in (13-63a) and (13-62b) (controversially) as in (13-63b). We ignore tense throughout.

(13-63) (a) $\text{break}_2'(w)(j)$
          (b) $\text{cause}'(j,\ THAT(\text{break}_1'(w)))$

Now we can state the three claims (I), (II), and (III) in terms of three alternative "meaning postulates" one could write. (See Carnap (1947) for the introduction of the term and Partee (1975) for its use to describe what Montague introduced as restrictions on possible interpretations.) One way to think of these meaning postulates is as capturing explicitly some aspects of the lexical semantics of the elements mentioned in the postulates; the cases linguists are generally most concerned to make explicit are those in which the given aspects of the lexical semantics play a crucial role in some general inference patterns, especially where whole families of lexical items participate in common inference patterns (as is the case with causative verbs.)

(13-64) MP I: $(\forall x)(\forall y)[\text{break}_2'(y)(x) \rightarrow \text{cause}'(x,\ THAT(\text{break}_1'(y)))]$
          MP II: $(\forall x)(\forall y)[\text{break}_2'(y)(x) \leftrightarrow \text{cause}'(x,\ THAT(\text{break}_1'(y)))]$
          MP III: $(\forall x)(\forall y)[\text{break}_2'(y)(x) \leftrightarrow CAUSE(x,\ THAT(\text{break}_1'(y)))]$

With respect to the relationship between meaning postulates and lexical rules, the most important difference among the three meaning postulates above is that between MP I and MPs II and III: only the latter two, involving full equivalence between the two sides, can be turned into lexical rules defining transitive *break* as the causative of intransitive *break*.

We will use MP II to illustrate how the conversion from meaning postulate to lexical rule can be done in such cases. First note that there is an asymmetry in the roles of break_2' and break_1' in the meaning postulate: the postulate implicitly gives us a definition of break_2' in terms of break_1' but not straightforwardly vice versa. To see how to turn the meaning postulate, already an implicit definition, into an explicit definition of break_2', look at break_2' as a function which applies to two arguments in turn. The right-hand side of the equivalence tells us what the value of that function is given interpretations of *cause'* and of break_1'. But that means the right-hand side is already perfectly suited to be the body of a lambda-expression; all we have to do is abstract in the right order on the two argument variables of break_2'. Which order? Well, since the transitive verb applies first to its direct object argument (the y argument in MP II), that should be the argument the first lambda-operator binds. (I.e. "first argument first" in the lambda-notation we are using. Be careful, since this is not always uniform across different notational versions of the lambda-calculus.) The result is the definition in (13-65).

(13–65) $\text{break}'_2 = \lambda y.\lambda x.\text{cause}'(x, THAT(\text{break}'_1(y)))$

All we then need to turn this into a lexical rule is to abstract away from the specific lexical items $break_1$, $break_2$ and cast this into a rule applying to a certain class of intransitive verbs to derive a causative transitive verb from them, with the similarly generalized form of (13-65) providing the corresponding interpretation rule.

(13–66) Lexical Rule For Causative Verb Formation (Assuming MP II)

Formation Rule: If α is an intransitive verb with such-and-such properties, then $F(\alpha)$ is a transitive verb. (F in English is mostly the identity function.)

Semantic Rule: The translation of the derived verb $F(\alpha)$ is $\lambda y.\lambda x.\text{cause}'(x, THAT(\alpha'(y)))$

The reader is invited to go back to the earlier applications of lambda abstraction mentioned in this subsection and try to see where the lambda-expressions come from. For the passive, for instance, it might be instructive to write down a biconditional statement stating the equivalence of the agent-less passive sentence to a corresponding active, and then see how the form of the lambda abstract given in the translation rule in (13-59) can be figured out from there. (Do not be discouraged if lambdas seem difficult and a bit mysterious at first; like many powerful tools, it takes time and practice before they feel natural to work with.)

Exercises

1. (a) Given the derivation tree for the following statements of SL according to the syntax given in (13-1) and (13-2).

   (i) $((\sim p \,\&\, q) \lor p)$

(ii) $(\sim (p \,\&\, q) \vee p)$

(iii) $\sim ((p \,\&\, q) \vee p)$

(b) Give the compositional semantic interpretation of the three trees of (1a), assuming that both atomic statements are true.

2. Assume the alternative syntax for SL, which has, besides the category for atomic statements, two other categories for connectives: *Neg* for negation which combines with only one statement at a time, and *Conn* for all four other connectives which combine with two statements at a time.

   (a) Write the two new syntactic rules for this syntax of SL

   (b) Give the derivation tree for the three statements given under 1a.

   To give SL with this syntax a compositional semantics we first have to interpret the connectives according to their truth tables as functions taking either one or a pair of truth values, which is/are the value(s) of their constitutive statement(s), and assigning a truth value. For instance, conjunction is interpreted by the following function:

   $$\langle 1, 1 \rangle \rightarrow 1$$
   $$\langle 1, 0 \rangle \rightarrow 0$$
   $$\langle 0, 1 \rangle \rightarrow 0$$
   $$\langle 0, 0 \rangle \rightarrow 0$$

   (a) Give the interpretations of the other connectives of SL as such functions.

   (b) Write the two compositional semantic rules for SL with this syntax. Hint: use the convention of $[\![P]\!]$ standing for the semantic interpretation of P.

   (c) Show how each of the statements of (1a) is interpreted compositionally according to the three trees you gave in (2b)).

3. (a) Give the trees and compositional interpretation of the following formulas of Predicate Logic, according to (13-8) and (13-9) given in section 13.1.2. Define your own model with two individuals and a non-empty interpretation of the predicates to use in the interpretation throughout this exercise which makes (i)-(iv) true.

   (i) $(\forall x)(\exists y)(P(x) \rightarrow R(x, y))$

  (ii) $(\exists y)(\forall x)(P(x) \rightarrow R(x,y))$
  (iii) $(\exists y)(P(y) \rightarrow (\forall x)(R(x,y))$
  (iv) $(\forall x)(\exists y)(P(y) \rightarrow R(x,y))$

 (b) Formulate four English sentences corresponding to (i)-(iv) which would best express their scope differences.

4. In (13-10) we define a formula or predicate logic as *true in a model* M if it is true for all assignments in M, and false otherwise. A common alternative definition is given in (13-10′) below.

 (13-10′) **(1)** For any formula φ, $[\![\varphi]\!]^{M} = 1$ (i.e. φ is true *simpliciter* with respect to M) iff for all assignments g, $[\![\varphi]\!]^{M,g=1}$.

   (2) For any formula ϕ, $[\![\varphi]\!]^{M} = 0$ iff for all assignments g, $[\![\varphi]\!]^{M,g'} = 0$.

   (3) Otherwise, $[\![\varphi]\!]^{M}$ is undefined.

 The two definitions give the same results for all *closed* formulas, but they give different results for some open formulas.

 (a) Find an open formula which comes out *true* under both definitions.

 (b) Find an open formula which comes out *false* under both definitions.

 (c) Find an open formula which comes out *false* according to (13-10) but undefined on this alternative (13-10′).

 (d) Are there any other cases, or does (c) exhaust the ways in which the results of the definitions can differ? State your reasons.

5. Give the derivation tree according to the SL syntax in (13-2) corresponding to the 'algebraic' tree in (13-20) and show its compositional derivation which makes it true in a simple model of you own choice.

6. Assume the following constants and variables

Type	Variables	Constants
e	$x, y, z,$	j, m
$\langle e,t\rangle$	P, Q	*walks, man*
$\langle e,\langle e,t\rangle\rangle$	R	*loves*
$\langle\langle e,t\rangle,t\rangle$	**P**	*someone, everyone*

 Check whether the following expressions are well-formed expressions

of TL. If so, specify their type. Draw derivation trees for at least three
of the wellformed ones.

Sample: (i) $\lambda x P(x)$ - yes, type $\langle e, t\rangle$
             (ii)   loves (m) - yes, type $\langle e, t\rangle$
             (iii) λP walks (P) - no

Derivation tree for (i):

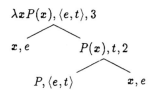

(a) λx loves $(m)(x)$

(b) $\lambda R R(m)(j)$

(c) someone(walks)

(d) $\lambda P P(j)$

(e) λx someone(x)

(f) $\lambda x (P(x) \& Q(x))$

(g) $\lambda P(P(j) \& P(m))$

(h) $(\lambda P P(j))(\text{walks})$

(i) $\lambda x \exists y$ loves $(x)(y)$

(j) $\lambda \mathbf{P}(\forall P(\mathbf{P}(P) \leftrightarrow P(j)))$
    ((j) has extra parentheses, do not judge it illformed on that ac-
    count)

7. Using the same variable-conventions as above, and the constants and
semantic interpretation of TLA given in 13.2.3, specify for each of the
following the type and a description of the semantic value for M and
g as given in (13-36).

Optional abbreviations: **Plus**(a, b) for **Plus**$(b)(a)$
                               gr(a, b) for **gr**$(b)(a)$

Sample: $(\lambda x \mathbf{gr}(x, 5))(8)$ - type: t, value: TRUE

(a) $(\lambda x \mathbf{gr}(x, 5))$

(b) $(\lambda x(\mathbf{odd}(x)\,\&\,\mathbf{gr}(x,5))(8)$

(c) $(\lambda x \mathbf{Plus}(x,3))(4)$

(d) $(\lambda x(\lambda y \mathbf{gr}(y,x)))(5)(8)$

(e) $(\lambda x(\lambda y \mathbf{gr})y,x))(5))(8)$

(f) $\lambda x \exists y(\mathbf{Plus}(y,y) = x)$

(g) $(\lambda P P(8))(\lambda x \mathbf{gr}(x,5))$

Hint: one of **(d)** and **(e)** is true, the other false.

Chapter 14

Generalized Quantifiers

14.1 Determiners and quantifiers

The universal and existential quantifiers of predicate logic introduced in Chapter 7 are in two major respects inadequate for the semantic analysis of the rich variety of quantification in natural languages. First of all, as we have seen in translating from English to predicate logic and as was pointed out again in Chapter 13, the syntactic structure of quantified formulas in predicate logic is completely different from the syntactic structure of quantified sentences in natural language. Quantifying expressions of natural language are typically full NPs, where the noun (CN) and possibly additional relative clauses provide essential restrictions on a quantifier. Not just the determiner or specifier of an NP binds dependent arguments or pronouns, but from a semantic point of view the appropriate scope-defining and binding category is the entire NP. It will prove useful for linguistic purposes (too) to distinguish between quantifying over domains and binding arguments of predicates — two jobs conflated by the two standard first-order quantifiers of predicate logic. Secondly, many forms of quantification in natural language are not expressible or definable in terms of the first-order logical quantifiers. For instance, the NP *more than half of the* CN is not expressible in terms of just first-order quantifiers, since its interpretation requires a one-to-one mapping between two finite or infinite sets dependent on a well-ordering by cardinality (see Barwise and Cooper (1981) for a complete proof).

These serious limitations of the analysis of quantification in any semantic framework restricted to a first-order language can be overcome by generalizing the notion of a quantifier to a higher-order concept: a *generalized quantifier* is a family of subsets of the domain of entities. Richard Montague initiated this higher-order analysis of quantification, as presented in the fragment of Chapter 13, for the logical quantifiers in his famous paper 'The Proper Treatment of Quantification in Ordinary English' (Montague (1974), p. 247-270), and recent research in model theoretic semantics has developed his insights considerably for linguistic purposes. Also genuinely new insights on the logical properties of quantifiers have been obtained, e.g., a new notion of first-order definability (see van Benthem (1986)). In this chapter the main linguistic results of the theory of generalized quantifiers are presented as an introduction to a very fruitful area of linguistic semantics where the mathematical methods of the previous chapters have found extensive empirical applications.

In the fragment of Chapter 13, NPs are defined categorially as terms, and they are interpreted in the semantics as generalized quantifiers. The semantic type of any term or NP is $\langle\langle e, t\rangle, t\rangle$, hence they all denote functions from sets of individuals to truth values. The fragment in Chapter 13 contained only the determiners *every* and *some*, translated in the formal language with lambda abstraction respectively as

$$\lambda Q \lambda P[\forall x[Q(x) \rightarrow P(x)]]$$

and

$$\lambda Q \lambda P[\exists x[Q(x) \,\&\, P(x)]]$$

In this functional perspective the subject NP denotes a function taking the interpretation of the VP in the sentence as argument. For instance, *every man walks* is true iff the set of walkers is a member of the family of sets interpreting *every man*.

Alternatively we may view the interpretation of this sentence in a 'flattened' version as a relation between sets, i.e., of type $\langle\langle\langle e, t\rangle, \langle e, t\rangle\rangle, t\rangle$. A determiner is then analyzed as a relation between the set of individuals interpreting the CN of the subject NP and the set of individuals interpreting the VP. This leads to the following general definition:

DEFINITION 14.1   *A determiner is a function D in a model* $\mathbf{M} = \langle E, [\![\ ]\!]\rangle$ *assigning to the domain of entities E a binary relation between subsets A and B.*

$$[\![\text{Det}[CN][VP]]\!]_E = [\![\text{Det}(A, B)]\!]_E = D_E AB$$

∎

In the following we first present the main notions in their flattened relational versions for ease of exposition, and discuss the relational analysis of quantifiers further in Section 4. Switching back and forth between a hierarchical functional perspective and a flattened relational analysis will prove heuristically useful since many of the results of the theory of relations of Chapter 3 can be brought to bear on generalized quantifier theory.

The methodological objectives and linguistic goals of the theory of generalized quantifiers are threefold:

(1) to provide a semantical characterization of the class containing all and only the possible determiners of natural language as a proper subset of the logically possible determiners, including a linguistically adequate classification of types of natural language determiners

(2) to explain distributional data of NPs in various contexts by notions definable in terms of properties of generalized quantifiers

(3) to analyze conditions on binding, scope-dependencies, inference and other informational dependencies between NPs and other categories as semantic constraints on the process of model theoretic interpretation as a formal model simulating human information processing with its cognitive constraints

The theory of generalized quantifiers proves to be a new framework for the semantic explanation of linguistic data which have been studied extensively in syntactic theory.

14.2 Conditions on quantifiers

In constructing generalized quantifiers as families of sets of entities or individuals in a domain there are four universal conditions which set initial restrictions on a linguistically useful notion of a quantifier. Although not all natural language quantifiers meet these conditions, they serve us here to carve out an initial domain of study, providing the foundation for a semantic analysis of quantification. Extensions of the simple cases to more complex forms of quantification, including context-dependent or intensional determiners, can be obtained by dropping one or more of these initial methodological assumptions.

For the interpretation of an NP the domain of entities E is never entirely relevant to the determination of its value, but rather just certain subsets of E are. For instance, when we want to check whether every man runs in a given model, we are not interested in the women or the books in that domain of interpretation. To express this rather obvious condition on the subsets which are relevant in verification of NPs we define a first general condition on determiners in generalized quantifiers:

C1. *Conservativity (the 'live-on' property)*

If $A, B \subseteq E$ then $D_E AB \leftrightarrow D_E A(A \cap B)$

A determiner that meets this condition is called *conservative* or is said to *'live on'* the set A. Subsets of the domain that contain no members of A, no things with the property interpreting the CN in the subject NP, i.e. any $(X - A) \subseteq E$, hence fall outside the interpretation of an NP.

English examples that illustrate this notion are the following equivalences

Many men run $\leftrightarrow$ Many men are men who run

Few women sneeze $\leftrightarrow$ Few women are women who sneeze

John loves Mary $\leftrightarrow$ John is John and loves Mary

The English expression *only*, for instance, which is sometimes (we think erroneously) considered to be a determiner, fails to be conservative. In evaluating for instance the sentence *Only athletes run* in a domain E we do have to consider the entire power-set of E, since the sentence is verified or falsified after we have determined of everything else in E whether it runs. This is an argument against treating *only* as a determiner, which finds additional support by the fact that other determiners may precede it, as in *the only boy*. The relatively free distribution of *only* in a sentence also sets it apart from the category of determiners. Consider

(14–1)

> Only athletes run / Every athlete runs
>
> Athletes only run / *Athlete every runs
>
> Athletes run only / *Athlete runs every

But note that some determiners may "float" more easily, e.g. *all*.

The second general condition on the class of generalized quantifiers that form our object of study is the requirement that extensions of the domain should not affect the interpretation of the determiner. For instance, if we know that some men walk in a given model, then adding more books to the domain of that model will not have any semantic effect. This condition on determiners is defined as:

C2. *Extension (Constancy)*

If $A, B \subseteq E \subseteq E'$ then $D_E AB \leftrightarrow D_{E'} AB$

Determiners that satisfy this condition are called *extensional* or *constant determiners*. In principle the interpretation of a determiner may vary with the extension of the domain of interpretation, but Extension says that in evaluating an NP the entities which fall outside the interpretation of the CN and outside the interpretation of the VP can be left out of consideration. This means that the determiners under consideration have to be independent of the size of the domain; they are insensitive to domain-extensions. In natural language there are, however, determiners which measure relative cardinalities and show an important dependence on the size of the domain; they are the context-dependent determiners like *many* or *more than half*. Although we return to context-dependent determiners below in section 5, it is easily seen that, for instance, there is at least one interpretation of *many men walk* which means that the number of men who walk exceeds the number of other things in the domain that walk. Under such a globally proportional interpretation of *many men*, addition of more things to the domain may change the truth value of the original sentence.

The two conditions Conservativity and Extension together permit suppression of the parameter E in the interpretation of an NP, which is defined as:

C1′. *Strong Conservativity*

If $A, B \subseteq E$ then $D_E AB \leftrightarrow D_A A(A \cap B)$

Strong conservativity tells us that the only sets which are relevant to the evaluation of a determiner are the CN-interpretation and the VP-interpretation. For a proof of the equivalence of conservativity plus extension to strong conservativity see Westerståhl (1985a).

The third universal condition on quantifiers requires that only the number of elements in the relevant sets determine the interpretation of a quantifier. To evaluate in a model M, for instance, whether several men walk we only need to know how many men there are and how many of them walk. It is not relevant who they actually are, since the interpretation of that sentence should not be affected if we were to substitute other men for the given ones. No quantifier hence may depend on a specific or particular choice of individuals in the domain, i.e. the quantifiers under consideration are 'topic neutral'. This condition is formulated as:

C3. *Quantity (Isom.)*

If F is a bijection from $\mathbf{M_1}$ to $\mathbf{M_2}$, then $D_{E_1}AB \leftrightarrow D_{E_2}F(A)F(B)$

Quantity requires sameness of interpretation up to isomorphic models. The requirement may be weakened to insensitivity to any permutation π on E or automorphism $F : \mathbf{M_1} \rightarrow \mathbf{M_1}$ of the domain of a given model, formulated as:

C3'. *Weak Quantity (Perm.)*

If π is a permutation of E, then $D_E AB \leftrightarrow D_E(\pi(A))(\pi(B))$

If we assume Constancy, then Quantity and Weak Quantity prove to be equivalent conditions (for a proof see Westerståhl (1985a)). Hence in the following we disregard this difference and assume Quantity as a constraint.

A quantifier $D(A)$ which meets Quantity is said to be a *quantitative* quantifier. Note that there is some potential terminological confusion here. Some authors (a.o. van Benthem) reserve the term 'quantifier' for those NP-interpretations that are conservative, extensional and quantitative, and others (a.o. Westerståhl) call this class the 'logical' quantifiers. We call here any NP-interpretation a (generalized) quantifier and use the universal conditions as properties of subsets of quantifiers.

Again there are expressions in English which are commonly considered to be determiners, but which fail to meet Quantity. This is not surprising, since in our ordinary use of language reference to specific objects and particular things often matters a great deal. In logic it is customary to obliterate all that is specific, and in setting the stage for the study of generalized quantifiers we chose to simplify matters first by disregarding specificity for the moment as it brings in complex contextual parameters.

Typical specific determiners which are sensitive to the choice of particular objects and let the interpretation of NPs vary across isomorphic models are the possessive determiners such as *John's, every man's*. One of the problems to solve in the interpretation of possessives is the fact that *John's book* should be interpreted equivalently to *the book of John* but *every man's book* should not necessarily be equivalent to *the book of every man.* See for more discussion van Benthem (1986), Keenan and Faltz (1985), Partee (1984).

The fourth and final universal condition on determiners requires that determiners must be active in the sense that they must have a detectable effect on different domains. The 'universal' determiner, which is true on any domain for any two sets, and the 'empty' determiner, false in every domain and every two sets, are excluded as trivial. This condition is formulated as:

C4. *Variation*

For each domain E there is a domain E' such that $E \subseteq E'$, A, B and $C \subseteq E'$, such that $D_{E'}AB$ and $\sim D_{E'}AC$

Variation says that, when you add entities to the domain, a set C can be found which is *not* related to A by the determiner. Hence natural language excludes determiners that just arbitrarily relate any or every two sets. A weaker condition may be called for when we do not want to exclude the interpretation of, for instance, *at least two* CN in a domain with only one single object.

C4'. *Non-triviality*

For non-empty domains E and E' there exist $A, B \subseteq E$ and $A', B' \subseteq E'$ such that $D_E AB$ and $\sim D_{E'} A'B'$

Again the difference between C4 and C4' may be disregarded for our purposes as both exclude the trivial quantifiers, and the precise strength of the conditions concerns primarily logicians who want to make the weakest possible general assumptions to obtain maximal proof-theoretic elegance.

Conservativity, Extension, Quantity and Variation together define a class of determiners which exhibit linguistically interesting semantic properties. We will study these properties in the next section of this chapter. As was already remarked above, these four conditions together require that the determiners under consideration depend only on the cardinality of two sets A and B, respectively the CN-interpretation and the VP-interpretation. If we assume finite domains, this allows tree-like representations of these determiners, called *number-theoretic trees*, which are outlined here just briefly, while relegating most results to the exercises. Letting $x = |A - B|$ and $y = |A \cap B|$, the tree is built by pairs $\langle x, y \rangle$ as in Figure 14-1.

$$
\begin{array}{lll}
x + y & = & 0 \\
      & = & 1 \\
      & = & 2 \\
      & = & 3
\end{array}
$$

				0,0		
			1,0		0,1	
		2,0		1,1		0,2
	3,0		2,1		1,2		0,3

etc.

Figure 14–1: The number-theoretic tree of
determiners

To illustrate the use of such number-theoretic trees briefly we can see directly that *every man walks* is true only on all right-most pairs on each line, since, for instance, if $x + y = 3$ all three elements must be in $A \cap B$, i.e. they all are men and walk. The same argument applies inductively to any number $x + y$. There are many other properties of determiners expressible in this number-theoretic tree, but these results make good exercises.

14.3   Properties of determiners and quantifiers

Assuming the four universal conditions of Conservativity, Extension, Quantity and Variation, we now turn to some linguistically useful semantic characterizations of the types of determiners which the NPs in this class may contain. Recent research has uncovered a host of interesting properties of determiners and quantifiers, and we can present here only some of the fundamental results.

The role of determiners and quantifiers in inferences is one of the central explananda of the theory of generalized quantifiers. The fundamental question here is how information expressed in natural language in inferential patterns is preserved or lost by manipulating models. The first property of determiners is based on increasing or decreasing the number of entities in the relevant sets A (CN-interpretation) and B (VP-interpretation). If we have the information that *some* men walk, adding more walkers to the interpretation will not change the initial assignment. But if we have the information that *no* man walks, adding more walkers to the interpretation may very well change it, because some of the walkers may turn out to be men. Similarly, in the first case, if we add more men we still maintain the information that some men walk. But, in the second case, if we add more men, the information that no man walks is not preserved. These facts are described by attributing to the determiners that allow such addition in either A or B the property of being respectively *left monotone increasing* (in A) or *right monotone increasing* (in B). The counterpart to increasing determiners are *monotone decreasing determiners*, again in either A (left) or B (right). For instance, if few men walk, and we restrict the set of men to a subset, it is still true that few men walk, since only fewer do walk then; so *few* is left monotone decreasing. And if we assume that no men walk, and take a subset of the walkers, that set cannot contain any men, so the information that no men walk is preserved and *no* is right monotone decreasing. The intuitive linguistic tests that discriminate the four different types of determiners are then the following entailments in which the determiner is the same in antecedent and consequent but either the CN- or the VP-interpretation is increased or decreased.

(1) **left monotone increasing**
   If $D\ CN_1\ VP$, then $D\ CN_2\ VP$ (where $CN_1 \subseteq CN_2$)
   e.g. If *several* women with red hair run, then *several* women run

(2) **right monotone increasing**
   If $D\ CN\ VP_1$, then $D\ CN\ VP_2$ (where $VP_1 \subseteq VP_2$)
   e.g. If *every* man walks fast, then *every* man walks

(3) **left monotone decreasing**
   If $D\ CN_1\ VP$, then $D\ CN_2\ VP$ (where $CN_2 \subseteq CN_1$)
   e.g. If *all* women run, then *all* women with red hair run

(4) **right monotone decreasing**
   If $D\ CN\ VP_1$, then $D\ CN\ VP_2$ (where $VP_2 \subseteq VP_1$)
   e.g. If *no* man walks, then *no* man walks fast

These four related properties of determiners are captured in the following set-theoretic definition.

P1. *Monotonicity*

left monotone increasing:	$(DAB\ \&\ A \subseteq A') \rightarrow DA'B$
right monotone increasing:	$(DAB\ \&\ B \subseteq B') \rightarrow DAB'$
left monotone decreasing:	$(DAB\ \&\ A' \subseteq A) \rightarrow DA'B$
right monotone decreasing:	$(DAB\ \&\ B' \subseteq B) \rightarrow DAB'$

Note that left monotone increasing determiners are also called *persistent*, and the left monotone decreasing ones *anti-persistent*.

A syntactically simple determiner which is increasing in the left argument (A) is increasing in the right hand argument (B), i.e., left monotone increasing simple determiners are also right monotone increasing. But left monotone decreasing simple determiners are not always also right monotone decreasing. This may be verified easily by considering the following entailments:

Some bald men walk fast $\rightarrow$ Some men walk

All men walk $\nrightarrow$ All bald men walk fast

The monotonicity properties of determiners provide a fundamental classification of inferential patterns. It in fact explains the power of the Square of Opposition of Syllogistic Logic (a pre-Fregean form of predicate logic) with the four traditional logical quantifiers *every, some, not every* and *no* (see van Eijck (1985)).

A simple linguistic constraint on coordination of NPs with conjunction and disjunction may now be formulated as follows:

> *Constraint on Coordination*: NPs can be coordinated by conjunction and disjunction iff they have the same direction of monotonicity.

Coordination of a decreasing determiner and an increasing one is hence excluded on semantic grounds, which conforms to the intuitive unacceptability of, e.g.,

*John or no student saw Jane

*All the women and few men walk.

Of course, coordination with the connective *but* requires NPs of different direction of monotonicity, but note that this coordination, contrary to conjunction and disjunction, does not allow iteration freely.

John but no student saw Jane

All the women but few men walk

*All the women, few men but several students walk

Conjunction preserves monotonicity, if it is interpreted as intersection of the two CN-sets. But disjunction does not preserve monotonicity, e.g., *all or no* is not monotone. Complex determiners are expressible equivalently as conjunctions of monotone determiners, even though they might themselves not be monotone, e.g., the non-monotone *exactly two* is equivalent to the monotone *at least two and at most two*.

To obtain a semantic universal stating that all syntactically simple natural language determiners (in the class meeting the four universal conditions on quantifiers) are characterized by a certain semantic property, we need a property which all right monotone determiners share with numerical determiners interpreted as *exactly n*. Such a weaker property is Continuity, formulated as:

P2. *Continuity*

$D_E \ A \ B_1$ and $D_E \ A \ B_2$ (where $B_1 \subseteq B \subseteq B_2$) $\rightarrow D_E \ AB$

Conjunction still preserves Continuity (the proof is an easy set-theoretic exercise). Now we can state the first empirical semantic universal of natural language determiners:

S1. *Universal on simple determiners* (van Benthem (1984))

Every simple determiner in a conservative, extensional and quantitative NP of any natural language is continuous.

The methodological role of such semantic universals is to demarcate the class of determiners that are realized in natural languages from the much wider class of all logically possible determiners. Semantic universals are hence of a genuinely empirical nature and make falsifiable linguistic claims.

We can state a general relation between increasing and decreasing determiners if we define external and internal negation of quantifiers as follows. Here Q_E is an abbreviation for $D_E(A)$.

DEFINITION 14.2 *If Q_E is defined in a model* M *with domain E, then:*

$$\sim Q_E = \{X \subseteq E \mid X \notin Q\}(external\ negation)$$

$$Q_E \sim = \{X \subseteq E \mid (E - X) \in Q\}(internal\ negation)$$

∎

External negation of an NP prefixes negation on the NP, e.g., *Not one man runs*. This should not be confused with full sentential negation, e.g., *It is not the case that one man runs*. Internal negation corresponds to VP-negation, e.g., *One man did not run*.

Now we can see that either kind of negation reverses the monotonicity direction of a quantifier. I.e., if Q is monotone increasing, then $\sim Q$ and $Q \sim$ are monotone decreasing, and if Q is decreasing, then $\sim Q$ and $Q \sim$ are increasing. To see that this is true, assume that Q is monotone increasing and suppose that $Y \in (Q \sim)$ and $X \subseteq Y$. Then $(E - Y) \in Q$ and $(E - Y) \subseteq (E - X)$, so $(E - X) \in Q$, hence $X \in (Q \sim)$. Now suppose $Y \in (\sim Q)$ and $X \subseteq Y$. Then $Y \notin Q$ so $X \notin Q$ so $X \in (\sim Q)$. The proof of the reversal of monotone decreasing quantifiers is similar. Also, as we may expect from the set-theoretic definitions, it is provable (a simple exercise!) that $Q = \sim\sim Q = Q \sim\sim$. From this correlation we may conclude that any decreasing simple quantifier is a negated form of an increasing simple one. This result may provide an explanation for the fact that not all NPs can be negated, e.g., acceptable external negations are:

(1) not every man

(2) not many men

(3) not a (single) man

whereas unacceptable are:

(4) *not few men

(5) *not no man

(6) *not John

Note first that only right monotone increasing quantifiers allow external negation. Instead of (4) and (5) one could as well use the simpler monotone increasing *many men* and *some men* respectively. To explain the unacceptability of (6) we define the new notion of a *dual* of a quantifier.

DEFINITION 14.3 *The* dual *of a quantifier Q_E is the quantifier $Q_{\widetilde{E}} = \{X \subseteq E \mid (E - X) \notin Q\}$. If $Q = Q^\sim$ then Q is called* self-dual. ∎

The NP *every man* turns out on this definition to be the dual of *some man*. We call determiners D and $D^\sim$ duals if the quantifiers in which they occur are duals. Furthermore for any $a \in E$, $\{X \subseteq E \mid a \in X\}$ is self-dual, so proper names, for instance, are self-dual. Now we can formulate the second semantic universal:

S2. *Universal on negation* (Barwise and Cooper (1981))
   If a language has a syntactic construction whose semantic interpretation is to negate a quantifier, then this construction is unacceptable with NPs with monotone decreasing or self-dual determiners.

This accounts for the unacceptability of (6). Another linguistic illustration of this duality between quantifiers in natural language is the following. For instance, *not many men did not leave* is often taken to be paraphrased by *quite a few men left*. Hence *quite a few* CN should be the dual of *many* CN. To show that this is untenable in general, we first prove a theorem of generalized quantifier theory.

THEOREM 14.1 *(Barwise and Cooper (1981))* If D is *right monotone increasing*, and DAB and $D^{\sim}AC$, then $B \cap C \neq \emptyset$. ∎

Proof: (reductio) Suppose $B \cap C = \emptyset$. Then $B \subseteq (E - C)$, so, by monotonicity, $DA(E - C)$. But then $(D \sim)AC$, so not $\sim (D \sim)AC$, resulting in a contradiction with the assumption $D^{\sim}AC$. ∎

Many is right monotone increasing (on a non-context-sensitive, i.e. extensional, interpretation); now in some model M, let $B = [\![\text{voted for Bush}]\!]$ and $C = [\![\text{voted for Dukakis}]\!]$. If *many men voted for Bush* and *quite a few men voted for Dukakis*, then by Theorem 14.1 we must accept that at least one man voted for Bush and for Dukakis! This shows that *many* and *quite a few* cannot simply be duals. Possibly a more context-sensitive notion of duality could solve this problem.

Duality is a fundamental aspect of both formal and natural languages. The familiar negation laws of predicate-logical quantifiers are a simple case of reversal of monotonicity direction, which we also call *polarity-reversal*. But in natural languages the correlation between negation and duality is much more pervasive. Negative polarity expressions, for instance, occur in various syntactic contexts, yet these *prima facie* disparate and almost stylistic phenomena can be given a universal semantic explanation (due to Ladusaw (1979)). The determiner *any* has been a notorious problem for semantic analysis, since it is sometimes equivalent to the universal *every*, which is called the free choice *any* as in *Any book is readable*. But there are contexts where it is not equivalent to universal quantification and in other contexts it is simply unacceptable. Closer scrutiny with a semantic eye of the acceptable contexts where it is not equivalent reveals that they can be all interpreted by monotone decreasing sets. Consider the data in (8).

(8) (a) John did not read any books
    (a′) *John read any books

(b) At most ten students who read anything passed
(b') *At least ten students who read anything passed
(c) It is difficult to find any book
(c') It is easy to find any book
(d) Before anyone enters, he must bow
(d') *After anyone enters, he must bow
(e) Never may anyone touch it!
(e') *Always may anyone touch it!
(f) If anyone can do it, (then) you can!
(f') Anyone can do it, so you can! (free choice 'any')
(g) John left without any books
(g') *John left with any books
(h) John left without having read any books
(h') *John left (with) having read any books
(i) Not reading any books makes life boring
(i') *Reading any books makes life boring

The data in (8) demonstrate polarity reversal across various categories, the first case of negative polarity and the primed case of positive polarity. We see that contexts that admit negative polarity items (n.p.) should be interpreted as monotone decreasing sets based on:

a) *verbs* for n.p. object NP

b) *head* NPs for relative clauses with n.p. NP

c) *adjectival phrases* for object n.p. NP in infinitival phrase

d) *locating temporal adverbs* for n.p. subject NP

e) *frequency temporal adverbial* for n.p. subject NP

f) *conditional* for n.p. subject NP

g) *preposition* for n.p. NP in PP

h) *preposition* for n.p. NP in gerund

i) *negation* for n.p. NP in nominalization

Note that in (8f) the negative polarity of the conditional antecedent conveys that if it can be done at all, you certainly can do it, i.e., the task is *difficult* to do; whereas the positive counterpart (8f') admits the free choice *any* but changes the meaning drastically to express that since everyone can do it, you can, i.e. the task is a very *easy* one. These facts show that monotone decreasing sets serve in the interpretation of expressions from all these different categories in a compositional model theoretic semantic theory, but it would lead too far for our present purposes to develop a fragment in detail.

There is another important semantic property of determiners which has been the subject of much recent linguistic research, i.e., the contrast between definite and indefinite NPs. The following definition captures a relevant semantic property:

DEFINITION 14.4

(i) *A determiner D is* positive strong *if for every model* $\mathbf{M}$ *and every $A \subseteq E$ if $D(A)$ is defined then DAA*

(ii) *A determiner D is* negative strong *if for every model* $\mathbf{M}$ *and every $A \subseteq E$ if $D(A)$ is defined then $\sim DAA$*

(iii) *If D is not positive or negative strong, it is* weak.

■

Examples of positive strong determiners are *every, all, both, most, the n;* negative strong is *neither,* and weak are *a, some, at least n, many, several, a few, few, no.* A simple linguistic test for strength of a determiner is to see whether a sentence of the form

$$DCN \begin{cases} \text{is a } CN \\ \text{are } CN\text{s} \end{cases}$$

comes out logically valid, contradictory or contingent. In the first case, the determiner is positive strong, in the second case negative strong and in the third case weak.

There is a simple theorem of generalized quantifier theory which shows that positive strong determiners always include the entire domain E.

THEOREM 14.2 *(Barwise and Cooper (1981))* *If D is a determiner in a conservative quantifier $D(A)$, then DAA iff DAE.* ■

Proof: Since $D(A)$ is conservative, DAE iff $DA(E \cap A)$, but $E \cap A = A$, and we know DAA. ∎

This theorem can be used to explain why only NPs with weak determiners are acceptable in so-called existential contexts with pleonastic subjects *there is/are* NP. For any positive strong determiner this context makes an uninformative tautology, whereas for negative strong ones it gives contradictions. Furthermore, only weak determiners can be used when we deny the existence of something with *there is not/are not* NP.

But, as was pointed out in Keenan (1987), it is not straightforward to extend Definition 14.4 of strong and weak determiners to n-place determiners, since it apparently makes the indefinite two-place determiners *as many CN as CN, more CN than CN* and *fewer CN than CN* strong (e.g. *as many students as students are students* is tautologous, *more students than students are students* contradictory). Nor does this analysis account for the fact that *There is every student* is plainly ungrammatical, whereas *Every student exists* may be trivially true but not ungrammatical. A more explanatory notion is the following (Keenan's work presents generalized quantifiers algebraically: for any two properties p, q, a determiner is interpreted as a function F from properties to sets of properties, i.e., DAB is written $q \in F(p)$. Intersection is meet and union is join in a Boolean algebra of properties. We limit ourselves here to extensional properties and give Keenan's definition in our notation. It is an interesting research question whether there are empirical arguments for or against using either set-theoretic or algebraic methods).

DEFINITION 14.5 *A determiner is* existential *iff either it is a basic existential determiner (i.e., DAB iff $D(A \cap B)E$ is true) or it is built up from basic existential determiners by Boolean combinations, composition of adjectives or the exception determiner operator but NP.* ∎

This notion accounts for the acceptability of the following sentences:

> There are fewer cats than dogs in the yard
> There are just as many female as male cats in the yard
> There is no cat but Felix (a cat) in the yard

Note also that determiners which do not meet Variation may be used ironically or with special meaning in such existential contexts, e.g. in:

> There are fewer than zero solutions to the problem

Look, there is either no or else at least one solution to the problem

Even though tautologies or contradictions may not by very informative from a logical point of view, a linguistic theory cannot ignore the fact that they can be used very meaningfully in perfectly acceptable sentences (see Keenan (1987)).

The relation discussed above between simple decreasing determiners and their positive simple counterparts can be specified here more precisely: there is a syntactically simple monotone decreasing determiner D iff there is a syntactically simple *weak non-cardinal* monotone increasing determiner D' (Barwise and Cooper (1981)). From this general correlation between simple decreasing and increasing determiners we may predict that no language will have syntactically simple determiners interpreted as *not most, not every, not the* or *not two*, since *most, every* and *the* are strong determiners and *two* is a weak cardinal determiner.

Furthermore, only NPs with existential or weak monotone increasing determiners seem acceptable antecedents of unbound anaphora which escape c-command domains, and can be unselectively bound by other quantifiers, as illustrated by the following sentences (see Heim (1982) and Reuland and ter Meulen (eds.) (1987) for recent research on indefiniteness):

(9) (a) Pedro owns *many/several/some donkeys*. He beats *them*.
    (a′) *Pedro owns *every donkey*. He beats *it*.
    (b) If Pedro owns *a donkey*, he beats *it*.
    (b′) *If Pedro owns *every donkey*, he beats *it*.
    (c) Every farmer who owns *a donkey*, beats *it*.
    (c′) *Every farmer who owns *every donkey*, beats *it*.

Definite determiners constitute a subset of the positive strong determiners, defined as follows:

DEFINITION 14.6 *A determiner is* definite *if in every model* M *where* $D(A)$ *is defined, there is a set* $B \neq \emptyset$, *such that* $D(A) = \{X \subseteq E \mid B \subseteq X\}$. ■

Note that for a definite determiner D the set $D(A)$ is the *principal filter* generated by B (see Chapter 11 for the general notion of a filter in a lattice). Determiners which are positive strong but not definite are *every, more than half* and *at least half.* Plural definite determiners are the only determiners that can be embedded in partitive constructions, as we can see from (10).

(10) (a) most of the children
      (a′) *most of some children
      (b) several of the five children
      (b′) *several of at least five children

Ladusaw (1982) added to this definiteness condition on determiners in partitives that the embedded plural NP must be interpreted collectively, since *one of both* is unacceptable although *both* is a filter generated by a set with two elements. *The two* is a collective determiner, but *both* is distributive, as can be seen from the fact that *both boys lifted the piano* means that the piano was lifted twice, whereas *the two boys lifted the piano* does not specify how many times the piano was lifted, as it is true also when the two boys once lifted the piano together, i.e., collectively. The analysis of plurals as generalized quantifiers presents intriguing semantic problems, many still open, which have been explored in Link (1983), (1984) using lattice-theoretic domains, Hoeksema (1983), and elsewhere. Other restrictions on determiners in partitives can also be described by semantic properties. For instance, in the general syntactic form of partitives

$$\text{Det}_1 \quad of \quad \text{Det}_2 \quad \text{Det}_3 \quad CN$$

Det_1 must be *pronominal*, i.e. a determiner which can be interpreted in isolation of any CN such as *some, several, none, the three* but not *every, the, a, no* (due to unpublished work of J. Hoeksema; see also Westerståhl (1985)). Possessive or demonstrative determiners are also pronominal, but they should already be excluded from Det_1 positions in partitives, since they do not occur in extensional and quantitative NPs. For the Det_2 position we find that only possessives, plural demonstratives and *the* are admissible, which are all definite once we allow context-sensitive filters (see Section 5 for context-sensitive determiners). Det_3 can be filled only with weak determiners which impose some measure or cardinality condition on the set A (the CN-interpretation). These results are typical descriptive semantic facts of generalized quantifier theory, for which further explanation should be sought in more procedural terms of verification of NPs in models, information processing, or complexity-measures of quantifiers and determiners.

Other recent results in generalized quantifier theory include extensions to many place determiners (*fewer men than women*) (Keenan and Faltz (1985), and Keenan and Moss in van Benthem and ter Meulen (1985)), exclusion determiners (*every man but John*), determiners which rely on some order-ing (*every other number*), adjectival and numerical determiners, temporal quantification, and comparatives for which we refer the reader to the further reading suggested for this chapter.

14.4 Determiners as relations

In presenting the main concepts of generalized quantifiers in the previous sec-tion, we switched back and forth between the functional perspective, in which the VP is interpreted as element of the second-order NP-interpretation, and the flattened relational perspective, where determiners are interpreted as re-lations between the sets A and B. In this section we focus on the relational perspective and study properties of relations as constraints on determiners, uncovering some important new semantic insights on the class of possible natural language determiners. (The relational analysis is extensively stud-ied in Zwarts (1983), whose exposition is followed closely in this section, and in van Benthem (1986).)

Let D be a binary relation in a model $\mathbf{M} = \langle E, [\![\ ]\!] \rangle$ on the sets $A, B, C \subseteq E$; the following list of properties of relations is useful for defining types of determiners.

reflexivity:	$D_E AA$
irreflexivity:	$\sim D_E AA$
symmetry:	$D_E AB \rightarrow D_E BA$
asymmetry:	$D_E AB \rightarrow \sim D_E BA$
anti-symmetry:	$D_E AB \,\&\, D_E BA \rightarrow A = B$
connectedness:	$D_E AB \vee D_E BA \vee A = B$
strong connectedness:	$D_E AB \vee D_E BA$
almost connectedness:	$D_E AB \rightarrow (D_E AC \vee D_E CB)$
transitivity:	$(D_E AB \,\&\, D_E BC) \rightarrow D_E AC$
euclideanness:	$(D_E AB \,\&\, D_E AC) \rightarrow D_E BC$
anti-euclideanness:	$(D_E AB \,\&\, D_E CB) \rightarrow D_E AC$
circularity:	$(D_E AB \,\&\, D_E BC) \rightarrow D_E CA$

For example, the determiner *every* is reflexive, transitive and anti-sym-met-ric, and its external negation *not every* is irreflexive, almost connected and connected. The numerical determiner *the n* is transitive, anti-symmetric but not reflexive. Symmetric determiners are *some, no, at least n, at most n, exactly n*. But we will see that other properties of relations like asymmetry, strong connectedness, euclideanness or circularity are not properties of possible determiners in natural languages.

We assume the four universal conditions on quantifiers Extension, Conservativity, Quantity and Variation set forth in Section 2 of this chapter. There are some useful theorems on equivalences between relational properties and set-theoretic inclusion of the sets A and B.

THEOREM 14.3 *The following pairs of statements are equivalent:*

(1) (i) D is reflexive
(ii) $A \subseteq B \rightarrow D\,AB$
(2) (i) D is irreflexive
(ii) $D\,AB \rightarrow A \nsubseteq B$
(3) (i) D is antisymmetric
(ii) $D\,AB \rightarrow A \subseteq B$
(4) (i) D is connected
(ii) $A \nsubseteq B \rightarrow D\,AB$

∎

Proofs:

(1) (i) → (ii) Assume D is reflexive, and take $A \subseteq B$. Then DAA and since $A \cap B = A$ also $DA(A \cap B)$. By Conservativity then DAB.

(1) (ii) → (i) follows directly from the reflexivity of inclusion.

(2) D is irreflexive iff $\sim D$ is reflexive. By (1) D is irreflexive iff $A \subseteq B \rightarrow \sim D\,AB$. Contraposition and double negation gives $D\,AB \rightarrow A \nsubseteq B$.

(3) (i) → (ii). Assume D is antisymmetric and take for some domain E, sets $A, B \subseteq E$ such that $D_E\,AB$. By Conservativity $D_E\,A(A \cap B)$. Extend E to E', and take $A' \subseteq E'$ such that $|A'| = |A|$ and $A \cap A' = A \cap B$. Then $D_E\,A(A \cap A')$ and by Extension $D_{E'}\,A(A \cap A')$. Conservativity gives $D_{E'}\,A\,A'$. Now consider a permutation π of E' which yields identical sets for $A \cap A'$ and $E' - (A \cup A')$ but permutes $A - A'$ with $A' - A$. Quantity gives us $D_{E'}\pi(A)\pi(A')$, i.e., $D_{E'}\,A'\,A$. So we have now $D_{E'}\,A\,A'$ and $D_{E'}\,A'\,A$, and antisymmetry of D gives $A = A'$. Since $A \cap A' = A \cap B$ it follows that $A \cap B = A$, so $A \subseteq B$.

(3) (ii) → (i). Assume (ii), let DAB and DBA. Then $A \subseteq B$ and $B \subseteq A$, so $A = B$.

(4) By definition D is connected iff $\sim D$ is antisymmetric. With (3) D is connected iff $\sim DAB \to A \subseteq B$. So D is connected iff $A \nsubseteq B \to DAB$.

∎

From these relational characterizations we can now prove that some properties of relations cannot be properties of natural language determiners, given the four universal conditions we have assumed on quantifiers. Such results demarcate the class of possible natural language determiners as a proper subset of the class of logically possible determiners.

THEOREM 14.4 *(van Benthem (1984)) There are no asymmetric determiners.*

∎

Proof. By definition of asymmetry, to show that there are no asymmetric determiners amounts to showing that there are no irreflexive antisymmetric determiners. Suppose D is irreflexive and antisymmetric, and assume DAB. From Theorem 14.3, (2) says that $A \nsubseteq B$ but (3) says that $A \subseteq B$. Contradiction! So D can only be the trivial empty determiner, but that violates Variety.

∎

As a corollary to Theorem 14.4 it follows that there exist no irreflexive and transitive determiners, since antisymmetry entails transitivity for determiners (see exercises). Since a binary relation which is irreflexive and transitive is called a strict partial ordering, we find that no determiners are strict partial orderings.

Similarly we can establish that no determiners induce a weak linear ordering on E (reflexive, transitive, anti-symmetric and connected), since there are no antisymmetric connected determiners.

THEOREM 14.5 *(Zwarts (1983)) There are no antisymmetric connected determiners.*

∎

Proof. Assume that some D is antisymmetric and connected. From Theorem 14.3, (4) tells us that $A \nsubseteq B \to DAB$ and (3) that $DAB \to A \subseteq B$. But then $A \nsubseteq B \to A \subseteq B$. Contradiction!

∎

In fact the only determiner which is reflexive and antisymmetric is the inclusion-determiner *every* (and its plural counterpart *all*), since it is evident from Theorem 14.3 (1) and (3) that for reflexive and antisymmetric

D, $D\,AB \leftrightarrow A \subseteq B$. Hence *every* is the only determiner which is reflexive, transitive and anti-symmetric, i.e. induces a weak partial ordering on E.

We prove two more non-existence results on natural language determiners here.

THEOREM 14.6 *(van Benthem) There are no symmetric and transitive determiners.*   ∎

Proof. Since transitive determiners are positive strong (see exercises), and Theorem 14.2 showed that positive strong determiners always include the entire domain E, we have $D\,AE$. Symmetry gives $D\,EE$, but that means that the only symmetric and transitive determiner is the trivial universal one, which violates Variation.   ∎

Since equivalence relations are reflexive, symmetric and transitive we can conclude from Theorem 14.6 that no natural language determiner will induce an equivalence relation on E. Since euclidean determiners must be symmetric and transitive (see Zwarts (1983)), we can also conclude that *a fortiori* there are no euclidean determiners in natural language.

THEOREM 14.7 *(van Benthem) There are no circular determiners.*   ∎

Proof. We show that circular determiners must be euclidean and hence cannot exist in natural language because of Theorem 14.6. The reasoning is similar to the proof of Theorem 14.1 (3) (i) → (ii). Assume D is circular and take for some domain E $A, B, C \subseteq E$ such that $D_E\,AB$ and $D_E\,AC$. By Conservativity $D_E A(A \cap B)$. Extend E to E', and take $A' \subseteq E'$ such that $|A'| = |A|$ and $A \cap A' = A \cap B$. Then $D_E A(A \cap A')$ and by Extension $D_{E'} A(A \cap A')$. Conservativity gives $D_{E'} A\,A'$. Now consider a permutation π of E' which yields identical sets for $A \cap A'$ and $E' - (A \cup A')$ but permutes $A - A'$ with $A' - A$. Quantity gives us $D_{E'} \pi(A)\pi(A')$, i.e. $D_{E'} A'\,A$. So we have now $D_{E'} A\,A'$ and $D_{E'} A'\,A$, and circularity of D gives $D_{E'} A\,A$ and by Extension $D_E A\,A$. From this together with the assumption that $D_E A C$ and circularity of D we infer $D_E C A$. Given $D_E A B$, the circularity of D gives us $D_E B C$, i.e., D must be euclidean.   ∎

More negative but also positive existence results on possible natural language determiners based on properties of relations can be found in Zwarts (1983).

14.5   Context and quantification

In studying the fundamental properties of NPs interpreted as generalized quantifiers we initially disregarded any form of context-dependence of the interpretation. Extension required NPs to be insensitive to domain extensions, and Quantity made us disregard all that is specific in reference and quantification. In this final section we indicate briefly how the theory may be extended to include the important forms of context-dependence found in natural language, while seeking to extend the explanatory power of this semantic analysis of quantification in terms of more dynamic processes of interpretation and evaluation. (The exposition is partly based on Westerståhl (1985a) and (1985b).)

How many is many? We already alluded to the fact that the determiner *many* violates Extension when interpreted by sets of a cardinality greater than a least number fixed by the size of the domain E:

$$many_E AB = many_E A(B \cap A) \text{ where } |(B \cap A)| \geq f(E)$$

Although Extension is clearly violated in this interpretation, Conservativity and Quantity are not. Let us call this interpretation $many^1$ for the moment.

Another interpretation of *many* compares the number of B's that are A's to some constant or normal frequency. For instance, in a class of twenty students we say that many students got an A, when we compare the number of A-grades to the average score in other classes over some period of time and find that five out of twenty is more than that average ratio. Suppose that by coincidence there are as many right-handed students as A-grade students, but they are not same individuals. In that situation *Many students got an A* is true, whereas *Many students are right-handed* is false, i.e. $D_E AB$ but $\sim D_E AC$ although $|A \cap B| = |A \cap C|$, violating Quantity. If we assume in addition that the students who got an A are the same individuals as the right-handed students, i.e. $D_E AB$ and $\sim D_E AC$ although $A \cap B = A \cap C$, we have a context where even Conservativity is violated.

What counts as many may depend on various contextual parameters. Although five A grades in a class of twenty might be considered many, if five out of twenty people are right-handed this is not considered to be many. Different contextual parameters are at stake in this example, and we should ask which properties of determiners are preserved under addition of which parameters. If we compare the cardinality of $B \cap A$ to some contextually fixed ratio of As, we get the following interpretation:

$$many_E^2 AB = many^2 A(A \cap B) \text{ where } |(A \cap B)| < c \cdot |A|$$

and c is here a contextual parameter which may be 1/4 for the A-students but 3/4 for right-handed students. This interpretation saves Conservativity, Extension and Quantity, but introduces an external parameter which must be given as input to the interpretation. If the dependence on the frequency of B's in the domain E should be represented explicitly, the following would be required:

$$many_E^3 AB = many^3 A(A \cap B) \text{ where } |(A \cap B)| > \frac{|B|}{|E|} \cdot |A|$$

Conservativity fails since E is now relevant to the interpretation, and hence Extension fails as well.

Finally *many* may be used to compare to the set of B's, rather than A's, as in the following examples from Westerståhl (1985a).

(1) Many winners of the Nobel prize in literature are Scandinavians

(2) Many Scandinavians have won the Nobel prize in literature

(3) Many Scandinavians are Nobel prize winners in literature

For (1) to be true a number of external parameters, like the distribution of nationality among Nobel prize winners in general, will have to be considered, hence the interpretation $many^2$ is appropriate. The sentence (2) is either equivalent to (1), or it counts among all Scandinavians the number of them who won the Nobel prize for literature, and that cannot turn out to be many. Sentence (3) expresses this latter interpretation of (2), which is obviously false. If (1) and one interpretation of (2) are equivalent, *many* in these contexts is symmetric, but, if it still is based on an asymmetry in the cardinalities of the respective sets, it must be interpreted as comparing to the set B, i.e. :

$$many_E^4 AB = many^4 A(A \cap B) \text{ where } |(A \cap B)| > c \cdot |B|$$

This interpretation satisfies Extension and Quantity, but not Conservativity. In Barwise and Cooper (1981) *many* in any of its interpretations is analyzed as requiring that $|B| \neq \emptyset$.

To gain more insight into the semantics of *many*, it should be contrasted to *most*, which appears to allow only two different interpretations. *Most*[1] compares the number of A's that are B's to the number of A's that are not B's, equivalent (on finite sets) to the complex determiner *more than half*.

$$most^1_E AB = most^1 A(A \cap B) \text{ where } |(A \cap B)| > |(A - B)|$$

This interpretation satisfies Conservativity, Extension and Quantity.

The other interpretation of *most* is related to the universal quantifier and gives it a meaning of *almost all*.

$$most^2_E AB = most^2 A(A \cap B) \text{ where } |(A \cap B)| > c \cdot |A|$$

Here c is again some contextually given parameter like in *many*[2], which determines in a given context how many counts as almost all. By using $\geq$ instead of $>$, *most*[2] A are B is always true when $A = \emptyset$, just as for the universal determiner, but *most*[1] A are B is always false when $A = \emptyset$. In terms of strength *most*[2] is positive strong, whereas *most*[1] is positive strong only when $A \neq \emptyset$. Let us call this property *almost positive strong*.

The following table summarizes our findings on *many* and *most* and lists their monotonicity properties.

	Ext.	Cons.	Quant.	Symm.	Rightincr.	Leftincr.
$many^1$	−	+	+	+	+	+
$many^2$	+	+	+	−	+	−
$many^3$	−	−	+	+	−	−
$many^4$	+	−	+	−	−	+
$most^1$	+	+	+	−	+	−
$most^2$	+	+	+	−	+	−

Figure 14–2: Properties of *many* and *most*

The definite determiner *the* shares the property of being almost positive strong with $most^1$. In fact, all definite positive strong determiners require that $|A| > 0$ in order to be interpretable in a model. Recall that a determiner D is *definite* if it is interpreted as the principal filter generated by a non-empty B in every model *in which* $D(A)$ *is defined*. The requirement that A is not empty is a *presupposition* of definite determiners on the models in which their interpretation is defined (see also de Jong and Verkuyl (1985) on the presuppositions of definite determiners). The set B determines the truth-conditions or the interpretation of the definite D, but the set A imposes a necessary pre-condition on a model for its interpretation: prior context must have introduced elements of the set A. Indefinite determiners like *three* or *few* which are weak and intersective do not carry such a presupposition on A, but their interpretation, which is always defined, requires A to be of a certain cardinality. Indefinite determiners serve to change the context so that A is of the required cardinality. But how do we represent such context-dependency in the notion of a generalized quantifier? Westerståhl (1985b) suggests relativizing all determiners to a context set $X \subseteq E$ by the following universal condition.

Restriction. $D_E^X AB \leftrightarrow D_E(X \cap A)B$.

Conservativity and Extension are preserved under this Restriction, and a local form of Quantity where the permutation is restricted to X may even be maintained as well. Many of the relational properties of determiners are preserved as well, but anti-symmetry, for instance, is not. Note that restriction to a context set X does not add another argument to a binary determiner, but serves to represent which elements of the large domain of entities E have been contextually given. Definite determiners are analyzed as context set indicators requiring $|X \cap A| > 0$, and indefinite determiners extend a given, possibly empty context set with new entities with property

A. The determiners which are neither definite nor indefinite, like the positively strong *more than half* or *every, each* and *all* together with their right monotone decreasing counterparts are truly quantitative over *E* and do not depend on any context set. Note that this notion of a context set solves a well-known problem concerning the uniqueness of the referent of a singular definite description: *A* may contain other elements besides those in the relevant context set $X \cap A$. E.g., interpreting *the dog is running in the yard* in a context where there are possibly more dogs around only requires $X \cap$ [dog] to contain a single dog, but $A \subseteq E$ may be of any non-empty cardinality.

In relation to this semantic analysis of definite and indefinite determiners as context-sensitive generalized quantifiers it is worth noting that quantifiers with definite determiners, whether plural or singular, have unique witness sets and quantifiers with indefinite determiners may have different witness sets.

DEFINITION 14.7 *A* witness set *of a conservative quantifier* $D(A)$ *is any* $W \subseteq A$ *such that* D AW. ∎

Since DAB with a definite monotone increasing determiner is interpreted as principal filter generated by *B*, the witness set *W* for $D(A)$ is always non-empty and unique. Furthermore this *W* is a singleton in case the relevant *CN* is morphologically marked as singular, and of cardinality 2 or more in case the relevant *CN* is morphologically marked as plural. Indefinite determiners introduce new elements of the domain into $X \cap A$, hence there may be several disjoint witness sets for a quantifier $D(A)$ with a weak determiner. The number marking of the *CN* again determines whether the witness set is a singleton or not, but the determiner itself may in addition impose an exact cardinality on $X \cap A$ and hence on any witness set for $D(A)$. In verifying a quantified sentence in a model we search for such witness sets, and if one is found, the statement is true in that model. Since quantifiers with definite determiners have only one witness set, the entire domain *E* may have to be searched in an attempted verification, whereas a quantifier with an indefinite determiner is verified as soon as one witness is found, and the domain may contain more such witness sets. From this fact we may predict that experimental verification of definite monotone increasing NPs requires in general more search time than indefinite monotone increasing NPs. Along these lines it may become feasible to give the theory of generalized quantifiers in natural language empirical foundations in psycholinguistic research.

Exercises

1. Explain and illustrate in a Venn diagram with two sets A and B in a domain E what the combined effects of the four universal conditions on quantifiers are.

2. Represent the following quantifiers and properties of quantifiers in the number-theoretic trees by describing the set of pairs which verify the quantifier by shading the appropriate area in the tree, and/or by describing the general pattern which the condition imposes on the tree.

   (a) no men
   (b) not all men
   (c) neither man
   (d) at most two men
   (e) at least one man
   (f) exactly one man or exactly three men do not walk (B = walkers)
   (g) Variation
   (h) Right monotone increasing
   (i) Symmetry

3. Determine the monotonicity properties of the following determiners: several, at most three, none, at least n, some (sing.), these, neither, every, all, each, infinitely many, a finite number of, most, many.

4. (a) Show with some examples of entailments for some simple left monotone increasing determiners that they are also:

      (i) right monotone increasing
      (ii) continuous

   (b) Construct an example of a complex English determiner which is left monotone increasing but not right monotone increasing.

5. Show in a model with four entities that *John's books* is not a quantitative quantifier, whereas *every book* is.

6. Prove set-theoretically that Variation is preserved under external and internal negation, (i.e. if Q meets Variation, then $\sim Q$ and $Q \sim$ do).

7. Prove that

   (a) if Q is monotone increasing, $Q^\sim$ is monotone increasing

   (b) for any Q, the dual of $Q^\sim$ is Q itself

   (c) for any Q, $Q^\sim \Leftrightarrow \sim(Q\sim) \Leftrightarrow (\sim Q)\sim$

   (d) if Q is self-dual, then $Q\sim \Leftrightarrow \sim Q$

8. Prove that every definite determiner is positive strong.

9. We define an *intersective* determiner as a determiner D for which in all models M and all $B \subseteq E : DAB \leftrightarrow D(A \cap B)B$.

   (a) Prove the following equivalences for intersective determiners:

   $$DAB \leftrightarrow D(A \cap B)E \leftrightarrow DBA$$

   (b) Give natural language examples of these semantic equivalences.

10. Prove in the relational analysis of determiners that

   (a) every antisymmetric determiner is transitive

   (b) every connected determiner is almost connected

   (c) every transitive determiner is positive strong
       (i.e. if $((D\,AB\;\&\;D\,BC) \to D\,AC)$ then $(D\,AB \to D\,AA)$)

Chapter 15

Intensionality

This chapter is of a somewhat different nature than the rest of this book, since it does not present mathematical tools for linguistic analysis, nor show successful applications of such tools to linguistic problems. It is concerned with some of the most difficult issues in philosophical and linguistic semantics which for a long time have been and still are central to the theory of meaning and interpretation of natural language. Various analyses of these issues have been proposed using different mathematical tools, but at least in the present state of the art there is no single account of these puzzles which is commonly received and recognized as the right solution. The core of these issues is outlined here without much formalization only to provide some initial understanding of what is at stake. In Section 3 a simple method is presented to analyze intensionality in natural language, and the discussion in subsequent sections may aid in appreciating the possibilities and limitations of different mathematical methods for linguistic analysis.

15.1   Frege's two problems

Two semantic puzzles which preoccupied Frege, the founder of modern logic, still constitute major foundational problems of contemporary linguistic and philosophical theories of meaning and interpretation. The first puzzle concerns the information expressed in identity statements with coreferential NPs. The classical discussion is based on the question why

(15-1) Hesperus is Phosphorus

would have been an informative identity statement to the Babylonian astronomers who did not know it was true, whereas

(15-2) Hesperus is Hesperus

would to them be completely uninformative, even though (15-1) and (15-2) are both true statements and the NPs, all proper names, corefer to the same object, the planet Venus. The same puzzle is also often formulated with complex referential NPs like definite descriptions, as in the informative

(15-3) The Morning Star is the Evening Star

and the uninformative

(15-4) The Morning Star is the Morning Star

If coreferential expressions have the same semantic value, they must be substitutable for each other in any context without changing its semantic value. Substitution of semantic equivalents is an important rule of inference in any logical system. But how can (15-1) and (15-3) then be informative, whereas (15-2) and (15-4) in which coreferential expressions are substituted are completely uninformative? If a semantic theory is to account for such facts it must allow coreferential expressions to have different semantic values. For this purpose Frege introduced the fundamental distinction between the *reference (Bedeutung)* of an expression and its *sense (Sinn)*. Proper names and other referential NPs may refer to the same object or individual, but they differ in their sense. Since we use natural language to communicate our thoughts, the meaning of any linguistic expression must at least in part be accessible to all its users. This objective part of meaning is what Frege called the sense of an expression. Identity statements are informative when they contain expressions with different senses, and they are true when their NPs are coreferential. Conditions of 'informativeness' hence cannot be identified with truth conditions. Perhaps there is more to the semantic value of an expression beyond its sense and reference, like its psychological associative power, connotation or 'color,' but that part of its meaning will be subjective and should be disregarded in semantics, according to Frege, for it cannot be the source of communicable information.

The sense of an expression determines its reference in different situations, but even when the reference of an expression in every situation is determined, this does not fix its sense uniquely. If we assume, as Frege did, that the reference of a sentence is its truth value, two sentences that necessarily have the same truth value in all situations, e.g.

(15-5) Robin won the race

(15-6) Everyone who did not compete or lost in the race has done something Robin did not do

still differ in their Fregean sense (the example is adapted from Bigelow (1978)). Similarly two distinct tautologies which are both always true may contain different information. In a proof, for instance, we use the logical laws and inference rules to construct a sequence of tautologies, yet new information is inferred from its premises. Reasoning in ordinary language is also based on the manipulation of old information to gain new information. If the semantics of natural language is to account for coreference, inference and reasoning, it should contain a mathematically satisfactory analysis of the Fregean notions of sense and reference.

The second problem Frege presented as a central question to semantics is related to the first one of informative identity statements. If such statements or any other two statements with the same truth values are embedded as sentential complements of certain verbs, the resulting statements may differ in truth value. For instance,

(15-7) Robin believes that Hesperus is Phosphorus

(15-8) Robin believes that Hesperus is Hesperus

(15-7) may be false, whereas (15-8) must be true even when Robin knows nothing of Babylonian astronomy, or when he is not even aware of what the name 'Hesperus' refers to. For Frege this meant that sentences embedded in *that*-clauses do not refer, as they ordinarily do, to their truth value but *refer indirectly*, i.e. they refer to their customary senses. Substitution of coreferential or equivalent expressions in such *that*-clauses does not preserve the truth value of the entire statement. Only if the believer knows that two NPs are coreferential can they be substituted in his belief reports.

Contexts where substitution of coreferential or equivalent expressions does not preserve reference are called *opaque*, as opposed to *transparent* contexts where the laws of predicate logic hold without restrictions. To

appreciate the extent of this semantic problem in natural language consider
the following versions of the same problem in different opaque contexts.

(15–9)   The Babylonian astronomers did not observe or compute that Hes-
         perus was the same planet as Phosphorus

(15–10) The Babylonian linguists did not realize that 'Hesperus' and 'Phos-
         phorus' are coreferential NPs, but they called Venus both 'Hespe-
         rus' and 'Phosphorus' (based on Soames (1985))

(15–11) Someone found out that the Morning Star and the Evening Star
         are the same planet

(15–12) John told me that the Babylonians referred to Venus as Hesperus
         or Phosphorus

(15–13) We know which planet the Morning Star or the Evening Star is,
         but the Babylonians did not know that

Another source of opacity was described originally in Quine (1956) and
based on belief reports grounded in perception. Ralph sees on one occasion
a man in a brown coat and says (of him) 'He is a spy.' On another occasion
Ralph sees a man in a grey coat and says (of him) 'He is not a spy.' Un-
beknownst to Ralph, what he sees on these two occasions is the same man
dressed in different coats. Ralph will report about the man he has seen with
the two sentences

(15–14) The man in the brown coat is a spy

and

(15–15) The man in the grey coat is not a spy

Since the two NPs corefer, (15-14) and (15-15) are contradictions. But
Ralph is not aware of their coreference, since from the two resource situations
in which he used the NPs to refer to an individual he saw, he did not gain
sufficient information to identify their referent as the same man. Someone

who is aware of this coreference would explicitly report Ralph's beliefs as contradictory by using a proper name (or demonstrative NP) to refer to the object of Ralph's beliefs. If the man is called Ortcutt, Ralph's beliefs would be described by

(15–16) Ralph believes of Ortcutt that he is and is not a spy.

The semantics of belief reports must on the one hand allow for people to have contradictory, incompatible or inconsistent beliefs, due to their misinformation or lack of information, but it must also be able to indicate on what grounds their beliefs are contradictory or incompatible. It must explain why Ralph believes (15-14) and (15-15), but does not assent to (15-16) nor to any other equivalent contradiction about the object of his beliefs, even though (15-16) is entailed by the conjunction of (15-14) and (15-15). This requires an account of the sense of expressions and the way their sense contributes compositionally to the reference of a *that*-clause in an opaque sentence-embedding construction.

From a more linguistic point of view we should note that NPs other than proper names or demonstratives inside opaque contexts cannot in general be extraposed without changing the interpretation of the entire statement. Consider the following existential constructions, disregarding tenses for the moment. If Ralph has reported his beliefs with (15-14) and (15-15), someone who heard him may express what Ralph said with (15-17) or (15-18), to which Ralph himself would still assent.

(15–17) Ralph believes that there is a man in a brown coat who is a spy and that there is a man in a grey coat who is not a spy

(15–18) There is a man in a brown coat of whom Ralph believes that he is a spy and there is a man in a grey coat of whom Ralph believes that he is not a spy

Since the definite NPs in Ralph's belief reports were grounded in his perception, we may infer with existential generalization to the existence of the individuals he saw, now using indefinite NPs to report what Ralph saw. Although (15-18) and (15-19) may seem (near) equivalents, and Ralph should assent to both, someone who knows that Ralph saw Ortcutt on both occasions will take (15-18) to be true but (15-19) to be false.

(15–19) There are two men and Ralph believes of the one that he is a spy
         and of the other that he is not a spy

Ralph cannot assent to two other sentences, (15-20) and (15-21), which
each entail (15-17), a sentence to which he did assent.

(15–20) There is a man of whom Ralph believes that he is and is not a spy

(15–21) Of Ortcutt Ralph believes that he is and is not a spy

These sentences all differ in their sense, express different thoughts as
Frege would say, but to provide a full-fledged compositional semantic analysis of these differences in terms of their information value is an assignment
that still constitutes a major open research problem. It requires a mathematically satisfactory account of equivalence of 'semantic value' which is
sufficiently fine-grained to explain when a statement expresses new information to someone in a particular context, and what that information is,given
the information that is already available to him.

To see why ordinary predicate logic cannot account adequately for opaque
contexts we should realize that they are characterized by

(15–22) (i) failure of substitution of predicate-logical equivalents
         (ii) failure of existential generalization

Although the example of Ralph's beliefs did admit of some forms of
existential generalization, because his own reports were grounded in his (non-
hallucinating) perception, NPs in opaque contexts in general do not admit
such existential generalization as we see in (15-22) and (15-23).

(15–23) (a) John wants to catch a fish and eat it
         (b) There is a fish that John wants to catch and eat

(15–24) (a) Every man seeks a woman who will always love him
         (b) For every man there exists a woman who will always love him
             if he seeks her

In a situation where (15-23a) is true there may not be a particular fish
that John wants to catch and eat, and from (15-24a) we cannot legitimately

infer that for every man there is a woman who will love him if he seeks her. Note that in each example any situation in which the (b) sentence is true must also verify the (a) sentence, so the (b) sentences entail the (a) sentences but not vice versa. The (a) sentences are hence semantically ambiguous, i.e. open to various interpretations, in a way that the (b) sentences are not. If opaque contexts like the (a) sentences are given an interpretation which is equivalent to their corresponding (b) sentences, we call this interpretation its *de re interpretation* (from Latin, about the 'res' (thing or object) itself), otherwise the interpretation of opaque contexts is called *de dicto* (literally, about what was said or about the word). In a compositional semantics these entailments will have to be reflected as a relation between the interpretation of the sentences, and the difference in their structure will be important. In predicate logic quantificational ambiguities are dissolved by differentiating the scope of quantifiers, but in models for opacity phenomena quantifier scope may depend not only on other quantifiers but also on the interpretation of the expressions that create the opacity.

15.2 Forms of opacity

Opacity phenomena are inherent to natural language, and in fact contribute importantly to the efficiency of communication in ordinary language use. One and the same expression may be used in different linguistic or extra-linguistic contexts and express different information. A disambiguated formal language is required for the purposes of formalization, abstract representation and mathematical analysis of the semantics of natural language, as we learned in practicing translations of English to predicate logic. Interpretation in mathematical models or translation to a formal language disambiguates natural language expressions, which is prerequisite for an account of reasoning and inference in ordinary language use. Our choice of mathematical methods should be determined by the kind of phenomena we want to study: for some quantificational ambiguities predicate logic is suitable, but for opacity phenomena different mathematical methods may provide analytical tools suited to different kinds of opacity.

In the previous section various kinds of opaque contexts were presented, and in this section we discuss more systematically but still informally what kinds of expressions in natural language may give rise to opacity.

The belief contexts in the previous section show that the epistemic verbs *to believe* and *to know* give rise to opacity. The examples were all based on sentential complements in *that*-clauses, but it is important to see that some epistemic verbs also allow other constructions which may be partly opaque as well. Consider the following sentences.

(15–25) Ralph believes a man in a brown coat to be spying

(15–26) Ralph knows Ortcutt but does not believe (that) he is a spy

Sentence (15-25) does not contain a *that*-clause, but the object NP and infinitival clause may well be interpreted de dicto, i.e. dependent on, or in the scope of the belief-verb. Sentence (15-26) shows that an epistemic verb may take an object NP which is an antecedent for a coreferential pronoun in a coordinated sentence containing another epistemic verb. Note that even when Ortcutt is indeed a spy, (15-26) may well be true. At least on some understanding of what it is to know someone, Ralph may know Ortcutt although he does not know or even believe everything that is true of him. The verb *to believe* behaves differently in this respect, since to believe someone is to believe that what he says is true. Belief *in* someone is again different, and borders on metaphoric use, but it is also opaque in that for instance (15-27)

(15–27) Ralph believes in a spy with a brown coat

means that Ralph believes that there is someone who is a spy and wears a brown coat, but in reality there maybe nobody who actually has these properties.

Although *to believe* and *to know* are typical epistemic verbs, this class of verbs that give rise to opacity is much larger and includes the stative *to be aware of*, and *to be conscious* of, besides action denoting verbs as *to find out*, *to compute*, *to calculate*, *to discover*, which are actions of gaining information and hence epistemic. These verbs belong to the same class on criteria that are semantic in nature; they do not necessarily enter in the same syntactic constructions. The non-equivalence of sentences (15-28) and (15-29) shows that coreferential NPs cannot be substituted in a context *find out who* NP *is*.

(15–28) Ralph found out who the man in the grey coat was

(15–29) Ralph found out who Ortcutt was

Similarly a *that*-clause reporting the content of a discovery or of a computation is opaque, as illustrated in (15-30), and the non-equivalent (15-31) and (15-32).

(15–30) An astronomer discovered that Hesperus and Phosporus are the same planet

(15–31) An astronomer computed that Hesperus is the planet Venus

(15–32) An astromer computed that Phosporus is the planet Venus

In (15-31) and (15-32) it becomes particularly clear that performing a certain operation on given objects is sensitive to the description of the objects, i.e. the way the input is given to the operation.

A class of opacity creating verbs which is closely related to the epistemic verbs is the class of perception verbs. However, certain constructions with perception verbs are transparent as we see from (15-34) and (15-35).

(15–33) Ralph sees that the man in the brown coat is spying

(15–34) Ralph sees the man in the brown coat spy

(15–35) Ralph sees Ortcutt spy

In (15-33) we cannot substitute the coreferential *Ortcutt* for the definite NP embedded in the *that*-clause reporting Ralph's perception. But in the naked infinitive constructions in (15-34) and (15-35) coreferential NPs can be substituted without distorting the content of the report. (see Barwise (1981), Higginbotham (1983) and Asher and Bonevac (1985) for more discussion). The class of perception verbs includes visual and auditory perception, but also verbs like *to notice*, or perhaps even *to catch*.

Epistemic verbs and perception verbs directly concern the information of a person or a 'system' , hence, for obvious reasons, communication verbs like *to tell, to say, to announce, to inform* and *to indicate* give rise to opaque constructions, not only in *that*-clauses. Consider the invalid inference in (15-36)

(15–36)   Ortcutt told Ralph about his profession
            Ortcutt is a professional spy
            ∴ Ortcutt told Ralph that he is a spy

Telling someone about or of something or telling him what something is brings in prime examples of opacity, as (15-36) shows, since for the first premise to be true Ortcutt may have told Ralph anything ranging from true stories about his adventurous life in Casablanca to tales about his cover-up occupation as real estate agent: the relation of someone telling something can be true without the relation truth-telling being true. The verb *to indicate* has interesting semantic properties of its own, but it does require a *that*-clause for a de dicto, opaque interpretation of what is indicated as the invalid (15-37) and the transparent, valid arguments in (15-38) and (15-38′) show.

(15–37)   The thermometer indicates that the temperature is
                ninety degrees Fahrenheit
            Ninety degrees Fahrenheit is the average summer
                temperature
            ∴ The thermometer indicates that the temperature is
                the average summer temperature

(15–38)   The thermometer indicates the temperature
            The temperature is ninety degrees Fahrenheit
            ∴ The thermometer indicates ninety degrees
                Fahrenheit

(15-38′)   The thermometer indicates ninety degrees Fahrenheit
            Ninety degrees Fahrenheit is the average summer
                temperature
            ∴ The thermometer indicates the average summer
                temperature

Besides the epistemic, perceptual and communication main verbs that give rise to opacity, the modal auxiliary verbs *may*, *must*, and *can* create well known opaque contexts, as well as the modal adverbials *possibly* and *necessarily* and the modal constructions with pleonastic subjects that take sentential complements *it is necessary that* and *it is possible that*. The logical aspects of modalities have been studied thoroughly in systems of *modal* or *intensional logic*, that were developed after the extensional systems of predicate logic. (See Hughes and Cresswell (1968) and van Benthem (1985)). The variety of such intensional systems cannot be discussed here, but in the next section it is briefly indicated what general characteristics make them useful tools for the semantic analysis of opacity phenomena in natural language.

In philosophical logic formal systems have also been designed for verbs of permission or obligation, called 'deontic' verbs (from the Greek *deon*-'duty') like *to permit*, or *to allow*, or the auxiliary verbs *may* and *must*. One important feature of such deontic verbs is that the rule of Addition (if p then $p \lor q$) which is valid in the logic of statements cannot be a rule of deontic logic, since the following argument is clearly intuitively invalid.

(15–39)   John may/is allowed to take a pear
──
   ∴. John may/is allowed to take an apple or a pear

In such deontic contexts disjunction apparently strengthens the information, rather than weakens it as it ordinarily does in transparent contexts and extensional inferences. Obviously, existential generalization is not valid either in deontic statements, since there is not necessarily a particular pear of which it is said that John may take it.

Related to the class of deontic verbs are the main psychological attitude verbs *to desire*, *to seek*, *to want* and *to search*. We have already seen some examples of opaque contexts with such verbs. Finally there are the intentional verbs which describe a mental state of the subject like *to try*, *to attempt*, *to plan*, including perhaps *to promise*. Note that intentions are not to be confused with intensions; the former are mental states a subject can be in, whereas the latter are properties of linguistic or logical expressions to which we return below. Often the epistemic and perceptual verbs together with the psychological attitude and intentional verbs are called the verbs of (psychological) attitudes.

This review of opacity phenomena in natural language is not intended as a comprehensive list, but it shows that natural language is far richer in expressive power than can be captured with the basic tools of ordinary predicate logic. The next section introduces some new methods to account for scope ambiguities in opaque contexts and some other opacity phenomena.

15.3   Indices and accessibility relations

In Section 12.5 the important idea of relativizing a predicate-logical truth definition to possible states of information was introduced in Kripke models as semantics for Heyting algebras. The same idea underlies the elementary system of intensional logic which is introduced in this chapter. Instead of the absolute notion of truth (or falsity) in a model that was defined for predicate logical formulas, we define here a notion of the truth value of a formula *relative to an index*. The syntax of the system of intensional logic will be specified here briefly, but we will not discuss its methods of proof. The usefulness of indexing truth values for natural language applications is illustrated with some examples of English expressions translated into a system of intensional logic, concentrating on the semantic aspects of the intensional logic.

Relativization of truth values to an index is a generalization of the information-states of Kripke models. An index can be understood as an epistemic state representing the information available to an agent, or as a 'possible world' , i.e., an alternative to the actual world representing a way things could have been otherwise, or as a mixture of such interpretations, or we can give it any other interpretation we want to depending on the kind of opacity to be explained by it. We will understand the notion of an index in the most general way here, leaving aside any metaphysical or philosophical reflection on its nature. For simplicity we start out taking indices as unanalyzed primitives of the model theory and add a set of indices to the predicate logical models.

If we assume that a sentence expresses a statement at an index, the truth value of that statement is either true or false at that index. We assume for simplicity that the reference of an expression is always determined, although an interpretation could be defined partially, leaving the reference of an expression undetermined at some indices. The Fregean reference of a sentence is hence defined as its truth value. We call the reference of any expression here its *extension*. To account for opacity the Fregean sense of a statement should also be defined. As a first approximation of Fregean senses let us define the *intension* of an expression as a function or an operation from the set of indices to the extensions of the expression. For simplicity we do not introduce in the syntax of the intensional logic a particular symbol for the intension of an English expression, as is common in Montague Grammar (see Dowty, Wall and Peters (1981)). Below it will become clear that this notion of an intension is not sufficiently fine-grained to account fully for Fregean senses, as it identifies the intensions of expressions that should have different semantic value or senses, since they are not substitutable in all contexts preserving informative content.

Instead of the partial order on information states that characterizes Kripke semantics for Heyting algebras, in intensional logic any relation may be defined on the set of indices. Such relations are called *accessibility relations*, representing which indices can be reached from a given index in a model. The accessibility relations characterize the structure of the models, and it is a sound methodological strategy to impose structure only when such is required for purposes of natural language semantics, i.e. depending on the nature of the opacity creating expressions.

The syntax of this system of intensional logic is a simple extension of predicate logic adding two operators that take formulas to produce new formulas. To define the set of formulas of intensional logic by extension of the recursive set of rules of predicate logic the following clause suffices:

(i) if φ is a formula then $\Box\varphi$ and $\Diamond\varphi$ are formulas.

Note that this syntactic clause generates for instance $(\forall x)\Box\varphi$, $(\exists x)\Box(\forall y)$ $\Diamond\varphi$, and the iterated $\Box\Box(\forall x)\varphi$ and $(\forall x)\Box\Diamond\varphi$.

Although the choice of semantic primitives is in principle open, we choose for simplicity to stay close to the predicate logical models and assume as primitives of the model theory a (non-empty) set of indices I, a domain of individuals or entities D, an accessibility relation $R \subseteq I \times I$, an interpretation function $[\![\ldots]\!]$ and a variable-assignment function g. An *intensional model* is then a quintuple $\mathbf{M}^I = \langle I, D, R, [\![\ldots]\!], g \rangle$. We define recursively the notion of the extension of a formula in a model, relative to the assignment g and an index i.

Let $\mathbf{M}^I$ be an intensional model, $i \in I$ and g a variable assignment, then an *extension* of an expression at an index i in the intensional model is defined as:

(i) for any constant c $[\![c]\!]^{\mathbf{M},g,i} \in D$

(ii) for any variable x $[\![x]\!]^{\text{M},g,i} = g(x) \in D$

(iii) if P is an n-ary predicate-letter, then $[\![P]\!]^{\text{M},g,i} \subseteq D^n$

(iv) if $P(t_1, t_2, \ldots, t_n)$ is a formula, then
$[\![P(t_1, t_2, \ldots, t_n)]\!]^{\text{M},g,i} = 1$ iff
$\langle [\![t_1]\!]^{\text{M},g,i} [\![t_2]\!]^{\text{M},g,i}, \ldots, [\![t_n]\!]^{\text{M},g,i} \rangle \in [\![P]\!]^{\text{M},g,i}$; 0 otherwise

(v) if φ and ψ are formulas, then
$[\![\sim \varphi]\!]^{\text{M},g,i} = 1$ iff $[\![\varphi]\!]^{\text{M},g,i} = 0$; 0 otherwise
$[\![\varphi \,\&\, \psi]\!]^{\text{M},g,i} = 1$ iff $[\![\varphi]\!]^{\text{M},g,i} = 1$ and $[\![\psi]\!]^{\text{M},g,i} = 1$; 0 otherwise
$[\![\varphi \vee \psi]\!]^{\text{M},g,i} = 1$ iff $[\![\varphi]\!]^{\text{M},g,i} = 1$ or $[\![\psi]\!]^{\text{M},g,i} = 1$; 0 otherwise
$[\![\varphi \rightarrow \psi]\!]^{\text{M},g,i} = 1$ iff $[\![\varphi]\!]^{\text{M},g,i} = 0$ or $[\![\psi]\!]^{\text{M},g,i} = 1$; 0 otherwise
$[\![\varphi \leftrightarrow \psi]\!]^{\text{M},g,i} = 1$ iff $[\![\varphi]\!]^{\text{M},g,i} = [\![\psi]\!]^{\text{M},g,i}$; 0 otherwise
$[\![(\forall x)\varphi]\!]^{\text{M},g,i} = 1$ iff for every $d \in D [\![\varphi]\!]^{\text{M},g'[x/d],i} = 1$; 0 otherwise
$[\![(\exists x)\varphi]\!]^{\text{M},g,i} = 1$ iff for some $d \in D [\![\varphi]\!]^{\text{M},g'[x/d],i} = 1$; 0 otherwise
$[\![\Box\varphi]\!]^{\text{M},g,i} = 1$ iff for every i' such that iRi' $[\![\varphi]\!]^{\text{M},g,i'} = 1$; 0 otherwise
$[\![\Diamond\varphi]\!]^{\text{M},g,i} = 1$ iff for some i' such that iRi' $[\![\varphi]\!]^{\text{M},g,i'} = 1$; 0 otherwise

Formulas with the new intensional operators $\Box$ and $\Diamond$ are interpreted as true by requiring truth of the remaining formula at all accessible indices or its truth at some accessible index respectively. This resembles the universal quantifier, and the existential quantifier now ranging over indices instead of ranging over individuals. These intensional operators consider the extension of an expression in their scope on indices accessible from the index of evaluation i. All the extensional predicate logical formulas are interpreted on i itself, but the extension of intensional formulas depends on extensions of subformulas at other indices.

As an illustration of this interpretation in an intensional model let us evaluate the quantified formula $\Diamond(\exists x)(Px \,\&\, \Box\, Qx)$ in

$$\text{M}^* = \langle \{i_0, i_1, i_2\}, \{d_0, d_1, d_2, d_3\},$$

$$R = \{\langle i_0, i_0 \rangle, \langle i_1, i_1 \rangle, \langle i_2, i_2 \rangle, \langle i_2, i_1 \rangle, \langle i_1, i_2 \rangle\}, [\![\ldots]\!], g \rangle$$

given that

$$
\begin{aligned}
[\![P]\!]^{\text{M}^*,g,i_0} &= \emptyset, & [\![Q]\!]^{\text{M}^*,g,i_0} &= \emptyset \\
[\![P]\!]^{\text{M}^*,g,i_1} &= \{d_2, d_3\}, & [\![Q]\!]^{\text{M}^*,g,i_1} &= \{d_0, d_3\} \\
[\![P]\!]^{\text{M}^*,g,i_2} &= \{d_0, d_3\}, & [\![Q]\!]^{\text{M}^*,g,i_2} &= \{d_1, d_2, d_3\}
\end{aligned}
$$

To evaluate a formula we pick an index of evaluation, say i_1, and see whether we can verify the formula.

$[\![\diamond(\exists x)(Px \ \& \ \Box\, Qx)]\!]^{M^*,g,i_1}$ is true iff at some i' iRi' and $(\exists x)(Px \ \& \ \Box\, Qx)$ is true; in M^I the indices i_1 and i_2 are accessible from i_1; let's pick i_1 and see whether we can verify the remaining formula.

$[\![(\exists x)(Px \ \& \ \Box\, Qx)]\!]^{M^*,g,i_1}$ is true iff for some g' which is like g except for assigning d to x, $[\![(Px \ \& \ \Box\, Qx)]\!]^{M^*,g'[x/d],i_1} = 1$.

There are in fact two objects in the extension of P at i_1, so there are two distinct assignments g' and g'' which verify the first conjunct Px. But do they also verify the second conjunct? If $g'(x) = d_2$ and $g''(x) = d_3$, then to verify $\Box\, Qx$, Qd_2 should be true at each index accessible from i_1, or Qd_3 should be true at each index accessible from i_1.

Since the indices i_1 and i_2 are accessible from i_1, but Qd_2 is not true at i_1, we rule out g' as route to verification, and check g''. Qd_3 is true at each accessible index since $d_3 \in [\![Q]\!]^{M^*,g,i_1}$ and $d_3 \in [\![Q]\!]^{M^*,g,i_2}$. So for the assignment $g''(x) = d_3$ we can verify the entire $[\![(Px \ \& \ \Box\, Qx)]\!]^{M^*,g''[x/d_3],i_1}$.

Given this recursive definition of the extension of an expression at an index in an intensional model, two expressions are called *coextensive at index i* iff they have identical extensions at i. Coreference of two NPs means that they are coextensive, so the notion depends on the index of evaluation. For instance, *the winner of the race* and *Robin* may be coreferential at some index, but not at others. We call two expressions *extensionally equivalent* in an intensional model when they have identical extensions at every index of that model. Two expressions are *logically equivalent* when they are extensionally equivalent in every possible intensional model. The strongest notion of equivalence says that two expressions are *intensionally equivalent,* when their intensions are identical, i.e., when their associated functions from or operations on the set of indices to the extensions at an index are identical. This notion of an intension is best understood dynamically as the procedure of computing the extension of an expression at an index. For instance, the process of computing the reference of *the winner of the race* must involve evaluating the predicates *winner* and *race*, but these steps do not play any role in the process of computing the reference of *Robin*. Hence when the two NPs *the winner of the race* and *Robin* are coreferential or even extensionally equivalent they are not intensionally equivalent. Since the intensional logic does not contain an expression for the intension of an expression this procedural character of intensions is not further analyzed in this model theory. Yet it is clear from the recursive definition of the extension of an expression in an intensional model by which procedure its extension is computed.

Now if we use these different notions of equivalence of expressions the
following criteria of substitutability can be defined.

1. Expressions which are coextensive at i are substitutable in a context
   with preservation of its extension only at i.

2. Expressions which are extensionally equivalent are substitutable in a
   context with preservation of its extension at any index in that model.

3. Expressions which are logically equivalent are substitutable in a context with preservation of its extension at any index in any model.

4. Expressions which are intensionally equivalent are substitutable in a
   context with preservation of its intension.

The translation of English to the intensional logic will not be carried
out here, but we assume that the opacity creating expressions discussed
in the previous section will always involve other indices besides the index
of evaluation in the determination of the extension of an expression. For
instance, to evaluate *John believes that Robin is the winner of the race* belief
is analyzed with an accessibility relation on indices, representing the different
epistemic alternatives John entertains and requiring that at least one of these
verifies the embedded statement.

Belief contexts require verification of the embedded expression at *some*
index which is related to the index of evaluation by the subject's epistemic
accessibility relation (cf. ◊). Knowledge contexts would require verification
of the embedded expression at *all* epistemically accessible indices (cf. □).
Similarly exploiting the universal and existential quantification over indices
in the analysis of opacity, modal necessities require verification at all accessible indices (cf. □), modal possibilities only at some (cf. ◊).

Some English examples which illustrate the four notions of substitutability are the following inferences.

(1) If we evaluate sentential complements of belief contexts at an index
related by an epistemic accessibility relation to the index of evaluation, i.e.,
interpret all predicate letters and NPs at that belief index, the following
inference is valid, since the second premise states that at that index the two
NPs are co-referential.

(15–40)   **John believes that Robin has red hair**
            John believes that Robin is the winner of the race
            ∴ **John believes that the winner of the race has red hair**

Note that this inferential pattern is only valid with definite, referential NPs in the premise stating the co-reference at the belief-index. The difference between valid (15-41) and invalid (15-42) is based on just the definiteness of the anaphoric reference in (15-41) to the referent of the indefinite NPs introduced in the first premise.

(15–41)   John believes that a man has red hair
           John believes that he is the winner of the race
           ∴. John believes that the winner of the race has red hair

(15–42)   John believes that a man has red hair
           John believes that a man is the winner of the race
           ∴. John believes that the winner of the race has red hair

(2) Proper names, if translated to logical constants as in predicate logic, have a constant reference according to the first clause in the definition of extensions in an intensional model. Kripke introduced the notion of a *rigid designator* for this semantic characteristic of proper names. Names do not contribute to the information expressed in a statement, but serve merely as 'pegs' for properties attributed to the referents. I.e., the extension of a proper name is the same entity of the domain at any index, so evaluating a proper name at any two indices gives the same extension. This means that a proper name in an opaque context can be extraposed outside the opacity creating expression to be evaluated at the index of evaluation without changing the truth value of the entire sentence.

(15–43)   John believes that Robin won the race
           ∴. Of Robin John believes that he won the race

Note that for (15-43) to be valid John himself does not necessarily report his beliefs with the proper name, but anyone describing John's beliefs with the first premise invites the inference. Because of this rigid designation of proper names, existential generalization is also valid when based on proper names. But for other NPs, including definite descriptions, no such inferences are valid, since their interpretation may vary at the accessible indices from the index of evaluation, as the invalidity of (15-44) and (15-45) show.

(15–44)   John believes that a man won the race
           ∴. Of a man John believes that he won the race

(15–45)   John believes that a man won the race
    ∴ There is a man of whom John believes that he won
         the race

(3) Since predicate logic is contained in the system of intensional logic as
defined above, the tautologies of predicate logic are also valid in intensional
logic, i.e., they are all logically equivalent, always true at any index in any
model. This means that an inference is valid in intensional logic when a
tautology is conjoined in an opaque context to a true premise.

(15–46)   John believes that Robin won the race
    ∴ John believes that Robin won the race and that he
         does or does not have red hair

    This is an unsatisfactory aspect of the simple system of intensional logic
we introduced here, since John may simply fail to have any beliefs about
Robin's hair color if he believes that Robin won the race. On the other
hand no rational person can fail to believe a tautology when he realizes
its necessary truth. If we maintain the ordinary logical notion of proof,
inferences preserve truth, but do not necessarily preserve intension. We
return to this problem below to suggest a solution.

(4) Finally there are intensionally equivalent equivalent expressions, which
are equivalent because their extension at any index is calculated in the same
way. To make this strong notion of equivalence precise a formal account
of the computational procedures used in determining extensions should be
given which specifies criteria of sameness for such procedures. We will not
do so here, but a simple example illustrates the main idea.

    We learned in Part B that conjunction can be viewed as a commuta-
tive operation on statements. Hence when determining the extension of a
conjunction the order in which the extension of each conjunct is computed
does not matter. In verifying $p \& q$ we may start with either p or q, knowing that the result will not be affected by our choice. Looking at predicate
logical operations in this intensional way the logical equivalence of $p \& q$ and
$q \& p$ should be attributed to their intensional equivalence. Some laws of
extensional logic may be viewed as determining sameness conditions on operations, especially those that merely permute the order of connectives or

their arguments (Associative, Distributive and Commutative Laws). On the other hand laws like the Complement Laws, De Morgan's Laws or the Conditional Laws are valid because of the particular truth-functional meaning we assigned to the connectives in this system of classical predicate logic, but there are extensional systems in which they would not be valid. If we would incorporate a formal definition of intensions along these procedural lines and define which logical laws were valid due to the intensional equivalence of their arguments, the following statements could be considered logically equivalent on the basis of intensional equivalence of conjunction. Premise and conclusion are interchangable in any context because they are 'informationally equivalent' and never give rise to informative identity statements.

(15–47)   John believes that Robin won the race and that
                   Robin has red hair
             ∴. John believes that Robin has red hair and that
                 Robin won the race

To account for the full variety of opacity phenomena discussed in the previous section more sophisticated intensional models would be required, but the examples illustrate how some aspects of these opaque contexts can be analyzed with these simple intensional models. It should be clear that the predicate logical laws of existential generalization and substitution of extensionally equivalent expressions do not hold universally in this interpretation in intensional models.

To conclude this section we discuss briefly some of the limitations of this formalization of intensional interpretations for natural language.

As we remarked earlier in this system of intensional logic the predicate-logical tautologies are all logically equivalent, although not necessarily also intensionally equivalent, and similarly for contradictions. This is partly due to the fact that we assumed that all functions are total, i.e. defined for all arguments. If that assumption were dropped it would become possible to distinguish functions that are logically equivalent when defined, but which are not defined for the same arguments. For instance, the truth value of the predicate-logical tautology *Robin did or did not win the race* would only be defined if the name *Robin* had a reference at the same index, i.e. if the domain contained someone called Robin. The interpretation of names could still be constant but partially defined, which is compatible with their being rigid designators. The interpretation of another tautology *Jane did or did not win the race* could similarly be partially defined, i.e. true at every index where *Jane* is interpreted. But the two tautologies would not necessarily be logically equivalent, for a model could be given which interpreted the two names at distinct sets of indices. Partial functions in semantic interpretations yield already an importantly finer-grained notion of logical equivalence.

The second problem with these simple intensional models concerns the interpretation of epistemic verbs which give rise to opaque contexts. Any logical consequence of what is believed by someone must be believed by him as well. For instance, if John believes that Robin won the race, then he must also believe that Robin won the race and that two plus two is four, assuming that names of numbers always refer. This issue is often called the problem of *logical omniscience*. What we know or believe is not ordinarily closed under its logical consequences, for we often discover new implications of information we have had for a long time. Only if totally defined functions with constant extensions were absolutely forbidden in an interpretation in intensional models could this problem be adequately, though not insightfully be solved. A more promising way would attempt to analyze the subject matter of beliefs and require that entailed beliefs must have the same subject matter. Another improvement would be to acknowledge the fact that on the one hand people have well understood beliefs which may be represented by a set of statements closed under some sufficiently fine-grained notion of logical consequence, but on the other hand they have a chunk of unanalyzed and only partially understood beliefs to be represented in a coarser way and not closed under any logical operation. The problem has not yet been solved in any definitive way for all epistemically opaque constructions which would still allow for people who have inconsistent beliefs to be rational in not just believing anything.

The third aspect in which these simple intensional models need improvement is the interpretation of proper names. Even when we let the functions interpreting proper names be partial, this still would not account for two natural facts: first, different people may have the same name and only a name in a sufficiently specific context can be said to refer uniquely, and second, people may use the same name intending to refer to the same individual when in fact they refer to distinct individuals, for instance, because they were wrongly introduced or forgot their true names. A proper solution would require major modifications in the intensional models: a formal representation of contexts and a general method to incorporate parameters of language use, in particular for cases in which speakers may hook up the same name to a different person. If functions interpreting expressions could be speaker-sensitive, we could explain how three communicative situations differ essentially although what two speakers say, respectively 'Robin has red hair' and 'Robin does not have red hair,' is exactly the same. In the first situation they would contradict each other, in the second they would merely refer to two different individuals called Robin, and in a third situation one of them or both could wrongly connect the name to the same individual or to different individuals.

The final point in which these intensional models are too simple is in their failure to account for genuine synonymous predicates. Although there are not too many examples in natural language of truly synonymous descriptive predicates, an interpretation would have to discriminate them, although they are logically equivalent and, if syntactically simple, even intensionally equivalent. For instance, John may believe that woodchucks are marmots, whereas he may not believe that groundhogs are marmots, although *woodchuck* and *groundhog* are synonyms. The only option open to repair this shortcoming is to assume a set of primitive properties, as extensions of predicates, instead of giving predicates an extensional set-theoretic interpretation as the set individuals in the domain with the property.

These suggestions to improve upon the intensional models outlined in this section are all currently subject of new research. Various formal accounts of interpretations are being developed motivated by these and other problems that were encountered with the simple intensional models. The interested reader is referred to the readings suggested for this chapter.

15.4 Tense and time

Another important linguistic application of relativizing extensions of expressions to indices is the interpretation of verbs, tenses and temporal adverbs. In this section some elementary aspects of the semantics of temporal reference are outlined briefly and we discuss what modifications the interpretation in intensional models requires in order to accommodate some aspects of temporal reference.

The simple past tense inflection on a verb, for instance, creates an opaque context, requiring the sentence to be interpreted in its present tense form at an index in the past of the index of evaluation. E.g., *Robin had red hair* is interpreted as true at an index i when there is an i' temporally located before i at which *Robin has red hair* is true. This means that for the interpretation

of tenses the set of indices is ordered by an asymmetric and transitive accessibility relation representing the passage of time. The tenses expressed by
inflection and the temporal auxiliary verbs require interpretation along this
temporal axis. Some classes of temporal adverbs are interpreted along this
line as quantifying in the meta-language over temporally ordered indices.
Always is a universal quantifier, *sometimes* an existential one and adverbs
of frequency like *often, every week* or *twice a week* require more complicated
forms of quantification over indices.

The set of temporal indices may be structured by additional assumptions motivated by linguistic considerations. Besides auxiliary verbs and the
inflectional morphology on VPs main verbs themselves describe changes in
the world called *events*. A sentence like *Robin won the race* describes an
event which took place over a period of time in the past of the index of
evaluation. When we consider the indices to represent periods of time of arbitrary length, rather than smallest 'points' or atomic moments, we may also
want to assume a symmetric temporal overlap relation on the indices and
construct smallest 'periods' as maximal sets of pairwise overlapping periods
(see van Benthem (1983), Kamp (1979) and (1980)).

The temporal adverb now has a special semantic function, since in any
context, transparent or heavily opaque, it refers to one and the same index,
the time of utterance, in an intensional model. Each intensional model
has to contain one designated index representing the current time, i.e. the
'now'-index, from which past and future coordinates are fixed. Consider for
instance

(15–48) You will once be grateful for what I tell you now

The future auxiliary verb takes the interpretation from the index of evaluation, the designated 'now'-index i_0, to a future index i_1, at which you *are*
grateful for what I *told* you at the original 'now' index i_0, not for what I tell
you at the new 'now'-index i_1 . So when tenses require the interpretation
to consider extensions at other indices, in any context the adverb *now* takes
the interpretation back to the designated index. A contextual parameter
'time of utterance' can be represented in an intensional model as a specially
selected index, and no matter at which index *now* is evaluated, its extension will always be that designated index. The difference between the two
sentences

(15–49) A child was born who would be king

(15–50) A child was born who will be king

can be analyzed by requiring for the interpretation of (15-50) that the 'now'-index be located between the past index at which *a child is born* is true and the future index at which *the child is king* is true, whereas the interpretation of (15-49) does not put any requirements on its location.

The 'now'-index is identified in each model with the time at which the evaluated statement is uttered. But each intensional model represents then in fact a static picture of the world at that time, and the past and future coordinates are fixed with respect to that index. If we want to do justice to the flow of time in an intensional model a series of indices would have to be designated as consecutive 'now'-indices. And to interpret a discourse consisting of temporally ordered utterances a chain of such 'now'-indices would be required within each model. This cannot be incorporated straightforwardly into a simple intensional model if what was once true could later become false in one and the same model, and hence any analysis of valid inference would be lost. The problem can be solved if we introduce in the formal language variables for the indices which can then be referred to and quantified over at the level of the object language. But a more satisfactory solution would take the need to represent contextual parameters seriously and define a context-sensitive notion of meaning and interpretation which does justice to the dynamics of context change and processing information. This would require syntactic and semantic adaptations which cannot be specified further here, but in current research several frameworks are developed in which events and periods as their temporal substratum constitute a domain of objects in the interpretation (see Dowty (1979), Kamp and Rohrer (1983), Lo Cascio and Vet (1986), and *Linguistics and Philosophy* 9.1)

The verbs which describe changing events create opaque contexts for some of their arguments. A by now classical form of opacity, known as Montague's 'temperature puzzle' is the following invalid inference:

(15–51)   **The temperature is ninety**
           The temperature rises
           ―――――――――――――――――――――
      ∴. **Ninety rises**

In this usage the verb *to rise* cannot have ordinary individuals in its extension, but must be interpreted as a property of intensional objects like functions or operations that determine extensions at an index. Verbs in the same semantic class include *to change, to decrease, to increase, to grow, to diminish.* In contrast to names of numbers, proper names of individuals apparently can take such change-denoting predicates notwithstanding their rigid designation. Rather than cop out of the puzzles by treating these verbs as lexically ambiguous, it would further our understanding of intensionality and opaque contexts considerably if we analyzed how changes in an individual must be distinguished from changes in measurable properties such as volume, size, weight, warmth or relative location.

Another class of verbs which create interesting opaque contexts is formed by verbs describing actions of creation or destruction, e.g. *to build, to write, to construct, to cook,* and *to destroy, to demolish, to devastate, to burn.* The object NPs of these verbs are opaque since the extension of these NPs gradually comes into existence or ceases to exist during the period at which the action takes place, and existential generalization cannot be valid in an unrestricted form. The progressive tense is typically used to describe such actions as they are going on. The interpretation of these verbs must hence add new objects to the domain of the interpretation, and withdraw objects or parts of them from it. The simple intensional models were based on one static domain of individuals which were taken to 'exist' at any index in the model. An analysis of this form of opacity must allow the domain of objects over which quantifiers range to depend on the index. Verbs of creation shift the index and add new objects to the domain, and verbs of destruction shift the index and drop objects from the domain. But if more structure is imposed on the domains to represent part-whole relations between objects and a related relation between events, the invalidity of the following inference can be analyzed

(15–52)   **John was writing a poem**
            ∴ John wrote a poem

and contrasted to the validity of the inference

(15–53)   **John was writing poetry**
            ∴ **John wrote poetry.**

These inferential patterns known as the *'Imperfective Paradox'* receive much attention in recent research on tense and aspect.

In early work on temporal reference by the logician H. Reichenbach (Reichenbach (1947)) used besides the time of utterance, and the index at which the event took place, a third temporal index, the *reference time* to represent the temporal 'point of view' of the speaker. The difference between the simple past tense sentence *Robin won the race* and the present perfect tense sentence *Robin has won the race* is accordingly analyzed by requiring the interpretation of the simple past tense to shift the reference time as well as the event time to a past index relative to the time of utterance, whereas the present perfect tense only shifts the event time, leaving the reference time at the time of utterance. Note, however, that not all simple past tense sentences shift the reference time but only those which describe 'bounded' or completed events. This leads into the semantic analysis of aspect and verb classes which is an important focus of ongoing research. In frameworks of dynamic interpretation the notion of reference time has come to be crucial in accounting for temporal dependencies and temporal anaphora (see Kamp and Rohrer (1983) and Partee (1984)).

15.5   Indexicality

In the previous section it was pointed out that in any linguistic context the temporal adverb *now* refers to a fixed contextual parameter, the time of utterance. The class of expressions in natural language which serve such a semantic function, the *indexical expressions*, is much larger and includes the personal pronouns *I*, *you*, and *we*, besides the locative expressions *here* and *there*. The *demonstrative* or *deictic* expressions *this*, *that*, *these*, *those*, and the deictic pronoun *he* are also often included in this semantic class.

The semantic interpretation of indexicals is essentially dependent on the extra-linguistic situation of use. An indexical refers in any linguistic context, i.e., on any index, directly to a value of a contextual parameter, e.g. *I* refers to the speaker who utters the sentence, *here* to the location of utterance and *that* to what is being pointed at by the speaker. But *I* cannot be interpreted synonymously with *the speaker* since the reference of a definite description is always dependent on the index. So on the one hand the reference of an indexical does not depend on its linguistic sentential context, on the other hand it shifts when the context of use changes. The value of a contextual parameter, i.e., who is the speaker at an index, where something is said and

what is being pointed at changes constantly. The context of use determines
the *content* of an indexical expression. For instance, when I say

(15–54) I am speaking

what I said differs from when you utter (15-54). The component of the
Fregean sense of an expression which determines how the content is determined by the context of use is called the *character* of the expression. This
is what competent speakers of a language have to know if they are to understand (15-54) in any context of use. The content of an expression may
be identified with what we called intension in the previous section, i.e., the
context-independent procedure which determines its extension at an index.
Now we may explain that any utterance of (15-54) is true, but that by utter-
ing (15-54) I am not expressing a logically necessary truth, but a contingent
statement, whose truth value varies from index to index. Non-indexicals
have a constant character and express the same content in every context.

To incorporate this account of the semantics of indexicals and their direct
reference to elements of the context of use, the interpretation by indexing the
extension of an expression in an intensional model is extended by contexts,
i.e. a set of contextual parameters representing elements of a context of use
and containing at least parameters for the speaker, the hearer, the utterance
time and the utterance location: context $c = \langle s_c, h_c, t_c, l_c \rangle$. Of course, the
set of contextual parameters can be extended upon need. This is called the
fleshing out strategy: supply contextual parameters when indexical linguistic
expressions refer to them.

In such a *double-indexing interpretation* the indexical *I*, for instance, is
interpreted by a function from contexts to the parameter s_c, the speaker at
that context, and the extension of s_c is determined at an index by identifying
it with the extension of the predicate *speaking* at that index. This explains
why

(15–55) The speaker is the one who is speaking

is an uninformative identity statement, whereas

(15–56) I am the one who is speaking

may express new information to others beside oneself.

Proper names interpreted as Kripkean rigid designators are expressions with constant contents. They are also independent of contextual parameters so their character is also constant. The identity statement

(15–57) I am Robin

is informative in two different ways: first, when it gives a hearer a new way of rigidly referring to the speaker when he is not present and second, when the hearer already has information about someone called Robin, but is not acquainted with him from his own experience. In the first case, the information stabilizes the character, in the second case it hooks up a stable content to the external context of use.

To provide a satisfactory mathematical modelling of these issues lies at the heart of contemporary research in the semantics of natural language. We have attempted to show that the tools offered in the first three parts of this book provide a choice of mathematical methods to tackle such problems in a linguistic theory of meaning and interpretation.

Exercises

1. If the intensional model M^* defined in Section 15.3 had an irreflexive accessibility relation, is the formula $[\![(\exists x)(Px \,\&\, \Box Qx)]\!]M^{*,g,i_1}$ still verifiable? If so, define the assignment.

2. Compute in M^* defined in Section 15.3 the truth value of
$$[\![(\exists x)(Px \,\&\, Qx) \to \Diamond(\forall x) \sim Px)]\!]M^{*,g,i_0}$$

3. If the following formulas are assumed to be valid in a system of intensional logic they characterize a property of the accessibility relation. Find out which property by drawing relational diagrams of small intensional models, making the formula true at each index and verifying it.

   (i) $\Box\varphi \to \varphi$

   (ii) $\Box\varphi \to \Box\Box\varphi$

   (iii) $\Diamond\Box\varphi \to \varphi$

Part E

LANGUAGES, GRAMMARS, AND AUTOMATA

Chapter 16

Basic Concepts

16.1 Languages, grammars and automata

At one level of description, a natural language is simply a set of strings—finite sequences of words, morpheme, phonemes, or whatever. Not every possible sequence is in the language: we distinguish the *grammatical* strings from those that are *ungrammatical*. A *grammar*, then, is some explicit device for making this distinction; it is, in other words, a means for selecting a subset of strings, those that are grammatical, from the set of all possible strings formed from an initially given alphabet or vocabulary.

In this chapter we will consider two classes of formal devices which can function as grammars in this very general sense: (1) automata, which are abstract computing machines, and (2) string rewriting systems, which generally bear the name "grammar" or "formal grammar". The latter will be familiar to linguists inasmuch as grammars in this sense have formed the basis of much of the work in generative transformational theory.

We begin by considering certain properties of strings and sets of strings. Given a finite set A, a *string on* (or *over*) A is a finite sequence of occurrences of elements from A. For example, if $A = \{a, b, c\}$, then *acbaab* is a string on A. Strings are by definition finite in length. (Infinite sequences of symbols are also perfectly reasonable objects of study, but they are not suitable as models for natural language strings.) The set from which strings are formed is often called the *vocabulary* or *alphabet*, and this too is always assumed to be finite. The length of a string is, or course, the number of occurrences of symbols in it (i.e., the number of tokens, not the number of types). The string *acbaab* thus is of length 6.

Because we are dealing with tokens of an alphabet, there is an important difference between the linearly ordered sequences we call strings and a linearly ordered set. If the set $A = \{a, b, c\}$ were linearly ordered, say, as $b \to a \to c$, each element of A would occupy a unique place in the ordering. In a string, e.g., *acbaab*, tokens of a, occur in the first, fourth, and fifth positions.

To be formal, one could define a string of length n over the alphabet A to be a function mapping the first n positive integers into A. For example, *acbaab* would be the function $\{\langle 1, a \rangle, \langle 2, c \rangle, \langle 3, b \rangle, \langle 4, a \rangle, \langle 5, a \rangle, \langle 6, b \rangle\}$. There is little to be gained in this case by the reduction to the primitives of set theory, however, so we will continue to think of strings simply as finite sequences of symbols. A string may be of length 1, and so we distinguish the string b of length 1 from the symbol b itself. We also recognize the (unique) string of length 0, the *empty string*, which we will denote e (some authors use Λ). Two strings are identical if they have the same symbol occurrences in the same order; thus, *acb* is distinct from *abc*, and strings of different length are always distinct.

An important binary operation on strings is concatenation, which amounts simply to juxtaposition. For example, the strings *abca* and *bac* can be concatenated, in the order mentioned, to give the string *abcabac*. Sometimes concatenation is denoted with the symbol "$\frown$" thus, $abca \frown bac$. Concatenation is associative since for any strings $\alpha, \beta, \gamma, (\alpha \frown \beta) \frown \gamma = \alpha \frown (\beta \frown \gamma)$, but it is not commutative, since in general $\alpha \frown \beta \neq \beta \frown \alpha$. The empty string is the identity element for concatenation; i.e., for any string α, $\alpha \frown e = e \frown \alpha = \alpha$.

Given a finite set A, the set of all strings over A, denoted A^*, together with the operation of concatenation constitutes a monoid. Concatenation is well-defined for any pair of strings in A^* and the result is a string in A^*; the operation is associative; and there is an identity element. $\langle A^*, \frown \rangle$ fails to be a group since no element other than e has an inverse: no string concatenated with a non-empty string x will yield the empty string. Since concatenation is not commutative, $\langle A^*, \frown \rangle$ is not an Abelian monoid.

A frequently encountered unary operation on strings is reversal. The reversal of a string x, denoted x^R, is simply the string formed by writing the symbols of x in the reverse order. Thus $(acbab)^R = babca$. The reversal of e is just e itself. To be formal, we could define reversal by induction on the length of a string:

Definition 16.1 *Given an alphabet A:*

(1) *If x is a string of length 0, then $x^R = x$ (i.e., $e^R = e$)*

(2) *If x is a string of length $k + 1$, then it is of the form wa, where $a \in A$ and $w \in A^*$; then $x^R = (wa)^R = aw^R$.*

∎

Concatenation and reversal are connected in the following way: For all strings x and y, $(x^\frown y)^R = y^R {}^\frown x^R$. For example,

$$(16\text{--}1) \quad (bca^\frown ca)^R = (ca)^R {}^\frown (bca)^R = ac^\frown acb = acacb$$

Given a string x, a *substring of x* is any string formed from continguous occurrences of symbols in x taken in the same order in which they occur in x. For example, *bac* is a substring of *abacca*, but neither *bcc* nor *cb* is a substring. Formally, y is a substring of x iff there exist strings z and w such that $x = z^\frown y^\frown w$. In general, z or w (or both) may be empty, so every string is trivially a substring of itself. (Non-identical substrings can be called *proper* substrings.) The empty string is a substring of every string; i.e., given x we can choose z in the definition as e and w as x so that $x = e^\frown e^\frown x$.

An initial substring is called a *prefix*, and a final substring, a *suffix*. Thus, *ab* is a (proper) prefix of *abacca*, and *cca* is a (proper) suffix of this string.

We may now define a *language* (over a vocabulary A) as any subset of A^*. Since A^* is a denumerably infinite set, it has cardinality $\aleph_0$; its power set, i.e., the set of all languages over A, has cardinality $2^{\aleph_0}$ and is thus non-denumerably infinite. Since the devices for characterizing languages which we will consider, *viz.*, formal grammars and automata, form denumerably infinite classes, it follows that there are infinitely many languages–in fact, non-denumerably infinitely many–which have no grammar. What this means in intuitive terms is that there are languages which are such motley collections of strings that they cannot be completely characterized by any finite device. The languages which *are* so characterizable exhibit a certain amount of order or pattern in their strings which allows these strings to be distinguished from others in A^* by a grammar or automaton with finite resources. The study of formal languages is essentially the investigation of a scale of complexity in this patterning in strings. For example, we might define a language over the alphabet $\{a, b\}$ in the following way:

(16-2) $L = \{x \mid x$ contains equal numbers of a's and b's (in any order)$\}$

We might then compare this language with the following:

(16-3) $L_1 = \{x \in \{a, b\}^* \mid x = a^n b^n (n \geq 0)\}$, i.e., strings consisting of some number of a's followed by the same number of b's
$L_2 = \{x \in \{a, b\}^* \mid x$ contains a number of a's which is the square of the number of b's$\}$

Is L_1 or L_2 in some intuitive sense more complex than L? Most would probably agree that L_2 is a more complex language than L in that greater effort would be required to determine that the members of a's and b's stood the "square" relation than to determine merely that they were equal. In other words, a device which could discriminate strings from non-strings of L_2 would have to be more powerful or more "intelligent" than a device for making the comparable discrimination for L.

What of L_1 and L? Here our intuitions are much less clear. Some might think that it would require a less powerful device to recognize strings in L reliably than to recognize strings in L_1; others might think it is the other way around or see no difference. As it happens, the particular scale of complexity we will investigate (the so-called Chomsky Hierarchy) does regard L_2 as more complex than L but puts L_1 and L in the same complexity class. At least this is so for the overall complexity measure. Finer divisions could be established which might distinguish L_1 from L.

One linguistic application of these investigations is to try to locate natural languages on this complexity scale. This is part of the overall task of linguistics to characterize as precisely as possible the class of (potential and actual) natural languages and to distinguish this class from the class of all language-like systems which could not be natural languages. One must keep clearly in mind the limitations of this enterprise, however, the principal one being that languages are regarded here simply as string sets. It is clear that sentences of any natural language have a great deal more structure than simply the concatenation of one element with another. Thus, to establish a complexity scale for string sets and to place natural languages on this scale may, because of the neglect of other important structural properties, be to classify natural language along an ultimately irrelevant dimension. Extend-

ing results from the study of formal languages into linguistic theory must
therefore be done with great caution.

16.2   Grammars

A formal grammar (or simply, grammar) is essentially a deductive system of
axioms and rules of inference (see Chapter 8), which generates the sentences
of a language as its theorems. By the usual definitions, a grammar contains
just one axiom, the string consisting of the *initial symbol* (usually S), and a
finite number of rules of the form $\psi \to \omega$, where ψ and ω are strings, and the
interpretation of a rule is the following: whenever ψ occurs as a substring
of any given string, that occurrence may be replaced by ω to yield a new
string. Thus if a grammar contained the rule $AB \to CDA$, we could derive
from the string $EBABCC$ the string $EBCDACC$.

Grammars use two alphabets: a *terminal alphabet* and a *non-terminal
alphabet*, which are assumed to be disjoint. The strings we are interested
in deriving, i.e., the sentences of the language, are strings over the terminal
alphabet, but intermediate strings in derivations (proofs) by the grammar
may contain symbols from both alphabets. We also require in the rules of
the grammar that the string on the left side not consist entirely of terminal
symbols. Here is an example of a grammar meeting these requirements:

(16–4) V_T (the terminal alphabet) $= \{a, b\}$
           V_N (the non-terminal alphabet) $= \{S, A, B\}$
           S (the initial symbol—a member of V_N)

$$
R \text{ (the set of rules)} = \left\{
\begin{array}{l}
S \ \to ABS \\
S \ \to e \\
AB \to BA \\
BA \to AB \\
A \ \to a \\
B \ \to b
\end{array}
\right\}
$$

A common notational convention is to use lower case letters for the terminal
alphabet and upper case letters for the non-terminal alphabet.

A derivation of the string *abba* by this grammar could proceed as follows:

(16–5) $S \Rightarrow ABS \Rightarrow ABABS \Rightarrow ABAB \Rightarrow ABBA \Rightarrow ABbA \Rightarrow$
           $aBbA \Rightarrow abbA \Rightarrow abba$

Here we have used the symbol "$\Rightarrow$" to mean "yields in one rule application." Note that *abba* is not subject to further rewriting inasmuch as it consists entirely of terminal symbols and no rule licenses rewriting strings of terminals. The sequence (16-5) is said to be a *derivation (of abba from S)*, and the string *abba* is said to be *generated by* the grammar. The *language generated by* the grammar is the set of all strings generated. Here are the formal definitions:

DEFINITION 16.2 *Let* $\Sigma = V_T \cup V_N$. *A (formal grammar G is a quadruple* $\langle V_T, V_N, S, R \rangle$, *where* V_T *and* V_N *are finite disjoint sets, S is a distinguished member of* V_N, *and R is a finite set of ordered pairs in* $\Sigma^* V_N \Sigma^* \times \Sigma^*$.   ∎

We have written $\psi \to \omega$ above for clarity instead of $\langle \psi, \omega \rangle$. The last condition simply says that a rule rewrites a string containing at least one non-terminal as some (possibly empty) string.

DEFINITION 16.3 *Given a grammar* $G = \langle V_T, V_N, S, R \rangle$, *a derivation is a sequence of strings* $x_1, x_2, \ldots, x_n$ $(n \geq 1)$ *such that* $x_1 = S$ *and for each* x_i $(2 \leq i \leq n)$, x_i *is obtained from* x_{i-1} *by one application of some rule in R.*   ∎

To be completely formal, we would spell out in detail what it means to apply a rule of R to a string. The reader may want to do this as an exercise.

DEFINITION 16.4 *A grammar G generates a string* $x \in V_T^*$ *if there is a derivation* $x_1, \ldots, x_n$ *by G such that* $x_n = x$.   ∎

Note that by this definition only strings of terminal symbols are said to be generated.

DEFINITION 16.5 *The language generated by a grammar G, denoted* $L(G)$, *is the set of all strings generated by G.*   ∎

The language generated by the grammar in the example of (16-4) is $\{x \in \{a, b\}^* \mid x$ contains equal numbers of a's and b's $\}$.

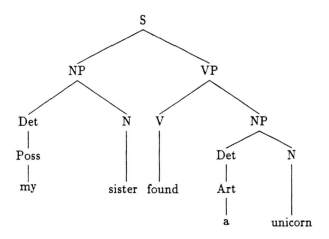

Figure 16–1: A typical constitutent
structure tree

16.3   Trees

When the rules of a grammar are restricted to rewriting only a single non-terminal symbol, it is possible to contrue grammars as generating *constituent structure trees* rather than simply strings. An example of such a tree is shown in Fig. 16-1.

Such diagrams represent three sorts of information about the syntactic structure of a sentence:

1. The hierarchical grouping of the parts of the sentence into constituents

2. The grammatical type of each constituent

3. The left-to-right order of the constituents

For example, Fig. 16-1 indicates that the largest constitutent, which is labeled by S (for Sentence), is made up of a constituent which is a N(oun) P(hrase) and one which is a V(erb) P(hrase) and that the noun phrase is composed of two constitutents: a Det(erminer) and a N(oun), etc. Further, in the sentence constituent the noun phrase precedes the verb phrase, the determiner precedes the noun in the noun phrase constituents, and so on. The tree diagram itself is said to be composed of *nodes*, or points, some of which are connected by lines called *branches*. Each node has associated with it a *label* chosen from a specified finite set of grammatical categories (S, NP, VP, etc.) and formatives (*my, sister,* etc.). As they are customarily drawn, a tree diagram has a vertical orientation on the page with the nodes labeled by the formatives at the bottom. Because a branch always connects a higher node to a lower one, it is an inherently directional connection. This directionality is ordinarily not indicated by an arrow, as in the usual diagrams of relations, but only by the vertical orientation of the tree taken together with the convention that a branch extends *from* a higher node *to* a lower node.

16.3.1   Dominance

We say that a node x *dominates* a node y if there is a connected sequence of branches in the tree extending from x to y. This is the case when all the branches in the sequence have the same orientation away from x and toward y. For example, in Fig. 16-1 the node labeled VP dominates the node labeled Art, since the sequence of branches connecting them is uniformly descending from the higher node VP to the lower node Art. The node labeled VP does not dominate the node labeled Poss, since the path by which they are joined first ascends from VP to S and then descends through NP and Det.

Given a tree diagram, we represent the fact that x dominates y by the ordered pair $\langle x, y \rangle$. The set of all such ordered pairs for a given tree is said to constitute the *dominance relation* for that tree. Dominance is clearly a transitive relation. If x is connected to y by a sequence of descending branches and y is similarly connected to z, then x dominates z because they are also connected by a sequence of descending branches, specifically, by the sequence passing through y. As a technical convenience, it is usually assumed that every node dominates itself, i.e., that the dominance relation is reflexive. Further, if x dominates y, then y can dominate x only if $x = y$; or in other words, dominance is antisymmetric. Thus, the relation of dominance is a weak partial ordering of the nodes of a tree.

If x and y are distinct, x dominates y, and there is no distinct node between x and y, then x *immediately dominates* y. In Fig. 16-1, the node labeled VP immediately dominates the node labeled V but not the node labeled *found*. A node is said to be the *daughter* of the node immediately dominating it, and distinct nodes immediately dominated by the same node are called *sisters*. In Fig. 16-1, the node labeled VP has two daughters, viz., the node labeled V and the rightmost node labeled NP. The latter two nodes are sisters. A node which is minimal in the dominance relation, i.e., which is not dominated by any other node, is called a *root*. In Fig. 16-1 there is one root, the node labeled S. Maximal elements are called *leaves*, and in Fig. 16-1 these are the nodes labeled by the formatives, *my*, *sister*, etc. Note that a tree diagram is ordinarily drawn upside down since the root is at the top and the leaves are at the bottom.

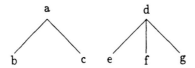

Figure 16–2: A multiply rooted "tree"

Mathematicians sometimes use the term *tree* for a configuration with more than one root, e.g., that shown in Fig. 16-2. For linguists, however, a tree is invariably singly rooted, the configuration in Fig. 16-2 being considered a "forest" of trees. We shall adhere to linguistic usage and accordingly we have the following condition:

The Single Root Condition: In every well-formed constituent structure tree there is exactly one node that dominates every node.

The root node is, therefore, a least element (and necessarily also a minimal element) in the dominance relation. We note, incidentally, that the Single Root Condition is met in the trivial case of a tree that has only one node, which is simultaneously root and leaf. The condition would not be met by an "empty" tree with no nodes at all, since it asserts that a node with the specified property exists in the tree.

16.3.2   Precedence

Two nodes are ordered in the left-to-right direction just in case they are not ordered by donimance. In Fig. 16-1 the node labeled V precedes (i.e., is to the left of) its sister node labeled NP and all the nodes dominated by this NP node; it neither precedes nor follows the nodes labeled S, VP, V, and *found*, i.e., the nodes that either dominate or are dominated by the V node. It is not logically necessary that the relations of dominance and left-to-right precedence be mutually exclusive, but this accords with the way in which tree diagrams are usually interpreted.

Given a tree, the set of all ordered pairs $\langle x, y \rangle$ such that x precedes y is said to define the *precedence relation* for that tree. To ensure that the precedence and dominance relations have no ordered pairs in common, we add the Exclusivity Condition:

The Exclusivity Condition: In any well-formed constituent structure tree, for any nodes x and y, x and y stand in the precedence relation P, i.e., either $\langle x, y \rangle \in P$ or $\langle y, x \rangle \in P$, if and only if x and y do not stand in the dominance relation D, i.e., neither $\langle x, y \rangle \in D$ nor $\langle y, x \rangle \in D$.

Like dominance, precedence is a transitive relation, but precedence is irreflexive rather than reflexive. The latter follows from the Exclusivity Condition, since for every node $x, \langle x, x \rangle \in D$ and therefore $\langle x, x \rangle \notin P$. If x precedes y, then y cannot precede x, and thus the relation is asymmetric. Precedence, therefore, defines a strict partial order on the nodes of the tree.

One other condition on the dominance and precedence relations is needed to exclude certain configurations from the class of well-formed trees. An essential characteristic of a tree that distinguishes it from a partially ordered set in general is that no node can have more than one branch entering it; i.e., every node has at most one node immediately dominating it. The structure shown in Fig. 16-3(a) has a node d with two immediate predecessors, b and c, and therefore it is not a tree. Another defining property of trees is that branches are not allowed to cross. Figure 16-3(b) illustrates the sort of structure that is forbidden. Both types of ill-formedness can be ruled out by adding the Nontangling Condition:

The Nontangling Condition: In any well-formed constituent structure tree, for any nodes x and y, if x precedes y, then all nodes dominated by x precede all nodes dominated by y.

The configuration in Fig. 16-3(a) fails to meet this condition because b precedes c, b dominates d, and c dominates d, and therefore d ought to precede d. This is impossible, however, since precedence is irreflexive. In Fig. 16-3(b), b precedes c, b dominates d, and c dominates e. Thus, by the Nontangling Condition, d should precede e, but in fact the reverse is true.

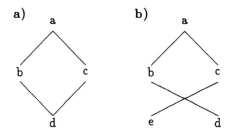

Figure 16–3: Structures excluded as trees by
the Nontangling Condition

16.3.3 Labeling

To complete the characterization of trees we must consider the labeling of the
nodes. It is apparent from Fig. 16-1 that distinct nodes can have identical
labels attached to them, e.g., the two nodes labeled NP. Since each node
has exactly one label, the pairing of nodes and labels can be represented
by a *labeling function L*, whose domain is the set of nodes in the tree and
whose range is a set (in syntactic trees, a set of grammatical categories and
formatives). The mapping is, in general, an *into* function. In summary, we
have the following definition:

DEFINITION 16.6 *A (constituent structure) tree is a mathematical configuration* $\langle N, Q, D, P, L \rangle$, *where*

> N *is a finite set, the set of* nodes
> Q *is a finite set, the set of* labels
> D *is a weak partial order in* $N \times N$, *the* dominance relation
> P *is a strict partial order in* $N \times N$, *the* precedence relation
> L *is a function from* N *into* Q, *the* labeling function

and such that the following conditions hold:

(1) $(\exists x \in N)(\forall y \in N)\langle x, y \rangle \in D$ (Single Root Condition)

(2) $(\forall x, y \in N)((\langle x, y \rangle \in P \vee \langle y, x \rangle \in P) \leftrightarrow (\langle x, y \rangle \notin D \,\&\, \langle y, x \rangle \notin D))$
(Exclusivity Condition)

(3) $(\forall w, x, y, z \in N)(((\langle w, x \rangle \in P \,\&\, \langle w, y \rangle \in D \,\&\, \langle x, z \rangle \in D) \rightarrow \langle y, z \rangle \in P)$
(Nontangling Condition)

∎

Given this definition, one can prove theorems of the following sort:

THEOREM 16.1 *Given a tree* $T = \langle N, Q, D, P, L \rangle$, *every pair of sister nodes is ordered by* P. ∎

Proof: Take x and y as sisters immediately dominated by some node z. By the definitions of 'sister' and 'immediate domination,' x, y, and z must all be distinct. As an assumption to be proved false, let x dominate y. Therefore, x must dominate z, since z immediately dominates y. But z also dominates x, and x and z are distinct, so this violates the condition that dominance is antisymmetric. Therefore, x cannot dominate y. By a symmetrical argument, we can show that y does not dominate x. Thus, $\langle x, y \rangle \notin D$ and $\langle y, x \rangle \notin D$, and by the Exclusivity Condition it follows that $\langle x, y \rangle \in P \lor \langle y, x \rangle \in P$; i.e., x and y are ordered by P. ∎

THEOREM 16.2 *Given a tree* $T = \langle N, Q, D, P, L \rangle$, *the leaves are totally ordered by* P. ∎

Proof: Let M be the set of leaves, and let R be the restriction of the relation P to the set M; i.e., $R = \{\langle x, y \rangle \in M \times M \mid \langle x, y \rangle \in P\}$. R is a strict partial order, since if there were any ordered pairs violating the conditions of irreflexivity, asymmetry, and transitivity in R, then because $R \subseteq P$, these pairs would also appear in P, and P would not be a strict partial order. By definition, a leaf dominates no node except itself, and therefore for every pair of distinct leaves x and $y, \langle x, y \rangle \notin D$ and $\langle y, x \rangle \notin D$. Thus, by the Exclusivity Condition $\langle x, y \rangle \in P \lor \langle y, x \rangle \in P$. Since x and y are leaves, $\langle x, y \rangle \in R \lor \langle y, x \rangle \in R$, by the definition of R, and thus R is connex. Therefore, R is a strict total order. ∎

Every statement about the formal properties of a constituent structure tree can be formulated in terms of the dominance and precedence relations and the labeling function. For example, one useful predicate on trees is that of *belonging to*. A node will be said to belong to the next highest S node that dominates it. Formally, the definition is as follows:

DEFINITION 16.7 *Given a tree* $T = \langle N, Q, D, P, L \rangle$, *node* x *belongs to node* y *iff*

(1) $x \neq y$

(2) $\langle y, x \rangle \in D$

(3) $\langle y, S \rangle \in L$

(4) $\sim (\exists w \in N)(\langle w, S \rangle \in L \ \& \ w \neq y \ \& \ w \neq x \ \& \ \langle y, w \rangle \in D \ \& \ \langle w, x \rangle \in D).$ ∎

Parts 2 and 3 of this definition specify that the node to which x belongs is labeled S and dominates x. Part 4 prohibits any S node from standing between x and y in the dominance relation, and part 1 excludes the case of an S node belonging to itself. To illustrate, let us consider the tree in Fig. 16-4.

The node Prn belongs to the circled S node since this is the next highest S node dominating it. Prn does not belong to the highest S (i.e., the root) of the tree because the circled S node is between the root and Prn in the dominance relation.

With this definition we can easily define some other predicates. Two nodes are called *clause mates* iff neither dominates the other and both belong to the same node. In Fig. 16-4 the nodes labeled *John* and *him* are clause mates since neither dominates the other and both belong to the circled S node. *Fred* and *him* are not clause mates since they do not belong to the same node, and Prn and *him* are not clause mates since Prn dominates *him*.

If we let $B\langle x, y \rangle$ denote 'x belongs to y,' we can state the definition of clause mates as follows:

DEFINITION 16.8 *Given a tree* $T = \langle N, Q, D, P, L \rangle$, *nodes* x *and* y *are clause mates iff* $\langle x, y \rangle \notin D \ \& \ \langle y, x \rangle \notin D \ \& \ (\exists z \in N)(\langle x, z \rangle \in B \ \& \ \langle y, z \rangle \in B.$ ∎

A node x is said to *command* a node y iff neither dominates the other and x belongs to a node z that dominates y (Langacker, 1969). In Fig. 16-4 the node labeled *Fred* commands the node labeled *him* since neither dominates the other and *Fred* belongs to the root node S, which also dominates *him*. The node *him* does not command *Fred*, however, since the node to which *him* belongs—the circled S node—does not dominate *Fred*. Note, further, that *John* commands *him* and vice versa. Formally, the definition is as follows

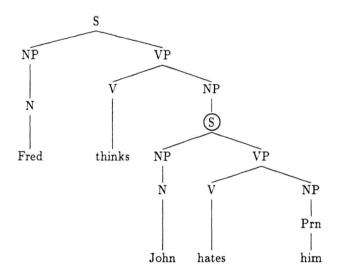

Figure 16–4: Tree illustrating the definitions
of 'belonging to' and 'command'

DEFINITION 16.9 *Given a tree $T = \langle N, Q, D, P, L \rangle$, node x commands node y iff $\langle x, y \rangle \notin D$ & $\langle y, x \rangle \notin D$ & $(\exists z \in N)(\langle x, z \rangle \in B$ & $\langle z, y \rangle \in D)$.* ∎

Problem: Prove that two nodes are clause mates iff each commands the other.

16.4   Grammars and trees

As we have said, if a grammar has only rules of the form $A \rightarrow \psi$, where A is a nonterminal symbol, there is a natural way to associate applications of such rules with the generation of a tree. For example, if the grammar contains the rule $A \rightarrow aBc$, we can associate this with the (sub)tree in Fig. 16-5.

in which A immediately dominates a, B, and c, and the latter three elements stand in the precedence relation in the order given. Further, if the grammar

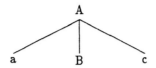

Figure 16–5.

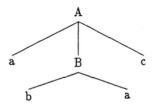

Figure 16–6.

also contains the rule $B \rightarrow ba$, we can apply this rule at the node labelled B in the preceding tree to produce the tree shown in Fig. 16-6.

Let us define the *yield* of a tree as the string formed by its leaves ordered according to the precedence relation. The yield of the tree in Fig. 16-6, for example, is *abac*; that of Fig. 16-5 is *aBc*. We can now say:

DEFINITION 16.10 *A grammar (having all rules of the form $A \rightarrow \psi$) generates a tree iff all the following hold:*

(i) *the root is labelled with the initial symbol of the grammar*

(ii) *the yield is a string of terminal symbols*

(iii) *for each subtree of the form* $\begin{array}{c} A \\ \overset{\triangle}{\alpha_1 \,\cdots\, \alpha_n} \end{array}$ *in the tree, where A immediately dominates $\alpha_1 \ldots \alpha_n$, there is a rule in the grammar $A \rightarrow \alpha_1 \ldots \alpha_n$.*

∎

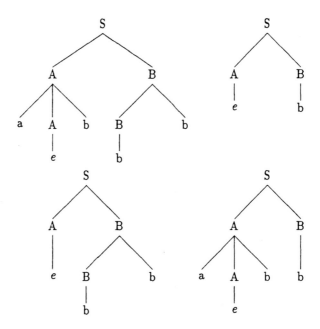

Figure 16–7.

Thus the grammar $G = \langle \{a, b\}, \{S, A, B\}, S, R \rangle$ where

$$R = \begin{cases} S \rightarrow AB & B \rightarrow Bb \\ A \rightarrow aAb & B \rightarrow b \\ A \rightarrow e \end{cases}$$

generates trees such as those in Fig. 16-7. We can further say that a string is generated by such a grammar iff it is the yield of some tree which is generated. The language generated is, as usual, the set of all strings generated. For grammars in which there is only a single symbol on the left side of each rule, this definition and the earlier definition of generation of a string turn out to be equivalent: a string is generated (by the earlier definition) iff it is the yield of some generated tree.

Problem: What language is generated by the above grammar?

Such grammars have interested linguists precisely because of the possibility of specifying a constituent structure tree for each string generated. In attempting to write such grammars for natural languages, however, linguists have noted that often such rules are not universally applicable but may be allowed only in certain contexts. For example, a rule rewriting Det(erminer) as *many* might be applied only if the following noun were a plural form. Such considerations led to the investigation of formal grammar rules of the form $A \rightarrow \psi/\alpha\_\beta$, where the "/" is read "in the context", and where "_" marks the position of the A. The interpretation of such a rule is that the symbol A can be replaced by the string ψ in a derivation only when the string α immediately precedes A and the string β immediately follows A. The context specifications are not necessarily exhaustive: additional symbols may occur to the left of the α and to the right of β. For example, if the rule were $A \rightarrow aBc/C\_Dc$, then the string $BECADcbA$ could be rewritten as $BECaBcDcbA$.

Such rules are called *context sensitive* in contrast to rules of the form $A \rightarrow \psi$, which are called *context free*. A context free rule, thus, is a context sensitive rule in which the context is null.

A context sensitive rule $A \rightarrow \psi/\alpha\_\beta$ can also be written as $\alpha A\beta \rightarrow \alpha\psi\beta$ in conformity with the schema for grammar rules generally. So long as we regard these grammars as string rewriting systems the notations are interchangeable: in either case we may replace A by ψ when we find the substring $\alpha A\beta$. However, if we want to think of context sensitive rules as generating trees, the two representations may not be equivalent. For example, the rule $CABD \rightarrow CAaBD$ could be construed either as $A \rightarrow Aa/C\_BD$ or as $B \rightarrow aB/CA\_D$, and the associated trees would obviously differ depending on whether an A node or a B node was expanded.

Another problem which arises is how the context restriction is to be satisfied by the tree. If we think of the rules as specifying how one tree is to be converted into the next in a derivation, then does a rule such as $A \rightarrow aBc/C\_D$ mean that the C and D must be *leaves* immediately to the left and right, respectively, of A when the rule is applied, or is it sufficient that the C *immediately precede* the A and the D *immediately follow*, without necessarily being leaves along with A? Under the latter interpretation, the following derivational step would be allowed, but by the former it would not.

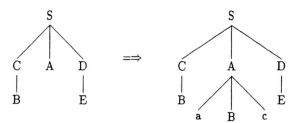

Note also that in the definition of tree derivation by means of context free rules in Def. 16-10 above, we essentially thought of the trees being somehow given in advance and then checked for well-formedness by the grammar rules. That is, the rules served as so-called "node admissibility conditions" rather than as directions for converting one tree into another. In the context free case, the two points of view are equivalent, but this is not the case for context sensitive rules. For example, the grammar

(16–6) $S \rightarrow AB$
$A \rightarrow a/\_b$
$B \rightarrow b/a\_$

will generate the tree

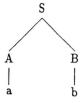

Figure 16–8.

if the rules are interpreted as node admissibility conditions but not if they are interpreted as tree generating rules (the problem being that the A cannot be rewritten until the B has, and vice versa.

16.5 The Chomsky Hierarchy

By putting increasingly stringent restrictions on the allowed forms of rules we can establish a series of grammars of decreasing generative power. Many such series are imaginable, but the one which has received the most attention is due to Chomsky and has come to be known as the Chomsky Hierarchy. At the top are the most general grammars of the sort we defined above in Section 16.2. There are no restrictions on the form of the rules except that the left side must contain at least one non-terminal symbol. (Actually, even this restriction could be eliminated in favor of one which says simply that the left side cannot be the empty string. The formulation we have chosen is essentially a technical convenience). Chomsky dubbed such grammars 'Type 0,' and they are also sometimes called unrestricted rewriting systems (urs). The succeeding three types are as follows:

Type 1: each rule is of the form $\alpha A \beta \rightarrow \alpha \psi \beta$, where $\psi \neq e$.

Type 2: each rule is of the form $A \rightarrow \psi$.

Type 3: each rule is of the form $A \rightarrow xB$ or $A \rightarrow x$

In the above α, β, and ψ are arbitrary strings (possibly empty unless otherwise specified) over the union of the terminal and non-terminal alphabets; A and B are non-terminals, and x is a string of terminal symbols.

Type 1 grammars are also called *context sensitive*; an equivalent formulation is to say that each rule is of the form $\psi \rightarrow \omega$, where ω is at least as long as ψ (i.e., the rules are "non-shrinking"). Type 2 grammars are called *context free*, and Type 3 grammars are called *regular* or *right linear* for reasons which will become apparent in the next section.

Note that these classes of grammars do not form a strict hierarchy in the sense that each type is a subclass of the one with the next lower number. Every Type 1 grammar is also a Type 0 grammar, but because rules of the form $A \rightarrow e$ are allowed in Type 2 grammars, these are not properly contained in Type 1. Type 3 grammars, however, are properly contained in the Type 2 grammars. It is nonetheless apparent, technical details concerning the empty string aside, that the hierarchy represents a series of generally increasing restrictions on the allowed form of rules.

The question then arises whether the languages generated by such grammars stand in an analogous relationship. We say that a language is of Type

n (n = 0, 1, 2, or 3) iff it is generated by some grammar of Type n. For example, we saw in Section 16.2 that $L = \{x \in \{a,b\}^* \mid x$ contains equal numbers of a's and b's$\}$ is of Type 0 inasmuch as it is generated by the grammar given in 16-4. But one might wonder whether it could also be generated by a grammar of some other type—say of Type 2. This is indeed the case; this language is generated by the following Type 2 grammar:

(16–7) $G = \langle \{a,b\}, \{S, A, B\}, S, R \rangle$ where

$$R = \begin{cases} S \to e & A \to a \\ S \to aB & A \to aS \\ S \to bA & A \to bAA \\ B \to b & B \to aBB \\ B \to bS & \end{cases}$$

This fact immediately establishes this language as Type 0 also, since every Type 2 grammar is perforce a Type 0 grammar. (It does not at the same time establish it as a Type 1 language since the given grammar is not Type 1, because of the rule $S \to e$. In fact, this language could not be Type 1 since Type 1 languages can never contain e.)

Is this language also Type 3? It turns out that it is not, but to prove this is not a simple matter. One must show somehow that *no* Type 3 grammar, however elaborate, can generate this language. We will consider techniques for proving such results in later sections.

Note that if one has two classes of grammars G_i and G_j such that G_i is properly contained in G_j, it does not necessarily follow that the corresponding classes of languages stand in the proper subset relation. Because every Type i grammar is also a Type $i+1$ grammar it *does* follow that every Type i language is also a Type $i+1$ language, i.e., $L_i \subseteq L_{i+1}$. But it might also be the case that every Type $i+1$ language happens to have some Type i grammar which generates it. In such a case L_i is a subset of L_{i+1} but not a proper subset. Among the earliest results achieved in the study of formal grammars and languages were proofs that the inclusions among the languages of the Chomsky hierarchy are in fact proper inclusions. Specifically,

(i) the Type 3 languages are properly included in the Type 2 languages;

(ii) the Type 2 languages not containing the empty string are properly included in the Type 1 languages;

(iii) the Type 1 languages are properly included in the Type 0 languages.

Some of the proofs will be sketched in the following chapters.

16.6   Languages and automata

As we mentioned at the beginning of this section, languages can also be characterized by abstract computing devices called automata. Ultimately we will define a hierarchy of automata and establish correspondences between them and the grammars of the Chomsky Hierarchy. This gives us yet another point of view from which to examine the notion of 'complexity of a language' which we hope eventually to put to use in characterizing natural language.

Before turning to the detailed study of the various classes of automata, it would be well to make a few general remarks about these devices.

An automaton is an idealized abstract computing machine—that is, it is a mathematical object rather than a physical one. An automaton is characterized by the manner in which it performs computations: for any automaton there is a class of *inputs* to which it reacts, and a class of *outputs* which it produces, the relation between these being determined by the *structure*, or internal organization of the automaton. We will consider only automata whose inputs and outputs are discrete (e.g., strings over an alphabet) rather than continuous (e.g., readings on a dial), and we will not deal with automata whose behavior is probabilistic.

Central to the notion of the structure of an automaton is the concept of a *state*. A state of an automaton is analogous to the arrangement of bits in the memory banks and registers of an actual computer, but since we are abstracting away from physical realizations here, we can think of a state as a characteristic of an automaton which in general changes during the course of a computation and which serves to determine the relationship between inputs and outputs. We will consider only automata which have a finite number of states (cf. a computer whose internal hardware at any given moment can be in only one of a finite number of different arrangements of 1's and 0's.)

An automaton may also have a *memory*. For the simplest automata, the memory consists simply of the states themselves. More powerful automata may be outfitted with additional devices, generally "tapes" on which the machine can read and write symbols and do "scratch work." Since the amount of memory available on such tapes is potentially unlimited, these machines can in effect overcome the limitations inherent in having only a finite number of states. We will see that the most powerful automata, Turing machines, are capable in principle of performing any computation for which an explicit set of instructions can be given.

Automata may be regarded as devices for computing functions, i.e., for pairing inputs with outputs, but we will normally view them as *acceptors*, i.e., devices which, when given an input, either accept or reject it after some finite amount of computation. In particular, if the input is a string over some alphabet A, then an automaton can be thought of as the acceptor of some language over A and the rejector of its complement. As we will see, it is also possible to regard automata as *generators* of strings and languages in a manner similar to grammars.

Chapter 17

Finite Automata, Regular Languages and Type 3 Grammars

17.1 Finite automata

A finite automaton (fa), or finite state automaton (fsa), is an abstract computing device that receives a string of symbols as input, reads this string one symbol at a time from left to right, and after reading the last symbol halts and signifies either acceptance or rejection of the input. At any point in its computation a fa is in one of a finite number of *states*. The computations of a fa are directed by a "program," which is a finite set of instructions for changing from state to state as the automaton reads input symbols. A computation always begins in a designated state, the *initial state*. There is also a specified set of *final states*; if the fa ends up in one of these after reading the input, it is accepted; otherwise, it is rejected.

It may help to visualize a finite automaton as composed of (1) a control box, which at any point in the computation can be in one of the allowed internal states, and (2) a reading head, which scans a single symbol of the input. In Fig.17-1 we have represented a fa in its initial state, q_0, at the beginning of its computation of the input string *abaab*.

Let us suppose further that the set of states for this fa is $\{q_0, q_1\}$ and that the set of final states is $\{q_1\}$. (We could have made the initial state a final state also, but we have not chosen to do so here.) We specify the program

Figure 17-1.

for this fa as a set of triples of the form (q_i, x, q_j), where q_i and q_j are states and x is a symbol of the alphabet—here, $\{a, b\}$. Instructions are interpreted in the following way: when the fa is in state q_i reading a symbol x on the input tape, it changes to state q_j (possibly identical to q_i) and advances the reading head one symbol to the right. The instruction for the now current state and symbol is then carried out, and the process is repeated until there are no more symbols to be read. Here are the instructions for our example:

(17–1) (q_0, a, q_0)
         (q_0, b, q_1)
         (q_1, a, q_1)
         (q_1, b, q_0)

Thus, from the initial situation shown in Fig. 17-1 the fa would first execute the instruction (q_0, a, q_0) and find itself in the following situation:

(17–2)

Now the instruction (q_0, b, q_1) is applied to produce:

(17–3)

and so on. You should now be able to verify that after reading the final symbol b, the fa is in state q_0, and since this is not a final state, the input is rejected. It should also be easy to determine that the input *ab* would be accepted, while *aa* is rejected.

Problem: Describe the set of all tapes accepted by this fa.

What would happen if the fa of our example were given the empty string as input? In such a case, the input tape has no symbols on it, and so no instructions can be applied—there being nothing to read. Thus, the initial situation is identical to the final situation, and since the initial state, q_0, is not a final state, this input is rejected. Note that to say that a machine accepts the empty string as part of its language is far different from saying that the language accepted is empty. The latter means that it accepts neither the empty string nor any other string. An automaton with no final states would, for example, accept no strings and thus would be said to accept the empty language.

One might wonder how a finite automaton would behave if there were no instruction applicable at a particular point or if there were more than one instruction which could be applied. Such questions will arise with the so-called *non-deterministic* automata, which we consider below. For now, we will be concerned only with *deterministic* fa's, in which there is one and only one instruction for each combination of state and scanned symbol. As the name suggests, the behavior of such an automaton is completely determined, given the input tape and the initial state.

17.1.1 State diagrams of finite automata

A convenient representation for a fa, called a *state diagram*, can be constructed in the following way. Each state is represented by a circle labelled with the name of the state. For each instruction (q_i, x, q_j) an arrow is drawn from the q_i circle to the q_j circle and labelled with symbol x. Final states are enclosed by an additional circle, and the initial state is marked by a caret. The state diagram for our example fa is shown in Fig. 17-2.

With such a diagram it is easy to trace the steps of a computation like that for *abaab* in the example above. The fa starts in state q_0 and returns to q_0 reading an *a*. The *b* takes it to state q_1; the next two *a*'s leave it in q_1; and the final *b* returns it to q_0. Since q_0 is non-final, the string is not accepted.

It is also somewhat easier to see from the state diagram than from the list of instructions in (17-1) that this fa accepts exactly the strings over the alphabet $\{a, b\}$ containing an odd number of *b*'s.

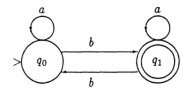

Figure 17–2.

17.1.2   Formal definition of deterministic finite automata

DEFINITION 17.1 *A deterministic finite automaton (dfa) M is a quintuple* $\langle K, \Sigma, \delta, q_0, F \rangle$, *where*

> *K is a finite set, the set of* states
>
> Σ *is a finite set, the* alphabet
>
> $q_0 \in K$, *the* initial state
>
> $F \subseteq K$, *the set of* final states
>
> δ *is a function from* $K \times \Sigma$ *into K, the* transition function *(or* next-state function*)*.   ∎

Note that the property of determinism is expressed in this definition by the fact that δ is a function; that is, for all $q \in K$ and all $\sigma \in \Sigma$, $\delta(q, \sigma)$ has a unique value.

   In order to express formally what it is for a dfa to accept an input string, we introduce the notion of a *situation* of a dfa. This is intended to be essentially a "snapshot" of the dfa and its input tape at any point during a computation. We represented situations above by diagrams such as Fig. 17-1, but we now want a more compact notation. The essential information to be captured is (1) the current state of the automaton; (2) the input tape; and (3) the position of the reading head. A convenient representation of this information is in the form of a triple (x, q, y), where q is the current state and x and y are the portions of the input string to the left and right of the reading head, respectively. In this notation, the symbol being scanned is the left-most symbol, if any, of y. Thus, the diagram in (17-3) would be represented as (ab, q_1, aab), and the sequence of situations in the computation of $abaab$ would be as follows:

(17-4) $(e, q_0, abaab) \vdash (a, q_0, baab) \vdash (ab, q_1, aab) \vdash (aba, q_1, ab) \vdash (abaa, q_1, b) \vdash (abaab, q_0, e)$

Here we have used the symbol $\vdash$ (the 'turnstile') to indicate that one situation leads to another by a single move of the automaton. We will define this formally below. Note that at the beginning of the computation the string to the left of the reading head is empty, and likewise for the string to the right at the end of the computation. In formal terms, a situation of a dfa is defined as follows:

DEFINITION 17.2 Given a dfa $M = \langle K, \Sigma, \delta, q_0, F \rangle$, a situation of M is a triple (x, q, y), where $q \in K$ and $x, y \in \Sigma^*$. ∎

This definition allows situations for a given M which are not actually attainable in the course of any computation by M. For example, (aa, q_1, abb) would be a situation of our example dfa, but it is not a situation which can be reached from the initial situation $(e, q_0, aaabb)$ by the given transition function of the automaton. It is convenient, nonetheless, to define the notion of situation in this overly broad way and to focus on attainable situations in our definition of acceptance.

Let us define, for a given dfa M, a binary relation on situations which we will call *produces-in-one-move*. Situation A produces situation B in one move just in case by applying one instruction in δ to A we produce situation B. Any two adjacent situations in (17-4) would stand in this relation, for example. Formally, we have:

DEFINITION 17.3 Given a dfa $M = \langle K, \Sigma, \delta, q_0, F \rangle$, a situation (x, q, y) produces *situation* (x', q', y') in one move iff (1) there is a $\sigma \in \Sigma$ such that $y = \sigma y'$ and $x' = x\sigma$ (i.e., the reading head moves right by one symbol), and (2) $\delta(q, \sigma) = q'$ (i.e., the appropriate state change occurs on reading σ). ∎

Problem: In general, is the produces-in-one-move relation reflexive? symmetric? transitive?

As noted above, we indicate by the turnstile that two situations stand in this relation; thus $(x, q, y) \vdash (x', q', y')$.

Once again, this definition is permissive in that it allows pairs of situations to stand in the produces-in-one-move relation whether or not either is attainable from some initial situation in the course of a computation. For example, in the dfa above, $(aa, q_1, abb) \vdash (aaa, q_1, bb)$, despite the fact that neither situation could arise from $(e, q_0, aaabb)$.

As a final step before giving a formal definition of acceptance, we extend the previously defined relation to a new binary relation: "produces in zero or more steps." We say that a situation A produces situation B in zero or more steps (or simply A produces B) iff there is a sequence of situations $S_0 \vdash S_1 \vdash \ldots \vdash S_k$ such that $A = S_0$ and $B = S_k$ ($k \geq 0$). (If $k = 0$, there is only one situation in the sequence, and $A = B$; thus, every situation produces itself in zero or more moves.) This relation is reflexive (as we have just seen) and transitive; in fact, it is in formal terms the *reflexive, transitive closure* of the produces-in-one-move relation. This is just the produces-in-one-move relation (for a given dfa) with enough pairs added to it to make it a reflexive and transitive relation. We will denote this relation by $\vdash^*$ ('turnstile star'). We may also add a subscript M to this or to the turnstile if necessary to emphasize the fact that the relation is defined with respect to a particular automaton M; thus, $\vdash_M$ or $\vdash^*_M$. Referring again to 17-4, we see

(17–5) $(a, q_0, baab) \vdash^* (aba, q_1, ab)$ and $(ab, q_1, aab) \vdash^* (ab, q_1, aab)$

but neither of these would be true if $\vdash^*$ were replaced by $\vdash$. Acceptance of a string by dfa is now easy to define formally:

DEFINITION 17.4 *Given a dfa* $M = \langle K, \Sigma, \delta, q_0, F \rangle$ *and a string* $x \in \Sigma^*$, M *accepts* x *iff there is a* $q \in F$ *such that* $(e, q_0, x) \vdash^*_M (x, q, e)$. ∎

And finally:

DEFINITION 17.5 *Given a dfa* $M = \langle K, \Sigma, \delta, q_0, F \rangle$, *the* language accepted by M, *denoted* $L(M)$, *is the set of all strings accepted by* M. ∎

17.1.3 Non-deterministic finite automata

We now consider what happens if we relax the requirement that the next move of a fa always be uniquely determined. Departures from determinism can occur in two ways:

(i) for a given state symbol pair, there may be more than one next state
(ii) for a given state symbol pair, there may no next state at all

There is an additional generalization from the deterministic case which, while
it is strictly speaking not a departure from determinism, is often included in
the definition of non-deterministic fa's:

(iii) transitions of the form (q_i, w, q_j) are allowed, where $w \in \Sigma^*$; i.e., the fa
can read a string of symbols in one move; and in particular,
(iv) transitions of the form (q_i, e, q_j) are allowed; i.e., the fa can change state
without moving the reading head.

An example of a non-deterministic fa which illustrates all four of these conditions is shown in Fig. 17-3.

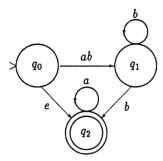

Figure 17–3.

The behavior of a non-deterministic fa is defined as follows: an input
tape is accepted iff there is *some* path through the state diagram which
begins in the initial state, reads the entire input, and ends in a final state.
In the fa of Fig. 17-3, for example, *abb* is accepted by virtue of the path from
q_0 (reading *ab*) to q_1 and then to q_2 (reading *b*). The fact that there is also a
path reading *abb* which ends in q_1 is irrelevant; only the existence of at least
one accepting path is required. On the other hand, *ba* is not accepted since
there is no path through the state diagram which succeeds in reading the
entire string. Likewise, *aba* is not accepted. Note, however, that the string
a is accepted by the path leading from q_0 to q_2 (reading no input) and then
again to q_2 (reading an *a*).

17.1.4   Formal definition of non-deterministic finite automata

Formally, a non-deterministic fa is identical to a dfa except that the transition function becomes a relation.

DEFINITION 17.6 *A non-deterministic finite automaton (nfa)* M *is a quintuple* $\langle K, \Sigma, \Delta, q_0, F \rangle$, *where* K, Σ, q_0, *and* F, *are as for a dfa, and* Δ, *the transition relation, is a finite subset of* $K \times \Sigma^* \times K$ *(i.e., a relation from* $K \times \Sigma^*$ *into* K *)*.   ∎

The fact that Δ is a relation, but not necessarily a function, allows for conditions (i) and (ii) above. The fact that it is a relation from $K \times \Sigma^*$ rather than from $K \times \Sigma$ allows for condition (iii) and its special case (iv). Because of the infiniteness of Σ^*, a relation from $K \times \Sigma^*$ to K is itself potentially infinite; we stipulate that it must be a *finite* subset of $K \times \Sigma^* \times K$ in order to retain the notion of a finite machine; i.e., an automaton with a finite number of states and a finite number of instructions in its program. Note that by this definition dfa's are a proper subclass of nfa's.

   The definitions of situation, produces-in-one-move, etc. are similar to those for dfa's.

DEFINITION 17.7 *A situation is any triple in* $\Sigma^* \times K \times \Sigma^*$. $(x, q, y) \vdash (x', q', y')$ *is true iff there exists a string* $z \in \Sigma^*$ *such that* $x' = xz$, $y = zy'$, *and* $(q, z, q') \in \Delta$.   ∎

DEFINITION 17.8 Produces, *i.e.,* $\vdash^*$, *is the reflexive, transitive closure of the* $\vdash$ *relation, and, as before, an nfa* M *accepts a string* $x \in \Sigma^*$ *iff* $(e, q_0, x) \vdash_M^* (x, q, e)$ *for some* $q \in F$.   ∎

The language accepted is, of course, the set of all strings accepted.

17.1.5   Equivalence of deterministic and non-deterministic finite automata

One might expect that when fa's are allowed the extra degrees of freedom inherent in non-determinism, significantly more powerful devices would be the result. Surprisingly, this is not the case. nfa's accept exactly the same class of languages as dfa's; or in other words, for every nfa there is an

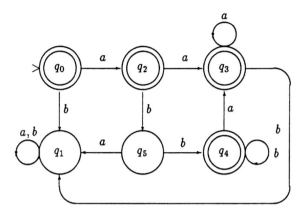

Figure 17–4.

equivalent dfa—equivalent in the sense that both accept exactly the same set of strings. (The equivalence in the other direction is trivial, every dfa being *a fortiori* a nfa.) An example of a dfa which is equivalent to the nfa in Fig. 17-3 is shown in Fig. 17-4.

A dfa will typically have more states that an nfa to which it is equivalent. The dfa works by essentially keeping track, in its states, of the *set* of states that the nfa could be in if it followed all possible paths simultaneously on a given input. There is in fact an algorithm for converting any nfa into an equivalent dfa, but it is too long to be included here. It can be found in Chomsky and Miller (1958), Rabin and Scott (1959), Hopcroft and Ullman (1979), and Lewis and Papadimitriou (1981).

In view of the equivalence of dfa's and nfa's, one might wonder why we bother to consider nfa's at all. For one thing, nfa's are generally easier to construct than dfa's. Thus, it might be simpler to show that a given language is of the sort accepted by a fa by devising an nfa which accepts it. We will in fact make use of this convenience in proving certain theorems about fa's below. For another thing, determinism and non- determinism are notions which arise in connection with other classes of automata to be considered later, and, as we will see, the two varieties are not always equivalent in these cases.

17.2   Regular languages

We will say that a language is a *finite automaton language* (fal) just in case
there is some fa which accepts it. We know, for example, that $\{x \in \{a,b\}^* \mid$
x contains an odd number of $b's\}$ is such a language by virtue of the fact
that we exhibited an fa accepting this language in Fig. 17-2 above. Consider,
however, the general problem of deciding whether a given language L is a fal
or not. Suppose we try to construct a fa accepting L, but all our attempts
result in failure. We would not be justified in concluding that L is *not* a fal,
of couse, since we might succeed in our attempts with renewed persistence or
perhaps a bit of luck. It would be useful if we had another way to characterize
this class of languages which does not depend on our ingenuity, or lack of it,
in constructing fa's. To that end, we define a class of languages, called *regular
languages*, which turn out to be provably identical to the class of fal's. Since
these languages are defined (recursively) by reference to operations on sets of
strings rather than to acceptance by automata, we have another interesting
and potentially useful approach to these languages. In the next section, we
prove a theorem which is used primarily to show that a given language is
not an fal. We will need a preliminary definition:

DEFINITION 17.9 *Given two sets of strings, A and B, the* concatenation *(or*
set product) of A and B, denoted $A \cdot B$ (or just AB), is the set of strings
$\{x^\frown y \mid x \in A \text{ and } y \in B\}.$ ■

For example,

(17–6)   if $A = \{a, b\}$ and $B = \{cc, d\}$, then $AB = \{acc, ad, bcc, bd\}$

Note that the concatenation of two sets of strings is itself a set of strings, in
contrast to the Cartesian product of two sets (of anything), which is a set of
ordered pairs. We should also note that, according to the definition, if one
of the sets is empty, the concatenation is also empty.

   Recall also that the notation A^* is used to denote the set of all strings
formed over the alphabet A. This is a special case of an operation called
closure or *Kleene star* on a set of strings: given a set of strings A, the Kleene
star or closure of A, denoted A^*, is the set formed by concatenating members
of A together any number of times (including zero) in any order and allowing
repetitions. For example,

(17-7) $\{a, bb\}^* = \{e, a, bb, aa, abb, bba, bbbb, aaa, aabb, abba, \ldots\}$.

Note that our original notation treated the members of the alphabet as strings of length 1. We are now ready to give the definition of the *regular languages*.

DEFINITION 17.10 *Given an alphabet* Σ:

1. $\emptyset$ *is a regular language.*

2. *For any string* $x \in \Sigma^*$, $\{x\}$ *is a regular language.*

3. *If* A *and* B *are regular languages, so is* $A \cup B$.

4. *If* A *and* B *are regular languages, so is* AB.

5. *If* A *is a regular language, so is* A^*.

6. *Nothing else is a regular language unless its being so follows from 1-5.*

■

For example,

(17-8) Let $\Sigma = \{a, b, c\}$. Then since aab and cc are members of Σ^*, $\{aab\}$ and $\{cc\}$ are regular languages. So is the union of these two sets, *viz.*, $\{aab, cc\}$, and so is the concatenation of the two, *viz.*, $\{aabcc\}$. Likewise, $\{aab\}^*$, $\{cc\}^*$, and $\{aab, cc\}^*$, are all regular languages, etc.

Another way to state the definition is to say that the regular languages (over a given alphabet) are just those which can be obtained from the empty language and the 'unit' languages (those containing just one string) by repeated application of the operations of union, concatenation, and Kleene star. Thus, to show that a given language is in fact regular, we indicate how it can be built up out of empty or unit languages by these operations. For example, the language $\{x \in \{a, b\}^* \mid x$ contains an odd number of b's$\}$ is a regular language since an equivalent representation of this language is $\{a\}^* \cdot \{b\} \cdot \{a\}^* \cdot (\{b\} \cdot \{a\}^* \cdot \{b\} \cdot \{a\}^*)^*$. In writing such expressions, it is usual to render them less cumbersome by suppressing the braces around sets and the dots in concatenation; extra parentheses can also be dispensed with in view of the associativity of union and concatenation. The previous expression in this pared-down notation would be: $a^*ba^*(ba^*ba^*)^*$. Such expressions are called *regular expressions*. We note also that the set of all strings in $\{a,b\}^*$ which contain exactly two or three b's is a regular language since it can be represented (as a regular expression) as $a^*ba^*ba^* \cup a^*ba^*ba^*ba^*$, or equivalently as $a^*ba^*ba^*(e \cup ba^*)$. Note, finally, that $\{e\}$ is a regular language since it is equal to $\emptyset^*$.

Having thus characterized the regular languages, we want to show that they are in fact identical to the finite automaton languages.

THEOREM 17.1 *(Kleene) A set of strings is a finite automaton language if and only if it is a regular language.*   ∎

We will sketch the proof of one half of this theorem; i.e., that every fal is a regular language. The proof of the converse is too complex to give here, but can be found in works such as Hopcroft and Ullman (1979) and Lewis and Papadimitriou (1981).

First, we show that the empty language and the unit languages (for a given Σ) are fal's. The empty language is accepted by the one-state fa in Fig. 17-5(a), and for each x in Σ^*, a fa of the form shown in Fig. 17-5(b) accepts the language $\{x\}$. (Note that these fa's are in general non-deterministic.)

a)   b)

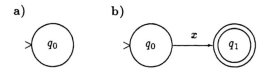

Figure 17–5.

Next we show that the fal's are closed under the operations of union, concatenation, and Kleene star. From this it will follow that the fal's are included in the regular languages.

We will indicate how, given any two fa's accepting languages L_1 and L_2, we can construct fa's accepting, respectively, $L_1 \cup L_2$, $L_1 L_2$, and L_1^*.

Suppose, for example, we are given the following fal's:

$L_1 = ab^*a$; that is, all strings beginning and ending with an a with any number of b's between them.

L_2 = all strings in $\{a, b\}^*$ containing exactly two b's.

These are fal's since they are accepted by the fa's in Figs. 17-6 and 17-7, respectively.

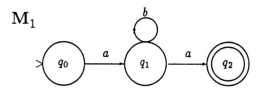

Figure 17–6.

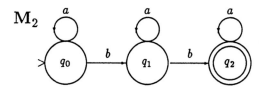

Figure 17–7.

To form a fa accepting the union of L_1 and L_2 we first relabel the states of one of the fa's so that all have distinct names—let us suppose that we add primes to the states of M_2. Now we introduce a new start state, q_0'', and establish e-transitions, i.e., changes of state reading the empty string, from q_0'' to the old start states, q_0 and q_0'. Everything else, including the final states, remains the same. The resulting automaton M_3 is shown in Fig. 17-8.

M_3 of course is non-deterministic. From its initial state it can go without reading any input to q_0, from which point it acts like M_1, or it can go to q_0' and then behave like M_2. Given a string x which is in $L_1 \cup L_2$, there will be an accepting path in M_3 corresponding to one (or both) of these possibilities. If x is not in $L_1 \cup L_2$, it is not accepted on any path in M_3.

It should not be difficult to see that the method of construction is general and can be applied to any two fa's. This is the basis of the proof that the

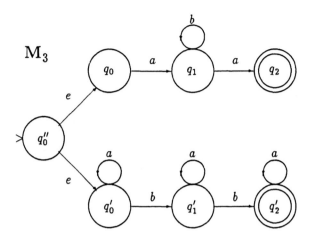

Figure 17–8.

fal's are closed under union.

The demonstration that the fal's are closed under concatenation is similar, except that the automata are hooked together "in series" rather than "in parallel." To construct a fa accepting $L_1 \cdot L_2$, we relabel the states of M_2, if necessary, to make them distinct from those of M_1 and then run e-transitions from all final states of M_1 to the initial state of M_2. Final states of M_1 now become non-final, but final states of M_2 remain. The result for our examples M_1 and M_2 above, would be as shown in Figure 17-9.

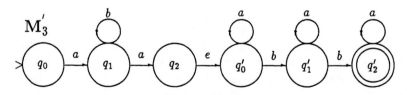

Figure 17–9.

M_3' accepts $L_1 \cdot L_2$ as follows. Given x, it will be accepted just in case $x = wz$, where w would be accepted by M_1 (in state q_2) and z would be accepted by M_2 (going from state q_0' to state q_2'.) If x is not in $L_1 \cdot L_2$, there will be no factorization of x into wz such that w would be accepted by M_1 and z accepted by M_2 and thus no accepting path through M_3'. Again, the method is general and does not depend on the particular characteristics of automata M_1 and M_2. Note, however, that if M_1 had more than one final state, we would have e-transitions from *each* of them to the initial state of M_2, and all these states would become non-final in the resulting fa.

Finally, we want to show that the fal's are closed under the Kleene star operation; that is, we want to take an automaton accepting L and convert it into an automaton accepting L^*. The strategy here is to establish e-transitions from all the final states back to the initial state so that the new fa can "recycle," accepting an input string $x_1 x_2 \ldots x_n$ just in case the original fa would have accepted x_1 and $x_2 \ldots$ and x_n. There is a slight difficulty, however, in connection with the acceptance of the empty string, which is of course a member of L^* for any language L.

One would naturally want to insure that e is accepted by making the initial state a final state if it isn't already. However, in certain cases this can lead to trouble. Consider, for example, the following fa accepting the language $a(b \cup baa)^* b$:

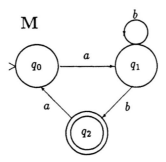

Figure 17–10.

If we were simply to add an e-transition from q_2 to q_0 so that the fa could "recycle" and make q_0 a final state, we would have:

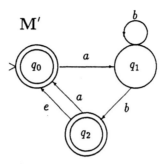

Figure 17-11.

M' accepts e, as required, but it also accepts aba, which is not in $(a(b \cup baa)^*b)^*$. Rather, what we should do is add a new initial state to M, which will also be a final state, and establish an e-transition from q_2 back to the *old* initial state, q_0:

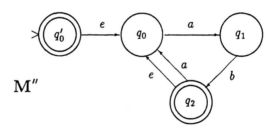

Figure 17-12.

Returning now to the examples M_1 and M_2 above, we see that this method of construction would produce the fa's in Fig. 17-13, accepting L_1^* and L_2^*, respectively.

This completes our informal demonstration that every finite automaton language is a regular language. As we have said, we will not attempt to show the converse here. It relies essentially on a procedure for extracting from any given fa a representation of the language it accepts. This representation can

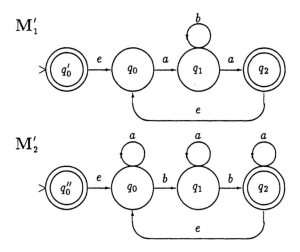

Figure 17–13.

be shown to involve only the empty and unit languages together with the operations of union, concatenation, and Kleene star, and thus, that every fal is a regular language.

17.2.1   Pumping Theorem for fal's

Consider an infinite fal L. By definition, it is accepted by some fa M, which, again by definition, has a finite number of states. But since L is infinite, there are strings in L which are as long as we please, and certainly L contains strings with more symbols than the number of states in M. Thus, since M accepts every string in L, there must be a loop in M—in particular, a loop which lies along a path from the initial state to some final state. In other words, in accepting a string longer than the number of states of M, M must enter some state more than once, and a path leading from such a state back to that state constitutes a loop along an accepting path.

Let x be the string of symbols which M reads on going from its initial state to the state at the beginning of some loop (call it q_i). Let y be the string read by M in going around the loop once, i.e., from q_i to the first re-entry to q_i. Finally, let z be the string read on going from q_i to some final state. Thus, xyz is accepted by M.

But now notice that any loop lying along an accepting path can be traversed any number of times—zero or more—and the result will still be an accepting path. Therefore, if M accepts xyz in the way indicated, it will also accept $xz, xyyz, xyyyz, \ldots$, in fact all strings of the form $xy^n z$ for $n \geq 0$. Finally, we observe that if L is an infinite language (so that there is no upper bound on sentence length), there has to be *some* loop along an accepting path in M such that $y \neq e$. Otherwise, M could not accept strings of length greater than the number of states of M. These observations are summarized in the following theorem, known as the Pumping Theorem (for fal's) because the string y is said to be "pumped", i.e., repeated with each traversal of the loop recognizing it.

THEOREM 17.2 *If L is an infinite fal over alphabet Σ, then there are strings $x, y, z \in \Sigma^*$ such that $y \neq e$ and $xy^n z \in L$ for all $n \geq 0$.*   ∎

As an example, consider the language

(17–9) $\{x \in \{a, b\}^* \mid x$ contains an odd number of b's $\}$

Since this is an infinite fal, the Pumping Theorem applies. Hence, there exist strings x, y, and z $(y \neq e)$ such that $xy^n z \in L$ for all $n \geq 0$. Many examples of such strings could be found; to take just one, let $x = e$, $y = bb$, and $z = ab$. Then it is true that $ab, bbab, bbbbab, bbbbbbab, \ldots$, are all in L; that is $(bb)^n ab \in L$ for all $n \geq 0$. For some choices of x, y, and z, this will not be true, but that doesn't matter: the theorem guarantees only that at least *one* choice for x, y, and z exists such that the specified condition holds.

The usefulness of this theorem lies in its application to languages which are not fal's. Suppose we have a language L which is infinite and for which we could somehow show that for *no* choice of x, y, and z $(y \neq e)$ whatsover is it the case that $xy^n z \in L$ for all $n \geq 0$. In such a situation we would be justified in concluding that L is *not* a fal. Here we are using the theorem in its contrapositive form. As stated, it is a conditional: If L is an infinite fal, then so-and-so. The contrapositive is: if not-so-and-so, then L is not an infinite fal. For example, consider the language

(17–10) $L = \{a^n b^n \mid n \geq 0\}$

and let us show that it is not a fal using the Pumping Theorem. If L were a fal, there would be some x, y, and z $(y \neq e)$ such that $xy^n z \in L$ for all $n \geq 0$. We show that no such x, y, and z exist.

The string xyz would have to be in L, so what could y consist of? It can't be empty, so it would have to consist of (1) some number of a's, or (2) some number of b's, or (3) some number of a's followed by some number of b's. It is easy to see that (3) is impossible because any string that contains more than one repetition of y, e.g., $xyyz$, will contain b's preceding a's—the b's at the end of the first y and the a's at the beginning of the next—which could not be a string in L. So such a choice of y is not pumpable.

What about case (1)? Here all the b's are contained in the z part, and as y is pumped, the number of a's in the string will increase while the number of b's remains constant. Thus, we will continually be producing strings which have more a's than b's in them, which cannot be in the language $a^n b^n$.

Case (2) is parallel, but here the number of b's outstrips the number of a's. These are the only logical possibilities for the choice of y, and since none meet the condition laid down in the Pumping Theorem, we conclude that no such x, y, z exist for this language. Conclusion: $a^n b^n$ is not a fal.

What we have just done, then, is to show that there is no fa accepting $a^n b^n$ without actually attempting to construct such an automaton.

One should also note that the Pumping Theorem does not yield particularly useful information when one shows that the consequent of the conditional is true. If we were to consider the language $L = \{x \in \{a,b\}^* \mid x$ contains equal numbers of a's and b's in any order $\}$ and observe that for $x = e$, $y = ab$, and $z = e$ it is the case that $xy^n z \in L$ for all $n \geq 0$, this would tell us nothing about whether L is a fal or not. Given $A \rightarrow B$ and B, we can conclude nothing about the truth or falsity of A. As it happens, the language just mentioned is *not* a fal. The moral is that the Pumping Theorem may be useful in showing that certain languages are not fal's but may not prove useful in other cases, even though the languages in question are in fact not fal's.

17.3 Type 3 grammars and finite automaton languages

We now want to examine the fal's from the point of view of grammars which generate them. Recall our previous discussion of formal grammars as consisting of V_T, the terminal vocabulary; V_N, the non-terminal vocabulary; S, the initial symbol; and R, a set of rules or productions. The various types of grammars differ in the form of productions they may contain, and here we want to focus our attention on Type 3 grammars, also called *right linear* grammars, in which each production is either of the form $A \rightarrow xB$ or $A \rightarrow x$, where A and B are in V_N and x is any string in V_T^*. That is, each rule of a Type 3 grammar has a single non-terminal on the left side, and on the right a string of terminals (possibly empty) followed by at most one non-terminal symbol. An example is shown in (17-11).

(17–11) $G = \langle V_T, V_N, S, R \rangle$, where $V_T = \{a, b\}$; $V_N = \{S, A, B\}$; and

$$R = \begin{cases} S \rightarrow aA \\ A \rightarrow aA \\ A \rightarrow bbB \\ B \rightarrow bB \\ B \rightarrow b \end{cases}$$

An example of a derivation by this grammar is shown in (17-12):

(17–12) $S \Rightarrow aA \Rightarrow aaA \Rightarrow aabbB \Rightarrow aabbbB \Rightarrow aabbbb$

The phrase-structure tree associated with this derivation is shown in Fig. (17-14).

It is evident from this tree why the Type 3 grammars are also called right linear: the non-terminal symbols form a single linear sequence down the right of the tree. (There is also a class of grammars called *left linear* in which every rule is of the form $A \rightarrow Bx$ or $A \rightarrow x$. The more general class of *linear* grammars has every rule of the form $A \rightarrow xBy$ or $A \rightarrow x$, i.e., the right side of each rule has at most one non-terminl symbol but it need not to be left-most or right-most in the string. What we will say here about right-linear grammars could equally well be formulated in terms of left-linear grammars—they are equivalent in generative capacity. Linear grammars, however, generate a larger class of languages.)

Note that in a derivation by a right-linear grammar there is exactly one non-terminal symbol at the right end of each string until the last one, at which point a rule of the form $A \rightarrow x$ is applied and the derivation terminates. This observation suggests an analogy to finite automata: the one non-terminal symbol at the right side of a string is like the state of a fa

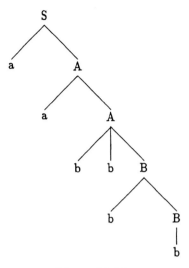

Figure 17–14.

in that the future course of the derivation or computation can depend only on the identity of that state or symbol and the given productions of the device in question. In particular, the past history, i.e., the string already read by the fa or the string already generated by the grammar, has no influence on the future course of events.

Let us then associate with each rule of a Type 3 grammar of the form $A \rightarrow xB$ a transition in a (non-deterministic) fa from state A to state B reading x. Further, let us associate each rule of the form $A \rightarrow x$ with a tranisition from state A reading x to a designated final state F. The initial state of the automaton will, of course, be S. Carrying out this construction for the grammar in (17-11) gives:

It should be reasonably easy to convince oneself that this fa accepts the same language as that generated by the grammar in (17-11). Moreover, the method is general and can be applied to any given Type 3 grammar to produce an equivalent fa. 'Equivalent,' of course, means that the language accepted by the fa is the same as the language generated by the Type 3 grammar.

On further consideration, we see that there is no reason why we should

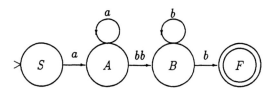

Figure 17–15.

consider fa's only as acceptors of languages. We might as well think of an
fa as a language generator which starts in an initial state, moves from state
to state emitting, or writing, symbols on an output tape, and halting at
will in either a final or non-final state. If the fa halts in a final state, the
output string is said to be generated; otherwise, it is not generated. The state
diagram of a fa is the same whichever way we want to look at it, and the same
language would be accepted by a given fa acceptor as that generated by the
fa regarded as generator. From this point of view, then, non-deterministic
fa's and Type 3 grammars are virtually isomorphic representations.

Problem: How could one construe a Type 3 grammar as accepting rather
than generating strings, i.e., how would the rules and derivations be interpreted?

What we have just argued (without giving a formal proof) is that every
Type 3 language is a fal. To show the converse is equally easy, but the
construction proceeds in the opposite direction. Given a fa, we use its instructions to create the rules of a Type 3 grammar in the following way. For
each transition $(q_i,\ x,\ q_j)$, we put in the grammar a rule $q_i \rightarrow xq_j$. Thus,
the states of the fa become non-terminal symbols of the grammar, and the
alphabet of the fa becomes the terminal alphabet of the grammar. Finally,
for each transition (q_i, x, q_j) where q_j is a final state, we also add to the
grammar the rule $q_i \rightarrow x$. If we carry out this construction on the fa in
(17-1), we get the following grammar:

(17–13) $G = \langle V_T, V_N, q_0, R \rangle$, where $V_T = \{a, b\}$; $V_N = \{q_0, q_1\}$; and

$$R = \begin{cases} q_0 \rightarrow a\,q_0 & q_1 \rightarrow b\,q_0 \\ q_0 \rightarrow b\,q_1 & q_0 \rightarrow b \\ q_1 \rightarrow a\,q_1 & q_1 \rightarrow a \end{cases}$$

A derivation of the string *aaba* by this grammar would be as follows:

(17–14) $q_0 \Rightarrow aq_0 \Rightarrow aaq_0 \Rightarrow aabq_1 \Rightarrow aaba$

The reader may find it instructive to compare this with an accepting computation for *aaba* by the fa in (17-1).

To be rigorous we would have to give a proof that the method of construction just outlined does indeed produce a grammar equivalent to the original fa, but we will not do so here since the equivalence is intuitively evident. The main point is that we now have three quite different characterizations of the same class of languages: the languages accepted (or generated) by (deterministic or non-deterministic) finite automata, the regular languages, and the languages generated by Type 3 grammars. It is always useful to view mathematical objects from different perspectives; our understanding is enhanced, and new methods of proof are opened up. We also come to realize that we are dealing with a coherent, and in some sense "natural" mathematical class.

17.3.1   Properties of regular languages

We also gain in understanding of mathematical objects when we ascertain their behavior under various sorts of operations. Since languages are sets, it is natural to ask how they behave when subjected to certain set-theoretic manipulations. We have already seen, for example, that the class of fal's (= regular languages = Type 3 languages) is closed under the operation of union: i.e., the union of any two fal's is also a fal. Similarly, we know that the fal's are closed under concatenation and Kleene star. What about the operations of complementation and intersection?

Given a regular language $L \in \Sigma^*$, its complement, i.e., $\Sigma^* - L$, is also regular. How can we show it? Given our equivalent characterizations of this class of languages, we can make use of whichever one is most convenient for what we want to prove. In this case, the desired result is easiest to show with finite automata.

Let M be a deterministic fa accepting L. Construct a new fa M' from M by interchanging final and non-final states. That is, M' is identical to M except that all final states are now non-final and vice versa. M' is also deterministic. Now M and M' read any input string in the same way, in the sense that for a given string they go through the same state transitions. The only difference is that when M accepts (ends in a final state), M' rejects (ends in a non-final state), and when M rejects, M' accepts. Thus, M' accepts the complement of L, which is therefore also a fal.

For example, applying this construction to the fa of (17-1), we obtain the following deterministic fa which accepts $\{x \in \{a,b\}^* \mid x$ contains an even number of b's$\}$. This is clearly the complement of the original language.

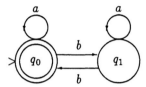

Figure 17–16.

Problem: Why wouldn't this procedure work in general if the original fa were not deterministic?

It now follows that the regular languages are also closed under intersection, since for any sets X and Y, $X \cap Y = (X' \cup Y')'$ by DeMorgan's Laws. In more detail, if X and Y are regular languages, then so are their complements, X' and Y', as we have just seen. The union of the latter, $X' \cup Y'$, is also regular, and the complement of the last set is also regular, i.e., $(X' \cup Y')'$, which is equal to $X \cap Y$.

Given then that the regular languages are closed under union, intersection and complementation, and that the empty language and Σ^* (for any given alphabet Σ) are regular, we have the result that the regular languages over any fixed alphabet form a Boolean algebra (see Ch. 12). This gives us some information about the class of regular languages but does not provide a complete characterization since there are other sets of languages which also form Boolean algebras (e.g., the set of *all* languages over a given alphabet) which are not regular.

Another frequently encountered problem concerning mathematical objects is this: What questions about them can be answered by algorithm? Or to put it another way, do there exist procedures which can be applied mechanically to any instance of one of these objects to yield an answer to a particular sort of question in a finite time?

An example of this sort of consideration as applied to finite automata would be: Given a fa M and a string x, can it be determined whether M accepts x or not? The answer in this case is yes. One procedure for answering this question would be the following. Given M, convert it to an equivalent deterministic fa M' (if M is not already deterministic.) There is an algorithm for performing this conversion, as we mentioned earlier. If $x \notin \Sigma^*$, we know it cannot be accepted, since it contains symbols not in the alphabet of M'. If $x \in \Sigma^*$, trace the computation of x by M'. There is a unique path through the state diagram of M' reading x which ends in some state q_i. If q_i is a final state, x is accepted; otherwise, x is rejected. Since the first part of the algorithm will yield an equivalent deterministic fa in a finite amount of time, the number of states of M being finite, and the second part will be accomplished in a finite number of steps, viz., the number of symbols of x, the procedure outlined is guaranteed to terminate after a finite time with the correct answer. This is an algorithmic solution to the so-called *membership question* for fal's.

Another example of a question about fa's which has an algorithmic solution is the *emptiness question*: given an fa M, does it accept any strings at all? One could proceed as follows. If M is not deterministic, make it so. The result is M', which necessarily has a finite number of states and a finite number of transitions. M' accepts at least one string just in case there is a path in its state diagram from the initial state to some final state. Furthermore, if there is any accepting path in M', there is an accepting path without loops in it. (Any path with loops can also be traversed by going through each loop zero times.) Since the number of states and state connections is finite, there are only a finite number of loop-free paths to examine to determine whether any ends in a final state. One could imagine systematic ways of looking at the paths, but the essential part here is not the relative efficiency of the process but only that it is a finite task. Thus, there is an algorithmic solution to the emptiness question for fa's.

Similarly, one might ask of a given fa, does it accept all strings in Σ^*? This can be reduced to the previous question by noting that Σ^* is the complement of $\emptyset$. Given M, make M deterministic if it isn't already, to produce M'. Interchange final and non-final states of M' to produce M''. Apply the algorithm for answering the emptiness question to M''. M'' accepts $\emptyset$ iff M' accepts Σ^*.

Problem: Given two fa's, M_1 and M_2, show that there is an algorithm for answering the question, is $L(M_1) \subseteq L(M_2)$ (Hint: $X \subseteq Y$ iff $(X \cap Y') = \emptyset$.)

Is there an algorithmic solution to the question of whether two fa's accept the same language?

17.3.2   Inadequacy of right-linear grammars for natural languages

Is English a regular language? We can prove that it is not, using the Pumping Theorem and the fact that regular languages are closed under intersection.

We assume that all the following are grammatical (although in some cases surely incomprehensible) English sentences:

(17–15) (1) The cat died.
         (2) The cat the dog chased died.
         (3) The cat the dog the rat bit chased died.
         (4) The cat the dog the rat the elephant admired bit chased died.
         etc.

These are all of the form:

(17–16) $(the + \text{common noun})^n$ (transitive verb)$^{n-1}$ intransitive verb

Let us take some finite set A of common noun phrases of the form $the +$ common noun:

(17–17) $A = \{\text{the cat, the dog, the rat, the elephant, the kangaroo},\ldots\}$

Let us also choose a finite set B of transitive verbs:

(17–18) $B = \{\text{chased, bit, admired, ate, befriended},\ldots\}$

Thus, the strings illustrated in (17-15) are all of the form:

(17–19) $x^n y^{n-1}$ died, where $x \in A$ and $y \in B$.

The language L consisting of all such strings, of which the sentences in (17-15) are members, is easily shown not to be regular. The proof uses the

Pumping Theorem and is very similar to the proof that $\{a^n b^n \mid n \geq 0\}$ is not regular.

L is the result of intersecting English (considered as a set of strings) with the *regular* language $A^* B^* \{died\}$. Since the regular languages are closed under intersection, if English were regular, L would be also. Thus, English is not regular.

The demonstration that English is not a finite automaton language was one of the first results to be achieved in the nascent field of mathematical linguistics (Chomsky, 1956; 1957, Chapter 3), although Chomsky did not use this particular method of proof, nor did he focus on the particular subset of English exemplified in (17-15). Rather, he pointed out that English has a certain number of constructions such as *either ... or*, *if ... then*, and the agreement between the subject of a sentence and the main verb, which can be thought of as obligatorily paried correspondences or *dependencies*. (In sentences of the form *Either S_1 or S_2*, we cannot substitute *then* or *and* for *or*, for example, and similarly, we cannot replace *then* in *If S_1 then S_2* by *and* or *or*, etc., and produce a grammatical sentence.) Further, these dependencies can be found in grammatical sentences nested one inside the other and to an arbitrary depth. Chomsky and Miller (1963) cite the following example in which the dependencies are indicated by subscripts:

(17-20) Anyone$_1$ who feels that if$_2$ so-many$_3$ more$_4$ students$_5$ whom we$_6$ haven't$_6$ actually admitted are$_5$ sitting in on the course than$_4$ ones we have that$_3$ the room had to be changed, then$_2$ probably auditors will have to be excluded, is$_1$ likely to agree that the curriculum needs revision.

This structure of nested dependencies finds an analog in the strings of a language like $\{x x^R \mid x \in \{a, b\}^*\}$ (recall that x^R denotes the reversal of the string x). In strings of this language, the ith symbol from the left must match the ith symbol from the right as indicated in the diagram of Fig. 17-17:

The language $x x^R$ can be shown not to be regular by first intersecting it with the regular language $a a^* b b a a^*$ to give $\{a^n b^2 a^n \mid n \geq 1\}$ and showing that the latter is not regular by means of the Pumping Theorem.

This result illustrates one sort of practical result that can sometimes be obtained from the study of formal grammars and languages. A linguistic theory proposes that the grammar of every natural language is drawn from some infinite class $\mathcal{G}$ of generative devices. (This is just to say that the

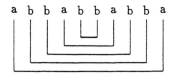

Figure 17–17.

linguistic theory specifies, as it should, the form that grammars may take.) Such a theory is supported, but not of course proven true, by each succesful prediction, i.e., whenever we are able to show that a grammar from $\mathcal{G}$ is adequate for some natural language. On the other hand, repeated failure to find an adequate grammar in $\mathcal{G}$ for, say, Swahili might raise doubts but would not suffice to prove the theory wrong. Since $\mathcal{G}$ is an infinite set, as it will be in all interesting cases, failure after a finite number of attempts may reflect only ineptness or bad luck. In certain cases, however, we may be able to demonstrate conclusively that a linguistic theory is inadequate for one or more natural languages, as we just did for the theory of right linear grammars vis-a-vis English. We are then justified in concluding that the theory is inadequate in principle and can be removed from consideration as a viable proposal.

Exercises

1. Consider the following state diagram:

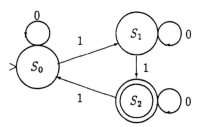

Figure 17–18.

(a) Which of the following strings are accepted by the machine?
  (i) 01011
  (ii) 0011
  (iii) 11001101
  (iv) 01010111111

(b) Describe as simply as possible the language accepted by the automaton.

2. Consider the following set of transition rules:

$(S_0, 0) \rightarrow S_0$ $(S_3, 0) \rightarrow S_0$
$(S_0, 1) \rightarrow S_1$ $(S_3, 1) \rightarrow S_4$
$(S_1, 0) \rightarrow S_2$ $(S_4, 0) \rightarrow S_0$
$(S_1, 1) \rightarrow S_3$ $(S_4, 1) \rightarrow S_5$
$(S_2, 0) \rightarrow S_0$ $(S_5, 0) \rightarrow S_0$
$(S_2, 1) \rightarrow S_1$ $(S_5, 1) \rightarrow S_5$
Final states: S_4, S_5.

(a) Draw a state diagram for this automaton.

(b) Describe the set of input strings accepted by the automaton.

(c) Draw a state diagram for an automaton which is equivalent to this one but which has four states.

3. Construct state diagrams for finite automata which accept the following languages using as few states as possible:

(a) The set of all strings containing a total of n 1's, where n is congruent to 1 (modulo 3) (i.e., the remainder when n is divided by 3 is 1).

(b) The set of all strings containing a total of exactly two 1's.

(c) The set of all strings which contain a block of at least three consecutive 1's, e.g.,
  010111001   but not   0101011011
  001111100   0011011000
  1101110111   1101100101

(Note that once such a block occurs, it is irrelevant what comes later.)

(d) The set of all strings which contain no block of more than one
consecutive 0 nor any block of more than one consecutive 1, e.g.,

0	but not	0101101
e		11
101		11010
101010		
0101		

(e) The set of all strings which contain the substring 101 anywhere
within them.

(f)* The set of all strings in which the total number of 0's is congruent
to the total number of 1's modulo 3 (see part (a) above).

4. Consider non-deterministic finite automata whose input alphabet is
{*the, old, man, men, is, are, here, and*}.

(a) Construct a state diagram for an automaton which accepts the
following language: {*the man is here, the men are here*}.

(b) Do the same for the following language: {*the man is here, the
men are here, the old man is here, the old men are here, the old
old man is here, the old old men are here,*...}.

(c) Construct a state diagram for an automaton which accepts all
the sentences in (b) plus all those formed by conjoining sentences
with *and*, e.g., *the old man is here and the old old men are here
and the men are here.*

5. (a) Construct a state diagram for an automaton which accepts the
terminal language of the following grammar. (The input alphabet
is {a, b, c}; it does not include S or C.)

$S \rightarrow SS$ $S \rightarrow bb$
$S \rightarrow aCa$ $C \rightarrow Cc$
$S \rightarrow bCb$ $C \rightarrow c$
$S \rightarrow aa$

(b) Draw a diagram for an automaton whose language is that of part
(a) plus the empty string.

6. Show how, given any finite automaton, you can construct an equivalent one which has no transition arrows leading to the initial state.

All automata asked for in exercises 7 and 8 may be non-deterministic, and of course must be finite state. The input alphabet is to be $\{0,1\}$.

7. (a) Construct an automaton A which accepts any string which contains no 1's.

   (b) Construct an automaton B which accepts any string which contains an odd number of 1's, with any number (including zero) of 0's.

   (c) Construct an automaton C which accepts the union $L(A) \cup L(B)$.

   (d) Construct an automaton D which accepts the complement $L(C)'$. (*Caution*: first find a deterministic equivalent of C.) Describe $L(D)$ in words.

8. (a) Construct an automaton A which accepts any string which contains *no* block of four or more consecutive 1's.

   (b) Construct an automaton B which accepts any string which contains no block of three or more consecutive 0's.

   (c) Construct an automaton C which accepts the intersection $L(A) \cap L(B)$.

9. Find a regular expression for the language of:

   (a) Exercise 4a. (above)

   (b) Exercise 4b.

   (c) Exercise 4c.

   (d) Exercise 3b.

   (e) Exercise 3e.

10. Draw a state diagram for a finite automaton corresponding to the following regular expressions.

    (a) 010^*1

    (b) $(010^*1)^*$

    (c) $(010^*1)^*1$

    (d) $(010^*1)^*1(0 \cup 1)^*$

    (e) $1(010^*1)^*$

(f) $1(010^{-}1)^{*}(0 \cup 1)^{*}$ (Hint: this one can be done by a simpler machine than any of the others.

11. Construct Type 3 grammars that generate each of the following languages. Assume a fixed terminal vocabulary $V_T = \{a, b\}$.

    (a) $L_1 = \{aa, ab, ba, bb\}$

    (b) $L_2 = \{x \mid x$ contains any number of occurrences of a and b in any order$\}$

    (c) $L_3 = \{x$ contains exactly two occurrences of a, not necessarily contiguous$\}$

    (d) $L_4 = \{x \mid x$ contains exactly one occurrence of a, or exactly one occurrence of b, or both$\}$

    (e) $L_5 = \{x \mid x$ contains an even number of a's and an even number of b's$\}$ (Zero counts as even.)

    (f) $L_6 = L_3 \cap L_5$

12. Construct finite automata (non-deterministic) accepting each of the languages in Exercise 11.

Chapter 18

Pushdown Automata, Context Free Grammars and Languages

18.1 Pushdown automata

We turn next to a class of automata which are more powerful than the finite automata in the sense that they accept a larger class of languages. These are the pushdown automata (pda's).

A pda is essentially a finite automaton with an auxiliary tape on which it may read, write, and erase symbols. This tape is organized as a *stack* or *pushdown store* similar in principle to the spring-loaded devices for holding plates seen in cafeterias. Both work on the basis of "last in, first out;" that is, the most recently added item is the first one to be removed. Items below the topmost ones cannot be reached without first removing items above them on the stack.

Pda's, like finite automata, read their input tapes from left to right and have a finite number of internal states. There is a designated initial state, and a set of final, or accepting, states. The transitions of a pda, however, allow the top symbol of the stack to be read and removed, added to, or left unchanged. We can represent these transitions schematically as $(q_i, a, A) \rightarrow (q_j, \gamma)$, where q_i and q_j are states, a is a symbol of the input alphabet, A is a symbol of the stack alphabet (which need not be the same as the input alphabet), and γ is a string of stack symbols. Such an instruction is interpreted as follows: when in state q_i, reading a on the input tape, and reading A at the top of the stack, go to state q_j and *replace A by the string* γ. If γ were, for example, the string BC, the A would be removed and BC added to the stack (in the order B first, C next) so that C would now become the top symbol on the stack. In case γ is e, the empty string, the net effect is to remove ("pop") A from the stack. The symbol next below A, if any, would then become the top symbol. If γ were, for example, AB, the effect would be to add ("push") a B on top of the A. If γ were A, the transition would leave the stack unchanged.

We also allow e to appear in the position of A in the above schema. In this case the transition does not depend on the contents of the stack since e can always be read at the top of the stack whatever it may actually contain. Note that the e here does *not* indicate that the stack must by empty. If $A = e$ and $\gamma = B$, for example, the transition would push B onto whatever was already on the stack.

The stack is assumed to be empty at the beginning of a computation with the pda in its initial state and the reading head positioned over the left-most symbol of the input. An input tape is accepted if the computation leads to a situation in which all three of the following are simultaneously true:

(i) the entire input has been read

(ii) the pda is in a final state

(iii) the stack is empty

One could define acceptance by empty stack or final state or, as we have done, by both, and the resulting classes of automata turn out to be equivalent. This choice is convenient for our purposes. The following is an example of a pda which accepts the language $\{a^n b^n \mid n \geq 0\}$:

(18–1) States: $K = \{q_0, q_1\}$
        Input alphabet: $\Sigma = \{a, b\}$
        Stack alphabet: $\Gamma = \{A\}$
        Initial state: q_0
        Final states: $F = \{q_0, q_1\}$

        Transitions: $\Delta = \begin{cases} (q_0, a, e) \rightarrow (q_0, A) \\ (q_0, b, A) \rightarrow (q_1, e) \\ (q_1, b, A) \rightarrow (q_1, e) \end{cases}$

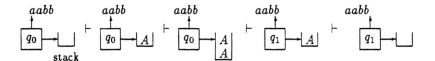

Figure 18–1.

Fig. 18-1 shows how this pda would accept input *aabb*.

Since the entire input is read and the pda halts in a final state with an empty stack, this input is accepted.

The reader should also be able to verify the following statements about the behavior of this pda:

(i) *ba* is rejected: the pda blocks in state q_0 and fails to read the entire input

(ii) *aaabb* is rejected: the pda halts in state q_1 with A on the stack

(iii) *aabbb* is rejected: the pda fails to read the last *b* since there is no A on the stack

(iv) *e* is accepted: the computation begins and ends in q_0 with an empty stack

This machine works by using its stack as a counter for keeping track of the number of *a*'s in the initial part of the input string. Once a *b* is found, it switches to state q_1 and begins popping an A from the stack for each *b* encountered. Only if the number of *b*'s equals the number of *a*'s will the stack be empty at the end (and the entire input string read).

Problem: Why is it necessary to go to a new state when the first *b* is encountered, i.e., why not stay in state q_0?

Here is an example of a pda which accepts the language $\{xx^R \mid x \in \{a,b\}^*\}$

(18–2) $K = \{q_0, q_1\}$, $\Sigma = \{a, b\}$, $\Gamma = \{A, B\}$,

  Initial state $= q_0$, $F = \{q_0, q_1\}$

$$\Delta = \left\{ \begin{array}{ll} (q_0, a, e) \to (q_0, A) & (q_0, b, B) \to (q_1, e) \\ (q_0, b, e) \to (q_0, B) & (q_1, a, A) \to (q_1, e) \\ (q_0, a, A) \to (q_1, e) & (q_1, b, B) \to (q_1, e) \} \end{array} \right\}$$

This machine works by putting an image of the left half of its input string on the stack (in the form of capital letters), and then, after non-deterministically "guessing" that the middle of the string has been reached, comparing each input symbol in the right half against the top symbol of the stack. If the symbols correspond, the stack symbol is removed; if not, the machine blocks. Since symbols come off the stack in the reverse of the order in which they went on, the stack will be emptied just in case the right half of the input is the reversal or "mirror image" of the left half.

This pda is non-deterministic since there is more than one move available to the automaton in certain situations. If, for example, it has just read an a in state q_0 (and therefore put an A on the stack) and is now reading another a, it could execute either the first or the third instruction above. The former corresponds to the "pushing" mode in which the image of the left half is being placed onto the stack; the latter corresponds to a decision that the middle of the string has just been encountered and that it is time to switch from pushing to popping mode. As with the finite automata, we say that a non-deterministic pda accepts if there exists *at least one* computational path on which the input is accepted; an input is rejected if there is no such accepting path. By this definition, the above machine accepts the language $\{xx^R \mid x \in \{a, b\}^*\}$.

The pda in (18-1), by contrast, is said to be deterministic, in that it has at most one move available to it for any situation. Unlike the finite automata, we do not insist that deterministic pda's have one move available for *every* situation; rather, that in no situation is more than one move allowed. One can determine from inspection of the instructions of a pda whether it is deterministic or properly non-deterministic. A pda is deterministic iff there are no two distinct instructions $(q_i, a, A) \rightarrow (q_j, \gamma)$ and $(q_i, a, A') \rightarrow (q_k, \delta)$ such that $A = A'$ or $A = e$ or $A' = e$. Thus, as with the finite automata, the deterministic machines are a proper subset of the non-deterministic.

The question then naturally arises as to whether deterministic and non-deterministic pda's are equivalent. The answer is that they are not, although it is not a simple matter to give a proof of this fact. We will simply note that this result agrees with our intuition that no deterministic pda could be devised to accept $\{xx^R \mid x \in \{a, b\}^*\}$, there being no way in general for a pda reading strictly left to right to tell with certainty when the center of the input string has been reached. In contrast, the language $\{xcx^R \mid x \in \{a, b\}^*\}$ in which the center of the string is marked by the c is easily acceptable by a deterministic pda.

It is often a matter of some practical interest to be able to tell whether a non-deterministic pda language is also accepted by some deterministic pda. This is so because many programming languages—languages used for writing instructions for computers to execute—belong to the class of non-deterministic pda languages. When programs are compiled, i.e., translated into sequences of 1's and 0's for execution by the computer, the compilation process is carried out by what is in effect a pda, and if this pda can be made deterministic, then the process can be made more efficient by avoiding backtracking or the pursuit of alternative paths. Most programming languages in current use are in fact deterministic pda languages (or nearly so), but it is an unfortunate fact that there is no way to tell in general whether any arbitrarily given non-deterministic pda language is also a deterministic pda language.

We end this section by giving formal definitions of pda's and the related notions of situation, acceptance, and so on. Note that in the following we have generalized the notion of a transition of a pda to allow the possibility that a *string* of input symbols and a *string* of stack symbols can be read on a single move. This does not affect the power of the automata and has the advantage of bringing the definitions into a form parallel to those for non-deterministic finite automata. A non-deterministic finite automaton will thus appear formally as a non-deterministic pda which never makes use of its stack.

DEFINITION 18.1 *A non-deterministic pushdown automaton is a sextuple* $\langle K, \Sigma, \Gamma, \Delta, s, F \rangle$, *where* K *is a finite set of states,* Σ *is a finite set (the input alphabet),* Γ *is a finite set (the stack alphabet),* $s \in K$ *is the initial state,* $F \subseteq K$ *is the set of final states, and* Δ, *the set of transitions, is a finite subset of* $K \times \Sigma^* \times \Gamma^* \times K \times \Gamma^*$. ∎

DEFINITION 18.2 *A situation of a pda is a quadruple* (x, q, y, z) *where* $q \in K$, $x, y \in \Sigma^*$, *and* $z \in \Gamma^*$. ∎

The intended interpretation is that the pda is in state q with x to the left of the reading head, y to the right of the reading head with the left-most symbol of y currently being scanned, and z *is* the contents of the stack.

DEFINITION 18.3 *Given a non-deterministic pda* M, *we say that situation* (x, q, y, z) *produces* (x', q', y', z') *in-one-move iff* $x' = x\alpha$, $y = \alpha y'$, $z = \gamma w$, $z' = \delta w$, *and* $(q, \alpha, \gamma) \rightarrow (q', \delta) \in \Delta$. ∎

DEFINITION 18.4 *Produces is the reflexive, transitive closure of the* produces-in-one-move *relation.*

These are denoted, as usual, by $\overset{*}{\vdash}_M$ *and* $\vdash_M$, *respectively.*   ∎

DEFINITION 18.5 *Given a pda* M, *a string* $x \in \Sigma^*$ *is accepted iff* (e, s, x, e) $\overset{*}{\vdash}_M (x, q, e, e)$ *for some* $q \in F$. *The language accepted by* M *is the set of all strings accepted.*   ∎

DEFINITION 18.6 *A pda is* deterministic *iff for no pair of distinct transitions,* $(q_i, x_i, \gamma_i) \rightarrow (q_j, \delta_j)$ *and* $(q_k, x_k, \gamma_k) \rightarrow (q_l, \delta_l)$ *is it the case that* $q_i = q_k$, *and* x_i *is a substring of* x_k *or vice-versa, and* γ_i *is a substring of* γ_k *or vice-versa.*   ∎

18.2   Context free grammars and languages

Non-deterministic pda's accept exactly the languages generated by context free (Type 2) grammars. Recall that in a context free grammar every rule is of the form $A \rightarrow \psi$, where A is a non-terminal symbol and ψ is any string, possibly empty, from the union of the terminal and non-terminal alphabets. It follows from this definition that every right-linear grammar is also a context free grammar, and therefore that the regular languages are contained in the context free languages. This containment is proper since, as we have seen, $\{a^n b^n \mid n \geq 0\}$ is not a regular language, but it can be generated by the simple context free grammar containing only the two rules $S \rightarrow aSb$ and $S \rightarrow e$.

The proof of the equivalence of context free languages and non-deterministic pda languages is too long and complex to give here. To give something of the flavor of this proof, we will show an algorithm for constructing from any given context free grammar an equivalent non-deterministic pda (but we will not prove formally that the constructed pda is actually equivalent). For the construction in the reverse direction—from non-deterministic pda to equivalent context free grammar—we refer the reader to Hopcroft and Ullman (1979) or Lewis and Papadimitriou (1981), which also contain references to the original sources.

Given a context free grammar $G = \langle V_N, V_T, S, R \rangle$, we construct an equivalent non-deterministic pda M as follows. The states of M are q_0 and q_1, with q_0 being the start state and q_1 being the only final state. The input alphabet is V_T and the stack alphabet $V_N \cup V_T$. The transitions of M are constructed out of the rules of G in the following way:

(i) M contains the instruction $(q_0, e, e) \rightarrow (q_1, S)$

(ii) For each rule of the grammar $A \rightarrow \psi$, M contains an instruction $(q_1, e, A) \rightarrow (q_1, \psi)$.

(iii) For each symbol $a \in V_T$, M contains an instruction $(q_1, a, a) \rightarrow (q_1, e)$.

As an example, let us take G to be as follows:

(18-3) $V_N = \{S\}$; $V_T = \{a, b\}$; $R = \{S \rightarrow aSb, S \rightarrow e\}$

(This is the grammar we referred to above which generates $\{a^n b^n \mid n \geq 0\}$.)

According to the construction procedure just given, M will contain the following:

(18-4) $K = \{q_0, q_1\}$; $\Sigma = \{a, b\}$; $\Gamma = \{S, a, b\}$; $s = q_0$; $F = \{q_1\}$;

$$\Delta = \left\{ \begin{array}{l} (q_0, e, e) \rightarrow (q_1, S) \\ (q_1, e, S) \rightarrow (q_1, aSb) \\ (q_1, e, S) \rightarrow (q_1, e) \\ (q_1, a, a) \rightarrow (q_1, e) \\ (q_1, b, b) \rightarrow (q_1, e) \end{array} \right\}$$

M accepts the input string $aabb$ by the following computation: $(e, q_0, aabb, e)$ $\vdash$ $(e, q_1, aabb, S)$ $\vdash$ $(e, q_1, aabb, aSb)$ $\vdash$ (a, q_1, abb, Sb) $\vdash$ $(a, q_1, abb, aSbb)$ $\vdash$ (aa, q_1, bb, Sbb) $\vdash$ (aa, q_1, bb, bb) $\vdash$ (aab, q_1, b, b) $\vdash$ $(aabb, q_1, e, e)$

M works by loading S onto its stack and then simulating a derivation there by manipulations which correspond to the rewriting rules of G. When a terminal symbol appears at the top of the stack, it is popped off if it matches the symbol being read on the input; otherwise the computation blocks. When a non-terminal appears at the top of the stack it is rewritten in a way licensed by the rules of G. Thus, M carries out what is in effect a left-most derivation (one in which the left-most non-terminal symbol is rewritten at each step) according to the grammar. If the derived terminal string matches the input, the stack will be emptied, the entire input read, and the string accepted.

Note that pda's constructed in this way will in general be non-deterministic since there may be in the grammar more than one rule rewriting some non-terminal A.

18.3   Pumping Theorem for cfl's

There is a Pumping Theorem for the cfl's which is similar in form to the
Pumping Theorem for fal's. It is useful primarily in showing that a particular
language is not context free.

The theorem makes use of the fact that a derivation by a cfg can be
naturally associated with a parse tree (see Section 16.4), and the fact that
the maximum width of any such parse tree is constrained by its height. Let
us see what this means in more detail.

Given a cfg G, there is some maximum number of symbols on the right
hand side of any rule. Suppose, for example, that no rule has a right hand
side longer than 4 symbols. This means that in one rule application, the
width of the tree (the number of symbols in its yield) can have increased
by at most 3. If each of the 4 symbols just introduced should happen to
be expanded into 4 symbols, then by these steps the single node could have
grown into 16 symbols, *but no more than 16 symbols.* If we define the height
of a tree to be the length of the longest path in it extending continuously
downward from the root, then what we have said is that (for a given grammar) the maximum width of a parse tree is bounded by its height. More
specifically, if n is the maximum length of a right side of the rules of G, then
the maximum width of a parse tree generated by G of height h is just n^h.
(It may in fact be considerably less than this, depending on the exact nature
of G, but we are interested here only in setting an upper bound.) To phrase
this another way, if a parse tree for some grammar G has width greater than
n^m, where n is the maximum length of the right side of rules of G, we can
be sure that the height of the tree is greater than m.

Let us now suppose that G has m non-terminal symbols in its alphabet.
If we find a parse tree generated by G of width greater than n^m, then there
must be some continuously descending path in the tree of length greater than
m, and thus some non-terminal symbol must appear at least twice along this
path (there being only m symbols to choose from). Let us represent this
situation by the diagram in Fig. 18-2.

The repeated non-terminal is called A. S dominates a terminal string
w, and so each non-terminal in the tree must also dominate some terminal
string. Let x be the terminal string dominated by the lower A, and vxy the
terminal string dominated by the upper A. (x must be a substring of this
string since, by hypothesis, the lower A is dominated by the upper A.) Let u
and z be terminal strings dominated by S to the left and right, respectively,

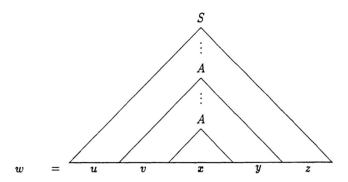

Figure 18–2.

of vxy. This general situation must obtain whenever there is a repeated non-terminal along some path in a parse tree.

But note that the lower subtree rooted by A could have stood in the place in the tree where the upper A-rooted tree stands. The rules of G are, after all, context free, so if it is possible to rewrite A in one position ultimately to yield x, the same is possible in any position in which A appears. Thus, the tree in Fig. 18-3 must also be generated by G.

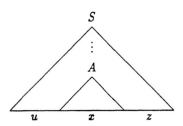

Figure 18–3.

Further, the lower A in Fig. 18-2 could have been rewritten as the upper one was, to produce the tree shown in Fig. 18-4.

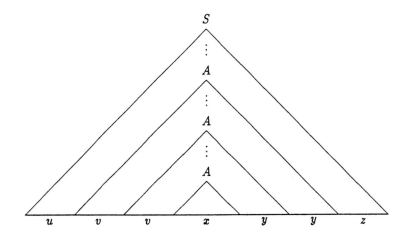

Figure 18–4.

Since we know that the derivation can be terminated by rewriting the lowest A, ultimately to give x, it follows that the string $uvvxyyz$ must also be generated by G. The process just illustrated could, of course, be carried out any finite number of times; thus, uv^ixy^iz is generated for all $i \geq 0$. We are now ready to state the Pumping Theorem for context free languages.

THEOREM 18.1 *If L is an infinite context free language, then there is some constant K such that any string w in L longer than K can be factored into substrings $w = uvxyz$ such that v and y are not both empty and $uv^ixy^iz \in L$ for all $i \geq 0$.* ■

Note that if L is an infinite language then it is guaranteed to contain strings longer than any given constant K. What is K? It is a number which depends on the grammar for L and which is big enough to ensure that any strings longer than K have derivation trees with a repeated non-terminal along some path. There is always such a K for any cfg since G contains a finite number of non-terminal symbols, and there is some maximum to the degree of branching allowed on the right sides of rules.

What about the stipulation that v and y are not both empty? If they were, we could get from A to A on a branch of a derivation tree without generating any terminal symbols either to the left or right. This situation could arise, since rules of the form $A \to B$, $B \to C$, $C \to A$ are allowed in a cfg. However, not all the non-terminals in the grammar could appear only in rules of this form or else the grammar could not generate an infinite language. That is, there must be *some* non-terminal symbol A which can be repeated along some path, i.e., $A \overset{*}{\underset{G}{\Rightarrow}} vAy$, such that not both v and y are empty, and further, such a non-terminal must appear in the derivation of any string longer than K.

Note that like the Pumping Theorem for fal's, this theorem is a conditional but not a biconditional. Given a language L, it is not particularly informative to find strings u, v, x, y, z such that $uv^i xy^i z \in L$ for all $i \geq 0$. Rather, we use the theorem in its contrapositive form: if there do not exist strings u, v, x, y, z such that..., then we can conclude that L is not an infinite cfl. Let us see how this can be done in the case of the language $L = \{a^n b^n c^n \mid n \geq 0\}$.

Suppose L were context free. Since it is infinite, the Pumping Theorem must apply, and there would be some constant K such that any string in L longer than K—let us choose $a^K b^K c^K$, for example—would be factorable into $uvxyz$ such that v and y are not both empty and the v and y are pumpable. We show that no such factorization can exist.

First, v cannot consist of both a's and b's, because when it is pumped, it would produce strings containing b's before a's, which cannot be in L. Similarly, v cannot consist of both b's and c's, and the same argument applies to the other pumpable term, y. Therefore, the only possibilities remaining are for v to consist of just a's or just b's or just c's. Then no matter how we choose y, the result of pumping v and y simultaneously gives strings not in L. Suppose, for example, that v consists of a's and y of b's. Then on pumping v and y the a's and b's increase but not the c's, and we get strings not in L. The other cases are similar. We conclude that there is no choice of u, v, x, y, z meeting the conditions of the Pumping Theorem for this language; therefore, L is not context free.

18.4   Closure properties of context free languages

Given the class of context free languages (identical to the non-deterministic pda languages), we want to investigate whether this class is closed under operations such as union, intersection, complementation, etc. We will see that unlike the fal's the cfl's are not so conveniently and tidily closed under all these operations.

Union: Given two cfg's $G_1 = \langle V_{N_1}, V_{T_1}, S_1, R_1 \rangle$ and $G_2 = \langle V_{N_2}, V_{T_2}, S_2, R_2 \rangle$, we form grammar G in the following way. If the non-terminals of G_1 and G_2 are not disjoint sets, we make them so (by appending primes to every symbol of G_2, say). The start symbol of G we take to be S, and G contains, in addition to R_1 and R_2, the rules $S \to S_1$ and $S \to S_2$. G is context free, and it generates $L(G_1) \cup L(G_2)$ since the start symbol may be either rewritten as S_1, whereupon G behaves like G_1, or as S_2, whereupon G behaves like G_2. A string $x \in (V_{T_1} \cup V_{T_2})^*$ is generated by G just in case it is generated by G_1 or by G_2 (or both). Since this method of construction is general (and, as the reader will have noted, quite similar to that used in showing that the fal's are closed under union; see Section 17.2), we conclude that the cfl's are closed under union.

Concatenation (or Set Product): The method of construction is similar to that for union except that instead of the two rules mentioned there we add to G the single rule $S \to S_1 S_2$. Thus, G will generate all strings of the form xy such that $x \in L(G_1)$ and $y \in L(G_2)$. Further, G will generate only such strings, and, again, since the method of construction is general, we conclude that the cfl's are closed under concatenation.

Kleene Star: Given $G = \langle V_N, V_T, S, R \rangle$, we construct G^* as follows: The start symbol of G^* is S', and G contains, in addition to all the rules in R, the rules $S' \to e$ and $S' \to S'S$. G^* generates all strings in $(L(G))^*$ since by application of the rules rewriting S', G^* produces strings S^n for all $n \geq 0$. Each such S can be rewritten to produce a string in $L(G)$, and e is produced by the rule $S' \to e$. Further, all strings in $(L(G))^*$ can be generated in this way. Thus, the cfl's are closed under Kleene star.

Problem: Why was it necessary to introduce the new start symbol S'? Why not just add the rules $S \to SS$ and $S \to e$?

Intersection: The cfl's are *not* closed under intersection. To see this, we note that the languages $\{a^i b^i c^j \mid i, j \geq 0\}$ and $\{a^k b^l c^l \mid k, l \geq 0\}$ are both context free. The former is generated by a grammar containing the rules:

(18–5) $S \to BC$
        $B \to aBb$
        $B \to e$
        $C \to cC$
        $C \to e$

and the grammar for the latter is similar. The intersection of these two languages, however, is $\{a^n b^n c^n \mid n \geq 0\}$, which we proved above by the Pumping Theorem not to be a context free language.

Recall in this connection what it means to say that a set is not closed under a certain operation. We have shown that the intersection of two cfl's is sometimes not a cfl. It is not claimed that the result is *never* a cfl. Indeed, this could not be so, since the regular languages are necessarily cfl's, and since the regular languages are closed under intersection, the result is regular, hence, context free.

Complementation: The cfl's are not closed under complementation. Given two cfl's L_1 and L_2 over some alphabet Σ, if their complements L_1' and L_2' (i.e., $\Sigma^* - L_1$ and $\Sigma^* - L_2$, respectively) were context free, then so would be their union, $L_1' \cup L_2'$. The complement of this, in turn, $(L_1' \cup L_2')'$, would also be context free, but this is equal by DeMorgan's Laws to $L_1 \cap L_2$, which is not necessarily context free. Hence, the complement of a cfl is not necessarily a cfl.

Intersection with a Regular Language: Although the intersection of two arbitrary cfl's L_1 and L_2 is not in general a cfl, it happens that if one of the languages is restricted to being regular, then the intersection is always a cfl. A demonstration of this fact is somewhat involved and depends on constructing a non-deterministic pda accepting $L_1 \cap L_2$ out of a pda accepting L_1 and a finite automaton accepting L_2. (The non-closure of cfl's under intersection implies that it is not in general possible to coalesce two non-deterministic pda's in this way.)

The closure of the cfl's under intersection with a regular language can be a convenience in showing certain languages not to be context free. For example, the language $L = \{x \in \{a, b, c\}^* \mid x$ contains equal numbers of a's, b's, and c's$\}$, although not context free, resists application of the Pumping Theorem. However, if L is first intersected with the regular language $a^* b^* c^*$, the result is $\{a^n b^n c^n \mid n \geq 0\}$, which we have shown not to be context free. Now if L were a cfl, its intersection with a regular language would also be a cfl; hence, L is not context free.

18.5   Decidability questions for context free languages

Context-free languages differ from fal's also in respect to which questions can be answered by algorithm. For the fal's we saw that there were algorithms for answering questions such as membership, emptiness, etc. We shall see that some of these questions have algorithmic solutions for the cfl's and some do not.

Membership: Given an arbitrary cfg G and an arbitrary string x, is x generated by G? One might propose an algorithm for answering this question of the following sort: Start producing derivations by G in some systematic fashion, discarding any whose last lines are longer than x. This will be some finite number of derivations. If x has not been generated by this point, it is not going to be.

As matters stand, this algorithm might not be successful for two reasons: first, the grammar may contain rules of the form $A \rightarrow e$, which allows derivations to become shorter. Thus, we cannot be sure that we can stop examining derivations when their last lines reach the length of x. A derivation might produce longer strings which then shrink to produce x. Second, because rules such as $A \rightarrow B$, $B \rightarrow C$, $C \rightarrow A$, etc. might be present in the grammar, derivations might continue indefinitely without their final strings getting any longer. This subverts our claim that we need to examine only a finite number of derivations to see if any generate x. The proposed algorithm would work, however, if we could somehow contrive to remove all rules of both types from a cfg while leaving the generative power of the grammar unchanged. We will now show that this can in fact be done.

If there is a rule $A \rightarrow e$ in the grammar, this rule can be dispensed with if we add more rules to the grammar in the following way. Whenever A appears on the right side of a rule we add another rule identical to it except that the A on the right is deleted. For example, given rules $A \rightarrow e$ and $B \rightarrow cAbBa$, we would add the rule $B \rightarrow cbBa$. Now what would have been accomplished by application of the first two rules in sequence can be accomplished by the last rule alone. The original rule is of course preserved since there may be other rules expanding A. We continue in this way for every rule containing an A on the right side, and repeat the process for every non-terminal which can be rewritten as e. (Note that if such a non-terminal appeared more than once on a right side, e.g., $B \rightarrow aAbAc$, we would add rules $B \rightarrow abAc$, $B \rightarrow aAbc$, and $B \rightarrow abc$.) This process must eventually come to an end since there are finitely many rules to begin with, there are a finite number of non-terminals, and a finite number of rules are added at each step. When we are done, we may remove all rules of the form $A \rightarrow e$ from the grammar since they are superfluous. The one exception is the rule $S \rightarrow e$, if it is present, which must be retained in order to generate the empty string as a member of the language. The presence of this rule will not interfere with the workings of our algorithm, however, since if there is a derivation of some non-empty string x which involves one or more applications of the rule $S \rightarrow e$, there will also be, after carrying out the procedure just outlined, a derivation of x which does not involve any applications of this rule. Thus, we can produce an equivalent cfg in which derivations are essentially non-shrinking.

What about rules of the form $A \rightarrow B$? These can be removed in the following way. Pick a rule of the form $A \rightarrow w$, where w is something other than a single non-terminal symbol. (If there are no such rules, the grammar generates no terminal strings and the membership question is settled at once.) Now for each non-terminal C distinct from A, determine whether $C \overset{*}{\underset{G}{\Rightarrow}} A$, i.e., whether C can be rewritten in some finite number of steps to give A. This can be done by examining all sequences $C, B_1, B_2, \ldots, B_n, A$ (where B_1, B_2, are single non-terminals) of length no more than the number of non-terminals in the grammar to see whether they are allowed by the grammar. The restriction on length of derivations is possible because if there is such a derivation with repeated symbols $C \Rightarrow \ldots \Rightarrow B_i \Rightarrow \ldots \Rightarrow B_i \Rightarrow B_j \Rightarrow \ldots \Rightarrow A$ then there is also a shorter one with the section between repetitions removed: $C \Rightarrow \ldots \Rightarrow B_i \Rightarrow B_j \Rightarrow \ldots \Rightarrow A$. Thus, the number of non-terminals fixes an upper bound on the length of such derivations, and we can effectively determine whether $C \overset{*}{\underset{G}{\Rightarrow}} A$. If so, then we add the rule $C \rightarrow w$ to the grammar, and thus the derivation $C \overset{*}{\underset{G}{\Rightarrow}} A \underset{G}{\Rightarrow} w$ can be replaced by the derivation $C \underset{G}{\Rightarrow} w$ directly. We continue this process for all rules of the form $A \rightarrow w$ ($w \notin V_N$) and all non-terminals distinct from A. When we have finished, all rules of the form $A \rightarrow B$ can be removed from the grammar without affecting the terminal strings generated.

Once all these steps have been carried out, the proposed algorithm for answering the membership question can be executed and is guaranteed to lead to an answer in a finite amount of time. No claim is made that this is particularly *efficient* way to answer the membership question, but we are not concerned with relative amounts of computational labor here—only with showing that the question can be answered in some finite amount of time by mechanical means.

Emptiness: Does an arbitrarily given cfg G generate any strings at all? There is an algorithm for answering this, the emptiness question, and it depends on the following observation. If G generates any terminal strings, it generates some terminal string with a parse tree which has no non-terminals repeated along any path. Refer again to Fig. 18-2 which we used in proving

the Pumping Theorem. If a parse tree for some terminal string has a repeated
non-terminal A along some path, the subtree rooted by the upper A could
be replaced by the subtree rooted by the lower A, and the result is also a
parse tree for a terminal string generated by the grammar (cf. Fig. 18-3).
Clearly all repeated occurrences of non-terminals could be removed in this
way. Thus, in order to see whether G generates any terminal strings, all
we have to do is examine the finite number of parse trees which contain no
repeated elements along any path. The exact number we need to look at
will depend on the number of non-terminals in the grammar and the degree
of branching allowed by the rules of G, but it will be finite. If no terminal
string has appeared as the yield of a tree by this point, none is ever going
to appear. This answers the emptiness question.

Undecidable questions: Many problems concerning context free languages
have no algorithmic solution. We cannot provide demonstrations of these
facts here since they require results from Turing machine theory, which we
have not yet examined. We will simply list some of the more important
undecidable questions:

a. Given an arbitrary context free grammar G, there is no algorithm for
determining:

   (i) whether $L(G) = V_T^*$, i.e., whether G generates all strings over the
   terminal alphabet
   (ii) whether the complement of $L(G)$, i.e., $V_T^* - L(G)$, is empty, infinite, regular, or context free.

b. Given two arbitrary context free grammars G_1 and G_2, there is no algorithm for determining:

   (i) whether $L(G_1) \subseteq L(G_2)$
   (ii) whether $L(G_1) = L(G_2)$
   (iii) whether $L(G_1) \cap L(G_2) = \emptyset$
   (iv) whether $L(G_1) \cap L(G_2)$ is infinite, regular, or context free.

Recall that the lack of a single algorithm for deciding every one of an infinite
class of cases does not preclude the possibility that for *certain* context free
grammars these questions might be answerable. In fact, for all context free
grammars which happen to be regular, there are algorithmic solutions to all
of the above questions, as we saw in Section 17.3.1.

18.6 Are natural languages context free?

In Section 17.3.2 we showed that English could not be a regular language. Could it or any other natural language be context free? This question has attracted considerable attention in the years since Chomsky first outlined the hierarchical categorization of formal languages (1963). The prevailing view has been that natural languages are not context free. Attempts to demonstrate this have usually centered on finding instances of so-called "cross-serial" dependencies of arbitrarily large size in some particular language. In a cross-serial dependency, items are linked in left-to-right order as shown in Fig. 18-5.

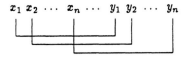

Figure 18-5.

(Compare this to the nested dependencies illustrated in Fig. 17-17.)

A language such as $\{xx \mid x \in \{a,b\}^*\}$ exhibits cross-serial dependencies (for strings of length $2n$ in the ith and $(n+i)^{th}$ symbols must match) and is not context free.

Pullum and Gazdar (1982) review the various attempts to establish that natural languages are not context free and find all of them either formally or empirically flawed. In the latter category are instances in which claims that certain forms are ungrammatical are unjustified and more probably involve semantic or pragmatic anomaly. A common formal mistake was to assume that because one has found a subset of a language which exhibits cross-serial dependency the language as a whole is thereby shown not to be context free. Note that the non-context free language $\{xx \mid x \in \{a,b\}^*\}$ is a subset of the context free (indeed, regular) language $\{a,b\}^*$.

Recently, however, evidence has appeared for the non-context freeness of Swiss German which seems unassailable on either formal or empirical grounds (Shieber, 1985). Swiss German, like its much studied cousin Dutch, allows cross-serial order in dependent clauses. Sentences like the following are grammatical:

(18–6)   Jan säit das mer em Hans es huus hälfed aastriiche
         John said that we Hans–Dat the house–Acc helped paint
         "John said that we helped Hans paint the house."

(18–7)   Jan säit das mer d'chind em Hans es huus lönd hälfe aastriiche
         John said that we the children – Acc Hans – Dat the house – Acc
         let help paint
         "John said that we let the children help Hans paint the house."

The NP's and the V's of which the NP's are objects occur in cross-serial order: in (18-7) *d'chind* ("the children") is the object of *lönd* ("let"), *em Hans*
is the object of *hälfe* ("help"), and *es huus* ("the house") is the object of *aastriiche* ("paint"). Furthermore, the verbs mark their objects for case: *Hälfe*
requires dative case, while *lönd* and *aastriiche* require accusative. Sentences
in which the case marking does not follow this restriction are uniformly rejected by native speakers as ungrammatical. (Since case marking is unlikely
to be accounted for semantically or pragmatically, this avoids the empirical
trap mentioned above.) It also appears that there are no limits other than
performance constraints on the length of such constructions in grammatical
sentences of Swiss German. Shieber then intersects Swiss German with the
regular language:

(18–8) $R =$ Jan säit das mer (d'chind)*(em Hans)* es huus haend wele
         (laa)* (hälfe)* aastriiche

         John said that we (the children)* (Hans)* the house have
         wanted to (let)*(help)* paint

(Here the *haend wele* ("have wanted to") is present in order to put all the
succeeding verbs in their infinitive forms. Schieber shows that this insertion
does not affect grammaticality judgments.)

The result of intersecting R and Swiss German is all sentences of the following
form:

(18–9) $L =$ Jan säit das mer (d'chind)^n(em Hans)^m es huus haend wele
         (laa)^n (hälfe)^m aastriiche

where the number of nouns in the accusative case matches the number of

verbs requiring this case and similarly for the dative case, and all accusative
case nouns (except the constant "es huus") precede all dative case nouns and
all accusative-case marking verbs precede all dative-case marking verbs. The
strings of this sublanguage of Swiss German are of the form $wa^n b^m xc^n d^m y$,
which can be shown to be non-context free by the Pumping Theorem. Since
the context free languages are closed under intersection with a regular language, this demonstrates fairly convincingly that Swiss German is not context free.

Note that the formal difficulty mentioned above has been avoided. The
sublanguage of Swiss German shown to be non-context free is not merely a
subset of the original but a subset obtained by intersection with a regular
language. The latter operation preserves context freeness while the operation
of simply selecting a subset in general does not.

Attempts to arrive at the corresponding results for Dutch could not succeed because Dutch does not have verbs with differing case-marking properties which can occur in arbitrarily long cross-serial dependent clauses.

Exercises

1. Construct context free grammars generating each of the following languages.

   (a) $L_1 = a^n b^m a^n (n, m \geq 1)$

   (b) $L_2 = a^n b^n a^m b^m (n, m \geq 1)$

   (c) $L_3 = \{x \mid x \in \{a, b\}^* \text{ and } x \text{ contains twice as many } b\text{'s as } a\text{'s } \}$

   (d) $L_4 = \{xx^R \mid x \in \{a, b\}^*\}$

   (e) $L_5 = \{x \in \{a, b\}^* \mid x = x^R\}$

2. Show that for every context free grammar there is an equivalent grammar in which all productions are of the form $A \rightarrow BC$ or $A \rightarrow a$
   (A, B, C in V_N, a in V_T). Such a grammar is said to be in *Chomsky
   Normal Form* (Chomsky, 1959).

3. Show by means of the Pumping Theorem that the following languages
   are not context free.

   (a) $\{a^{n^2} \mid (n \geq 1)\}$

   (b) $\{a^n \mid n \text{ is prime (i.e., divisible only by 1 and by itself)}\}$

4. Given a language L we define the *reversal* of L, denoted L^R, as $\{x^R \mid x \in L\}$, where x^R is the reversal of x. Show that the context free languages are closed under reversal.

5. Construct a deterministic pda which accepts the language $(ab)^n(cd)^n$ for all $n \geq 1$. (The parentheses are not part of the language nor do they indicate optionality; they are used in the expression above only for grouping.)

6. Construct a deterministic pda which accepts every string of the form xc, where x is a string of a's and b's of length 0 or more in which the total number of a's is exactly equal to the total number of b's.

7. Construct a non-deterministic pda which accepts every string which is of the form $a^n b a^n$ or of the form $a^{2n} b a^n$ for all $n \geq 1$.

8. Is the union of the languages of two determinsitc pda's necessarily the language of some deterministic pda? Justify your answer.

9. Show by means of the Pumping Theorem for context free languages that $a^i b^j c^{\max(i,j)}$ is not context free, where $\max(i,j)$ is the larger of i and j.

Chapter 19

Turing Machines, Recursively Enumerable Languages and Type 0 Grammars

19.1   Turing machines

We have seen that a pushdown automaton can carry out computations which are beyond the capability of a finite automaton, which is perhaps the simplest sort of machine able to accept an infinite set of strings. At the other end of the scale of computational power is the Turing machine (after the English mathematician, A. M. Turing, who devised them), which can carry out any set of operations which could reasonably be called a computation.

Like the previous classes of automata, a Turing machine can be visualized as having a control box, which at any point is in one of a finite number of states, an input tape marked off into squares with one symbol of the input string being inscribed on each square, and a reading head which scans one square of the input tape at a time. The Turing machine, however, can write on its input tape as well as read from it, and it can move its reading head either to the left or to the right. As before, a computation is assumed to begin in a distinguished initial state with the reading head over the leftmost symbol of the input string. We also assume that the tape extends infinitely to the left and right and that all tape squares not occupied by symbols of the input string are filled by a special "blank" symbol #.

The moves of a Turing machine (henceforth, TM) are directed by a finite set of quadruples of the form (q_i, a_j, q_k, X), where q_i and q_k are states, a_j is a symbol of the alphabet, and X is either an alphabet symbol or one of the special symbols L or R. Such a quadruple is interpreted in the following way: if the TM is in state q_i scanning a_j, then it enters state q_k (possibly identical to q_i) and if X is a symbol of the alphabet, it *replaces* a_j by that symbol. If X is L or R, then a_j is left unchanged and the reading head is moved one square to the left or right, respectively.

In the formulation we shall adopt, TM's are assumed to be deterministic; i.e., for each state and each alphabet symbol there is at most one move allowed. We do not insist that there be a move for every state-symbol pair (this is similar to the formulation of deterministic pda's), and so if the TM reaches a point in its computation at which no instruction is applicable, it *halts*.

We note that a TM may in general read and write the blank symbol # and thus may extend its computation into portions of the tape beyond that originally occupied by the input string. Since it is not necessarily blocked by the #'s surrounding the input, one possibility open to a TM, but not to fa's or pda's, is that it might compute forever. This is an important property of TM's, as we shall see.

For example:

(19–1) The set of states K is $\{q_0, q_1\}$; the alphabet Σ is $\{a, b, \#\}$; the initial state is q_0; the set of instructions δ is written with an arrow between left and right halves for clarity:

$(q_0, a) \rightarrow (q_1, b)$
$(q_0, b) \rightarrow (q_1, a)$
$(q_0, \#) \rightarrow (q_1, \#)$
$(q_1, a) \rightarrow (q_0, R)$
$(q_1, b) \rightarrow (q_0, R)$

This machine scans an input string from left to right, changing a's to b's and b's to a's, until it encounters the first #. It then rewrites the # as #, changes state to q_1 and halts (since there is no instruction beginning $(q_1, \#)$). Since a # is sure to be found eventually, this TM has the property of halting on all inputs. Note, however, that if it had also contained the instruction $(q_1, \#) \rightarrow (q_1, R)$, then it would compute forever once it had reached the string of #'s to the right of the input. The same result could also be achieved by the instruction $(q_1, \#) \rightarrow (q_1, \#)$, except that instead of scanning endlessly to the right, the TM would stay on one tape square forever reading and writing #.

(19–2) Example of computation:

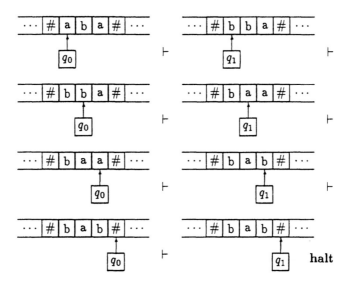

We have not designated the states of a TM as final or non-final. It would be perfectly feasible to do so and to define acceptance of an input string in terms of halting in a final state. It will be slightly more convenient, however, to say that a string is accepted if, when it is given to the machine in the standard starting configuration, it causes the TM to halt after some finite number of moves; otherwise, it is rejected (i.e., the TM never halts). In (19–3) we give a machine which accepts all strings in $\{a, b\}^*$ which contain at least one a and which rejects, i.e., computes forever, when given anything else in $\{a, b\}^*$. (Note that we are here concerned only with strings in $\{a, b\}^*$ not $\{a, b, \#\}^*$. TM's are assumed always to be able to read and write the # symbol, but we will ordinarily confine ourselves to strings over alphabets which do not contain #. A TM which accepts some language in $\{a, b\}^*$ may give bizarre results when given a string not in this alphabet, but that doesn't matter. We are only concerned with its behavior when given inputs from the relevant set.)

(19-3) $M = \langle K, \Sigma, s, \delta \rangle$; $K = \{q_0, q_1\}$; $\Sigma = \{a, b, \#\}$; $s = q_0$;

$$\delta = \begin{cases} (q_0, a) \rightarrow (q_1, R) \\ (q_0, b) \rightarrow (q_0, R) \\ (q_0, \#) \rightarrow (q_0, R) \\ (q_1, a) \rightarrow (q_1, R) \\ (q_1, b) \rightarrow (q_1, R) \end{cases}$$

This machine scans left to right and stays in state q_0 so long as it sees b's. Once it encounters an a, it changes to state q_1 and continues rightward in this state until the first $\#$ and then halts. It if meets the first $\#$ in state q_0, it scans right forever.

19.1.1 Formal definitions

DEFINITION 19.1 *A Turing machine M is a quadruple $\langle K, \Sigma, s, \delta \rangle$, where K is a finite set of states, Σ is a finite set (the alphabet) containing $\#$, $s \in K$ is the initial state, and δ is a (partial) function from $K \times \Sigma$ to $K \times (\Sigma \cup \{L, R\})$.* ∎

A situation of a TM will be a quadruple of the form (x, q, a, y), where q is the current state, a is the symbol being scanned, and x and y are the strings to the left and right, respectively, of the reading head *up to the beginnings of the infinite strings of $\#$'s.* This last provision is necessary to insure that a situation is uniquely specified. The TM in (19-2) is in situation (e, q_0, a, ba) at the beginning of the computation and in $(bab, q_1, \#, e)$ when it halts.

DEFINITION 19.2 *A situation of a TM $M = \langle K, \Sigma, s, \delta \rangle$ is any member (x, q, a, y) of $\Sigma^* \times K \times \Sigma \times \Sigma^*$ such that x does not begin with $\#$ and y does not end with $\#$.* ∎

We omit the formal definition of the *produces-in-one-step* relation, $\vdash_M$, on pairs of situation since it is rather complex when specified in full detail. Note that one must allow for cases such as the following: the TM is in situation $(abb, q, \#, e)$, as shown in Fig. 19-1, and executes the instruction $(q, \#) \rightarrow (q', L)$. The resulting situation is (ab, q', b, e), as in Fig. 19-2, where the $\#$ originally being scanned has joined the infinite string of $\#$'s to the right and has thus dropped out of the formal specification of the situation.

In a similar vein, if the instruction had been $(q, \#) \rightarrow (q', R)$, the resulting situation would be $(abb\#, q', \#, e)$ with a # taken from the string of #'s to the right and placed under the reading head.

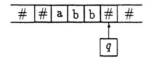

Figure 19-1.

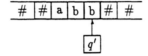

Figure 19-2.

Given the produces-in-one-step relation, we define the *produces* relation, $\vdash_M^*$ as its reflexive transitive closure.

DEFINITION 19.3 *Given a TM $M = \langle K, \Sigma, s, \delta \rangle$ and Σ_1, a subset of Σ which does not contain #, we say that M accepts a string $x = a_1 a_2 \ldots a_n \in \Sigma_1^*$ iff $(e, s, a_1, a_2 \ldots a_n) \vdash_M^* (y, q, b, y')$, where y and y' are strings in Σ^*, $b \in \Sigma$, and there is no instruction in δ beginning (q, b) (i.e., M has halted). (In case $x = e$, the initial situation is $(e, s, \#, e)$.)* ∎

DEFINITION 19.4 *A TM M accepts a language $L \in \Sigma_1^*$ iff M accepts all strings in L and rejects (i.e., fails to halt on) all strings not in L.* ∎

Note that we have defined acceptance so that it holds only of strings and languages defined over alphabets not containing #. This is primarily a technical convenience.

DEFINITION 19.5 *We say that a language is* Turing acceptable *iff there is some TM which accepts it.*   ∎

In virtue of Example (19-3) above, we can say that the language $L = \{x \in \{a,b\}^* \mid x$ contains at least one $a\}$ is Turing acceptable. In fact, all the regular languages and the deterministic and non-deterministic pda languages are Turing acceptable. (It should not be too difficult to imagine how one would go about constructing a TM to mimic the behavior of a fa or a pda.) Are there any languages, then, which are not Turing acceptable? There are, but it is not easy to exhibit one. We will return to this important question below.

We have seen that a given TM might not halt on certain inputs—indeed, we make use of this property in characterizing rejection of an input string. But this presents us with a problem. Suppose we have set a TM to computing on some input and it has not yet halted. Can we tell in general whether it is going to halt eventually or whether it is going to compute forever? This is the renowned Halting Problem for Turing machines, and we will show in a later section that there is, in general, *no* way to tell—at least if we mean by "a way to tell" some explicit procedure which can be computed mechanically by, say, a Turing machine. Another way to formulate the Halting Problem is this: Could we take any TM which accepts a language L and convert it into a machine which halts on all inputs (over the relevant alphabet) and signals its acceptance or rejection of the input by, say, the state it is in (or some special symbol printed on the tape, etc.)? Let us, in fact, make the following definition:

DEFINITION 19.6 *A TM* $M = \langle K, \Sigma, s, \delta \rangle$ *with some designated set* $F \subseteq K$ *of* final *states, decides a language* $L \subseteq \Sigma_1^*$, *(where* $\Sigma_1 \subseteq \Sigma$ *and does not contain* #*) iff for all* $x \in \Sigma_1^*$, *M halts in a final state if* $x \in L$ *and M halts in a non-final state if* $x \notin L$.   ∎

DEFINITION 19.7 *We say that a language is* Turing decidable *iff there is some TM which decides it, in the sense just defined.*   ∎

It is not difficult to convert the TM of Example (19-3) above into one which decides, rather than accepts, the language $L = \{x \in \{a,b\}^* \mid x$ contains at least one $a\}$—simply remove the instruction $(q_0, \#) \to (q_0, R)$ and designate q_1 as the only final state. The question is whether such a conversion can always be carried out. If so, then every Turing acceptable language is Turing decidable. and, provided that the conversion can be carried out "mechanically", i.e., algorithmically, the Halting Problem is solvable. Since this turns out not to be so, we will have to conclude that there are Turing acceptable languages which are not Turing decidable. Again, most of the languages one ordinarily encounters as examples in formal language theory are Turing decidable, so one must look further afield to find one which is not.

Note that the implication in the opposite direction is easy to establish: every Turing decidable language is Turing acceptable. Given a TM which decides a language L, it is a simple matter to convert it into a TM which computes forever just in case the original machine would have halted in a non-final state. (Just add instructions which rewrite symbols as themselves while staying in the same state).

Turing machines are probably most often viewed not as language acceptors but as devices which compute functions. The initial input string is the argument for the function, and the expression on the tape when the machine halts (if it halts) is taken to be the value of the function at that argument. For example, the TM of (19-1) computes the function $f : \{a, b\}^* \to \{a, b\}^*$ such that when $f(u) = v$, v is like u with a's and b's interchanged. If the TM does not halt for a certain input, the function is not defined at that argument. Thus, TM's in general compute partial functions, but a TM which halts for all inputs in some set A computes a total function from A to its range. A TM which decides a language $L \subseteq \Sigma_1^*$, in the sense just defined, computes the characteristic function of L. A TM which accepts L computes a different function—one which is defined for all strings in L and undefined for all other strings in Σ_1^*.

By coding natural numbers as strings—say, in binary or in a unary encoding in which n a's represent the natural number n—we can let TM's serve a computers of functions from natural numbers to natural numbers. We can then ask whether functions such as $f(x) = x^2$ or $f(x) = x!$ are computable by Turing machine (they are, in fact, as are most of the functions ordinarily encountered). We can generalize this approach to functions of k arguments by letting the initial string given to the TM be, say, k blocks of a's of appropriate size separated by #'s. The TM which computes the addition function on natural numbers, for example, would start with $\ldots \#\# a^n \# a^m \#\# \ldots$ on its tape and end with $\ldots \#\# a^{n+m} \#\# \ldots$

Functions which are computable by Turing machine are called *partial recursive functions* (*partial*, because the TM may not halt for all arguments and thus may leave some values of the function undefined). The Turing computable functions which happen to be total functions ought to be called "total recursive functions," but aren't. They're called simply *recursive functions*. A recursive function, thus, is a function which can be computed by a Turing machine which halts on all inputs in the domain of the function.

A TM may also be regarded as a device for generating, rather than accepting or deciding, a set of strings. Let a TM be given as input some encoding of a natural number (say, n a's representing n) and let it compute until it halts, if it does. The contents of its tape between the infinite strings of #'s is some string over the alphabet of the TM (which may contain more than a's, of course), and this string is said to be generated by the TM. The set of all such strings generated, given all the natural numbers as inputs, is said to be the set *recursively enumerated* by the TM. A set is said to be *recursively enumerable* (abbreviated *r.e.*) if there is some TM which recursively enumerates it in the way just described.

It turns out that a set of strings is r.e. just in case it is Turing acceptable. That is, if A is recursively enumerated by some TM T, there is a TM T' which accepts A, and conversely. (We will omit the proof of this result.)

Note also that a set which is recursively enumerated constitutes the range of a partial recursive function from the natural numbers to the set of all strings over the alphabet of A. In fact it is inessential here that the domain be the natural numbers—any denumerably infinite set would do. Thus, we can say that a set is recursively enumerable if it is the range of some partial recursive function. The following three statements, therefore, are equivalent:

(19–4)   (i) A is accepted by some TM.
         (ii) A is the range of some partial recursive function.
         (iii) A is recursively enumerated by some TM.

19.2   Equivalent formulations of Turing machines

There are many ways in which Turing machines can be defined which turn out to be equivalent in computational power. The input tape can be stipulated to be infinite in one direction only, or the machine can be endowed with any finite number of tapes which extend infinitely in one or both directions, or the machine may have one multiple-track tape with multiple reading heads. It may even be regarded as operating on an n-dimensional grid extending infinitely in all dimensions, so long as n is a finite number.

Even making a TM non-deterministic does not change its capabilities in any essential way. Suppose a non-deterministic TM had k distinct moves allowed from any given situation. Then from the initial situation there could be at most k possible situations after one step, at most k^2 after two steps, ..., at most k^n after n steps of the computation. A deterministic TM could keep track of all of these (at some expenditure of tape and time). If there is a halted computation by the non-deterministic machine, it occurs in some finite number of steps r. The deterministic machine will therefore discover this fact after having examined at most k^r possible situations—again, a finite number—and can then halt. A language accepted by some non-deterministic TM can therefore be accepted by a deterministic TM.

What seems to be essential to the formulation of a Turing machine, therefore, is that it has a finite number of states, a finite alphabet, a finite number of instructions, and an unbounded amount of computational space available to it.

19.3   Unrestricted grammars and Turing machines

An unrestricted (or Type 0) grammar $G = \langle V_T, V_N, S, R \rangle$ is one in which the only limitation on the form of the rules is that the left side contain at least one non-terminal symbol. Thus, letting upper case letters be non-terminals and lower case letters be terminals as usual, $aAbb \rightarrow ba$, $aAbB \rightarrow e$, and $A \rightarrow bCaB$ would all be allowed rules in such a grammar. Rules such as $ab \rightarrow ba$, $b \rightarrow BA$, or $e \rightarrow aA$ would be excluded. Note that because more than one symbol may be replaced in Type 0 rules, it is in general not possible to associate a phrase structure tree with a derivation in such a grammar.

Type 0 grammars can generate languages which are not context free. Here, for example, is an unrestricted grammar generating $\{x \in \{a, b, c\}^* \mid x$ contains equal numbers of a's, b's, and c's $\}$ which, as we have seen, is not a cfl.

(19–5) $G = \langle \{a, b, c\}, \{S, A, B, C\}, S, R \rangle$, where

$$R = \begin{cases} S & \rightarrow SABC & AC \rightarrow CA & A \rightarrow a \\ S & \rightarrow e & CA \rightarrow AC & B \rightarrow b \\ AB & \rightarrow BA & BC \rightarrow CB & C \rightarrow c \\ BA & \rightarrow AB & CB \rightarrow BC & \end{cases}$$

This grammar works by producing strings of the form $(ABC)^n$ then permuting non-terminals freely by means of the rules $AB \rightarrow BA$, etc. Finally,

non-terminals are rewritten as the corresponding terminals. Here is a derivation of *cabbca*.

(19–6) $S \Rightarrow SABC \Rightarrow SABCABC \Rightarrow ABCABC \Rightarrow ACBABC \Rightarrow$
$CABABC \Rightarrow CABBAC \Rightarrow CABBCA \Rightarrow \ldots \Rightarrow cabbca$

And here is a Type 0 grammar generating the non-context free language
$\{xx \mid x \in \{a,b\}^*\}$:

(19–7) $G = \langle \{a,b\}, \{S,S',A,B,\#\}, S, R \rangle$, where

$$R = \begin{cases} S \rightarrow \#S'\# & Aa \rightarrow aA & \#a \rightarrow a\# \\ S' \rightarrow aAS' & Ab \rightarrow bA & \#b \rightarrow b\# \\ S' \rightarrow bBS' & Ba \rightarrow aB & A\# \rightarrow \#a \\ S' \rightarrow e & Bb \rightarrow bB & B\# \rightarrow \#b \\ & & \#\# \rightarrow e \end{cases}$$

Here is a derivation of *abaaba*:

(19–8) $S \Rightarrow \#S'\# \Rightarrow \#aAS'\# \Rightarrow \#aAbBS'\# \Rightarrow \#aAbBaAS' \Rightarrow$
$\#aAbBaA\# \Rightarrow \#abABaA\# \Rightarrow \#abAaBA\# \Rightarrow \#abaABA\# \Rightarrow$
$a\#baABA\# \Rightarrow a\#baAB\#a \Rightarrow \ldots \Rightarrow aba\#\#aba \Rightarrow abaaba$

This grammar works by generating sequences of aA's and bB's between $\#$'s
as endmarkers and then letting the non-terminals migrate to the right, where
they can hop over the $\#$ and become terminals. The terminals in the left
half similarly hop over the left end marker, and when the two $\#$'s meet in
the middle they are erased.

The languages generated by the Type 0 grammars are exactly the languages accepted by Turing machines, i.e., the r.e. sets. We will not give
detailed proofs of this equivalence here but will simply suggest how the
proofs are constructed.

Given a Type 0 grammar G generating $L(G)$ a TM M accepting $L(G)$
can be constructed as follows. M is non-deterministic and has two tapes.
Its input is given on the first tape where it is stored intact throughout the
computation. The instructions of M essentially mimic the rules of G. The
initial symbol S is placed on the second tape, and M proceeds to rewrite
as G would. After the application of each rule, M compares the contents of
the second tape with the input on tape 1. If they match, M halts, and thus
accepts its input. If they do not match, M continues applying rules of G to

the string on tape 2, and if no rule is applicable, M cycles endlessly in some fashion. Clearly, if there is a derivation of the input string by G, there will be some computation by M which discovers this fact and thus M will halt and accept. If there is no such derivation, M computes forever, as required.

The simulation in the reverse direction—making a Type 0 grammar mimic a Turing machine—depends essentially on the fact that a situation of a TM can be regarded simply as a finite string of symbols and that to get from one situation to the next, some substring of these symbols is rewritten as some other string. For example, a TM instruction of the form $(q, a) \rightarrow (q', b)$ would correspond to the grammar rule $qa \rightarrow q'b$. Thus, situation (aab, q, a, bb) becomes (aab, q', b, bb) in one move by the machine, and, correspondingly, the string $aabqabb$ is rewritten as $aabq'bbb$ by the grammar. Left-moving and right- moving TM instructions require somewhat more complicated grammar rules to cover all possibilities. The details are tedious and not too instructive. Now, given a TM M which accepts language $L(M)$, we first convert it to a machine M' which behaves like M up to the point at which M would halt. M', however, replaces all non-blank symbols on its tape by #'s, then writes S, and halts in some designated state q_1. Thus, M' accepts $L(M)$ also but does so in such a way that it always halts in situation (e, q_1, S, e).

We now construct G so that it simulates the moves of M' in reverse. The initial symbol of G is S', and it first rewrites S' as $q_1 S$. Then, mimicking the moves of M' in reverse it can arrive at the string $q_0 x$, where q_0 is the initial state of M' and x was the input accepted. Now all G has to do is to erase q_0, thereby generating x. The only complication here is that we don't want to erase q_0 unless it is part of an initial situation of M'; i.e., q_0 might be entered at other points in the computation by M', and we don't want to erase it in these cases. This difficulty can be taken care of by adding new states to M' to insure that once it has left its initial state q_0 it never enters it again in the course of any computation. With this repair, the grammar G generates exactly the strings accepted by M' (and M). Thus, we can add a fourth equivalent statement to those given in (19-4) above:

(iv) A is generated by some unrestricted grammar.

19.4 Church's Hypothesis

An *algorithm* is a fixed, deterministic procedure which can be applied mechanically to yield a result within a finite amount of time. For example, there is an algorithm for finding the square root of any positive number to any desired number of decimal places. Algorithms are normally designed to apply to a *class* of problems, not to a single problem. The algorithm for finding square roots can be applied in the same way to *any* positive number—we do not have to hunt for a new procedure for every case.

Some classes of problems do not have algorithmic solutions. There is no algorithm, for example, for supplying proofs for theorems of geometry. To find a proof for a given theorem often requires some ingenuity, skill, and even luck, whereas algorithms, by definition, demand only simple clerical abilities.

The definition of algorithm given above is not mathematically precise, relying as it does on such intuitive notions as "mechanical." In the 1930's, a number of attempts were made to find a precise, formal characterization of the notion of algorithm as applied to mathematical problems. The Turing machine was the result of one such attempt. It is clear that a Turing machine satisfies our intuitive notion of what an algorithm should be; a TM which computes a function, for example, determines the value at any agrument in a fixed, deterministic, mechanical way and in a finite amount of time. The question then arises whether all things which we would intuitively call algorithms can be formulated as Turing machines. The conjecture that this is indeed the case has been given the name *Church's Thesis* or *Church's Hypothesis* (after the logician Alonzo Church). It is not a theorem, since it relates a mathematical construct—the Turing machine—to an intuitive, imprecise notion—an algorithm. It is nonetheless widely believed to be correct. The evidence in its favor arises basically from the fact that all independent attempts to characterize the notion of algorithm by mathematicians such as Kleene, Post, Markov, Church, and others turned out to be equivalent to the Turing machine. Rogers (1967) calls this the Basic Result in Recursive Function Theory:

> The classes of partial functions (and hence total functions) obtained by the characterization of Turing, Kleene, Church, Post, Markov, and certain others, are identical, i.e., are just one class.

Further support for Church's Hypothesis comes from the fact that modifications and enrichments to the definition of a Turing machine which keep intact our view of it as a mechanical computing device with a finite number of states and instructions but with a potentially unlimited amount of space for computation, always produce an equivalent device.

These results suggest that the characterizations are not purely arbitrary but do in fact define a natural concept, i.e., sets which are recognizable, or functions which are computable, by algorithm. If we accept Church's Hypothesis, then, we may add a fifth equivalent statement to the list in (19-4) above.

(v) There is an algorithm for recognizing strings in A.

19.5   Recursive versus recursively enumerable sets

A Turing machine which accepts a set A halts eventually whenever given a member of A as input but fails to halt when given a non-member of A. If we accept Church's Hypothesis, this means that an algorithm may work in such a way that it yields an answer in a finite amount of time for all members of a particular class but may yield no result for things not in the class. It may happen, however, that there exist algorithms for recognizing not only all members of A but also one for recognizing all members of $\Sigma^* - A$, i.e., the complement of A. When this is so, A is called a *recursive set*. To state the definition formally in terms of Turing machines, a set A is recursive iff both A and A' are recursively enumerable (= Turing acceptable). It now follows that the recursive sets are just the Turing decidable languages defined above. Recall that a language is Turing decidable if there is some TM which halts on all inputs over the relevant alphabet and signals whether or not the input was in the language. As we have seen, it is a simple matter to convert a TM which decides L into one which accepts L (or into one which accepts L') by causing it to compute forever on negative outcomes. Conversely, if we were given two TM's, one accepting L and one accepting L', we could construct a TM for deciding L by having it simply alternate the instructions of the two machines on two copies of the input. One of these will eventually halt, since by assumption both L and L' are Turing acceptable, and then our composite machine can signal whether the input was in L or L'. Thus it decides L.

Analogous remarks could be made about computation of functions rather than recognition of sets. The functions which are algorithmically computable are, by Church's Hypothesis, just the parital recursive functions. If the function is properly partial and not total, the algorithm will yield no value at arguments for which the function is not defined. If the function is total, however, the algorithm yields a value at each argument. As we have seen, a TM which decides a language in effect computes the characteristic function of that language. The recursive sets, then, are just those which have recursive characteristic functions. The recursively enumerable sets have characteristic functions which are partial recursive functions. We may summarize our statements about recursive sets as follows:

(19-9)   The following statements are equivalent:

   (i) A is a recursive set

   (ii) A is Turing decidable

   (iii) Both A and A' are recursively enumerable

   (iv) A has a characteristic function which is (total) recursive.

We do not yet officially know, of course, whether there are actually any r.e. sets which are not recursive. We turn our attention to this matter in the next section.

19.6   The universal Turing machine

Since a Turing machine is defined as a finite set of quadruples together with a designated initial state (the set of states and the alphabet are implicit in the quadruples), it is possible to enumerate all possible Turing machines. To be somewhat more explicit, we might code the states and alphabet symbols as sequences of 1's and separate them by 0's. A complete coding for a Turing machine might, then, look something like this:

We might also agree on a fixed order of listing the quadruples so that each TM has a unique representation in this coding scheme. We could now enumerate TM's by listing them with machines with the smallest number of quadruples first in increasing order according to their encodings interpreted as a binary number. Thus we have a one-to-one correspondence between TM's and the natural numbers. (Incidentally, this fact shows us that there must be languages which are not Turing acceptable simply by considering the cardinalities of the sets involved. Given a finite alphabet A, there are $\aleph_0$ strings in A^*. There are $2^{\aleph_0}$ subsets of A^*, i.e., languages over the alphabet A. By Cantor's Theorem, $2^{\aleph_0} > \aleph_0$ and since there are only $\aleph_0$ Turing machines, there is an uncountable infinity of languages over any given alphabet which are not Turing acceptable.)

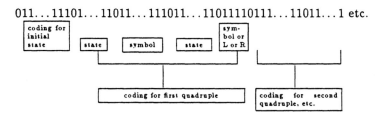

Figure 19–3.

Let us also assume that input strings are encoded into 1's and 0's in some fixed fashion. We may also assume without loss of generality that whatever output a TM leaves on its tape can also be encoded into 1's and 0's. Let us denote by $E(M)$ an encoding of a Turing machine M and by $E(x)$ the encoding of an input string x. It now turns out that there is a TM U, the universal Turing machine, which can take as input $E(M)E(x)$ and mimic the behavior of M on x. That is, if M halts on x, U halts given $E(M)E(x)$ and leaves on its tape an encoding of whatever output M would have left when it halted; if M does not halt on x, then U does not halt on $E(M)E(x)$.

We will not attempt to give the construction of U here, but it can be thought of as a three-tape machine which keeps on its tapes (1) the encoded instructions of M, (2) an encoded version of the non-blank portion of the tape M would have at each point in its computation, and (3) an encoded representation of the current state. U consults tape 3 for the current state, examines tape 2 to see which symbol is under the reading head (of M) and then consults tape 1 to find the instruction beginning with that state and symbol. If none is found, M would have halted, and U halts. If one is found, U makes the appropriate changes to tape 2, changes the state on tape 3 and repeats the cycle.

To dispel any possible air of mystery surrounding the universal Turing machine, let us point out that simulating the moves of any given TM on any given input tape falls under the class of procedures which can be carried out in purely mechanical fashion. (Think what would be involved if you were asked to carry out this task yourself.) It is therefore executable by a

Turing machine. The universal character of the machine arises from the fact
that all Turing machines and input tapes are given an encoding over a fixed
alphabet (here, 1's and 0's, although any convenient alphabet would do).
Thus U needs to be programmed only to find instructions and carry them
out on tapes all coded in the same way.

Another way of formulating what we have just said is that the language
$\{E(M)E(x) \mid M$ accepts $x\}$ is Turing acceptable. This is a language over
the alphabet $\{1,0\}$, and it is accepted by the Turing machine U (actually, a
slight variant of U which first checks to see if the string which it has received
as input is in fact of the right form to be a TM encoding followed by a string
encoding; this again is an easily arranged mechanical procedure.)

19.7   The Halting Problem for Turing machines

We are now ready to address the problem mentioned above, namely, the
problem of deciding for an arbitrarily given TM and an arbitrarily given
input string whether the TM will ever halt on that input. Given our method
of encoding TM's and input strings, it is easy to state the halting problem
in terms of Turing acceptable and Turing decidable languages. We have just
seen that the language

(19–10) $L = \{E(M)E(x) \mid M$ accepts $x\}$

is a Turing acceptable language. Thus, in order to determine whether M
halts given x, simply give the encoding of M and the encoding of x to
(modified) U. If M halts on x, U will also. But now if M does not halt on
x, U doesn't halt either. We want to know if there is some way to tell that
M will *not* halt on x when that is the case. In other words, is L *Turing
decidable*? Is there some TM which will halt and say yes if M halts on x,
and will halt and say no when M does not halt on x?

We will show that this cannot be the case. Assume L is Turing decidable
by some TM M_L. Since L is decidable for all $E(M)$ and $E(x)$, it will be
decidable in the special case in which x happens to be $E(M)$ itself. It may
seem strange to give a Turing machine its own encoding as an input tape,
but since this encoding is just a long string of 1's and 0's, there is nothing
in principle to prevent us from doing so. That is, the following language L_1
is Turing decidable if L is:

(19–11) $L_1 = \{E(M) \mid M \text{ accepts } E(M)\}$

It would in fact be decided by a TM M_1 which first encodes its input and copies it directly to the right of the original and then behaves like M_L.

But now, since L_1 is decidable, it follows that its complement is decidable and hence, Turing acceptable; i.e., there is a TM, call it M^*, which accepts L_1'.

(19–12) $L_1' = \{x \in \{0,1\}^* \mid x \text{ is not a TM encoding, or else } x \text{ is the encoding}$
       of a TM T and T does not accept $E(T)$ (i.e., x)$\}$

We now ask whether the encoding of M^* itself is in L_1'; that is, is M^* a machine which does not accept its own encoding as input?

First case: $E(M^*) \in L_1'$. Then $E(M^*)$ is one of the strings accepted by M^*, by the assumption that M^* accepts L_1'. So M^* accepts $E(M^*)$. But because $E(M^*) \in L_1'$, it is the encoding of a Turing machine which does *not* accept its own encoding, i.e., M^* does not accept $E(M^*)$. Contradiction.

Second case: $E(M^*) \notin L_1'$. Then $E(M^*)$ is *not* a string accepted by M^*, by the assumption that M^* accepts L_1'. So M^* does not accept $E(M^*)$. Therefore, M^* is a TM which does not accept its own encoding; therefore $E(M^*)$ is a member of L_1'. Contradiction.

Since $E(M^*)$ must either be in L_1' or not in L_1', and either assumption leads to a contradiction, we conclude that there is no such machine as M^*; thus, L_1' is not Turing acceptable (our first example of a set of this sort). But the Turing acceptability of L_1' was implied by its Turing decidability, which in turn was implied by the Turing decidability of L_1. Therefore, we conclude that L_1 cannot be Turing decidable after all. Finally, L_1's Turing decidability was implied by the assumed Turing decidability of L. Thus, we conclude that L is not Turing decidable, and the Halting Problem for Turing machines is not decidable by Turing machine; hence, given Church's Hypothesis, not decidable by algorithm.

Note that in the process of proving the undecidability of the Halting Problem, we have exhibited a set which is not Turing acceptable (namely, L_1') and sets which are Turing acceptable but not Turing decidable (namely, L and L_1). We can thus state the following:

THEOREM 19.1 *There are sets which are not recursively enumerable.* ∎

THEOREM 19.2 *There are sets which are recursively enumerable but not recursive.* ∎

As we have seen, these are not ordinary garden variety sets. The latter are exemplified by the set of all encodings of TM's which accept their own encodings as input; the former by the set of all Turing machines (in encoded form) which do not accept their own encodings as input. However, having established a foothold in this territory we can use these sets to discover others of their class. We may also use the undecidability of the TM Halting Problem to prove that other problems are undecidable as well. For example, we will show the following problem for Turing machines to be undecidable:

Problem: For an arbitrarily given TM M, does M halt given e, the empty string, as input?

We first express the problem as a language:

(19–13) $L_2 = \{E(M) \mid M \text{ accepts } e\}$

and ask whether there is a TM M_2 which *decides* this language. We show that there is not, and the proof technique is to show that if such a machine existed then it could be modified to produce a machine which decides the Halting Problem. Since the latter cannot exist, neither can M_2.

Suppose we have M_2, which by hypothesis decides L_2. We show how to use M_2 to construct a machine M, which decides L, where L is the language of the Halting Problem:

(19–14) $L = \{E(M)E(x) \mid M \text{ accepts } x\}$

First of all, for any given TM M and any given input string x, one can modify M so that if it is started on the empty tape it will first write x on it and then proceed as M would have, given x. Call this modified machine M_x. M_x first checks to see if its input is the empty tape. (If not, it runs forever in some fashion.) If so, it writes x (a finite string, so this is done by some finite set of instructions added to M) and then positions its reading head for the start of a computation and executes the moves of M thereafter.

Now if we assume that we have a machine M_2 which decides L_2, then it will work, in particular, if it is given the encoding of any machine M_x

constructed in the way just described. (M_2 works for *any* TM encoding; it will work if that encoding happens to be the encoding of M_x.) But notice that M_x accepts e just in case M accepts x. That is, M_x halts, given the empty string as input, iff M halts given x. Therefore a machine which decides whether M_x halts given e could be used in effect to decide whether M halts given x. This has been shown to be impossible so there is no such machine as M_2, and language L_2 is therefore not Turing decidable.

A whole host of problems concerning Turing machines turn out to be undecidable: whether an arbitrarily given TM ever enters a particular state, whether it halts on any inputs at all, whether it halts on every input, whether it ever writes a particular symbol on its tape, etc. These and other undecidability results can, in turn, be used to establish undecidability results in other areas. For example, the undecidability of the TM Halting Problem can be used to establish the undecidability of another problem called the Post Correspondence Problem. This can then be used in showing that certain problems concerning context free grammars and languages are undecidable. For example, it is undecidable, given two arbitrary cfg's G_1 and G_2 whether $L(G_1) = L(G_2)$, whether $L(G_1) \cap L(G_2) = \emptyset$, whether $L(G_1) \subseteq L(G_2)$, whether $L(G_1)$ is inherently ambiguous, etc.

One should note carefully that none of these undecidability results imply that for a particular TM, a particular cfg, etc. there is no way to determine whether it halts given the empty string, whether it is inherently ambiguous, etc. We have seen examples of TM's, e.g., in (19-1), which can be shown, quite easily in fact, to halt given the empty string. What the undecidability result says is that there is no single, generally applicable algorithm which is guaranteed to work for every TM (or every arbitrarily given pair of cfg's, etc.)

It is also worth noting that in view of the correspondence shown above between TM's and unrestricted grammars, the undecidability results for TM's can be carried over immediately to grammars. Thus, there is no algorithm for determining for an arbitrarily given Type 0 grammar G whether G generates any strings, whether G generates the empty string, whether G generates all strings in Σ^*, etc.

Exercises

1. Construct a Turing machine that accepts any tape written on the vocabulary $\{0, 1\}$ and converts every contiguous string of two or more 1's

to 0's. Everything else is left unchanged. For example, the input tape
$\cdots\#01011011101\#\cdots$ should end up as $\cdots\#01000000001\#\cdots$.

2. Construct a Turing machine with three states $\{q_0, q_1, q_2\}$, initial state
   q_0, that begins with an input tape consisting entirely of blanks and
   halts with exactly three contiguous 1's on the tape.

3. Consider the following Turing machine: $M = \langle\{q_0, q_1\}, \{a, b, \#\}, q_0, \delta\rangle$
   where
   $$\delta = \left\{\begin{array}{l} (q_0, a) \;\rightarrow\; (q_0, R) \\ (q_0, \#) \rightarrow (q_1, a) \\ (q_1, a) \;\rightarrow\; (q_1, L) \\ (q_1, \#) \rightarrow (q_0, a) \end{array}\right\}$$

   (a) Write the first twelve situations of the machine M if it starts in
       the situation $(e, q_0, a, \#\#a)$.

   (b) Describe verbally what machine M will continue to do after this
       much has been done.

   (c) Will it ever halt?

   (d) Will it use only a finite amount of tape?

   (e) Are there any squares of the tape that it will scan only a finite
       number of times?

   (f) What will machine M do if started in another situation?

4. (a) Make up a simple Turing machine which never halts no matter
       what the initial tape sequence is. Give both the quadruples and
       a verbal description of its behavior. Let the machine be allowed
       to start scanning at any square but always start in state q_0.

   (b) Similarly, make up a Turing machine which always halts eventu-
       ally.

5. Tell whether the following functions are total or only partial. A function is considered to be undefined if it would yield a value outside the
   set on which it is specified.

   (a) Addition on the set of all even integers.

   (b) Addition on the set of all prime numbers.

   (c) Set union on the set $\{\{0\}, \{1\}, \{2\}, \{0, 1\}\}$

6. Describe informally an algorithm for converting an integer in binary notation to decimal notation.

7. Write a Type 0 grammar generating the language $\{a^{2^n} \mid n \geq 0\}$.

8. Show that the following problem for Turing machines is undecidable: For an arbitrarily given TM M, does M accept at least one string? (Hint: Show that if a TM existed which decided the language $\{E(M) \mid M$ accepts at least one string$\}$, it could be modified to produce a machine deciding L_2 in (19-13).)

Chapter 20

Linear Bounded Automata, Context Sensitive Languages and Type 1 Grammars

20.1 Linear bounded automata

A linear bounded automaton (lba) is, in effect, a Turing machine whose computations are restricted to the amount of tape on which the input is written. We can imagine it as consisting of a finite set of states, a finite alphabet (including special right- and left- endmarkers [and]), a designated initial state, and a finite set of instructions of the same form as the quadruples for Turing machines. We assume, however, that the input to an lba is given between the designated endmarkers, i.e., as [w] and that the lba has no instructions which allow it to move past these endmarkers or to erase or replace them. Thus, the tape head can move only in the portion of the tape originally occupied by w, although an equivalent formulation of lba's sets the limit on usable tape not as *equal* to the length of the input but rather as a *linear function* of the length of the input. (A linear function in a variable x is of the form $ax + b$, where a and b are constants. Plotting values of $ax + b$ for each value of x on graph paper gives a straight line, whereas plots of functions involving x^2, x^3, etc. gives curves.) This is the source of the name for these automata—the allowed computational space is bounded by a linear function of the length of the input string.

Lba's are thus placed between pda's and TM's. They can read and write, and move left and right on the input tape like TM's, but TM's have a potentially unlimited amount of tape available for computation. A pda, on the other hand, uses a maximum amount of tape for its pushdown store which is a linear function of the length of the input. (This is not obvious given the way we have formulated pda's since a pda could cycle endlessly on e-transitions adding more and more symbols to its pushdown store. It can be shown, however, that each pda can be turned into an equivalent pda which always reads to the end of its input and which does not loop endlessly on e-transitions. Such a pda uses at most an amount of pushdown storage which is a linear function of the length of its input.) But pda's lack the power of lba's to move left and right and thus to have access to any portion of the "memory" encoded on the tape during a computation.

Lba's come in deterministic and non-deterministic varieties, defined in ways analogous to the corresponding types of Turing machines, but it is not known whether they are equivalent. That is, given language L accepted by some non-deterministic lba, we don't know in general whether there is some deterministic lba which also accepts L. This problem has remained open for many years despite the efforts of a good many talented and energetic people to solve it.

20.1.1   Lba's and context sensitive grammars

Recall that a context sensitive grammar (csg) is one in which every rule has the property that the right side is at least as long as the left side. In particular, rules of the form $\alpha \rightarrow e$ are excluded, and therefore the empty string cannot be generated as part of any context sensitive language. (An equivalent formulation states that every rule is of the form $\alpha A \beta \rightarrow \alpha \psi \beta$, where A is a non-terminal, α, β, and ψ are strings over $(V_T \cup V_N)^*$, and $\psi \neq e$. See Section 16.4)

Except for the matter of the empty string, the languages accepted by non-deterministic lba's are the languages generated by csg's. We will simply sketch here how this equivalence is established and refer the reader to Hopcroft and Ullman (1979, pp. 225-6) for details.

Given a csg G, we can construct a non-deterministic lba M to simulate derivations by G. M is given an input string w embedded between the endmarkers; i.e., $[w]$, and it sets up a work space to the right of the input of length equal to the length of w where it inserts the start symbol S. M then non-deterministically carries out a derivation from S according to the rules of G, checking after each step to see if the contents of the work space equal w. If so, M halts and accepts; if not, M continues the derivation.

If there is a derivation of w by G, it will be found by M, and, furthermore, it will be found by some computation which uses no more than the allotted amount of work space. Since rules of G are "non-shrinking," no line of a derivation is shorter than the preceding one. Thus, no derivation of w by G contains a line longer than w, and the derivation can be carried out by M on an amount of tape which is a linear function of (roughly, double) the length of the input.

The construction in the other direction—simulating the moves of an lba in reverse by a csg—is similar to that for Turing machines and Type 0 grammars. However, because of the restriction that rules cannot make strings shorter, a problem arises in getting rid of the boundary symbols and the symbol for the state of the automaton. This can be accomplished by coding sequences of symbols as complex non-terminals; for details, see the section in Hopcroft and Ullman (1979) referred to above. Another matter which must be attended to is that the grammar cannot generate e even if the lba accepts it; i.e., if L is accepted by a non-deterministic lba M, $L - \{e\}$ is generated by the corresponding csg G.

20.2 Context sensitive languages and recursive sets

Every language generated by a context sensitive grammar is a recursive set of strings in the sense defined above in connection with our discussion of recursive and recursively enumerable sets. That is, for every context sensitive language, there is a Turing machine which decides it. We will show this— appealing to Church's Hypothesis—by sketching an algorithm for deciding any csl. It would not be very difficult to give this algorithm explicitly in the form of a TM.

Given a csg G and a string x, we decide whether or not $x \in L(G)$ as follows. Construct all derivations beginning with S and whose last lines are no longer than the length of x. If any line in a derivation is repeated, the derivation can be disregarded, since, if there is a derivation of x beginning with S, there is one with no repeated lines. The number of derivations whose last lines are no longer than the length of x and which contain no repeated lines is a finite number. We simply examine this finite list of derivations to see if any end in x. If none do, we can be sure that x is not generated by G since derivations of x cannot contain lines longer than x. This follows from the fact that rules of a csg never decrease the number of symbols in succeeding lines of a derivation. (Note that the possibility of such a decision procedure for Type 0 languages is precluded by the possibility that rules in such grammar may decrease the number of symbols. As a consequence, we cannot in general fix an upper bound on the length of a derivation of a string of given length by a Type 0 grammar. This reasoning does not *prove* that no decision procedure can be found for Type 0 languages—although in fact there is none, as we have seen—only that we cannot arrive at one by enumerating derivations.)

The context sensitive languages do not exhaust the recursive languages; there are recursive languages which are not csl's. There is a sense in which this is trivially true since some recursive languages contain e, and no csl's do. But even if we consider the class of all csl's together with the class of all csl's with e added (which are just the non-deterministic lba languages), there are still recursive languages which are not in this class. We show this with respect to lba's for simplicity.

Like a TM, a non-deterministic lba could be encoded as a string over the alphabet $\{0,1\}$. We can then enumerate lba's in the same fashion as we did for TM's—say, shortest encodings first and with encodings of the same length being arranged in increasing order when interpreted as a binary number. Thus, we have an enumeration of lba's:

(20–1) $M_1, M_2, \ldots, M_i, \ldots$

We also construct an enumeration of input strings (for example by coding them in the alphabet $\{0,1\}$ and arranging them in the order of increasing binary number of the encoding).

(20–2) $x_1, x_2, \ldots, x_i, \ldots$

We construct the language L in the following way:

(20–3) $L = \{x_i \mid$ and x_i is not accepted by $M_i\}$

That is, w is in L iff its encoding is not accepted by the lba at the corresponding position in the enumeration. This language is not an lba language since it is not accepted by any of the lba's in the enumeration. Given any M_j, it cannot accept L because there is a string, namely x_j, which is in L iff it is not accepted by M_j. Thus, L differs from the languages accepted by each of the lba's in at least one string.

L is nonetheless recursive. There is a procedure for determining for any string w whether or not it is in L. Encode w in the prescribed manner into 0's and 1's, and find it in the enumeration. This can be done, since the encodings of the x_i's are listed in order of increasing length and within strings of the same length in increasing order of size as a binary number. Having located w in the enumeration, we get its index (by counting from the beginning) and find the corresponding lba in the enumeration of lba's. We then determine by the algorithm referred to above whether the selected lba accepts w or not. If it does, $w \notin L$; if not, $w \in L$. Thus L is a recursive language which is not the language accepted by any non-deterministic lba.

20.3 Closure and decision properties

The csl's are closed under the operations of union and intersection, but it is not known whether they are closed under complementaiton (this is essentially the problem of determining whether deterministic and non-deterministic lba's are equivalent). They are closed under concatenation but not under Kleene star, inasmuch as L^* must contain e, and no csl does. The csl's, however, are closed under *positive closure* L^+, defined as $L^* - \{e\}$. They are also closed under intersection with a regular language. We omit the demonstrations of these results here; the interested reader may consult Hopcroft and Ullman (1979, Chapter 11) and references therein for more details.

Although the membership question is decidable for csl's, almost all the other standard question turn out to be undecidable:

(i) Is $L = \emptyset$?

(ii) Is $L = \Sigma^*$?

(iii) Is $L_1 = L_2$?

(iv) Is $L_1 \subseteq L_2$?

(v) Is $L_1 \cap L_2 = \emptyset$?

Exercises

1. Construct context sensitive grammars for each of the following languages.

   (a) $a^n b^n c^n (n \geq 1)$

   (b) $\{x \in \{a, b, c\}^* \mid x$ consists of an equal number (≥ 1) of a's, b's, and c's$\}$

   (c) $\{xx \mid x \in \{a, b\}^+\}$ (i.e., all non-empty strings in $\{a, b\}^*$ with identical left and right halves.)

Chapter 21

Languages Between Context Free and Context Sensitive

Most investigators supposed from the time that the Chomsky hierarchy was first established that natural languages, considered as string sets, would fall somewhere between the context free and the context sensitive languages and, further, that they would lie in some sense "close" to the context free class. On the one hand, the context sensitive languages seemed much too inclusive, containing as they do species such as $\{a^n b^{n!}\}$ ($n!$ is n factorial, i.e., $1 \times 2 \times 3 \times \ldots \times n$) and $\{a^n : n \text{ is prime}\}$, which seem unlikely candidates for any sort of linguistic model. On the other hand, a large part of natural language syntax seems to be handled quite nicely by a CFG, and the aspects which seem to cause languages to fall outside the CFL class (as string sets) could be considered rather isolated and infrequent. After all, it took nearly thirty years to find one completely convincing example of a natural language which was not context free.

Such considerations spawned work on the formal languages which would be, in Aravind Joshi's phrase, "mildly context sensitive." In the following sections we will survey very briefly a few of these whose formal properties have been most thoroughly investigated.

535

21.1   Indexed grammars

According to Hopcroft and Ullman (1979, p. 389) "of the many generalizations of context free grammars that have been proposed, a class called 'indexed' appears the most natural in that it arises in a wide variety of contexts." An indexed grammar (IG) differs from a context free grammar in that nonterminal symbols may carry a sequence of indices chosen from an initially specified finite set, and its productions allow for adding or removing these indices in the course of a derivation. We write $A[i,j,k]$ for the nonterminal symbol A bearing the index sequence $[i,j,k]$. Indices can be added or removed from the left end of the sequence, and there is no upper bound on the length. Thus, an index sequence is like a pushdown stack attached to a nonterminal. Further, when a rule of the ordinary CF form, e.g., $A \to aBcdC$, is applied, the index sequence on A, if any, is copied onto each of the nonterminals on the right, i.e., B and C. Terminal symbols never bear indices. If A is rewritten as a string containing no nonterminals, e.g., $A \to bc$, the indices on A simply disappear.

Productions may also be of the form $A[i] \to \alpha$, where i is an index and α is any string, in which case the rule can only be applied to a nonterminal A bearing index i at the left of its index sequence, and if α contains any nonterminals, then the sequence on A with i removed is copied onto each of them. For example, the rule $A[i] \to BaC$ could be applied to the indexed nonterminal $A[i,j,k]$ to produce $B[j,k]aC[j,k]$. The rule could not be applied to $A[j,k]$ or $A[j,i]$, for example, since neither index sequence has i at the left. Thus, rules of the ordinary CF form $A \to \alpha$ are accompanied by index copying, while rules of the form $A[i] \to \alpha$ are "pop and copy" rules.

Finally, rules of the form $A \to B[i]$ add index i at the left of the sequence already present on A and copy the result onto B (a "push and copy" rule). Such rules have only a single nonterminal on the right because we don't want to allow the possibility of pushing different indices and copying onto different nonterminals; i.e., $A \to B[i]C[j]$ is not allowed. We are following here the formulation in Hopcroft and Ullman (1979, pp. 389-390) with slight notational changes. Different but equivalent formulations can be found in Aho (1968), Salomaa (1973, pp. 257-259) and Gazdar (1985). Thus, the IG's properly include the CFG's, since a CFG can be regarded as an IG in which all index sequences are empty. That the CFL's are a proper subset of the index languages (IL's) is shown by the following IG generating the non-context free language $\{a^n b^n c^n : n \geq 0\}$:

$$G = \langle V_T, V_N, I, S, R \rangle, \text{ where}$$
$$V_T = \{a, b, c,\}; \; V_N = \{S, T, A, B, C\};$$
$$I = \{i, j\}, \text{ the set of indices;}$$
$$R = \{S \to T[j] \quad A[i] \to aA \quad A[j] \to e$$
$$T \to T[i] \quad B[i] \to bB \quad B[j] \to e$$
$$T \to ABC \quad C[i] \to cC \quad C[j] \to e\}$$

Fig. 21-1 is a derivation tree for $a^2 b^2 c^2$.

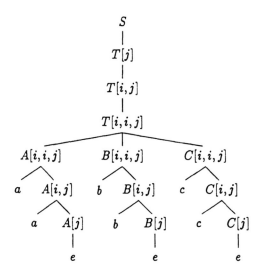

Figure 21-1.

Note that it is necessary to use an index distinct from i as a "bottom of stack" marker in this grammar. Because of the convention that index sequences disappear when the right side of a production contains no nonterminals, if we had only the rules $A[i] \to aA$ and $A[i] \to a$ rewriting A, then $A[i, i]$ could give rise either to a or aa.

The grammar containing the following rules generates $\{xx : x \in \{a, b\}^*\}$:

$$S \to T[k] \quad F[i] \to aF \quad G[i] \to aG$$
$$T \to T[i] \quad F[j] \to bF \quad G[j] \to bG$$
$$T \to T[j] \quad F[k] \to e \quad G[k] \to e$$
$$T \to FG$$

A derivation tree for *abbabb* appears in Fig. 21-2.

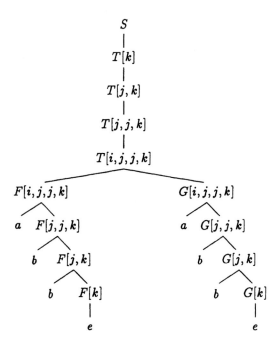

Figure 21–2.

In the first example, indices are used as counters to ensure that the numbers of a's, b's, and c's are all equal; in the second, the indices constrain the rewriting sequence so that the two halves of the string are identical. The following grammar (henceforth we give just the rules) combines elements of both techniques to generate $\{a^n b^m c^n d^m : m, n \geq 0\}$, which exhibits the kind of cross-serial dependencies found in Swiss German (Sec. 18.6 above):

$$S \rightarrow T[k] \quad A[i] \rightarrow aA \quad C[i] \rightarrow cC$$
$$T \rightarrow T[j] \quad A \rightarrow B \quad C \rightarrow D$$
$$T \rightarrow T' \quad B[j] \rightarrow bB \quad D[j] \rightarrow dD$$
$$T' \rightarrow T'[i] \quad B[k] \rightarrow e \quad D[k] \rightarrow e$$
$$T' \rightarrow AC$$

Fig. 21-3 is a derivation tree for *abbcdd*.

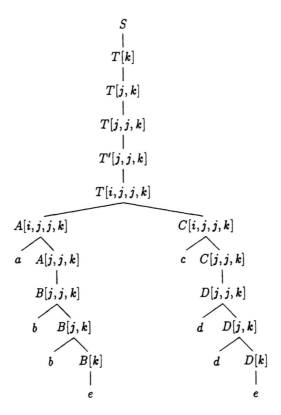

Figure 21-3.

It is worth noting here that alternative grammars are possible for the preceding examples, some of which will produce very different derivation trees. For example, the following grammar also generates $\{a^n b^n c^n : n \geq 0\}$ with the derivation tree for $a^2 b^2 c^2$ in Fig. 21-4.

$$
\begin{array}{lll}
S \to T[j] & A[i] \to aA & B[i] \to bBc \\
T \to T[i] & A[j] \to e & B[j] \to e \\
T \to AB & &
\end{array}
$$

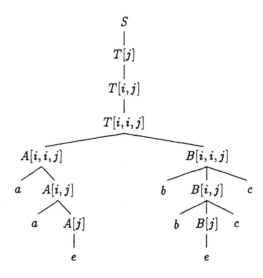

Figure 21–4.

The context free languages can of course be generated by IL's without indices, but it is also possible to use the power of the indices to generate CFL's with right- (or left-) linear derivation trees. See, for example, the following IG, with an accompanying derivation in Fig. 21-5, which generates strings in $a^n b^n$ with a right-linear rather than a center-embedded tree structure:

$$
\begin{array}{lll}
S \to A[k] & A \to aT & B[i] \to bB \\
T \to A[i] & A \to B & B[k] \to e
\end{array}
$$

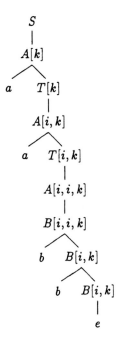

Figure 21–5.

Aho (1968) was in fact able to prove that the languages generated by IG's with entirely right-linear or left-linear tree structures were exactly the CFL's. Gazdar (1985) suggests that this fact may be of linguistic significance, citing examples of nested dependencies which appear to require a right- or left-linear rather than a center-embedded constituent structure (e.g., nested comparative constructions and unbounded dependencies in the Scandinavian languages).

The IL's have an equivalent characterization in terms of automata, viz., the nondeterministic "nested" stack automata. A stack automaton is like a PDA which, in addition to popping and pushing symbols at the top, can also enter its stack in "read-only" mode, moving up or down without writing or erasing any symbols. A nested stack automaton has the further capability of creating stacks inside its stack, stacks inside these stacks, etc., but it can only empty a stack after all stacks within it are empty.

It can be shown that the IL's (without e) are contained in the context-sensitive languages and that the containment is proper. That is, we have:

(21-1) CFL's $\subset$ IL's $\subset$ CSL's

Examples of CSL's which are not IL's are $\{a^{n!} : n \geq 1\}$ and $\{(\$w)^{|w|} : w \in \{a, b\}^*\}$ (Hayashi, 1973). The language $\{w \in \{a, b, c\}^* : w$ contains equal numbers of a's, b's, and c's$\}$ is conjectured by Marsh (1985) to be non-IL (we have already seen that it is CS). The language $\{a^n b^{n^2} : n \geq 1\}$ is IL, however, and is generated by the following grammar (modified from Salomaa (1973)):

$$
\begin{array}{llll}
S \rightarrow T[k] & A[i] \rightarrow aA & Z[i] \rightarrow bZ & B[i] \rightarrow bBZZ \\
T \rightarrow T[i] & A[k] \rightarrow a & Z[k] \rightarrow b & B[k] \rightarrow b \\
T \rightarrow AB & & &
\end{array}
$$

Fig. 21-6 is the derivation tree for $a^3 b^9$.

The IL's are closed under such operations as union, concatenation, intersection with a regular set, and Kleene closure, but they are not closed under intersection or complementation. There exists an algorithm for deciding whether the language generated by an arbitrary IG is empty.

Gazdar and Pullum (1985, pp. 11) state that "no phenomena are known which would lead one to believe that the NLs [natural languages] fall outside [the ILs'] purview... The indexed languages thus provide us, at least for the moment, with a kind of upper bound for syntactic phenomena." This is of course in the context of the assumption that languages are being regarded as string sets.

21.2 Tree adjoining grammars

Tree adjoining grammars (TAG's) were devised by Joshi and his coworkers (Joshi, Levy, and Takahashi, 1975) as limited extensions of CFG's. They occupy, in terms of weak generative capacity, a position between CFG's and indexed grammars; i.e.,

(21-2) CFL's $\subset$ TAL's $\subset$ IL's

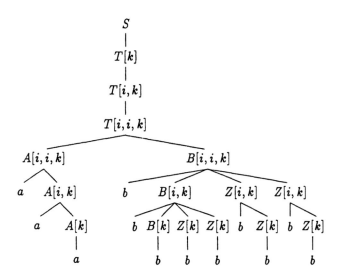

Figure 21–6.

A TAG, unlike the grammars we have seen thus far, does not generate sentences by rewriting strings of symbols; rather, it begins with a finite set of initial trees, which can be enlarged by recursively inserting at appropriate positions one of a finite number of auxiliary trees. For example, if the following is an initial tree,

(21-3) $\alpha\ =\ S$

and β is an auxiliary tree

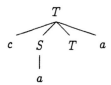

then β can be "adjoined" to α by

1) excising the subtree rooted by T from α giving

2) placing β in the position just vacated giving

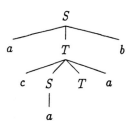

3) reattaching the excised subtree at the position of the T node in β giving

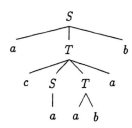

In a TAG initial trees are always sentential in that they are rooted by S and have a string of terminals as their yield. Auxiliary trees can have any nonterminal symbol as root and must have that same symbol occurring once in its yield (on its "frontier"), all the rest being terminals. Although not part of the formal definitions, the intent is that both initial and auxiliary trees be "minimal". Initial trees should contain no repeated non-terminals along any path, and auxiliaries should contain no repetitions of the nonterminal labeling the root node and the node at the frontier (the "foot" node) on the path connecting the two.

Given a tree γ containing a nonterminal node X, and an auxiliary tree β with X as root (hence with X as the only nonterminal on its frontier), we can represent the operation of adjunction schematically as in Fig. 21-7.

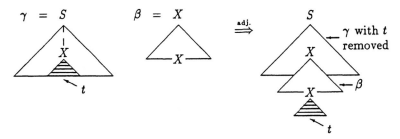

Figure 21–7.

(The similarities between the generation of trees by a TAG and the decomposition of derivation trees employed in the proof of the Pumping Theorem for CFL's is evident.)

Formally, a TAG $G = \langle I, A \rangle$ is composed of finite sets of initial and auxiliary trees, I and A, respectively. The *set of trees generated* by G is the set of trees obtainable from any tree in I by repeated (possibly zero) applications of adjunction using trees from A. The *language generated*, $L(G)$, is the set of terminal strings on the trees generated by G.

Not surprisingly, for every CFG there is a strongly equivalent TAG (one which generates exactly the same strings with the same tree structures). In fact, given any CFG there is a procedure for constructing a TAG which is strongly equivalent to it. Strong equivalence implies weak equivalence of course, so the CFL's are included in the TAL's. There are, however, TAG's for which no strongly equivalent CFG exists (see Joshi, 1985, pp. 211-2, for an example), and, moreover, there are TAL's which are not weakly CF. Since the TAL's are such a modest extension of the CFL's, it is difficult to exhibit a simple example of a non-CF TAL. The following is from Joshi (op. cit., pp. 212-3):

(21–4) $L_1 = \{wc^n : n \geq 0$ and w is a string of a's and b's such that (i) the number of a's = the number of b's = n, and (ii) for any initial substring of w, the number of a's is $\geq$ the number of b's$\}$

L_1 can be thought of as made from the language $\{(ab)^n c^n\}$ by displacing some of the a's to the left. Thus, $aabaabbbcccc$ is in L_1 but $aababbbacccc$ is not. L_1 is not CF since its intersection with $a^* b^* c^*$ is $\{a^n b^n c^n\}$. But L_1 is generated by the following TAG:

(21–5)   I: $\alpha = S$

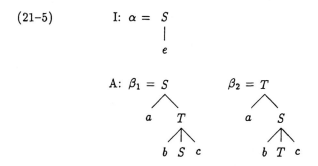

The derivation of the tree for $aabbcc$ appears in Fig. 21-8.

$\{a^n b^n c^n : n \geq 0\}$ is an example of an indexed language which cannot be generated by a TAG. If there were a TAG generating this language, each of its initial trees would have to contain an equal number of a's, b's, and c's in order (recall that all initial trees are sentential and therefore have yields which are in the language). Further, each auxiliary tree also would have to have equal numbers of a's, b's, and c's (because each adjunction of an auxiliary tree also produces a sentential tree) with all a's preceding b's, which precede all c's. But then adjunction cannot avoid mixing the order of the elements and thus some strings not in the language will be generated.

Joshi (1985) shows that an extension of the theory of TAG's to include local context-dependence for adjunction of auxiliary trees yields a class of

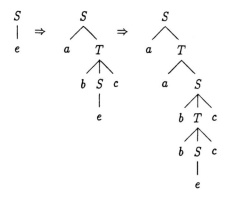

Figure 21–8.

grammars which can generate such languages as $\{a^n b^n c^n\}$ and $\{ww : w \in \{a,b\}^*\}$. These grammars are also of interest since with a suitable notion of linking defined between pairs of nodes in trees it appears that structures with cross-serial dependencies can be generated. The languages of the extended TAG's still do not equal the full class of indexed languages since languages such as $\{a^{2^n} : n \geq 0\}$ are beyond their range. This is evident from the fact that in any TAG (context restrictions are not relevant here) during an application of adjunction a terminal string can be increased in length by only the number of terminal symbols in an auxiliary tree. The result is that the growth in length of terminal strings for any TAL is represented by a series of linear progressions, none of which grows as fast as the exponential growth rate of strings in a^{2^n}. It has been shown, however, (Vijay-Shankar, 1987) that the TAL's are weakly equivalent to a restricted class of indexed languages, viz., those generated by IG's whose rules limit the inheritance and manipulation of index sequences to a single nonterminal daughter on the right side of the rule. Gazdar (1985) points out that such a restriction make IG's of limited interest as natural language grammars since conjunction constructions would seem to require the inheritance of index sequences by multiple daughter nodes.

The TAL's are closed under union, concatenation, Kleene star, and intersection with regular languages, but not under intersection or complementation.

21.3   Head grammars

Pollard (1984) proposed an extension of CFG's in which each string contains a distinguished symbol called the *head* of that string. In formal terms, a headed string can be thought of as a pair consisting of a string and a natural number (up to the length of the string) indicating the position of the head. Two headed strings can be concatenated, in which case one of the heads becomes the head of the resulting string, and there are "wrapping" operations as well in which a string is split at its head and a second string inserted. A normal form theorem due to Roach (1987) guarantees that Head Grammars (HG's) need only two concatenation operations (in which the left, resp. the right, head becomes head of the result) and four wrapping operations (the second string is inserted either left or right of the head of the first, and either the first or second head becomes the new head).

Formally, a HG is a quadruple $\langle V_N, V_T, S, P \rangle$, where V_N and V_T are finite sets of non-terminal and terminal symbols, respectively; S, the initial symbol, is a member of V_N; and P is a set of productions of the form

$$A \rightarrow \alpha_1$$
$$\text{or } A \rightarrow f(\alpha_1 \ldots \alpha_n)$$

where $A \in V_N$; α_i is either a nonterminal or a headed string; and f is a concatenation or a wrapping operation of the sort just mentioned.

The languages generated by HG's, Head Languages (HL's), are included in the TAL's (Weir, Vijay-Shankar, and Joshi, 1986). The inclusion in the reverse direction has not yet been demonstrated owing to technical difficulties arising from the notion of the 'headed empty string.' This has led Joshi, et al. to define a closely related class of grammars, the so-called Modified Head Grammars (MHG's) in which these difficulties are avoided and which are provably equivalent in weak generative capacity to TAG's. Strings in MHG's have, instead of heads, a designated position between symbols where the string can be split and a second string inserted. A "split string" is denoted $w_1 \uparrow w_2$, where w_1 and w_2 are in V_T^*, and in a MHG there are just three operations: two concatenations and one wrapping.

$$C_1(w_1 \uparrow w_2, u_1 \uparrow u_2) \;=\; w_1 \uparrow w_2 u_1 u_2$$
$$C_2(w_1 \uparrow w_2, u_1 \uparrow u_2) \;=\; w_1 w_2 u_1 \uparrow u_2$$
$$W(w_1 \uparrow w_2, u_1 \uparrow u_2) \;=\; w_1 u_1 \uparrow u_2 w_2$$

The form of the productions and the rest of the formalism otherwise remain as in HG's except that the α_i can be either a nonterminal or a split string.

Here is an example of a MHG generating the language $\{a^n g b^n f c^n h \mid n \geq 0\}$.

$V_T = \{a, b, c, f, g, h\}; \; V_N = \{S, S_1, S_2, S_3\};$
$P = \quad S \rightarrow W(S_1, f \uparrow) \qquad S \rightarrow W(S_2, f \uparrow)$
$\qquad\quad S_1 \rightarrow C_2(a \uparrow, S_3) \qquad S_2 \rightarrow g \uparrow h$
$\qquad\quad S_3 \rightarrow W(S_1, b \uparrow c) \quad S_3 \rightarrow W(S_2, b \uparrow c)$

Here is a derivation of $aagbbfcch$:

$S \Rightarrow W(S_1, f \uparrow) \Rightarrow W(C_2(a \uparrow, S_3), f \uparrow) \Rightarrow$
$\quad W(C_2(a \uparrow, W(S_1, b \uparrow c)), f \uparrow) \Rightarrow$
$\quad W(C_2(a \uparrow, W(C_2(a \uparrow, S_3), b \uparrow c), f \uparrow) \Rightarrow$
$\quad W(C_2(a \uparrow, W(C_2(a \uparrow, W(S_2, b \uparrow c)), b \uparrow c), f \uparrow) \Rightarrow$
$\quad W(C_2(a \uparrow, W(C_2(a \uparrow, W(g \uparrow h, b \uparrow c)), b \uparrow c), f \uparrow) \Rightarrow$
$\quad W(C_2(a \uparrow, W(C_2(a \uparrow, gb \uparrow ch), b \uparrow c), f \uparrow) \Rightarrow$
$\quad W(C_2(a \uparrow, W(agb \uparrow ch, b \uparrow c), f \uparrow) \Rightarrow$
$\quad W(C_2(a \uparrow, agbb \uparrow cch), f \uparrow) \Rightarrow$
$\quad W(aagbb \uparrow cch, f \uparrow) \Rightarrow aagbbf \uparrow cch$

The split marker is ignored in the final string, so the grammar is taken as generating $aagbbfcch$.

The HL's are included in the MHL's, but the converse has not been shown, again because of the difficulty mentioned above concerning the headed empty string. The differences between HG's and MHG's, however, are marginal, and the systems are equivalent in all important respects. Thus, MHG's, TAG's and IG's restricted to inheritance of indices by a single non-terminal daughter (IG(1)'s) form a stable class of weakly equivalent grammars in the "mildly context sensitive" domain.

21.4   Categorial grammars

Categorial grammars are based on the work of Ajdukiewicz (1935) on semantic categories of logical languages and were proposed has a system of
syntactic description for natural languages by Bar-Hillel (1953). Montague's
work in natural language semantics assumes a categorial syntax, and this in
part has led to a revival of interest in such systems.

The fundamental idea in a categorial grammar (CG) is that lexical items
may be assigned not only to basic categories such as N and V, but also to
complex categories like S/VP, V/(NP/S), etc. Sequences of categories can
be reduced by a kind of "cancellation" rule of the form $A/B\ B \Rightarrow A$. That
is, if x is of category A/B and y is of category B, then the sequence xy is
of category A. A "backward cancellation" rule, $B\ A\backslash B \Rightarrow A$, is ordinarily
included as well. To take a natural language example, *Mary* might be of
category S/VP and *sleeps* of category VP; then *Mary sleeps* would be of
category S. Further, if *often* were assigned category VP/VP, the sequence
Mary often sleeps would be reduced to category S by the following sequence
of steps:

S/VP	VP/VP	VP	$\Rightarrow$	S/VP	VP	$\Rightarrow$	S
Mary	often	sleeps		Mary	often sleeps		Mary often sleeps

The same information could be represented as a tree structure:

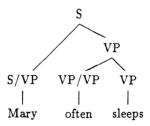

Notice that in a CG the paucity of syntactic rules is compensated for by
the complexity of the syntactic categories to which constituents belong. In
some sense, CG's code their syntactic operations into their lexicons. One of
the advantages of such a system lies in the close correspondence of syntactic
and semantic structures. Parallel to syntactic reduction of categories X/Y

and Y to X is the semantic operation of applying a function (from Y-type things to X-type things) to an argument (of type Y) to produce a value (of type X). It is for this reason that the reduction rules are often referred to as rules of (forward and backward) Function Application. (See the discussion in Chapter 13 where this is applied to natural language semantics.)

The formal definitions of what might be termed a classical, bi-directional CG would be as follows:

We assume a finite alphabet V_A of category symbols. The set C of all category symbols is then given by:

(1) For all $x \in V_A$, $x \in C$.

(2) If x and y are in C, then so are (x/y) and $(x \backslash y)$.

(3) Nothing else is in C.

A CG then is a quadruple $G = \langle V_T, V_A, S, F \rangle$ where

V_T is a finite set of terminal symbols

V_A is as above

S is a designated member of V_A

F is a function from V_T to $\wp(C)$; i.e., a function assigning to each terminal symbol a set of categories from C.

We define the binary relation $\Rightarrow$, "reduces in one step to", on pairs of category sequences as follows:

For any categories X, Y in C and any finite sequences of categories α and β,

$$\alpha\ X/Y\ Y\ \beta \Rightarrow \alpha X \beta$$

$$\alpha\ Y\ X \backslash Y\ \beta \Rightarrow \alpha X \beta$$

The relation $\overset{*}{\Rightarrow}$ "reduces to (in zero or more steps)" is the reflexive transitive closure of $\Rightarrow$.

A string $w \in V_T^*$ is *generated* by G iff $w = w_1 \ldots w_n$ and there is some sequence of categories $C_1 \ldots C_n$ such that $F(w_i) = C_i$ for all $1 \leq i \leq n$, and $C_1 \ldots C_n \overset{*}{\Rightarrow} S$. In other words, $w_1 \ldots w_n$ is generated iff there is some choice of category assignments by F to the symbols in $w_1 \ldots w_n$ which reduces to S.

Example: $G = \langle V_T, V_A, S, F \rangle$ where
$$V_T = \{a, b\}; \; V_A = \{S, B\}; F(a) = \{S/B\}; F(b) = \{B, B \setminus S\}$$

The string a^3b^3 is generated as indicated by the derivation tree in Fig. 21-9.

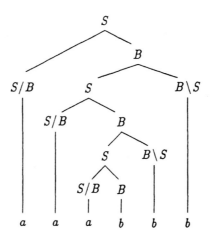

Figure 21-9.

CG's have been shown to be identical to CFG's in weak generative capacity (Bar-Hillel, Gaifman, and Shamir, 1960). The proof is constructive; from any given (basic, bi-directional) CG, a weakly equivalent CFG can be constructed, and vice versa.

More recent work in categorial grammar has focused on systems with expanded sets of reduction rules. Some of those most frequently encountered are:

(21-6)   1. $X/Y\;Y/Z \Rightarrow X/Z$ Function Composition
         2. $(X/Y)\setminus Z \Rightarrow (X\setminus Z)/Y$ Commutativity
         3. $X \Rightarrow Y/(Y\setminus X)$ Type raising
         4. $X/Y \Rightarrow (X/Z)/(Y/Z)$ "Geach Rule"

These rules also have corresponding forms with / and \ interchanged; e.g.,

$Y \backslash Z \, X \backslash Y \Rightarrow X \backslash Z$ (Backward Function Composition)

A system containing all the rules in (21-6) (in both forward and backward versions) together with the two standard rules of Function Application was proposed by Lambek (1958) and has come be known as the Lambek Calculus. Van Bentham (1988) has shown that a particular variety of this calculus (in which categories are non-directional, i.e., both $X \mid Y \, Y \Rightarrow X$ and $Y \, X \mid Y \Rightarrow X$ are valid) generates the permutation closure of the CFL's. The permutation closure of a language L is the set of strings obtained by taking every string L and permuting its symbols in every possible way. For example, the permutation closure of $\{a^n b^n \mid n \geq 0\}$ is $\{x \in \{a,b\}^* \mid x$ contains equal numbers of a's and b's$\}$. Both these languages happen to be CF, but the permutation closure of a CFL is not always CF. For example, $\{(abc)^n \mid n \geq 0\}$ is CF (indeed regular), yet its permutation closure $\{x \in \{a,b,c\}^* \mid x$ contains equal numbers of a's, b's, and c's$\}$ is not CF. Thus the languages of the non-directional Lambek calculus include some non-CF languages and do not include all CF languages. Weir and Joshi (1988) report that CG's with directional categories, forward and backward Function Application, and a generalized form of (forward and backward) Function Composition are weakly equivalent to TAG's, and thus also to MHG's and IG(1)'s.

A number of CG systems based on the work of Ades and Steedman (1982) and others have been investigated by Friedman and her co-workers (Friedman et al., 1982). These systems have unidirectional, parenthesis-free categories (parenthesization is assumed to the left) and a variety of function application and function composition rules. Some systems generate the CFL's, others a subset of the CFL's, and still others, depending on the particular inventory of reduction rules, generate languages which are "mildly context sensitive". At least all CSL's discovered thus far in the languages of these systems are generated by IG(1)'s, which as we saw above are weakly equivalent to TAG's and MHG's, and have CF-like growth functions.

The whole area of CG's and their mathematical properties is one currently under active investigation, and it would be premature to try to give a more thorough summary. A representative collection of recent work in CG can be found in Oehrle, Bach, and Wheeler (eds.) (1988).

Chapter 22

Transformational Grammars

One of the most important developments in the mathematical study of grammars of linguistic interest was the work of Peters and Ritchie (1973) and Ginsburg and Partee (1969) on the so-called "standard theory" transformational grammars of the sort outlined in Chomsky (1965).

The syntactic component of a transformational grammar consists of two parts: (1) a base component, which is a CFG or CSG, and (2) a transformational component, composed of an ordered set of transformational rules. The base generates an infinite class of trees by recursion through the initial symbol S. Each such tree serves as an input to the transformational rules, each of which defines a mapping from trees to trees. The transformational rules are assumed to be linearly ordered, the output of one forming the input to the next. If a given transformational rule cannot apply to a particular tree, the tree is left unchanged and the next rule in the sequence is considered.

In this version of transformational grammar, the transformational rules are assumed to apply in accordance with the principle of the *transformational cycle*. This specifies that the entire sequence of transformational rules applies first to the lowest S-rooted subtrees (those that properly contain no S-rooted subtrees). A single pass through all the transformational rules is said to constitute a *cycle*. Subsequent cycles take as their domains successively larger S-rooted subtrees, until finally on the last cycle the domain of application of the rules is the entire tree.

The tree that is the final output of the transformational rules is called a *surface structure*.

Transformational rules perform elementary operations of (i) deletion, (ii) substitution, and (iii) adjunction, but for our purposes here it suffices to observe only that deletion is constrained by a principle of *recoverability*. More specifically, any item deleted by a transformation must either leave behind a copy in a specified place in the tree or else be a fixed lexical item mentioned in the specification of the transformation.

Not every phase marker generated by the base need be mapped into a well-formed surface structure by the transformational component. For example, a special boundary symbol #, which is placed on both sides of every S by the rules of the base, may be erased by the application of certain transformational rules. If a phrase marker that is the final output of the transformational component contains any instance of #, it is not a well-formed surface structure, and the phrase marker that formed the original input is said to have been *filtered out* by the transformational rules.

A transformational grammar with this property is called a transformational grammar *with filtering*. On this view, then, a transformational grammar is a device for pairing base trees with well-formed surface structures. The language generated by the grammar is the set of all strings that appear as a sequence of leaves of some well-formed surface structure tree.

Peters and Ritchie showed that a transformational grammar formalized in this way with a context-sensitive grammar as its base has the same weak generative capacity as the type 0 grammars. That is, the languages generated by context-sensitive based transformational grammars are just the recursively enumerable sets.

The proof, which we only outline here, proceeds by showing first, for any given context-sensitive based transformational grammar G, how to construct a Turing machine that accepts all and only the terminal strings in $L(G)$. Thus, every transformational language is a r.e. set. The converse is proved in the following way. If L is a r.e. set, then there is some type 0 grammar G_0 generating L. Next, a type 1 grammar G_1 is constructed from G_0 such that for every x if $x \in L(G_n)$, $xb^m \in L(G_0)$ for some integer m, and conversely. This is done by taking each rule in the type 0 grammar whose right side is shorter than its left side and adding a sufficient number of b's (a special symbol not occurring in L) to make the rule "no-shrinking." Then rules are added which permute the b's with the other symbols, allowing the b's to migrate to the right side. Thus G_1 generates all the strings in $L(G_0)$ (equal to L) followed by some number of occurrences of b. From G_1 it is possible by using some results of Kuroda (1964) to construct an equivalent type 1 grammar G_1' in which every string xb^m generated is assigned the sort of tree structure shown in Fig. 22-1, where $x = \alpha_1 \ldots \alpha_{n-1}\alpha_n$, and

A, A', A'', A''' etc., are nonterminals distinct from S. G_1' is then taken as the base of a transformational grammar whose only transformational rule is to delete an occurrence of b if it is the rightmost terminal symbol of the sentence being processed on that cycle. Since this is the deletion of a fixed terminal symbol in a fixed position, it meets the condition on recoverability of deletions. Thus, the transformational component takes as input a tree of the form given in Figure 22-1 and deletes all occurrences of b (together with the nonterminals dominating each b) to produce a tree having $x = \alpha_1 \ldots \alpha_{n-1}\alpha_n$ as it leaves. This transformational grammar, therefore, generates all and only the strings of the original recursively enumerable set L.

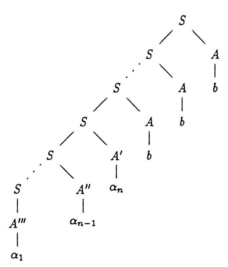

Figure 22-1.

Peters and Ritchie were able to show that transformational grammars still generate all r.e. sets even if the base is made context free rather than context sensitive. With a context-free base, however, the filtering effect of the transformational component must be used extensively; this feature is not needed at all for context-sensitive based transformational grammars to generate the r.e. sets.

These results raise serious difficulties for the standard theory. Since it is commonly supposed that natural languages are properly included in the recursive sets, which are, in turn, properly included in the r.e. sets, transformational grammars, by this formulation, are capable of generating sets of strings that are not possible natural languages. One of the goals of linguistic theory is to give a precise characterization of the notion 'possible grammar of a natural language,' and thus this version of the theory of transformational grammar is shown to fail to meet this goal by virtue of being too broad, i.e., allowing too large a class of grammars.

The nonrecursiveness of transformational languages was shown by Peters and Ritchie (1971) to arise solely from the fact that for any arbitrarily given transformational grammar G, there is no upper bound on the number of S-rooted subtrees that can occur in the base phrase marker underlying x. This is a consequence of the fact that the theory allows the transformational rules to pare down base phrase markers containing a large number of component S trees to produce very short strings without violating the condition on recoverability of deletion. In order for transformational grammars to generate only recursive sets they would have to be restricted in such a way that for any given grammar and any given sentence there is a procedure for determining the maximum number of cycles that could be involved in the derivation of the sentence by the grammar. This would be assured if transformational grammars had, for example, what Peters (1973) has termed the Survivor Property: "if ϕ is the input domain of any cycle ... and ψ is the output from that cycle, then ψ contains more terminal nodes than any subpart of ϕ on which the transformational cycle operated earlier in the derivation." Peters argued that existing transformational grammars did exhibit this property (with some minor exceptions which do not affect the overall result), a claim challenged by Wasow (1979), who argued that existing grammars could be shown to meet the weaker Subsistence Property (obtained by replacing "more" in the above condition by "no fewer.") This latter property had been shown in unpublished work by Myhill to be sufficient to guarantee the generation of only recursive languages.

The insufficiently restricted state the theory allowed an even more disturbing conclusion to be drawn: Given the sort of data that linguists ordinarily consider relevant, the Universal Base Hypothesis (the conjecture that the grammars of all natural languages have the same base rules) could not be proved false. The essential part of the argument comes in showing that even the trivial base component consisting of just two right-linear rules,

(22-1) 1. $S \rightarrow S\#$
       2. $S \rightarrow a_1 a_2 \ldots a_n b\#$

together with a small number of transformational rules, suffice to generate any recursively enumerable language on the alphabet $\{a_1, a_2, \ldots, a_n\}$. From this it is relatively straightforward to show that there are an infinite number of such trivial "universal bases." This result still holds when the grammar is constrained to be 'descriptively adequate,' in the sense that it give the intuitively correct results with respect to grammaticality, ambiguity, and paraphrase. Thus, given the powerful nature of the standard theory, certain propositions such as the Universal Base Hypothesis, whose truth value ought to depend on the facts of natural language, turn out to be trivially true.

Results such as these provide a particularly convincing demonstration of the importance of finding precise mathematical formulations of the grammars allowed by a linguistic theory, for it is only with the aid of such formulations that the consequences of the theory can be carefully investigated. Without them, we have little hope of being able to prove a theory wrong, much less of seeing wherein it fails and how it might possibly be corrected.

Appendix E-I

The Chomsky Hierarchy

Figure E.I-1 shows the inclusion relations that hold among the formal languages considered in this section (this is essentially the Chomsky Hierarchy). Tables E.I-1 and E.I-2 are a summary of closure and decision properties for these classes of languages.

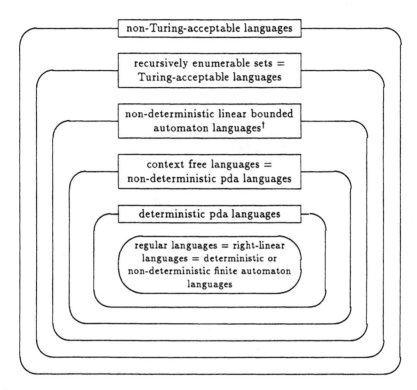

The non-Turing-acceptable languages

recursively enumerable sets =
Turing-acceptable languages

non-deterministic linear bounded
automaton languages[†]

context free languages =
non-deterministic pda languages

deterministic pda languages

regular languages = right-linear
languages = deterministic or
non-deterministic finite automaton
languages

[†] The context sensitive languages are the non-deterministic linear bound automaton languages$-\{e\}$. It is not known whether the deterministic linear bounded automaton languages are equal to the non-deterministic lba languages or are a proper subset.

Figure E.I–1: Inclusion relations of the
classes of formal languages

Class of languages	Operation					
	$\cup$	$\cap$	complementation	$\bullet$	$*$	$\cap$ with a regular language
Regular	yes	yes	yes	yes	yes	yes
Det. pda	no	no	yes	no	no	yes
Context free	yes	no	no	yes	yes	yes
Context sensitive	yes	yes	?	yes	no[†]	yes
Recursive	yes	yes	yes	yes	yes	yes
Recursively enumerable	yes	yes	no	yes	yes	yes

[†] The context sensitive languages do not contain e and therefore are never equal to Σ^*

Table E.I–1: Summary of closure properties
of classes of formal languages

Class of languages	Question					
	$x \in L(G)$?	$L(G) = \emptyset$?	$L(G) = \Sigma^*$?	$L(G_1) \subseteq L(G_2)$?	$L(G_1) = L(G_2)$?	$L(G_1) \cap L(G_2) = \emptyset$?
Regular	yes	yes	yes	yes	yes	yes
Det. pda	yes	yes	yes	no	?	no
Context free	yes	yes	no	no	no	no
Context sensitive	yes	no	yes[‡]	no	no	no
Recursive	yes	no	no	no	no	no
Recursively enumerable	no	no	no	no	no	no

[‡] This case is trivially decidable (the answer is always no) because the context sensitive languages do not contain e.

Table E.I–2: Summary of decidability
properties of classes of formal languages

Appendix E-II

Semantic Automata

Since the earliest days of modern generative linguistics the theory of automata and their relation to formal grammars has been a cornerstone of syntactic linguistic theories, but recently semantic applications have been developed by Johan van Benthem for 'quantifier automata'. In this section the main idea is outlined and illustrated, but for proofs of the advanced theorems the interested reader is referred to van Benthem (1986), chapter 8.

A *generalized quantifier* is interpreted as a functor $D_E AB$ which assigns to each domain E a binary relation between its subsets A and B (see Chapter 14). In the procedural view of quantifiers the determiner D of the NP takes as input a list of members of A marked for their membership in B and either accepts or rejects the list. In its mathematical formulation a determiner D is presented with finite sequences of 0's and 1's, where 0 stands for members of $A - B$ and 1 for members of $A \cap B$, respectively. The output of D is either 'yes' or 'no', depending on whether or not $D_E AB$ is true for the sequence read.

Examples:

   Every AB is recognized by the finite state machine in Fig. E.II-1. **Every AB** is true iff $|A - B| = 0$, so the **Every** automaton should accept all and only those sequences consisting of only 1's.

   In all figures S_0 is the initial state, and the square state always marks an accepting state, so in Fig. E.II-1 S_0 is also the accepting state. For instance, for **every man walks** the 1's represent men who walk and the 0's men who do not walk. The automaton accepts only 1's, i.e., whenever $A \subseteq A \cap B$. The negated quantifier **not every AB** is obtained by reversing the accepting and rejecting states of the **every** automaton.

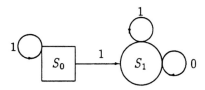

Figure E.II–1: **Every** automaton

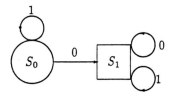

Figure E.II–2: **Not every** automaton

The **not every** automaton accepts sequences that consist of at least one A that is not in B. Reversal of accepting and rejecting states in finite state automaton for a determiner gives in general the automaton for the (externally) negated determiner. The automaton for **at least one (some)**, the dual of **every**, should accept any sequence containing at least one 1, i.e., one A that is also in B. It exchanges 1 and 0 in the initial state of the **every** automaton and reverses its accepting and rejecting states.

To complete the traditional Square of Opposition the **no** automaton, the negation of the **at least (some)** automaton, reverses its accepting and rejecting states, and accepts only sequences consisting of only 0's.

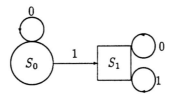

Figure E.II–3: **At least one (some)**
automaton

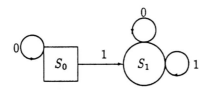

Figure E.II–4: **No automaton**

Comparison to the tree of numbers

There is a clear relation between the finite state automata for these determiners and their tree of numbers representation (see Chapter 14). In a
tree of numbers a node $\langle x, y \rangle$ corresponds to x 0's and y 1's in the input
for the automaton, since $x = |A - B|$ and $y = |A \cap B|$. The tree for **every**
shows that only the right most pair of numbers on each line is not in the
quantifier. The trees for **at least one (some)** and **no** are related in exactly
the same way. Thus we see that negation of a quantifier reverses the tree
pattern and switches accepting and rejecting states.

From a given tree the corresponding automaton can be derived by a
reduction algorithm. Let us look at the example for **at least one** first.
Nodes in the tree are first identified with states, connected by adding 0's
or 1's, and accepting states are indicated by squares. This can be shown
equivalent to the simpler automaton in figure E.II-3 by the reductions in

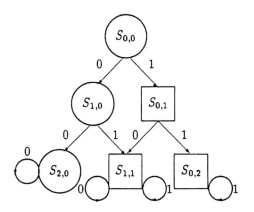

Figure E.II–5: The **at least one** tree of
numbers turned into an automaton

Fig. E.II-6.

The procedure which turns a tree into an automaton is specified as:

(i) look at the downward triangle generated by a node $\langle x, y \rangle$

(ii) turn it into a $+/-$ pattern

(iii) if it is identical to the triangle pattern of the node above and to the
right, it should correspond to the same state as that one

(iv) if it is identical to the node up and left, it is the same state as that
one

(v) the minimum number of states should be the number of distinct
triangle patterns in the tree

This procedure may not be completely general for arbitrarily complex determiners, but it works well for the limited cases we consider here. Here is
one more complicated example for **exactly two AB**.

In Figure E.II-7 the square states are the accepting states again, and
the bold face states represent the four states needed for the automaton,
corresponding to the four different triangle patterns in Fig. E.II-8. The
exactly two automaton is shown in Fig. E.II-9.

(1) mark all accepting states with ⊞ —all rejecting states with ⊟

(2) the configuration:

corresponds to the **acceptance for ever after-state**

(3) the configuration:

corresponds to the **rejection for ever after-state**

(4) the configuration:

corresponds to the **acceptance with 0-state**

(5) the configuration:

corresponds to the **rejection with 0-state**

(6) the configuration:

corresponds to the **acceptance with 1-state**

(7) the configuration:

corresponds to the **rejection with 1-state**

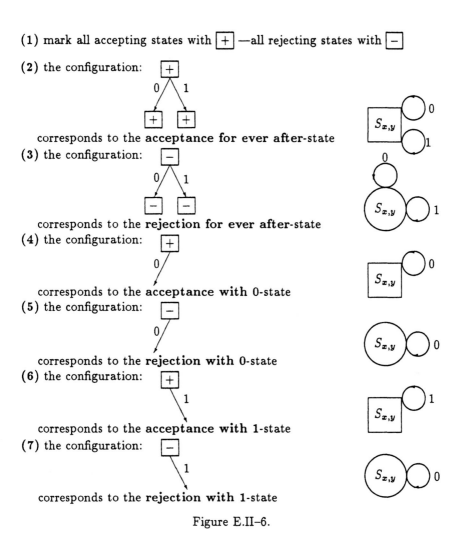

Figure E.II–6.

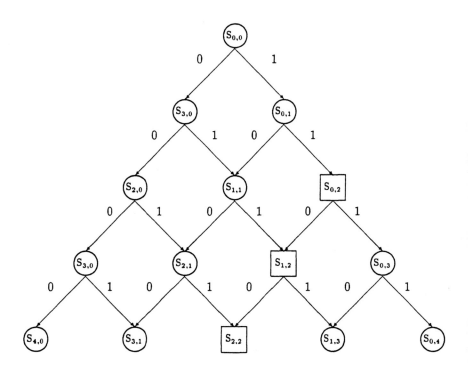

Figure E.II–7: The tree/automaton for
exactly two

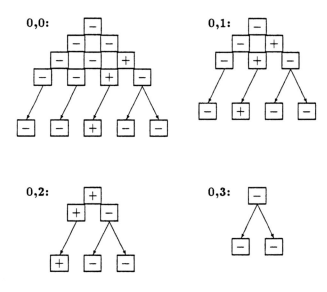

Figure E.II-8.

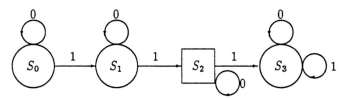

Figure E.II-9.

Higher order quantifiers

The determiner most is not recognized by any finite state machine; this follows from the Pumping Lemma. The language for most is context free so it can be recognized by pushdown automaton. The idea is that the stack stores the values read, and that complementary pairs 0,1 or 1,0 of the top stack symbol and the symbol being read are erased as they occur. When the entire sequence has been read the stack should only contain 1's. This is slightly liberal version of a pushdown automaton accepting with a non-empty stack, but it can be turned into a normal pushdown automaton with some additional encoding.

It turns out that higher order quantifiers may need context free languages, but, for instance, the higher order quantifier **an even number of** is recognized by a finite state machine. The following theorem characterizes the first-order definable determiners.

THEOREM E.II.1 *(van Benthem (1986)) All and only all first-order definable quantifiers are computable by permutation-invariant and acyclic finite state machines.* ■

Permutation-invariance means that any permutation in the order of 1's and 0's of an accepted or rejected list is accepted or rejected, and an automaton is acyclic when it contains no non- trival loops between states. A proportional determiner like **at least two-thirds** is essentially context free. A pushdown automaton for it keeps track of two top stack positions, comparing them with the next symbol read. If it reads 1 with 1,0 or 0,1 on top two positions of the stack it erases that top and continues. Likewise if it reads 0 with 1,1 on top. In the other cases the symbol read is stored on top of the stack. When the entire sequence is read, the automaton checks if the stack contains only 1's, and if so, it recognizes the sequence.

Many other determiners can be recognized by finite state or pushdown automata. It turns out that natural language determiners venture rarely, if at all, beyond the context free realm. For the proofs and more substantial arguments the interested reader is referred to van Benthem (1986).

Exercises

1. Design finite state automata for:
    (a) **at least three AB**
    (b) **all but one AB**
    (c) **an even number of AB**
    (d) **almost all AB** (in the sense of 'with at most finitely many exceptions')

Review Exercises

1. Consider the following grammar G:

    $S \rightarrow N$ seems certain

    $S \rightarrow$ I am right

    $N \rightarrow$ that S

   (a) List three members of $L(G)$.

   (b) Abbreviating so that $\Sigma = \{s, c, i, a, r, t\}$, construct a push down automaton which accepts $L(G)$.

2. For each language below, construct a non-deterministic finite state automaton which accepts all and only the specified strings. In all cases the input alphabet $\{0, 1\}$.

   (a) The terminal language of the following grammar:

    $S \rightarrow 0A$

    $S \rightarrow 1B$

    $A \rightarrow 0A$

    $A \rightarrow 1B$

    $B \rightarrow 1A$

    $B \rightarrow 1$

   (b) The set of all strings two or more symbols long whose first and last symbols are identical.

   (c) The set whose regular expression is $(01)^*1^*1$.

3. Find a regular expression for:

   (a) The language of problem 2a above.

   (b) The intersection of the languages of 2b and 2c.

(c) The set of all strings of 1's and 0's in which every substring of consecutive 1's is of even length.

e.g.

include:	but not:
011001111000	00100
0000	00110111
1111	01
0111111	111

4. Construct a Turing machine which operates with the alphabet $\{\#, a, b\}$ which when started in q_0 will move to the right until it encounters an a, change the a into an b, then move left until it encounters a different b, change that b into an $\#$, and halt. If there is no a to the right of the initially scanned square, or if there is such an a but no b to its left, the machine will never halt.

Solutions to

selected exercises

CHAPTER 1

1. (a) t; (b) f; (c) f; (d) t; (e) f; (f) t; (g) t; (h) f; (i) f; (j) t; (k) f;
(l) t; (m) f; (n) t; (o) f; (p) f; (q) f; (r) t

2. (a) yes; (b) no; (c) yes; (d) $\{\{S\}\}$

3. (a) *Rule:* 1. $5 \in A$
           2. If $x \in A, x + 5 \in A$
       Property: $A = \{x \mid x$ is positive and x is a multiple of $5\}$
   (b) *Property:* $B = \{x \mid x + 3$ is a positive multiple of $10\}$
       or $B = \{x \mid x$ is a positive integer whose last digit is $7\}$
   (c) *Rule:* 1. $300 \in C$
           2. If $x \in C$ and $x < 400, x + 1 \in C$
   (d) *Rule:* 1. $3 \in D$
           2. $4 \in D$
           3. If $x \in D, x + 4 \in D$
       or 1. $3 \in D$
           2. If $x \in D$ and x is odd, $x + 1 \in D$
           3. If $x \in D$ and x is even, $x + 3 \in D$
       Property: $D = \{x \mid x$ is a positive multiple of 4 or
                   $x + 1$ is a positive multiple of $4\}$

(e) *Rule:* 1. $0 \in E$

          2. If $x \in E$, then $x + 2 \in E$

          3. If $x \in E$, then $-x \in E$

(f) *Property:* $F = \{x \mid x = \frac{1}{2^n}$ where n is a non-negative integer$\}$

5. (c) $\{\emptyset\}$; (d) $\{\{\emptyset\}, \emptyset\}$;

    (e) $\{\emptyset, \{\{a\}\}, \{\{b\}\}, \{\{a,b\}\}, \{\emptyset\}, \{\emptyset, \{\{a\}\}, \{\emptyset, \{b\}\}, \{\emptyset, \{a,b\}\}, \{\{a\}, \{b\}\}, \{\{a\}, \{a,b\}\}, \{\{b\}, \{a,b\}\}, \{\emptyset, \{a\}, \{b\}\}, \{\emptyset, \{a\}, \{a,b\}\}, \{\emptyset, \{b\}, \{a,b\}\}, \{\{a\}, \{b\}, \{a,b\}\}, \{\emptyset, \{a\}, \{b\}, \{a,b\}\}\}$

6. (a) $\{a,b,c,2\}$, (b) $\{a,b,c,2,3,4\}$, (c) $\{a,b,c,\{c\}\}$, (d) $\{a,b,\{a,b\}, \{c,2\}\}$, (e) $\{b,c\}$, (f) $\{a,b\}$, (g) $\{a,b\}$, (h) $\{c\}$, (i) $\emptyset$, (j) $\emptyset$, (k) $\emptyset$, (l) $\{c,2,3,4\}$, (m) $\emptyset$, (n) $\{2\}$, (o) $\{a,b,\{c\}\}$, (p) $\emptyset$, (q) $\{\{a,b\}, \{c,2\}\}$

7. (a) $\{a,b,c,2\}$, (b) $\{a,b,c,2\}$, (c) $\{a\}$, (d) $\{2\}$, (e) $\{2\}$, (f) $\{a,b,c,2, 3,4,\{c\}\}$, (g) $\{2,3,4,\{a,b\}, \{c,2\}\}$, (h) $\{2,3,4,\{a,b\}, \{c,2\}\}$, (i) $\emptyset$, (j) U, (k) $\{b,c,2\}$, (l) $\{2\}$, (m) U, (n) U

8. (a) (i) $\{a,b,c,d\}$; (ii) $\{c\}$; (iii) $\{a,b,c,d\}$; (iv) $\emptyset$; (v) $\{c,d\}$; (vi) $\emptyset$; (vii) $\{a,b\}$

    (b) (i) no; (ii) yes

9. (b) 1. $A \cap (B - A)$

       2. $A \cap (B \cap A')$ Compl.

       3. $(B \cap A') \cap A$ Comm.

       4. $B \cap (A' \cap A)$ Assoc.

       5. $B \cap (A \cap A')$ Comm.

       6. $B \cap \emptyset$ Compl.

       7. $\emptyset$ Ident.

11. (b) 1. $(A \cup B) - (A \cap B)$

        2. $(A \cup B) \cap (A \cap B)'$ Compl.

        3. $(A \cup B) \cap (A' \cup B')$ DeM.

        4. $((A \cup B) \cap A') \cup ((A \cup B) \cap B')$ Distr.

        5. $(A \cap A') \cup (B \cap A') \cup (A \cap B') \cup (B \cap B')$ Distr. (twice)

        6. $\emptyset \cup (B \cap A') \cup (A \cap B') \cup \emptyset$ Compl. (twice)

        7. $(B \cap A') \cup (A \cap B')$ Ident. (twice)

        8. $(B - A) \cup (A - B)$ Compl. (twice)

        9. $(A - B) \cup (B - A)$ Comm. (twice)

    (c) $(X \cup Y) - (X \cap Y) = (Y \cup X) - (Y \cap X)$ by the commutativity of union and intersection.

(d) (i) $\emptyset$, (ii) A', (iii) A, (iv) $B - A$, (v) $A \cup B$

(e)
1. $(A - B) + (B - A)$
2. $((A - B) \cup (B - A)) - ((A - B) \cap (B - A))$ Def. of $A + B$
3. $(A + B) - ((A - B) \cap (B - A))$ Def. of $A + B$
4. $(A + B) - ((A \cap B') \cap (B \cap A'))$ Compl.
5. $(A + B) - (A \cap A' \cap B \cap B')$ Assoc., Comm.
6. $(A + B) - \emptyset$ Compl., Ident.
7. $(A + B) \cap \emptyset'$ Compl.
8. $(A + B) \cap U$ Compl.
9. $(A + B)$ Ident.

(f)
1. $(A + B) \subseteq B$
2. $(A + B) \cup B = B$ Cons. Prin.
3. $((A \cup B) - (A \cap B)) \cup B = B$ Def. of $A + B$
4. $((A \cup B) \cap (A \cap B)') \cup B = B$ Compl.
5. $((A \cup B) \cap (A' \cup B')) \cup B = B$ DeM.
6. $((A \cup B) \cup B) \cap ((A' \cup B') \cup B) = B$ Distr.
7. $(A \cup (B \cup B)) \cap (A' \cup (B' \cup B)) = B$ Assoc. (twice)
8. $(A \cup B) \cap (A' \cup U) = B$ Idemp., Ident.
9. $(A \cup B) \cap U = B$ Ident.
10. $A \cup B = B$ Ident.
11. $A \subseteq B$ Cons. Prin.

CHAPTER 2

1. (a) (i) $\{\langle b,2 \rangle, \langle b,3 \rangle, \langle c,2 \rangle, \langle c,3 \rangle\}$;
   (ii) $\{\langle 2,b \rangle, \langle 2,c \rangle, \langle 3,b \rangle, \langle 3,c \rangle\}$;
   (iii) $\{\langle b,b \rangle, \langle b,c \rangle, \langle c,b \rangle, \langle c,c \rangle\}$;
   (iv) $\{\langle b,2 \rangle, \langle b,3 \rangle, \langle c,2 \rangle, \langle c,3 \rangle, \langle 2,2 \rangle, \langle 2,3 \rangle, \langle 3,2 \rangle, \langle 3,3 \rangle\}$;
   (v) $\emptyset$ (since $A \cap B = \emptyset$);   (vi) same as $A \times B$
   (b) (i) True; (ii) False; (iii) False, $\langle c,c \rangle \in (A \times A)$; (iv) True;
   (v) True; (vi) True; (vii) True
   (c) (i) $\mathrm{dom}(R) = A$, $\mathrm{ran}(R) = \{b,2,3\}$;
   (ii) $R' = \{\langle b,c \rangle, \langle b,3 \rangle, \langle c,b \rangle, \langle c,c \rangle\}$,
       $R^{-1} = \{\langle b,b \rangle, \langle 2,b \rangle, \langle 2,c \rangle, \langle 3,c \rangle\}$;
   (iii) No.

2. In relations from A to B each of a, b, and c can be paired with 1, with 2, with both 1 and 2, or with neither, i.e., in four possible ways. Therefore there $4 \times 4 \times 4 = 64$ distinct relations. In functions from A to B each of a, b, and c can be paired with 1 or 2, i.e., in two possible ways. Therefore, there are $2 \times 2 \times 2 = 8$ distinct functions. Six of these are onto (only $\{(a,1),(b,1),(c,1)\}$ and $\{(a,2),(b,2),(c,2)\}$ are not onto). Since none of these are one-to-one and onto, none have inverses that are functions. There are 8×8 distinct relations from B to A of which $3 \times 3 = 9$ are functions. None are onto, six are one-to-one, and none have inverses that are functions.

3. (a) $R_2 \circ R_1 = \{\langle 1,2 \rangle, \langle 1,4 \rangle, \langle 1,3 \rangle, \langle 2,2 \rangle, \langle 2,4 \rangle, \langle 2,3 \rangle, \langle 3,4 \rangle, \langle 4,2 \rangle, \langle 4,3 \rangle, \langle 4,4 \rangle\}$, $R_1 \circ R_2 = \{\langle 3,4 \rangle, \langle 3,1 \rangle, \langle 1,1 \rangle, \langle 1,2 \rangle, \langle 1,4 \rangle, \langle 2,4 \rangle, \langle 2,3 \rangle, \langle 2,1 \rangle, \langle 1,3 \rangle\}$
   (b) $R_1^{-1} \circ R_1 = \{\langle 1,1 \rangle, \langle 1,2 \rangle, \langle 1,4 \rangle, \langle 2,1 \rangle, \langle 2,2 \rangle, \langle 2,4 \rangle, \langle 3,3 \rangle, \langle 3,4 \rangle, \langle 4,4 \rangle, \langle 4,3 \rangle, \langle 4,2 \rangle, \langle 4,1 \rangle\}$

CHAPTER 3

1. (a)(ii) irreflexive, non-symmetric, non-transitive
   Note: In considering transitivity, it can be misleading to consider only triples of *distinct* elements, as this example shows. For if a is the brother of b (aBb) and bBc, and a, b, c are all distinct, a must indeed be the brother of c. But consider a pair of brothers: aBb and bBa; now it is false that a is the brother of a, as one would have to conclude if the relation were transitive.

2. (a) Irreflexive (no utterance forms a minimal pair with itself), symmetric, nontransitive (e.g., $\langle$ cat, bat $\rangle$ and $\langle$ bat, bag $\rangle$ are minimal pairs but not $\langle$ cat, bag $\rangle$), and nonconnected;
   (d) Irreflexive or reflexive (depending on how the term 'allophone' is interpreted), symmetric, transitive (if "phonemic overlap" is excluded, otherwise nontransitive) and nonconnected. If one takes the view that it is reflexive, symmetric, and transitive, then A is an equivalence relation that partitions the set of English phones into equivalence classes corresponding to the ("taxonomic") phonemes of English;
   (e) Reflexive, symmetric, transitive, and nonconnected (in general). Each equivalence class contains all the sets that have the same numbers of members;

3. (a) R_1 and R_1^{-1}: reflexive, antisymmetric, nontransitive, nonconnected; R_1': irreflexive, nonsymmetric, nontransitive, nonconnected; R_2 and R_2^{-1}: irreflexive, asymmetric, transitive, connected; R_2': reflexive, antisymmetric, transitive, connected; R_3 and R_3^{-1}: nonreflexive, symmetric, nontransitive, nonconnected; R_3': nonreflexive, symmetric, nontransitive, nonconnected; R_4 and R_4^{-1}: reflexive, symmetric, transitive, nonconnected; R_4': irreflexive, symmetric, intransitive, nonconnected; R_4 ($= R_4^{-1}$) is an equivalence relation. The partition induced in A is $\{\{1,3\},\{2,4\}\}$
(b) $\{\langle 1,1 \rangle, \langle 2,2 \rangle, \langle 3,3 \rangle, \langle 4,4 \rangle, \langle 2,3 \rangle, \langle 3,2 \rangle\}$
(c) 15

4. The fallacy lies in ignoring the if-clause in the definition of symmetry: *if aRb, then bRa*. The "proof" takes aRb for granted, so a counterexample can be constructed by finding a relation R which is symmetric and transitive on a certain set S where for some a, a does not bear the relation R to *any* member of S. Such an example is the following: Let S be the set of all humans and let R be defined by 'aRb if and only if a and b have the same parents and those parents have at least two children'. Then an only child does not bear R to anyone, including himself. (A simpler R might be 'has the same oldest brother as', but it could be objected that the relation is simply not defined, rather than failing to hold among people who have no older brothers.)

5. (a) $R = \{\langle 1,1 \rangle, \langle 2,2 \rangle, \langle 3,3 \rangle, \langle 5,5 \rangle, \langle 6,6 \rangle, \langle 10,10 \rangle, \langle 15,15 \rangle, \langle 30,30 \rangle, \langle 1,2 \rangle, \langle 1,3 \rangle, \langle 1,5 \rangle, \langle 1,6 \rangle, \langle 1,10 \rangle, \langle 1,15 \rangle, \langle 1,30 \rangle, \langle 2,6 \rangle, \langle 2,10 \rangle, \langle 2,30 \rangle, \langle 3,6 \rangle, \langle 3,15 \rangle, \langle 3,30 \rangle, \langle 5,10 \rangle, \langle 5,15 \rangle, \langle 5,30 \rangle, \langle 6,30 \rangle, \langle 10,30 \rangle, \langle 15,30 \rangle\}$, which is reflexive, antisymmetric, transitive, and nonconnected.
(b) 1 is minimal and least; 30 is maximal and greatest.

CHAPTER 4

1. There is one-to-one correspondence of every set with itself—for example, the identity function. Thus, the relation of equivalence of sets is reflexive. If f is a one-to-one correspondence from A to B, then f^{-1} is a one-to-one correspondence from B to A. Therefore, the relation is symmetric. If f and g are one-to one correspondences from A to B and

from B to C, respectively, then $g \circ f$ is a one-to-one correspondence from A to C. (This can be easily shown by an indirect proof.) Thus, the relation is transitive.

2. The set can be denoted $\{10^1, 10^2, 10^3, 10^4, \ldots\}$.

4. The cardinality is $\aleph_0$. A 1–1 correspondence between the set of all sentences of English and the natural numbers could be established as follows: First, arrange all the sentences into groups according to the number of symbols in their written form, and order these groups linearly starting with the group of the shortest sentences. Within each group, arrange the sentences alphabetically (using some arbitrary convention for the punctuation marks and space). This procedure puts all the sentences into a single linear order, and thus establishes a 1–1 correspondence between the sentences and the natural numbers.

5. The hotelkeeper uses his intercom to ask each guest to move into the room whose number is twice the number of his present room. That leaves all the odd numbered rooms empty, so each football player can double the number on his shirt and subtract one to find his room number.

6. (a) The turtles can be numbered as follows:

Since the turtles can be effectively listed, so can the corresponding monotheistic sects, and the cardinality of the set of such sets is therefore $\aleph_0$;

(b) Taking the preceding enumeration, it is clear that each sect corresponds to a subset of the set of all natural numbers; the atheistic sect corresponds to $\emptyset$, the monotheistic sets to singleton sets. The set of all sects therefore can be put in one-to-one correspondence with $\mathcal{P}(N)$ and thus has cardinality $2^{\aleph_0}$.

7. (a) Let $A = \{1, 2, 3, \ldots\}$ and $B = \{0\}$.

(b) Let $A = \{0, 1, 2, \ldots\}$ and $B = \{a, b\}$. The set $\{\langle 0, a \rangle, \langle 0, b \rangle,$

$\langle 1,a \rangle, \langle 1,b \rangle, \langle 2,a \rangle, \langle 2,b \rangle, \ldots \}$ is mapped 1–1 onto $\{0,1,2,3,\ldots\}$ by $f(n,a)=2n$, $f(n,b)=2n+1$.
(c) Let $A=\{0,2,4,6,\ldots\}$ and $B=\{1, 3,5,7,\ldots\}$.
(d) Let $A = \{0,1,2,3,\ldots\}$ and let B be the set of "primed" integers $\{0',1',2',3',\ldots\}$ disjoint from A. $A \times B$ is equivalent to $A \times A$, which has cardinality $\aleph_0$.

REVIEW PROBLEMS, PART A

1. (a) A_4; (b) $\emptyset$; (c) A_5; (d) A_4

2. Sample answers:
   (a) Let aRb be $a+b = 5$ or $\mid a - b \mid = 1$ or $a \times b = 24$ or '$a+b$ is odd'.
   (b) Let aRb be $a > b$ or '$a - b$ is positive'.

3. (a) Antisymmetric, transitive, reflexive
   (b) Yes. If $n \in N$, $n = \{0,1,2,3,\ldots,n-1 \}$. If $x \in n$, x is a natural number smaller than x. Then since all the members of x are natural numbers smaller than x, they are also smaller than n and therefore members of n. Hence x is a subset of n. It is a proper subset, i.e., not equal to n, because x was given as a member of n, and the members of n do not include n itself.

5. (a) The set of all members could be represented graphically in a family tree diagram:

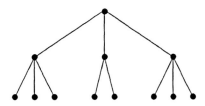

where left-to-right order of branches from a single node represents oldest-to-youngest order among brothers. Then the nodes can be effectively enumerated proceeding top-to-bottom and left-to-right:

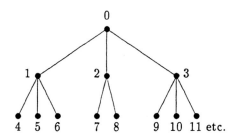

(b) Assume that the set of all clubs is denumerably infinite, so that the clubs could be listed as $C_0, C_1, C_2, C_3, \ldots$. Then define a new club C^* by the membership requirement:

$$\text{man}_i \in C^* \text{ if and only if } \text{man}_i \notin C_i$$

Since C^* is thereby made distinct from every club in the putative listing, the listing could not have been complete, i.e., no complete effective enumeration is possible.

6. (asterisked entries are discussed below)

	PO	SO	WO
(a)	yes	yes	no
(b)	yes	yes	no
(c)	yes	yes	no*
(d)	no*	no	no
(e)	yes	yes	yes
(f)	yes	no*	no
(g)	yes	yes	yes*
(h)	yes	yes	no*

(c) It is easy to be misled into thinking that the negative rational numbers with 0 are well-ordered by the relation $\geq$, because the *whole* set does have a first element, namely 0. But well-ordering requires that *every subset* have a first element, and there are in this case infinitely many subsets that do not. Consider, for example, the subset consisting of all the negative rational numbers less than -1. There is no first (i.e. largest) number in that set, since for any rational number x which is less than -1 it is possible to find another rational number y which is larger than x but still smaller than -1;

(d) The set is not even partially ordered, because two distinct strings may have the same length—i.e., antisymmnetry does not hold;

(f) The ordering looks like this:

$$0, 2, 4, 6, 8, \ldots$$

$$1, 3, 5, 7, 9, \ldots$$

with no relation holding between any evens and any odds. This sort of ordering satisfies the partial ordering definition, but fails to meet the linear-ordering requirement that R hold in some direction between every pair of elements.

(g) The ordering looks like this:

$$0, 2, 4, 6, 8, 10, \ldots, 1, 3, 5, 7, 9, \ldots$$

This is a well-ordering; every subset has a first element, which will be the smallest even number in the subset, if there are any, and otherwise the smallest odd number in the subset;

(h) The ordering looks like this:

$$\ldots, 9, 7, 5, 3, 1, 0, 2, 4, 6, 8, \ldots$$

This is not a well-ordering, since any subset which includes infinitely many odd numbers will lack a first member.

7. If $|A| \geq |B|$ and $|B| \geq |C|$, there are functions $f: A \to B$ and $g: B \to C$ which are onto B and C, respectively. We prove that $g \circ f$ is an onto function (from A to C). Assume that it is not onto. Then there is some $z \in C$ such that for no $x \in A$, $(g \circ f)(x) = z$, i.e., $g(f(x)) = z$. But g is onto C, and thus there is some $y \in B$ such that $g(y) = z$. Thus it must be that there is no $x \in A$ such that $f(x) = y$. But this contradicts the assumption that f is onto B. Therefore, $g \circ f$ is onto C, and $|A| \geq |C|$.

PART B

CHAPTER 6

1. (Other proposition letters may be used, other interpretations may be argued for, and other equivalent symbolizations are possible for any given interpretation.)

(a) j = John is in that room, m = Mary is in that room, $j \vee m$

(b) a = the fire was set by an arsonist, e = there was an accidental explosion in the boiler room, $(a \vee e) \,\&\, \sim(a \,\&\, e)$, or equivalently, $a \leftrightarrow \sim e$

(c) r = it rains, p = it pours:
(1) If the statement means that every rainstorm is a big one, then "when" must be translated as "if and only if", since it can't pour without raining: $r \leftrightarrow p$
(2) In the famous salt advertisement, the second "it" refers to salt, which presumably can also pour when it isn't raining, $r \to p$

(d) s = Sam wants a dog, a = Alice prefers cats, $s \,\&\, a$. (The difference between "but" and "and" relates to the content of the conjoined sentences, not their truth values)

(e) l = Steve comes home late, s = Steve has had some supper, r = we will reheat the stew:
(1) If one interprets the "if" as "if and only if", then the proposition can be symbolized as $(l \,\&\, \sim s) \leftrightarrow r$
(2) Under the interpretation that the stew may be reheated in any case, then the symbolic form is $(l \,\&\, \sim s) \to r$

(f) c = Clarence is well educated, r = Clarence can read Chuvash, $c \to r$

(g) c = this cat goes, i = I go, $c \vee i$, or equivalently $\sim c \to i$ (The statement might also be taken to mean $\sim c \leftrightarrow i$.)

(h) m = Marsha goes out with John, b = John shaves off his beard, d = John stops drinking, $m \to (b \vee d)$ (The statement might also be taken to mean $m \leftrightarrow (b \,\&\, d)$.)

(i) n = negotiations commence, b = Barataria ceases all acts of aggression against Titipu, $n \to b$

2. (a) j = John is going to the movies, b = Bill is going to the movies, t = Tom is going to the movies, $j \& b \& \sim t$

(b) s = Susan likes squash, t = Susan likes turnips, $\sim (s \lor t)$ or equivalently, $\sim s \& \sim t$

(c) p = Peter is going to the party, f = Fred is going to the party, i = I am going to the party, $\sim (p \lor f) \to \sim i$ or equivalently, $(\sim p \& \sim f) \to \sim i$

(d) l = Mary has gotten lost, a = Mary has had an accident, h = Mary will be here in five minutes, $(\sim l \& \sim a) \to h$ or equivalently, $\sim (l \lor a) \to h$

(e) b = a bear frightened the boys, w = a wolf frightened the boys, $b \lor w$

(f) p = a party would have amused the children, s = a softball game would have amused the children, $p \& s$. (Perhaps $p \lor s$ could be argued for, but under the natural interpretation that either one would have amused them, then one is saying both that a party would have amused them and that a softball game would have amused them.)

3. (b) False; **(d)** True; **(f)** False

4. (a) and **(b)** are logically equivalent.

5. (b) $p : 1, q : 0$, or $p : 0, q : 1$;

(d) $p : 1, q : 0, r : 0$ or $1, s : 1$;

(e) $p : 1, q : 0, r : 1, s : 1$, or $p : 0, q : 1, r : 1, s : 1$

6. (a) tautology; **(b)** contingent; **(c)** tautology; **(d)** contradiction; **(e)** contingent

7. (a) $p \to q$ can be defined as $\sim (p \& \sim q)$

(b) $p \& q$ can be defined as $\sim (\sim p \lor \sim q)$

(c) $p \leftrightarrow q$ can be defined as $(p \to q) \& (q \to p)$

8. (a)

1.	$\sim p \lor (p \& q)$	
2.	$(\sim p \lor p) \& (\sim p \lor q)$	Distr.
3.	$(p \lor \sim p) \& (\sim p \lor q)$	Comm.
4.	$T \& (\sim p \lor q)$	Compl.
5.	$(\sim p \lor q) \& T$	Comm.
6.	$\sim p \lor q$	Ident.

(b) $\sim p$; **(c)** F; **(d)** $\sim p$; **(e)** T

9. (a)
1. $p \to q$
2. $q \to r$
3. $\sim r$
4. $\sim q$ 2,3, M.T.
5. $\sim p$ 1,4, M.T.

(d)
1. $p \to \sim q$
2. $r \to q$
3. $\sim r \to s$
4. | p Auxiliary Premise
5. | $\sim q$ 1,4, M.P.
6. | $\sim r$ 2,5, M.T.
7. | s 3,6, M.P.
8. $p \to s$ 4-7, C.P.

(f)
1. $p \vee (q \,\&\, r)$
2. $\sim t$
3. $(p \vee q) \to (s \vee t)$
4. $\sim p$
5. $(p \vee q) \,\&\, (p \vee r)$ 1, Distr.
6. $p \vee q$ 5, Simpl.
7. $s \vee t$ 3,6, M.P.
8. s 2,7, D.S.
9. $p \vee r$ 5, Simpl.
10. r 4,9, D.S.
11. $r \,\&\, s$ 8, 10, Conj.

(h)
1. $\sim p \to q$
2. $r \to (s \vee t)$
3. $s \to \sim r$
4. $p \to \sim t$
5. | r Auxiliary Premise
6. | $s \vee t$ 2,5, M.P.
7. | $\sim s$ 3,5, M.P.
8. | t 6,7, D.S.
9. | $\sim p$ 4,8, M.T.
10. | q 1,9, M.P.
11. $r \to q$ 5-10, C.P.

(i)
1. $p \rightarrow (q \& r)$
2. $q \rightarrow s$
3. $r \rightarrow t$
4. $(s \& t) \rightarrow \sim u$
5. u
6. p Auxiliary Premise
7. $q \& r$ 1,6, M.P.
8. q 7, Simpl.
9. s 2,8, M.P.
10. r 7, Simpl.
11. t 3,10, M.P.
12. $s \& t$ 9,11, Conj.
13. $\sim u$ 4,12, M.P.
14. $u \& \sim u$ 5,13, Conj.
15. $\sim p$ 6-14, Indirect Proof

(l)
1. p
2. $(p \& q) \vee (p \& r)$
3. $(p \vee q) \rightarrow \sim r$
4. $p \vee q$ 1, Addn.
5. $\sim r$ 3,4, M.P.
6. $p \& (q \vee r)$ 2, Distr.
7. $q \vee r$ 6, Simpl.
8. q 5,7, D.S.
9. $p \& q$ 1,8, Conj.
10. $(p \& q) \vee (\sim p \& \sim q)$ 9, Addn.
11. $p \leftrightarrow q$ 10, Bicond.

10. (a) valid, B = the butler killed the baron, K = the cook killed the baron, C = the chauffeur killed the baron, S = the stew was poisoned, Q = there was a bomb in the car:

1. $B \vee K \vee C$
2. $(K \rightarrow S) \& (C \rightarrow Q)$
3. $\sim S \& \sim B$
4. $\sim B$ 3, Simpl.
5. $K \vee C$ 1,4, D.S.
6. $K \rightarrow S$ 2, Simpl.
7. $\sim S$ 3, Simpl.
8. $\sim K$ 6,7, M.T.
9. C 5,8, D.S.

(b) Valid; (c) Invalid (recall that 'p only if q' is represented logically as $p \to q$); (d) Valid; (e) Invalid (let it be false that the segment is voiceless and let all the other elementary propositions be true).

11. (a) R is an equivalence relation since
(1) it is reflexive: $x \leftrightarrow x$ is always true
(2) it is symmetric: whenever $x \leftrightarrow y$ is true, $y \leftrightarrow x$ is true (since they have the same truth tables)
(3) it is transitive: if $x \leftrightarrow y$ is true; $y \leftrightarrow z$ is true, then $x \leftrightarrow z$ is true; otherwise, if $x \not\leftrightarrow z$, then for some assignment of truth values to elementary statements there would be some y which is both true and false.

(b) $\{p, (p \lor p), (p \,\&\, (q \lor \sim q)), (p \lor (q \,\&\, \sim q))\}$
$\{(p \lor q), (\sim q \to p), (\sim p \to q)\}$
$\{(p \lor \sim p), (p \to (q \to p)), (p \lor (q \lor \sim q))\}$

12. (a)

	TRUE			FALSE	
1.	$p \to (q \to r)$			$p \,\&\, \sim q$	
	$\sim(\sim p \lor r)$				
2.				$\sim p \lor r$	
3.				$\sim p$	
4.				r	
5.	p				
6.	$6._1\ q \to r$	$6._2$	$6._1$	$6._2\ p$	
		======		======	
7.	$7._{11}\ r$	$7._{12}$	$7._{11}$	$7._{12}\ q$	
	======		======		
8.	$8._{121}$	$8._{122}$	$8._{121}\ p$	$8._{122}\ \sim q$	
	======		======		
9.		$9._{122}\ q$		$9._{122}$	
		======		======	

All the subtableaux close, so the tableau closes, and the argument is shown to be valid.

(c)

	TRUE	FALSE
1.	$((p \rightarrow q) \& (s \vee t))$ $(t \rightarrow q)$	$((p \rightarrow q) \vee \sim(s \rightarrow q))$
2.	$(p \rightarrow q)$	
3.	$(s \vee t)$	
4.		$(p \rightarrow q)$
		======
5.		$\sim(s \rightarrow q)$

This tableau remains open.

13. (a) (i) KKApqAqrAps, (ii) CKNpCNpqq, (iii) CApqKErsp

   (b) (i) $p \vee ((\sim p \& \sim q) \rightarrow (p \& (q \leftrightarrow r)))$
      (ii) $(\sim (((((p \leftrightarrow q) \leftrightarrow r) \& s) \vee p) \& q) \vee r) \& s$
      (iii) $\sim ((((p \leftrightarrow q) \& r) \vee s) \rightarrow t)$

   (c) NApq $\Leftrightarrow$ KNpNq, NKpq $\Leftrightarrow$ ANpNq

CHAPTER 7

1. (a) $(\forall x)(B(x) \vee W(x))$: $B(x)$ – 'x is black', $W(x)$ – 'x is white'

   (c) $(\forall x)(D(x) \rightarrow Q(x))$: $D(x)$ – 'x is a dog', $Q(x)$ – 'x is a quadruped'

   (e) $(\forall x)(\exists y)L(x,y)$: $L(x,y)$ – 'x loves y'

   (g) $(\exists x)(\forall y)L(x,y)$: $L(x,y)$ – 'x loves y'

   (i) $(\forall x)(L(x,x) \rightarrow (x = j))$: $L(x,y)$ – 'x loves y', j – 'John'

   (k) $(\forall x)((W(x) \& L(g,x)) \rightarrow (K(g,x) \vee M(g,x)))$:
      $W(x)$ – 'x is a woman', $L(x,y)$ – 'x loves y',
      g – 'you', $K(x,y)$ – 'x kisses y', $M(x,y)$ – 'x loses y'

   (m) $(\forall x)((P(x) \& M(x,h)) \rightarrow L(x,h))$:
      $P(x)$ – 'x is a person', h – 'New York', $L(x,y)$ – 'x loves y',
      $M(x,y)$ – 'x lives in y'

   (o) $(\forall x)(\sim L(x,h) \rightarrow \sim N(x,h))$:
      $L(x,y)$ – 'x loves y', h –'New York', $N(x,y)$ – 'x knows y'

   (q) $(\forall x)(\forall y)((F(y,x) \& G(x,y,g) \rightarrow (\exists z)(H(z,y) \& I(g,z,x)))$
      $F(x,y)$ – 'x is a finger of y', $G(x,y,z)$ – 'x gives y to z',
      $H(x,y)$ – 'x is the whole hand of which y is a finger',
      $I(x,y,z)$ – 'x takes y from z', g – 'he'

(s) $((\exists x)N(x) \rightarrow (\forall x)A(x))$:
$N(x)$ – 'x is noisy', $A(x)$ – 'x is annoyed'

(t) $\sim(\exists x)N(x) \,\&\, A(j)$:
$N(x)$ – 'x made noise', $A(x)$ – 'x was annoyed', j – 'John'

(v) $(\forall x)(A(x) \rightarrow B(x))$:
$A(x)$ – 'x causes bad accidents',
$B(x)$ – 'x is a drunk driver under 18'

(x) $(\forall x)(A(x) \rightarrow B(x))$:
$A(x)$ – 'x is drunk', $B(x)$ – 'for x to drive is risky'

2. (a) $\sim(\exists x)(P(x) \,\&\, (\forall y)(Q(y) \rightarrow A(x,y)))$

(b) $(\forall x(Q(x) \rightarrow (\exists y)(P(y) \,\&\, A(y,x)))$

(d) $(\exists x)(P(x) \,\&\, (\forall y)(Q(y) \rightarrow\sim A(x,y)))$, although 'some people' might also be taken to mean not 'at least one person' but 'at least two persons'.

(e) $L(x,y)$ – 'x likes y', $(\forall x)(L(x,\text{Mary})) \leftrightarrow \sim I(x,\text{Mary}))$

(g) $T(x,y)$ – 'x attempted y',
$(\forall x)((P(x) \,\&\, (\exists y)(Q(y) \,\&\, A(x,y))) \rightarrow (\exists z)(Q(z) \,\&\, T(x,z)))$

3. (a) x in $P(x)$ bound, last x and the y free; (b) x free, y and z bound; (c) everything bound; (d) first x bound, everything else free; (e) everything bound

4. (a) (1) Yes. Applying (7-24) to $(\forall z)$ in the translation gives

$$(\forall z)((\forall x)(\exists y)F(y,x) \,\&\, (O(z) \rightarrow I(z))).$$

Then $(\forall x)$ and $(\exists y)$ can be moved outside by the following sequence of equivalences. Note first that $P \,\&\, Q \Leftrightarrow \sim(P \rightarrow \sim Q)$. Thus, $(\forall x)P(x) \,\&\, Q \Leftrightarrow \sim((\forall x)P(x) \rightarrow \sim Q) \Leftrightarrow$
$\sim(\exists x)(P(x) \rightarrow \sim Q)$ (by Law 11) $\Leftrightarrow$
$(\forall x) \sim(P(x) \rightarrow \sim Q)$ (by Law 1''') $\Leftrightarrow$
$(\forall x)(P(x) \,\&\, Q)$.
The steps for $(\exists y)$ are similar.

(2) No. Applying (7-24) in reverse to $(\forall z)$ in (2) gives

$$(\exists y)(\forall x)(F(y,x) \,\&\, (\forall z)(O(z) \rightarrow I(z)))$$

which says 'There is something which is everything's father, and all odd numbers are integers'.

(3) Yes. Applying Law 6 to (1).

(b) **(1)** No. (1) is equivalent by Law 9 to $B(a) \rightarrow (\forall x) \sim (M(x) \rightarrow H(x))$, which is equivalent by the steps noted in the answer to (a,1) to $B(a) \rightarrow (\forall x)(M(x) \& \sim H(x))$, which says 'If Adam is a bachelor, then everything is a man and a non-husband', or loosely, 'If Adam is a bachelor, then everyone is a bachelor'.
(2) Yes. Apply Law 10 to (2), then Law 1.
(3) No. 'It's not the case that if Adam is a bachelor then all men are husbands.' (N.B. This is equivalent to: 'Adam is a bachelor and not all men are husbands.')
(4) Yes.

(c) **(1)** Yes (by equivalences concerning $\rightarrow$, &, and $\sim$).
(2) Yes, (by Law 12).

5. (a) $(\forall x)(I(x) \rightarrow (\exists y)(I(y) \& L(y,x)))$,
$(\forall x)(\exists y)(I(x) \rightarrow (I(y) \& L(y,x)))$,
$\sim(\exists x)(I(x) \& \sim(\exists y)(L(y,x))$
(and many others; such listings are never exhaustive)

(b) $((\forall x)(P(x) \rightarrow O(x)) \lor (\exists y)(I(y) \& \sim O(y)))$,
$(\exists y)((\forall x)(P(x) \rightarrow O(x)) \lor (I(y) \& \sim O(y)))$,
By various applications of commutativity and Laws 9-12:
$(\forall x)(\exists y)((P(x) \rightarrow O(x)) \lor (I(y) \& \sim O(y)))$,
$(\exists y)(\forall x)((P(x) \rightarrow O(x)) \lor (I(y) \& \sim O(y)))$
(Note that this is one case in which the order of universal and existential quantifiers is immaterial; the reason is that there are no two-place predicates relating x and y.)

(c) $((\exists x)(P(x) \& \sim O(x)) \rightarrow (\forall y)((P(y) \& G(y,7)) \rightarrow O(y)))$. It is natural to try an alphabetic change of variable and a reinterpretation of $\rightarrow$ in terms of $\sim$ and $\lor$, in hopes of leading to an application of Law 3. However, once we get to: $((\forall x) \sim (P(x) \& \sim O(x)) \lor (\forall x)((P(x) \& G(x,7)) \rightarrow O(x)))$, we see that only Law 4, which is not an equivalence, will apply. With two variables, we can apply Laws 9 and 12 to get: $(\forall x)(\forall y)((P(x) \& \sim O(x)) \rightarrow ((P(y) \& G(y,7)) \rightarrow O(y)))$

(d) $(\forall x)(H(x) \rightarrow M(x)) \rightarrow M(s)$,
$(\exists x)((H(x) \rightarrow M(x)) \rightarrow M(s))$,
$\sim M(s) \rightarrow (\exists x)(H(x) \& \sim M(x))$, etc.

6. (a) $(((\exists x)A(x)\,\&\,(\exists x)B(x)) \to C(x))$

     1. $(((\exists y)A(y)\,\&\,(\exists z)B(z)) \to C(x))$ alph. variant

     2. $(\sim((\exists y)A(y) \to \sim(\exists z)B(z)) \to C(x))$ put in terms of $\sim$, $\to$

     3. $(\sim(\forall y)(A(y) \to \sim(\exists z)B(z)) \to C(x)$ Law 12

     4. $(\sim(\forall y)(A(y) \to (\forall z)\sim B(z)) \to C(x))$ Law 1

     5. $(\sim(\forall y)(\forall z)(A(y) \to \sim B(z)) \to C(x))$ Law 9

     6. $((\exists y)(\exists z)\sim(A(y) \to \sim B(z)) \to C(x))$ Law 1 (2x)

     7. $(\forall y)(\forall z)(\sim(A(y) \to \sim B(z)) \to C(x))$ Law 12 (2x)

     8. $(\forall y)(\forall z)((A(y)\,\&\,B(z)) \to C(x))$

(b) $(\forall x)A(x) \leftrightarrow (\exists x)B(x)$

     1. $\sim(((\forall x)A(x) \to (\exists y)B(y)) \to \sim((\exists w)B(w) \to (\forall z)A(z)))$

                              alph. variants and in terms of $\sim$, $\to$

     2. $\sim((\exists x)(\exists y)(A(x) \to B(y)) \to \sim(\forall w)(\forall z)(B(w) \to A(z)))$

                              Laws 9, 10, 11, 12

     3. $\sim((\exists x)(\exists y)(A(x) \to B(y)) \to (\exists w)(\exists z)\sim(B(w) \to A(z)))$

                              Law 1

     4. $\sim(\forall x)(\forall y)(\exists w)(\exists z)((A(x) \to B(y)) \to \sim(B(w) \to A(z)))$

                              Laws 10 and 12

     5. $(\exists x)(\exists y)(\forall w)(\forall z)\sim((A(x) \to B(y)) \to \sim(B(w) \to A(z)))$

                              Law 1

     6. $(\exists x)(\exists y)(\forall w)(\forall z)((A(x) \to B(y))\,\&\,(B(w) \to A(z)))$

7. (a)   1. $\sim(\exists x)(P(x)\,\&\,Q(x))$

        2. $(\exists x)(P(x)\,\&\,R(x))$

        3. $P(w)\,\&\,R(w)$ 2, E.I.

        4. $(\forall x)\sim(P(x)\,\&\,Q(x))$ 1, Quant. Neg.

        5. $\sim(P(w)\,\&\,Q(w))$ 4, U.I.

        6. $\sim P(w) \lor \sim Q(w)$ 5, DeM.

        7. $P(w)$ 3, Simpl.

        8. $\sim Q(w)$ 6,7, D.S.

        9. $R(w)$ 3, Simpl.

       10. $R(w)\,\&\,\sim Q(w)$ 8,9, Conj.

       11. $(\exists x)(R(x)\,\&\,\sim Q(x))$ 10, E.G.

(e) 1. $(\forall x)(P(x) \rightarrow Q(x))$
 2. $R(a)$
 3. $P(a)$
 4. $P(a) \rightarrow Q(a)$ 1, U.I.
 5. $Q(a)$ 3,4, M.P.
 6. $R(a) \,\&\, Q(a)$ 2,5, Conj.
 7. $(\exists x)(R(x) \,\&\, Q(x))$ 6, E.G.

(f) 1. $(\forall x)((P(x) \lor Q(x)) \rightarrow R(x))$
  2. $(\forall x)((R(x) \lor S(x)) \rightarrow T(x))$
  3. | $P(v)$ Auxiliary Premise
  4. | $(P(v) \lor Q(v)) \rightarrow R(v)$ 1, I.U.
  5. | $P(v) \lor Q(v)$ 3, Addn.
  6. | $R(v)$ 4,5, M.P.
  7. | $(R(v) \lor S(v)) \rightarrow T(v)$ 2, U.I.
  8. | $R(v) \lor S(v)$ 6, Addn.
  9. | $T(v)$ 7,8, M.P.
 10. $P(v) \rightarrow T(v)$ 3-10, C.P.
 11. $(\forall x)(P(x) \rightarrow T(x))$ 10, U.G.

8. (c) $D(x) = x$ is a duck, $O(x) = x$ is an officer, $P(x) = x$ is (one of) my poultry, $W(x) = x$ waltzes

 1. $(\forall x)(D(x) \rightarrow \sim W(x))$
 2. $(\forall x)(O(x) \rightarrow W(x))$
 3. $(\forall x)(P(x) \rightarrow D(x))$
 4. $P(v) \rightarrow D(v)$ 3, U.I.
 5. $D(v) \rightarrow \sim W(v)$ 1, U.I.
 6. $P(v) \rightarrow \sim W(v)$ 4,5, H.S.
 7. $O(v) \rightarrow W(v)$ 2, U.I.
 8. $\sim W(v) \rightarrow \sim O(v)$ 7, Cond.
 9. $P(v) \rightarrow \sim O(v)$ 6,8, H.S.
 10. $(\forall x)(P(x) \rightarrow \sim O(x))$ 9, U.G.

9. (a)

	TRUE	FALSE	$D = \{a, \ldots\}$
1.	$\sim(\exists x)F(x)$	$(\forall x)\sim F(x)$	
2.		$(\exists x)F(x)$	
3.		$\sim F(a)$	
4.	$F(a)$		
5.		$F(a)$	
	======	======	

(b)

	TRUE	FALSE	$D = \{a, b\}$
1.	$(\forall x)(\exists y)R(x, y)$	$(\exists y)(\forall x)R(x, y)$	
2.	$(\exists y)R(a, y)$		
3.		$(\forall x)R(x, a)$	
4.	$R(a, a)$		
5.		$R(a, a)$	
	======	======	
6.		$R(b, a)$	
7.	$(\exists y)R(b, y)$		
8.	$R(b, a)$		
	======	======	
9.	$R(b, b)$		
10.		$R(a, b)$	

So a counterexample consists of a model with a universe of discourse $D = \{a, b\}$ and an extension $R = \{\langle a, a\rangle, \langle b, b\rangle\}$

(c)

	TRUE	FALSE	$D = \{a, \ldots\}$
1.	$(\exists y)(\forall x)R(y, x)$	$(\forall x)(\exists y)R(y, x)$	
2.	$(\forall x)R(a, x)$		
3.	$R(a, a)$		
4.		$(\exists y)R(y, a)$	
5.		$R(a, a)$	
	======	======	
6.		$(\exists y)R(y, b)$	
7.		$R(a, b)$	
8.		$R(b, b)$	
		======	
9.	$R(a, b)$		
	======		

10. (a)

	1.	$V_1 \subseteq V_2 \,\&\, V_2 \subset V_3$	Auxiliary Premise
	2.	$V_2 \subset V_3$	1, Simpl.
	3.	$V_2 \subseteq V_3 \,\&\, V_2 \neq V_3$	2, Def. of $\subset$
	4.	$V_2 \subseteq V_3$	3, Simpl.
	5.	$V_1 \subseteq V_2$	1, Simpl.
	6.	$V_1 \subseteq V_2 \,\&\, V_2 \subseteq V_3$	4,5, Conj.
	7.	$V_1 \subseteq V_3$	6, (7-54)
	8.	$V_1 = V_3$	1, Auxiliary Premise
	9.	$V_1 \subseteq V_3 \,\&\, V_3 \subseteq V_1$	8, (7-52)
	10.	$V_3 \subseteq V_1$	9, Simpl.
	11.	$V_3 \subseteq V_1 \,\&\, V_1 \subseteq V_2$	5,10, Conj.
	12.	$V_3 \subseteq V_2$	11, (7-54)
	13.	$V_2 \subseteq V_3 \,\&\, V_3 \subseteq V_2$	4,12 Conj.
	14.	$V_2 = V_3$	13, (7-52)
	15.	$V_2 \neq V_3$	3, Simpl.
	16.	$V_2 = V_3 \,\&\, V_2 \neq V_3$	14,15, Conj.
	17.	$V_1 \neq V_3$	8-16, Indirect Proof
	18.	$V_1 \subseteq V_3 \,\&\, V_1 \neq V_3$	7,17, Conj.
	19.	$V_1 \subset V_3$	18, Def. of $\subset$
	20.	$(V_1 \subseteq V_2 \,\&\, V_2 \subset V_3) \to V_1 \subset V_2$	1-19, Conditional Proof
	21.	$(\forall X, Y, Z)((X \subseteq Y \,\&\, Y \subset Z) \to$ $X \subset Z)$	20, U.G.

11. (a) Assume $x \in (A - B)$. Then $x \in A$ and $x \notin B$, from which it follows that $x \in A$. Therefore, if $x \in (A - B)$, then $x \in A$. Thus, $(A - B) \subseteq A$. (b) If $A = B$, then $(A - A) \cup (A - A) = \emptyset \cup \emptyset = \emptyset$. If $(A - B) \cup (B - A) = \emptyset$, then both $A - B = \emptyset$ and $B - A = \emptyset$ (otherwise the union could not equal $\emptyset$). $A - B = \emptyset$ means $\sim (\exists x)(x \in A \,\&\, x \notin B)$, which by Quant. Neg., DeM., and Cond. is equivalent to $(\forall x)(x \in A \to x \in B)$, i.e., $A \subseteq B$. Similarly, $B - A = \emptyset$ is equivalent to $B \subseteq A$. Thus, $A = B$. (e) If $x \in \wp(A) \cup \wp(B)$ then $x \in \wp(A)$ and $x \in \wp(B)$. $x \in \wp(A)$ iff $x \subseteq A$ and $x \in \wp(B)$ iff $x \subseteq B$. If $x \subseteq A$ and $x \subseteq B$, then $x \subseteq A \cap B$, and thus $x \in \wp(A \cap B)$. The converse is proved by taking these steps in the opposite order.

CHAPTER 8

1. Assume that *atomic statement* is defined as in (8-7).
   Base: Every atomic statement is a Pwff (Polish well-formed formula).
   Recursion: For all α and β, if α and β are Pwff's, then so are

   (a) $N\alpha$, (b) $A\alpha\beta$, (c) $K\alpha\beta$, (d) $C\alpha\beta$, (e) $E\alpha\beta$

   Restriction: Nothing else is a Pwff.

2. $f(0) = 2, f(n) = (f(n-1))^2$;
   $f(0) = 2$
   $f(1) = (f(0))^2 = 2^2 = 4$
   $f(2) = (f(1))^2 = 4^2 = 16$
   $f(3) = (f(2))^2 = 16^2 = 256$
   $f(4) = (f(3))^2 = 256^2 = 65,536$

4. The power set of the set with zero members, $\emptyset$, is $\{\emptyset\}$, which has
   one member. Since $2^0 = 1$, this establishes the base. To prove the
   induction step, let A_{k+1}, a set with $k + 1$ members, be formed from
   A_k, a set with k members, by the addition of some element x not in A_k;
   i.e., $A_{k+1} = A_k \cup \{x\}$. Let $B_1, B_2, \ldots, B_{2^k}$ be the 2^k members of $P(A_k)$.
   $P(A_{k+1})$ contains all these sets plus the sets formed by taking $B_{2^k} \cup \{x\}$.
   This makes an additional 2^k set. Thus, $P(A_{k+1})$ has $2(2^k) = 2^{k+1}$
   members. The desired result now follows by Mathematical Induction.

6. The induction fails in going from 1 to 2 as the reader can verify by
   letting n take on the value 1 in the induction step.

7.

1. $p\to(q\to p)$ (A1)

2. $((\sim q\to \sim p)\to(p\to q))\to$
$\quad\quad\quad (\sim p\to((\sim q\to \sim p)\to(p\to q)))$ 1, (R2)
   (Subst. $(\sim q\to \sim p)\to(p\to q)$ for p and $\sim p$ for q)

3. $(\sim p\to \sim q)\to(q\to p)$ (A3)

4. $(\sim q\to \sim p)\to(p\to q)$ 3, (R2)
   (Subst. p for q and q for p)

5. $\sim p\to((\sim q\to \sim p)\to(p\to q))$ 2,4, (R1)

6. $(p\to(q\to r))\to((p\to q)\to(p\to r))$ A2

7. $(\sim p\to((\sim q\to \sim p)\to(p\to q)))\to$
$\quad\quad\quad ((\sim p\to(\sim q\to \sim p))\to(\sim p\to(p\to q)))$ 6, (R2)
   (Subst. $\sim p$ for p, $(\sim q\to \sim p)$ for q, and $(p\to q)$ for r)

8. $(\sim p\to(\sim q\to \sim p))\to(\sim p\to(p\to q))$ 5,7, (R1)

9. $\sim p\to(\sim q\to \sim p)$ 1, (R2)
   (Subst. $\sim p$ for p and $\sim q$ for q)

10. $\sim p\to(p\to q)$ 8,9, (R1)

8. The alphabet is $(p,\,',\,N,\,A,\,K,\,C,\,E)$; the axioms are the elementary propositions as defined in (8-7); the productions are:

$$x \;\to\; Nx$$
$$x,y \;\to\; Axy$$
$$x,y \;\to\; Kxy$$
$$x,y \;\to\; Cxy$$
$$x,y \;\to\; Exy$$

where x and y are any strings on the alphabet. An equivalent semi-Thue system has a basic alphabet as above, an auxiliary alphabet $\{Q,R\}$, and axiom set $\{Q\}$, and productions:

$$Q \;\to\; NQ$$
$$Q \;\to\; AQQ$$
$$Q \;\to\; KQQ$$
$$Q \;\to\; CQQ$$
$$Q \;\to\; EQQ$$
$$Q \;\to\; R$$
$$R \;\to\; R'$$
$$R \;\to\; p$$

9. $A = \{J, K\}, B = \{a\}, S = \{J, K\};$

$$P: \quad \alpha J\beta \quad \rightarrow \quad \alpha Jaa\beta$$
$$\alpha J\beta \quad \rightarrow \quad \alpha\beta$$
$$\alpha K\beta \quad \rightarrow \quad \alpha Kaaa\beta$$
$$\alpha K\beta \quad \rightarrow \quad \alpha\beta$$

where α, β are any strings on $(A \cup B)^*$.

11. If the axiom had not been independent, it would be provable from the remaining axioms. But then its deletion from the set of axioms would have no effect on the total system: anything that could be proved before could still be proved. If that is not the case, the axiom must have been independent.

12. (c) "0" is interpreted as +1; "is a natural number" as "is a power of -2"; "successor of x" as "-2 times x". Thus the sequence is viewed as having the form: $(-2)^0, (-2)^1, (-2)^2, (-2)^3, \ldots$

13. (a) In this model, the "lines" are not the sides or diagonals of the rectangle, but rather pairs of vertices, by Axiom 1.

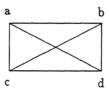

(b) Consider an arbitrary point p. By Axiom 2 there is at least one other point; call it q. By Axiom 3, there is a line containing p and q; call it L_1. By Axiom 4, there exists a point not in L_1; call it r. By Axiom 3 again, there is a line containing p and r; call it L_2. Thus p is in at least two lines, L_1, and L_2.

(c) Assume the empty set is one of the lines. Consider any point p: by (b) above, p is in at least two distinct lines L_1 and L_2. But then Axiom 5 is violated, because p is a point not in the empty line, but L_1 and L_2 are both lines containing p and disjoint from the above empty line.

(d) This was proved in the course of proving (b) above.

(e) No, because Axioms 2 and 3 together contradict the new axiom.

REVIEW PROBLEMS, PART B

1. If $P \leftrightarrow Q$ is true, then either P and Q are both true or P and Q are both false. In either case $P \vee \sim Q$ is true.

2. Other valid derivations are possible in all the following examples:

(a) 1. p
     2. q
     3. $p \,\&\, q$ 1,2, Conj.
     4. $(p \,\&\, q) \vee r$ 3, Addn.

(b) 1. $p \leftrightarrow q$
     2. $(p \to q) \,\&\, (q \to p)$ 1, Bicond.
     3. $(q \to p) \,\&\, (p \to q)$ 2, Comm.
     4. $q \to p$ 3, Simpl.
     5. $\sim q \vee p$ 4, Cond.

(c) 1. $p \to (q \to \sim\sim r)$
     2. $p \,\&\, \sim r$
     3. p 2, Simpl.
     4. $q \to \sim\sim r$ 3,1, M.P.
     5. $q \to r$ 4, Compl.
     6. $\sim r \,\&\, p$ 2, Comm.
     7. $\sim r$ 6, Simpl.
     8. $\sim q$ 7,5, M.T.

(d) 1. $p \vee q$
     2. $\sim p \vee r$
     3. $\sim q$
     4. $q \vee p$ 1, Comm.
     5. p 4,3 D.S.
     6. $p \to r$ 2, Cond.
     7. r 5,6, M.P.

(e) 1. $p \& (q \rightarrow (r \lor \sim\sim s))$
    2. q
    3. p 1, Simpl.
    4. $q \rightarrow (r \lor \sim\sim s)$ 1, Comm. Simpl.
                                 (2 steps)
    5. $r \lor \sim\sim s$ 2,4, M.P.
    6. $\sim\sim s \lor r$ 5, Comm.
    7. $s \lor r$ 6, Compl.
    8. $p \& (s \lor r)$ 3,7, Conj.

(f) 1. $\sim(p \lor \sim q)$
    2. $r \lor p$
    3. $\sim p \& \sim \sim q$ 1, De M.
    4. $\sim p$ 3, Simpl.
    5. $p \lor r$ 2, Comm.
    6. r 5,4, D.S.
    7. $\sim \sim q$ 3, Comm. Simpl.
                            (2 steps)
    8. q 7, Compl.
    9. $q \& r$ 8,6, Conj.

(g) 1. $p \rightarrow q$
    2. $p \rightarrow (q \rightarrow r)$
    3. $q \rightarrow (r \rightarrow s)$
    4. | p Auxiliary premise
    5. | q 4,1, M.P.
    6. | $q \rightarrow r$ 4,2, M.P.
    7. | r 5,6, M.P.
    8. | $r \rightarrow s$ 5,3, M.P.
    9. | s 7,8, M.P.
  10. $p \rightarrow s$ 4-9, Conditional proof

(h) 1. $r \to (p \lor s)$
    2. $q \to (s \lor t)$
    3. $\sim s$
    4. $\sim p \,\&\, \sim t$ Auxiliary premise
    5. $\sim p$ 4, Simpl.
    6. $\sim p \,\&\, \sim s$ 5,3, Simpl.
    7. $\sim (p \lor s)$ 6, DeM.
    8. $\sim r$ 7,1, M.T.
    9. $\sim t$ 4, Comm. Simpl.
  10. $\sim s \,\&\, \sim t$ 3,9, Conj.
  11. $\sim (s \lor t)$ 10, DeM.
  12. $\sim q$ 11,2, M.T.
  13. $\sim r \,\&\, \sim q$ 8,12, Adjunction
  14. $(\sim p \,\&\, \sim t) \to (\sim r \,\&\, \sim q)$ 4-13 Conditional proof

(i) 1. $p \to q$
   2. $\sim q \,\&\, r$
   3. p Auxiliary premise
   4. q 3,1, M.P.
   5. $\sim q$ 2, Simpl.
   6. $q \,\&\, \sim q$ 4,5, Conj.
   7. $\sim p$ 3-6, Indirect Proof

(j) 1. $p \lor q$
   2. $r \,\&\, \sim p$
   3. $\sim q$ Auxiliary premise
   4. p 1,3, D.S.
   5. $\sim p \,\&\, r$ 2, Comm.
   6. $\sim p$ 5, Simpl.
   7. $p \,\&\, \sim p$ 4, 6, Conj.
   8. q 3-7, Indirect Proof

(k) 1. $p \leftrightarrow (\sim q \to r)$
     2. $\sim r \,\&\, \sim(s \to q)$
     3. | p Auxiliary premise
     4. | $(p \to (\sim q \to r))$ 1, Bicond.
        | $\&\, ((\sim q \to r) \to p)$
     5. | $p \to (\sim q \to r)$ 4, Simpl.
     6. | $\sim q \to r$ 3,5, M.P.
     7. | $\sim(s \to q)$ 2, Comm. Simpl.
     8. | $s \,\&\, \sim q$ 7, Cond., Compl., DeM.
     9. | $\sim q$ 8, Comm. Simpl.
    10. | r 9,6, M.P.
    11. | $\sim r$ 2, Simpl.
    12. | $r \,\&\, \sim r$ 10,11, Conj.
    13. $\sim p$ 3-12, Indirect Proof

3.   1. $r \,\&\, (p \lor q)$ Premise
         2. $\sim(p \,\&\, r)$ Premise
         3. $\sim(q \,\&\, r)$ Premise
         4. r 1, Simpl
         5. $\sim p \lor \sim r$ 2, DeM.
         6. $\sim r \lor \sim p$ 3, Comm.
         7. $r \to \sim p$ 6, Cond.
         8. $\sim p$ 4,7, M.P.
      9-12. $\sim q$ analogous to 5-8
        13. $\sim p \,\&\, \sim q$ 8,12, Conj.
        14. $\sim(p \lor q)$ 13, DeM.
        15. $p \lor q$ 1, Comm., Simpl.

Since 14 is the negation of 15 and both are derived from the premises, the premises are inconsistent.

6. (a) $(\forall x)(hx \to qx) \,\&\, (\exists y)(qy \,\&\, \sim hy)$ or
       $(\forall x)(hx \to qx) \,\&\, (\exists x)(qx \,\&\, \sim hx)$ or
       $(\forall x)(hx \to qx) \,\&\, (\exists x) \sim(qx \to hx)$ or
       $(\forall x)(hx \to qx) \,\&\, \sim(x)(qx \to hx)$ (or yet others);

   (b) Let Ixy: x is identical with y, Pxy: x is a phonemic transcription of y, Ux: x is an utterance, $(\forall x)(\forall y)[(Ux \,\&\, Uy \,\&\, \sim Ixy) \to (\forall z)(\forall w)((Pzx \,\&\, Pwy) \to \sim Izw))]$
       or $(\forall x)(\forall y)(\forall z)(\forall w)((Ux \,\&\, Uy \,\&\, \sim Ixy \,\&\, Pzx \,\&\, Pwy) \to \sim Izw)$

(or any other logically equivalent expression);

7. (b) $D(x) = x$ is a cab driver, $H(x) = x$ is a head waiter, $S(x) = x$ is surly, $C(x) = x$ is churlish

1. $(\forall x)((D(x) \lor H(x)) \to (S(x) \& C(x)))$
2. $D(v)$ Aux. Premise
3. $D(v) \lor H(v)$ 2, Addn.
4. $(D(v) \lor H(v)) \to (S(v) \& C(v))$ 1, U.I.
5. $S(v) \& C(v)$ 3,4, M.P.
6. $S(v)$ 5, Simpl.
7. $D(v) \to S(v)$ 2-6, Cond. Proof
8. $(\forall x)(D(x) \to S(x))$ 7, U.G.

PART C

CHAPTER 9

1. (a) The universal set U, the union of all the sets in the collection, is the (two-sided) identity.

   (b) If U is a member of the collection, then it is the only element with an inverse; viz., itself.

2. (a) ϕ is the (two-sided) identity element for union. ϕ is the only element with an inverse; viz., itself.

   (b) ϕ is also the (two-sided) identity element for symmetric difference (for all A, $A + \phi = \phi + A = A$). Every set A is its own inverse ($A + A = \phi$).

3. Let I_1 be a (two-sided) identity for union. Then for all A, $A \cup I_1 = I_1 \cup A = A$, by definition. Let I_2 be another (two-sided) identity and $I_1 \neq I_2$. But when $A = I_2$ we have, $I_2 \cup I_1 = I_1 \cup I_2 = I_2$. But since I_2 is also an identity, $I_1 \cup I_2 = I_1$, contradicting the assumption that $I_1 \neq I_2$.

CHAPTER 10

1. Consider the group operation table, or "multiplication table," for addition modulo 4:

+ mod 4	0	1	2	3
0	0	1	2	3
1	1	2	3	0
2	2	3	0	1
3	3	0	1	2

Closure is shown by the fact that every cell of the table if filled with an element of the set $\{0, 1, 2, 3\}$. Associativity must be verified by exhaustion (or else by a general argument, which in this case would take even longer, since the best general argument would go by way of proving associativity for addition over *all* the integers). The fact that 0 is the unique identity element is evident from the fact that the 0-column and the 0-row match the outside column and row respectively, and no other rows or columns do. The fact that 1 and 3 are inverses of each other and that 2 and, of course, 0 are each their own inverses can be seen from the position of the 0's in the table.

2. (a) No; e.g. $7 \circ 3 \equiv 10 \pmod{11}$, and 10 is not in the set, so the closure property fails.
   (b) Yes, if it's associative, which in fact it is.
   (c) No, a is the identity element; c is its own inverse, but has d as an additional "right-inverse," i.e. $c \circ d = a$, which violates the uniqueness condition on inverses (Corollary 10.2); in addition, d has no "right-inverse," which violates part of axiom G4. Also, the operation is not associative.
   (d) Yes. (Remember to check associativity.)
   (e) No. The identity element is $\emptyset$, but no sets other than $\emptyset$ have inverses.
   (f) No. (g) Yes. (h) No.

3. (a) The convention for multiplication tables is that the entry in the ath row and the bth column shows $a \circ b$, not $b \circ a$. This makes a difference

for non-commutative operations like this one.

	$a \circ b$	I	R	R'	R''	H	V	D	D'
	I	I	R	R'	R''	H	V	D	D'
	R	R	R'	R''	I	D	D'	V	H
	R'	R'	R''	I	R	V	H	D'	D
a	R''	R''	I	R	R'	D'	D	H	V
	H	H	D'	V	D	I	R'	R''	R
	V	V	D	H	D'	R'	I	R	R''
	D	D	H	D'	V	R	R''	I	R'
	D'	D'	V	D	H	R''	R	R'	I

(columns: b)

(b) $\langle\{I, R, R', R''\}, \circ\rangle$, $\langle\{I, R', H, V\}, \circ\rangle$,$\langle\{I, R', D, D'\}, \circ\rangle$;
(c) The sets are $\{I, R'\}$, $\{I, H\}$, $\{I, V\}$, $\{I, D\}$, $\{I, D'\}$. The operation tables all look alike:

	I	X
I	I	X
X	X	I

(d) $\langle\{I, R', H, V\}, \circ\rangle$ and $\langle\{I, R', D, D'\}, \circ\rangle$. It turns out that *any* correspondence which maps I onto I is an isomorphism in this case, e.g., $I \to I$, $R \to R'$, $H \to D$, $V \to D'$, or $I \to I$, $R' \to D$, $H \to D'$, $V \to R'$, etc.
(e) For the subgroup $\langle\{I, R, R', R''\}, \circ\rangle$, the only non-trivial automorphism is $I \to I$, $R \to R''$, $R' \to R'$, $R'' \to R$. For the other two subgroups, any of the non-I elements can correspond to any other, so there are actually five different non-trivial automorphisms for each of them, of which the following is one example for $\langle\{I, R', H, V\}, \circ\rangle$: $I \to I$, $R' \to V$, $H \to R'$, $V \to H$.
(f) For the subgroup $\langle\{I, R, R', R''\}, \circ\rangle$ and any of the subgroups $\langle\{I, X\}, \circ\rangle$, the only possible homomorphism is $I \to I$, $R' \to I$, $R \to X$, $R'' \to X$.
It may be useful to see why some other correspondences do *not* give homomorphisms. Consider, for instance, the correspondence $f(I) = I$, $f(R) = R'$, $f(R') = R'$, $f(R'') = R'$. This is not a homomorphism because, for instance, $R \circ R' = R''$ but $f(R) \circ f(R') = R' \circ R' = I$, and $I \neq f(R'')$. For either of the other two subgroups, the one with $\{I, R', H, V\}$ or the one with $\{I, R', D, D'\}$, there are several possible

homomorphisms with any of the $\{I,X\}$ subgroups. They all have the
following form: Let I and any other one element correspond to I, and
let the other two elements correspond to X, e.g., for $\langle\{I,R',H,V\},\circ\rangle$
and $\langle\{I,D\},\circ\rangle$, one possible homomorphism is $I \rightarrow I$, $R' \rightarrow I$,
$H \rightarrow D, V \rightarrow D$.

4. It must be a subset because the original group had to contain an iden-
    tity element; by definition the identity element is included, associativ-
    ity is automatic for subsets of groups, and since the identity element
    is its own inverse, all the group axioms are satisfied.

5. (a) No. The second and third group axioms are satisfied, but 2, 3, and
    4 lack inverses, and $2 \circ 3 = 0$, which is not a member of the set.
    (b) Multiplication is associative, the set is closed under it, 1 is the
    identity element, $2^{-1} = 4$, $3^{-1} = 5$, $6^{-1} = 6$.
    (c) $\langle\{1\},\times \bmod 7\rangle$, $\langle\{1,6\},\times \bmod 7\rangle$, $\langle\{1,2,4\},\times \bmod 7\rangle$.
    (d) $\langle\{0,1,2,3,4,5\},+ \bmod 6\rangle$. Correspondence:

$$\begin{array}{llll}
0 \rightarrow 1 & & 0 \rightarrow 1 & \\
1 \rightarrow 3 & & 1 \rightarrow 5 & \\
2 \rightarrow 2 & \text{or} & 2 \rightarrow 4 & \text{(no others)} \\
3 \rightarrow 6 & & 3 \rightarrow 6 & \\
4 \rightarrow 4 & & 4 \rightarrow 2 & \\
5 \rightarrow 5 & & 5 \rightarrow 3 &
\end{array}$$

(e) Condition: n must be a prime number.

6. S must be a group to be a subgroup of S'. The only further condition
    to be met is that the set of S be a subset of the set of S'', and that
    follows from the transitivity of "is a subset of," plus the fact that the
    subset relation must hold between the sets of S and S' and between
    those of S' and S''.

7. (a) Examples: the set of all positive rationals of the form $1/n$, or the
    set of all positive integers, or the set of all rational numbers equal to
    or greater than 1.
    (b) It is a semigroup and a monoid, but not a group because 0 has no
    inverse.

8. Symmetric difference can easily be shown to be commutative and asso-
    ciative either by set-theoretic equalities or by Venn diagrams. It is not

idempotent since $A + A = \emptyset$. $\emptyset$ is the two-sided identity element, and every set is its own inverse. $\langle P(A), + \rangle$ is an Abelian group of order 4.

10. (a) 1. $a + b = a + c$ — Premise
2. $-a + (a + b) = -a + (a + c)$ — By D2, a has an additive inverse $-a$ and addition is well-defined and unique
3. $(-a + a) + b = (-a + a) + c$ — By D2, $+$ is *associative*
4. $0 + b = 0 + c$ — Def. of inverse, 0 is the additive identity
5. $b = c$ — Def. of additive identity

(b) 1. $a + 0 = a$ — Def. of identity
2. $a \circ (a + 0) = a \circ a$ — Uniqueness of multiplication (i.e. if $a + 0$ and a are the same element, then there is a single element which is that element multiplied by a)
3. $a \circ (a + 0) = a \circ a + a \circ 0$ — Distributive law
4. $a \circ a + a \circ 0 = a \circ a$ — 2,3, Transitivity of $=$
5. $-(a \circ a) + (a \circ a + a \circ 0) = -(a \circ a) + a \circ a$ — Existence of add. inverse, Uniqueness of addition
6. $(-(a \circ a) + a \circ a) + a \circ 0 = -(a \circ a) + a \circ a$ — Associativity of $+$
7. $0 + a \circ 0 = 0$ — Def. of inverse
8. $a \circ 0 = 0$ — Def. of identity

The proof that $0 \circ a = 0$ is similar. $0 \circ a = 0$ also follows directly from $a \circ 0 = 0$.

(c) (1) Associativity of +
    (2) Distributive law
    (3) Def. of inverse
    (4) By the theorem of problem b.
    (5) Distributive law
    (6) Def. of inverse
    (7) By the theorem of problem b.
    (8) From 4, 7, by symmetry and transitivity of $=$.

11. Given: $a < b$ and $b < c$. Then $a + b < b + c$, by the addition law. Since $-b = -b$,

$$(a + b) + (-b) < (b + c) + (-b) \quad \text{by the addition law}$$
$$a + (b + (-b)) < ((-b) + b) + c \quad \text{by assoc. and comm.}$$
$$a + 0 < 0 + c \quad \text{by def. of inverse}$$
$$a < c \quad \text{by def. of 0}$$

13. (a) To show: every positive integer n has the property that for all m, $a^m \circ a^n = a^{m+n}$

  (i) To show that 1 has that property:
$$a^m \circ a^1 = a^m \circ a \quad \text{(by def.)}$$
$$= a^{m+1} \quad \text{(by def.)}$$

  (ii) To show that if k has the property, then $k + 1$ must have it:
$$a^m \circ a^k = a^{m+k} \quad \text{conditional premise}$$
$$a^m \circ a^{k+1} = a^m \circ (a^k \circ a) \quad \text{by def.}$$
$$= (a^m \circ a^k) \circ a \quad \text{by assoc. of } \circ \text{ in integral domains}$$
$$= a^{m+k} \circ a \quad \text{by the conditional premise}$$
$$= a^{(m+k)+1} \quad \text{by def.}$$
$$= a^{m+(k+1)} \quad \text{by assoc. of } + \text{ in ordinary arithmetic}$$

From (i) and (ii) the conclusion follows by the principle of mathematical induction.

(b) We will use induction on n. $P(n)$: for all m, $(a^m)^n = (a^n)^m$

  (i) for $n = 1$: $(a^m)^1 = a^m \quad \text{(by def.)}$
$$= (a^1)^m \quad (\text{since } a = a^1, \text{ by def.})$$

  (ii) To show that $P(k) \rightarrow P(k+1)$:

$$
\begin{aligned}
(a^m)^k &= (a^k)^m && \text{conditional premise} \\
(a^m)^{k+1} &= (a^m)^k \circ a^m && \text{by def.} \\
&= (a^k)^m \circ a^m && \text{by the conditional premise} \\
&= (a^k \circ a)^m && a^n \circ b^n = (a \circ b)^n \\
& && \text{(theorem proved in text)} \\
&= (a^{k+1})^m && \text{by def.}
\end{aligned}
$$

Since $P(1)$ holds and $P(k) \rightarrow P(k+1)$, it follows from the principle of mathematical induction that $P(n)$ holds for all n.

CHAPTER 11

1. 11-1 and 11-2 are lattices; in 11-3 there is no lub for $\{a,b\}$, nor any glb for $\{c,d\}$.

2. (i) (a), (b), and (c) are posets; (d) and (e) are not transitive.
   (ii) (a) is a semilattice; (b) and (c) are not lattices.

4. Let the poset $A = \langle A, \geq \rangle$ be a meet semilattice. Set $a \wedge b = \inf\{a,b\}$. Then the algebra $A^a = \langle A, \wedge \rangle$ is a semilattice.

   (a) For all a, $a \wedge a = a$ (idempotent), since $\inf\{a,a\} = a$.
   (b) For all a, b, $a \wedge b = b \wedge a$ (commutative), since $\inf\{a,b\} = \inf\{b,a\}$.
   (c) Let $d = \inf\{a, \inf\{b,c\}\}$ and $e = \inf\{\inf\{a,b\}, c\}$. Then $d \leq a$ and $d \leq \inf\{b,c\}$. Therefore, $d \leq b$ and $d \leq c$. Since $d \leq a$ and $d \leq b$, $d \leq \inf\{a,b\}$. And since $d \leq c$, $d \leq \inf\{\inf\{a,b\},c\}$; i.e., $d \leq e$. Similarly, $e \leq d$; thus, $d = e$. Hence, $a \wedge (b \wedge c) = (a \wedge b) \wedge c$ (associativity).

6. Suppose $(D1)$ holds. Then
$$
\begin{aligned}
a \vee (b \wedge c) &= (a \vee (a \wedge c)) \vee (b \wedge c) && (L4) \\
&= a \vee ((a \wedge c) \vee (b \wedge c)) && (L2) \\
&= a \vee ((c \wedge a) \vee (c \wedge b)) && (L1) \\
&= a \vee (c \wedge (a \vee b)) && (D1) \\
&= a \vee ((a \vee b) \wedge c) && (L1) \\
&= (a \wedge (a \vee b)) \vee ((a \vee b) \wedge c) && (L4) \\
&= ((a \vee b) \wedge a) \vee ((a \vee b) \wedge c) && (L1) \\
&= (a \vee b) \wedge (a \vee c) && (D1)
\end{aligned}
$$
So $(D2)$ also holds. A similar proof shows that if $(D2)$ holds, so does $(D1)$.

7. By Theorem 11-8, a^* has a unique complement in a complemented distributive lattice. Since $a^* \wedge a = 0$ and $a^* \vee a = 1$, a is the complement of a^*, i.e., $a = (a^*)^*$.

8. Interchange $\wedge$ and $\vee$, 0 and 1 in the proof of Th. 11-11.

9. Th. 11.8:
$$
\begin{aligned}
a^* &= a^* \wedge 1 & &\text{def. of 1 and } \wedge \\
&= a^* \wedge (a \vee b^*) & &\text{def. of compl. } (C1) \\
&= (a^* \wedge a) \vee (a^* \wedge b^*) & &D1 \\
&= 0 \vee (a^* \wedge b^*) & &C2 \\
&= a^* \wedge b^* & &\text{def. of 0 and } \vee
\end{aligned}
$$

Th. 11.9:
$$
\begin{aligned}
d &= d \wedge c & &RC2, \text{ def of } \vee \text{ and } \wedge \\
&= d \wedge (b \vee d') & &RC2 \\
&= (d \wedge b) \vee (d \wedge d') & &D1 \\
&= d \wedge d' & &RC1, \text{ def of } \vee
\end{aligned}
$$

CHAPTER 12

1. If $a \wedge b = 0$
then
$$
\begin{aligned}
a^* &= a^* \vee (a \wedge b) \\
&= (a^* \vee a) \wedge (a^* \vee b) \\
&= 1 \wedge (a^* \vee b) \\
&= a^* \vee b; \text{hence } a^* \ge b
\end{aligned}
$$
If $a \vee b = 1$
then
$$
\begin{aligned}
a^* &= a^* \wedge (a \vee b) \\
&= (a^* \wedge a) \vee (a^* \wedge b) \\
&= 0 \vee (a^* \wedge b) \\
&= a^* \wedge b; \text{hence } a^* \le b
\end{aligned}
$$
So $b = a^*$.

2. (Idempotent Law) For all $a \in B$, $a \cup a = a$ and $a \cap a = a$

Proof:
1. $a = a \cup 0$ B4
2. $a = a \cup (a \cap a^*)$ B5
3. $a = (a \cup a) \cap (a \cup a^*)$ B3
4. $a = (a \cup a) \cap 1$ B5
5. $a = a \cup a$ B4

$a \cap a = a$ can be proved similarly

3. (i) If $a = 0$, the set of join-irreducible elements $S(a) = \{x \mid x \leq a\} = \emptyset$, and 0 is the lub of the empty set.

(ii) Let $P(n)$ be the statement that every element is the join of some join-irreducible elements if the number of elements $x \leq a$ in the finite Boolean lattice L is n.

$P(n)$ is trivially true if a is join-irreducible.

If a is not join-irreducible and not 0, then $a = x \vee y$, where $x < a$ and $y < a$. So $n(x) < n(a)$ and $n(y) < n(a)$. By induction on n, it follows that x and y are joins of join-irreducible elements: $x = \bigvee_{S(a)} n(x)$ and $y = \bigvee_{S(a)} n(y)$, so $a = \bigvee n(x) \vee \bigvee n(y)$.

4. Suppose $a \leq b \vee c$, then
$$
\begin{aligned}
a &= (b \vee c) \wedge a \\
&= (b \wedge a) \vee (c \wedge a) \text{ (distributivity)} \\
&= (b \wedge a) \text{ or} \\
&= (c \wedge a) \text{ since } a \text{ is join-irreducible}
\end{aligned}
$$
So $a \leq b$ or $a \leq c$.

5. (i) If L has 1, then a is its own relative pseudo-complement, since by definition for all $x \in L$, $x \leq a \Rightarrow a$ iff $x \wedge a \leq a$, so $a \leq a \Rightarrow a$.

(iii) For all $x \in L$, $x \leq a \Rightarrow b$ iff $a \wedge x \leq b$; since $a \wedge b \leq b$ we infer $b \leq a \Rightarrow b$ (provided $a \Rightarrow b$ exists).

6. Since the lattice if finite, it has 0. Given a, b, define
$$
C = \{c \mid a \wedge c \leq b\} = \{c_1, c_2, c_3, \ldots, c_k\}
$$

Let c_0 be the lub of C, so $c_0 = c_1 \vee c_2 \vee \ldots \vee c_k$.

Then, if $a \wedge c \leq b$, also $c \leq c_0$.

Conversely, if $c \leq c_0$
$$
\begin{aligned}
a \wedge c \leq a \wedge c_0 &= a \wedge (c_1 \vee c_2 \vee \ldots \vee c_k) \\
&= (a \wedge c_1) \vee \ldots \vee (a \wedge c_k) \text{ (distributivity)}
\end{aligned}
$$

But $a \wedge c_i \leq b$ for each i, $1 \leq i \leq k$. Therefore, $a \wedge c_0 \leq b$. Hence $a \wedge c \leq b$. Thus c_0 satisfies the conditions on $a \Rightarrow b$. So the lattice is a Heyting lattice.

REVIEW EXERCISES, PART C

2. For instance, $\mathbf{P} = \langle\{0,1,2,3,4\}, +\bmod 5\rangle$

3. Care must be taken in this problem to remember that $x + (y - 3)$ is defined as a *single* operation on two elements x and y. Thus to check associativity it must be verified that

$$((x + (y - 3)) + (z - 3)) = (x + (y + (z - 3)) - 3))$$

which turns out to be true because both sides can be reduced to $(x + +y + z) - 6$. The identity element is 3 and the inverse of x is $6 - x$.

4. (a) The only finite one is $\langle\{0\}, +\rangle$. All the others consist of all the mutiples of any one integer, e.g. $\{0, 2, -2, 4, -4, \ldots\}, \{0, 10, -10, 20, -20, \ldots\}$, etc.

(b) $\langle\{0\}, +\rangle$ certainly is not. All of the others are. To set up an isomorphism between the group with all integers and the group with all multiples of a, let $n \rightarrow an$. This correspondence is clearly one-one, and preserves addition, since

$$an_1 + an_2 = a(n_1 + n_2)$$

5. There are only two: $\quad$
$$\begin{array}{ll} 0 \rightarrow I & \quad 0 \rightarrow I \\ 1 \rightarrow R & \quad 1 \rightarrow R'' \\ 2 \rightarrow R' & \quad 2 \rightarrow R' \\ 3 \rightarrow R'' & \quad 3 \rightarrow R \end{array}$$

6. A non-Abelian group of order 6.

7. (a) Every string is a conjugate of itself since $x = x^\frown e = e^\frown x$. Conjugacy is symmetric by the definition. To prove transitivity, let x and y be conjugate and also y and z. Then for some t, u, v, w, $x = t^\frown u, y = u^\frown t, y = v^\frown w$, and $z = w^\frown v$. Case 1: let $u = v$ and $t = w$. Then $x = t^\frown u = w^\frown v = z$; thus x and z are conjugate because they are identical. Case 2: let u be shorter than v; that is, there is some r such that $u^\frown r = v$. Since $y = v^\frown w = u^\frown r^\frown w = u^\frown t$, it follows that $r^\frown w = t$. Therefore, $x = t^\frown u = r^\frown w^\frown u$, and $z = w^\frown v = w^\frown u^\frown r$; thus x and z are conjugate. Case 3: let u be longer than v; that is, for some s, $v^\frown s = u$. Since $y = u^\frown t = v^\frown s^\frown t = v^\frown w$, it follows that

$w = s\frown t$. Therefore, $x = t\frown u = t\frown v\frown s$, and $z = w\frown v = s\frown t\frown v$; thus, x and z are conjugate. This exhausts the possible cases. This relation partitions A^* into equivalence classes, each class containing all the strings that are conjugates of each other. A string of length n may be the only string in its equivalence class ($aaaa$, for example, is conjugate only with itself) or there may be as many as n strings in the class ($abca$ for example, is conjugate with itself and with $bcaa$, $caab$, and $aabc$).

(b) Let x and y be conjugates. Therefore, $x = uv$ and $y = vu$, for u and v. The string u is a string such that $x\frown u = u\frown y$, since $x\frown u = u\frown v\frown u = u\frown y$.

8. (1) (a) all; (b) all but G4; (c) Yes

(2) (a) none: G1 not, because $2 - 4 \neq$ a non-neg. integer, G2 not, because $(9 - 5) - 4 = 0$, $9 - (5 - 4) = 8$, G3 not, because there is no e such that for all x, both $x - e = x$ and $e - x = x$, G4 not, because G3 not; (b) all but G4; (c) no; D1 not, D2 not

(3) (a) all; (b) all but G4 (5 has no inverse); (c) no: D4 not, because $5 \cdot 2 = 10 \pmod{25}$ and $5 \cdot 7 = 10 \pmod{25}$, but $2 \neq 7 \pmod{25}$

(4) (a) only G2: G1 not, because $1 + 10 = 0 \pmod{11}$, and $0 \notin A$; G3 not, because $0 \notin A$; G4 not, because G3 not; (b) all; (c) no: D1 not, D2 not

(5) (a) only G2; (b) all; (c) no: D1 not, D2 not

(6) (a) only G2: G1 not, because $2/3 + 2/3 = 4/3$, $4/3 \notin A$, G3 not, because $0 \notin A$, G4 not, because G3 not; (b) only G1 and G2; (c) no: D1 not, D2 not, D3 not

(7) (a) all; (b) G3 not, because for no x does $3 \odot x = 3$, G4 not — only G1 and G2; (c) D3 not, D4 not, because $3 \odot 4 = 3 \odot 5 = 0$, but $4 \neq 5$

9. (a) $(a + b) \cdot (c + d)$
$$\begin{aligned} &= [(a + b) \cdot c] + [(a + b) \cdot d] \\ &= [c \cdot (a + b)] + [d \cdot (a + b)] \quad \text{D3 (commut.)} \\ &= (c \cdot a + c \cdot b) + (d \cdot a + d \cdot b) \quad \text{D5} \\ &= (a \cdot c + b \cdot c) + (a \cdot d + b \cdot d) \quad \text{D3} \end{aligned}$$

(b) $-0 + 0 = -0$ because $x + 0 = x$ for all x (G3)
$-0 + 0 = 0$ because $-x + x = 0$ for all x (G4)
hence $-0 = 0$ because $-0 + 0$ must have a single value (G1)

(c) 1. $a \cdot b = 0$ premise
     2. | $a \neq 0$ auxiliary premise
     3. | $a \cdot 0 = 0$ Problem 10(b) in Chapter 10
     4. | $b = 0$ 1,3 cancellation law (D4)
     5. $a \neq 0 \supset b = 0$ cond. proof
     6. $\sim a \neq 0 \lor b = 0$ 5, conditional law
     7. $a = 0 \lor b = 0$ double neg.

(d) 1. $-a + -(-a) = 0$ Inverse law
     2. $-a + a = 0$ Inverse law
     3. $-(-a) = a$ 1,2, problem 10(a) in Chapter 10

10. (a) Yes. $|x| \cdot |y| = |x \cdot y|$ and we can show the new system is also a group.
    (b) No. $-2 \rightarrow 2$, $-4 \rightarrow 4$, $8 \rightarrow -8$ but $-2 \cdot -4 = 8$ while $2 \cdot 4 \neq -8$.
    (c) No. $2 \rightarrow 4$, $3 \rightarrow 6$, $6 \rightarrow 12$ but $2 \cdot 3 = 6$ while $4 \cdot 6 \neq 12$.
    (d) Yes. $1/x \cdot 1/y = 1/x \cdot y$ and the new system is a group.
    (e) Yes. $x^2 \cdot y^2 = (x \cdot y)^2$ and the new system is a group.

11.* (a) **Reflex:** for all a, $a^{-1} \cdot a = e$ & $e \in S$;
     Sym: given $a^{-1} \cdot b \in S$, does it follow that $b^{-1} \cdot a \in S$?
     $$(b^{-1} \cdot a) \cdot (a^{-1} \cdot b) = b^{-1} \cdot (a \cdot a^{-1}) \cdot b$$
     $$= b^{-1} \cdot e \cdot b$$
     $$= b^{-1} \cdot b$$
     $$= e$$
     Since $(b^{-1} \cdot a) \cdot (a^{-1} \cdot b) = e$, $b^{-1} \cdot a$ is the inverse of $a^{-1} \cdot b$. Therefore $b^{-1} \cdot a$ must also be in S.
     Trans: given $a^{-1} \cdot b \in S$, $b^{-1} \cdot c \in S$ then
     $$(a^{-1} \cdot b) \cdot (b^{-1} \cdot c) \in S = a^{-1} \cdot (b \cdot b^{-1}) \cdot c$$
     $$= a^{-1} \cdot e \cdot c$$
     $$= a^{-1} \cdot c \text{ so } a^{-1} \cdot c \in S$$
     It is an equivalence relation. One of the equivalence classes is $\{x \mid x \in S\}$. The others can vary from case to case. For example, for $G =$ the symmetries of the square and $S = \{I, H\}$, the equivalence classes are:
     $$E_1 = \{I, H\}$$
     $$E_2 = \{R', V\}$$
     $$E_3 = \{D, R\}$$
     $$E_4 = \{D', R''\}$$

But for the same G and $S = \{I, H, V, R'\}$:
$$E_1 = \{I, H, V, R'\}$$
$$E_2 = \{D, D', R, R''\}$$

(b) Reflex: $a + (-a) = 0$ and 0 is even,
Sym: if $a + (-b) = c$ and c is even, then $b + (-a) = -c$ which is also even,
Trans: if $a + (-b)$ is even and $b + (-c)$ is even, then $a + (-c)$ is even because it is the sum of two even numbers, $a + (-b)$ and $b + (-c)$,

Equivalence classes:

$$E_1 = \{x \mid x \text{ is odd }\} \quad \text{(because the difference}$$
of any two odd numbers
is even)

$$E_2 = \{x \mid x \text{ is even }\};$$

(c) Reflex: $a + (-a) = 0$ *not* odd: no,
Sym: if $a + (-b) = c$ is odd, so is $b + (-a) = -c$,
Trans: if $a + (-b)$ is odd and $b + (-c)$ is odd, $a + (-c)$ is not odd, $a + (-c) = (a + (-b)) + (b + (-c)) = \text{odd} + \text{odd} = \text{even}$: No *not* an equivalence relation;

12. (a)

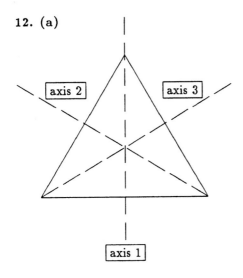

I
R 120° clockwise
R 240° clockwise
D_1 flip in axis 1
D_2 flip in axis 2
D_3 flip in axis 3

$x \cdot y$	I	R	R'	D_1	D_2	D_3
I	I	R	R'	D_1	D_2	D_3
R	R	R'	I	D_2	D_3	D_1
R'	R'	I	R	D_3	D_1	D_2
D_1	D_1	D_3	D_2	I	R'	R
D_2	D_2	D_1	D_3	R	I	R'
D_3	D_3	D_2	D_1	R'	R	I

(with y labelling the columns and x labelling the rows)

(b) $\{I, R, R'\}, \{I, D_1\}, \{I, D_2\}, \{I, D_3\}, \{I\}$

(c)

$$\left.\begin{array}{l} I \\ R \\ R' \\ D_1 \\ D_2 \\ D_3 \end{array}\right\} \to I$$

$$\left.\begin{array}{l} I \\ R' \\ R \\ D_1 \end{array}\right\} \to I \qquad \left.\begin{array}{l} D_2 \\ D_3 \end{array}\right\} \to D_1$$

14. (a) $a \le b$ iff $a \Rightarrow b = 1$.

(c) $b \wedge a \le a \wedge b$, and $c \le a \Rightarrow b$ iff $a \wedge c \le b$, so $a \le b \Rightarrow (a \wedge b)$.

PART D

CHAPTER 13

1. (a) tree (ii) (b) interpretation (ii)

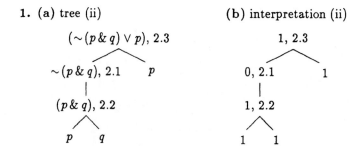

2. (b) tree (ii)　　　　　　　　　　　**(e)** interpretation (ii)

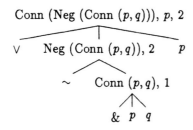

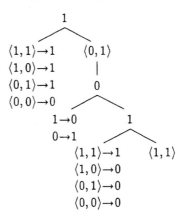

3. (a) A possible model making all four formulas true is:

$\mathbf{M} = \langle D, F \rangle$ where $D = \{a, b\}$
$F(P) = \{a\}$
$F(R) = \{\langle a, a \rangle, \langle b, a \rangle\}$
with assignment given $g(x) = a$ and $g(y) = b$.

Note that although (iii) is logically equivalent to (iv), the interpretation process is quite different.

(b) (i) Every student kissed someone.
(ii) There is someone whom every student kissed.
(iii) & (iv) If someone/anyone is a student then everyone kissed him, i.e., Everyone kissed every student.

5. Take a very simple model where your choice of statement for γ is true. The entire statement-schema could be instantiated by e.g., $((\sim (p \rightarrow q)) \vee r)$, but the choice of statement constants is yours.

7. (b) t, FALSE, **(d)** t, TRUE (convert $5\,/\,x$, $8\,/\,y$), **(e)** t, FALSE(convert $5\,/\,y$, $8\,/\,x$), **(g)** t, TRUE

CHAPTER 14

1.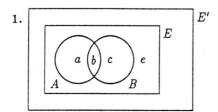

Conservativity: only a and b matter to DAB.
Extension: E and E' are irrelevant to DAB.
Quantity: only the cardinalities a, b, c, e matter to DAB.
Variety: $D(A) \not\subseteq \wp(E) - \emptyset$.
Cumulative effect: $D(A)$ is completely specified by the set of all pairs $\langle a, b \rangle$, the cardinalities of A and B.

2. (a)

(b)

(c)

(d)

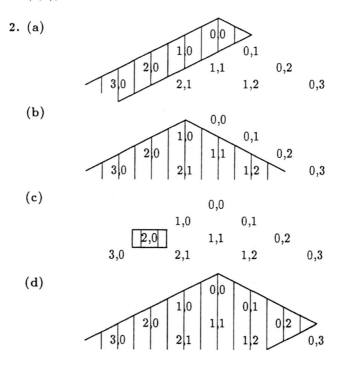

(e)

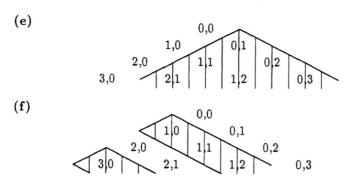

(f)

(g) Some part(s) of the tree must be shaded.
(h) Any node to the right of a node in $D(A)$ is itself in $D(A)$.
(i) If $\langle a,b \rangle$ belongs to $D(A)$ then $\langle 0,b \rangle$ belongs to $D(A)$.

3.

	right		left	
	↑	↓	↑	↓
several	+	−	+/?	−
at most 3	−	+	−	+
none	−	+	−	+
at least n	+	−	+	−
some	+	−	+	−
these	+	−	−	−
neither	−	+	−	−
every	+	−	−	+
all	+	−	−	+
each	+	−	−	+
infinitely many	+	−	+	−
a finite number of	−	+	−	+
most	+	−	−	−
many	+	−	−	−

See section 5 for *most* and *many*.

4. (a) (i) Some men walk fast → some men walk.
   Several students failed the final test → several students failed
   a test.
   Infinitely many numbers are even primes → infinitely many
   numbers are prime.
   (ii) Some men sing, dance and laugh → some men sing and laugh.
   At least five students got A's on their midterms and finals →

at least five students got A's on their finals.

(b) $|E| \geq 2, D(A) = \{X \subseteq E | A \cap X \neq \emptyset$ and $A - X \neq \emptyset\}$
$D(A)$ means 'some but not all A's'. If $A \subseteq B$, $D(A) \subseteq D(B)$, so D
is left monotone increasing. But D is not right monotone increasing
since $E \notin D(A)$ for all A.

5. Model should show mapping $\pi : A \to A'$ where at least one $a \in A \cap X$,
$\pi(a) \notin A \cap X$, if X is the set of entities owned by John.

6. Suppose Q_E meets Variation, i.e. $X \in Q_{E'}$ and $\sim Y \in Q_{E'}$ for some
$X, Y \subseteq E'$. $\sim Q_E =_{def} \{Z \subseteq E | Z \notin Q_E\}$. By Extension $\sim Z \in Q_{E'}$.
For $Q \sim$ similarly.

7. (a) We know that if Q is monotone increasing, $Q \sim$ and $\sim Q$ are
monotone decreasing, and if Q is monotone decreasing, $Q \sim$ and $\sim Q$
are monotone increasing. Since $Q^{\sim} = \sim (Q \sim)$ it follows by double
negation that if Q is increasing, $Q^{\sim}$ is.
(d) If $Q = Q^{\sim}$, $X \in Q \leftrightarrow (E - X) \notin Q$. So if for some $Y \subseteq$
E, $(E - Y) \in Q$ then $Y \notin Q$ and if $Y \notin Q$ then $(E - Y) \in Q$.

8. Since D is definite, $D(A)$ is the principal filter generated by some
$B \subseteq E$. DAE by definition of principal filter, so by theorem 14.2
DAA. Note that $DAB \to DAA$ is the relational definition of positive
strength, also called the property of *quasi-reflexivity*.

9. (a) (i) $DAB \leftrightarrow D(A \cap B)E$:
$DAB \leftrightarrow DA(A \cap B)$ (conservativity) $\leftrightarrow D(A \cap (A \cap B))$
$(A \cap B)$ (intersective) $\leftrightarrow D(A \cap B)(A \cap B)(A \cap B = A \cap (A \cap$
$B)) \leftrightarrow D(A \cap B)E$ (Theorem 14.2) □
(ii) $DAB \leftrightarrow DBA$:
$DBA \leftrightarrow D(A \cap B)E$ (by 9.(a)(i)) and $DAB \leftrightarrow D(A \cap B)E$
(by (a)(i)) so $DBA \leftrightarrow DAB$. □
(b) Some students walk → some walkers are students → some walking
students are individuals. (There exist walking students.)

10. (a) $DAB \& DBC$, so $A \subseteq B$ and $B \subseteq C$ by theorem 14.3, so $A \subseteq C$.
By Conservativity $DA(A \cap B)$, so DAA, since $A \cap B = A$. But then
also $DA(A \cap C)$, since $A \cap C = A$. So by Conservativity DAC. □
(b) If D is connected, $\sim D$ is antisymmetric by definition of connectedness. With the result of (a), $\sim D$ is transitive. So D is almost-
connected by definition of transitivity. □

(c) Suppose $D_E AB$ and D transitive. By Conservativity $D_E A(A \cap B)$. Take $E' \supseteq E$ and $A' \subseteq E'$ such that $|A'| = |A|$ and $A \cap A' = A \cap B$. Clearly $D_E A(A \cap A')$, and with Extension $D_{E'} A(A \cap A')$. With Conservativity $D_{E'} AA'$. Take π a permutation of E' which leaves $A \cap A'$ and $E' - (A \cup A')$ intact, but interchanges $A - A'$ and $A' - A$. Quantity gives $D_{E'} \pi(A) \pi(A')$, i.e. $D_{E'} A'A$. Since D is transitive, $D_{E'} AA'$ and $D_{E'} A'A$ imply $D_{E'} AA$, and Extension gives $D_E AA$. $\square$

CHAPTER 15

1. $g''(x) = d_3$, since Pd_3 is true at i_2 which is the only index accessible from i_1 if we drop all reflexive pairs from R, and Qd_3 is true at i_1, the only remaining accessible index for i_2.

2. Evaluating $(\exists x)Px$ at i_0 gives 0, so the entire antecedent is false at i_0, and the whole formula hence must be true at i_0.

3. (a)

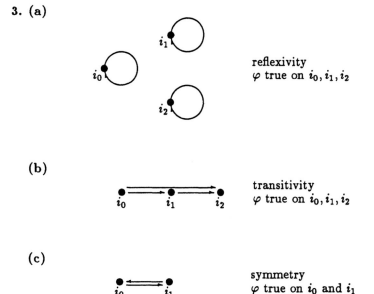

reflexivity
φ true on i_0, i_1, i_2

(b)

transitivity
φ true on i_0, i_1, i_2

(c)

symmetry
φ true on i_0 and i_1

PART E

CHAPTER 17

1. (a) (ii), (iii), (iv); (b) The set of all strings containing a total of n 1's, where $n \equiv 2$ (modulo 3)

2. (c)

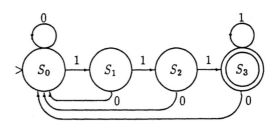

3. (a)

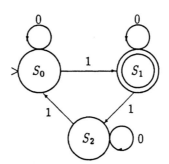

(b)

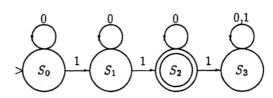

(c)

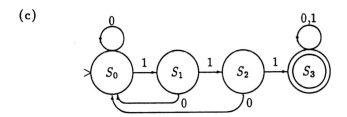

(d)

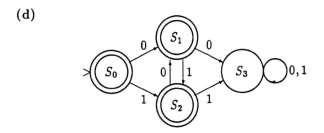

(e)

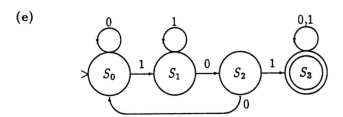

(f)

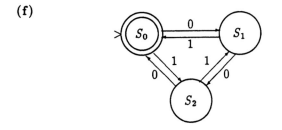

4. (c)

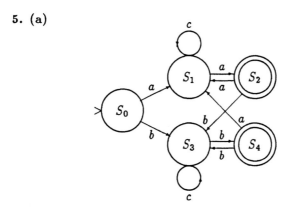

5. (a)

(b)

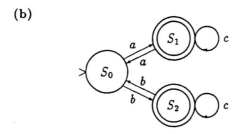

6. (a) Duplicate the states of the original machine, and duplicate all the
transitions except those leading to S_0. Add a new state S_0'. Wherever
the original machine had a transition from a state S_i into S_0, labelled
a, let the new automaton have a transition from S_i into S_0', labelled
a. If the original automaton had a loop transition on S_0, add a loop
transition on S_0' instead. For every other transition from S_0 to a state

S_j, add a transition from S_0' to S_j, with the same label. If S_0 was a final state, make S_0' a final state as well. The resulting automaton starts in S_0, but for the rest of the computation, S_0' plays the role previously played by S_0.

7. (a)

(b)

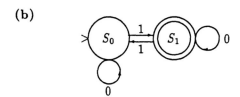

(c)

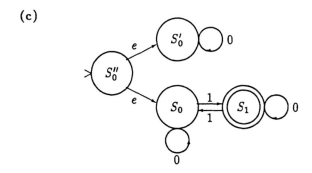

(d) A deterministic equivalent of C is:

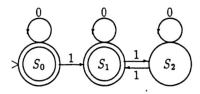

The complement construction then gives us D:

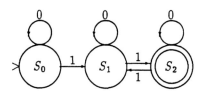

D accepts any string containing a positive even number of 1's.

8. (a)

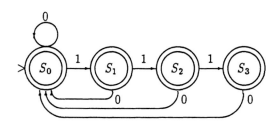

(b)

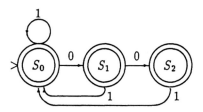

(c)

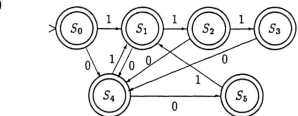

9. (a) the (man is ∪·men are) here
  (b) the old* (man is ∪ men are) here
  (c) the old* (man is ∪ men are) here (and the old* (man is ∪ men

   are) here)*
(d) $0^*10^*10^*$
(e) $(0 \cup 1)^*101(0 \cup 1)^*$ or (corresponding to the automaton given as
   the answer to the original problem) $(0^*11^*00)^*0^*11^*01(0 \cup 1)^*$

10. (a)

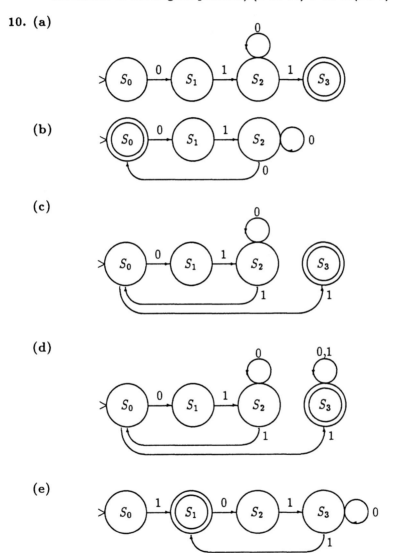

(b)

(c)

(d)

(e)

(f)

11. (a) $S \to aa$ (b) $S \to e$ (c) $S \to aA$ $A \to a$ $B \to b$
    $S \to ab$ $S \to aS$ $S \to bS$ $A \to aB$ $B \to bB$
    $S \to ba$ $S \to a$ $A \to bA$
    $S \to bb$ $S \to bS$
                      $S \to b$

(d) $S \to a$ $A \to bA$ $C \to aC$ (e) $S \to e$ $A \to aS$ $B \to bA$
    $S \to b$ $A \to aB$ $C \to bD$ $S \to aA$ $A \to a$ $B \to aC$
    $S \to aC$ $A \to a$ $C \to b$ $S \to bC$ $A \to bB$ $C \to aB$
    $S \to bA$ $B \to bB$ $D \to aD$ $C \to bS$
                 $B \to b$ $D \to a$ $C \to b$

(f) $S \to bA$ $A \to bS$ $C \to bB$
    $S \to aB$ $A \to aC$ $C \to aE$
                 $B \to bC$ $D \to bE$
                 $B \to aD$ $E \to bD$
                 $B \to a$ $E \to b$

12. (a) (a, q_0, q_1) (c) (b, q_0, q_0) (e) (a, q_0, q_1) (a, q_3, q_2)
       (b, q_0, q_1) (a, q_0, q_1) (a, q_1, q_0) (b, q_3, q_0)
       (a, q_1, q_2) (a, q_1, q_2) (b, q_1, q_2) (b, q_0, q_3)
       (b, q_1, q_2) (b, q_1, q_1) (b, q_2, q_1) $F = \{q_0\}$
       $F = \{q_2\}$ (b, q_2, q_2) (a, q_2, q_3)
                             $F = \{q_2\}$

CHAPTER 18

1. (a) $S \to aSa$ (b) $S \to AA$ (c) $S \to aBB$ $A \to aS$ $B \to bS$
    $S \to aBa$ $A \to aAb$ $S \to bAB$ $A \to bBAA$ $B \to aBBB$
    $B \to bB$ $A \to ab$ $S \to bBA$ $A \to bABA$
    $B \to b$ $S \to e$ $A \to bAAB$

2. Any rules which are already of the form $A \to a$ or $A \to BC$ can be left unchanged. Remove all rules of the form $A \to B$ by the procedure outlined in Sec. 18.5. For each rule of the form $A \to \alpha_1 \alpha_2 \ldots \alpha_n$, where $n \geq 2$ and one or more of the α_i is a terminal symbol, replace each occurrence of such an α_i by a new nonterminal A_i that occurs nowhere else and add the rule $A_i \to \alpha_i$ (which is of the allowed form). The right sides of all rules now consist either of a single terminal symbol or else a string of two or more nonterminals. Each remaining rule of the form $A \to B_1 B_2 \ldots B_n$ $(n \geq 3)$ is now replaced by the rules $A \to B_1 C_1$, $C_1 \to B_2 C_2, \ldots, C_{n-1} \to B_{n-1} B_n$, where $C_1, C_2, \ldots, C_{n-1}$ are new nonterminals that occur nowhere else in the grammar. All rules are now of the required form. Clearly for every derivation of a terminal string in the original grammar there is a derivation of that string in the new grammar and conversely.

3. (b) If L is context free, then for some sufficiently long string $w \in L$, there exist u, v, x, y, z such that $w = uvxyz$, v and y not both e, and $uv^i xy^i z \in L$ for all $i \geq 0$. Let $u = a^p$, $v = a^q$, $x = a^r$, $y = a^s$, $z = a^t$, and call $b = p + r + t$ and $c = q + s$. Then $b + ic$ must be prime for all $i \geq 0$. When $i = bc^2$, $b + ic = b + (bc^2)c = b + bc^3 = b(1 + c^3) = b(1+c)(1-c+c^2)$. Since $c \geq 1$, $(c+1) \geq 2$ and thus $b + bc^3$ is divisible by 2 or some large integer. This establishes that $b + bc^3$ could not be prime unless it happened to equal 2. However, in this case $b = 1$ and $c = 1$, and it is obviously false that $1 + i \cdot 1$ is prime for all integral values of i. Therefore a^n (n prime) is not type 2.

4. If L is generated by a cfg G, construct G' by reversing the right sides of all rules of G. G' generates L^R.

5. $M = \langle K, \Sigma, \Gamma, \Delta, s, F \rangle$
   $K = \{q_0, q_1\}$ $\Delta = \{(q_0, ab, e) \to (q_0, A)$
   $\Sigma = \{a, b, c, d\}$ $(q_0, cd, A) \to (q_1, e)$
   $\Gamma = \{A\}$ $(q_1, cd, A) \to (q_1, e)\}$
   $s = q_0$
   $F = \{q_1\}$

6. $\Delta = \{(q_0, e, e) \rightarrow (q_1, \$)$
$\qquad (q_1, a, \$) \rightarrow (q_1, A\$)$
$\qquad (q_1, b, \$) \rightarrow (q_1, B\$)$
$\qquad (q_1, a, A) \rightarrow (q_1, AA)$
$\qquad (q_1, b, B) \rightarrow (q_1, BB)$
$\qquad (q_1, a, B) \rightarrow (q_1, e)$
$\qquad (q_1, b, A) \rightarrow (q_1, e)$
$\qquad (q_1, c, \$) \rightarrow (q_1, e)\}$
$\quad F = \{q_1\}$

7. The machine will store the number of a's preceding the b. Then it
will make a choice of whether to start checking off 1 or 2 a's from the
storage tape with each new a of the input tape. Once made, the choice
must stay consistent for the rest of the computation.
$$\Delta = \{(q_0, a, e) \rightarrow (q_0, A)$$
$$\qquad (q_0, b, e) \rightarrow (q_1, e)$$
$$\qquad (q_0, b, e) \rightarrow (q_2, e)$$
$$\qquad (q_1, a, A) \rightarrow (q_1, e)$$
$$\qquad (q_2, aa, A) \rightarrow (q_2, e)\}$$
$$F = \{q_1, q_2\}$$

8. No. Problem 7 provides a counterexample.

9. Choose $a^k b^k c^k$ in L. Then if L is context free, there exist u, v, x, y, z,
($|vy| \geq 1$) such that $uvxyz = a^k b^k c^k$ and $uv^n x y^n z \in L$ for all $n \geq 0$.
But if so, then neither v nor y can contain more than one type of letter
since "pumping" would produce a string with b's preceding a's, or c's
preceding b's. Therefore, the only remaining possibilities are:
$\qquad$ 1) both v and y in a^*,
$\qquad$ 2) both v and y in b^*,
$\qquad$ 3) both v and y in c^*,
$\qquad$ 4) v in a^* and y in b^*,
$\qquad$ 5) v in a^* and y in c^*, or
$\qquad$ 6) v in b^* and y in c^*,
provided, of course, that not both v and y are empty. But in cases 1-4
"pumping" v and y produces a string not in L since the a's, b's, and c's
will not be in the required proportion of i a's, j $b's$, and $\max(i, j)$ c's.
In case 5, if $y = e$, then it is like case 1; if $v = e$, then it is like case 3; if
neither v nor y is empty then $n = 0$ ("pumping" zero times) produces

a string not in L. Case 6 is similar. Therefore, no such u, v, x, y, z exist, and L is not context free.

CHAPTER 19

1. $\delta = \{(q_0, 0) \to (q_0, R)$
$(q_0, 1) \to (q_1, R)$
$(q_1, 0) \to (q_0, R)$
$(q_1, 1) \to (q_2, L)$
$(q_2, 1) \to (q_3, 0)$
$(q_3, 0) \to (q_4, R)$
$(q_4, 1) \to (q_3, 0)$
$(q_4, 0) \to (q_0, R)\}$
$s = q_0$

2. $\delta = \{(q_0, \#) \to (q_1, 1)$
$(q_1, 1) \to (q_1, R)$
$(q_1, \#) \to (q_2, 1)$
$(q_2, 1) \to (q_2, R)$
$(q_2, \#) \to (q_0, 1)\}$
$s = q_0$

3. (a)

q_0	a	$\#$	$\#$	a	
a	q_0	$\#$	$\#$	a	
a	q_1	a	$\#$	a	
q_1	a	a	$\#$	a	
q_1	$\#$	a	a	$\#$	a
a	q_1	a	a	$\#$	a
a	q_0	a	a	$\#$	a
a	a	q_0	a	$\#$	a
a	a	a	q_0	$\#$	a
a	a	a	q_1	a	a
a	a	q_1	a	a	a
a	q_1	a	a	a	a

(b) The machine moves back and forth along the tape; each time it encounters an $\#$ it changes it to a and reverses direction; (c) No; (d) No; (e) No; (f) Same as (b)

4. (a) $M = \langle \{q_0, q_1\}, \{a, \#\}, \delta, q_0 \rangle$
$\delta = \{(q_0, \#) \to (q_0, R)$
$(q_0, a) \to (q_1, R)$
$(q_1, \#) \to (q_1, R)$
$(q_1, a) \to (q_1, R)\}$
(b) $M = \langle \{q_0, q_1\}, \{a, \#\}, \delta, q_0 \rangle$
$\delta = \emptyset$

5. (a) Total, since the sum of any two even numbers is even.
   (b) Partial. There are some prime numbers whose sum is prime ($2+5 = 7, 2 + 11 = 13$), but unless one of the primes is 2, both primes will be odd, and their sum will then be even, and hence divisible by 2, i.e. not prime.
   (c) Partial.

6. Reading the digits from right to left, multiply the first digit by $2^0(= 1)$, the second by 2^1, and so on; in general the nth digit is to by multiplied by 2^n. Then add the resulting numbers to get the result, e.g. $101 \Rightarrow (1 \times 2^0) + (0 \times 2^1) + (1 \times 2^2) = 1 + 0 + 4 = 5$.

7. $G = \langle\{[,],A,D,S,a\},\{a\},R,S\rangle$
   $R = \{S \rightarrow [A],$
   $\quad\quad [\rightarrow [D,$
   $\quad\quad DA \rightarrow AAD,$
   $\quad\quad D] \rightarrow],$
   $\quad\quad [\rightarrow e,$
   $\quad\quad] \rightarrow e,$
   $\quad\quad A \rightarrow a\}$

8. Given arbitrary M, modify it so that it first erases its input tape and then proceeds as M would (on the resulting empty tape). Call this machine M'. Then M' accepts its input (in fact, all inputs) iff M accepts e. Thus, a TM which decided whether an arbitrary TM accepts at least one input could be applied to M' to decide, in effect, whether M accepts e. Since the latter is impossible, the problem is undecidable.

CHAPTER 20

1. (a) $S \rightarrow aSBc$
   $\quad\quad S \rightarrow aBc$
   $\quad\quad cB \rightarrow Bc$
   $\quad\quad aB \rightarrow ab$
   $\quad\quad bB \rightarrow bb$
   (b) Replace the rule $S \rightarrow e$ by $S \rightarrow ABC$ in the grammar of (19-5).

(c) $S \to aa$ $Aa \to aA$ $A'A \to aA'$
      $S \to bb$ $Ab \to bA$ $A'B \to aB'$
      $S \to aAS'$ $Ba \to aB$ $B'A \to bA'$
      $S \to bBS'$ $Bb \to bB$ $B'B \to bB'$

      $S' \to aAS'$ $AA \to aA'$ $A'A'' \to aa$
      $S' \to bBS'$ $AB \to aB'$ $A'B'' \to ab$
      $S' \to aA''$ $BA \to bA'$ $B'A'' \to ba$
      $S' \to bB''$ $BB \to bB'$ $B'B'' \to bb$

APPENDIX E II

1. (c)

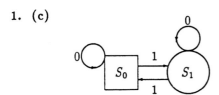

An *even number of* automaton.
Note that there is a non-trivial loop between S_0 and S_1, so this automaton is cyclic.

(d)

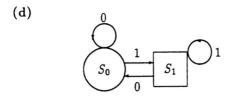

Almost all automaton.
Note that this automaton is not permutation invariant.

REVIEW PROBLEMS, PART E

1. (a) I am right;

That I am right seems certain;

That that that I am right seems certain seems certain seems certain.

(b) For example:

$K = \{q_0, q_1\}, \Sigma = \{s, c, i, a, r, t\}, \Gamma = \{t\}, F = \{q_0\}$

$\Delta = \{(q_0, t, e) \rightarrow (q_0, t)$

$(q_0, iar, e) \rightarrow (q_1, e)$

$(q_1, sc, t) \rightarrow (q_1, e)\}$

2. (b)

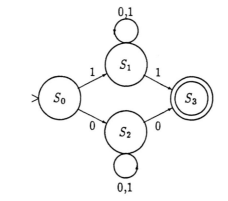

(c)

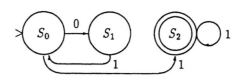

3. (a) $(0^*11)^*0^*11$ or $0^*11(0^*11)^*$;

(b) 111^* or 1^*11 or 11^*1;

(c) $(0^*(11)^*0^*)^*$

4. $K = \{q_0, q_1, q_2, q_3\}, \Sigma = \{a, b, \#\}, s = q_0$

$\delta = \{(q_0, b) \rightarrow (q_0, R)$

$\quad (q_0, \#) \rightarrow (q_0, R)$

$\quad (q_0, a) \rightarrow (q_1, b)$

$\quad (q_1, b) \rightarrow (q_2, L)$

$\quad (q_2, a) \rightarrow (q_2, L)$

$\quad (q_2, \#) \rightarrow (q_2, L)$

$\quad (q_2, b) \rightarrow (q_3, b)\}$

Bibliography

PART A

Introductory textbook:
Halmos, P. R.: 1960, *Naive Set Theory*, Princeton, N.J., Van Nostrand.

Set Theory, Paradoxes and Foundations:
Anderson, A. R. (ed.): 1964, *Minds and Machines*, Englewood Cliffs, N.J., Prentice-Hall.
Barwise, J. and J. Etchemendy: 1987, *The Liar: An Essay on Truth and Circularity*, New York, Oxford University Press.
Cohen, P.: 1966, *Set Theory and the Continuum Hypothesis*, New York, Benjamin.
Copi, I. M.: 1971, *The Theory of Logical Type*, London, Routledge & Kegan Paul.
Dauben, J. W.: 1979, *Georg Cantor: His Mathematics and Philosophy of the Infinite*, Cambridge, M.A., Harvard University Press.
Fraenkel, A. and Y. Bar-Hillel: 1973, *Foundations of Set Theory*. 2nd edition, Amsterdam, North-Holland.
Gödel, K.: 1940, *The Consistency of the Axiom of Choice and of the Generalized Continuum Hypothesis with the Axioms of Set Theory*, Princeton University Press.
Hofstadter, D. R.: 1979, *Gödel, Escher, Bach: An Eternal Golden Braid*, New York, Vintage Books.
Kunen, K: 1980, *Set Theory: An Introduction to Independence Proofs*, Amsterdam, North-Holland.
Martin, R. L.: 1984, *Recent Essays on Truth and the Liar Paradox*, New York, Oxford University Press.
Moore, G. H.: 1982, *Zermelo's Axiom of Choice. Its origins, development and influence*, New York/Heidelberg/Berlin, Springer Verlag.
Quine, W. van Orman: 1963, *Set Theory and Its Logic*, Cambridge, M.A., Harvard University Press.
Quine, W. van Orman: 1966, *The Ways of Paradox*, New York, Random House.
Russell, B.: 1919, *Introduction to Mathematical Philosophy*, London, Allen and Unwin.
Smullyan, R.: 1978, *What Is the Name of This Book?*, Englewood Cliffs, N.J., Prentice-Hall.
Zadeh, L. A.: 1987, *Fuzzy Sets and Applications: Selected Papers*, New York, Wiley.

PART B

Introductory textbooks:
Copi, I. M: 1965, *Symbolic Logic*. 2nd edition. New York, Macmillan.
Jeffrey, R. C.: 1967, *Formal Logic: Its Scope and Limits*, New York, McGraw-Hill.
Kalish, D. and R. Montague: 1964, *Logic*, New York, Harcourt, Brace and World.
Mates, B.: 1972, *Elementary Logic*, 2nd edition, New York, Oxford University Press.
Thomason, R. H.: 1970, *Symbolic Logic*, New York, Macmillan.
An innovative method for learning predicate logic on a Macintosh computer: J. Barwise and J. Etchemendy, *Tarski's World*. Available from Kinko's Courseware 1987.

Mathematical logic, axiomatization and metatheory:
Barwise, J. (ed.): 1977, *Handbook of Mathematical Logic*, Amsterdam, North-Holland.
Bell, J. L.: 1978, *Boolean-valued Models and Independence Proofs in Set Theory*, Oxford, Clarendon Press.
Bell, J. L. and M. Machover: 1977, *A Course in Mathematical Logic*, Amsterdam, North-Holland.
Beth, E.: 1962, *Formal Methods, An introduction to symbolic logic and to the study of effective operations in arithmetic and logic*, Dordrecht, Reidel.
Beth, E.: 1970, *Aspects of Modern Logic*, Dordrecht, Reidel.
Boolos, G. and R. Jeffrey: 1980, *Computability and Logic*, 2nd edition, Cambridge, England, Cambridge University Press.
Chang, C. C., and Keisler, H. J.: 1973, *Model Theory*, New York, American Elsevier and Amsterdam, North-Holland.
Davis, M.: 1965, *The Undecidable*, Hewlett, N.Y., Raven Press.

Davis, M. and E. J. Weyuker: 1983, *Computability, Complexity and Languages. Fundamentals of Theoretical Computer Science*, New York/London, Academic Press.

Gamut, L. T. F.: *Logica, Taal en Betekenis*, vol. 1 and 2 (in Dutch), Spectrum, Utrecht (English translation to appear with the University of Chicago Press).

Gödel, K: 1962, *On Formally Undecidable Propositions*, New York, Basic Books.

Kleene, S. C.: 1967, *Mathematical Logic*, New York, Wiley.

Kneale, W. and M. Kneale: 1962, *The Development of Logic*, Oxford, Clarendon Press.

Kreisel, G., and Krivine, J. L.: 1967, *Elements of Mathematical Logic: Model Theory*, Amsterdam, North-Holland.

Landman, F.: 1986, *Towards a Theory of Information. The status of partial objects in semantics*, Dordrecht, Foris.

Malitz, J.: 1979, *Introduction to Mathematical Logic. Set-theory, Computable Functions, Model theory*, N.Y., Springer Verlag.

Peano, G: 1973, *Selected Works of Giuseppe Peano*, ed. and transl. by H. C. Kennedy, Toronto, University of Toronto Press.

Quine, W. van Orman: 1972, *Methods of Logic*, 3rd edition, N.Y., Holt, Rinehart and Winston, Inc.

Rasiowa, H. and R. Sikorski: 1970, *The Mathematics of Metamathematics*, 3rd edition, Warszawa, Panstwowe Wydawn.

Robinson, A.: 1965, *Introduction to Model Theory and to the Metamathematics of Algebra*, 2nd edition, Amsterdam, North-Holland.

Shoenfield, J. R.: 1967, *Mathematical Logic*, Reading, M.A., Addison-Wesley.

Smullyan, R.: 1961, *Theory of Formal Systems*, Princeton, N.J., Princeton University Press.

Tarski, A. M.: 1956, *Logic, Semantics, Mathematics*, Oxford, Oxford University Press.

Tarski, A. M. and R. M. Robinson: 1953, *Undecidable Theories*, Amsterdam, North-Holland.

Tarski, A. M. and J. C. C. McKinsey: 1948, *A Decision Method for Elementary Algebra and Geometry*, 2nd edition, Berkeley, U.C. Press.

PART C

Abbott, J. C.: 1969, *Sets, Lattices and Boolean Algebras*, Boston, Allyn & Bacon.

Birkhoff, G.: 1961, *Lattice Theory*, Providence, R.I., A. M. S. Colloquium, vol. 25.

Birkhoff, G. and S. MacLane: 1977, *A Survey of Modern Algebra*, New York, Macmillan.

Gill, A.: 1976, *Applied Algebra for the Computer Sciences*, Englewood Cliffs, N.J., Prentice-Hall.

Grätzer, G.: 1968, *Universal Algebra*, New York, Van Nostrand.

Grätzer, G.: 1971, *Lattice-theory. First concepts and distributive lattices*, San Francisco, Freeman and Co.

MacLane, S.: 1971, *Categories for the Working Mathematician*, Berlin, Springer.

MacLane, S. and G. Birkhoff; 1979, *Algebra*, 2nd edition, New York, Macmillan.

Scott, D. S.: 1972, 'Continuous lattices', in: *Toposes, Algebraic Geometry and Logic*, F. W. Lawvere (ed.), 97–136, Berlin, Springer.

PART D

Ajduciewicz, K.: 1935, *Die syntaktische Konnexität*, Studia Philosophica 1.

Asher, N. and D. Bonevac: 1985, 'How extensional is extensional perception?', *Linguistics and Philosophy* 8.2, 203–228.

Barendregt, H.: 1984, *The Lambda Calculus. Its syntax and semantics*, North-Holland, Amsterdam/New York/Oxford.

Barwise, J.: 1981: 'Scenes and other situations', *The Journal of Philosophy* 78, 369–397.

Barwise, J. and R. Cooper: 1981, 'Generalized quantifiers and natural language', *Linguistics and Philosophy* 4.

Barwise, J. and J. Perry: 1983, *Situations and Attitudes*, Cambridge, Bradford Books.

Bäuerle, R., U. Egli and A. von Stechow (eds.): 1979, *Semantics from Different Points of View*, Berlin, Springer.

van Benthem, J.: 1983, *The Logic of Time*, Dordrecht, Reidel.

van Benthem, J.: 1985, *A Manual of Intensional Logic*, Chicago, the University of Chicago Press.

van Benthem, J.: 1986, *Essays in Logical Semantics*, Dordrecht, Reidel.

van Benthem, J. and A. ter Meulen (eds.): 1985, *Generalized Quantifiers in Natural Language*, Dordrecht Foris.

Bigelow, J.: 1978, 'Believing in semantics', *Linguistics and Philosophy* **2.1**, 101–144.

Chellas, B.: 1980, *Modal Logic: An Introduction*, Cambridge, Cambridge University Press.

Church, A.: 1941, *The Calculi of Lambda Conversion*, Princeton University Press, Princeton.

Cooper, R.: 1983, *Quantification and Syntactic Theory*, Dordrecht, Reidel.

Cooper, R. and T. Parsons: 1976, 'Montague grammar, generative semantics and interpretive semantics', in Partee (ed.), *Montague Grammar*, New York, Academic Press, 311–362.

Cresswell, M. J.: 1973, *Logics and Languages*, London, Methuen.

Cresswell, M. J.: 1985, *Structured Meanings*, Cambridge, MIT Press.

Davidson, D. and G. Harman (eds.): 1972, *Semantics of Natural Language*, Dordrecht, Reidel.

Dowty, D.: 1979, *Word Meaning and Montague Grammar*, Dordrecht, Reidel.

Dowty, D., R. Wall and S. Peters: 1981, *Introduction to Montague Semantics*, 2nd edition, Dordrecht, Reidel.

Dummett, M.: 1973, *Frege. Philosophy of Language*, London, Duckworth.

van Eijck, J.: 1985, 'Generalized quantifiers and traditional logic' in van Benthem and ter Meulen (eds.), 1–19.

Frege, G.: 1960, *Translations from the Philosophical Writings of Gottlob Frege*, P. Geach and M. Black (eds.), 2nd edition, Oxford, Blackwell.

Gabbay, D. and F. Guenthner (eds.): 1983–7, *Handbook of Philosophical Logic*, vol. I–IV, Dordrecht, Reidel.

Gallin, D.: 1975, *Intensional and Higher-Order Modal Logic. With Applications to Montague Semantics*, North-Holland Publ./Elsevier Publ., Amsterdam, New York.

Gamut: 1982, *Logica, Taal en Betekenis*, vol. 1 and 2, Het Spectrum: Aula Pockets, De Meern. English translation forthcoming in 1989 with the University of Chicago Press.

Gärdenfors, P. (ed.): 1987, *Generalized Quantifiers. Linguistic and logical approaches*, Dordrecht, Reidel.

Gazdar, G., E. Klein, G. Pullum and I. Sag: 1985, *Generalized Phrase Structure Grammar*, Harvard University Press, Cambridge.

Geach, P.: 1962, *Reference and Generality*, Ithaca, N.Y., Cornell University Press.

Halvorsen, P.-K. and Ladusaw, W.: 1979, 'Montague's "Universal Grammar": An introduction for the linguist', *Linguistics and Philosophy* 3, 185–223.

Henkin, L.: 'A theory of propositional types', *Fundamenta Mathematica* **52**, 323–344.

Higginbotham, J.: 1983, 'The logic of perceptual reports: an extensional alternative to Situation Semantics', *The Journal of Philosophy* **80**, 100–127.

Hintikka, K. J. J.: 1969, *Models for Modalities*, Dordrecht, Reidel.

Hintikka, K. J. J.: 1975, *The Intentions of Intentionality and Other New Models for Modalities*, Dordrecht, Reidel.

Hoeksema, J.: 1983, 'Plurality and conjunction', in ter Meulen (ed.) (1983), 63–83.

Hughes, G. E. and M. J. Cresswell: 1968, *An Introduction to Modal Logic*, London, Methuen.

Hughes, G. E. and M. J. Cresswell: 1984, *A Companion to Modal Logic*, London, Methuen.

Janssen, T. M. V.: 1983, *Foundations and Applications of Montague Grammar*, Ph.D. Dissertation, Mathematical Centre, Amsterdam.

de Jong, F. and H. Verkuyl: 1985, 'Generalized quantifiers: the properness of their strength', in van Benthem and ter Meulen (1985), 21–43.

Kamp, H.: 1971, 'Formal properties of "now"', *Theoria* **31**.

Kamp, H.: 1979, 'Events, instants and temporal reference', in R. Bäuerle *et al.* (eds.), *Semantics from Different Points of View*, Berlin, Springer Verlag, 376–417.

Kamp, H.: 1980, 'Some remarks on the logic of change', in Chr. Rohrer (ed.), *Time, Tense and Quantifiers*, Tuebingen, Niemeyer Verlag.

Kamp, H. and C. Rohrer: 1983, 'Tense in texts', in R. Bäuerle *et al.* (eds.), *Meaning, Use and Interpretation of Language*, Berlin, de Gruyter, 250–269.

Kaplan, D: 1978, 'Dthat', in P. Cole (ed.), *Syntax and Semantics*, vol. 9, New York, Academic Press.

Kaplan, D: 1979, 'On the logic of demonstratives', in P. French *et al.* (eds.), *Contemporary Perspectives in the Philosophy of Language*, Minneapolis, University of Minnesota Press.

Linguistics and Philosophy **9.1**, Feb. 1986, special issue 'Tense and Aspect in Discourse', D. Dowty (ed.).

Keenan, E. (ed.): 1974, *Formal Semantics of Natural Language*, Cambridge, Cambridge University Press.

Keenan, E. and L. Faltz: 1985, *Boolean Semantics for Natural Language*, Dordrecht, Reidel.

Keenan, E. and J. Stavi: 1986, 'A semantic characterization of natural language determiners', *Linguistics and Philosophy* 9, 253–326.

Keenan, E.: 1987, 'A semantic definition of "indefinite NP"', in Reuland and ter Meulen (eds.), 286–317.
Ladusaw, W.: 1979, *Polarity Sensitivity as Inherent Scope Relations*, Ph.D. Diss. University of Texas, Austin.
Ladusaw, W.: 1982, 'Semantic constraints on the English partitive construction', in D. Flickinger *et al.* (eds.), *Proceedings of the First West Coast Conference on Formal Linguistics*, Dept. of Linguistics, Stanford University, 231–242.
Lewis, D. K.: 1973, *Counterfactuals*, Oxford, Basil Blackwell.
Lindstrom, P.: 1966, 'First order predicate logic with generalized quantifiers', *Theoria* 32, 186–195.
Link, G.: 1979, *Montague Grammatik I: Die Logische Grundlagen*, Wilhelm Fink, München.
Link, G.: 1983, 'The logical analysis of plurals and mass terms, a lattice-theoretic approach', in R. Bäuerle *et al.* (eds.) (1983), *Meaning, Use and Interpretation of Language*, Berlin, de Gruyter, 302–323.
Link, G.: (1984), 'Hydras. On the logic of relative constructions with multiple heads', in F. Landman and F. Veltman (eds.) (1984), *Varieties of Formal Semantics*, Dordrecht, Foris, 245–258.
Lo Cascio, V. and C. Vet (eds.): 1986, *Temporal Structure in Sentence and Discourse*, Dordrecht, Foris.
Loux, M. J., (ed.): 1979, *The Possible and the Actual*, Ithaca, N.Y., Cornell University Press.
May, R.: 1985, *Logical Form. Its structure and derivation*, MIT Press.
ter Meulen, A. (ed.): 1983, *Studies in Modeltheoretic Semantics*, Dordrecht, Foris.
Montague, R.: 1974, *Formal Philosophy*, R.H. Thomason (ed.), New Haven, Yale University Press.
Mostowski, A.: 1957: 'On a generalization of quantifiers', *Fundamenta Mathematicae* 44, 12–36.
Partee, B. Hall: 1975, 'Deletion and variable binding', *Linguistic Inquiry* 6, 203–300.
Partee, B. H.: 1979, 'Semantics – mathematics or psychology?' in *Semantics from Different Points of View*, R. Bäuerle *et al.* (eds.), Berlin, Springer, 1–14.
Partee, B. H.: 1984, 'Compositionality', in F. Landman and F. Veltman (eds.), *Varieties of Formal Semantics*, Dordrecht, Foris, 281–312.
Quine, W. van Orman: 1953, *From a Logical Point of View*, 2nd edition (1961), Cambridge, Harvard University Press.
Quine, W. van Orman: 1956, 'Quantifiers and propositional attitudes', *The Journal of Philosophy* 53, 177–187.
Reichenbach, H.: 1947, *Elements of Symbolic Logic*, New York, MacMillan.
Reuland, E. and A ter Meulen (eds.): 1987, *The Representation of Indefiniteness, Current Studies in Linguistics*, Cambridge, MIT Press.
Scott, D.: 1969, *Models for the lambda-calculus*, ms. (unpublished) 53 pp.
Scott, D.: 1980, 'Lambda-calculus: some models some philosophy', in Barwise, J. *et al.* (eds.), *The Kleene Symposium*, North-Holland, Amsterdam/New York.
Soames, S.: 1985, 'Lost innocence', *Linguistics and Philosophy* 8.1, 59–71.
Turing, A.: 1937, 'Computability and lambda-definability', *Journal of Symbolic Logic* 2, 153–163.
Vendler, Z.: 1968, *Linguistics in Philosophy*, Ithaca, Cornell University Press.
Westerståhl, D.: 1984, 'Some results on quantifiers', *Notre Dame Journal of Formal Logic* 25, 152–170.
Westerståhl, D.: 1985a, 'Logical constants in quantifier languages', *Linguistics and Philosophy* 8, 387–413.
Westerståhl, D.: 1985b, 'Determiners and context sets', in van Benthem and ter Meulen (eds.): (1985), 45–71.
Zwarts, F.: 1983, 'Determiners: a relational perspective', in ter Meulen (ed.) (1983), 37–62.

PART E

Textbooks:

Arbib, M. A.: 1969, *Theories of Abstract Automata*, Englewood Cliffs, New Jersey, Prentice-Hall.
Brainerd, W. S. and L. H. Landweber: 1974, *Theory of Computation*, New York, John Wiley & Sons.
Cohen, D. I. A.: 1986, *Introduction to Computer Theory*, New York, John Wiley & Sons.
Gill, A.: 1963, *Introduction to the Theory of Finite-State Machines*, New York, McGraw-Hill.
Ginsburg, S.: 1962, *An Introduction to Mathematical Machine Theory*, Reading, Massachusetts, Addison-Wesley Publ. Co.
Ginsburg, S.: 1966, *The Mathematical Theory of Context-Free Languages*, New York, McGraw-Hill.
Gross, M. and A. Lentin: 1970, *Introduction to Formal Grammars*, New York, Heidelberg, and Berlin, Springer-Verlag.
Harrison, M. A.: 1965, *Introduction to Switching and Automata Theory*, New York, McGraw-Hill Book Co.
Hopcroft, J. E. and J. D. Ullman: 1979, *Introduction to Automata Theory, Languages, and Computation*, Reading, Massachusetts, Addison–Wesley Publ. Co.

Lewis, H. R. and C. H. Papadimitriou: 1981, *Elements of the Theory of Computation*, Englewood Cliffs, New Jersey, Prentice-Hall.

Minsky, M. L.: 1967, *Computation: Finite and Infinite Machines*, Englewood Cliffs, New Jersey, Prentice-Hall.

Nelson, R. J.: 1968, *Introduction to Automata*, New York, John Wiley & Sons.

Rogers, H., Jr.: 1967, *Theory of Recursive Functions and Effective Computability*, New York, McGraw-Hill.

Salomaa, A.: 1969, *Theory of Automata*, Oxford, Pergamon Press.

Salomaa, A.: 1973, *Formal Languages*, New York, Academic Press.

Collections:

Davis, M. (ed.): 1965, *The Undecidable: Basic Papers on Undecidable Propositions, Unsolvable Problems and Computable Functions*, Hewlett, New York, Raven Press.

Dowty, D. R., L. Karttunen, and A. M. Zwicky (eds.): 1985, *Natural Language Processing: Theoretical, Computational and Psychological Perspectives*, New York, Cambridge Univ. Press.

Luce, R. D., R. R. Bush, and E. Galanter (eds.): 1963, *Handbook of Mathematical Psychology*, Vol. 2, New York, John Wiley & Sons.

Luce, R. D., R. R. Bush, and E. Galanter (eds.): 1965, *Readings in Mathematical Psychology*, Vol. 2, New York, John Wiley & Sons.

Manaster-Ramer, A. (ed.): 1987, *Mathematics of Language*, Amsterdam, John Benjamins.

Moore, E. F. (ed.): 1964, *Sequential Machines: Selected Papers*, Reading, Massachusetts, Addison-Wesley Publ. Co.

Oehrle, R. T., E. Bach, and D. Wheeler (eds.): 1988, *Categorial Grammars and Natural Language Structures*, Dordrecht, Reidel.

Shannon, C. E. and J. McCarthy (eds.): 1956, *Automata Studies*, Princeton, New Jersey, Princeton Univ. Press.

Savitch, W. J., E. Bach, W. Marsh, and G. Safran-Naveh (eds.): 1987, *The Formal Complexity of Natural Languages*, Dordrecht, Reidel.

Other books and articles:

Ades, A. E. and M. J. Steedman: 1982, 'On the order of words', *Linguistics and Philosophy* 4, 517–558.

Aho, A. V.: 1968, 'Indexed grammars – an extension of context-free grammars', *Journal of the Association for Computing Machinery* No. 15, No. 4, 647–671.

Ajdukiewicz, K.: 1935, 'Die syntaktische Konnexität', *Studia Philosophica* 1, 1–27. English translation in Storrs McCall (ed.) (1967), *Polish Logic*, Oxford, Oxford Univ. Press.

Bar-Hillel, Y.: 1953, 'A quasi-arithmetical notation for syntactic description', *Language* 29, 47–58.

Bar-Hillel, Y., C. Gaifman, and E. Shamir: 1960, 'On categorial and phrase structure grammars', *Bulletin of the Research Council of Israel* 9, 1–16. Reprinted in Bar-Hillel, Y.: 1964, *Language and Information: Selected Essays on their Theory and Application*, Reading, Massachusetts, Addison-Wesley Publ. Co.

van Benthem, J.: 1986, *Essays in Logical Semantics*, Dordrecht, Reidel.

van Benthem, J.: 1988, 'The Lambek calculus', in Oehrle, Bach, and Wheeler (eds.), pp. 35–68.

Chomsky, N.: 1956, 'Three models for the description of language', *IRE Transactions on Information Theory* 2, No. 3, 113–124. A corrected version appears in Luce, Bush, and Galanter (eds): 1965.

Chomsky, N.: 1957, *Syntactic Structures*, The Hague, Mouton & Co.

Chomsky, N.: 1959, 'On certain formal properties of grammars', *Information and Control* 2, No. 2, 137–167.

Chomsky, N.: 1963, 'Formal properties of grammars', in Luce, Bush, and Galanter (eds.), pp. 323–418.

Chomsky, N.: 1965, *Aspects of the Theory of Syntax*, Cambridge, Massachusetts, MIT Press.

Chomsky, N. and G. A. Miller: 1958, 'Finite-state languages', *Information and Control* 1, 91–112. Reprinted in Luce, Bush and Galanter (eds.): 1965.

Chomsky, N. and G. A. Miller: 1963, 'Introduction to the formal analysis of natural languages', in Luce, Bush and Galanter (eds.) (1963), pp. 269–321.

Davis, M.: 1958, *Computability and Unsolvability*, New York, McGraw-Hill.

Friedman, J., D. Dai, and W. Wong: 1986, 'The weak generative capacity of parenthesis-free categorial grammars', proceedings of the 11th International Conference on Computational Linguistics.

Friedman, J. and R. Venkatesan: 1986, 'Categorial and non-categorial language', proceedings of the 24th Meeting of the Association for Computational Linguistics.

Gazdar, G.: 1985, 'Applicability of indexed grammars to natural languages', Report No. CSLI-85-34, Center for the Study of Language and Information, Stanford University.

Gazdar, G. and G. K. Pullum: 1985, 'Computationally relevant properties of natural languages and their grammars', *New Generation Computing* 3, 273–306; also appeared as Report CSLI-85-24, Center for the Study of Language and Information, Stanford University.

Ginsburg, S.: 1975, *Algebraic and Automata-Theoretic Properties of Formal Languages*, Amsterdam, North-Holland.

Ginsburg, S. and B. H. Partee: 1969, 'A mathematical model of transformational grammar', *Information and Control* 15, 297–334.

Ginzburg, A.: 1968, *Algebraic Theory of Automata*, New York, Academic Press.

Hayashi, T.:1973, 'On derivation trees of indexed grammars – an extension of the uvwxy theorem', publ. of the Research Institute for Mathematical Sciences, Kyoto University, Vol. 9, pp. 61–92.

Joshi, A. K.: 1985, 'How much context-sensitivity is necessary for characterizing structural descriptions – tree adjoining grammars', in Dowty, Karttunen, and Zwicky (eds.).

Joshi, A. K., L. Levy, and M. Takahashi: 1975, 'Tree adjunct grammars', *Journal of the Computer and System Sciences* 10, No. 1, 136–163.

Kuroda, S. Y.: 1964, 'Classes of languages and linear bounded automata', *Information and Control* 7, 207–223.

Lambek, J.: 1958, 'The mathematics of sentence structure', *American Mathematical Monthly* 65, 154–170.

Langacker, R. W.: 1969, 'On pronominalization and the chain of command', in D. A. Reibel and S. A. Schane (eds.), *Modern Studies in English: Readings in Transformational Grammar*, Englewood Cliffs, New Jersey, Prentice-Hall.

Marsh, W. E.: 1985, 'Some conjectures on indexed languages', paper presented to the Association for Symbolic Logic Meeting, Stanford Univ., July 15–19.

Peters, P. S., Jr.: 1973, 'On restricting deletion transformations', in Gross, Halle, and Schützenberger, *The Formal Analysis of Natural Languages*, The Hague, Mouton.

Peters, P. S., Jr. and R. W. Ritchie: 1973, 'On the generative power of transformational grammars', *Information Sciences* 6, 49–83.

Pollard, C.: 1984, *Generalized Phrase Structure Grammars, Head Grammars, and Natural Language*, Ph.D. Dissertation, Stanford University.

Pullum, G. K. and G. Gazdar: 1982, 'Natural languages and context-free languages', *Linguistics and Philosophy* 4, 471–504. Reprinted in Savitch, Bach, Marsh, and Safran-Naveh (eds.).

Rabin, M. O. and D. Scott: 1959, 'Finite automata and their decision problems', *IBM Journal of Research and Development* 3, No. 2, 114–125.

Roach: 1987, 'Formal properties of head grammars', in A. Manaster-Ramer (ed.).

Shieber, S. M.: 1985, 'Evidence against the context-freeness of natural language', *Linguistics and Philosophy* 8, 333–343. Reprinted in Savitch, Bach, Marsh, and Safran-Naveh (eds.).

Vijay-Shankar, K.: 1987, *A Study of Tree Adjoining Grammars*, Ph.D. Dissertation, University of Pennsylvania.

Wasow, T.: 1978, 'On constraining the class of transformational languages', *Synthese* 39, 81–104. Reprinted in Savitch, Bach, Marsh, and Safran-Naveh (eds.).

Weir, D. J. and A. K. Joshi: 1988, 'Combinatory categorial grammars: generative power and relationship to linear context-free rewriting systems', proceedings of the 26th Meeting of the Association for Computational Linguistics.

Weir, D. J., K. Vijay-Shanker, and A. K. Joshi: 1986, 'The relationship between tree adjoining grammars and head grammars', proceedings of the 24th Meeting of the Association for Computational Linguistics.

General collections and readers:

Bernacerraf, P. and H. Putnam (eds.): 1964, *Philosophy of Mathematics: Selected Readings*, Englewood Cliffs, N.J., Prentice-Hall.

Copi, I. M. and J. A. Gould: 1967, *Contemporary Readings in Logical Theory*, New York, Macmillan.

van Heijenoort, J.: 1967, *From Frege to Gödel*, a sourcebook in Mathematical Logic 1879–1931, Cambridge, M.A., Harvard University Press.

Kline, M.: 1972, *Mathematical Thought from Ancient to Modern Times*, New York/Oxford, Oxford University Press.

Martinich, A. P. (ed.): 1985, *The Philosophy of Language*, New York/Oxford, Oxford University Press.

Index

Studies in Linguistics and Philosophy

1. H. Hiż (ed.): *Questions.* 1978   ISBN Hb: 90-277-0813-4; Pb: 90-277-1035-X
2. W. S. Cooper: *Foundations of Logico-Linguistics.* A Unified Theory of Information, Language, and Logic. 1978   ISBN Hb: 90-277-0864-9; Pb: 90-277-0876-2
3. A. Margalit (ed.): *Meaning and Use.* 1979   ISBN 90-277-0888-6
4. F. Guenthner and S.J. Schmidt (eds.): *Formal Semantics and Pragmatics for Natural Languages.* 1979   ISBN Hb: 90-277-0778-2; Pb: 90-277-0930-0
5. E. Saarinen (ed.): *Game-Theoretical Semantics.* Essays on Semantics by Hintikka, Carlson, Peacocke, Rantala, and Saarinen. 1979   ISBN 90-277-0918-1
6. F.J. Pelletier (ed.): *Mass Terms: Some Philosophical Problems.* 1979   ISBN 90-277-0931-9
7. D. R. Dowty: *Word Meaning and Montague Grammar.* The Semantics of Verbs and Times in Generative Semantics and in Montague's PTQ. 1979   ISBN Hb: 90-277-1008-2; Pb: 90-277-1009-0
8. A. F. Freed: *The Semantics of English Aspectual Complementation.* 1979   ISBN Hb: 90-277-1010-4; Pb: 90-277-1011-2
9. J. McCloskey: *Transformational Syntax and Model Theoretic Semantics.* A Case Study in Modern Irish. 1979   ISBN Hb: 90-277-1025-2; Pb: 90-277-1026-0
10. J. R. Searle, F. Kiefer and M. Bierwisch (eds.): *Speech Act Theory and Pragmatics.* 1980   ISBN Hb: 90-277-1043-0; Pb: 90-277-1045-7
11. D. R. Dowty, R. E. Wall and S. Peters: *Introduction to Montague Semantics.* 1981; 5th printing 1987   ISBN Hb: 90-277-1141-0; Pb: 90-277-1142-9
12. F. Heny (ed.): *Ambiguities in Intensional Contexts.* 1981   ISBN Hb: 90-277-1167-4; Pb: 90-277-1168-2
13. W. Klein and W. Levelt (eds.): *Crossing the Boundaries in Linguistics.* Studies Presented to Manfred Bierwisch. 1981   ISBN 90-277-1259-X
14. Z. S. Harris: *Papers on Syntax.* Edited by H. Hiż. 1981   ISBN Hb: 90-277-1266-0; Pb: 90-277-1267-0
15. P. Jacobson and G. K. Pullum (eds.): *The Nature of Syntactic Representation.* 1982   ISBN Hb: 90-277-1289-1; Pb: 90-277-1290-5
16. S. Peters and E. Saarinen (eds.): *Processes, Beliefs, and Questions.* Essays on Formal Semantics of Natural Language and Natural Language Processing. 1982   ISBN 90-277-1314-6
17. L. Carlson: *Dialogue Games.* An Approach to Discourse Analysis. 1983; 2nd printing 1985   ISBN Hb: 90-277-1455-X; Pb: 90-277-1951-9
18. L. Vaina and J. Hintikka (eds.): *Cognitive Constraints on Communication.* Representation and Processes. 1984; 2nd printing 1985   ISBN Hb: 90-277-1456-8; Pb: 90-277-1949-7
19. F. Heny and B. Richards (eds.): *Linguistic Categories: Auxiliaries and Related Puzzles.* Volume I: Categories. 1983   ISBN 90-277-1478-9
20. F. Heny and B. Richards (eds.): *Linguistic Categories: Auxiliaries and Related Puzzles.* Volume II: The Scope, Order, and Distribution of English Auxiliary Verbs. 1983   ISBN 90-277-1479-7
21. R. Cooper: *Quantification and Syntactic Theory.* 1983   ISBN 90-277-1484-3

Volumes 1–26 formerly published under the Series Title: Synthese Language Library.

Studies in Linguistics and Philosophy

22. J. Hintikka (in collaboration with J. Kulas): *The Game of Language*. Studies in Game-Theoretical Semantics and Its Applications. 1983; 2nd printing 1985
ISBN Hb: 90-277-1687-0; Pb: 90-277-1950-0

23. E. L. Keenan and L. M. Faltz: *Boolean Semantics for Natural Language*. 1985
ISBN Hb: 90-277-1768-0; Pb: 90-277-1842-3

24. V. Raskin: *Semantic Mechanisms of Humor*. 1985
ISBN Hb: 90-277-1821-0; Pb: 90-277-1891-1

25. G. T. Stump: *The Semantic Variability of Absolute Constructions*. 1985
ISBN Hb: 90-277-1895-4; Pb: 90-277-1896-2

26. J. Hintikka and J. Kulas: *Anaphora and Definite Descriptions*. Two Applications of Game-Theoretical Semantics. 1985   ISBN Hb: 90-277-2055-X; Pb: 90-277-2056-8

27. E. Engdahl: *Constituent Questions*. The Syntax and Semantics of Questions with Special Reference to Swedish. 1986   ISBN Hb: 90-277-1954-3; Pb: 90-277-1955-1

28. M. J. Cresswell: *Adverbial Modification*. Interval Semantics and Its Rivals. 1985
ISBN Hb: 90-277-2059-2; Pb: 90-277-2060-6

29. J. van Benthem: *Essays in Logical Semantics* 1986
ISBN Hb: 90-277-2091-6; Pb: 90-277-2092-4

30. B. H. Partee, A. ter Meulen and R. E. Wall: *Mathematical Methods in Linguistics*. 1990
ISBN Hb: 90-277-2244-7; Pb: 90-277-2245-5

31. P. Gärdenfors (ed.): *Generalized Quantifiers*. Linguistic and Logical Approaches. 1987
ISBN Hb: 1-55608-017-4; Pb: 1-55608-018-2

32. R. T. Oehrle, E. Bach and D. Wheeler (eds.): *Categorial Grammars and Natural Language Structures*. 1988   ISBN Hb: 1-55608-030-1; Pb: 1-55608-031-X

33. W. J. Savitch, E. Bach, W. Marsh and G. Safran-Naveh (eds.): *The Formal Complexity of Natural Language*. 1987   ISBN Hb: 1-55608-046-8; Pb: 1-55608-047-6

34. J. E. Fenstad, P.-K. Halvorsen, T. Langholm and J. van Benthem: *Situations, Language and Logic*. 1987   ISBN Hb: 1-55608-048-4; Pb: 1-55608-049-2

35. U. Reyle and C. Rohrer (eds.): *Natural Language Parsing and Linguistic Theories*. 1988   ISBN Hb: 1-55608-055-7; Pb: 1-55608-056-5

36. M. J. Cresswell: *Semantical Essays*. Possible Worlds and Their Rivals. 1988
ISBN 1-55608-061-1

37. T. Nishigauchi: *Quantification in the Theory of Grammar*. 1990
ISBN Hb: 0-7923-0643-0; Pb: 0-7923-0644-9

38. G. Chierchia, B.H. Partee and R. Turner (eds.): *Properties, Types and Meaning*. Volume I: Foundational Issues. 1989   ISBN Hb: 1-55608-067-0; Pb: 1-55608-068-9

39. G. Chierchia, B.H. Partee and R. Turner (eds.): *Properties, Types and Meaning*. Volume II: Semantic Issues. 1989   ISBN Hb: 1-55608-069-7; Pb: 1-55608-070-0
Set ISBN (Vol. I + II) 1-55608-088-3; Pb: 1-55608-089-1

Further information about our publications on *Linguistics* are available on request.
Kluwer Academic Publishers – Dordrecht / Boston / London

Printed in the United States
82909LV00001B/43-48/A

9 789027 722454